Mastering VMware Horizon 6

Unlock the advanced features and full power of VMware Horizon 6 to deliver the industry's most comprehensive end-to-end user experience

Peter von Oven

Barry Coombs

BIRMINGHAM - MUMBAI

Mastering VMware Horizon 6

First published: March 2015

Production reference: 1240315

Published by Packt Publishing Ltd.
Livery Place
35 Livery Street
Birmingham B3 2PB, UK.

ISBN 978-1-78439-923-8

www.packtpub.com

Credits

Authors
Peter von Oven
Barry Coombs

Reviewers
Biswapati Bhattacharjee
Bruce Bookman
Joe Jessen
Craig Kilborn
Raimundo Rodulfo
Sunil Sarat

Commissioning Editor
Ashwin Nair

Acquisition Editor
Greg Wild

Content Development Editor
Mohammed Fahad

Technical Editor
Mohita Vyas

Project Coordinator
Danuta Jones

Copy Editors
Shambhavi Pai
Vikrant Phadke
Adithi Shetty
Sameen Siddiqui

Proofreaders
Simran Bhogal
Stephen Copestake
Joanna McMahon

Indexer
Rekha Nair

Graphics
Sheetal Aute

Production Coordinator
Shantanu N. Zagade

Cover Work
Shantanu N. Zagade

About the Author

Peter von Oven is an experienced technical consultant and has spent the last 20 years of his IT career working with customers and partners, designing technology solutions aimed at delivering true business value. During his career, Peter was involved in numerous large-scale enterprise projects and deployments. He has presented at key IT events and has worked in senior presales roles for some of the giants of IT. Over the last 9 years, Peter has used his skills and experience within the desktop virtualization market. Today, he is a subject matter expert in end user computing at VMware in the UK, and is also the systems engineering manager for the partner and general business SE team.

Peter got his first taste of writing when assisting with some of the chapters in the book *Building End-User Computing Solutions with VMware View*. This led him to author three Packt Publishing titles: *VMware Horizon Mirage Essentials*, *VMware Horizon View Essentials*, and *VMware Horizon Workspace Essentials*, coauthored by Peter Bjork and Joel Lindberg.

Acknowledgments

There are a couple of people I want to thank for the support they have given me during the writing of this book. Firstly, and most importantly, I would like to thank my wife and two daughters for their continued support when I spent evenings and weekends slaving over the keyboard. Secondly, thanks to the Packt Publishing team for giving me the opportunity to write this book and for their support, which has yet again been outstanding. Finally, I'd also like to say a big thank you to my coauthor, Barry, for his support and time in getting this title published.

About the Author

Barry Coombs is the presales director for Computerworld Systems, a UK-based, virtualization-focused value-added reseller. He has been focusing on virtualization, storage, and end-user computing technologies as a customer, consultant, and architect for the last 8 years. Previously, Barry was a member of a team supporting internal and customer solutions and projects for a software house. This role brought with it a variety of experiences, particularly with Microsoft, Citrix, and VMware technologies.

In his current role, Barry manages a team of technical architects and is actively involved in engaging with customers and designing solutions to meet their needs. He also works with his technical director to set implementation standards and act as a point of technical escalation. Barry is responsible for identifying new technologies and speaking at and hosting customer-focused events surrounding virtualization, storage, and end-user computing.

Barry has been awarded VMware's vExpert award for contributions to the VMware community every year since 2010. He is also part of the VMUG leadership team for South West UK and has a VMware-focused blog, `http://virtualisedreality.com/`. He is active on Twitter (`@virtualisedreal`), particularly reporting live from many industry-related events.

This is Barry's second book on end-user computing technologies. He was a coauthor of *Building End-User Computing Solutions with VMware View* published in 2012.

Acknowledgments

I would like to thank my wife, Laura, for all the support she has given me during the process of writing this book, particularly through a very busy and challenging year. I would also like to thank the team at Packt Publishing, without whom this book wouldn't have been possible.

Special thanks should also be given to Nimble Storage for the loan of a Nimble CS200 array and Computerworld Systems LTD for the loan of the virtual infrastructure utilized while I was working on and writing this book. Nimble Storage is a proven storage partner for Horizon View through VMware's Fast Track 2.0 program. Nimble Storage is unique in the way it is designed, utilizing Intel processors instead of spindles to drive performance, alongside SSDs for read cache and high-capacity disks for storage, making it an ideal choice for your VDI solution.

About the Reviewers

Biswapati Bhattacharjee is a seasoned professional in the field of information technology. So far, he has played many roles in various domains in his professional life, ranging from quality engineering, performance benchmarking, presales technical, and project management to customer interaction, ISV partner management, and technical consultancy. He is a speaker at VMworld. He can be found on LinkedIn at `www.linkedin.com/in/biswapatibhattacharjee/`.

I would like to thank my wife, Chandrima, for her continuous encouragement and support and our lovely daughter, Bidushi, who never fails to inspire me.

I also want to thank my parents, Gauri and Nishithendu, for always believing in me and my brothers, Basudeb and Vivekananda, for their guidance.

I take this opportunity to express my gratitude to all the people who have been instrumental in the successful completion of this book review. This work would not have been possible without my extended family: my sisters-in-law, Pompa and Nivedita; my niece, Satakshi; my nephew, Vishok; my brother-in-law, Chitrarath; and my parents-in-law, Ratna and Chinmoy.

Bruce Bookman is a software and hardware veteran from Silicon Valley, who has held roles ranging from frontline technical support to director of software quality assurance. He is currently with Oracle as a QA architect on the Exalogic private cloud team. He is the author of technical articles covering virtualization on developer.com and has created and delivered extensive technical training on virtualization and other topics. Bruce has received a number of recognitions for his customer advocacy and dedication to customer success.

Joe Jessen is a veteran of the IT industry and has held roles in private organizations, vendors, and consulting organizations. He has been involved in application and desktop virtualization since 1996, setting the strategic direction for global organizations with their infrastructure and end user computing initiatives.

Joe recently spent 5 years as an industry analyst, focusing on virtualization. He is currently working for a large hardware and software manufacturer, focusing on desktop virtualization solutions. His analysis and papers can be found at `http://dabcc.com/` and `http://www.virtualizationpractice.com/`.

Joe was also the technical reviewer for *VMware Horizon View 5.3 Design Patterns and Best Practices, Packt Publishing* and *VMware Horizon View 6 Desktop Virtualization Cookbook, Packt Publishing*. You can follow him on Twitter at `@JoeJessen`. You can view his LinkedIn profile at `http://linkedin.com/in/joejessen`, and his website is at `http://www.solutions101.us`. He currently resides at Fairfield, Connecticut, with his wife, Rosanne, and their two children.

Craig Kilborn is a solutions architect with SCC, who enjoys helping customers achieve success with virtualization and VDI. His experience has spanned a number of roles, including first-, second-, and third-line support for his current focus, which is the design, installation, and configuration of multisite vSphere and Horizon View infrastructures.

Craig holds various active industry certifications, including VMware Certified Advanced Professional, and is recognized as a VMware vExpert. In his spare time, he shares his insights on VMware-related technologies on his independent blog (`vmfocus.com`) and through Twitter at `@Craig_Kilborn`.

Raimundo Rodulfo is a technology manager, electrical and electronics engineer, and project manager, with over 22 years of experience in telecommunications, information technology, and electronics industries, including positions of leadership in USA and Latin America. He is currently the assistant chief information officer of a local government organization in Florida, USA. Previously, he has held technical and managerial positions with Bellsouth, Siemens, NCR, Choice One Telecom and USA Telephone and has worked on projects with Agilent, Motorola, Lucent Technologies, Alcatel, Microsoft, Cisco, CheckPoint, VMWare, and other organizations. He has managed multiple full-cycle enterprise infrastructure projects, engineered systems and applications, and business operations for various organizations. Raimundo has participated as revision team lead and balloting group member in the IEEE, ISO, and IEC engineering standards working groups, developing standards and guidelines for the engineering and management of systems, electronic appliances, software, websites, and service information. He is an active member and participant of the IEEE, NSPE, FES, PMI, IIBA, CIO/CISO/CDO governing bodies, and several other professional organizations. He holds several professional licenses and certifications, such as Professional Engineer (P.E.), Certified Virtualization Expert (CVE), Information Technology Infrastructure Library (ITIL), and Project Management Professional (PMP), among other credentials.

Thanks to the staff at Packt Publishing (project coordinators, editors, and so on) for inviting me to participate in this project and guiding me through the process.

Sunil Sarat is the vice president of cloud and end user transformation services at an India-based global hybrid IT infrastructure services provider. He has played a key role in setting up and running this practice, dealing with emerging technologies such as public/private cloud, hybrid IT, enterprise mobility, VDI, app virtualization, and associated transformation services. His role is to strategize, create, roll out, and manage services in these technology areas.

Sunil is a technology and business leader, with varied experience in handling diverse functions such as innovation/technology, service delivery, transition, presales/solutions, and automation. He has authored white papers, blogs, and articles on various technology- and service-related areas. He reviews technical books and is a speaker at cloud-related events.

Sunil holds various industry certifications in the areas of computing, storage, and security, and he also holds an MBA in marketing.

www.PacktPub.com

Support files, eBooks, discount offers, and more

For support files and downloads related to your book, please visit `www.PacktPub.com`.

Did you know that Packt offers eBook versions of every book published, with PDF and ePub files available? You can upgrade to the eBook version at `www.PacktPub.com` and as a print book customer, you are entitled to a discount on the eBook copy. Get in touch with us at `service@packtpub.com` for more details.

At `www.PacktPub.com`, you can also read a collection of free technical articles, sign up for a range of free newsletters and receive exclusive discounts and offers on Packt books and eBooks.

`https://www2.packtpub.com/books/subscription/packtlib`

Do you need instant solutions to your IT questions? PacktLib is Packt's online digital book library. Here, you can search, access, and read Packt's entire library of books.

Why subscribe?

- Fully searchable across every book published by Packt
- Copy and paste, print, and bookmark content
- On demand and accessible via a web browser

Free access for Packt account holders

If you have an account with Packt at `www.PacktPub.com`, you can use this to access PacktLib today and view 9 entirely free books. Simply use your login credentials for immediate access.

Instant updates on new Packt books

Get notified! Find out when new books are published by following `@PacktEnterprise` on Twitter or the *Packt Enterprise* Facebook page.

Table of Contents

Preface

VMware Horizon View is the platform to deliver centralized, virtual desktop machines hosted on a server running a hypervisor, and located in a data center. The end user then connects remotely to their virtual desktop machine from their endpoint device such as a Windows laptop, Apple Mac, or tablet device.

This technology was first introduced by VMware in 2002, and has developed and matured to become the mainstream technology that we know today as Virtual Desktop Infrastructure (VDI).

VDI provides users the freedom to work in a way that suits them, by freeing them from the restrictions of not having to be in the office, but also allowing them the choice of device they use making them more productive, and ultimately your business more agile.

From an IT administrator's perspective, it allows you to centrally manage your desktop environment, from being able to manage desktop images, to the ease of adding and removing user entitlements, all controlled from a single management console.

Horizon 6 with Horizon View version 6.1 is VMware's latest virtual desktop solution, designed to centralize and virtualize your desktop environment using the market leading virtualization features and technology within VMware's Software Defined Data Center (SDDC) portfolio.

Horizon View 6 builds upon this technology platform, and today goes far beyond just VDI in delivering a rich user experience, enabling BYOD, flexible working, enhanced security, application delivery, and end-to-end management.

Delivering an end user experience requires a different approach from other infrastructure-based initiatives, and getting this right is the key for a project to have a successful outcome, and this book will show you how to succeed.

What this book covers

Chapter 1, Introduction to VMware Horizon 6, covers an introduction to what VDI is, and how it compares to other VDI type technologies. We will then cover a brief history of the VMware VDI story, followed by an overview of the latest solution.

Chapter 2, An Overview of Horizon View Architecture and its Components, will introduce you to the architectural components that make up the core VMware Horizon solution, concentrating on the virtual desktop elements of Horizon View Standard and the functionality of brokering virtual desktop machines.

Chapter 3, Design and Deployment Considerations, will introduce you to design and deployment techniques to take into consideration when undertaking your VMware Horizon project. We will discuss techniques to prove the technology and understanding how it will work inside your business, methods to assess your user's existing workload and how to use this information to help design your VMware Horizon Solution.

Chapter 4, Installing and Configuring Horizon View, will cover the installation process of the core Horizon View components, such as the Connection Server, Security Server, and replica server. Following the installation, we will start to configure the base elements of a Horizon View installation.

Chapter 5, Securing Horizon View with SSL Certificates, covers the aspect of VMware Horizon View, and in particular, how we deliver secure communication to the end user client, and also the different infrastructure components within the data center. We will start with an overview of what an SSL certificate is, and then how to create and issue a certificate before configuring Horizon View to use it.

Chapter 6, Building and Optimizing the Desktop Operating System, covers how to create and configure the virtual desktop machines after building the Horizon View infrastructure and its components, and then build the desktop operating system on them, configuring it so that it is running at its optimum performance level to run in a virtual environment.

Chapter 7, Managing and Configuring Desktop Pools, covers how Horizon View uses the concept of desktop pools to create a collection of virtual desktop machines for specific use cases, which in turn are allocated to the end users. In this chapter, we will look at the process to configure the different types of desktop pools.

Chapter 8, Fine-tuning the End User Experience, covers one of the key tasks in building the best user experience possible, which is to start fine-tuning the performance and experience for the end user's session with their virtual desktop machine. In this chapter, we will look at the tuning techniques and the pre-built Group Policy objects that can be applied to create that experience.

Chapter 9, Managing User Profiles with View Persona Management, introduces you to Horizon View Persona Management, what it is, and why you would want to deploy it. We will then examine how it is driven by Standard Active Directory Group Policy finishing with an in depth look at the policies available.

Chapter 10, Delivering Remote Applications with Horizon Advanced, dives deeper into the key feature of Horizon Advanced Edition, and looks at how Horizon View publishes an application directly into the Horizon View Client, without the need of having to launch a full virtual desktop machine. We will walk through the installation and configuration process to get our first set of Horizon View published applications available to the end users.

Chapter 11, Delivering Session-based Desktops with Horizon View, covers the other half of View's remoting capabilities and looks at how Horizon View can deliver session-based desktops from a Microsoft RDSH infrastructure.

Chapter 12, View Client Options, covers how the View Client is used to receive and display the virtual desktops and applications on the end user's device. In this chapter, we will look at the options for the View Client, both hardware and software, and discuss the various options and why you would choose one method over another.

Chapter 13, Upgrading to Horizon View 6, covers all the things you need to consider before upgrading and will then take you through the upgrade process. This chapter is designed for those that are currently running a previous version of Horizon View and are looking to upgrade to the latest version.

Chapter 14, Horizon 6 Advanced Edition, covers some of the additional features that are part of the Horizon Advanced Edition, namely VMware Mirage and VMware Workspace Portal.

Chapter 15, Introduction to App Volumes, will show you how to get up and running to the point of delivering your first set of applications. App Volume is one of the newest features of Horizon Enterprise Edition following the VMware acquisition of Cloud Volumes. App Volumes provides real-time application delivery.

Chapter 16, Introduction to VSAN for VDI, covers an overview of the VMware Virtual SAN (VSAN) technology, how it is architected, and how you create a VSAN-enabled cluster ready to use for your VDI users.

Chapter 17, Troubleshooting, covers some troubleshooting techniques and methods for use within Horizon View rather than going through a list of problems and issues.

What you need for this book

To get the most out of this book, you should have some experience of working as a desktop administrator with skills and knowledge around building and designing Microsoft Windows-based desktop environments. You should also be familiar with the VMware vSphere platform (ESXi and vCenter Server) and be comfortable with building and configuring virtual machines as well as configuring storage and networking for use in a virtual infrastructure.

Throughout this book, you have the opportunity to follow step-by-step practical guides in deploying Horizon View in an example lab environment. If you want to work through the practical examples, you will need the following software:

- VMware Horizon View Version 6.1
- vSphere 5.5 U1 (or vSphere 6 if you are going to deploy vGPU)

You can download a trial copy of Horizon View 6.1 from the following link:

`https://my.vmware.com/web/vmware/info/slug/desktop_end_user_computing/vmware_horizon_6/6_0`

You will also need the following software to build virtual machines and deploy applications:

- Microsoft Windows Server 2008 R2 64-bit
- Microsoft Windows 7 Professional 32-bit or 64-bit
- Microsoft Windows 8.1
- Microsoft SQL Express
- Adobe Reader

Who this book is for

If you are a desktop administrator or part of a project team looking at deploying a virtual desktop and/or application delivery solution, or take advantage of some of the latest features, then this book is perfect for you and your ideal companion in helping to deploy a solution to centrally manage and virtualize your desktop estate using Horizon View 6.

You will need to have some experience in desktop management using the Microsoft Windows desktop and server operating systems, and general Windows applications, as well as be familiar with the Active Directory, SQL, and VMware vSphere infrastructure (ESXi and vCenter Server) technology.

Conventions

In this book, you will find a number of text styles that distinguish between different kinds of information. Here are some examples of these styles and an explanation of their meaning.

Code words in text, database table names, folder names, filenames, file extensions, pathnames, dummy URLs, user input, and Twitter handles are shown as follows: "Allows Windows applications to be packaged, distributed, and executed as single `.exe` or `.msi` files on either physical or virtual machines."

Any command-line input or output is written as follows:

```
defaults read com.vmware.rtav
```

New terms and **important words** are shown in bold. Words that you see on the screen, for example, in menus or dialog boxes, appear in the text like this: "Click on **Start** and then click on **Run...**."

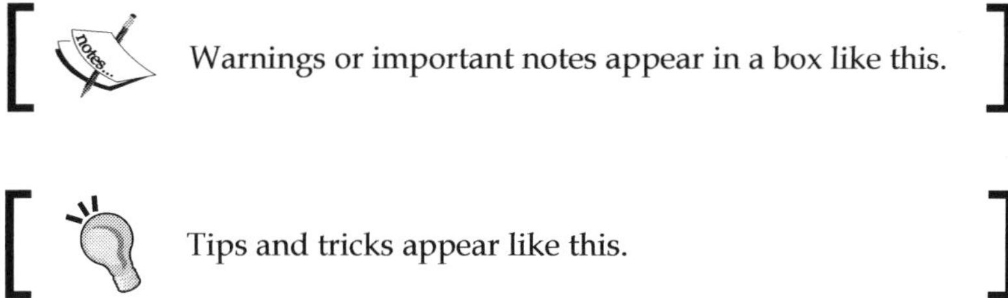

[Warnings or important notes appear in a box like this.]

[Tips and tricks appear like this.]

Reader feedback

Feedback from our readers is always welcome. Let us know what you think about this book—what you liked or disliked. Reader feedback is important for us as it helps us develop titles that you will really get the most out of.

To send us general feedback, simply e-mail `feedback@packtpub.com`, and mention the book's title in the subject of your message.

If there is a topic that you have expertise in and you are interested in either writing or contributing to a book, see our author guide at `www.packtpub.com/authors`.

Customer support

Now that you are the proud owner of a Packt book, we have a number of things to help you to get the most from your purchase.

Errata

Although we have taken every care to ensure the accuracy of our content, mistakes do happen. If you find a mistake in one of our books—maybe a mistake in the text or the code—we would be grateful if you could report this to us. By doing so, you can save other readers from frustration and help us improve subsequent versions of this book. If you find any errata, please report them by visiting `http://www.packtpub.com/submit-errata`, selecting your book, clicking on the **Errata Submission Form** link, and entering the details of your errata. Once your errata are verified, your submission will be accepted and the errata will be uploaded to our website or added to any list of existing errata under the Errata section of that title.

To view the previously submitted errata, go to `https://www.packtpub.com/books/content/support` and enter the name of the book in the search field. The required information will appear under the **Errata** section.

Piracy

Piracy of copyrighted material on the Internet is an ongoing problem across all media. At Packt, we take the protection of our copyright and licenses very seriously. If you come across any illegal copies of our works in any form on the Internet, please provide us with the location address or website name immediately so that we can pursue a remedy.

Please contact us at `copyright@packtpub.com` with a link to the suspected pirated material.

We appreciate your help in protecting our authors and our ability to bring you valuable content.

Questions

If you have a problem with any aspect of this book, you can contact us at `questions@packtpub.com`, and we will do our best to address the problem.

1

Introduction to VMware Horizon 6

VMware Horizon 6 is the foundation of VMware's **End User Computing** (**EUC**) solution. It first came to the market 12 years ago, when server virtualization was becoming a more mature and prevalent technology and VMware applied the same principles that it used in server virtualization, and applied them to desktops, by virtualizing and centralizing the management and deployment.

Before we get into discussing product specifics, let's define what we mean when we talk about **Virtual Desktop Infrastructure** or **VDI**, and then take a brief stroll down memory lane and look at where and how this started.

What is Virtual Desktop Infrastructure?

When we talk about Virtual Desktop Infrastructure, or VDI as it's more commonly referred to, we typically describe a solution whereby the desktop operating system is hosted as a virtual machine running on a **hypervisor** that in turn, is part of the data center server infrastructure. This is also sometimes referred to as a **Hosted Virtual Desktop** (**HVD**). This is shown in the following diagram:

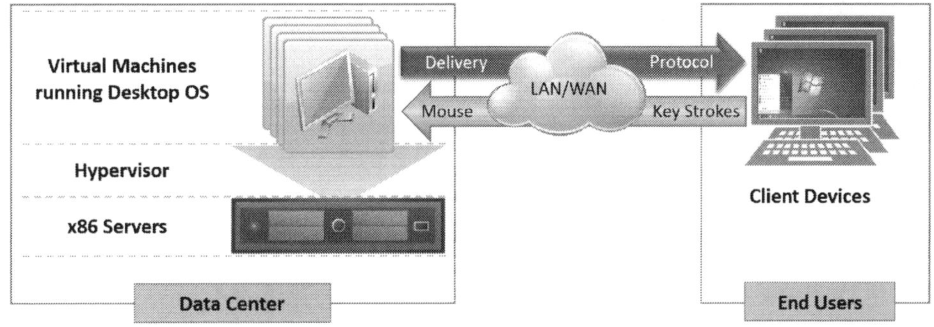

A user connects to their desktop remotely from a client device (a PC or mobile device) using an optimized delivery protocol and a connection broker. No data leaves the data center but screenshot updates are sent over the network. It's like watching a smart TV with the pictures broadcast to your television from the television studios, rather than the actors performing the show in your lounge, and you interact with the TV via the remote control.

From an architectural perspective, the virtual desktop typically gets built on-demand, bringing together the different components that make up a full desktop. The operating system, user profile, desktop policies, and applications are all treated as separate components, abstracted from the underlying machine, and are then delivered back together to create a user's desktop experience. This is sometimes referred to as a composite desktop and is shown in the following diagram:

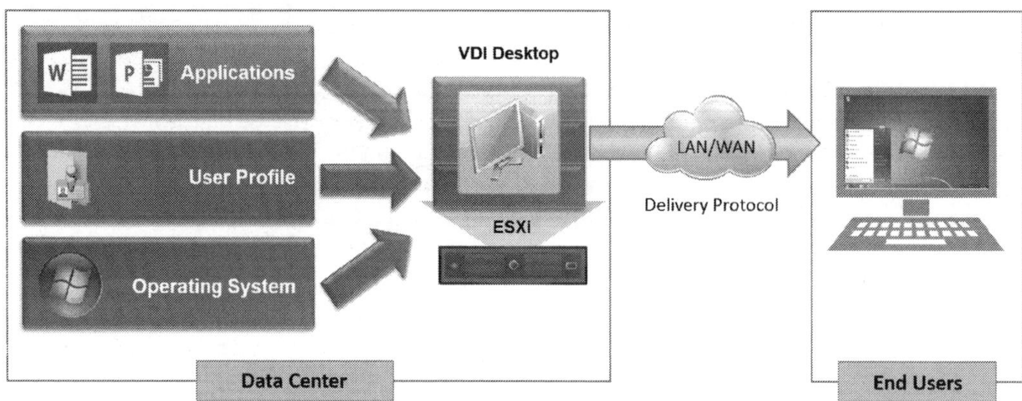

VDI sometimes get confused with **Server Based Computing** (**SBC**) or **Remote Desktop Services** (**RDS**). So what are the differences between these technologies and VDI (if any)?

Let's take SBC/RDS first, as these are the technologies that have probably been around the longest. In fact, you could probably trace these back as far as the 1950s, with the introduction of mainframe technology that was designed to deliver centralized computer power running the applications, with users connecting to the applications using a green-screen-type terminal, which was more or a less just a screen with a keyboard:

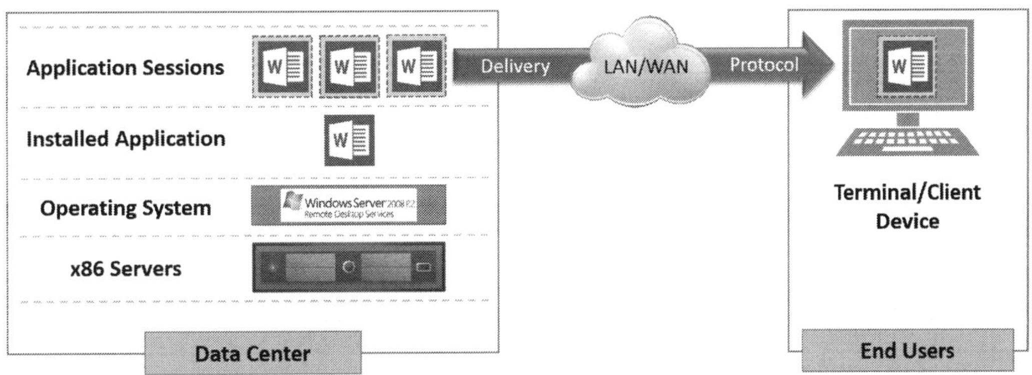

As shown in the previous diagram, SBC or RDS is seemingly not that different from VDI. You are connecting to an application that is installed on a server and running in a separate, protected session for each user who connects to it. The difference is that it is hosted on x86-based servers running a multi-user operating system instead of being a separate instance of the operating system. A user would connect to a session via a terminal or thin client. In fact, SBC is sometimes referred to as thin-client computing.

You could also be connecting to an operating system running in the same way, in that the operating system, like the applications described earlier, is also running in a separated, protected individual user session. This is the key difference between VDI and SBC. In an RDS environment, users are leveraging shared resources and single instances of applications, whereas, in a VDI environment, the resources are dedicated, and each user has their own instance of the operating system and applications.

The benefits of deploying VDI

By virtualizing your end-user desktop estate into a centrally managed service, you can deliver benefits not only to the IT administrators, but also to the users. Some of these are detailed as follows:

- **Security and compliance**: No data actually leaves the data center unless the IT department has specifically configured a policy to allow it, such as the ability to connect a USB pen drive. All that gets transmitted to the client devices are the screenshots of the virtual desktop, with keyboard and mouse interactions being sent back to the virtual desktop. It's a bit like having a remote control for your desktop.

- **Centralized and simplified management**: Centralized desktops equal centralized management. Now that the desktops are virtualized and hosted in the data center, it is much easier to perform tasks such as updating and patching an operating system or installing new applications. The virtual desktops are all created from a single gold image that is maintained and updated centrally so you don't have to visit every physical machine. You can simply update the image, recreate the virtual desktops with a few mouse clicks, and, hey presto, all users get the new updated version. You can also troubleshoot the environment more easily, without the need for a desk visit.
- **Flexibility and agility**: By having desktops hosted on a virtual platform, allows you to scale up and scale down much more easily, without the need to necessarily purchase more physical desktops. You could use thin-client devices or allow users to connect from their own devices. Environments can be spun up quickly, and also taken down just as easily, to accommodate seasonal workers or contractors working on specific projects. Users now have access to their virtual desktops wherever they are and no longer need to be in the office, at a desk, or have a PC to access their corporate desktop. They can continue to be productive even with inclement weather, traffic, or other events preventing them from getting to the office.
- **Mobile and BYOD from anywhere**: Virtual desktop clients enable mobile devices, tablets, and noncorporate-owned devices to connect securely to corporate desktops. Following the flexible working theme, users can now choose a device that suits them to access their corporate desktop. Whether it be a tablet, smart phone, or a non-Windows platform, users can still access their corporate desktop securely from remote locations.
- **Operational cost savings**: Implementing a virtual desktop environment and adopting operational best practices around image, patch, and profile management with centralized application deployment will result in saving **operational expenditure** (**OPEX**), compared to traditional desktop management. **Capital expenditures** (**CAPEX**) are still required to support the virtual desktop environment. One of the things I hear all the time is that deploying VDI will reduce costs. The thing to point out is that yes, it will reduce OPEX, but typically, the CAPEX at the beginning of a VDI project will be higher as you deploy the infrastructure. Overall, though, the costs will reduce through savings in the management of the solution, and you will not be caught in the typical three-year-PC-refresh cycle trap.

A brief history of VMware and VDI

The concept of virtualizing Windows desktops or the idea of VDI has been around since as early as 2002, when VMware customers started virtualizing desktop workloads and hosting them on VMware Server and **ESX** servers in the data center. As there was no concept of a connection broker at that time, customers simply connected using the RDP protocol directly to a dedicated desktop virtual machine running Windows XP.

It wasn't until 2005 that VMware first showed the idea of having the concept of a connection broker. By demonstrating a prototype at VMworld, VDI entered the limelight, raising the profile of the technology. It was also at the same event that companies such as Propero showed their version of a connection broker. Propero would later become the Horizon View Connection Server.

In early 2006, VMware launched the VDI alliances program with a number of technology vendors, such as Citrix, HP, IBM, Sun, and Wyse Technology, joining this program (`http://www.vmware.com/company/news/releases/vdi`).

By 2007, the prototype connection broker was introduced to customers to help with the development, before it was given to the VMware product organization to productize it and turn it into a real product. The released product was called **Virtual Desktop Manager 1.0 (VDM)**. The year 2007 was a busy year, and it also saw VMware acquire Propero for $25 million, to accelerate their connection broker development, leading to the VMworld announcement and release of VDM 2.0 in January 2008.

After the release of VDM 2.0 in early 2008, a second release came at the end 2008 along with a new name: VMware View 3.0. This was also the year that Citrix entered the VDI market.

VMware View 4.0 was released in 2009 and was the first version to include the PCoIP protocol from Teradici. PCoIP delivered a much richer user experience than RDP.

In 2010, VMware View 4.5 was released with new features such as local mode (offline desktops), PCoIP enhancements, Windows 7 support, and the ability to tier storage. This was also the year that VMware talked publically about the biggest VDI reference case to date with Bank of Tokyo Mitsubishi, who deployed 50,000 virtual desktop machines. You can read the case study at `http://tinyurl.com/oua28bh`.

The following year, in 2011, VMware View 4.6 was released with two notable new features. First was the iPad client, which allows a user to connect to their virtual desktop session on an iPad, using the PCoIP protocol. The second new feature was the PCoIP Secure Gateway function for the View Security Server, which allows users to connect to their virtual desktop without needing a VPN connection.

Later the same year, View 5.0 was released with more new features, aimed at improving the end-user experience, the key one being the introduction of Persona Management that allowed a user's profile to be independent from the virtual desktop. When a user logs in via the same profile to any virtual desktop, their profile is delivered on-demand. View 5.0 also introduced 3D graphic support using the latest vSphere 5.0 platform, as well as some major enhancements to the PCoIP protocol.

Although only a point release in May 2012, View 5.1 had a number of significant enhancements, especially around storage, with the introduction of the View Storage Accelerator, View Composer Array Integration, and the ability to scale the hosting infrastructure up to a 32-node cluster when using NFS storage. This version also added Radius two-factor authentication, improved USB device support, a standalone View Composer, and the ability support profile migration from XP to Windows 7 as well as from physical desktops to virtual desktops with Persona Management.

In March 2013, VMware View 5.2 was released, and to bring it in line with VMware's launch of the brand launch of Horizon (launched at the same time), it was renamed to Horizon View 5.2. In this release, there were a number of new features based on end-user experience, such as support for unified communications with Microsoft Lync 2013, hardware-accelerated graphics with **Virtual Shared Graphics Acceleration** (**vSGA**), and Windows 8 support. One of the biggest updates came in the form of a feature pack that allowed a user to access their desktop in an HTML 5 browser using the VMware Blast protocol.

A second release, later in 2013 with Horizon View 5.3, saw the introduction of **Virtual Dedicated Graphics Acceleration** (**vDGA**) that allowed a virtual desktop to have dedicated access to a GPU in the host. It is also the first release to support Windows Server 2008 R2 as the virtual desktop machine, meaning you can "skin" the operating system to look like a desktop. The main reason for this was that there is no **Service Provider License Agreement** (**SPLA**) for Windows 7, so the license agreement doesn't allow you to deploy Windows 7 as a virtual desktop until you purchase a Microsoft **Virtual Desktop Access** (**VDA**) license. In this model, you do not require a VDA license per user. The other advantage is that Windows Server 2008 Datacenter Edition allows you to have unlimited virtual machines. It's licensed on a per-CPU model. It's worth noting that we are running the Windows Server operating system as a replacement to the desktop operating system and not as a desktop session.

Finally, Horizon Mirage support was added to manage full clone desktops.

The final 5.x release arrived in 2014, with Horizon View 5.3.1 adding support for **Virtual SAN (VSAN)**. The timeline is shown pictorially in the following diagram:

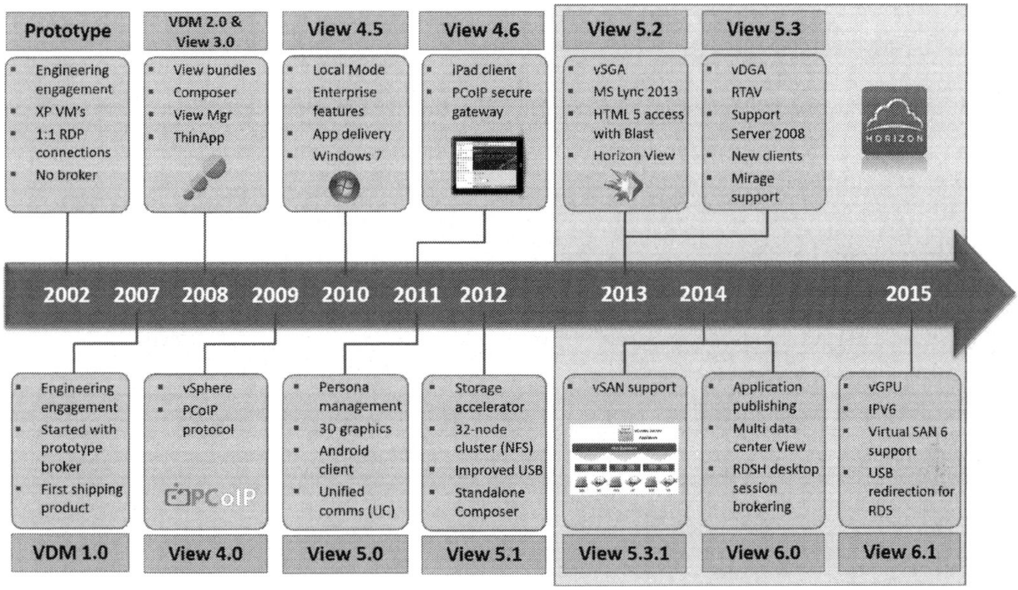

That brings us right up-to-date and to the latest version, VMware Horizon 6. In the next section, we will look at VMware Horizon 6 in more detail.

VMware Horizon 6

VMware Horizon 6 is the next generation of VMware's EUC vision and strategy to deliver desktop computing environments and publishing applications. In the previous sections, we have discussed some of the differences between VDI and SBC RDS, and the advantages of the two solutions. However, now Horizon 6 offers the ability to deliver VDI desktops, published applications, and session-based desktops from one platform.

Following on from the VMware acquisition of AirWatch, VMware now has two distinct brands:

- Horizon for desktop computing
- AirWatch for enterprise mobility management

This book focuses on the brand Horizon, the solution for the delivery of desktops and applications as centralized services.

VMware Horizon 6 was announced on April 9, 2014 with the latest 6.1 version being released on March 12, 2015 and comes packaged in three different editions.

In the next section, we will cover the different product editions for Horizon 6.

The VMware Horizon 6 product family

There are three different editions within the Horizon 6 portfolio, each with a different theme, with each successive edition adding to the previous edition. The themes are as follows:

- Application delivery
- Desktop management (physical and virtual) and infrastructure
- Management and automation

The three editions are described in the following section.

Horizon View Standard Edition

With Horizon View Standard Edition, you have the core VDI solution and all of its features, along with the licensing for the hosting infrastructure-vSphere and vCenter for desktop. Also included is ThinApp, VMware's application virtualization/packaging solution, that allows you to extract applications from the underlying OS and deliver them independently.

Horizon Advanced Edition

With Horizon Advanced Edition, the theme is all about application delivery and management. This is the first edition that includes application publishing as part of the View solution; this allows an application running on a Microsoft RDSH back end to be published via the VMware View client using the PCoIP protocol. This feature means that a user can now just have an individual application delivered to their client device rather than on a full-blown desktop.

The Advanced Edition also includes VMware Mirage to deliver centralized image management with the ability to manage View desktops and offline desktops delivered to a Mac or Windows laptop. For a detailed overview of VMware Mirage, you can read *VMware Horizon Mirage Essentials, Peter von Oven, Packt Publishing.*

Also included in this edition is an application catalog and a brokering functionality. The catalog allows users to select applications from a central catalog of entitled applications. The brokering feature is delivered using VMware Workspace and allows the brokering of ThinApp packages, SaaS-based applications, XenApp-published applications, and Microsoft Office 365.

The final component of Advanced Edition is the inclusion of VSAN for desktops.

Horizon Enterprise Edition

Horizon Enterprise Edition builds on the previous two versions and adds features to deliver operations management and automation functionality. This includes vRealize Operations for Horizon and vCenter Orchestrator with a plugin for desktops.

One of the biggest additions to the Enterprise Edition is AppVolumes, which gives you the ability to deliver just-in-time applications to a virtual desktop.

The table in the following screenshot details the features available in each edition:

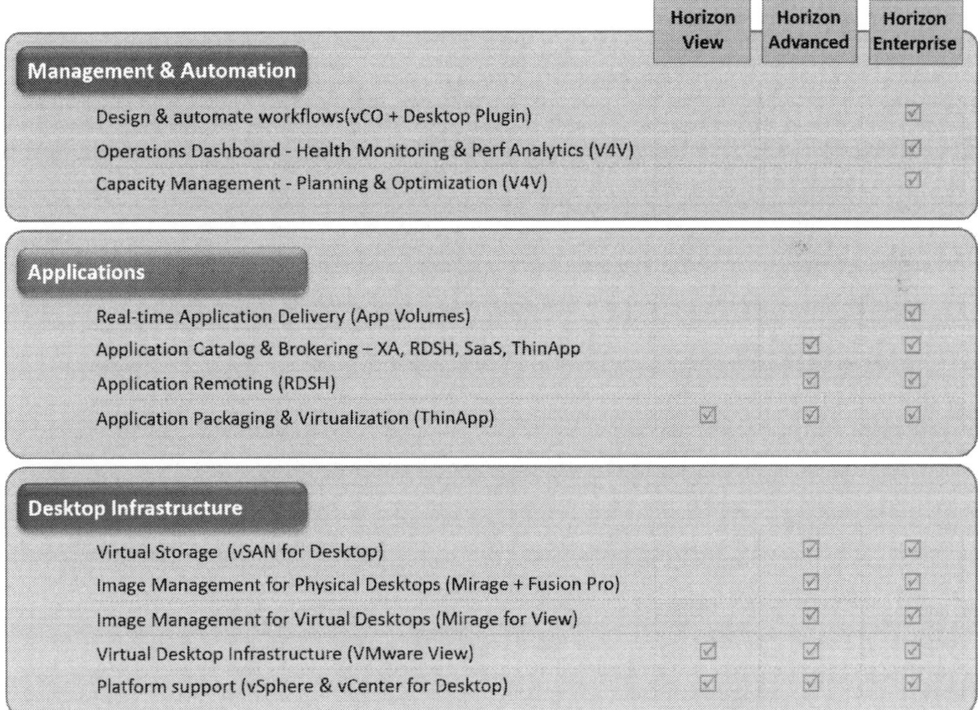

	Horizon View	Horizon Advanced	Horizon Enterprise
Management & Automation			
Design & automate workflows(vCO + Desktop Plugin)			☑
Operations Dashboard - Health Monitoring & Perf Analytics (V4V)			☑
Capacity Management - Planning & Optimization (V4V)			☑
Applications			
Real-time Application Delivery (App Volumes)			☑
Application Catalog & Brokering – XA, RDSH, SaaS, ThinApp		☑	☑
Application Remoting (RDSH)		☑	☑
Application Packaging & Virtualization (ThinApp)	☑	☑	☑
Desktop Infrastructure			
Virtual Storage (vSAN for Desktop)		☑	☑
Image Management for Physical Desktops (Mirage + Fusion Pro)		☑	☑
Image Management for Virtual Desktops (Mirage for View)		☑	☑
Virtual Desktop Infrastructure (VMware View)	☑	☑	☑
Platform support (vSphere & vCenter for Desktop)	☑	☑	☑

In this book, we will be covering all three of the Horizon 6 editions.

Summary

In this chapter, we had a look at what VDI is and covered some of the history of where it all began for VMware, demonstrating that VMware was, and still is, at the forefront of virtual desktop and application delivery.

We then went on to discuss the latest release, VMware Horizon 6.0, and the three different editions that are available, namely: Horizon View, Horizon Advanced, and Horizon Enterprise.

In the next chapter, we will take a deep dive into the technology of View and start looking at the architecture.

2

An Overview of Horizon View Architecture and its Components

In this chapter, we will introduce you to the architecture and architectural components that make up the core VMware Horizon solution, concentrating on the virtual desktop elements of Horizon with Horizon View Standard.

This chapter will cover the core Horizon View functionality of brokering virtual desktop machines that are hosted on the VMware vSphere platform. Application publishing will be covered in *Chapter 10, Delivering Remote Applications with Horizon Advanced*, and session-based desktops will be covered in *Chapter 11, Delivering Session-based Desktops with Horizon View*.

In this chapter, we will discuss the role of each of the Horizon View components and explain how they fit into the overall infrastructure and the benefits they bring, followed by a deep-dive into how Horizon View works. We will also cover some of the third-party technologies that integrate into Horizon View, such as antivirus solutions, storage acceleration technologies, and high-end graphics solutions that help deliver a complete solution.

After reading this chapter, you will be able to describe each of the components and what part they play within the solution. We will also look at some of the best practices and individual use cases for some of the optional components.

Introducing the key Horizon components

To start with, we are going to introduce, at a high level, the main components that make up the Horizon View product. In the following chapters, we will discuss these in a lot more detail, along with other integrated components and complementary technologies.

All of the VMware Horizon components described are included as part of the licensed product, and the features that are available to you depend on whether you have the View Standard Edition, the Advanced Edition, or the Enterprise Edition.

Horizon licensing also includes ESXi and vCenter licensing to support the ability to deploy the core hosting infrastructure. You can deploy as many ESXi hosts and vCenter Servers as you require to host the desktop infrastructure.

The key elements of Horizon View are outlined in the following diagram:

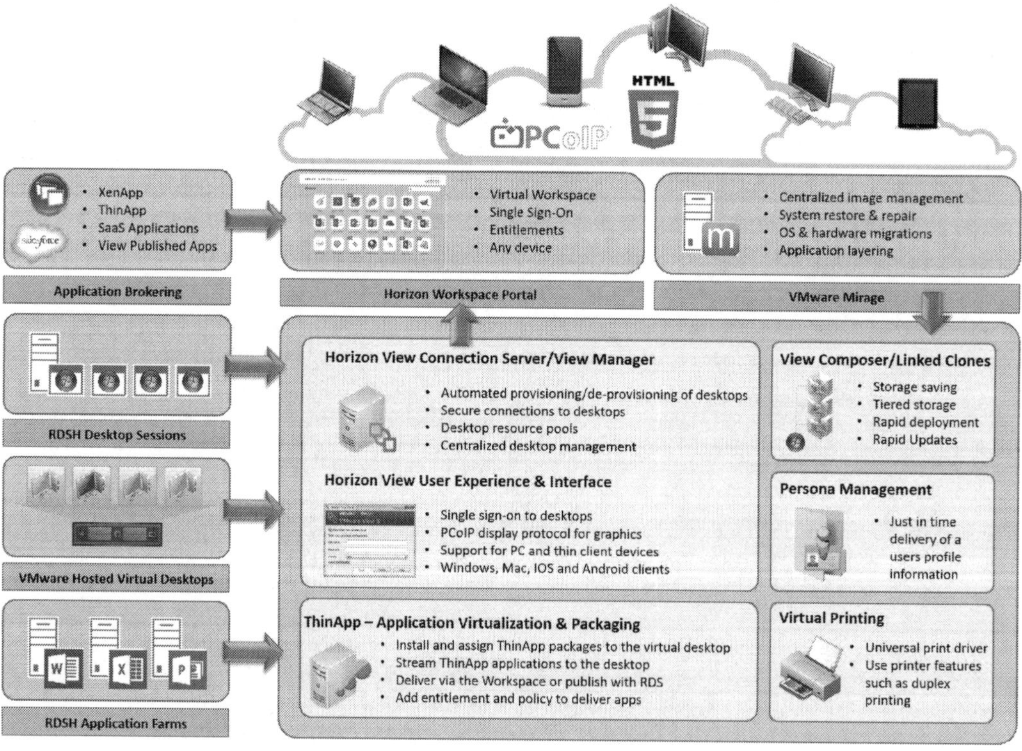

In the next section, we are going to start drilling down deeper into the architecture of how these high-level components fit together and how they work.

A high-level architectural overview

In this chapter, we will cover the core Horizon View functionality of brokering virtual desktop machines that are hosted on the VMware vSphere platform. Application publishing will be covered in *Chapter 10, Delivering Remote Applications with Horizon Advanced*, and session-based desktops will be covered in *Chapter 11, Delivering Session-based Desktops with Horizon View*.

The Horizon View architecture is pretty straightforward to understand, as its foundations lie in the standard VMware vSphere products (ESXi and vCenter). So, if you have the necessary skills and experience of working with this platform, then you are already halfway there.

Horizon View builds on the vSphere infrastructure, taking advantage of some of the features of the ESX hypervisor and vCenter Server. Horizon View requires adding a number of virtual machines to perform the various View roles and functions. An overview of the View architecture is shown in the following diagram:

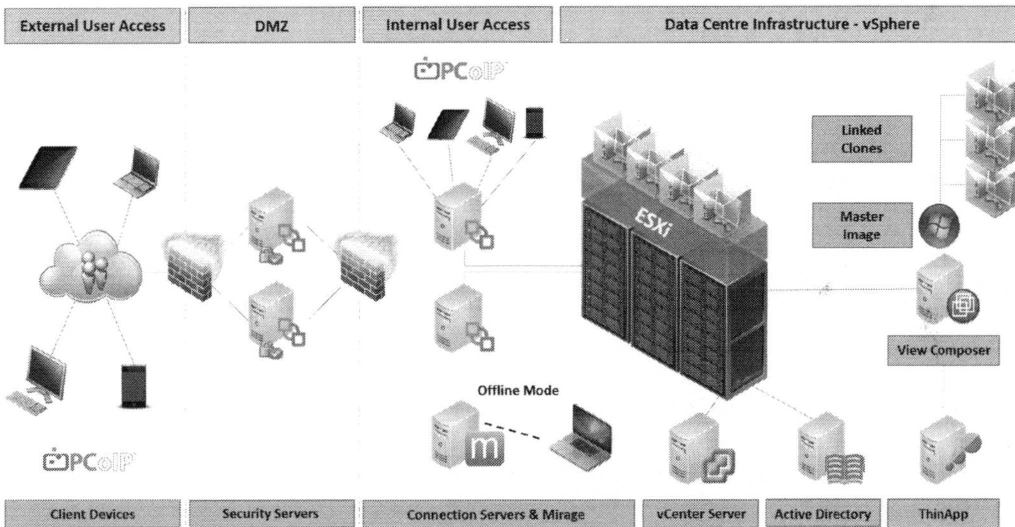

View components run as applications that are installed on the Microsoft Windows Server operating system, so they could actually run on physical hardware as well. However, there are a great number of benefits available when you run them as virtual machines, such as delivering HA and DR, as well as the typical cost savings that can be achieved through virtualization.

The following sections will cover each of these roles/components of the View architecture in greater detail.

The Horizon View Connection Server

The Horizon View Connection Server, sometimes referred to as Connection Broker or View Manager, is the central component of the View infrastructure. Its primary role is to connect a user to their virtual desktop by means of performing user authentication and then delivering the appropriate desktop resources based on the user's profile and user entitlement. When logging on to your virtual desktop, it is the Connection Server that you are communicating with.

How does the Connection Server work?

A user typically connects to their virtual desktop from their device by launching the View Client. We will discuss browser-based access to a virtual desktop later on in this chapter.

Once the View Client has launched, the user enters the address details of the View Connection Server, which in turn responds by asking them to provide their network login details (their **Active Directory** (**AD**) domain username and password).

It's worth noting that Horizon View now supports different AD function levels. These are detailed in the following screenshot:

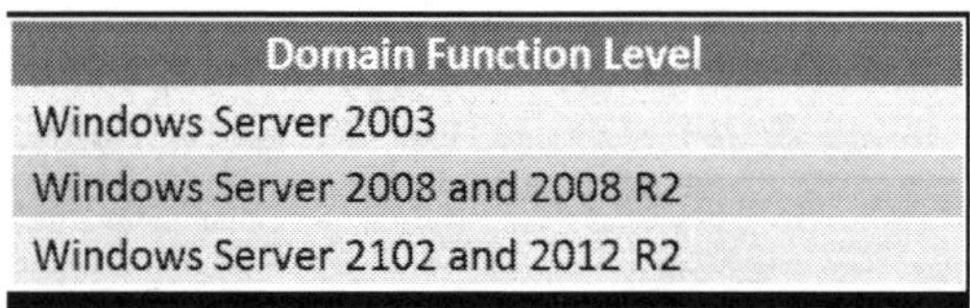

Domain Function Level
Windows Server 2003
Windows Server 2008 and 2008 R2
Windows Server 2102 and 2012 R2

Based on their entitlements, these credentials are authenticated with AD and, if successful, the user is able to continue the logon process. Depending on what they are entitled to, the user could see a launch screen that displays a number of different desktop shortcuts available for login. These desktops represent the desktop pools that the user has been entitled to use. A pool is basically a collection of virtual desktops; for example, it could be a pool for the marketing department where the desktops contain specific applications/software for that department. Desktop pools are discussed in *Chapter 7, Managing and Configuring Desktop Pools*.

Once authenticated, the View Manager makes a call to the vCenter Server to create a virtual desktop machine and then vCenter makes a call to View Composer (if you are using linked clones) to start the build process of the virtual desktop if there is not one already available. Once built, the virtual desktop is displayed/delivered within the View Client window, using the chosen display protocol (PCoIP or RDP).

The process is described in detail in the following diagram:

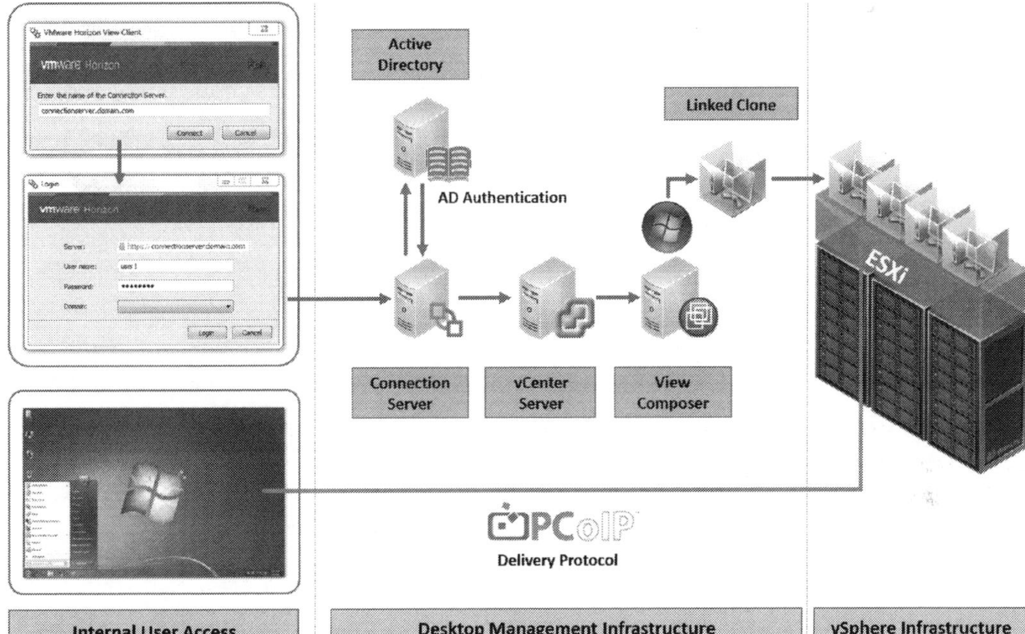

There are other ways to deploy VDI solutions that do not require a connection broker, and allow a user to connect directly to a virtual desktop; fact, there might be a specific use case for doing this such as having a large number of branches, where having local infrastructure allows trading to continue in the event of a WAN outage or poor network communication with the branch.

VMware has a solution for what's referred to as a "Brokerless View": the VMware Horizon View Agent Direct-Connection Plugin. However, don't forget that, in a Horizon View environment, the View Connection Server provides greater functionality and does much more than just connecting users to desktops, as we will see later in this chapter.

The Horizon View Connection Server runs as an application on a Windows Server that, which in turn, could either be a physical or a virtual machine. Running as a virtual machine has many advantages; for example, it means that you can easily add high-availability features, which are key if you think about them, as you could potentially have hundreds of virtual user desktops running on a single-host server.

Along with managing the connections for the users, the Connection Server also works with vCenter Server to manage the virtual desktop machines. For example, when using linked clones and powering on virtual desktops, these tasks might be initiated by the Connection Server, but they are executed at the vCenter Server level.

Minimum requirements for the Connection Server

To install the View Connection Server, you need to meet the following minimum requirements to run on physical or virtual machines:

- **Hardware requirements**: The following screenshot shows the hardware required:

Hardware Requirements	Required	Recommended
Processor	Pentium IV 2.0GHz or higher	4 CPU's
Networking	1 or more 10/100Mbps NICs	1Gbps NIC
Memory	4GB or higher	10 GB for 50 or more desktops

- **Supported operating systems**: The View Connection Server must be installed on one of the following operating systems:

Operating System	Version	Edition
Windows Server 2008 R2	64-Bit	Standard & Enterprise
Windows Server 2008 R2 SP1	64-Bit	Standard & Enterprise
Windows Server 2012 R2	62-Bit	Standard & Enterprise

The Horizon View Security Server

Horizon View Security Server is another instance and another version of the View Connection Server but, this time, it sits within your DMZ so that you can allow end users to securely connect to their virtual desktop machine from an external network or the Internet. As you will see in *Chapter 4, Installing and Configuring Horizon View,* the installation process is almost the same as the View Connection Server but, here the Security Server role is selected from the drop-down menu of the different roles.

You cannot install the View Security Server on the same machine that is already running as a View Connection Server or any of the other Horizon View components.

How does the Security Server work?

The user login process at the start is the same as when using a View Connection Server for internal access but, now we have added an extra security layer with the Security Server. The idea is that users can access their desktop externally without unnecessarily needing a VPN on the network first.

The process is described in detail in the following diagram:

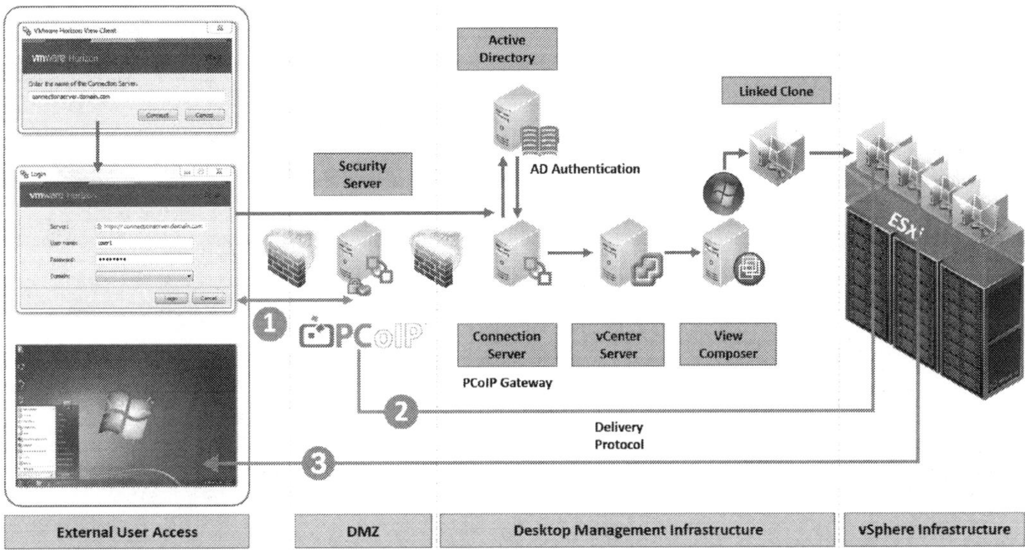

The Security Server is paired with a View Connection Server that is configured by the use of a one-time password during installation. It's a bit like pairing your phone's Bluetooth with the hands-free kit in your car. We will cover this in the *Installing of the Security Server* section in *Chapter 4, Installing and Configuring Horizon View.*

When the user logs in from the View Client, they access the View Connection Server, which in turn authenticates the user against AD. If the View Connection Server is configured as a PCoIP gateway, then it will pass the connection and addressing information to the View Client. This connection information will allow the View Client to connect to the View Security Server using PCoIP. This is shown in the diagram by the green arrow (**1**). The View Security Server will then forward the PCoIP connection to the virtual desktop machine, (**2**) creating the connection for the user. The virtual desktop machine is displayed/delivered within the View Client window (**3**) using the chosen display protocol (PCoIP or RDP).

The Horizon View Replica Server

The Horizon View Replica Server, as the name suggests, is a replica or copy of a View Connection Server that is used to enable high availability to your Horizon View environment. Having a replica of your View Connection Server means that, if the Connection Server fails, users are still able to connect to their virtual desktop machines.

You will need to change the IP address or update the DNS record to match this server if you are not using a load balancer.

As with the View Security Server, you will see, in *Chapter 4, Installing and Configuring Horizon View*, that the installation process is again almost the same as the View Connection Server but, this time, you select the Replica Server role from the drop-down menu with the different role options.

How does the Replica Server work?

So, the first question is, what actually gets replicated? The View Connection Broker stores all its information relating to the end users, desktop pools, virtual desktop machines, and other View-related objects, in an **Active Directory Application Mode** (**ADAM**) database. Then, using the **Lightweight Directory Access Protocol** (**LDAP**) (it uses a method similar to what AD uses for replication), this View information gets copied from the original View Connection Server to the Replica Server.

As both, the Connection Server and the Replica Server are now identical to each other, if your Connection Server fails, then you essentially have a backup that steps in and takes over so that end users can still continue to connect to their virtual desktop machines.

Just like with the other components, you cannot install the Replica Server role on the same machine that is running as a View Connection Server or any of the other Horizon View components.

Persistent or nonpersistent desktops

In this section, we are going to talk about the different types of desktop assignments that can be deployed with Horizon View; these could also potentially have an impact on storage requirements (covered in the next section), and also the way in which desktops are provisioned to the end users.

One of the questions that always get asked is about having a dedicated (persistent) or a floating desktop assignment (nonpersistent). Desktops can either be individual virtual machines, which are dedicated to a user on a 1:1 basis (as we have in a physical desktop deployment, where each user effectively has their own desktop), or a user has a new, vanilla desktop that gets provisioned, personalized, and then assigned at the time of login and can be chosen at random from a pool of available desktops. If you remember, back in *Chapter 1, Introduction to VMware Horizon 6*, we talked about building the composite desktop. This is the model that is used to build the user's desktop. The two options are described in more detail as follows:

- **Persistent desktop**: Users are allocated a desktop that retains all of their documents, applications, and settings between sessions. The desktop is statically assigned the first time that the user connects and is then used for all subsequent sessions. No other user is permitted access to the desktop.
- **Nonpersistent desktop**: Users might be connected to different desktops from the pool, each time that they connect. Environmental or user data does not persist between sessions and is delivered as the user logs on to their desktop. The desktop is refreshed or reset when the user logs off.

In most use cases, a nonpersistent configuration is the best option, the key reason is that, in this model, you don't need to build all the desktops upfront for each user. You only need to power on a virtual desktop as and when it's required. All users start with the same basic desktop, which then gets personalized before delivery. This helps with concurrency rates. For example, you might have 5,000 people in your organization, but only 2,000 ever login at the same time; therefore, you only need to have 2,000 virtual desktops available. Otherwise, you would have to build a desktop for each one of the 5,000 users that might ever log in, resulting in more server infrastructure and certainly a lot more storage capacity. We will talk about storage in the next section.

The other thing that we often see some confusion over is the difference between dedicated and floating desktops, and how linked clones fit in. Just to make it clear, linked clones and full clones are not what we are talking about when we refer to dedicated and floating desktops. Cloning operations refer to how a desktop is built, whereas the terms persistent and nonpersistent refer to how a desktop is assigned to a user.

Dedicated and floating desktops are purely about user assignment and whether they have a dedicated desktop or one allocated from a pool on-demand. Linked clones and full clones are features of Horizon View, which uses View Composer to create a desktop image for each user from a master or parent image. This means, regardless of having a floating or dedicated desktop assignment, the virtual desktop machine could still be a linked or full clone.

So, here's a summary of the benefits:

- It is operationally efficient. All users start from a single or smaller number of desktop images. Organizations reduce the amount of image and patch management.
- It is efficient storage-wise. The amount of storage required to host the nonpersistent desktop images will be smaller than keeping separate instances of unique user desktops.

In the next section, we are going to cover an in-depth overview of Horizon View Composer and linked clones, and the advantages the technology delivers.

Horizon View Composer and linked clones

One of the main reasons a virtual desktop project fails to deliver, or doesn't even get out of the starting blocks, is heavy infrastructure down to storage requirements. The storage requirements are often seen as a huge cost burden, which can be attributed to the fact that people are approaching this in the same way they would approach a physical desktop environment's requirements. This would mean that each user gets their own dedicated virtual desktop and the hard disk space that comes with it, albeit a virtual disk; this then gets scaled out for the entire user population, so each user is allocated a virtual desktop with some storage.

Let's take an example. If you had 1,000 users and allocated 250 GB per user's desktop, you would need *1,000 * 250 GB = 2.5 TB* for the virtual desktop environment. That's a lot of storage just for desktops and could result in significant infrastructure costs that could possibly mean that the cost to deploy this amount of storage in the data center would render the project cost-in effective, compared to physical desktop deployments.

A new approach to deploying storage for a virtual desktop environment is needed and this is where linked clone technology comes into play. In a nutshell, linked clones are designed to reduce the amount of disk space required, and to simplify the deployment and management of images to multiple virtual desktop machines—a centralized and much easier process.

Linked clone technology

Starting at a high level, a clone is a copy of an existing or parent virtual machine. This parent **virtual machine (VM)** is typically your gold build from which you want to create new virtual desktop machines. When a clone is created, it becomes a separate, new virtual desktop machine with its own unique identity. This process is not unique to Horizon View; it's actually a function of vSphere and vCenter, and in the case of Horizon View, we add in another component, View Composer, to manage the desktop images. There are two types of clones that we can deploy, a full clone or a linked clone. We will explain the difference in the next sections.

Full clones

As the name implies, a full clone disk is an exact, full-sized copy of the parent machine. Once the clone has been created, the virtual desktop machine is unique, with its own identity, and has no links back to the parent virtual machine from which it was cloned. It can operate as a fully independent virtual desktop in its own right and is not reliant on its parent virtual machine.

However, as it is a full-sized copy, be aware that it will take up the same amount of storage as its parent virtual machine, which leads back to our discussion earlier in this chapter about storage capacity requirements. Using a full clone will require larger amounts of storage capacity and will possibly lead to higher infrastructure costs.

Before you completely dismiss the idea of using full clone virtual desktop machines, there are some use cases that rely on this model. For example, if you use VMware Mirage to deliver a base layer or application layer, it only works today with full clones, dedicated Horizon View virtual desktop machines.

If you have software developers, then they probably need to install specialist tools and a trust code onto a desktop, and therefore, need to "own" their desktop. Or perhaps, the applications that you run in your environment need a dedicated desktop due to the way the applications are licensed.

Linked clones

Having now discussed full clones, we are going to talk about deploying virtual desktop machines with linked clones.

In a linked clone deployment, a delta disk is created and then used by the virtual desktop machine to store the data differences between its own operating system and the operating system of its parent virtual desktop machine. Unlike the full clone method, the linked clone is not a full copy of the virtual disk. The term linked clone refers to the fact that the linked clone will always look to its parent in order to operate, as it continues to read from the replica disk. Basically, the replica is a copy of a snapshot of the parent virtual desktop machine.

The linked clone itself could potentially grow to the same size as the replica disk if you allow it to. However, you can set limits on how big it can grow, and should it start to get too big, then you can refresh the virtual desktops that are linked to it. This essentially starts the cloning process again from the initial snapshot.

Immediately after a linked clone virtual desktop is deployed, the difference between the parent virtual machine and the newly created virtual desktop machine is extremely small and therefore reduces the storage capacity requirements compared to that of a full clone. This is how linked clones are more space-efficient than their full clone brothers.

The underlying technology behind linked clones is more like a snapshot than a clone, but with one key difference: View Composer. With View Composer, you can have more than one active snapshot linked to the parent virtual machine disk. This allows you to create multiple virtual desktop images from just one parent.

Best practice would be to deploy an environment with linked clones so as to reduce the storage requirements. However, as we previously mentioned, there are some use cases where you will need to use full clones.

One thing to be aware of, which still relates to the storage, is that, rather than capacity, we are now talking about performance. All linked clone virtual desktops are going to be reading from one replica and therefore, will drive a high number of **Input /Output Operations Per Second (IOPS)** on the storage where the replica lives. Depending on your desktop pool design, you are fairly likely to have more than one replica, as you would typically have more than one data store. This in turn depends on the number of users who will drive the design of the solution. We will cover this in detail in *Chapter 3, Design and Deployment Considerations*.

In Horizon View, you are able to choose the location where the replica lives. One of the recommendations is that the replica should sit on fast storage such as a local SSD.

Alternative solutions would be to deploy some form of storage acceleration technology to drive the IOPS. Horizon View also has its own integrated solution called **View Storage Accelerator** (**VSA**) or **Content Based Read Cache** (**CBRC**). This feature allows you to allocate up to 2 GB of memory from the underlying ESXi host server that can be used as a cache for the most commonly read blocks. As we are talking about booting up desktop operating systems, the same blocks are required; as these can be retrieved from memory, the process is accelerated.

Another solution is **View Composer Array Integration** (**VCAI**), which allows the process of building linked clones to be offloaded to the storage array and its native snapshot mechanism rather than taking CPU cycles from the host server.

There are also a number of other third-party solutions that resolve the storage performance bottleneck, such as Atlantis Computing and their ILIO product, Nutanix, Nimble, and Tintri to name a few others. In the next section, we will take a deeper look at how linked clones work.

How do linked clones work?

The first step is to create your master virtual desktop machine image, which should contain not only the operating system, core applications, and settings, but also the Horizon View Agent components. This virtual desktop machine will become your parent VM or your gold image. We will cover the build process in *Chapter 6, Building and Optimizing the Desktop Operating System*.

This image can now be used as a template to create any new subsequent virtual desktop machines.

> The gold image or parent image cannot be a VM template.

An overview of the linked clone process is shown in the following diagram:

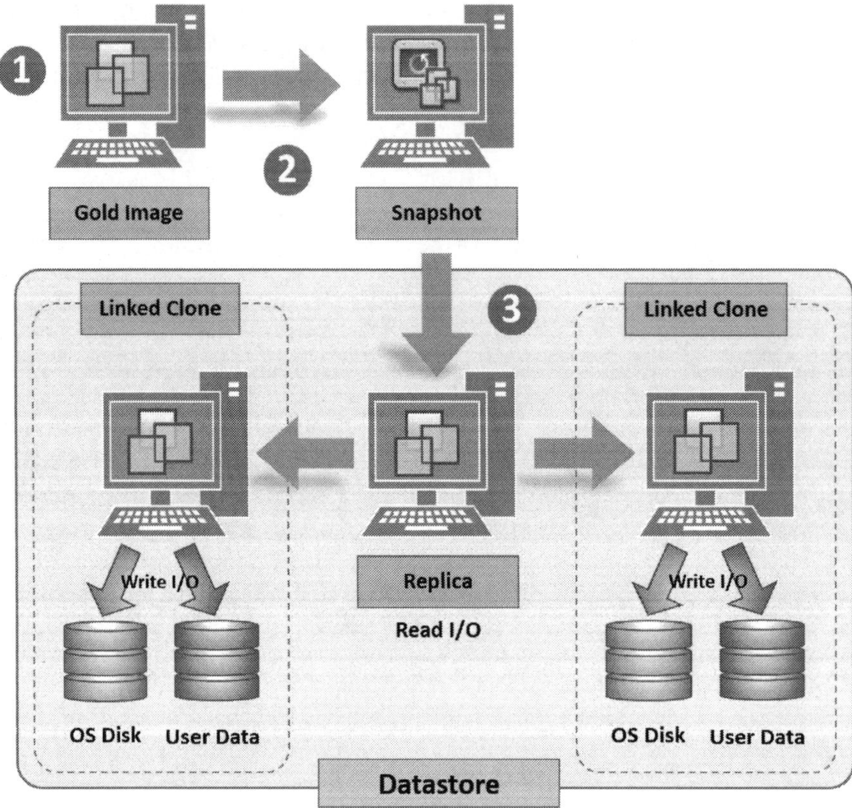

Once you have created the parent virtual desktop or gold image (**1**), you then take a snapshot (**2**). When you create your desktop pool, this snapshot is selected and will become the replica (**3**) and will be set to be read-only. Each virtual desktop is linked back to this replica; hence the term linked clone. When you start creating your virtual desktops, you create linked clones that are unique copies for each user.

> Try not to create too many snapshots for your parent VM. I would recommend having just a handful, otherwise this could impact the performance of your desktops and make it a little harder to know which snapshot is which.

What does View Composer build?

During the image building process, and once the replica disk has been created, View Composer creates a number of other virtual disks, including the linked clone (operating system disk) itself. These are described in the following sections.

Linked clone disk

Not wanting to state the obvious, the main disk that gets created is the linked clone disk itself. This linked clone disk is basically an empty virtual disk container that is attached to the virtual desktop machine as the user logs in and the desktop starts up.

This disk will start off small in size, but will grow over time, depending on the block changes that are requested from the replica disk by the virtual desktop machine's operating system. These block changes are stored in the linked clone disk, and this disk is sometimes referred to as the delta disk, or differential disk, due to the fact that it stores all the delta changes that the desktop operating system requests from the parent VM. As mentioned before, the linked clone disk can grow to the maximum size, equal to the parent VM but, following best practice, you would never let this happen. Typically, you can expect the linked clone disk to only increase to a few hundred MBs. We will cover this in the Linked clone processes section later.

The replica disk is set as read-only and is used as the primary disk. Any writes and/ or block changes that are requested by the virtual desktop are written/read directly from the linked clone disk.

It is a recommended best practice to allocate tier-1 storage, such as local SSD drives, to host the replica, as all virtual desktops in the cluster will be referencing this single read-only VMDK file as their base image. Keeping it high in the stack improves performance, by reducing the overall storage IOPS required in a VDI workload. As we mentioned at the start of this section, storage costs are seen as being expensive for VDI. Linked clones reduce the burden of storage capacity but they do drive the requirement to derive a huge amount of IOPS from a single LUN.

Persistent disk or user data disk

The persistent disk feature of View Composer allows you to configure a separate disk that contains just the user data and user settings, and not the operating system. This allows any user data to be preserved when you update or make changes to the operating system disk, such as a recompose action.

It's worth noting that the persistent disk is referenced by the VM name and not username, so bear this in mind if you want to attach the disk to another VM.

This disk is also used to store the user's profile. With this in mind, you need to size it accordingly, ensuring that it is large enough to store any user profile type data such as Virtual Desktop Assessments. This is another reason why it's a good idea to run a desktop assessment, as we will cover in *Chapter 3, Design and Deployment Considerations*, so that you can build up a picture of what your user desktop profiles and user data requirements look like.

Disposable disk

With the disposable disk option, Horizon View creates what is effectively a temporary disk that gets deleted every time the user powers off their virtual desktop machine.

If you think about how the Windows desktop operating system operates and the files it creates, there are several files that are used on a temporary basis. Files such as Temporary Internet files or the Windows pagefile are two such examples. As these are only temporary files, why would you want to keep them? With Horizon View, these type of files are redirected to the disposable disk and then deleted when the VM is powered off.

Horizon View provides the option to have a disposable disk for each virtual desktop. This disposable disk is used to contain temporary files that will get deleted when the virtual desktop is powered off. These are files that you don't want to store on the main operating system disk as they would consume unnecessary disk space. For example, files on the disposable disk are things such as the pagefile, Windows system temporary files, and VMware log files.

Note that here we are talking about temporary system files and not user files. A user's temporary files are still stored on the user data disk so that they can be preserved. Many applications use the Windows temp folder to store installation CAB files, which can be referenced post-installation. Having said that, you might want to delete the temporary user data to reduce the desktop image size, in which case you could ensure that the user's temporary files are directed to the disposable disk.

Internal disk

Finally, we have the internal disk. The internal disk is used to store important configuration information, such as the computer account password, that would be needed to join the virtual desktop machine back to the domain if you refreshed the linked clones. It is also used to store Sysprep and Quickprep configurations details. We will cover Quickprep in *Chapter 6, Building and Optimizing the Desktop Operating System.*

In terms of disk space, the internal disk is relatively small, averaging around 20 MB. By default, the user will not see this disk from their Windows Explorer, as it contains important configuration information that you wouldn't want them to delete.

Understanding the linked clone process

There are several complex steps performed by View Composer and View Manager and that occur when a user launches a virtual desktop session. So, what's the process to build a linked clone desktop, and what goes on behind the scenes? When a user logs into Horizon View and requests a desktop, View Manager, using vCenter and View Composer, will create a virtual desktop machine. This process is described in the following sections.

Creating and provisioning a new desktop

An entry for the virtual desktop machine is created in the **Active Directory Application Mode** (**ADAM**) database before it is put into provisioning mode:

1. The linked clone virtual desktop machine is created by View Composer.
2. A machine account created in AD with a randomly generated password.
3. View Composer checks for a replica disk and creates one if one does not already exist.
4. A linked clone is created by the vCenter Server API call from View Composer.
5. An internal disk is created to store the configuration information and machine account password.

Customizing the desktop

Now that you have a newly created, linked clone virtual desktop machine, the next phase is to customize it.

The customization steps are as follows:

1. The virtual desktop machine is switched to customization mode.
2. The virtual desktop machine is customized by vCenter Server using the `customizeVM_Task` command and is joined to the domain with the information you entered in the View Manager console.
3. The linked clone virtual desktop is powered on.
4. The View Composer Agent on the linked clone virtual desktop machine starts up for the first time and joins the machine to the domain, using the `NetJoinDomain` command and the machine account password that was created on the internal disk.
5. The linked clone virtual desktop machine is now Sysprep'd. Once complete, View Composer tells View Agent that customization has finished, and View Agent tells View Manager that the customization process has finished.
6. The linked clone virtual desktop machine is powered off and a snapshot is taken.
7. The linked clone virtual desktop machine is marked as provisioned and is now available for use.

When a linked clone virtual desktop machine is powered on with the View Composer Agent running, the agent tracks any changes that are made to the machine account password. Any changes will be updated and stored on the internal disk.

In many AD environments, the machine account password is changed periodically. If the View Composer Agent detects a password change, it updates the machine account password on the internal disk that was created with the linked clone.

This is important, as a the linked clone virtual desktop machine is reverted to the snapshot taken after the customization during a refresh operation. For example, the agent will be able to reset the machine account password to the latest one.

The linked clone process is depicted in the following diagram:

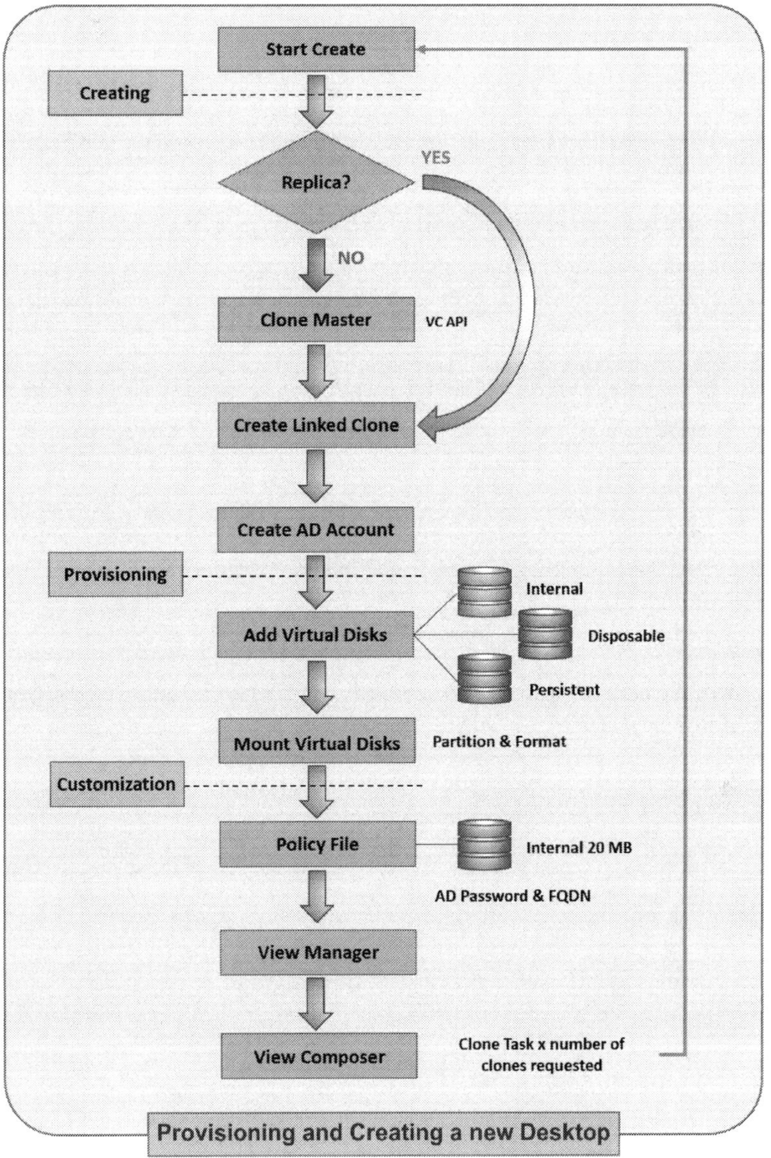

Additional features and functions of linked clones

There are a number of other management functions that you can perform on a linked clone disk from View Composer; these are outlined in this section and are needed in order to deliver the ongoing management of the virtual desktop machines.

Recomposing a linked clone

Recomposing a linked clone virtual desktop machine or desktop pool allows you to perform updates to the operating system disk, such as updating the image with the latest patches, or software updates. You can only perform updates on the same version of an operating system, so you cannot use the recompose feature to migrate from one operating system to another, such as going from Windows XP to Windows 7.

As we covered in the *What does View Composer Build?* section, we have separate disks for items such as user's data. These disks are not affected during a recompose operation, so all user-specific data on them is preserved.

When you initiate the recompose operation, View Composer essentially starts the linked clone building process over again; thus, a new operating system disk is created, which then gets customized and a snapshot, such as the ones shown in the preceding sections, is taken.

During the recompose operation, the MAC addresses of the network interface and the Windows SID are not preserved. There are some management tools and security-type solutions that might not work due to this change. However, the UUID will remain the same.

The recompose process is described in the following steps:

1. View Manager puts the linked clone into maintenance mode.
2. View Manager calls the View Composer resync API for the linked clones being recomposed, directing View Composer to use the new base image and the snapshot.
3. If there isn't a replica for the base image and snapshot yet, in the target datastore for the linked clone, View Composer creates the replica in the target datastore (unless a separate datastore is being used for replicas, in which case a replica is created in the replica datastore).

4. View Composer destroys the current OS disk for the linked clone and creates a new OS disk linked to the new replica.
5. The rest of the recompose cycle is identical to the customization phase of the provisioning and customization cycles.

The following diagram shows a graphical representation of the recompose process. Before the process begins, the first thing you need to do is update your **Gold Image** (**1**) with the patch updates or new applications you want to deploy as the virtual desktops.

As described in the preceding steps, the snapshot is then taken (**2**) to create the new replica, **Replica V2** (**3**). The existing OS disk is destroyed, but the **User Data** disk (**4**) is maintained during the recompose process:

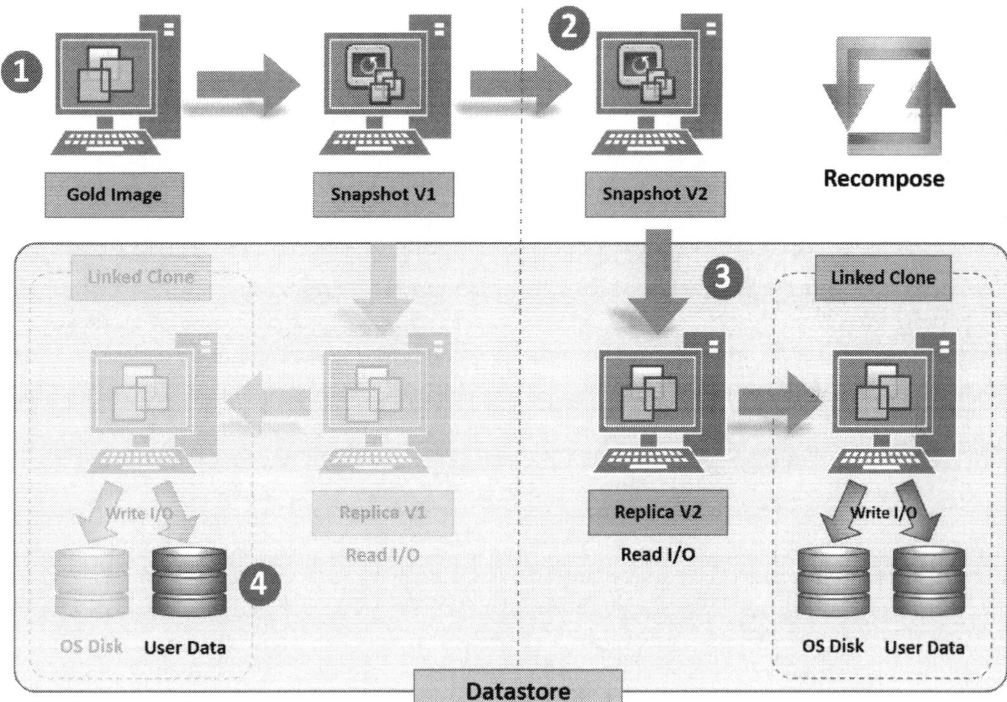

Refreshing a linked clone

By carrying out a refresh of the linked clone virtual desktop, you are effectively reverting it to its initial state, when its original snapshot was taken after it had completed the customization phase. This process only applies to the operating system disk and no other disks are affected.

An example use case for refresh operations would be recomposing a nonpersistent desktop two hours after logoff, to return it to its original state and make it available for the next user.

The refresh process performs the following tasks:

1. The linked clone virtual desktop is switched into maintenance mode.
2. View Manager reverts the linked clone virtual desktop to the snapshot taken after customization was completed: - `vdm-initial-checkpoint`.
3. The linked clone virtual desktop starts up, and View Composer Agent detects if the machine account password needs to be updated. If not, and the password on the internal disk is newer than the one in the registry, the agent will update the machine account password using the one on the internal disk.

One of the reasons why you would perform a refresh operation is if the linked clone OS disk starts to become bloated. As we previously discussed, the OS-linked clone disk could grow to the full size of its parent image. This means it would be taking up more disk space than is really necessary, which kind of defeats the objective of linked clones. The refresh operation effectively resets the linked clone to a small delta between it and its parent image.

The following diagram shows a representation of the refresh operation:

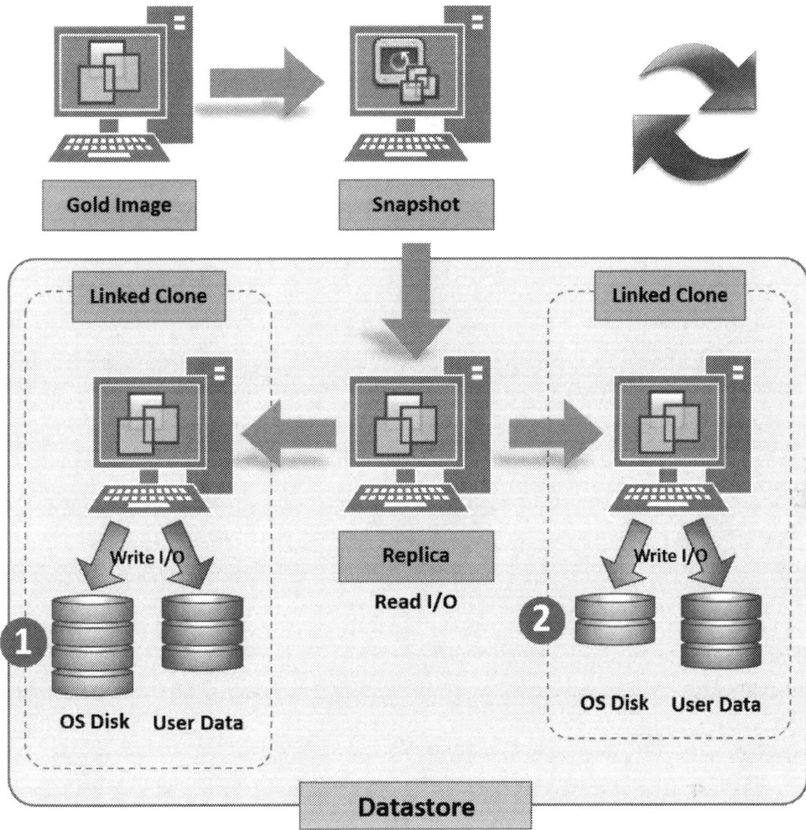

The linked clone on the left-hand side of the diagram (**1**) has started to grow in size. Refreshing reverts it back to the snapshot as if it was a new virtual desktop, as shown on the right-hand side of the diagram (**2**).

Rebalancing operations with View Composer

The rebalance operation in View Composer is used to evenly distribute the linked clone virtual desktop machines across multiple datastores in your environment. You would perform this task in the event that one of your datastores was becoming full while others have ample free space. It might also help with the performance of that particular datastore. For example, if you had 10 virtual desktop machines in one datastore and only two in another, then running a rebalance operation would potentially even this out and leave you with six virtual desktop machines per datastore.

> You must use the View Administrator console to initiate the rebalance operation in View Composer. If you simply try to vMotion any of your virtual desktop machines, then View Composer will not be able to keep track of them.

On the other hand, if you have six virtual desktop machines on one datastore and seven on another, then it is highly likely that initiating a rebalance operation will have no effect, and no virtual desktop machines will be moved, as doing so has no benefit. A virtual desktop machine will only be moved to another datastore if the target datastore has significantly more spare capacity than the source.

The rebalance process is described in the following steps:

1. The linked clone is switched to maintenance mode.
2. Virtual machines to be moved are identified based on the free space in the available datastores.
3. The operating system disk and persistent disk are disconnected from the virtual desktop machine.
4. The detached operating system disk and persistent disk are moved to the target datastore.
5. The virtual desktop machine is moved to the target datastore.
6. The operating system disk and persistent disk are reconnected to the linked clone virtual desktop machine.
7. View Composer resynchronizes the linked clone virtual desktop machines.
8. View Composer checks for the replica disk in the datastore and creates one if one does not already exist as per the provisioning steps covered earlier in this chapter.
9. As per the recompose operation, the operating system disk for the linked clone gets deleted and a new one is created and then customized.

The following diagram shows the rebalance operation:

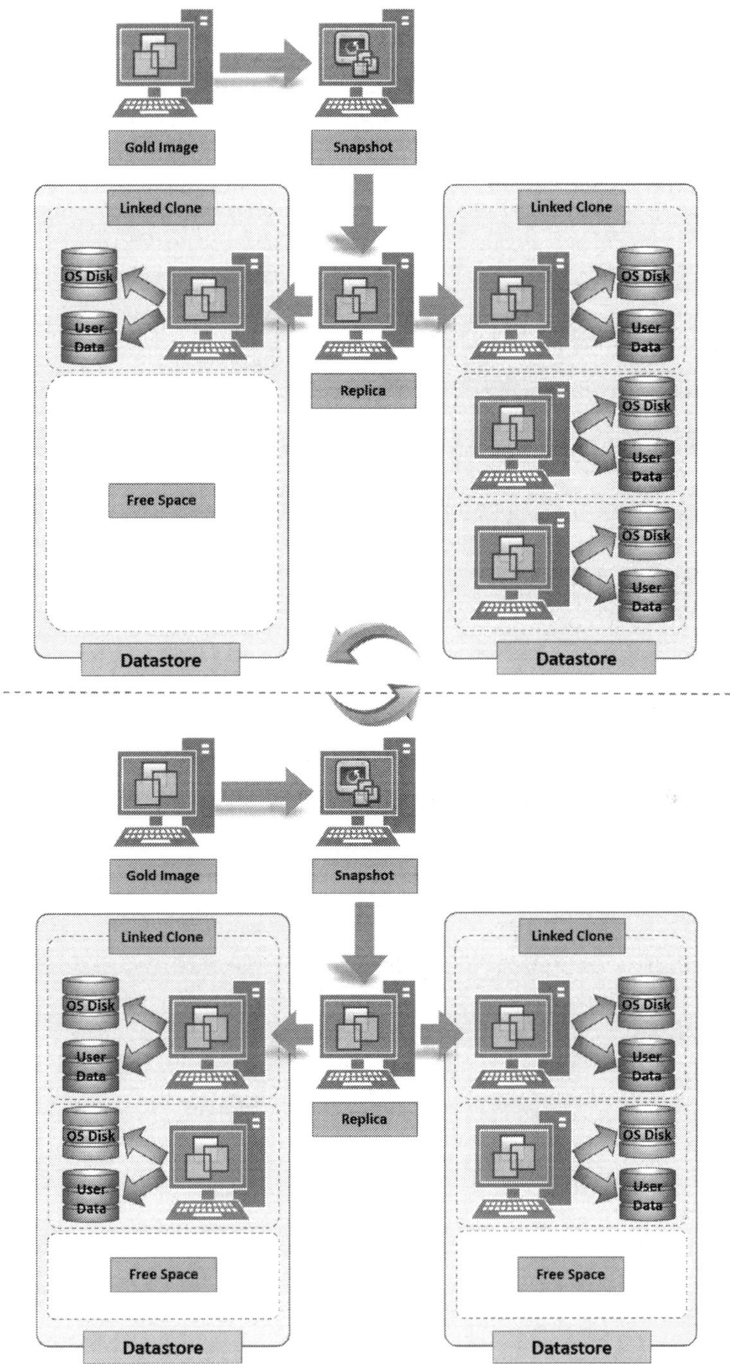

View Persona Management

Let's start with a little bit about the background and history behind View Persona Management. **View Persona Management** was originally a technology product called **Virtual Profiles** and was acquired by VMware from RTO Software in 2010. It was first introduced with View 5.0, and it allows you to configure user profiles so that they dynamically synchronize with a remote profile repository that is located on a file server in the data center. Its purpose is to manage user profiles within a virtualized desktop environment.

More information about the acquisition can be found at `http://www.vmware.com/files/pdf/VMware-RTO-acquisition-FAQ.pdf`.

What is View Persona Management?

VMware View Persona Management was first introduced with View 5.0, and it allows you to configure user profiles that dynamically synchronize with a remote profile repository located on a file server in the data center.

Why do we need to manage user profiles differently in VDI?

In a VDI solution, one of the key benefits is the way the virtual desktop is either built on-demand or delivered from a pool of prebuilt, floating desktops and then delivered back to the user. The typical deployment model is the floating model, which basically means that the user doesn't actually own their desktop.

When they log in, they could have any desktop delivered to them from a pool of available virtual desktop machines. This means that the virtual desktop that is delivered would not be personalized to that particular user. It would just be a standard vanilla build of the operating system and applications.

This is where View Persona Management comes into play and delivers the user's profile to the floating virtual desktop they have been assigned, effectively making it theirs.

When we talk about the desktop being built on-demand, we are referring to how a desktop is put together from several different components. The desktop can be broken down into three components: the operating system, applications, and the user's personalization or profile, essentially the bit that makes the desktop yours. As a user logs on, all these pieces come together to deliver the end user desktop experience. In this particular example, we are talking about the user's profile. This is shown in the following diagram:

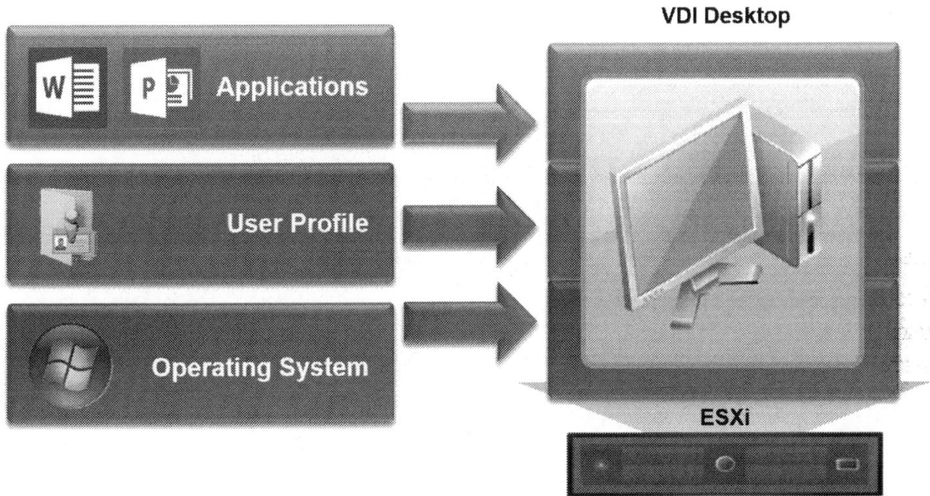

In this section, we will have a detailed look at View Persona Management to manage the user profile element and the key benefits it delivers. A deep dive into a technical overview and details on how to configure View Persona Management can be found in *Chapter 9, Managing User Profiles with View Persona Management*.

The benefits of Persona Management

At high levels, View Persona Management provides the following features:

- Fast loading of user personalization settings, with just-in-time retrieval of user profile data
- Little or no infrastructure required—just a file share or the use of an existing folder redirection structure
- Profile consistency maintains personalization between sessions
- Efficient architecture with no dependency on Windows roaming user profiles
- Multiplatform support for Windows XP, Windows Vista, Windows 7, and Windows 8.x

In addition to the preceding features, View Persona Management also helps reduce virtual desktop TCO by giving organizations the ability to deploy more stateless desktops over persistent desktops. In some deployments, users were placed in dedicated pools solely to retain their profile settings, which added to the cost and complexity in management. On the subject of cost, as Persona Management is integrated as part of Horizon View, you don't need to purchase additional third-party products.

While on the subject of management, there are no additional components to set up or install, as everything is driven by Active Directory Group Policy; in terms of scalability, again, as there are no infrastructure overheads such as databases, scaling does not cause any problems.

Printing from a Horizon View virtual desktop

A question that often comes up when deploying a VDI solution is, how do you manage printing? As your virtual desktop is now effectively running on a server in the data center, does that mean that, when you hit the print button, your print job comes out there? What about printer drivers? Typically, your desktop has the driver installed for the printer that is nearest to you, or it might be a locally attached printer. Does that mean you need to install every possible printer driver onto your virtual desktop machines? Luckily, the answer to these questions is no, and in this section, we will cover how VMware Horizon View manages printing.

Bundled within Horizon View is an OEM virtual printing solution, ThinPrint, which is OEM'd from a company called Cortado. ThinPrint allows your end users to print either to a network-based printer or to a local printer that is attached from the user's end-point device to their virtual desktop machine via USB redirection. We will cover USB device management in the next section.

To answer the question about the printer drivers that must be installed, ThinPrint uses a single, virtual print driver that replaces all other print drivers. You can still install a specific print driver if necessary, for use cases where your printer has some additional features or functionalities. However, the virtual print driver provides support for most multifunctional printers, supporting features such as double-sided printing.

The other question centered around location; where your print job actually prints is also addressed with ThinPrint, which provides a location-based printing feature that allows you to map to a printer that is nearest to your end-point device.

Installing the virtual printing components

There are two key components to the virtual printing solution that gets installed as part of the Horizon View installation process; they are as follows:

- **The .print Engine**: This gets installed as part of the Horizon View Agent installation on the virtual desktop machine. It includes the virtual print driver.
- **The .print Client**: This gets installed as part of the Horizon View Client on the end-point device and provides information on available printers and also receives print jobs from the engine component.

Managing USB devices

We are all used to plugging USB devices into our laptops and desktop machines. If you are working in a VMware Horizon View environment, you might want to continue using your USB devices within that virtualized desktop. USB device redirection is a functionality, built into Horizon View, that allows the USB device to be physically connected to the end-point device while working as if it's connected to the virtualized desktop.

USB Device support in Horizon View

There isn't a list that details every single device that works within Horizon View, as that would be one very long list and it would be impractical to test everything out there, given the number of USB devices on the market.

In general, most USB devices should work in a Horizon View environment, as all it essentially does is redirect the USB traffic from the View Client running on the end-point device to the View Agent running on the virtual desktop machine. A complete list of "validated" devices does not exist; if there are any questions about the functionality of a particular device, you should contact the USB device manufacturer.

There might be some devices that will not work, purely due to the nature and the behavior of the device itself—for example, some security devices that check the physical properties of the machine or device they are plugged into. We used to classify USB webcams as unsupported devices. However, with the introduction of **Real Time Audio Video** (**RTAV**), these devices are now supported. We will cover this later on in this chapter.

In the next section, we will talk about how you can select which USB devices get redirected by using USB filtering.

Filtering supported USB devices

In some circumstances, you might not want to allow users to have the ability to plug in external USB devices and redirect them to their virtual desktop machine. The question is, do you allow users to plug USB devices into their physical desktops?

Horizon View has a feature that can prevent USB devices from being redirected to the user's virtual desktop machine. You can apply this by using a policy on the end-point device, the virtual desktop, or by means of an Active Directory Group Policy. For example, your organization might want to prevent USB memory sticks from being used as this would give the user the ability to copy data from the virtual desktop machine (one of the reasons for the deployment of VDI is so that data is centralized and doesn't leave the data center).

You can create specific filters to include devices (by manufacturer or by type) that you want to allow, but block all others. So, if you have a corporate, standard-type device, it will be allowed. You could even go to the next level and choose a particular model of device while blocking any other devices even though they are from the same vendor.

Managing multifunction USB devices

In your environment, you might also have some USB devices that each have several different functions while still using a single USB connection. For example, a multimedia keyboard could have a touchpad mouse, speakers, a fingerprint reader, and the keyboard itself.

Horizon View supports a function known as device splitting. This allows you to just redirect certain components of that device rather than the entire device. With our multimedia example, you might want to leave the mouse as a local device on the end point while redirecting the fingerprint reader to allow secure login to the virtual desktop machine.

ThinApp application virtualization

ThinApp is an agentless application virtualization or application packaging solution that decouples applications from their underlying operating systems. It's designed to eliminate application conflict, streamline application delivery, and improve management. ThinApp licenses are included with the Horizon View license and can be used on both physical and virtual desktops, therefore providing a mechanism to deliver applications across all of your desktop models, your entire end user estate.

How does application virtualization work?

ThinApp encapsulates applications into a package consisting of a single .EXE or .MSI file and abstracts them from the following:

- The host operating system
- Any traditionally installed applications already running on the system
- All other virtual applications running on the system

Applications are run in a virtual environment with minimal or zero impact on the underlying operating system, virtual filesystem, and Virtual Registry. Easily deployed, upgraded, managed, and retired

When you create a ThinApp package, you are basically capturing all the application files, registry settings, and filesystem changes that an application requires for it to run. It also captures its own agent as part of the process, so the end-client device requires nothing to be installed, unless you deliver your ThinApp packages using the Workspace Portal.

Once packaged, the application can be deployed (either streamed or installed) onto the virtual desktop machine or even a physical desktop. The only requirement ThinApp packages have in order to run, is an underlining Windows operating system, physical or virtual. When running, it's important to note that the package makes no changes to the operating system of the machine it's running on.

There are no requirements for additional back-end infrastructure components, and all your ThinApp-packaged applications are stored on a file share on a file server. This means that you can centrally manage and easily update your packages so that all users will receive the updates the next time they launch the application.

To summarize, ThinApp does the following:

- Allows Windows applications to be packaged, distributed, and executed as single `.exe` or `.msi` files on either physical or virtual machines
- Builds process links, a **Virtual Operating System** (**VOS**) with a compressed embedded filesystem and registry into a single file
- Requires no pre-installed software on the end user machine (unless using the Workspace Portal for entitlements)
- Provides a zero footprint on the underlying OS
- Necessitates no traditional installation or changes to the local OS registry or filesystem
- Requires no backend server infrastructure other than a file share to store your ThinApp packages

For more details on ThinApp, you can read *VMware ThinApp 4.7 Essentials*, by *Peter Björk, Packt Publishing*.

Antivirus software for virtual desktops

In a traditional desktop model, an antivirus scanning model agent is installed, runs on every desktop, and is responsible for the performance of antivirus detection scans while maintaining and updating the definition files containing information about the latest malware.

This model works well in the physical desktop world but presents some challenges when running in a virtual desktop environment. When a detection scan starts, every virtual desktop's resource usage will increase significantly. This will result in end-user performance degradation, and the desktop host server will become resource-bound. That's fine on a physical desktop but now in VDI it's the server hosting the desktops that is going to become resource-bound. When recomposing desktops or building them on-demand, the desktops will have to download the definitions file each time, taking up network bandwidth and storage capacity. One last thing you need to take into consideration is the memory footprint of the typical desktop AV software that gets installed on each virtual desktop. You will need to allocate more memory to run the agents and scanning process.

Let's say you have a vSphere host server running maybe 100 virtual desktops or so; what if, at 12:00 noon on Thursday, they all kick off a virus scan? That host is likely to become 100% utilized very quickly, both for CPU and storage I/Os, with the result being unresponsive desktops. Instead of affecting one user's desktop, you have now affected 100 users' desktops. You could schedule the scans so that they don't all happen at once but, ideally, you need to look at alternative methods that are designed to work more specifically with a virtual desktop infrastructure.

Secondly, if we are recomposing desktops or building them on-demand, we have to download the definitions file every time, which not only takes up network bandwidth but also unnecessary storage capacity.

So, what is required is a new approach to antivirus protection, specifically designed for virtual desktop infrastructure.

With VMware vSphere 5.5, VMware introduced a product called vShield Endpoint that addresses the problems inherent in antivirus scanning in large scale virtual desktop implementations. In a Horizon View deployment, vShield Endpoint consolidates and offloads all antivirus operations into one centralized **security virtual appliance** (**SVA**).

VMware has partnered with antivirus software vendors to provide this bundled solution to antivirus problems in a VDI environment. VMware partners supply the dedicated SVA, which integrates with the vShield Endpoint programmable interfaces to protect VMware virtual desktops against viruses and other malware. Instead of installing the antivirus agents on each individual virtual desktop, you connect one virtual appliance to each virtual machine host.

VMware works with the following partners who have integrated their antivirus solutions with vShield Endpoint:

- Bitdefender
- Kaspersky
- McAfee
- Sourcefire
- Symantec
- Trend Micro

VMware vShield Endpoint delivers the following features:

- Improved virtual desktop performance by not creating antivirus storms, which prevents scanning storms from occurring.
- Scanning and defining file updates are centralized using a virtual appliance.
- Freed up resources on virtual desktop machines by eliminating the need for AV agents on the virtual desktop images.
- No agent to install or update on the virtual desktop machines. The driver is contained within the VMware Tools installation.
- It has an always-on protection. As antivirus signature updates are processed by the SVA, desktops receive the latest protection as soon as they are powered on.
- Any changes to the antivirus software are configured only in the virtual appliance, not in each desktop. You can change the configurations for the antivirus solution in the virtual appliance without reconfiguring the desktop driver. All changes are made to the virtual appliance instead.
- Simple substitution of antivirus vendors. You can add or change partner solutions by adding or removing the virtual appliances. You do not need to reconfigure the desktop driver.

VMware vShield Endpoint architecture

There are two main components of **vSheild Endpoint**. As we previously discussed, instead of installing the antivirus software on each virtual desktop machine, you install SVA and the vSheild Endpoint driver. You will need one SVA per ESXi host server, and each virtual machine to be protected requires only a small footprint. The vShield Endpoint driver is installed on the desktop image, which is part of the VMware Tools installation for the virtual machine:

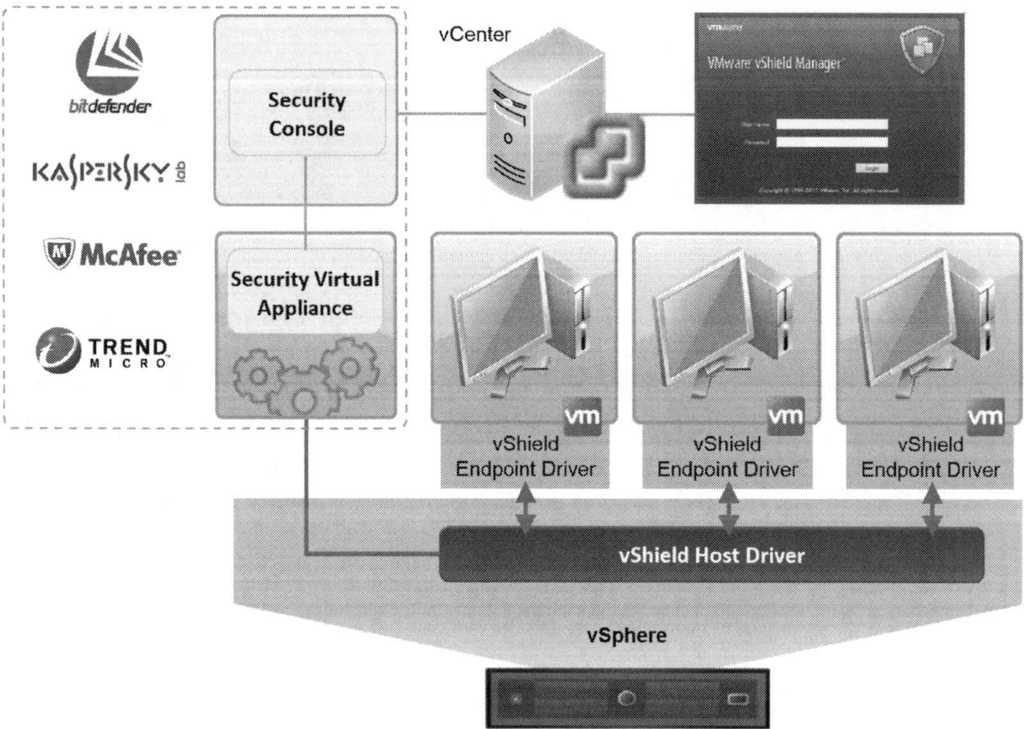

IT administrators can centrally manage VMware vShield Endpoint through the included **VMware vShield Manager** console, which in turn is integrated with VMware **vCenter** Server. Isolating the antivirus scanning engine on a virtual appliance makes it easier to protect the scanning engine than if it were placed on every virtual machine. In addition, detailed logging of activity from the antivirus or anti-malware service satisfies auditor compliance requirements.

PCoIP Protocol – delivering the desktop experience

One of the most important elements of a virtual desktop solution is how you get the screen contents of the virtual desktop machine running in the data center delivered to the user's end point device, which they are connecting from. To do this, VMware Horizon View uses the **PC-over Internet Protocol (PCoIP)**. In this section, we are going to cover what the PCoIP protocol is and how it works in delivering the end user experience.

An introduction to PCoIP

PCoIP is a high-performance display protocol designed and developed by Teradici (`www.teradici.com`). It has been purpose-built to deliver virtual desktops over the LAN or WAN and to provide end users with the best, feature-rich desktop experience.

With PCoIP, the entire screen content is compressed, encrypted, and encoded in the data center before transmitting only the pixels across a standard IP network to PCoIP-enabled endpoint devices (such as zero clients) that use the hardware-based Teradici Terra 1 or Terra 2 chipset, or to Windows, Mac, or tablet devices running the software-based View Client. The key is that no data ever leaves the data center; it's kind of like watching TV where just the pictures are sent from the studio to your TV set at home rather than having the actors in the corner of your lounge.

PCoIP supports high-resolution, full-frame rates, 3D graphics, HD media, multiple displays (up to four, depending on the endpoint device), and high-definition audio. As we discussed earlier in this chapter, PCoIP also supports USB peripheral redirection.

Unlike some legacy display protocols that were built just to deliver applications, PCoIP was designed and built from the ground up, specifically to deliver a full desktop experience, taking advantage of Teradici-based zero clients with an integrated graphics acceleration technology built into the silicon on these devices.

PCoIP ensures the best user experience, regardless of the end user location, whether that is on the LAN or even across a WAN. It dynamically adapts based on the network conditions and user policy.

In the next sections, we are going to cover how PCoIP renders images and how it adapts dynamically to the network environment.

PCoIP host rendering

So lets start by taking a look at how the different rendering models work. With a desktop PC, the applications, operating system, and graphics drivers work together locally to deliver the best performance on that PC. This is local client rendering.

If we move to a client rendering model, we now introduce a network between the components. Images are now sent across the network to the endpoint device, where they are processed locally using the resources of that endpoint device. Using this model introduces degradation of the application performance as it travels across the network from the host server to the client and you would still need a fairly powerful Windows-based endpoint device.

So what about host rendering? In a host rendering scenario, the desktop PC environment that we previously described is pretty much the same. However, the PC is now running as a virtual desktop machine. This means that applications will work as they normally would on a physical desktop PC and the rendering is done at the host end. PCoIP then works by encrypting just the pixels on the virtual desktop machine running the View Agent, and then sends them to the endpoint device running the View Client or to a zero client device running Teradici hardware, where the decoding takes place.

Using this model, you can easily deploy lower-powered, non-Windows devices such as zero clients, as the applications have no dependencies on the endpoint on which they run.

Multi-codec support with PCoIP

If you look at how an image is built up and how the content is rendered, some of the components of the image might require the use of different codecs to display the image, depending on what type of image it is. For example, you would use a different codec to display text from one that you would use to display videos.

PCoIP has the ability to analyze these different media image components and apply the appropriate codec for each pixel before compressing, encrypting, and sending the pixels to the endpoint device for decoding. Working in this way allows PCoIP to transmit the pixels more efficiently, which ultimately means less bandwidth and better performance. It also means that you can control the image content quality that is being delivered. We will talk about it in the next section.

Controlling the image quality

The quality of the image that PCoIP delivers can be controlled through the Active Directory Group Policy to deliver the appropriate image quality, depending on the use case. The image is built progressively from, what is termed, a perceptually lossless image to a lossless image, with the latter delivering a high-fidelity, pixel-perfect image. For example, would you really need to build a pixel-perfect image if you were just running Microsoft Word?

The important thing to remember is that the quality of the image will have an impact on the bandwidth required to deliver it. We will cover these controls in more detail in *Chapter 8, Fine-tuning the End User Experience*.

Dynamic networking capabilities

As we briefly mentioned in the previous section, image quality settings for PCoIP can be easily configured using Active Directory Group Policy. We will cover this in more detail in *Chapter 8, Fine-tuning the End User Experience*. To manage bandwidth use, PCoIP's adaptive encoders automatically adjust image quality on congested networks, based on the limits you set in the policy, and then resume maximum image quality when the network is no longer congested. As PCoIP doesn't transfer any data and just the pixels, it makes sense to use a real-time **User Datagram Protocol** (**UDP**), rather than a TCP protocol (the same protocol as **Voice over IP** or **VoIP**), to ensure a responsive and interactive remote-user experience. This reduces the overall bandwidth requirement and delivers the best interactive user experience based on the network bandwidth available at the time.

UDP does not employ error-checking or correction, and therefore removes any overheads in processing the checking and correcting. The lack of retransmission delays that you would find with a TCP protocol means that it is ideal for streaming media. For the end user experience, these delays translate to jerky movements, most commonly experienced when watching video content.

Other display protocols

There are a couple of other mainstream desktop protocols. The main protocols available today are Microsoft **Remote Desktop Protocol** (**RDP**) and Citrix **Independent Computing Architecture** (**ICA**). These are described in more detail in the following sections.

The Remote Desktop Protocol (RDP)

The RDP protocol was developed for Microsoft and is used primarily to connect to a remote machine, a server, desktop, or virtual machine using TCP IP. RDP is now more commonly known as Remote Desktop Connection. You probably use it on a daily basis to connect remotely to your server infrastructure.

When you connect to the remote desktop or machine, you are essentially connecting to a terminal service component, which then relays the screen content back to the client, along with key strokes and mouse movements.

The Independent Computing Architecture (ICA) protocol

ICA is another display protocol that is used by Citrix in its products XenDesktop and XenApp. It is similar in design to other protocols, in that it is used to deliver screen content and keyboard strokes to a client device over a TCP IP network connection.

You connect using an ICA client, such as Citrix Receiver, installed on your endpoint device. This loads an ICA file containing the details of the remote system you are connecting to and any properties to apply to that session.

What about HDX? HDX is not actually a protocol or a technology, but rather a marketing brand for **High Definition Experience**. **HDX** encompasses a number of Citrix technologies that describe the entire user experience rather than concentrating on just the protocol element. You will also see some subbrands fall under HDX, such as HDX MediaStream, HDX RealTime, and HDX 3D.

Which protocol to use – PCoIP or RDP?

Now that we have a good understanding of PCoIP and some of the other available protocols, why would we choose PCoIP? The most compelling reason to go with PCoIP is the fact it uses the UDP protocol, which is much better suited to streaming media, and therefore lends itself perfectly to the characteristics of virtual desktop delivery. As we discussed, UDP is not concerned with how the data ends up on the endpoint device; it's only concerned with the speed of delivery and how quickly it gets there. On the other hand, RDP uses TCP as its protocol, which is widely used across the Internet. The key difference with TCP is that it is concerned with how the data is being received. TCP requests an acknowledgement from the endpoint device as to whether or not it has received all of the packets successfully. If the endpoint device does not receive what it was expecting, then it replies, asking TCP to either stop sending packets or to narrow the amount that it receives. UDP just keeps sending and is much speedier, simply because there is no acknowledgement packet back from the endpoint device.

PCoIP also leverages host rendering. The image is rendered on the server host to provide the framework in which the host transmits only the pixels across the network, without being concerned about the applications or responses from the client. This allows you to deploy the thinnest of endpoint devices, such as thin or zero clients. The job of the zero client is purely to receive the pixels, decode them, and then display them on the screen of the endpoint device.

PCoIP is also far more configurable with regard to bandwidth settings, allowing you to configure image quality depending on the connection speed and use case (what task the user is doing). Bandwidth is the main cause in most, if not all, display-related end user experience issues within a virtual desktop infrastructure.

The dynamic and adaptive nature of PCoIP on the bandwidth that is available helps during times when there are constraints on the network. If there is ample bandwidth available, then it can leverage the additional bandwidth to deliver the best experience possible with higher-quality images; but when there is network congestion, it can turn down the image quality until the bandwidth becomes available again.

However, there are still some cases where PCoIP won't be the appropriate protocol to use. The one we see most of the time is when the required network ports are being blocked by corporate policy. When you connect to your Horizon View session with the View Client, you initiate the connection on port 443 (or 8443 if you are using the Blast Gateway).

When your desktop is displayed back to you, PCoIP uses UDP port 4172 to send the pixels. This port is sometimes blocked, as it's not typically used. The result of this port being blocked is that, even though you will be able to log on to your virtual desktop via the View Client and everything looks OK, you will just receive a black screen. The black screen is due to the pixels being blocked as they are sent. In this example, the workaround is to access the desktop from an HTML5-enabled browser. We will cover this in *Chapter 8, Fine-tuning the End User Experience*.

The key take-away here is to engage with your networking and security teams when planning how users connect to their virtual desktop machines and looking at the requirements.

In the next section, we are going to discuss some of the options available to assist in optimizing the processing of the protocol and how to connect to physical machines.

PCoIP offload with the Teradici Apex 2800

In addition to the software solutions discussed in the previous sections, Teradici also offers a server offload card called Apex 2800. This PCI card is installed into the servers hosting the virtual desktops.

The first thing to say about this card is that it is not a **Graphics Processing Unit** (**GPU**) card. I often hear some confusion around this, and users assume that, by adding an Apex card, you would get the OpenGL and DirectX capabilities; but this is not the case. You might well improve the overall experience and performance, but you will not be adding additional GPU features and functionalities.

The objective of this card is purely to take the load from the CPU in the host when processing image encoding operations. Offloading image encoding to a hardware encoding card reduces peaks in CPU utilization, ensuring a consistent user experience across all users, regardless of task and activity level. In cases where the CPU is being starved off cycles, the offload function enables applications to run more smoothly. If you compare it to something such as **TCP Offload Engine** or the **TOE** card used in the IP storage world for iSCSI. It's much better to use hardware-based cards than it is to use software initiators.

Freeing up CPU cycles and the overall load on the servers' CPU will potentially result in better consolidation ratios of the virtual desktops; that is, more virtual desktops per host server. Typically, you will see an increase of 1.2 times.

The Teradici host card for physical workstations

Teradici also has a solution for physical workstations to leverage the PCoIP protocol, the PCoIP Remote Workstation card. This card is not actually for virtual desktop sessions; instead, it allows you to add a Teradici host card into a physical workstation, connect to your workstation, and send remote graphics, audio, and USB from the workstation to a PCoIP-enabled endpoint device, such as a zero client. Think of it as picking up your desktop PC and put it into the data center, and then running a very long video, mouse, and keyboard cable to it. This use case is typically deployed for high-powered rack mount workstations or PC's.

Although, in reality, the pixels are sent over the network. So where does that fit in with Horizon View? Quite simply, the connection to the physical desktop is managed using Horizon View and the Connection Server to broker the session in the same way you would connect to a virtual desktop machine.

Hardware-accelerated graphics for Horizon View

Early versions of virtual desktop technology faced challenges when it came to delivering high-end graphical content, as the host servers were not designed to render and deliver the size and quality of images required for such applications.

Let's start with some history and background to this subject. Technology to support high-end graphics was released in several phases, with the first support for 3D graphics released in vSphere 5, with View 5.0 using software-based rendering. This gave us the ability to support things such as Windows Aero feature, but it was still not powerful enough for some of the really high-end use cases due to this being a software feature.

The next phase was to provide a hardware-based GPU virtualization solution that came with vSphere 5.1 and allowed virtual machines to share a physical GPU by allowing virtual machines to pass through the hypervisor layer to take advantage of a physical graphics card installed in the host server.

If we had this conversation about 12-18 months ago and you had a use case that required high-end graphics capabilities, then virtual desktops would not have been a viable solution. As we just discussed, in a VDI environment graphics will be delivered using a virtualized, software-based graphics driver as part of the hypervisor. Also, don't forget that, as we are now using servers to host the virtual desktops, we are using the power of the graphics card in the server, and servers aren't renowned for their high-end graphics capabilities and have limited GPU power, as typically, all a server needs to do is display a management console.

That has all changed now. With the release of View 5.2 back in 2013, the ability to deliver hardware-accelerated graphics became a standard product feature with the introduction of **Virtual Shared Graphics Acceleration** (**vSGA**), which was then followed with the launch of **Virtual Dedicated Graphics Acceleration** (**vDGA**). We will discuss these two technologies in the next sections of this chapter and also touch on the next installment of graphics capabilities in Horizon View, with the announcement of **Virtual Graphics Processing Unit** (**vGPU**).

Virtual Shared Graphics Acceleration – vSGA

The vSGA allows for multiple virtual desktop machines to share a physical GPU card that is installed into the ESXi host server hosting those virtual desktops.

In this model, the virtual desktop machines do not have direct access to a dedicated physical GPU card. The VMware SVGA 3D graphics driver is installed on the virtual desktop's operating system. SVGA is a VMware driver that provides support for DirectX 9.0c and OpenGL 2.1. Graphics commands from user sessions are intercepted by this driver and sent to the hypervisor, which controls the GPU. In this configuration, the NVIDIA driver is installed in the vSphere hypervisor rather than the virtual desktop machine's own operating system.

The following diagram shows an overview of vSGA architecture:

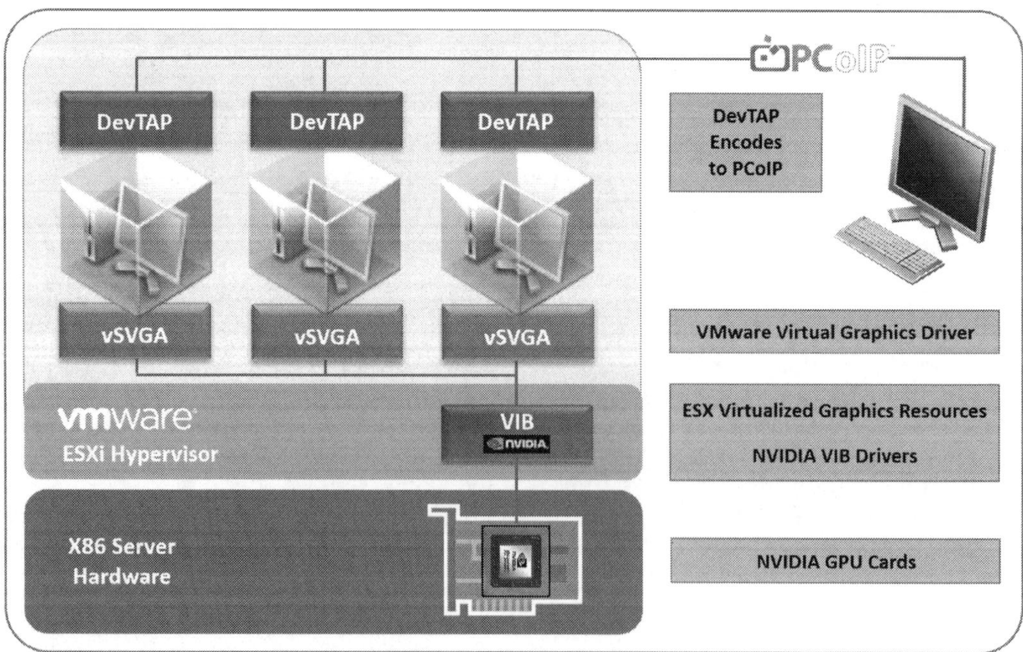

There are a number of configuration and support options to consider, which we will cover in the next sections.

vSGA-supported configurations

vSGA will support OpenGL 2.1- and DirectX 9-based applications running either on Windows 7 or 8 virtual desktop machines, virtualized on VMware vSphere 5.1 and greater, using one of the following NVIDIA GPU cards:

- Quadro 4000, 5000, and 6000
- Tesla M2070-Q
- Grid K1 and K2

There is also a hardware compatibility list that details which servers support these graphic cards. The compatibility guide can be found at `http://www.vmware.com/resources/compatibility/search.php?deviceCategory=io`.

How many virtual desktops are supported with vSGA?

This is a question that gets asked when talking about delivering hardware-based graphics within a Horizon View environment, so in this section, let's spend some time understanding this. Within Horizon View, you create different desktop pools depending on the use case, as we will cover in *Chapter 7, Managing and Configuring Desktop Pools*. One of the desktop pools will be configured to use high-end graphics as typically, you would not give all users access to a hardware-based GPU.

So to answer the question, the number of virtual desktops you can allocate to a GPU is dependent on the amount of **video memory** (**VRAM**) that you allocate to each virtual desktop. The thing to bear in mind is that the resources are shared and therefore normal VMware virtualization rules apply. The first thing to note is how memory is shared.

Half of the video memory allocated to a virtual desktop machine is allocated from the GPU card's memory and the other half is from the host server's memory. When sizing your host servers, you need to ensure that you have enough memory configured in the server to allocate this as video memory.

Based on this and with the number of virtual desktops supported based on the amount of allocated VRAM), let's look at how that works out. So, the default amount of VRAM allocated to a virtual desktop machine is 128 MB. So, in this example, 64 MB will come from the GPU and the other 64 MB from the host server. If you then take a GPU card that has 4 GB of VRAM onboard, you will be able to support 64 virtual desktops (4 GB or 4096 MB divided by 64 MB from the GPU = 64 virtual desktop machines).

Within Horizon View, you can allocate a maximum of 512 MB of VRAM per virtual desktop machine. If you apply this to the preceding example using the same 4 GB GPU card, you now reduce the number of supported virtual desktops down to 16 (4 GB or 4096 MB divided by 256 MB from the GPU = 16 virtual desktop machines).

We stated previously that normal VMware virtualization rules apply, so let's explain exactly what that means. Basically, what happens when you cannot fulfil a virtual desktop machine's specification and there are insufficient resources? It won't boot or power on, right? It's the same for GPU configuration. If you configure a desktop pool with more virtual desktop machines than you can support on that GPU, then they will not boot.

If you do happen to configure more virtual desktop machines in a pool where you probably cannot guarantee the GPU resources to be available, set the **Hardware 3D** setting in the View Administrator console to **Automatic**. Doing this allows Horizon View to revert to the software-based 3D rendering in order to deliver the virtual desktop machines.

Within Horizon View, you can create different desktop pools, depending on the use case, as we will cover in *Chapter 7, Managing and Configuring Desktop Pools*. One of the desktop pools will be configured to use high-end graphics, as typically, you will not give all users access to a hardware-based GPU.

Virtual Dedicated Graphics Acceleration – vDGA

While vSGA works on a shared basis, vDGA allows for an individual virtual desktop machine to have dedicated access to a physical GPU card installed in the ESXi host server. This allows the virtual desktop machine to have a higher level of graphic performance, making it perfect for such use cases as CAD/CAM applications, as it supports NVIDIA CUDA, DirectX (9, 10, and 11), and OpenGL 4.4.

The following diagram shows the architecture for vDGA:

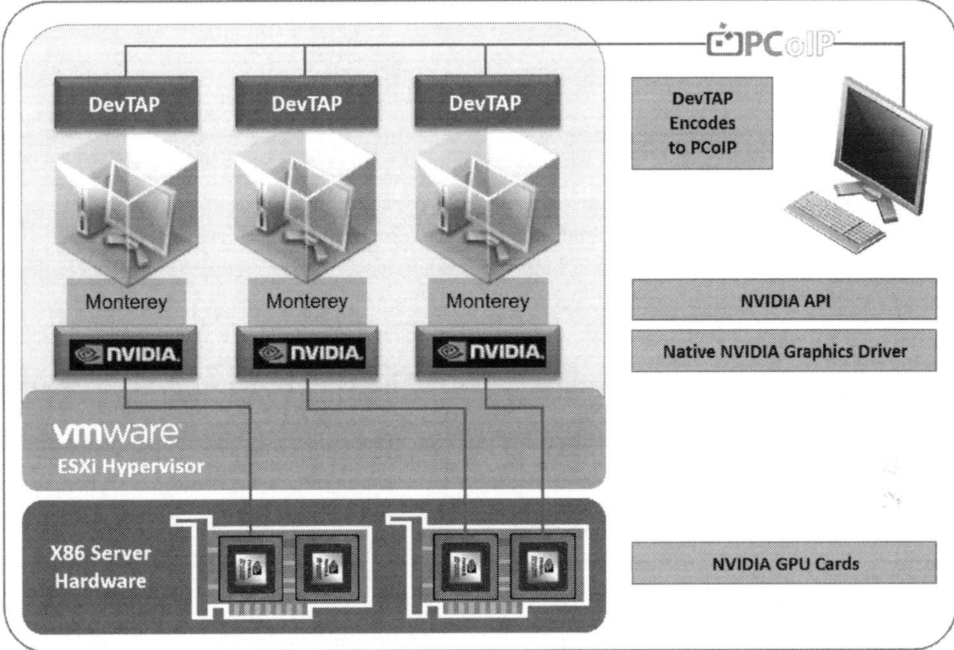

The vDGA makes use of a feature called VMDirectPath I/O pass-through, or sometimes referred to as PCI pass-through, which allows the virtual desktop machine to pass through the hypervisor layer and directly access the hardware in the host server. In this case, the hardware in question is the NVIDIA GPU cards.

> As a virtual desktop machine is mapped directly to a GPU on a one-to-one basis, you cannot use vSphere features such as HA, DRS, or vMotion.

How many virtual desktops are supported with vDGA?

Unlike vSGA, which is limited by the amount of memory on the GPU card, vDGA is limited purely by the number of GPUs or GRID cards you can physically fit into the host server. This is dependent on your server vendor and what they support.

Server vendors offer NVIDIA GRID-enabled servers that are prebuilt and, therefore, this technology is only available from the OEM channel. The primary reason is that servers require additional power and cooling components to drive the GRID cards.

For example, an NVIDIA GRID K2 GPU card has two GPUs on-board, which would mean that you can allocate four virtual desktop machines to this card. Depending on your server hardware platform, you could install more than one card, therefore increasing the number of users that have access to a hardware-enabled GPU in their virtual desktop.

vDGA-supported configurations

The following GPU cards are supported with vDGA:

- Quadro 2000, 4000, 5000, and 6000
- Quadro 1000M and 3000M
- Tesla M2070-Q
- GRID K1 and K2

The compatibility guide can be found at `http://www.vmware.com/resources/compatibility/search.php?deviceCategory=io`.

Virtual GPU

In the previous sections we have talked about two different models for delivering high-end graphics. There are a couple of draw backs with each solution. With vSGA you get the scalability in terms of the number of users that can use the GPU card, however because it does not use the native NVIDIA graphics driver some of the ISV's will not certify their applications running on this solution.

The answer was to use vDGA which does use the native NVIDIA graphics driver. The drawback here is scalability and cost. Having a virtual desktop machine dedicated to a GPU, with only a handful of GPU's available in each host server made for a quite expensive solution.

So what we need is a solution that takes the best of both worlds, a solution that takes the shared approach, yet uses the native NVIDIA graphics drive.

That solution is **Virtual GPU** (**vGPU**) and was launched as part of the Horizon 6 Version 6.1 release. The following screenshot shows the architecture for vGPU:

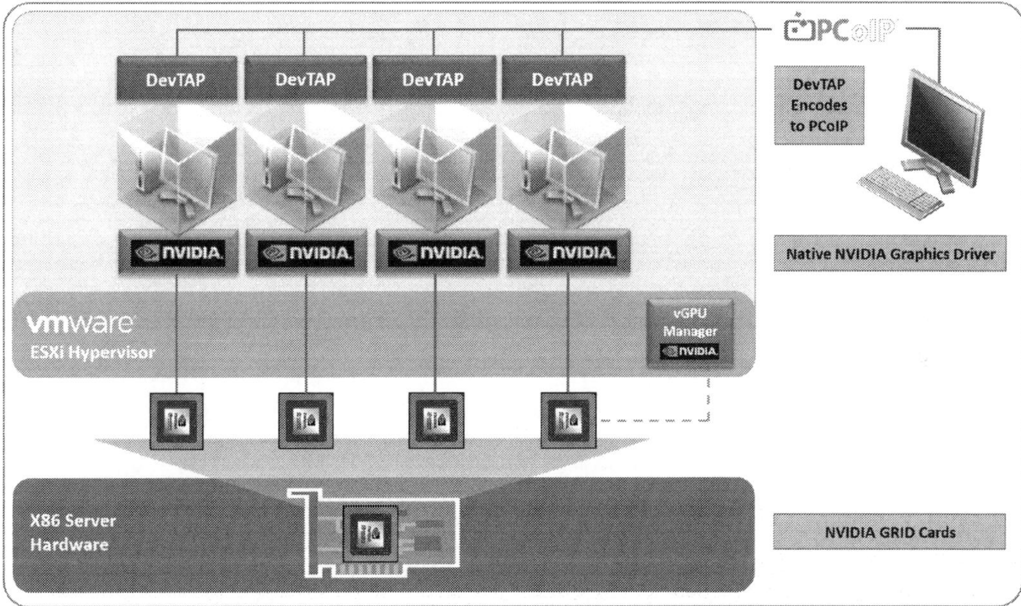

In this model we have the native NVIDIA driver installed in the virtual desktop machines, which then has direct access to the NVIDIA GRID card in the host servers. The GPU is then effectively virtualized and time-sliced, with each virtual desktop machine having a slide of that time.

vGPU is only available with VMware vSphere 6 and Horizon View 6.1.

How many virtual desktops are supported with vGPU?

With vGPU the number of supported users/virtual desktop machines is based on different profiles. These profiles are detailed in the following screenshot and it also gives you the number of users, number of supported monitors, and so on:

Configuration	vGPU Profile	Graphics Memory	Max Monitors	Max. Resolution	Max Users per GRID
NVIDIA GRID K2	K280Q	4GB	4	2560 x 1600	2
	K260Q	2GB	4	2560 x 1600	4
	K240Q	1GB	2	2560 x 1600	8
	K220Q	512MB	2	2560 x 1600	16
NVIDIA GRID K1	K180Q	4GB	4	2560 x 1600	4
	K160Q	2GB	4	2560 x 1600	8
	K140Q	1GB	2	2560 x 1600	16
	K120Q	512MB	2	2560 x 1600	32

As with the vDGA and vSGA solutions you need to check that you have the correct supported hardware. In addition you need to check that your applications are supported. You can find the current list of supported applications by following the link to the NVIDIA website at: `http://www.nvidia.com/object/grid-isv-tested-applications.html`.

Unified communications support

Like high-end graphics, if we had a conversation about running a unified communications solution or VoIP session on a VDI desktop about 12-18 months ago, I would have described it as Kryptonite for VDI! Although it technically works, the first call might have an acceptable performance, but adding more users would ultimately bring the servers to their knees with the amount of traffic generated and resources required to conduct the calls. Eventually, the experience would have become completely unusable. **Unified comms** was not a good use case for VDI.

However, this has all changed and you can now happily use a unified communications solution with your virtual desktop. There was always a great use case to deploy Unified comms with VDI; it just never worked. For example, within a call center environment with the ability to provide a DR solution or allow users to work from home during a snow day.

So why didn't it work? Quite simply, it was because, when you placed a VoIP call from your virtual desktop, the call would go over the PCoIP protocol, causing bandwidth issues and making your desktop perform slowly, and also putting additional load on the servers in the data center in having to process the call. This is detailed in the following diagram, which shows how it was before and the result afterwards.

To solve these issues and to enable a working solution, VMware concentrated on three key areas and delivered the following new features/enhancements:

- Offloading media processing to the client device by removing the load that was placed on the server in the data center
- Optimized point-to-point media delivery, eliminating the hairpin effect
- High-quality UC VoIP and video with QoS

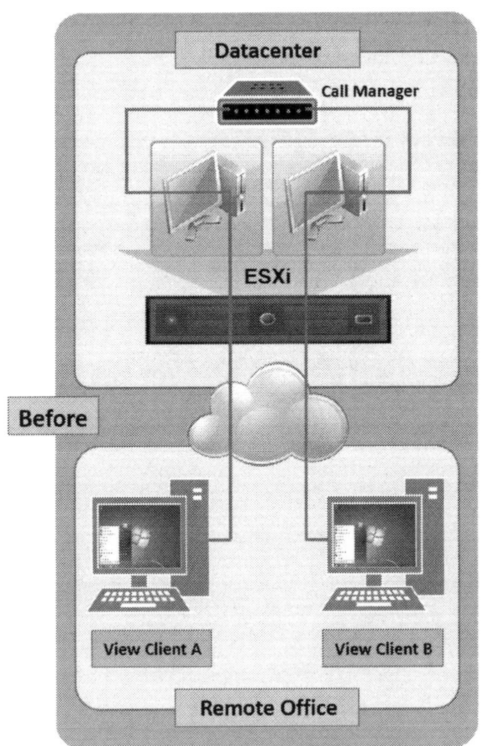

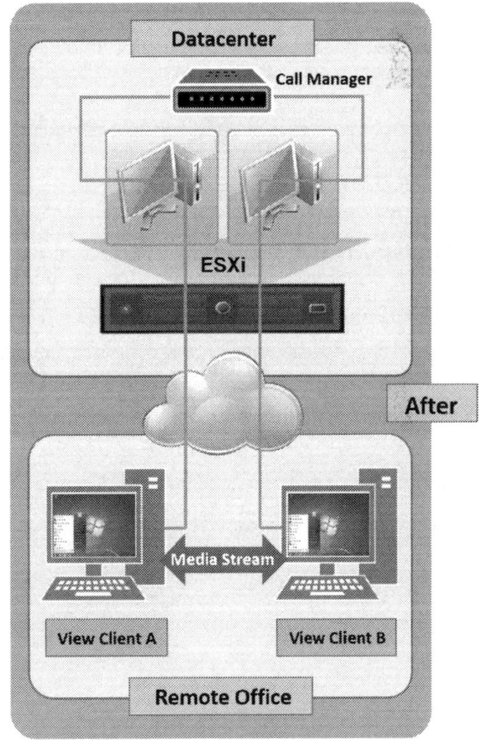

How does unified communications work now?

A **Remote Procedure Call** utilizes a virtual channel to allow the different components of a softphone, running on a virtual desktop machine, to communicate and pass voice and video data to other softphone components in the client device. This is out-of-band communication.

The call control stack (an SIP stack if using SIP signaling) communicates with the call control server or call manager to register or establish the call.

A media engine on the client device performs the encoding and decoding of voice and video streams into native voice and video codecs and then streams the VoIP/ video stream directly to the other endpoint (as directed by the call manager server), therefore setting up a peer-to-peer call and not going through the data center. This now eliminates the hairpin effect.

Currently, VMware supports solutions from Cisco, Mittal, Avaya, and Microsoft Lync 2013. We will cover the Microsoft Lync solution in the next section.

Support for Microsoft Lync 2013

Horizon View provides certified support for Microsoft Lync 2013. This includes full support for VoIP and video, using RDP and PCoIP protocols. The following diagram shows the process of how the client works:

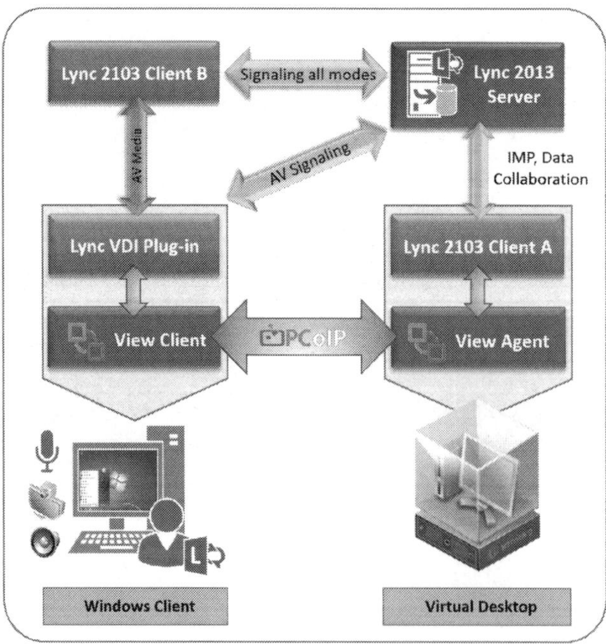

To enable Lync, you need to ensure that the Lync VDI plug-in is installed along with the View client and Microsoft Lync 2013 client on the end point device. Currently, only a 32-bit client is available. VMware has implemented Microsoft's **Dynamic Virtual Channels** (**DVC**) inside the PCoIP protocol to enable this feature. DVC provides the communication path between the virtual desktop machine and the client endpoint.

Real-Time Audio Video

Following on from the unified communications support, the next question we hear concerns support for plugging in a USB webcam and using it with a virtual desktop.

The issue

Like unified communications and VoIP, using a webcam or using audio in and audio out on a virtual desktop machine was not initially supported due to the high bandwidth requirements these types of devices require, therefore resulting in poor performance. Any redirection of these types of devices was previously handled with the USB redirection feature of the PCoIP protocol.

This is how audio in worked, but audio in using a 3.5 mm jack socket did not work at all. Audio out did work using the PCoIP audio redirection feature, which was much better than using a USB redirection.

The problem is that you can't split a USB audio device such that the audio out functionality remains local to the client and audio in is redirected. So, using a USB headset in a VoIP-type application required the entire headset to be forwarded to the guest.

How does RTAV fix this issue?

Real-Time Audio Video (**RTAV**) does not forward audio and webcam devices using USB. Instead, the devices are left local to the client, and audio/images are pulled from the local devices. The audio/images are then encoded and delivered to the guest virtual machine, and then decoded. A virtual webcam and a virtual microphone are installed in the guest virtual machine, which then plays the received audio/video. You will see **VMware Virtual Microphone** and **VMware Virtual Webcam** in the device manager of your virtual desktop machine.

RTAV can support the following:

- Webcams and audio in at the same time—for example, VoIP video-conference-type applications such as Google Talk and Skype
- Audio-in only (without video)—for example, VoIP applications
- A webcam on its own—for example, webcam-monitoring-type applications and user photo-taking

The RTAV feature only works when using the PCoIP protocol. It does not work with RDP.

View Clients

In this section, we are going to quickly touch on the Horizon View Client as it is an important component of the solution and the way you receive your virtual desktop machine's screenshots remotely.

The View Client is basically where your virtual desktop machine's screen is decoded and displayed on an endpoint device. There are two distinct types of View Clients, a software-based version, which is installed on the user's endpoint device, and a hardware-based version, which uses zero clients.

We will cover the View Client options in more detail in *Chapter 12, View Client Options*.

Summary

In this chapter, we discussed the Horizon View architecture and the different components that make up the complete solution. We covered the key technologies, such as how linked clones work to optimize storage, and then introduced some of the features that go toward delivering a great end user experience, such as delivering high-end graphics, unified communications, profile management, and how the PCoIP protocol delivers the desktop to the end user. Now that you understand these features and components, how they work, and how they fit into the overall solution, in the upcoming chapters, we will be taking a deeper look at how to configure them.

3

Design and Deployment Considerations

In this chapter, we will introduce you to the design and deployment techniques to be taken into consideration when undertaking your VMware Horizon project.

We will discuss suggested techniques to prove the technology and understand how it needs to work inside your business, methods to assess users' existing workloads, and how to use this information to help design your VMware Horizon solution.

Once we fully understand what it is we need to achieve for the business, we will dive deep into design considerations for your Horizon View solution, including, but not limited to, ESXi host design, memory and CPU allocations, the dos and don'ts, storage considerations, thin clients, and more.

Understanding your business requirements

Before jumping ahead into your Horizon project, take a step back and ensure that you document what you are actually trying to achieve. More often than not, it can be very easy to get carried away with the technology, the installation, and configuration such that the end goal is lost. Start by writing a document of requirements listing the business needs, the current problems, the vision, and any compromises and assumptions. As you progress through your project, you should use this document to keep yourself set on the end goal.

In the following sections, we will discuss some methods that will help you understand where the business is today, and this will help you ensure that the end solution will meet the documented needs that you have discovered at the start of your project.

Desktop assessments

A desktop assessment will allow you to granularly understand how your users are using their current desktop solution, whether this be an existing virtual desktop, shared desktop solution, or physical desktop. With a desktop assessment, we are trying to understand many different aspects of the desktop environment; when these metrics are collected, we are able to use these to help us make design decisions. It is likely that the findings of your desktop assessment will feed into the business case for your new Horizon solution.

Methods

There are a number of different third-party products on the market that you can use to conduct a desktop assessment, and you are often able to use the services of a partner to assist with this process rather than purchase any specific software yourselves to conduct the process. Two of the most well-known solutions in this space would be Lakeside Software's SysTrack and Liquidware Labs' Stratusphere UX.

Whatever solution you decide to use, ensure it is designed for the process of desktop assessment specifically and not server virtualization. These are two completely different areas, and while you could probably use desktop assessment software to plan your server virtualization project, it simply would not work the other way around.

What do your users actually do?

While working in an IT department, we often have a good level of understanding of the tasks our users undertake and the software they use to achieve these tasks on a daily basis. However, this can usually be a lot more complex than it might first appear.

By undertaking a desktop assessment, we gather a granular level of understanding about the processes, applications, and experience our users are getting from their existing desktops. This will likely include the applications they use or probably don't use, including the installed versions, capacity and performance requirements, and user experience metrics, such as login times and application load times.

Applications

Understanding the applications in use is going to be a key element moving forward. This will have an impact on many areas, including the number of pools, pool design, application virtualization, and potentially on whether the desktop we are going to assign to the user can be nonpersistent or do we need to allocate a persistent desktop.

Alongside the preceding metrics, we are often able to fully understand the current situation of our desktop estate; it will not be unfamiliar to find many disparate versions of software, meaning potential security risks and many key applications actually crashing on a regular basis. This is some great information to help you build a business case for change and to help you prioritize your rollout to the users with the biggest security holes or the worst user experience.

Performance

If you don't undertake a desktop assessment, it is likely that your desktops might be sized in one of two ways. The first would be by sizing your desktops based on the manufacturer's minimum recommendations, which will potentially be the most cost effective, but is likely to cause you the most amount of problems. The flip side would be to base your desktops on the software manufacturer's recommended specifications. While your users might end up happy with this solution, it is likely that this is going to cost you the most and potentially mean that you will fail to get sign off for your project.

By undertaking a desktop assessment, we can actually understand what the performance curves look like throughout the working day; you are likely to see many dips and spikes throughout the day, such as login storms, AV scans, logoff storms, and other metrics, such as increased Internet usage during lunch breaks. If you work in an education environment, you might see many login and logoff storms during the day. It is important to understand this, as you will need to ensure your solution is designed to meet these requirements. This information can be used to help guide you when sizing the relevant desktop pools, but do be aware of what you are going to be changing within the desktops between the assessments and VDI desktops. This might include moving from XP to Windows 7, or moving to a desktop that has been heavily optimized in comparison to an OEM installation of Windows.

User experience

Above all else, what matters is user experience, which is the measurement of how good or how poor the user's experience of using their desktop actually is. When you undertake a server virtualization project, if done correctly, the users will probably not even realize it has happened. With a desktop virtualization or any EUC work project, it is most likely that they will realize a change has happened and we need to ensure that this is for the project to be a success.

The measurements of user experience will be wide and varied, but these will include elements such as boot time, login time, application load time, page load time, and application failures.

As you are progressing through the proof of concept, pilot, and tuning processes, you want to ensure that the user experience is improving; failing to take user experience into consideration will result in definite failure.

Floor walks, interviews, and department champions

While the desktop assessment process is a key element in any EUC project, this should not replace the need to interact with your users; the benefit of human involvement is that you are able to pick up elements that simply would not be possible with software alone.

Start by simply walking through your office, noting what the users are doing, what applications they are using, what accessories, how many screens, if they are using laptops or PCs, and so on.

Once you have this high level of understanding, consider booking meetings with key business leaders in each department to understand their needs, requirements, and the problems they have with their desktops today. You should also start considering who your department champions are going to be!

What are department champions?

If you are going to make a short list of take-away considerations from this book, departmental champions should be one of them. A departmental champion is a user who is going to be your go-to in the department for everything to do with their department's desktop, design, testing, and support. These people do not need to be IT experts, but should have a desire to help you improve their desktop experience. You will use these people to help you with the design of their desktops; they will be your first port of call to test their desktops and test again after you have listened to feedback.

By using a department champion, you have in from someone in the department straight away. They will have a sense of pride over what is being rolled out and will be there to help you sculpt the desktop and will be the user on your side to help explain why certain decisions have been made.

Considering your options and choosing your technologies

With VMware Horizon, there is no one-product-fits-all solution to your users' needs, so it is important to consider the use cases and match the different use cases to the different technologies within VMware Horizon. Once you have collected the key information from the methods mentioned earlier, it is important to come to a conclusion on which technology is going to meet the users' needs the best. We have two technologies available to us to deliver the desktops to our users with Horizon, Horizon View or Horizon Mirage. We are then able to layer applications over the top of these desktops using Mirage application layers or Horizon Workspace. In the next section, we will discuss some sample scenarios and the decisions we could make based upon these scenarios.

Scenario 1

We have a number of users based in a call center utilizing a Windows desktop to access a customer relationship database. They are also using a web browser to access an intranet page. These users work set hours in a shift pattern across the call center, and they work in a hot desk fashion, utilizing whichever device is available.

Recommendation

This would seem to be the ideal scenario for a Horizon View VDI desktop. With such a simple use case, we might actually decide to deliver these users' desktops through Horizon View with a Microsoft RDS server to allow greater levels of consolidation and potential cost savings. Due to the specifics of the use case, we would limit access to the pool using tags configured on the desktop pool and the View Connection Servers. The CRM client could be installed onto the base image or RDS server, or alternately, could be delivered by ThinApp.

Scenario 2

There are a number of engineering users who need access to a desktop, both online and offline. When offline, they will be utilizing bespoke software to program machinery; often, this work is carried out in areas of poor mobile signal. They rarely come into the office, but do work from home once or twice a week where they have good Internet access. They also need access to a job allocation system when they have access to the Internet. At present, this is accessed via connecting to a work VPN and running a Windows client application on their laptops. They would like to be able to adopt iPads to access the job allocation system but are restricted by the need to use the Windows client.

Recommendation

This scenario highlights the exact type of user that does not suit a VDI desktop alone. Previously, if we had tried to make VDI work in this scenario, it would not have lead to a good user experience. With the diversity available to us now in Horizon Suite, we are able to use the individual components to deliver a solution that can be seamless to the user and offer them a genuine productivity advantage. In this scenario, we would be looking to centralize and manage the desktops using Horizon Mirage. This would allow us to not only locally store a copy of the devices in the case of failure or loss, but also allow us to update and deliver new software when a connection to the Mirage server is available over the Internet. However, there is a key requirement to access an online application in the form of the job allocation system; we could, of course, deliver this in the same way as it is delivered today, but we could also consider delivering this through Horizon View and a published application. This would give the advantage of this application being accessible through a variety of devices, without the complexity of a second desktop that VDI would bring. We could also consider AirWatch by VMware to manage the iPad devices.

Scenario 3

In this scenario we have a marketing department with 10 users, all using desktop PCs with dual screens running Windows XP. Across these desktops are a number of matching applications, but each desktop also has a few individual applications that have been installed by IT for users over the years. They are now looking to start making use of a number of SaaS applications and services such as WebEx, and would also like to have the ability to work from home.

Recommendation

With the end of support for XP, we are going to want to move these users to Windows 7. As such, we are going to want to check the compatibility of their applications with Windows 7, and where possible, we will want to try and standardize the applications as much as possible without affecting the user. Where there are applications that don't support Windows 7, we could see if VMware ThinApp would allow us to virtualize the application on a Windows XP desktop for us to subsequently run on Windows 7. As the user has no offline requirements, this would seem a good fit for VDI, and as there is a large commonality across the desktops, we should try and see how a nonpersistent-linked clone pool would work for these users. We would deliver the common applications by installing these applications in the base image and delivering the individual applications where possible via ThinApp and Horizon Workspace.

Horizon Workspace would also allow the single sign on access to the SaaS applications and services. Finally, as the users' desktops would now be virtualized, they would be able to use their own personal devices to connect into the corporate desktop from home.

Scenario 4

There is a small CAD department with 10 users utilizing Autodesk AutoCAD 2014. They last purchased five workstations with new high-end graphics cards a year ago for half the users. The users must have access to install their own software and keep a lot of data locally while they are working on designs.

Recommendation

We have a number of options in this scenario. With Horizon View 6 and NVidia GRID graphics cards, it is likely that we would be able to offer these users a good experience on a correctly configured virtual desktop. With AutoCAD 2014, it is likely the users will need access to the GPU in a dedicated mode, meaning with a single K1 card, you could have four entry-level users, or with a K2 card, you could have two high-end users. As half the workstations have recently been refreshed, we would recommend these be kept in use until they are due to be replaced, but we use Horizon Mirage for data protection and to manage updates and software rollout. For the remaining users, we should consider dedicated, full-clone desktops inside View along with a K1 or K2 card. These desktops would be managed with Horizon Mirage the same as the physical machine, but as they are VDI desktops, they would offer the ability for thin clients to be deployed on the office floor rather than expensive workstations. It might also offer extended options for remote working in the future if required. It is recommended that this scenario is heavily tested during the **proof of concept** (POC) and pilot stages to understand the type of card required along with the CPU and memory resources.

Conclusions

We have been able to demonstrate that there is no one-size-fits-all solution that can be used over some diverse businesses. If we were to try and wedge some of these scenarios into a single solution, it would result in a poor user experience. With the Horizon Suite, we are not only able to have commonality across the solutions for the users and administrators, but are also able to offer a diverse range of solutions to meet the users' requirements.

Implementation strategy (test, test, and test again)

A correct and well-planned implementation strategy will serve you well, and as you move between stages of the solution, you should be gaining momentum, meaning you are getting closer to your goals of meeting your business requirements and improving the users' experience.

Proof of concept

A POC should do exactly what it says on the tin; this is your opportunity to download the software, install it, and prove that you can do what you need to with the software. Often this might take place prior to or alongside a desktop assessment, and you will probably initially be using the manufacturer's trial licenses to allow you to do this. The POC should be open-minded and should allow you to get a base layer of understanding as to whether you are going to achieve your business objectives. By the end of the POC, you will probably have got some of your departmental champions to connect to some desktops and give you initial feedback on the solution so you can start tuning into their needs.

Pilot

This is when your project is stepping up a notch; you have a high-level understanding that the software is going to let you achieve your goals and you are going to start rolling out desktops to get an understanding of the users' thoughts, as you test and tune the solution to meet your objectives. You will, at this time, probably have at least some investment into dedicated licensing, if not hardware. You will initially start by continuing to roll out, tune, and recreate desktops for your department champions until they are at a stage where they feel they could swap to the virtual desktop full-time to continue giving you feedback. Initially, they might simply connect to their desktop from the Horizon View software clients on their PC, and this would give you a good opportunity to assess the thin clients you might be looking to use. As the testing and tuning process continues, and the issues become lesser, you can then agree to rollout the desktops to a limited amount of pilot users to continue this process. Continually during this process, you should be measuring your success alongside your starting objectives, aiming to get a User Acceptance Test completed prior to full production rollout.

Production

This is where things get really serious; you have tested your solution, proved the concept, piloted with a subset of your users, built a business case, and signed off. Now is the time to start rolling out to your agreed user base. This will happen in a number of ways, but initially, I would suggest starting this slowly and gathering momentum over time. By gathering momentum in this way, you are able to guarantee success, and less tuning is required along the way.

Horizon View pod and block architecture

We are going to start by discussing a key concept of Horizon View design, that is, **pod** and **block architecture**.

VMware's pod and block architecture allows you to grow a single site to 10,000 users. This is achieved by creating separate Horizon View blocks that scale into a pod to give you one large, unified virtual desktop environment. Now, you might be reading this thinking, "I only have 500 desktops to create in my environment so this does not matter to me", but I would urge you to carry on and understand the design principle. If you are creating a VDI solution for 500 desktops, you will still be utilizing the concepts within the pod and block architecture, but you will only be creating one pod and one block.

Inside the pod, the Horizon View Connection Servers are configured in a cluster, and replicate their data using Microsoft's lightweight directory services and the **Java Message Service (JMS)**. VMware recommends a limit of seven View Connection Servers in a pod; these are installed as one per block plus two extra for availability and/or external connectivity.

Within each block, there are a number of ESXi hosts, a vCenter, and a View Composer instance along with the supporting SQL database, as well as shared storage that can either be exclusive to the block or shared across multiple blocks. All the blocks in the architecture are connected together by a switched network and all management components run in the management block. If you are starting out with one block in your pod, you will want to ensure that you have at least two View Connection Servers for resilience.

You should note that VMware does not support configuration of blocks across a WAN link as the JMS utilized for communication is very susceptible to network latency. However, using Horizon 6, VMware now supports Cloud Pod Architecture, which allows you to further scale out and provide high availability across multiple sites. We will discuss this later in this chapter.

The following image shows the high-level overview of the Horizon View block and pod architecture. When implemented in production, the users connect to the View Connection Servers or security servers via third-party load balancers:

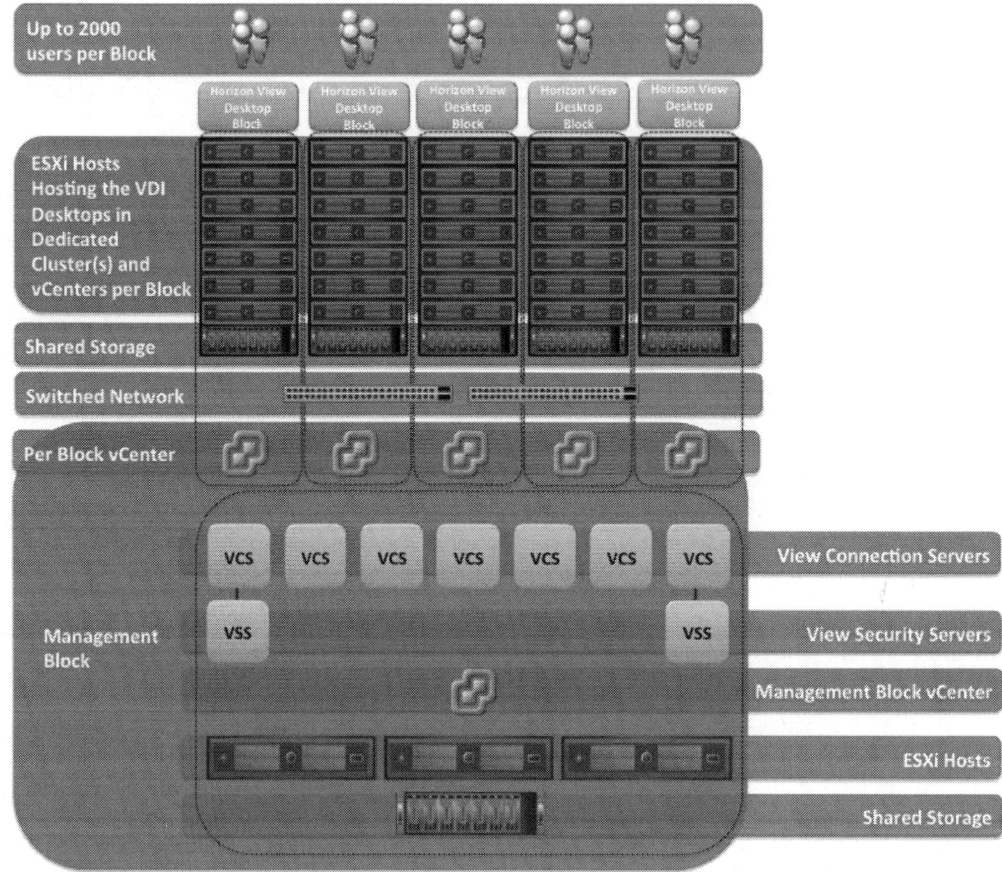

It should be noted that as of View 5.2, it is possible to scale a block up to 10,000 users when there are multiple Connection Servers used to overcome the 2,000 connection limit of View Connection Servers. However, this would result in a large single point of failure in the vCenter Server itself, as big as you should be considering the risk to your business by that component failing and design your architecture accordingly. It would be recommended by VMware that, where possible, you limit your pods to 2,000 users to limit the risk of failure.

With a single vCenter, we will also be limited to the amount of concurrent operations that we are able to undertake. This will be of major significance, for example, when powering up a large number of desktops or recomposing a large number of pools. If we have multiple vCenter Servers in this scenario, we will be able to further increase the amount of parallel operations that could happen across the vCenter Servers rather than the serial nature of a single vCenter.

Cloud Pod Architecture

The Cloud Pod Architecture is new in Horizon 6 and it allows you to federate up to four pods over two sites and up to a maximum of 20,000 desktops.

When connecting multiple pods in this manner, it will give you the ability to entitle users across pools on both pods and sites. So if you currently have scaled past a single pod, either for scale on one site or to deliver a view environment on multiple sites, it will now allow you to administer users through a global user entitlement layer. We are now also able to deliver users' DR desktops, in the event of failure, through the global user entitlement layer. We are able to configure the scope to set whether View shows users' resources based only locally to them on the same site, but across pods, or in all pods across both sites:

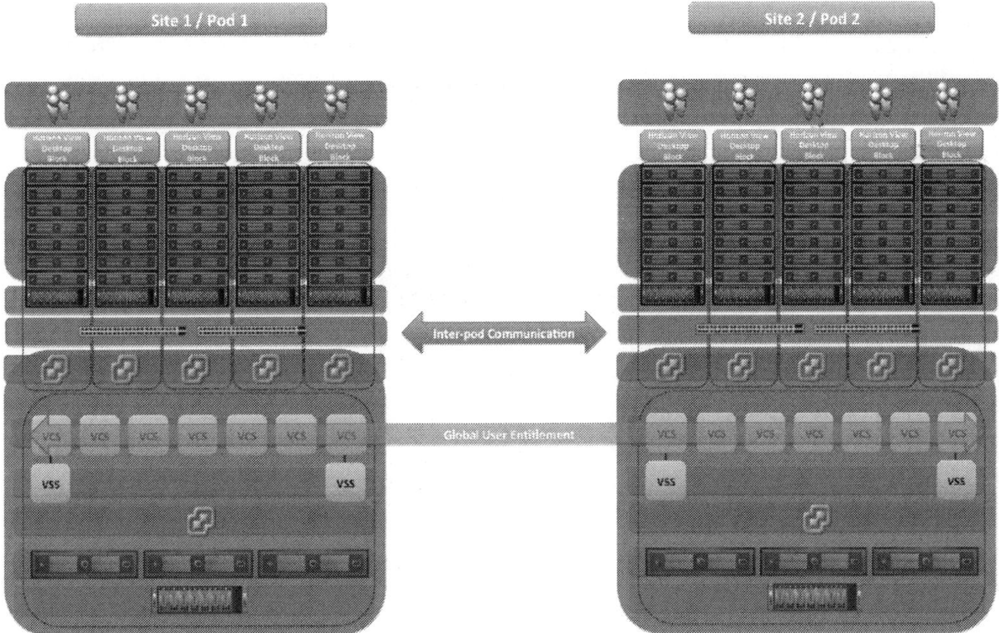

Microsoft Active Directory Lightweight Service and the new **View Interpod API (VIPA)** are used for interpod communications. VIPA is enabled when you enable the Cloud Pod Architecture from the command line on the View Connection Servers. VIPA is used when desktops are launched, to send health information and to find existing desktops and more.

By default, when a user connects to Horizon View and they have a global entitlement, there will be a preference applied by the global entitlement to utilize desktops at the local site rather than across a secondary site where possible. However, this is fully customizable by the administrator when creating the global entitlement as well as a wealth of other options. An example on some of these options is discussed ahead in the chapter.

With the scope configuration options, we are able to select the behavior of users' desktop connections in the Cloud Pod:

- **Any**: This allows View to look for any desktops that are part of the global entitlement in any pod
- **Site**: This allows View to look only for desktops that are part of the global entitlement in any pod within the same site as the user
- **Local**: This allows View to look only for desktops that are in the local pod that the user is connected to

You are also able to configure elements such as the **from home** option, which will cause View to look for desktops in a user's home site when a user has been preconfigured with a home site.

Along with configuring the Cloud Pod Architecture, you will need to utilize third party load balancing technologies to allow the benefits of this technology to be seamless to the end users. But this now gives us a way of unifying our multiple View deployments that previously would have been separate entities. We will look at how this is configured in the later chapters, but it should be noted that, at present, the Cloud Pod Architecture is managed only from the command line.

vSphere design for Horizon View

Between your POC and pilot, you are likely to start thinking about the design of the infrastructure to help you build a business case. Following the POC and the pilot, you will be looking to ratify your design to ensure the design still meets the requirements based upon your findings.

vSphere design

In this book, we aren't going into the intricacies of how to install and configure your ESXi hosts. However, we will briefly discuss the recommendations on how you should configure vCenter, your hosts, and clusters within your Horizon View environment.

It is technically possible to run your Horizon View and Server virtual environments from one infrastructure, with one vCenter and one or more clusters of ESXi hosts. By doing this, it can create a number of points of contention and a lot of difficulty during the time of upgrades.

We have two key areas when it comes to the Horizon View environment, first, the components that are required to run the Horizon View environment, such as the vCenter, View Composer, and View Connection Server, and second, the virtual desktops themselves. We recommend that these two components be separated physically onto different ESXi hosts; this minimizes the risk of there being performance issues with the server components during heavy use periods or large desktop provision processes. We would also recommend that the Horizon View components be separated onto a different vCenter from your production vSphere environment, by separating the Horizon components into a separate vCenter. This will mean less clash of priorities and prerequisites when it comes to upgrading either environment.

The following diagram shows an example of how your virtual environments could be designed:

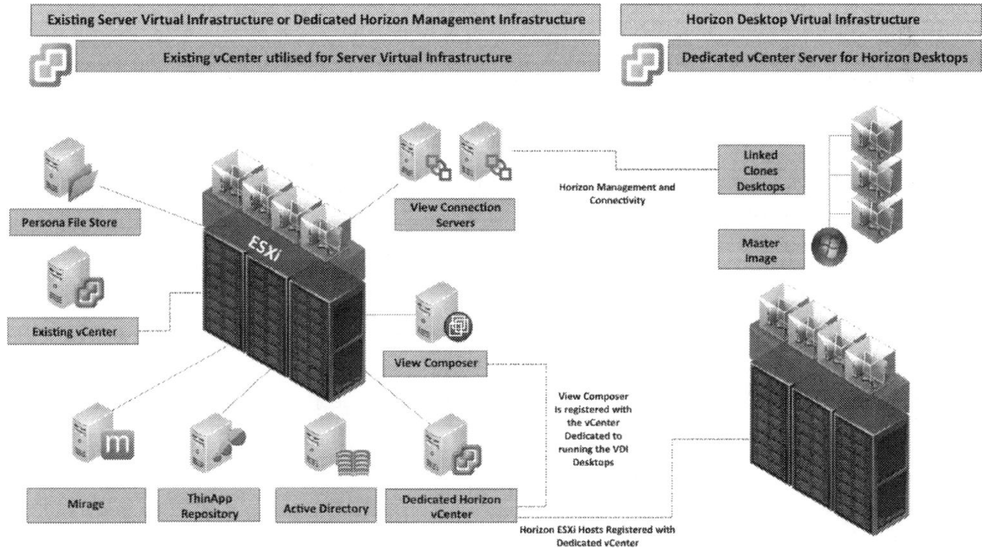

Configuration maximums

When building any VDI infrastructure, we can sometimes very quickly and easily reach the configuration maximums that have been set by the manufacturer for any given product. When it comes to vSphere and vCenter, there are a number of maximums that we should be aware of.

The following is a selection of configuration maximums for vSphere 5.5 that might affect your vSphere design for VDI. If you will be deploying vSphere 6 within your environment you will want to note the new maximums such as the increased cluster size but ensure you check for the latest compatibility with Horizon View prior to installing vSphere 6:

Item	Maximum
Maximum number of connections for a single connection server (PCoIP or RDS)	2000
Maximum number of connection for 7 connection servers (PCoIP or RDS)	10000
Blast Secure Gateway connections to remote desktops using HTML Access	2000
Maximum number of desktops in a cloud pod	20000
Maximum number of pods in a cloud pod architecture	4
Maximum number of sites in a cloud pod architecture	2
Maximum View Connection Servers in a cloud pod architecture	20
Machine name character limit including auto generated numbers	15
Clusters per desktop pool	1
Hosts per cluster with vSphere 5.1 or higher	
Limited to VMFS5 and NFS datastores or VSAN with vSphere 5.5 Update 1	32
Maximum monitors with PCoIP	4
Maximum monitors with 3D Rendering enabled	2
Maximum monitors with RDP 7	16

You will also need to keep in mind the Horizon View specific maximums that are discussed later in this chapter. Don't forget that these maximums are not goals to try and hit but maximum limits. When designing your architecture, you should also keep in mind what is the risk of losing an individual component such as vCenter.

ESXi hosts

We are going to cover some recommendations on the sizing and quantities of hosts that might be required within your infrastructure.

As with any virtual infrastructure, we want to ensure that redundancy is included. This means ensuring that your chosen servers have redundant power supplies, RAID hard disks or mirrored SD cards for ESXi, and multiple network cards for network failovers in the case of a card or switch failure. You are also going to examine how many hosts are likely to be required within our environment and then add the relative amount of hosts to allow for the *N+* capacity that you require. In most environments, this will be *N+1*, meaning you will have the number of hosts you require to run your virtual desktops and one additional to allow for failover of desktops in the case of host failure.

CPU and memory

Now let's look at some recommendations for your CPU and memory.

Overcommitting resources

As a rule of thumb, never over commit memory in a VDI environment. This can have many knock-on effects if memory is not granted when required, which will ultimately affect user experience. As such, you might wish to set up a reservation for memory on your desktop VMs to 100 percent of the memory required. This will result in the swap file not needing to be created and a reduction in storage space required.

When it comes to CPUs, while it would be nice to also not have an over commitment, this would simply not be affordable. CPU over commitment, if done carefully and not pushed too far, can usually be allowed with little to no effect on the end users.

However, how far is not too far is the question. This will generally depend on the type of workload you will see within your environment. If you look at various resources on the Internet, you will find different answers to this question, with some claiming figures of more than 10 **virtual CPUs** (**vCPUs**) per physical core. The only true way to find out what is going to be acceptable in your environment is by reviewing the CPU Ready figure; you can review this metric via vCenter, ESXTOP, or similar tools. When reviewing the CPU Ready figures, you should initially be looking to ensure that you are keeping CPU Ready below 5 percent per vCPU for the desktops in your environment. Your environment might be able to accept CPU Ready higher than 5 percent, but this should only be after testing during your POC and pilot stages. Generally, if CPU Ready is as high as 10 percent per vCPU, the environment is going to struggle enough to affect the user experience considerably.

CPU and memory sizing

The number of hosts required for your Horizon View infrastructure is usually dictated by the number of desktops required, the amount of CPU and RAM these desktops require, what over commit ratio you can allow for the CPU within your infrastructure, and how much CPU and memory can you include on your chosen hosts. When taking all of that into consideration, you are looking to include the amount of memory and CPU cores across the infrastructure that allows you to balance these in a cost-effective fashion without too much wastage.

When selecting your host, you should also consider what effect it would have on the business if that one host was to fail. As such sometimes, you might consider hosts with two physical CPUs to be a better design decision than four, and as the number of cores per CPU increase, there are less cores per CPU than more.

Ensure within your calculations that you are considering the overheads ESXi requires to be able to run your virtual machines, as well as memory to be dedicated as graphics memory to virtual machines if required.

The following screenshot lists typical values of overheads (in MB) required per VM:

Memory (MB)	1 vCPU	2 vCPU	3 vCPU	4 vCPU
256	20.29	24.28	32.23	48.16
1024	25.90	29.91	37.86	53.82
4096	48.64	52.72	60.67	76.68

Resource: VMware vSphere Resource Management Guide 5.5

Network

There are generally two considerations for the networking in your ESXi hosts, 1 GB or 10 GB. No matter what, you will always want to ensure you have at least two multiport network cards to separate your traffic to allow the resilient network design that you require. As to whether you require 1 GB or 10 GB for the VM LAN traffic within your infrastructure, it completely depends on the use case. If you are streaming a lot of HD media into your VDI desktops, then 10 GB might well be required.

Graphics

A lot of information has already been covered regarding the hardware and software graphics offload and accelerating options in *Chapter 2, An Overview of Horizon View Architecture and its Components*.

The requirements for graphics in your environment should be carefully considered and tested during the POC and pilot stages of your VDI project. You will consider all of the elements mentioned in *Chapter 2, An Overview of Horizon View Architecture and its Components*, and decide what is then required with regard to PCI cards in your ESXi hosts. The requirement for PCI cards for graphics acceleration or offloading will affect the hardware you choose for your ESXi hosts due to the limitations of some of these cards with regard to power and cooling, along with the number of PCIe slots available.

NVidia has a list of supported servers, with the numbers of cards these servers might house, listed at `http://bit.ly/eucbook2_3_1`.

Storage

We could probably write a whole book on storage considerations, designs, and options with regard to your VDI environment. Storage is probably among the most important areas to get right, the first most obvious reason is that you don't want to end up with insufficient storage for your planned rollout, and the second reason is failure to specify a storage solution that is going to meet your performance requirements will leave you with unhappy users and a failed project.

Capacity

Your first consideration will be how much storage you need for your Horizon View environment. You will need to consider where the relative elements of your virtual infrastructure are to be located. The first and easy bit is going to be totaling the required space for any server components. Often, the server components will live on the same storage device as the rest of your virtual infrastructure, and the desktops will live on a dedicated storage device. However, this is not compulsory and will depend on the type of storage you are utilizing and the levels of separation you desire. You will then need to understand the required storage for your desktops based upon the technologies being used to deploy the desktops, such as linked clones, linked clones with persistent disks, or full clones.

With linked clones, you need to have an understanding of the growth of the linked clone between the refresh and recompose operations. The following figure gives an example of some areas for consideration with regard to storage for a typical desktop pool utilizing linked clones and persistent disks:

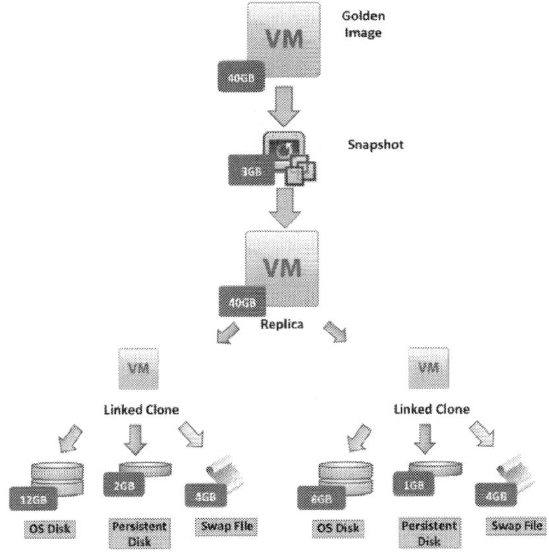

We recommend that during your POC and pilot stages, you collect this type of storage usage information. Once you have this information, you will be able to use a spreadsheet to create a model to predict the storage utilization and you can grow your environment. The following screenshot depicts a sample excel spreadsheet outlining the storage requirement across 3 desktop pools:

Desktop Pool	Golden Image Size	Linked Clone or Full Clone?	Replica Size	Swap File	Persistent Disk Per Desktop	Number of Desktops	Space per Desktop	Total Space (GB)
Administration	40GB	Linked Clone	40GB	2GB		200	12GB	2880
Managers	60GB	Full Clone		4GB		20	40GB	940
Marketing	40GB	Linked Cline	40GB	4GB	10GB	30	20GB	1100
Total								4920

During the proof of concept we have been able to understand the capacity required per desktop for the linked clones. This is a key component to understanding the overall capacity required for the solution moving forward.

Performance

Once you are aware of how much capacity you require for you Horizon View environment, you are able to start considering your performance needs. As always, it is recommended that you understand your performance requirements during the POC and pilot stages and use this to size your storage. When examining your virtual environment, you are looking to keep the read and write latency as low as possible to guarantee a good user experience. The amount of latency acceptable will depend greatly on the workload of your users and the tolerances of the applications they are using. However, keeping average latency as low as 25 ms will often deliver a good user experience for your users.

However, we will talk around typical values seen in real-world scenarios and the common pitfalls when sizing storage performance for a VDI environment. The first point to understand is to never believe a marketing document or white paper that tells you that your VDI environment requires between 5-15 IOPS per user. In real life, scenarios such as this are often far from good and will result in unhappy users. In most typical physical desktops, the users will have at least a single SATA 7.2 K disk that is capable of 80 IOPS. In a more modern desktop, they might even have an SSD drive capable of many hundred, if not thousands, of IOPS. In real-life scenarios, we have found that sizing sample workloads between 30-50 IOPS will deliver more realistic results, which will deliver a suitable user experience. Once again, we highly recommend reviewing and testing what will work for your users during the POC and pilot stages.

During the POC and pilot stages, utilize the performance graphs available in vCenter and ESXTOP to understand the utilization per desktop and the relative latency figures.

The first point of consideration is to understand the type of storage workload we see in VDI environments. Commonly, overlooked VDI workloads are typically more intensive than similarly sized server workloads. To understand this statement, we need to understand what makes up a typical server workload and VDI workload. Within a server-based environment, we will typically see that a usage of 70-80 percent reads to the remaining writes. This is important due to the overhead of RAID and the effect this will have on storage performance. With a smaller amount of writes to reads, the storage solution needed to deliver the performance will typically be able to contain less disks or, at least, slow performing disks than a solution with higher writes, even if the overall IOPS are the same. With VDI workloads, we can often flip these figures on their head with a login storm and steady state IOPS being made up with as high as 70 percent writes. This can and will have a major effect on the storage required to run our VDI environment.

The following graph depicts a sample storage environment depicting a sample workload as the desktops are booted. Users log in and then continue to use the desktops. On the vertical axis, we can see inputs and outputs per second, and on the horizontal axis, we can see time. As we can see, the boot storm is heavily read intensive, with the login storm and steady state being heavily write-intensive:

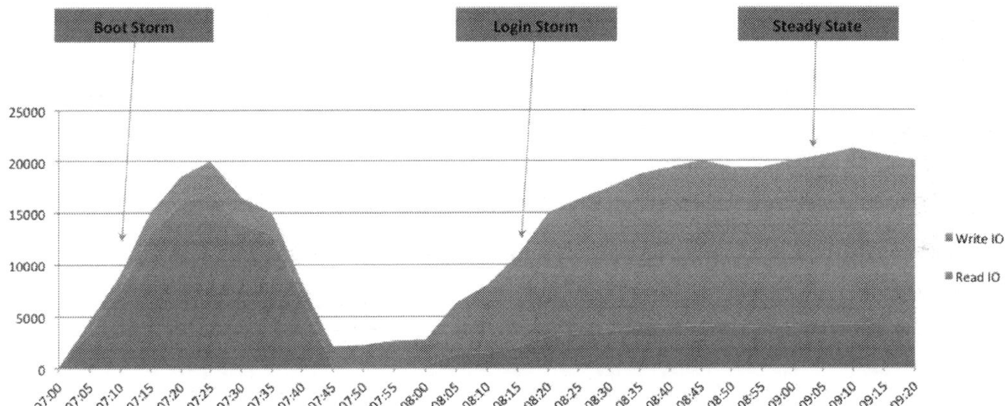

Once you understand what performance and capacity you require for your VDI environment, you are able to browse the marker to understand what solution will work for you. Quite often, hybrid flash and spinning disk solutions offer the lowest cost per GB while delivering suitable performance in a VDI environment.

Horizon View offers a number of ways to configure your storage on a per-pool basis, meaning your options are by no means limited to what type of storage you are able to use. When you are configuring your View Pool, you get the option to separate the replica from the OS disk. This means, if you have a tier of SSD storage that is optimized for reads, you get the opportunity to place the replica on this storage while placing the linked clones on a suitable alternative storage. You are also able to make use of local storage for your virtual machines. When configuring linked clones and utilizing storage, your replica will be placed on each local datastore selected. Ensure you have considered the availability of the desktops if you do use local storage.

Horizon View design specifics

There are a number of concepts we need to ensure we understand while designing our Horizon View infrastructure.

Configuration maximums

Alongside the configuration maximums listed earlier in this chapter for vSphere, we need to be aware of the specific configuration maximums for Horizon View. We have listed some of the more important ones to consider when building your View environment:

Item	Maximum
Maximum number of connections for a single connection server (PCoIP or RDS)	2000
Maximum number of connection for 7 connection servers (PCoIP or RDS)	10000
Blast Secure Gateway connections to remote desktops using HTML Access	800
Maximum number of desktops in a cloud pod	20000
Maximum number of pods in a cloud pod architecture	4
Maximum number of sites in a cloud pod architecture	2
Maximum View Connection Servers in a cloud pod architecture	20
Machine name character limit including auto generated numbers	15
Clusters per desktop pool	1
Hosts per cluster with vSphere 5.1 or higher	
Limited to VMFS5 and NFS datastores or VSAN with vSphere 5.5 Update 1	32
Maximum monitors with PCoIP	4
Maximum monitors with 3D Rendering enabled	2
Maximum monitors with RDP 7	16

Networking

There are a number of considerations when understanding the network requirements for your Horizon View environment. We will need to understand the use cases for our desktops and where our users will be connecting from. Some of these elements will be out of our control, such as the users' Internet connection when connecting from external sources. Other elements, such as available bandwidth and quality of service on the internal network, are very much under your control.

Bandwidth considerations

VMware have previously posted the sample figures seen in the following diagram for bandwidth-sizing guidelines for VMware View. As you can see, the amount of bandwidth required for the desktop connectivity is directly related to the users' activity, as well as the monitor configuration. You are also able to control and optimize the bandwidth usage by tuning the PCoIP protocol. You can read about this in *Chapter 8, Fine-tuning the End User Experience*.

While the bandwidth considerations for the LAN should not be a problem for most networks, serious consideration and understanding should be given to the requirements for users connecting over the WAN, including but not limited to branch offices:

Scenario	Average Required Bandwidth
Basic office productivity desktop: typical office applications with no video, no 3D graphics, and the default Windows and Horizon View settings	100 to 150Kbps
Optimized office productivity desktop: typical office applications with no video, no 3D graphics, with Windows desktop settings optimized and Horizon View optimized	50 to 100Kbps
Virtual desktops utilizing multiple monitors, 3D, Aero, and Office 2010	400 to 600Kbps
User running 480p video, depending upon the configured frame rate limit and the video type	2Mbps

The preceding figures are based on information from VMware's architectural planning guides.

Load balancers

A key requirement for Horizon View is the need of load balancers to use between View Connection Servers. This not only allows you to scale your solution, but also offers high availability, should there be a failure.

It should be noted that there is no load balancer functionality included within Horizon View. As such, you will require third-party load balancers. It is possible to make use of Microsoft **Network Load Balancing** (**NLB**) on a small scale and proof of concept deployments, but as your solution starts moving on from POC to pilot stage, you should consider the need for dedicated physical or virtual load balancers.

When selecting a load balancer, you need to ensure it is able to offer session persistence. This ensures the connected user is already directed to the same View Connection Server or View Security Server during their session. You should also ensure that the load balancing solution that is implemented is highly available.

The following diagram shows how a typical load balancing solution for Horizon View would be configured:

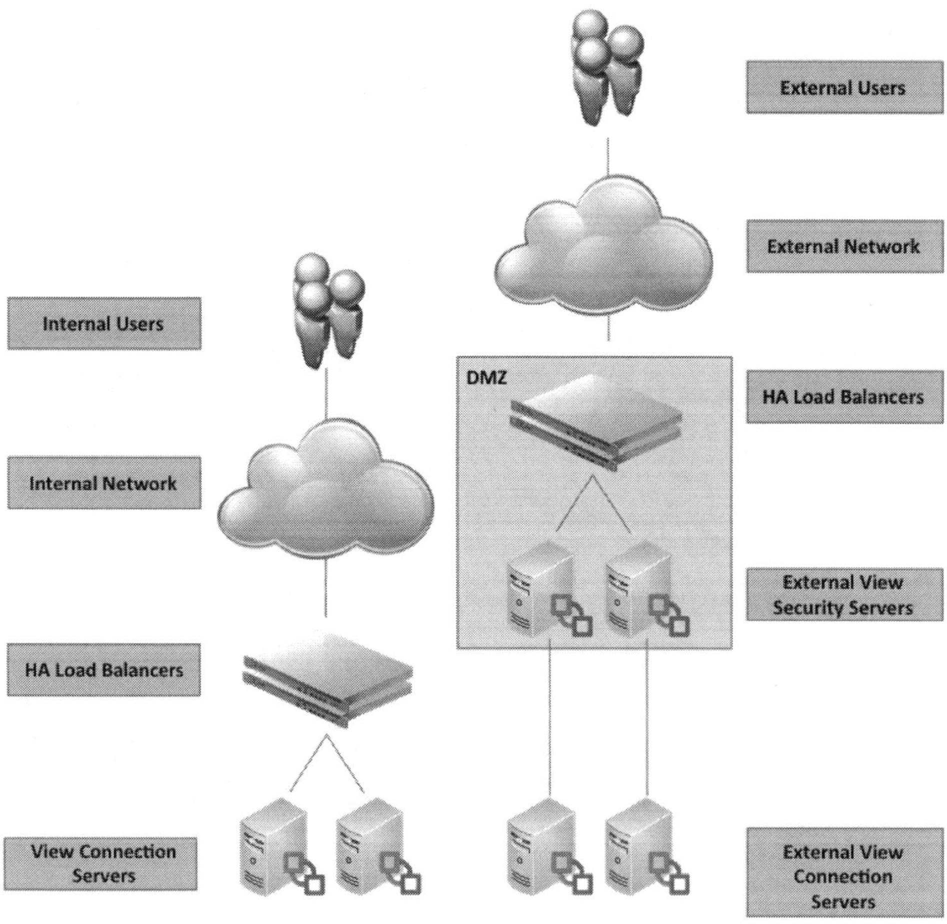

As we can see, there are multiple VMware Horizon Connection Servers configured for internal and external connections. The internal Connection Servers are load balanced behind an HA pair of load balancers. Externally, there are two View Connection Servers, each paired with a dedicated View Security Server, and the security servers are then load balanced by a dedicated HA pair of load balancers.

Remote Desktop Server design considerations

With Horizon View 6, VMware now supports Microsoft RDS as first-class desktop sources, meaning they now fully support PCoIP, whereas previously, while they have been supported as desktop sources, they only support RDP. Along with the supported RDS as a desktop source we are now able to use RDS servers to present published applications to our users. We will go into these two elements in detail in *Chapter 10, Delivering Remote Applications with Horizon Advanced* and *Chapter 11, Delivering Session-based Desktops with Horizon View*. We are going to concentrate on the design considerations for RDS-based designs here.

Horizon View uses the concept of farms to place together hosts that provide a common set of applications or desktops for users. When you are creating applications or desktop pools, you will point them at the specific farms that you have created. A farm might contain anywhere between 1 and 200 RDS hosts.

With Horizon View, the RDS servers are able to be either physical or virtual. An important point to consider when designing your RDS servers in a virtual environment is to ensure you do not over commit virtual CPUs to the underlying physical CPUs. In the following diagram, we will try and illustrate why:

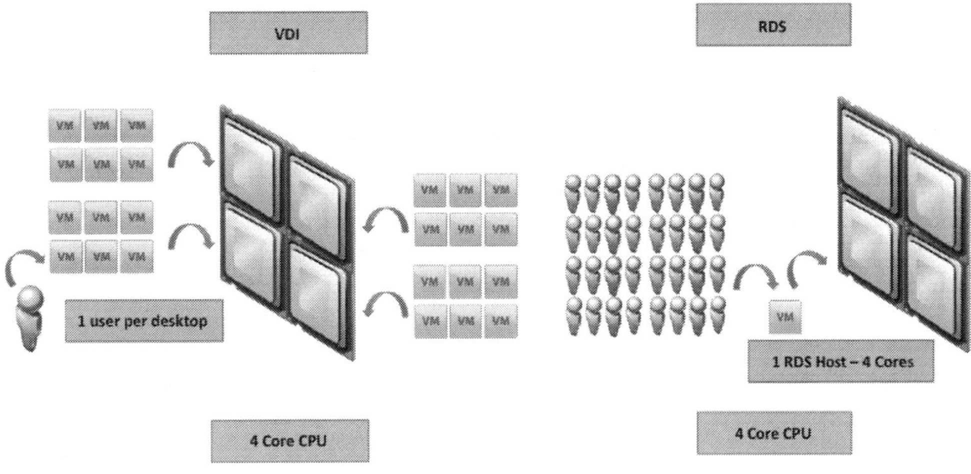

With VDI, we are able to achieve good levels of consolidation by over allocating virtual CPUs to physical cores. With RDS, we achieve good levels of consolidation by over allocating users to physical or virtual cores. If we, in turn, over allocate virtual CPUs to physical CPUs, it will ultimately result in poor performance for your users. As ever, we don't want to design memory over allocation into our design as standard.

If we are utilizing RDS for published applications, you need to consider the design with regard to application deployment. Will all of our applications be deployed on one server farm or are there going to be separate server farms for different applications? We need to consider the resource, CPU memory, and disk required for each of our RDS servers depending on their workload.

Consideration should also be made on how many PCoIP connections are required based on your application and desktop design. In the following diagram, we can see that the user has a View desktop and they are running one set of applications from **Server Farm A** and one set of applications from **Server Farm B**. In total, this user will be utilizing three **PCoIP** connections, one for the View desktop, one for all the applications in **Server Farm A**, and one to allow the applications in **Server Farm B**. As such, we need to be sure that we understand the maximum connections for one View Connection Server and decide how we are going to scale our solution to meet the needs of the design:

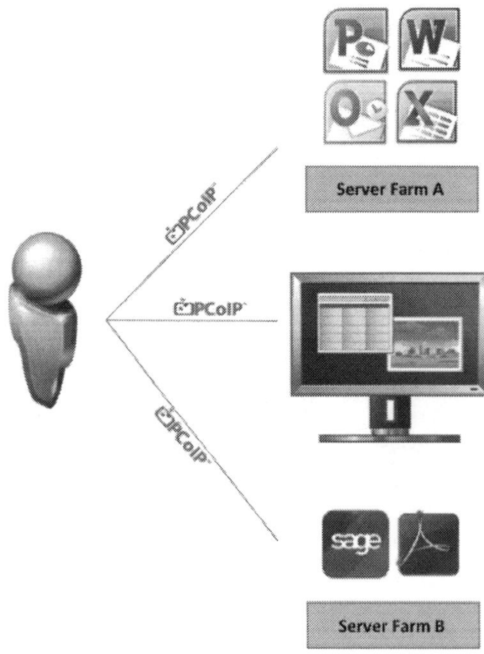

We shouldn't forget that we can also use Horizon Workspace to deliver published applications to virtual or physical desktops. So your VDI or RDS desktops could be in a completely separate View environment to that of your hosted applications.

Supporting infrastructure design

Outside of the virtual infrastructure itself there are a number of other components that you will have to consider when it comes to designing a Horizon View solution. We would recommend you use migration to a new desktop solution as an opportunity to review all components associated with your users' experience of their desktops. There are also a number of third-party services that Horizon View is reliant on.

SQL/Oracle

Microsoft SQL or Oracle are key components for View Composer and the View events database. Without the Composer database being available, View is unable to undertake any provisioning or recompose operations. As such, you might wish to consider the availability of the database server and split the environment up as per the block architecture, to use multiple database servers at one per block. You should also ensure you have regular and up-to-date backups of the View Composer database in the case of loss or corruption.

File servers

File servers are often overlooked when it comes to creating your Horizon View environment but often play a critical role in the overall functionality of the VDI environment.

The following image illustrates some of the components for which you may be relying on a file server:

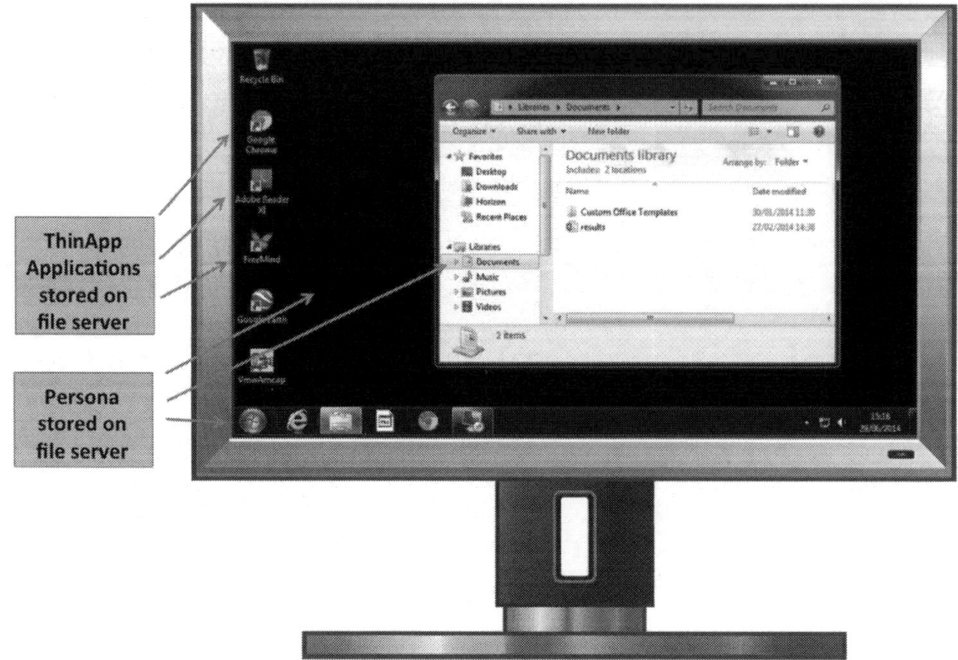

First of all, let's size your file server for performance, ensure that your file server has sufficient RAM and CPU to meet the demands, particularly at peak times, monitor the utilization of your file server, and ensure you grow it as required. The performance of the disks associated with your file server will also be critical.

With your applications and Personas being saved on the file servers, we need to consider the effect of these resources being unavailable when the users are trying to use their desktops. In the case of the streamed applications, ThinApp will not be loaded or might fail midway through using an application if the file server goes offline. With the Persona on the file server, this could have a severe impact on the users accessing their data or there may be unconsidered effects, such as the application data being unable to load or reduced performance of the desktop.

As such, the availability of file servers needs to be a serious consideration if you plan on using a shared storage device that supports CIFS shares. You could consider storing these files on this device, otherwise a clustered file server could probably be considered to ensure availability. Of course, these decisions need to be taken alongside the business needs. If your View environment is going to be small initially and your file server is stored on a virtual environment, the built-in HA functionality might be enough for your requirements.

IP addressing

Often overlooked in a VDI rollout are IP addressing, subnets, and DHCP requirements. Quite often, in a large company, you are going to use multiple subnets across the business as you separate areas with VLANs. When you slowly start scaling your deployment, it can sometimes be easy to forget that your subnets or DHCP scopes won't be large enough until it is too late and you run out of addresses. As such, we should consider how we are going to configure our VDI desktops with regard to our IP schemes. By default, through the View Administrator, it is only possible to assign each pool a single network tag. As such, when the desktops are rolled out, they will use the same network tag that the golden image is configured to use. However, it is possible to configure multiple network tags to pools via the View PowerCLI, which we will discuss in *Chapter 7, Managing and Configuring Desktop Pools*.

On the subject of IP addressing, it's important to note that if you want to use IPv6 then you will need to deploy Horizon 6 Version 6.1. You must also use either IPv4 or IPv6 and not a mixed mode as that is not supported. It's also worth noting that not all Horizon 6 features that are supported in an IPv4 environment are supported in an IPv6 environment.

Antivirus

Antivirus can often be the nemesis of a good VDI design. If the antivirus solution is not configured in a way that is understanding to the shared nature of the VDI solution, it can often be the cause of large performance issues across the environment.

The first consideration with any optimized desktop solution is to ensure you optimize your antivirus solution to be considerate to the use cases of the users and the applications that they are using. With a VDI solution, we often want to deliver just the right amount of resources to ensure it meets the users' needs while not over-delivering resources that can have a knock-on effect to the overall cost of our solution. We have personally seen in VDI environments with antivirus configuration issues, that double the CPU, RAM, and disk resources that are required. Clearly, this could have a massive effect on the cost of our solution and, ultimately, our ability to deliver the project.

Second, full desktop scans need to be considered. First of all, you should consider whether full scans are required at all on desktops that are being refreshed on a daily basis. If full AV scans are a defined requirement, ensure that they are run out of hours and staggered across the desktops. Simultaneous starting scans across all the desktops will affect the RAM, CPU, and IOPS being consumed, and potentially cause knock-on effects across the environment.

Wherever possible, consider utilizing an antivirus product that can integrate with the vShield Endpoint, as covered in *Chapter 2, An Overview of Horizon View Architecture and its Components*. If it is not possible to utilize the vShield Endpoint, ensure you have considered how the linked clone desktops are going to receive their updates to the virus signatures and antivirus updates on their own, between recompose operations. Without a process to handle this every time the desktop is refreshed between recompose operations, all the virus signatures and antivirus updates have to be updated each time. This could be daily, and as time goes by, could begin to be a considerable size when calculated across all desktops. You will also want to ensure that when installing the AV in your golden image, you run a full AV scan to allow an index file to be created. Failing to do this with many AV products will effectively result in a full scan having to run on each desktop between recompose operations.

Group policy

As ever, group policy has a major affect on your desktops, irrespective of whether they are physical or virtual. When designing any EUC solution, there are three main areas you should consider when designing your group policies, namely, functionality, lockdown, and performance.

Functionality

Group policy can be your best friend, particularly when implementing nonpersistent desktops. Correctly configured, you should be looking to use group policy to configure first-use settings for your desktops and Microsoft applications, alongside the obvious login scripts and mapped drives.

Lockdown

Using group policy to lockdown desktops can offer an advantage in a VDI environment, again, particularly for nonpersistent desktops where you don't want users saving documents in areas that won't be redirected, or customizations that probably won't be saved. Our advice would be, in a new VDI environment, try and not use the implementation of your new VDI infrastructure as an opportunity to introduce new strict lockdowns while implementing VDI itself. Often, when these kinds of stringent lockdowns are implemented at the same time as VDI, the VDI solution will be blamed for any disruptions or reduction in user experience caused by the new lockdowns. Our advice would be, if a new stringent lockdown policy is required, either try and implement it on the physical desktops prior to the migration to VDI, or implement the VDI solution first before introducing the new lockdowns. You will also find that it can be difficult to troubleshoot where a problem may reside by introducing too many changes at once.

Performance and management

We aren't going to use this book to write about the A to Z regarding configuration of group policy for optimal performance. There are already a number of resources on the Internet and multiple topics on this subject. We would recommend that you ensure to keep on top of your group policies, ensuring old unnecessary policies are removed wherever possible. Use a functional design, where you group together GPOs into functional groups but don't take them to the nth degree by creating a GPO per setting. This will ensure ease of management and will reduce the performance effect when changes are made.

As this book is not dedicated to group policy, we would recommend checking out the galore of information on the Internet regarding group policy best practices.

Key Management Server

To ensure seamless license activation between recompose operations of Windows and Office, a Microsoft **Key Management Server** (**KMS**) is imperative to your VDI design. Your desktop will find the KMS via DNS or via manual assignment, which you can preconfigure into the base image and will then be assigned the relevant keys to gain activation.

Microsoft KMS is quickly and easily configured as a role within Windows 2012 and earlier versions of Windows. As part of the configuration, you will need your KMS license key from Microsoft. This key will be input during configuration, and your KMS will need to be activated by Microsoft over the Web or via the phone. Once the role is configured, you are ready to start rolling out and activating your desktops with KMS. However, you should be aware that there is a threshold for activations prior to KMS coming to life of 25 client machines. So, if you want to give this a try, ensure your first pool is larger than 25 machines. Once the threshold has been reached, you will be able to activate single machines one at a time, if required.

If you wish to activate Microsoft Office products using the KMS server, you also need to install the Microsoft Office 2013 Volume License Pack on your KMS server. This can be downloaded from the Microsoft Download Center.

Printing

Printing is often a black art, and working with any VDI or RDS, this can often be complicated further. Included with Horizon View is the ThinPrint technology that allows a number of configurations when it comes to printing from your desktop pools. We covered ThinPrint in some detail in *Chapter 2, An Overview of Horizon View Architecture and its Components*.

However, we have often found that the simplest solution across the board is to implement a follow me printing solution. With a solution such as PaperCut, users print to a virtual follow me printer. They are then able to release the document to the printer from a localized **Release Station** or compatible printer, which has been explained in the following diagram:

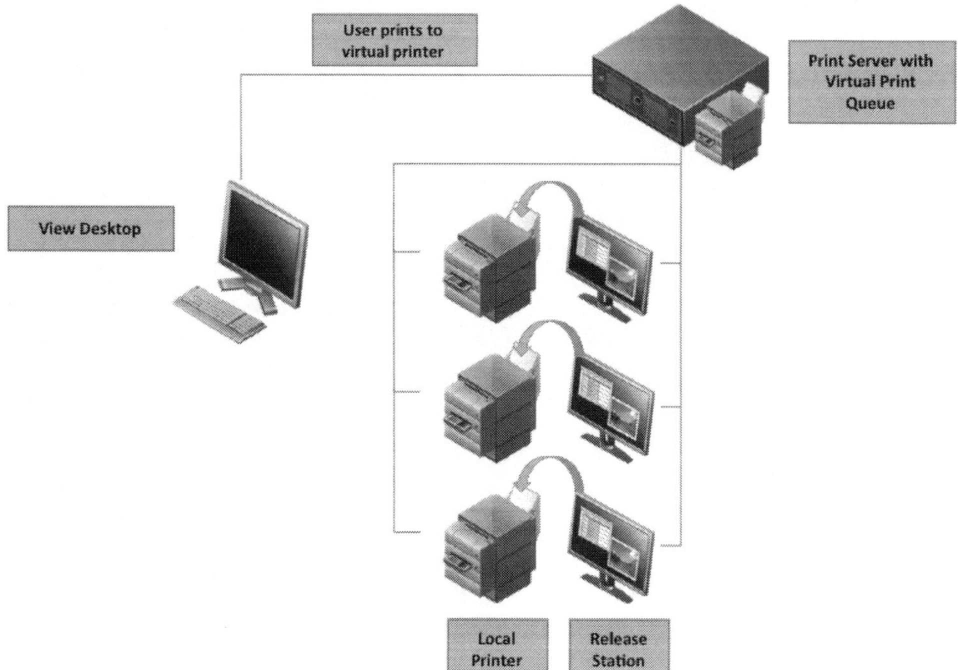

Thin clients

We are going to talk in great detail about thin clients in *Chapter 12, View Client Options*. However, it is important to understand that not all thin clients are built the same way; you need to ensure that for each specific use case, you have considered the thin client requirements and selected the appropriate thin client. It is also important to consider how you are going to manage the thin clients. Please refer to *Chapter 12, View Client Options*, for more detail in this area.

Desktop design

You might think that once you have spent the time considering and designing all the elements mentioned earlier, that the hard work is over. Realistically, it has only just begun. Your VDI solution, without the desktops, is just a VI, and the design and functionality of the desktops is critical to a successful implementation. There are a great number of choices we need to make around the design for the desktops within Horizon View. This will be affected by the way the users need to use the desktops and is likely to have a knock-on effect on the way you are going to manage the desktops and the resources the desktops require.

Pool design

You will want to design your desktop pools based on the similarities between the desktops that will allow you to group desktops together. We will utilize the information collected by the desktop assessment and other sources to start designing how your pools are going to look. While analyzing this data, you are going to look for similarities between the applications and use cases, and make decisions based on the following information on how you will design these pools. You are going to look wherever possible to have the smallest number of pools to ease the ability to maintain the environment, but you will also not want to take this to the nth degree, as trying to recompose ridiculously large pools could be difficult and might affect performance. As you can see, this is going to be a very careful balancing act to get the pool design correct.

Desktop sizing

The following is a list of some recommendations for base desktop sizing collected from a number of different VMware documents. Obviously, the resource required for the desktops will be greatly effected by the applications being used within the desktops as well:

Scenario	Recommended starting RAM	Recommended starting CPU
Windows XP 32-bit	1GB	1vCPU
Windows 7 32-bit	1GB	1vCPU
Windows 7 64-bit	2GB	2vCPU
Windows 8	2GB	2vCPU
High definition or full screen video in use	2-4GB	2vCPU
Desktops with hardware accelerated graphics		2vCPU

Linked clone versus full clone

As we have already discussed in *Chapter 2, An Overview of Horizon View Architecture and its Components*, there are two types of desktop images that we can use, linked clones or full clones. To recap briefly, linked clones are created by replicating a golden image into a thin provisioned replica VM. This VM will be the same size as the used space within the golden image; all reads come from this VM and no matter how many desktops we have within the pool within limits, each desktop will have a delta disk for writes that will continue to grow until the linked clone is recomposed, refreshed, or deleted. With a full clone, it does exactly what it says on the tin and will represent a copy of the golden image itself and consume the same amount of space.

As such, to save space on our storage device where possible, we will want to utilize linked clones. However, there are a few important use cases where using linked clones will simply not make sense, such as:

- **VMware Mirage Integration**: With Horizon View 6 and the previous versions, if you like to make use of VMware Mirage to protect data on desktops, to layer applications, or to maintain the desktop images, you will need to utilize dedicated full clone desktops.
- **Desktops where regular refresh or recompose is not possible**: The concept of linked clones relies on the fact that you will be able to refresh or recompose the desktops on a regular basis. If you have a desktop, you will simply not be able to achieve this. Due to use case or configuration issues, the linked clones will soon bloat to full size. There will be little or no benefit of using linked clones.

As we can see, while linked clones are possibly the most attractive from the outside and we should be able to use them widely, they are not always going to be possible or the right design choice. When your design utilizes full clone desktops, you should be considering your storage design carefully in line with this design choice. There are many storage manufacturers that offer re-duplication, compression, and single-instance storage that allows you to minimize the storage impact of this type of desktop.

Persistent versus nonpersistent

Along with deciding whether you are going to use linked clones or full clones, you will also need to decide whether you are going to use persistent or nonpersistent desktops. With persistent desktops, the user is allocated a desktop, either manually or automatically, and will always be directed to that desktop when connecting to their desktop pool. With nonpersistent desktops, the users will be directed to any desktop in the given pool. In a lot of designs, linked clone desktops will be configured as nonpersistent and full clone desktops as persistent; but this is not always the case and will come down to your use case.

Our advice would be, wherever possible, utilize nonpersistent desktops in association with View Persona Management and group policy, to configure the desktops. If your design allows this, it will offer you the easiest way to maintain and refresh the desktops with minimal effect to the users. If your design does not allow this, consider your use case carefully, if you do have to configure persistent desktops due to some value of data or a configuration held within the desktop; consider whether a full clone persistent desktop managed by Horizon Mirage for protection and maintenance might be a better approach.

Offline desktops

An offline desktop is a desktop that will be used when there is no network connection at all, either LAN or WAN based. Previous versions of View had the ability to utilize the transfer server to download a copy of your View desktop to run directly in the View client in offline mode, which acts as a type 2 hypervisor. When you come back on the network, you are able to upload the desktop changes back to the virtual environment. The process of doing this is not overly complicated, but it is time consuming for the user to wait for the download and upload operations to happen. As such, while often investigated and implemented during POC, it very rarely made it into production and when it did, it was realistically used only in a small number of use cases.

VMware has discontinued the transfer server role in Horizon 6. For these use cases, VMware now recommends utilizing Horizon Mirage; you could simply allocate the user with a laptop and manage it with Mirage, allow them to use their own laptop and download a desktop VM to their laptop utilizing Fusion Pro, or let the user run in a hybrid mode utilizing a physical laptop managed by Mirage and also use View with a desktop or published app where appropriate.

Desktop layers

The key to a flexible desktop design is being able to build and customize the desktops in layers. By achieving this, the desktops can not only be more flexible to allow one base image to be used for many more users or pools, but also allow you to configure more linked clone desktop pools that will assist in maintenance. The following image depicts a users desktop and where all the key elements are being controlled and managed:

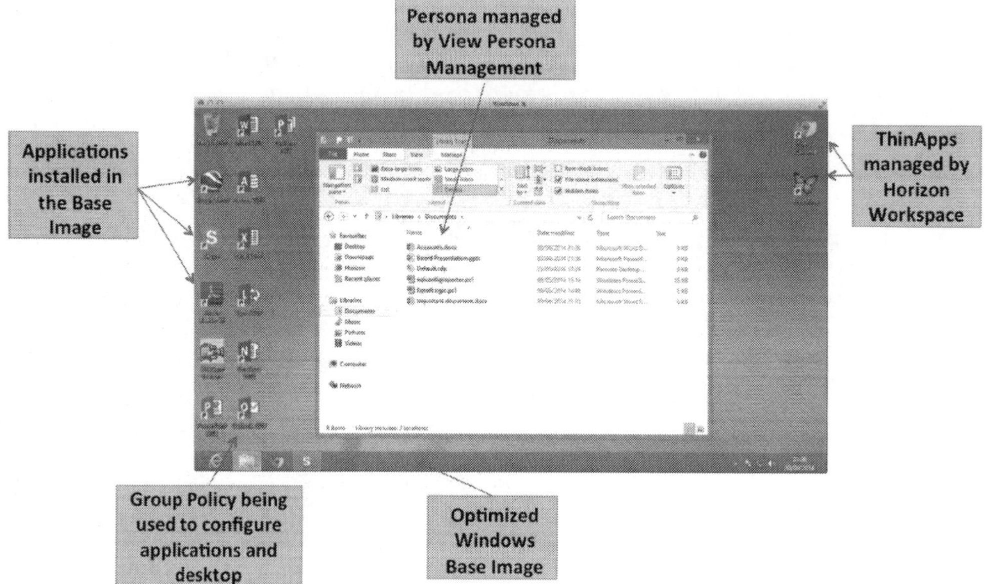

Base layer

Your base layer will consist of an optimized operating system and be configured to the needs of your business. Agents such as the View agent and AV will be installed into the base image along with select applications. You will need to make a decision as to what applications should be installed into the base image and which ones are going to be streamed in by other means. Often, the applications that will get installed into the base image will be applications that are used across the organization or a complete pool, such as the Microsoft Office suite. You will also want to consider the nature of the application; if the application is unable to be virtualized with ThinApp, as it contains drivers, or integrate with the shell, these applications will also need to be installed in your base layers.

Applications

Select applications can be streamed into your VDI desktops and effectively layered on top of the base image. By default, there is only one way to achieve this with Horizon View alone. This is by the method of encapsulating your applications into ThinApp packages and allocating these applications using the View Manager to select pools. However, there is no way in View to allocate the ThinApp packages to individual users, which would be a normal use case. This is where Horizon Workspace could be integrated. With Horizon Workspace, we are able to layer ThinApp packages, SaaS applications, and XenApp-published applications onto our View desktops or physical desktops on a per-user or per-security group basis.

Persona/profiles

Finally, let's look to overlaying the Persona or user's profile on top of the desktop. Think of the Persona as everything that makes the desktop personal; for example, application settings, the contents of my documents, and icons on the desktop. There are a number of ways to achieve this from redirected profiles, to group policy, to View Persona Management, and to third-party products (such as AppSense DesktopNow or RES Workspace Manager). Wherever possible, keeping the solution as simple as possible and not having to combine third-party products is often the easiest way to reduce the management overheads. However, depending on the levels of customization for your users, you might need to introduce some of the products mentioned to achieve this level of customization.

With View Persona Management, the users' profiles are redirected by a set of group policies to a dedicated file server. When a user logs into their VDI desktop, elements of the profile are downloaded from the file server to the VDI desktop as they are required. As such, once a file has been called from the profile, it is cached on the local VDI desktop for future use. Any changes to the profile are stored locally on the VDI desktop, but periodically uploaded back to the file server.

We are going to cover View Persona Management in *Chapter 9, Managing User Profiles with View Persona Management*.

Disaster recovery and backup

As with any solution, fully understanding the backup and disaster recovery options is highly important. With Horizon View, we have many areas where we should understand the backup and recovery options as well as the options available to us if a DR event should occur.

Backup and recovery options

There are a number of elements that we need to ensure are backed up when it comes to our Horizon View solution; they are summarized as follows:

- View Connection Servers
- View Security Servers
- Microsoft Lightweight Directory Service
- View Composer Database
- vCenter Database
- vCenter
- File servers containing ThinApps and View Persona Data
- Golden images
- Full clone and persistent desktop images

As you can see, there are a number of areas that we need to ensure are protected on a daily basis if not more often.

Through View Administrator, you are able to configure the scheduled backup of the LDAP repository and the View Composer Database. These will be backed up to the location on your View Connection Servers at `C:\Programdata\VMWare\VDM\backups`.

You should ensure that these backup files are regularly backed up to an external backup solution. We will look into the configuration and restoration of the View LDAP repository and View Composer Database in *Chapter 4, Installing and Configuring Horizon View*.

It is highly recommended that all server components be protected by backup software, such as Veeam Backup and Replication or VMware Data Protection. As previously mentioned, you could consider protecting and maintaining your full clones with Horizon Mirage.

Disaster recovery options

Due to the integration of Horizon View with View Composer and vCenter, it is not recommended or supported to replicate View environments from production to a DR site. Likewise, Horizon View is not supported for use with VMware SRM. We need to ensure that we have designed the DR strategy for our Horizon View environment in a different manner.

There are a number of ways we could consider offering DR for View, but we will speak about one option here.

First, we need to think of the components that are important to our View environment, usually these are as follows:

- Users' Personas
- ThinApp applications
- Golden images
- Full clone desktops

If we have these components available at DR, we can start recovering our View environment at DR with relative ease. We will configure a dedicated View environment at the DR site, preconfigured with the needed vCenters, View Connection Servers, and View Security Servers. We then need to understand what we need to do to roll out the VDI solution customized for our business needs in a DR event. As the users' Personas and ThinApp applications are located on a file server of device file, we can consider using technology such as Microsoft **Distributed File System Replication** (**DFSR**) or similar from the filer vendors. This allows us to have a copy of the Persona and ThinApps at both the production and disaster recovery sites.

Once we have our ThinApps and Persona at the DR site, we need to understand how we are going to deliver the desktops. As the desktops will be rolled out from the golden images, we should consider replicating the golden image from production to DR utilizing replication integrated into the storage device. We can even do something as primitive as exporting our golden image as an **Open Virtualization Format** (**OVF**) and moving to the DR site. We are then able to recompose the pools from this golden image at the DR site whenever the golden image is updated. With regard to full clone desktops, as these are just standard VMs, we could simply consider replicating these directly from the SAN and utilizing SRM to mount them online at the DR site ready to be added back into Horizon View.

Finally, we should think about how users are going to connect to our DR site in the event of a failure. This could be something as simple as getting the users to connect to a different address, such as `drdesktop.eucbook.com`, or we could make use of global load balancing technology to direct the regular URL to the DR site.

As you can see, there isn't a simple solution to build a DR site for your Horizon View solution, but if we break it down to its component level, we can easily configure a solution that will work to deliver the desktops and relevant files for our users, should the need arise. We can also consider utilizing the Cloud Pod Architecture to help enable the cross-site management of users between production and DR.

VMware is also able to deliver desktops as a service as part of their vCloud Hybrid Service. We could consider utilizing this technology in some way to offer DR for our on-premises Horizon View environment.

Full solution scenario

We wanted to give an example of a real-life scenario at the end of this chapter to give you the opportunity to put into action some of the elements covered within the chapter. You will see our mock scenario if you read through it and make some notes about the elements that you would be configuring and how you would design the architecture. We have then briefly covered what our consideration would be after the scenario.

Requirement scenario

Our company has approximately 5,500 employees over two main sites, Silverstone, UK and Franco champs, Belgium. Our company specializes in the sale, design, and distribution of products for the motorsport industry.

They have completed an initial proof of concept with the Horizon Suite and would like to understand a high-level design for these products, prior to moving ahead with a pilot.

Across the two sites, the users can be separated as follows:

- **Managers and directors**: They utilize a variety of business applications, and all of these users are equipped with laptop devices and work from a variety of locations. An important aspect for these users is to be able to work while traveling on a plane as well the Eurostar. They also require the ability to install their own applications when required. Being managers of the company, these users are allowed to choose their own devices from a selection of premium Microsoft Windows devices. The following screenshot gives an overview of the specification of the current devices in use and the performance utilization of these devices:

Manager / Director typical desktops	UK – 50, Belgium 250
CPU	4 Core CPU
Average CPU Utilization	20%
RAM	8GB
Average RAM Utilization	50%
HD	256GB SSD
HD Usage	80%
95th Percentile IOPS	100
Number of Screens	1

- **Project managers**: They manage internal projects for the business. These users use laptop devices supplied by the business and need access to the corporate desktop in whichever location they work. They are only able to complete their work when they have an Internet connection and can connect to the office. All of their documents are saved on a dedicated file share system. The following screenshot gives an overview of the specification of the current devices in use and the performance utilization of these devices:

Project Managers typical desktops	UK – 100, Belgium 500
CPU	2 Core CPU
Average CPU Utilization	60%
RAM	4GB
Average RAM Utilization	70%
HD	80GB 7.2K SATA
HD Usage	50%
95th Percentile IOPS	25
Number of Screens	2

- **Call center workers**: They utilize one main CRM application, and this application is utilized for all call management, order processing, and by the customer services team for warranty replacements. All users also require access to the Microsoft Office Suite of products. The call center is one of two departments still on Windows XP and will need to be moved to Windows 7. The following screenshot gives an overview of the specification of the current devices in use and the performance utilization of these devices:

Call Center Workers typical desktops	UK – 1000, Belgium 3000
CPU	1 Core CPU
Average CPU Utilization	50%
RAM	1GB
Average RAM Utilization	50%
HD	80GB 7.2K SATA
HD Usage	50%
95th Percentile IOPS	15
Number of Screens	1

- **Design department**: They utilize Solid works across both sites. At present, they have difficulty sharing workloads between the countries because of the size of the files that are created. Due to this, it is not feasible to pass the files back and forth with ease between countries. When they render their workloads, it requires a large amount of processing power and it is not unusual for their CPUs to hit 100 percent usage at these times. They need the ability to install their own desktops and store a lot of files locally to their desktops. The following screenshot gives an overview of the specification of the current devices in use and the performance utilization of these devices:

Design Department typical desktops	UK – 200, Belgium 200
CPU	4 Core CPU
Average CPU Utilization	90%
RAM	16GB
Average RAM Utilization	100%
HD	256GB SSD
HD Usage	50%
95th Percentile IOPS	150
Number of Screens	2

- **Accounts department**: They use a Bespoke finance application across both sites. The servers for this application are based in Belgium, and the UK-based users often complain about the performance of this application. This application is only supported on XP at present and is currently being rewritten by a new development company, but this is not scheduled for completion for another two years. The following screenshot gives an overview of the specification of the current devices in use and the performance utilization of these devices:

Accounts Department typical desktops	UK – 10, Belgium 40
CPU	1 Core CPU
Average CPU Utilization	30%
RAM	2GB
Average RAM Utilization	50%
HD	80GB
HD Usage	50%
95th Percentile IOPS	30
Number of Screens	1

Between the two sites are two dedicated links delivery with 1 GB bandwidth in a highly available manner.

They require a solution that is able to offer DR failover for the UK site to Belgium and vice versa, for 50 percent of the entire workforce in the case of a site failure.

Based on the preceding information, consider what would be your high-level design for the solution. What elements will affect your design and what likely resources would you require? In the next sections you will find some of our thoughts on the design considerations for this scenario.

Scenario design considerations

We will now discuss some of the considerations we would have undertaken as a design for the preceding scenario.

The following screenshot represents the types of desktops and the amounts for both sites. This takes into consideration the requirement of offering 50 percent redundancy for each site:

	UK	Belgium	UK with Belgium DR	Belgium with UK DR
Managers / Directors	50	250	175	275
Project Managers	100	500	350	550
Call Center	1000	3000	2500	3500
Design Depertment	200	200	300	300
Accounts	10	40	30	45
Total	1360	3990	3355	4670

Pod and block architecture

One of our first considerations is going to be how we are going to architect this solution over all. With the number of users mentioned earlier, we are looking at implementing a number of blocks at each site, but there won't be a requirement of any more than one pod at any one site.

As there are two physically separate sites, and because we want cross-site DR, we want to implement the new Cloud Pod Architecture to simplify the entitlement of desktops in the DR scenario. There might also be a number of other benefits of the Cloud Pod Architecture in this design, such as being able to entitle the CAD users' desktops from each other's sites to enable easier collaboration on projects.

In the UK, we look at implementing a minimum of two blocks with four View Connection Servers. This equates to one Connection Server for each block and two View Connection Servers for external connectivity between two load balanced View Security Servers. In Belgium, there would be a minimum of three blocks with five Connection Servers, one server for each block and two for external connectivity, paired with two load balanced Security Servers.

Storage performance considerations

We would clearly need much more information to understand the overall storage requirement. For example, the read to write ratios and the final capacities required. However, based on the preceding information, we require a solution that can deliver in approximately 100,000 IOPS at each site. As such, we are likely to consider a hybrid SAN technology such as VMware's VSAN. The main benefit with the VSAN technology is that we could grow the storage along with the hosts in a linear fashion from the pilot stage through to a staged production rollout. This will also give us the ability to easily scale the solution in the future.

Manager's desktops

As these users have a strict use case of being able to use their laptops offline, we would recommend Horizon Mirage for these users. If required, they could also utilize a View desktop of View-published applications for the managers to be able to use data center-connected applications when out of the office, where they have an Internet connection available.

Project managers

The project managers would be given a linked clone, nonpersistent desktop pool, and this pool would be configured to refresh on logout to ensure it is always kept up to date and free of problems. Based on the current configuration and utilization, we will be looking to configure these desktops with dual core CPUs and 4 GB of memory. The project managers could keep their existing desktops or we could consider thin client laptops due to the nature of their work, which can only be completed when they have a connection back to the corporate head office.

Call center workers

The call center workers are also likely to utilize a linked clone, nonpersistent desktop pool like the project managers. As we want to move these users to Windows 7, we have to carefully review the resources required for their desktops. We might need to increase their RAM to 2 GB from the existing 1 GB, and their CPU to 2 vCPU from 1 core.

Design department

With the design department, we need to be very careful while specifying the resource for their infrastructure. As they require the ability to be able to install their own applications and store data locally, we will provision these users with dedicated full clone desktops. VMware Mirage will be used to centralize the data not only for protection purposes, but also to manage the operating system and software updates. We will look to provision the desktops with the same 16 GB RAM and 4 vCPUs per desktop. We need to be very careful with CPU over commit as to not affect the performance of their rendering operations. During the pilot stage, we will see how high we can feasibly get away with, but due to the nature of their workloads, this could be as low as 2 vCPUs per physical core, if not 1:1. Each ESXi host would be configured with an NVidia GRID K1 or K2 card, and it is likely they will need to be used in a dedicated mode to work with the Solid Words application.

Accounts department

With the accounts department, we need to focus on the two main concerns, the first is the performance of the accounts application in the UK connecting to the server in Belgium, and the second is the fact the application will only run on XP at present. With regard to the application performance, we could consider hosting the UK users' desktops in Belgium and offer failover for all users in the UK. Clearly, DR for the accounts server needs to be taken into consideration as much as any other server needs to be considered. With regard to the application compatibility, we can see whether we are able to ThinApp this application on a Windows XP PC and then run the application on Windows 7. That failing, we might need to continue using Windows XP for the accounts users until the application compatibility is sorted.

Summary

In this chapter, we have covered a number of design considerations to design a Horizon View solution. We have learned the importance of understanding your business and users' needs. When designing, any EUC solution that users experience is of utmost importance. When it comes to technical considerations, we need to keep the VMware block and pod architecture at the forefront in our mind when designing the solution. A well-designed solution will give careful consideration to the needs of the desktops when sizing and selecting storage, and the over allocation of CPU memory for our infrastructure. Most importantly, we should have a much better understanding of why not all VDI solutions are the same, and we need to carefully consider many aspects for our VDI solution.

In the next chapter, we will cover the installation and configuration of Horizon View.

4

Installing and Configuring Horizon View

In this chapter, we will cover the installation process of the core Horizon View components, such as the Connection Server, Security Server, and Replica Server. Following the installation, we will start configuring the base elements of a Horizon View installation.

Preparing Active Directory

Horizon View requires **Active Directory** (**AD**) for authentication of users and desktops. We are also going to make use of group policy in later chapters to control and tune many aspects of users' desktops.

Horizon View 6.1 is compatible with the following AD-functional domain levels:

- Windows 2003
- Windows 2008 and Windows 2008 R2
- Windows 2012 and Windows 2012 R2

When deploying your View Connection Servers, they either need to be in the same domain as the desktops that you are going to deploy or in a domain with a two-way transitive trust to the domain where your desktops will be located.

Active Directory accounts

We recommend that you also take this opportunity to create a number of user accounts that will be needed across your installation.

These accounts will include service accounts for your View Connection Server Services and Composer Services. You need an AD account to be used by View to log in and manage components within your vCenter, and a user for View Composer to manage the creation of computer accounts in AD.

A vCenter user

You will need an AD user to allow View to connect to your vCenter Server. This account should also be added as a local admin on the vCenter Server, as we will be using Composer to create linked clone desktops. Once you have created your user within AD, you will need to give this user permission in your vCenter Server. The following screenshot lists the permissions required by this user:

Required Group	Required Privilege
Folder	• Create Folder • Delete Folder
Datastore	• Allocate Space • Browse Datastore • Low Level File Operation

Virtual Machine	• Configuration
	    • All
	• Inventory
	    • All
	• Snapshot Management
	    • All
	• Interaction
	    • Power Off
	    • Power On
	    • Reset
	    • Suspend
	• Provisioning
	    • Customize
	    • Deploy Template
	    • Read Customization Specifications
	    • Clone Virtual Machine
	    • Allow Disk Access

Resource	• Assign Virtual Machine to Resource Pool • Migrate Powered off Virtual Machine
Global	• Act as vCenter Server • Enable Methods • Disable Methods • System Tag
Host	• Configuration • Advanced Settings
Network	• All

To add the user to your vCenter, we will first start by creating a new role specifically for our View vCenter User, as follows:

1. From inside the **vmware vSphere Web Client** dialog box, select **Roles** (**1**) from the **Home** screen, as shown in the following screenshot:

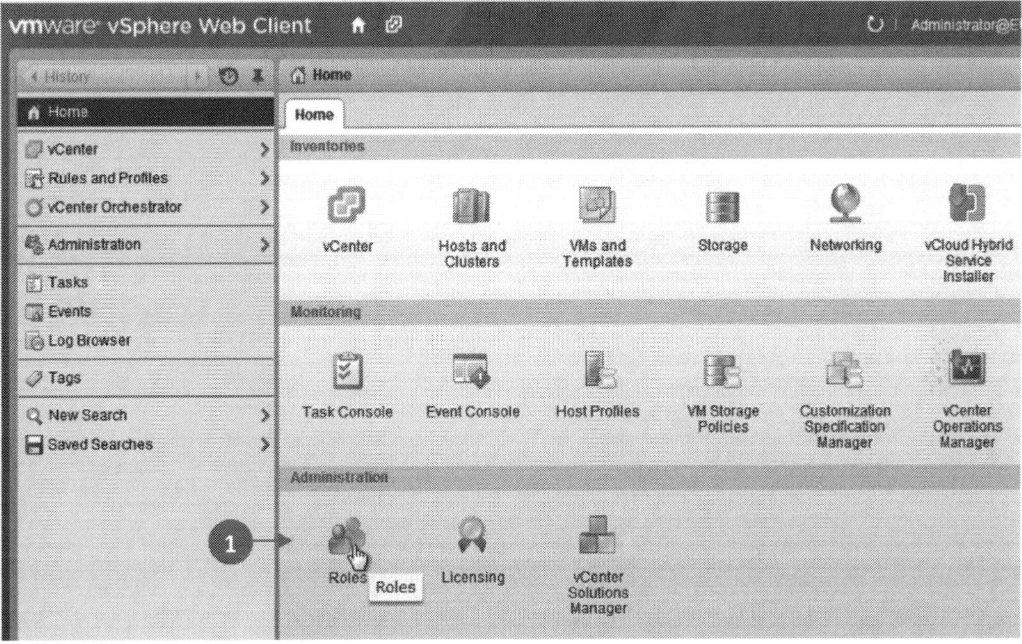

2. We are now going to create a new role by clicking the green **+** (**1**) symbol at the top left and typing in a role name in the **Role name** box (**2**). Then, expand the **Host** and **Configuration** sections. Check the boxes to select the relevant privileges to match the required privileges that we covered previously, as shown in the following screenshot:

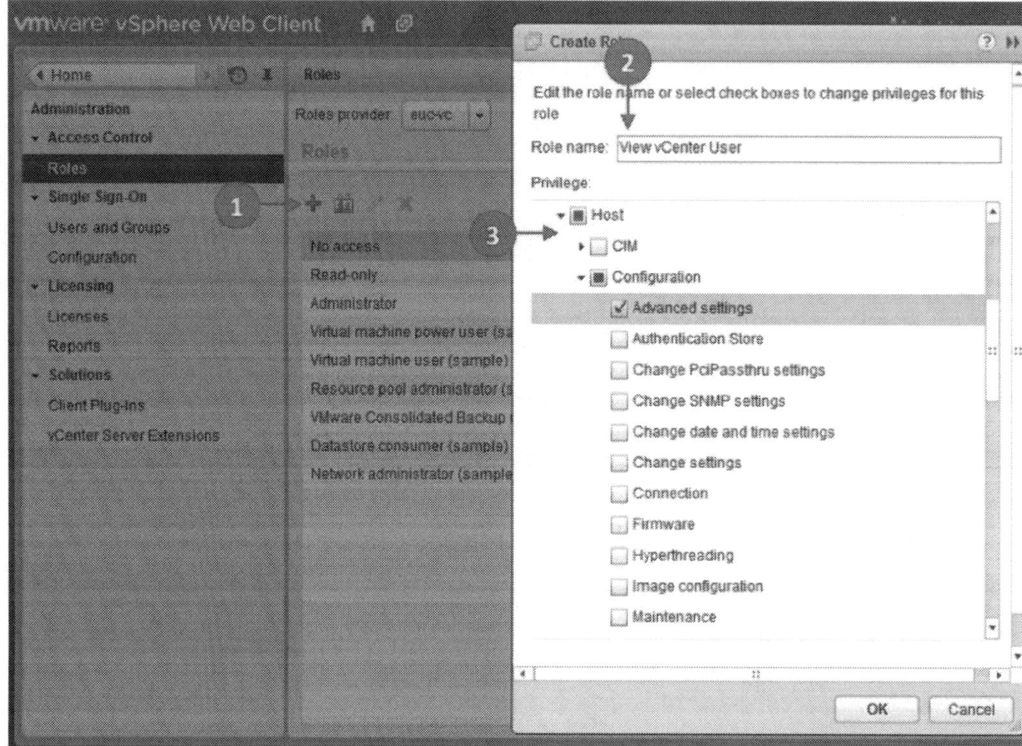

3. We are then going to browse into the inventory in the **vmware vSphere Web Client** dialog box and right-click on the **euc-vc** vCenter Server. From this menu, click on **All vCenter Actions** and **Add Permission... (1)**, as shown in the following screenshot:

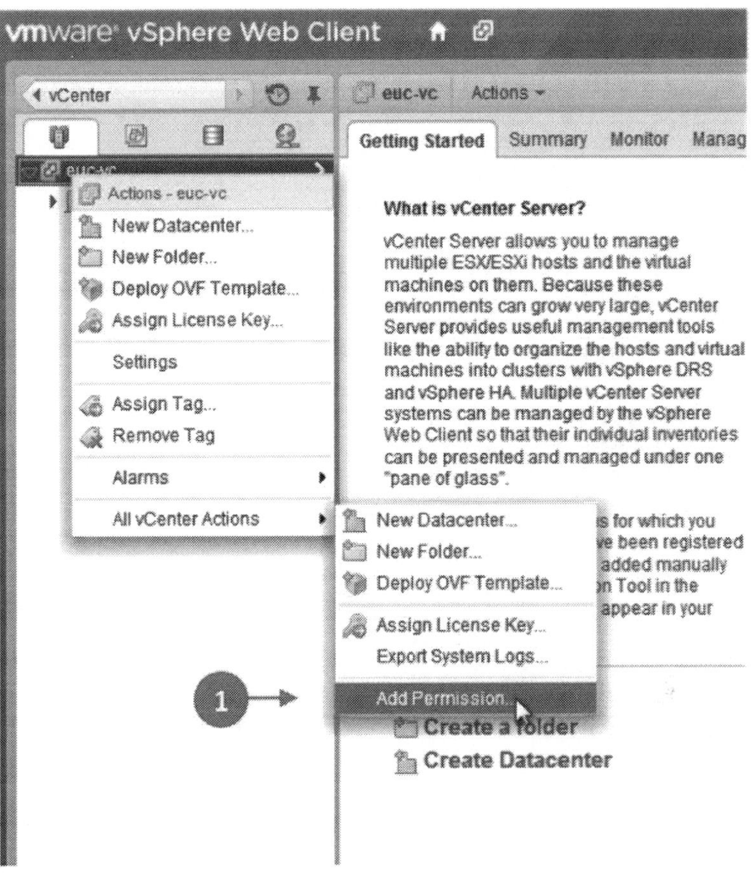

4. We are now able to select the role we just created and assign the **ViewVCUser** user to it so that the View Connection Server has an account that allows it to connect to the vCenter Server, as shown in the following screenshot:

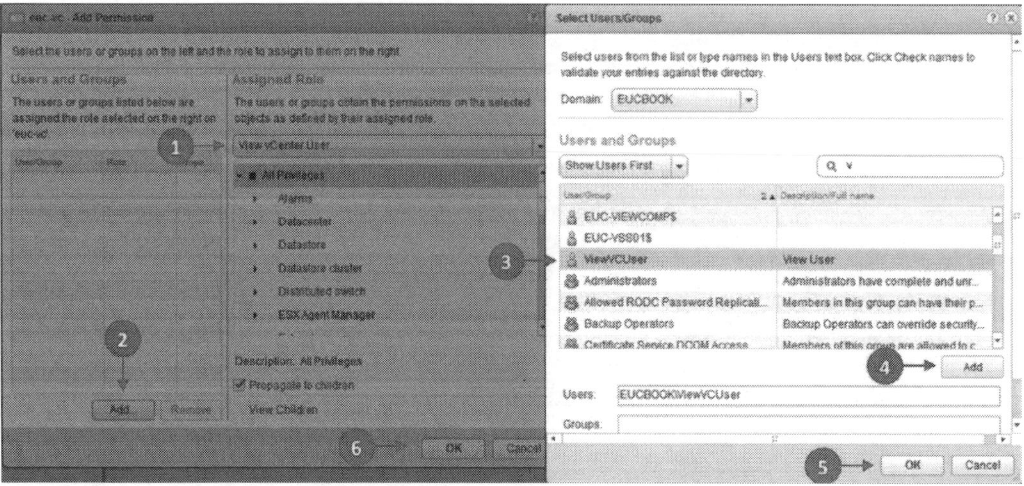

5. From the drop-down menu (**1**), select the **View vCenter User** option and click on **Add...** (2). In the **Select Users/Groups** dialog box, ensure that the domain reflects your domain and then search for the user account **ViewVCUser** (3). Click on the **Add** button (**4**), and then click on **OK** (**5**). Finally, click on **OK** (6) in the **Add Permission** dialog box to complete the task.

View Composer user

You will also require an AD user for your View Composer account, as this account will be responsible for the addition and deletion of computer accounts for your clones linked to the domain. The following are the required AD permissions this user should have:

- List contents
- Read all properties
- Write all properties
- Read permissions
- Reset password
- Create computer objects
- Delete computer objects

The permissions for this account need to apply at the root domain level for the AD container and all child objects of the container. You will also need to ensure that you have advanced features selected when creating this user. You will use this account later to configure View Administrator for the View Composer connection.

Organizational units for View desktops

At this time, you should also be considering creating organizational units with your View desktops. We should place these in dedicated OUs to allow you to easily configure specific group policies based on the requirements of the pool being created.

System requirements

We are going to start by assuming you already have a vCenter in place that you wish to use for your Horizon View environment. You can use a Windows or Linux appliance-based vCenter in conjunction with Horizon View.

View Composer

View Composer can either be installed directly onto a Windows vCenter, or alternatively, it can be installed on a standalone Windows Server. The following screenshot lists the requirements to be aware of when creating a server for your View Composer installation:

Component	Supported Configuration

Supported Operating Systems	• Windows Server 2008 R2 (64 bit)
	  • Standard
	  • Enterprise
	• Windows Server 2008 R2 SP1 (64 bit)
	  • Standard
	  • Enterprise
	• Windows Server 2012 R2 (64 bit)
	  • Standard

Processor	• **Required**
	  • 1.4 GHz or faster Intel 64 or AMD 64 processor with 2 CPUs
	• **Recommended**
	  • 2GHz or faster and 4 CPUs

Networking	• **Required**
	  • One or more 10/100Mbps network interface cards (NICs)
	  • Static IP Address
	• **Recommended**
	  • 1Gbps NICs

Memory	• **Required**
	  • 4GB or higher (50 desktops or under)
	  • 8GB or higher (Over 50 desktops)
	• **Recommended**
	  • 8GB or higher

Disk space	• **Required**
	  • 40GB
	• **Recommended**
	  • 60GB

SQL Server (When used in conjunction with vCenter 5.5)	• Microsoft SQL Server 2012 Express • Microsoft SQL Server 2012 (SP1) Standard and Enterprise • Microsoft SQL Server 2008 (R2 SP2), Standard and Enterprise • Oracle 11g Release 2, Standard, Standard ONE, and Enterprise [11.2.0.3]

View Connection Server, replica, and security server

The View Connection Server and related components are all installed on dedicated Windows Servers. The following screenshot lists the requirements to be aware of when creating a server for these roles:

Component	Supported Configuration

Supported Operating Systems	• Windows Server 2008 R2 (64 bit)
	  • Standard
	  • Enterprise
	• Windows Server 2008 R2 SP1 (64 bit)
	  • Standard
	  • Enterprise
	• Windows Server 2012 R2 (64 bit)
	  • Standard

Processor	• **Required**
	  • Pentium IV 2.0GHz processor or higher
	• **Recommended**
	  • 4 CPUs

Networking	• **Required**
	  • 100Mbps network interface cards (NICs)
	• **Recommended**
	  • 1Gbps NICs

Memory	• **Required**
	  • 4GB or higher (50 desktops or under)
	  • 10GB or higher (Over 50 desktops)
	• **Recommended**
	  • 10GB or higher

Disk space	• **Required**
	  • 40GB
	• **Recommended**
	  • 60GB

vCenter Server	• **Recommended (Please check compatibility matrix for other supported versions)** • vCenter 5.5 Update 1
ESXi	• **Recommended (Please check compatibility matrix for other supported versions)** • ESXi 5.5 Update 1

IP addressing and DNS requirements

For your Horizon View installation, there are going to be a number of requirements for the IP addresses and DNS names of the various components inside your environment. We have summarized the typical requirements around IP and DNS for a small Horizon View environment.

As you can see in the following table, we suggest that load balancers are utilized to load balance connections between the internal View Connection Servers and also between the external View Security Servers.

In a smaller environment, you might decide to go with only one View Security Server; in which case you would require the external DNS name rather than the load balancer. The following screenshot lists the IP addressing and DNS requirements:

	Internal IP Address Required	Internal DNS Name Required	External IP Address Required	External DNS Name Required	Network
VMware vCenter Server	Yes	Yes	No	No	Production
View Composer Server	Yes	Yes	No	No	Production
SQL Server	Yes	Yes	No	No	Production
View Connection Server 1	Yes	Yes	No	No	Production
View Connection Server 2	Yes	Yes	No	No	Production
Internal Load Balancer	Yes	Yes	No	No	Production
View Connection Server 1 (External)	Yes	Yes	No	No	Production
View Connection Server 2 (External)	Yes	Yes	No	No	Production
View Security Server 1	Yes	Yes	No	No	DMZ
View Security Server 2	Yes	Yes	No	No	DMZ
External Load Balancer	Yes	Yes	Yes	Yes	DMZ

Server template

Our recommendation is to create a template inside vCenter to be used to create your Horizon servers. This will allow for quick and uniform deployment of your servers. When creating your template, you should be considering which operating systems you are going to use from the preceding list of supported operating systems. Our recommendation is, wherever possible, use the latest supported operating system to avoid compatibility issues in the future. Your template should be installed with all the latest operating systems, patches, and updates to the required supported versions. You can also use this as an opportunity to install any other agents, such as antivirus, if supported by your vendors.

Installing the View Composer Server

We will start our installation of Horizon View by installing the View Composer Server. In our example lab, vCenter has already been installed, and for this book, we are going to use the vCenter appliance. As a result of this, we will need to install View Composer on a dedicated Windows Server as it's a Windows-based application.

In the following screenshot, you can see that we have already deployed a virtual machine from our template to meet the requirements for View Composer. Our virtual machine has been configured with an 8-GB RAM, 4 vCPUs, and a 60-GB hard disk. This machine has been given a static IP address and has been added to the AD domain:

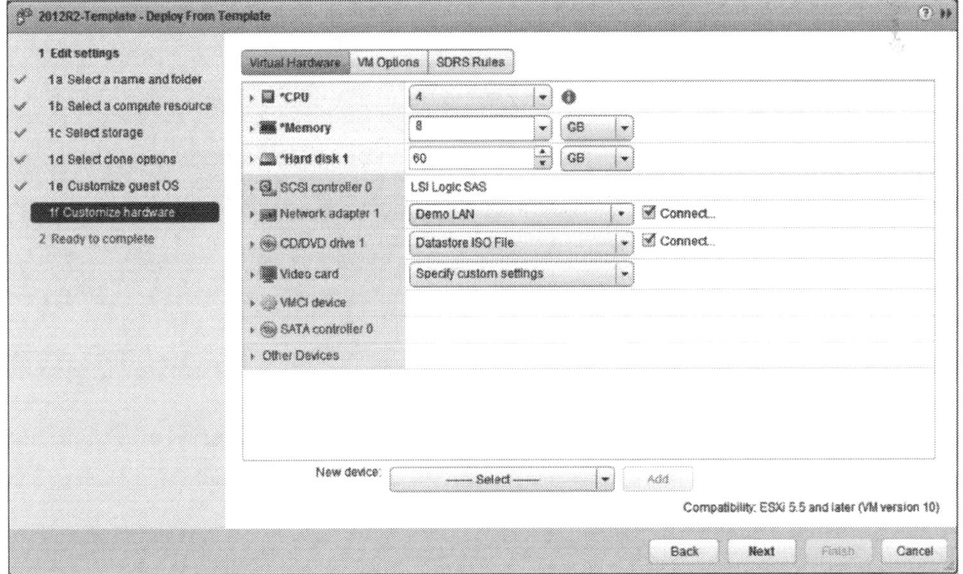

For ease in our lab, we have installed Microsoft SQL on this server. In a production environment, you want to separate the SQL server instance into dedicated SQL servers. This allows you to ensure the database is protected in line with your company's SQL protection and availability policies, and also ensure there are sufficient resources for all components. There might also be some cost saving on SQL licensing. Ensure you keep checking the latest compatibility lists to ensure the version of SQL you are going to use is supported.

First of all, we will need to configure a SQL user and a SQL database for use with View Composer.

Inside the SQL management studio, we will start by creating a new SQL login:

1. Browse to the **Security** folder and expand it. Click on **Logins** (**1**) and then right-click and select **New Login** (**2**), as shown in the following screenshot:

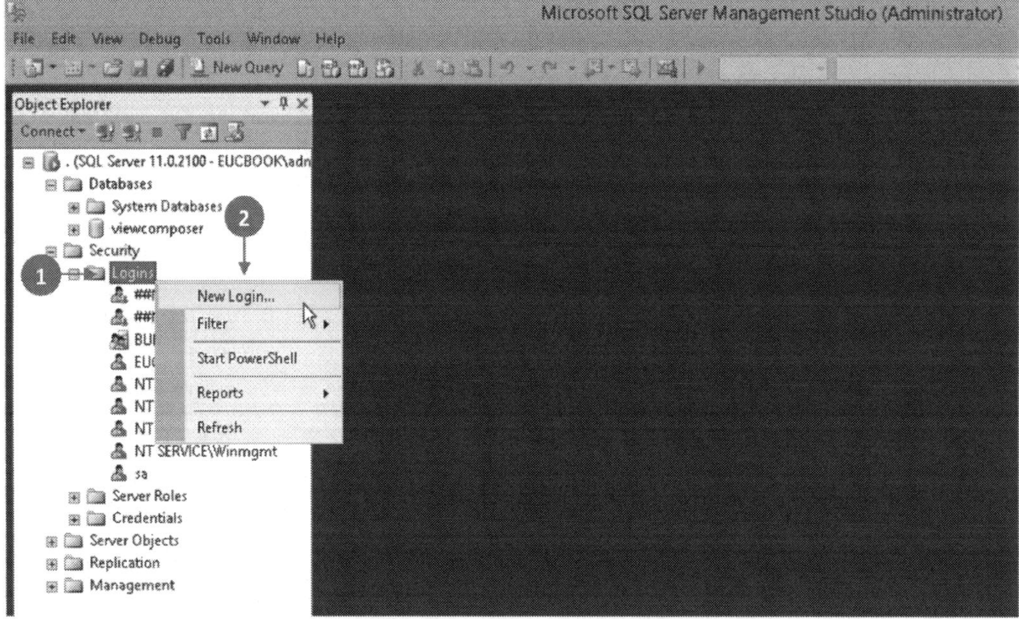

If you are using a SQL server that is located on the View Composer Server, for example, in a test environment, you can use Windows authentication or SQL authentication. If you are using a separate SQL server as recommended, you can use SQL authentication.

2. First, you will need to create a new login ID, as shown in the following screenshot:

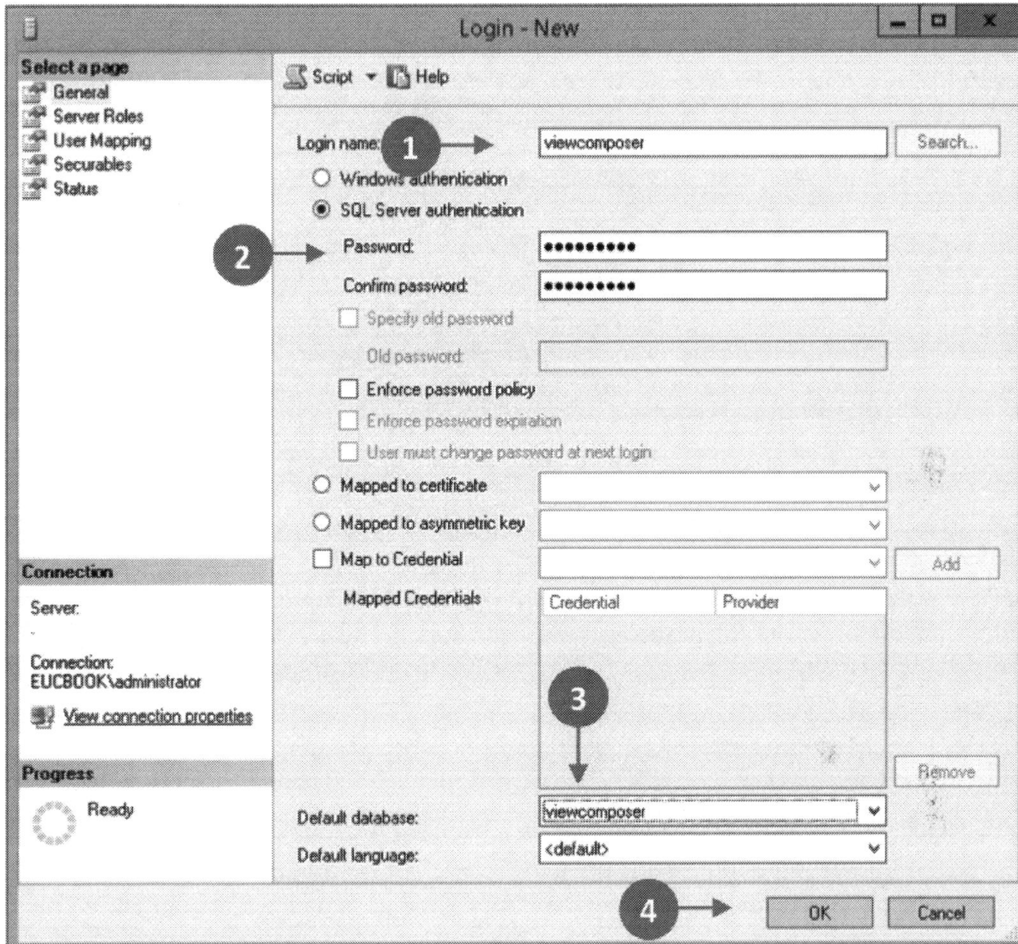

3. Enter **Login name** (**1**), and **Password** (**2**). Ensure you un-tick **Enforce password policy**, **Enforce password expiration**, and **User must change password at next login**.
4. For the time being, we are going to leave the default database as master. We will need to ensure we change this to our Composer database when it is created. Ensure you document the details used for this account for future reference and upgrades.

5. Now that we have created the login account, let's move on and create the database for View Composer. In the **Databases** folder (**1**) in the **Microsoft SQL Server Management Studio(Administrator)** dialog box, right-click and select **New Database...** (**2**):

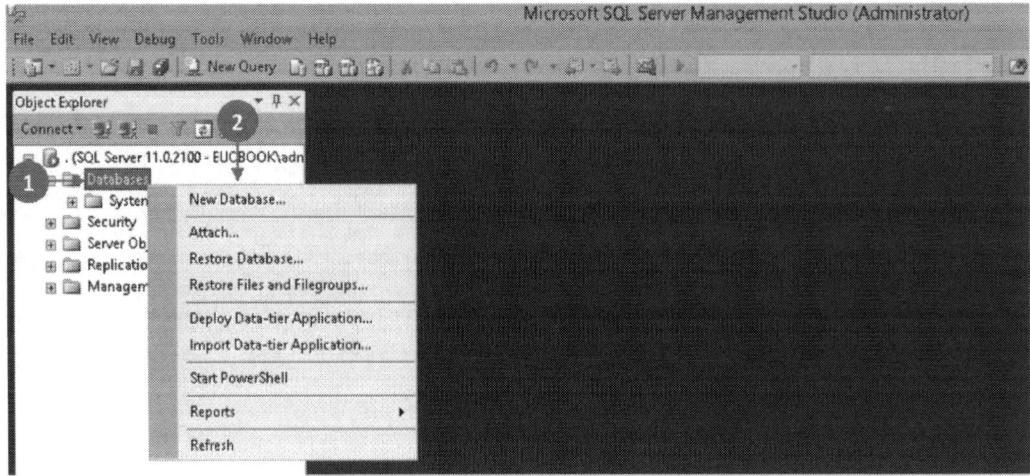

You will have to name the database and select the user we created earlier as the owner of the database. We recommend you work with your DBAs to ensure all other settings for this database are configured as per your guidelines.

Consideration needs to be given to the location of the database, log files, and the recovery model.

6. Finally, once this is created, ensure you select the `viewcomposer` database to be the default database for the login you created earlier, to avoid any issues. This is also a good time to set up your SQL maintenance plan to ensure your database is protected as shown in the following screenshot:

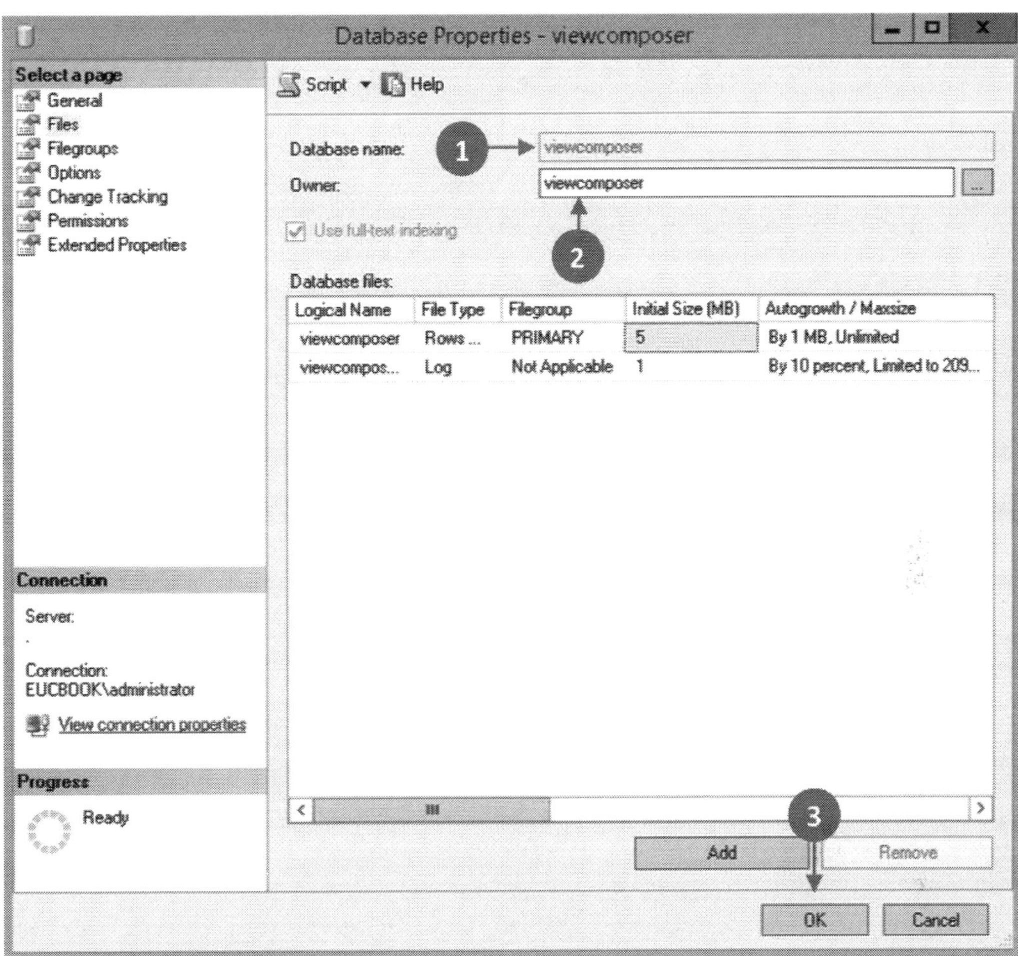

You can take this time to also create the View Events database; details for this can be found later in this chapter.

7. You are now in a position to start the installation of View Composer onto your server. As you will see in the following screenshot, we have downloaded all the relevant components of Horizon View to a single location to ensure the installation is as easy as possible. Before we start the installation, ensure you are logged into the server as an administrator with full permissions. For the installation of View Composer, we are going to execute the file `VMware-viewcomposer-6.X.X-XXXXXXX.exe`:

Name	Date modified	Type	Size
VMware-Horizon-View-Extras-Bundle-3.3...	18/03/2015 13:57	Compressed (zipp...	2,694 KB
VMware-Horizon-View-HTML-Access-2....	18/03/2015 13:58	Compressed (zipp...	1,869 KB
VMware-personamanagement-6.1.0-250...	18/03/2015 13:56	Application	12,478 KB
VMware-personamanagement-x86_64-6....	18/03/2015 13:56	Application	18,387 KB
VMware-viewagent-6.1.0-2509441	18/03/2015 13:54	Application	122,825 KB
VMware-viewagent-direct-connection-6....	18/03/2015 13:57	Application	13,719 KB
VMware-viewagent-direct-connection-x...	18/03/2015 13:57	Application	15,144 KB
VMware-viewagent-x86_64-6.1.0-2509441	18/03/2015 13:56	Application	161,800 KB
VMware-viewcomposer-6.1.0-2506641	18/03/2015 13:57	Application	32,084 KB
VMware-viewconnectionserver-x86_64-6....	18/03/2015 13:53	Application	175,837 KB

8. You will need to work through the installation wizard initially by starting the installation. Click on **Next >** after reading and accepting the **end-user license agreement (EULA)**:

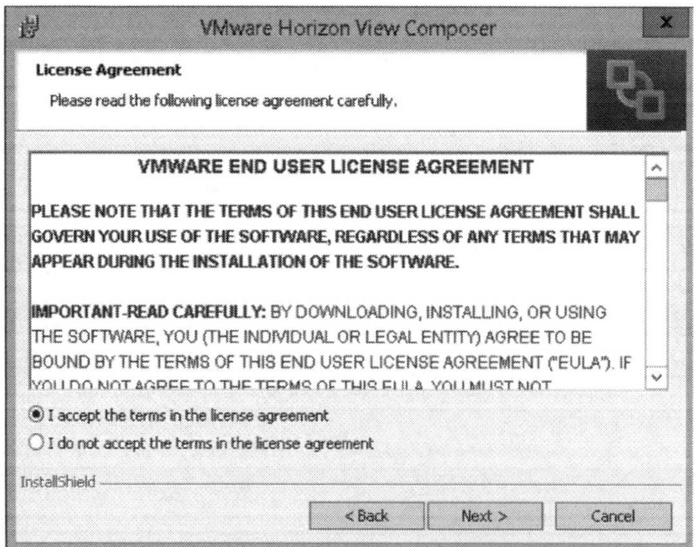

9. You will now select where we are going to install VMware View Composer in our lab. You have one drive with sufficient space within your environment. You will need to follow the guidelines set out by your business about the location for applications and other aspects:

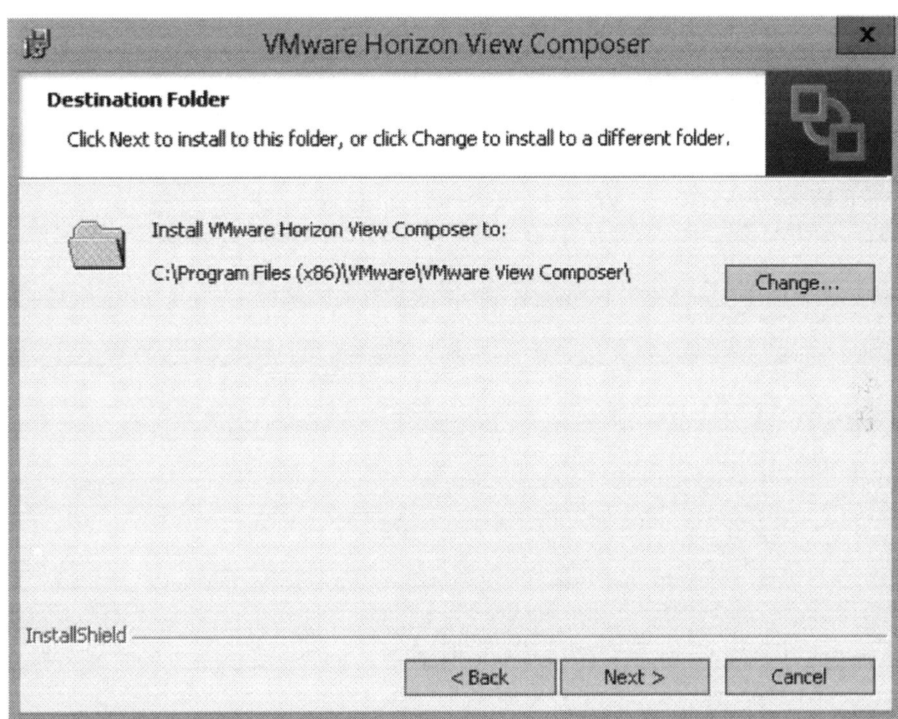

10. You are now in a position to create the ODBC DSN to connect to the View Composer database with the credentials we created earlier. If you aren't installing Composer on the same server as the SQL server, you might need to download and install the relevant SQL native driver from Microsoft's website.

11. From inside the installation Wizard, we select the **ODBC DSN Setup...** button (**1**). This will load the relevant window for us to create our DSN. Ensure you select the **System DSN** tab (**2**) and then select **Add...** (**3**), as shown in the following screenshot:

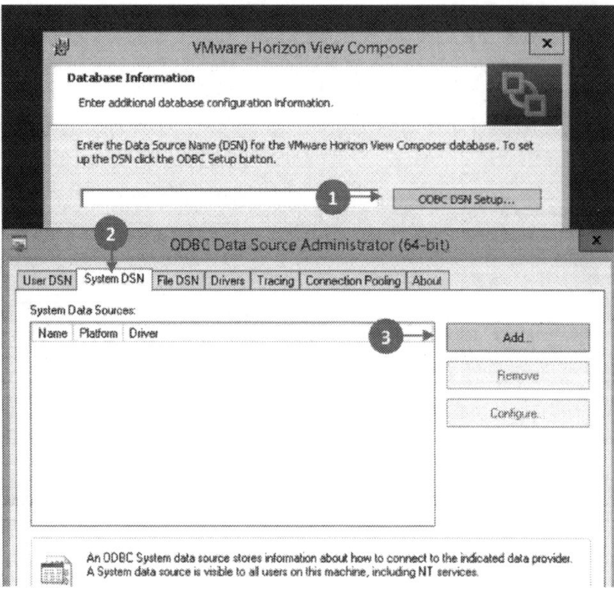

12. You will now see the DSN wizard appear on screen; select **SQL Native Client 11.0** (**1**). If you do not see this, you will need to install the relevant SQL server native client first. Click on **Finish** (**2**):

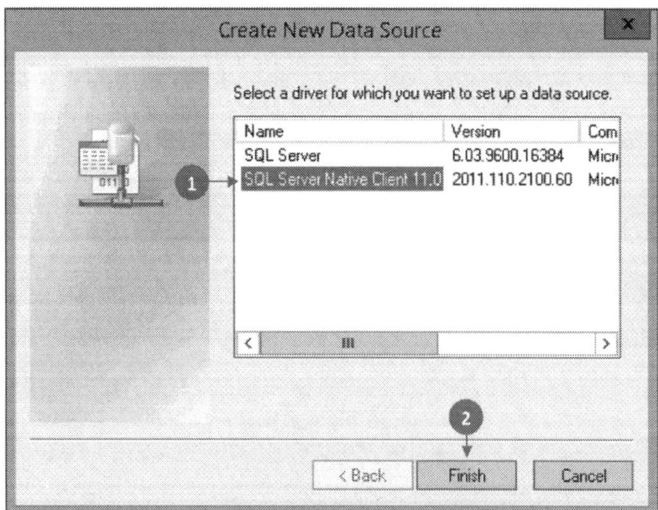

13. In the **Name** box (**1**), name the DSN something meaningful and either select our SQL server from the list or type the name of the SQL server in the SQL **Server** dialog box (**2**). In our environment, we have simply typed a period (`.`), which indicates it is the local server:

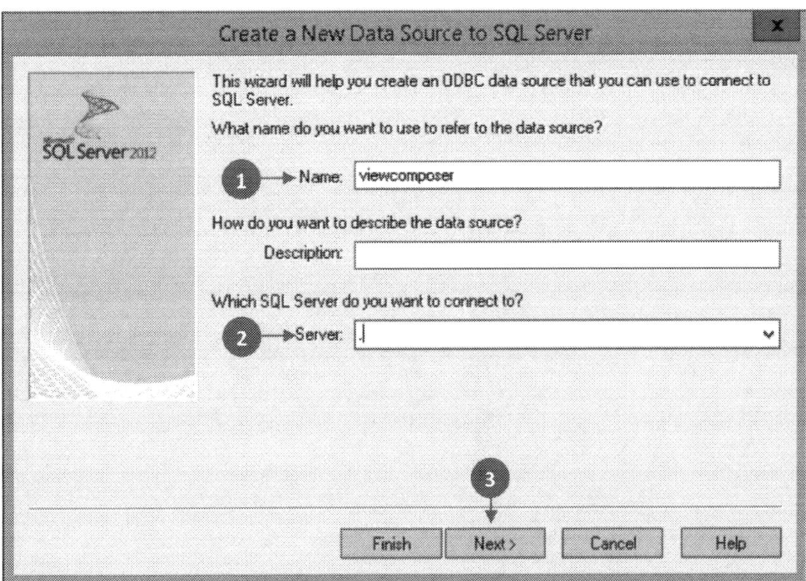

14. On the next screen, ensure you set the default database to the `viewcomposer` database you created earlier. This shouldn't be necessary if you set it to be the default database for the user, but we prefer to be double sure to ensure you do not update the wrong database. Enter the database name in the box (**1**) and then click on **Next >**:

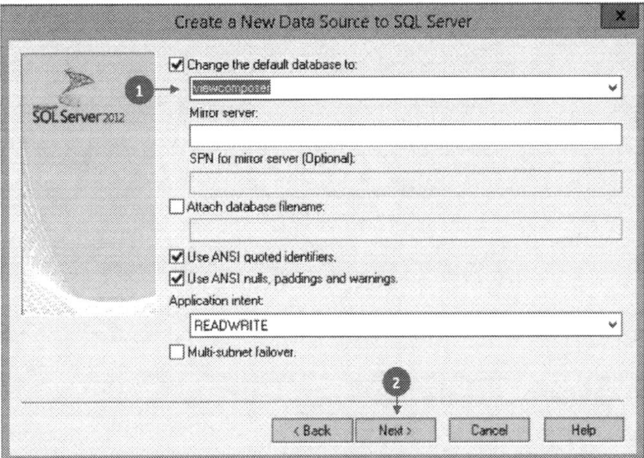

15. At the end of the DSN wizard, you should always ensure you have completed a test of the connection. This will ensure there aren't going to be any connectivity issues as we progress through the installation of View Composer:

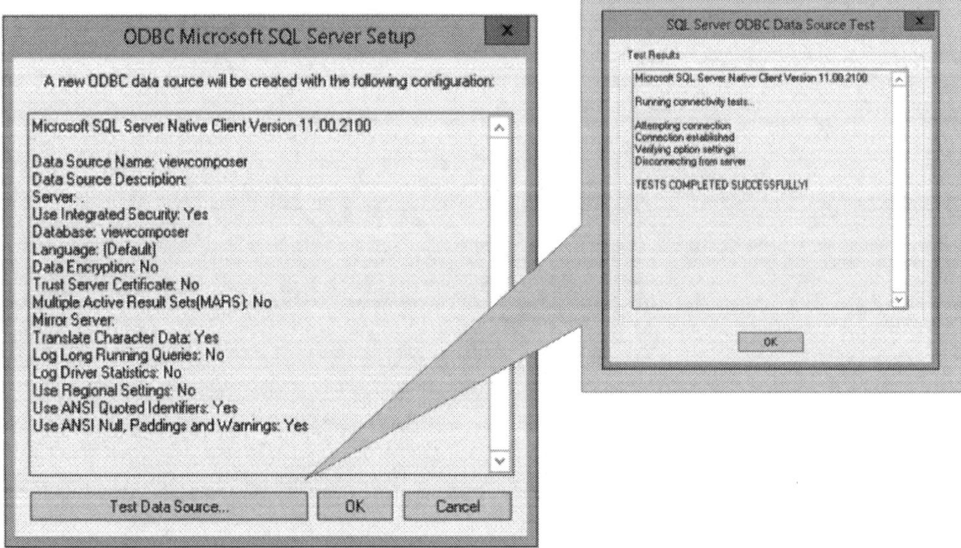

16. You now need to re-enter the credentials into the installation wizard for our DSN:

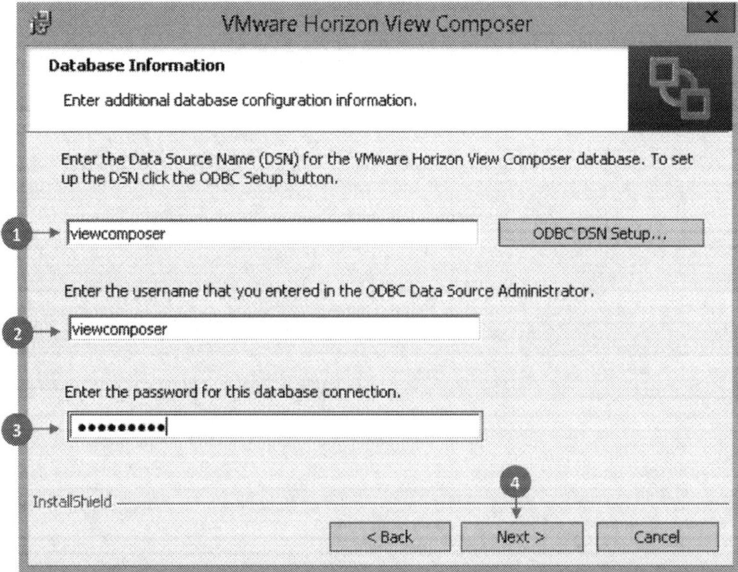

17. As you continue through the wizard, you will configure the **Simple Object Access Protocol** (**SOAP**) port. This is utilized by View to communicate with Composer in an XML format, as well as to have the option of configuring SSL; we will cover SSL configuration in *Chapter 5, Securing Horizon View with SSL Certificates*.
18. So for the time being, note your **SOAP Port** (we wouldn't recommend changing this, unless there was a specific reason to do so) and click on **Next >** as shown in the following screenshot:

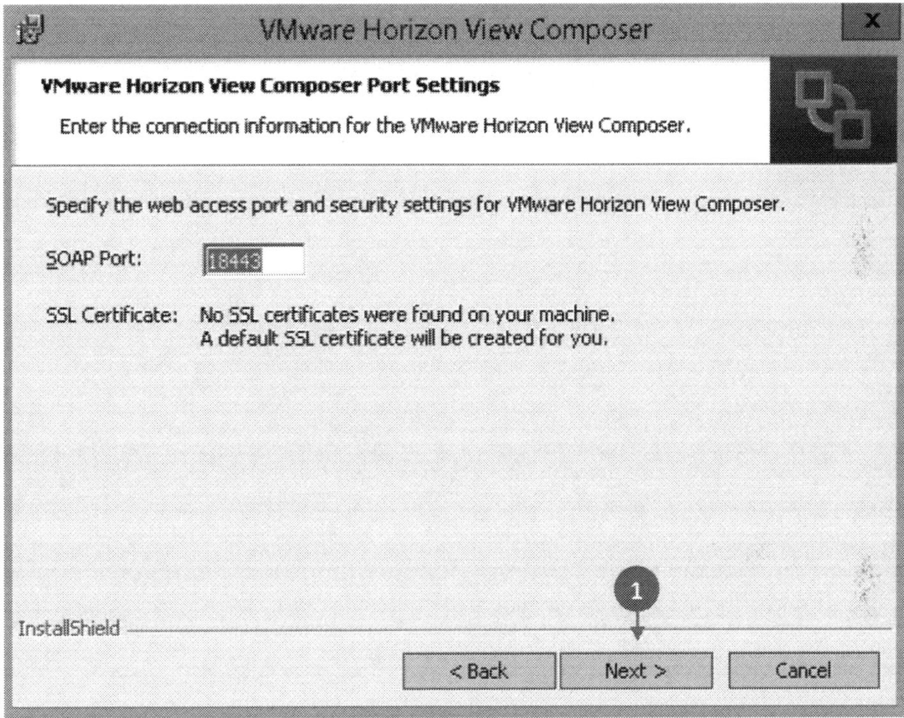

19. You are now ready to complete the installation of View Composer, so click on **Install** (**1**) to start the process:

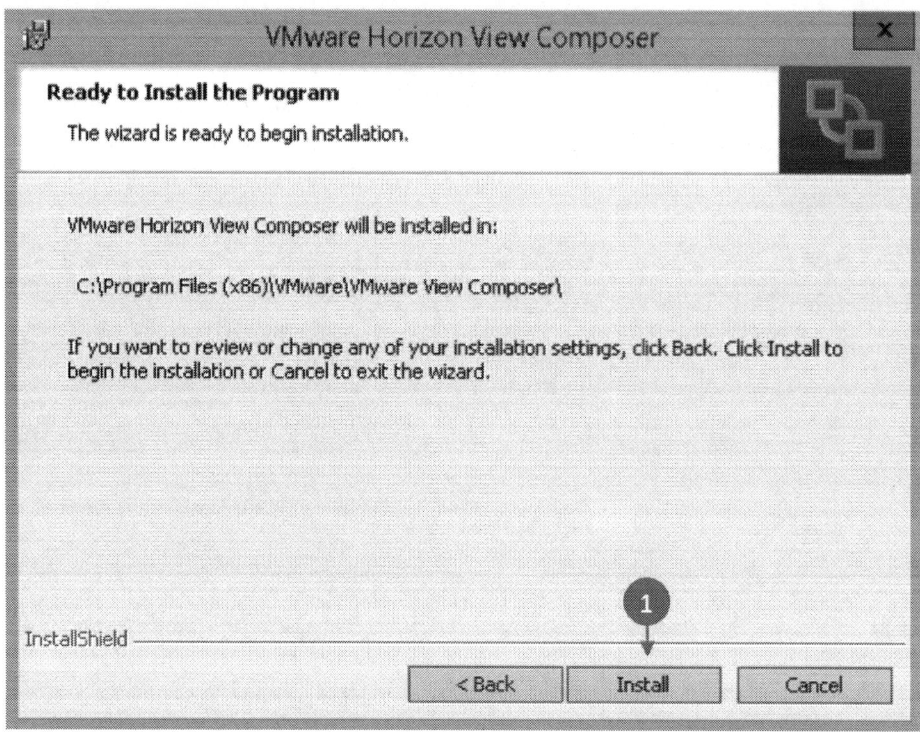

20. If, for any reason, the installation of View Composer fails, installation logs are held in the Composer Server at `%TEMP%\vminst.log_date_timestamp`.
21. Additionally, there are MSI logs created, which can be found at `%TEMP%\vmmsi.log_date_timestamp`.
22. You should now hopefully be in a position where your installation has been successful. You will see the following **Installer Completed** message in the **VMware Horizon View Composer** dialog box. Click on **Finish** (**1**) to complete the installation process:

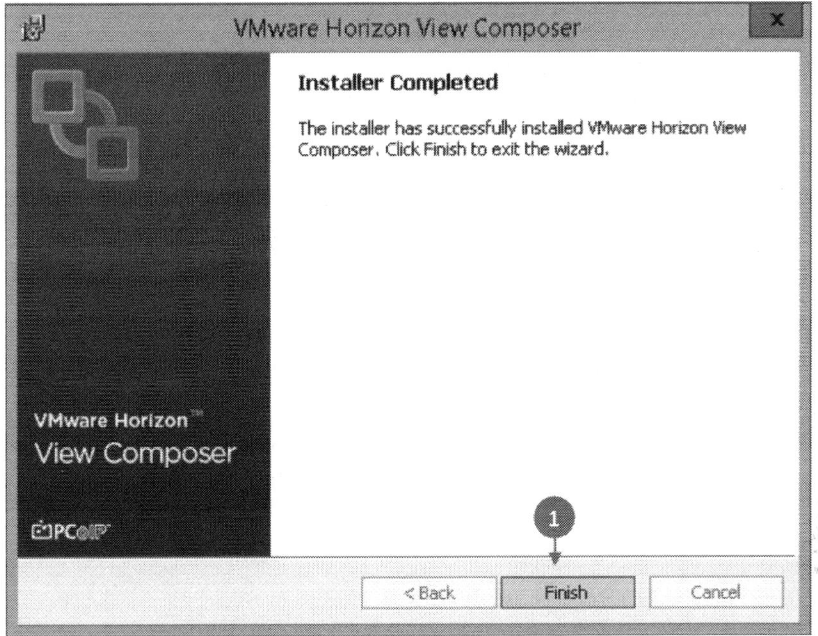

23. It's worthwhile at this point to check through the log files and, for good measure, reboot the server.
24. As the View Composer does not have a user interface, it can be very difficult at this stage to check that composer has installed correctly. To double check, browse to **Services** of the Windows, you should see that the **VMware Horizon View Composer** service has been registered and is now running:

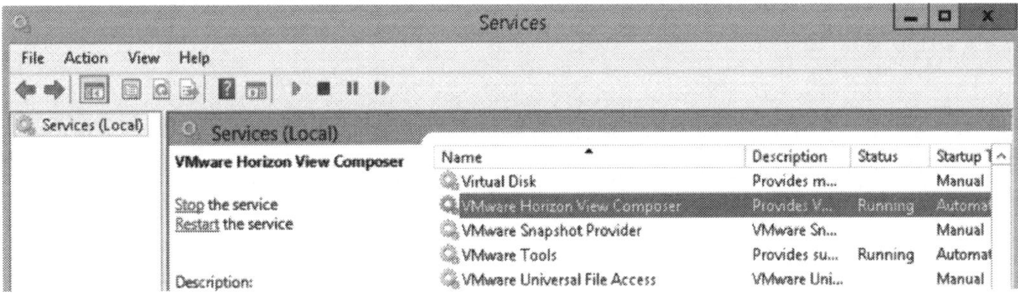

Installing the Connection Server

You will now move on to deploy the first View Connection Server in your infrastructure. You will need to roll out a virtual machine from your template to meet the requirements for the View Connection Server. Our virtual machine has been configured with a 10-GB RAM, 4 vCPUs, and a 60-GB hard disk. This machine needs to be given a static IP address and be added to the active directory domain.

Once you have the virtual machine ready, you will be able to install the Connection Server.

From our files, we are going to execute the `VMware-viewconnectionserver-x86_64-6.X.X-XXXXXXX.exe` file to start the installation:

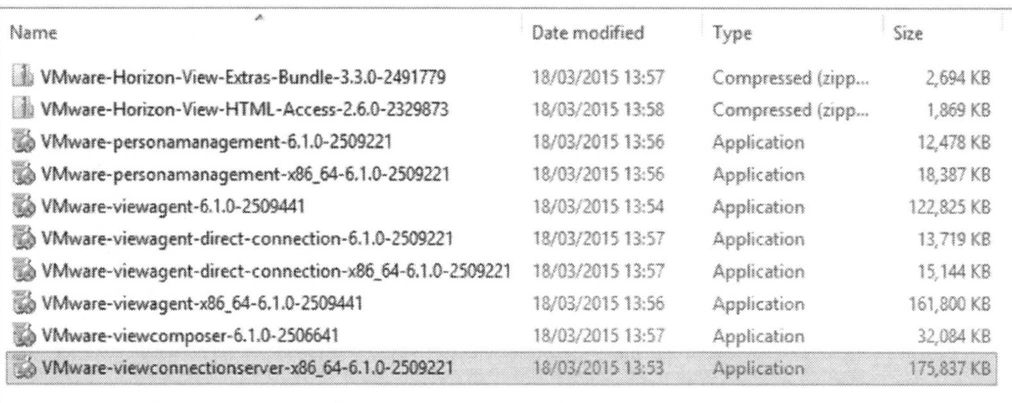

Name	Date modified	Type	Size
VMware-Horizon-View-Extras-Bundle-3.3.0-2491779	18/03/2015 13:57	Compressed (zipp...	2,694 KB
VMware-Horizon-View-HTML-Access-2.6.0-2329873	18/03/2015 13:58	Compressed (zipp...	1,869 KB
VMware-personamanagement-6.1.0-2509221	18/03/2015 13:56	Application	12,478 KB
VMware-personamanagement-x86_64-6.1.0-2509221	18/03/2015 13:56	Application	18,387 KB
VMware-viewagent-6.1.0-2509441	18/03/2015 13:54	Application	122,825 KB
VMware-viewagent-direct-connection-6.1.0-2509221	18/03/2015 13:57	Application	13,719 KB
VMware-viewagent-direct-connection-x86_64-6.1.0-2509221	18/03/2015 13:57	Application	15,144 KB
VMware-viewagent-x86_64-6.1.0-2509441	18/03/2015 13:56	Application	161,800 KB
VMware-viewcomposer-6.1.0-2506641	18/03/2015 13:57	Application	32,084 KB
VMware-viewconnectionserver-x86_64-6.1.0-2509221	18/03/2015 13:53	Application	175,837 KB

Here's how you will start the installation:

1. The installation needs to be done in the same way that you installed View Composer, by clicking on **Next >** to start the installation and accepting the EULA. You will then select the location in which you are going to install the View Connection Server to meet your company's guidelines for application installations on servers. Again, we will install View Connection Server on our `C:` drive in our example:

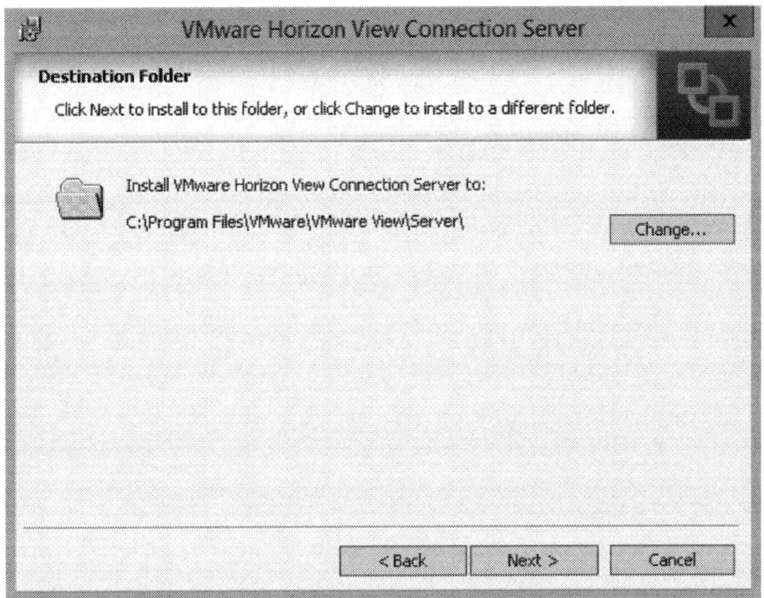

2. As this is your first View Connection Server, select View Standard Server from the list. Note, we have also chosen to **Install HTML Access** option along with our standard server. This will allow users to access their desktops using the Blast Protocol and an HTML 5 web browser. You also have the option of choosing which IP protocol to use, either IPv4 or IPv6:

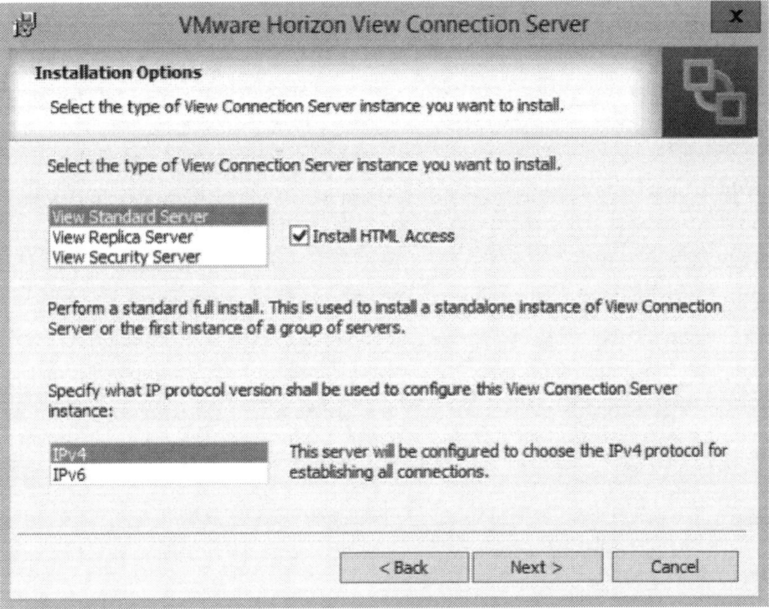

3. On the next screen of the wizard, we are asked to configure a data recovery password. This password will be used to protect your View Connection Server backups of the ADAM database. You will need this password if you ever need to recover these files, so it is of utmost importance that you document the password that has been used to protect these backups.
4. In the event of you not remembering the password, it is possible to get the recovery tool to prompt you for a reminder. So, where possible, ensure the password reminder will serve without giving away what the password is:

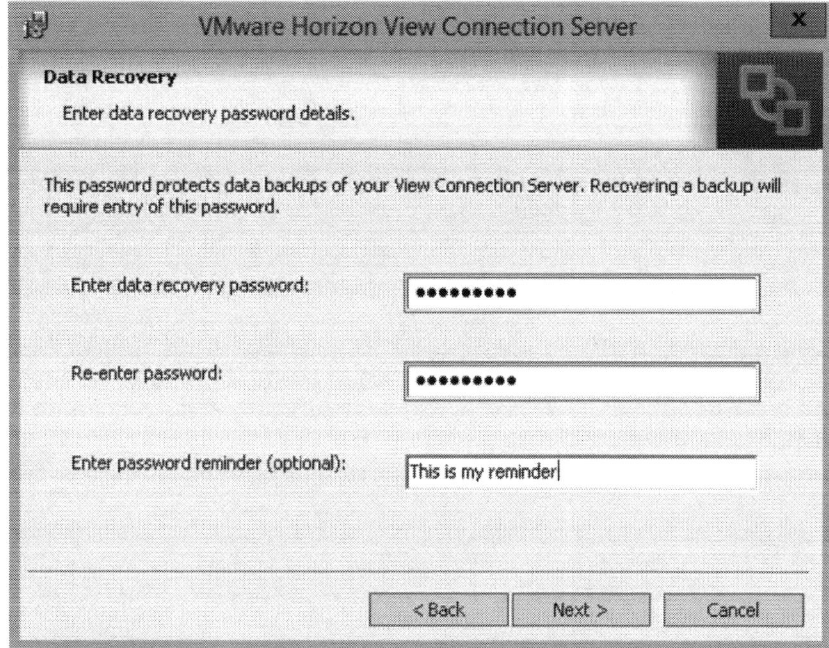

5. You will now need to select whether you are happy for the installation wizard to configure Windows Firewall with the specific ports required for Horizon View.

Please note that Windows Firewall is a requirement for Horizon View, specifically for security server to Connection Server communication. So under no circumstances should you disable the Windows Firewall service on your View servers. We recommend allowing Windows Firewall to be configured automatically, noting down the required ports where needed and clicking on **Next >**.

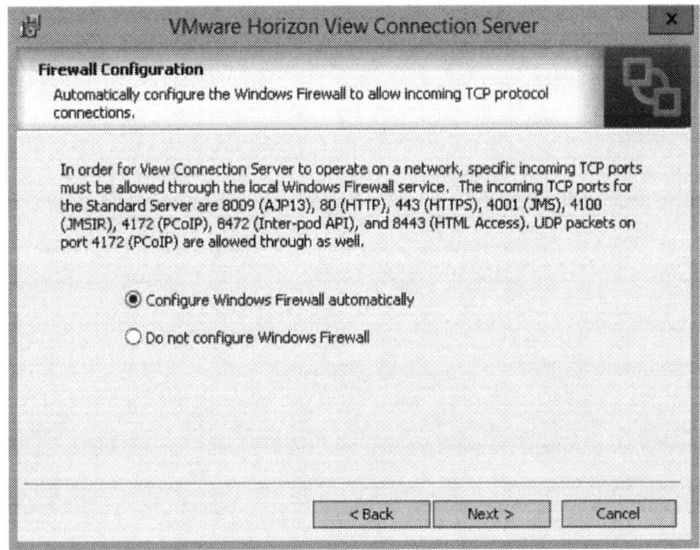

6. You now need to configure which users on your domain or on the local server are going to be configured as your first View Administrators. For ease, we have selected only the domain administrator in our configuration. In your environment, we would recommend creating a security group and including the required domain admin accounts to be part of this security group. We are then able to add additional users later, if required, through the View Administrator:

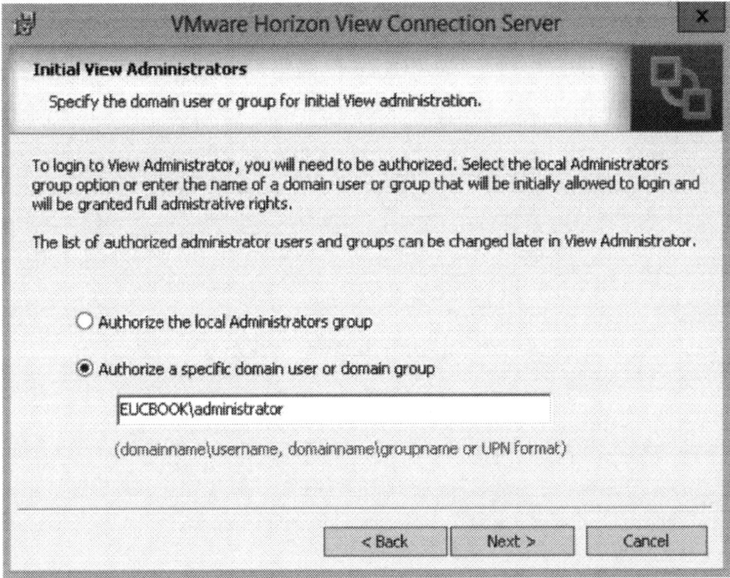

You will get the option of participating in the customer experience program. This program is completely anonymous and allows VMware to improve the user experience of their products by collecting usage statistics.

7. If you wish to participate, check the relevant box and complete the three on-screen questions prior to moving on. If you don't wish to participate, simply click on **Next >**.
8. You can opt in or opt out of the experience program at a later date. This is achieved by navigating to **View Configuration | Product Licensing and Usage | Customer Experience Program** in the **View Administrator**:

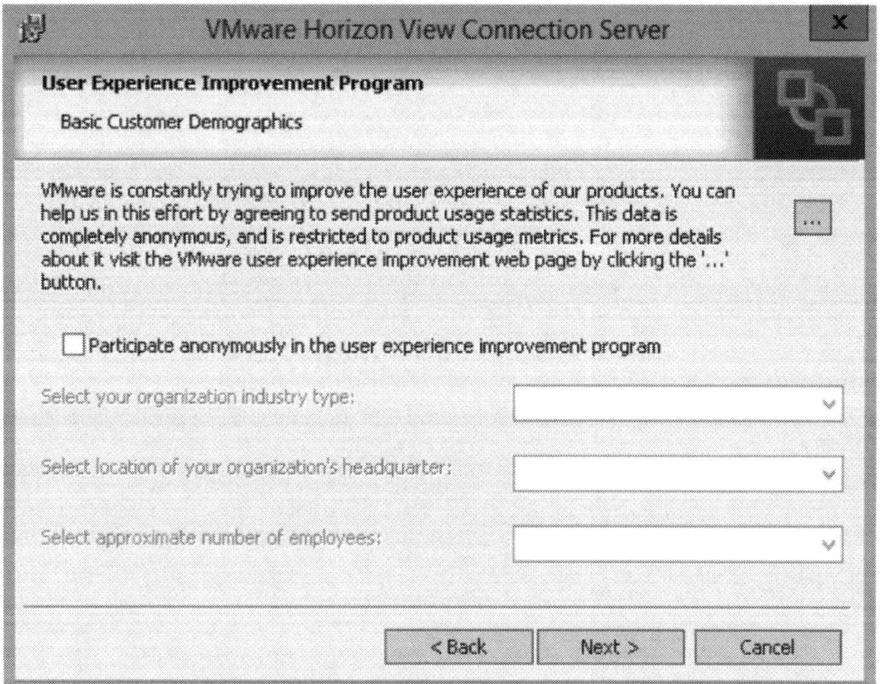

You are now in a position where you can complete the installation.

9. Once again, if the installation fails for any reason, the installation logs are held in the Connection Server at `%TEMP%\vminst.log_date_timestamp`.
10. Additionally, there are MSI logs created, which can be found at `%TEMP%\vmmsi.log_date_timestamp`.

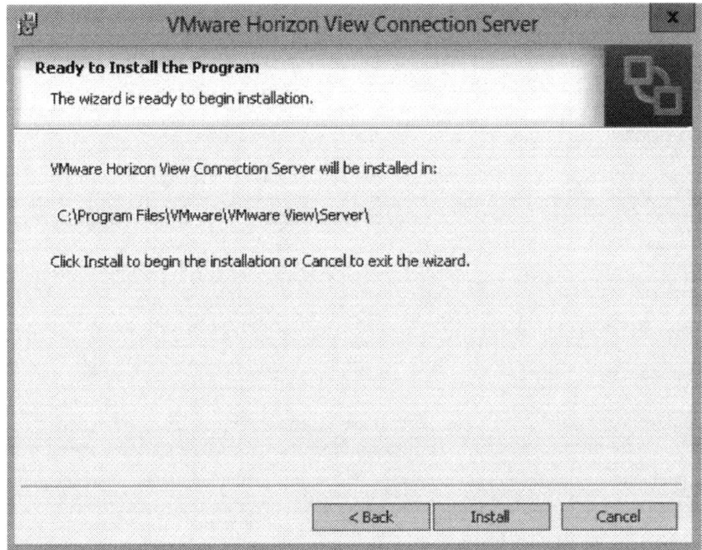

11. You will now hopefully be in a position where you have had a successful installation of your first Horizon View Connection Server. As you finish the installation, you will be prompted to **Show the readme file** listing your next steps. We recommend that you review this document; it mainly discusses the importance of valid SSL certificates in the Horizon View installation, which we will cover in *Chapter 5, Securing Horizon View with SSL Certificates*:

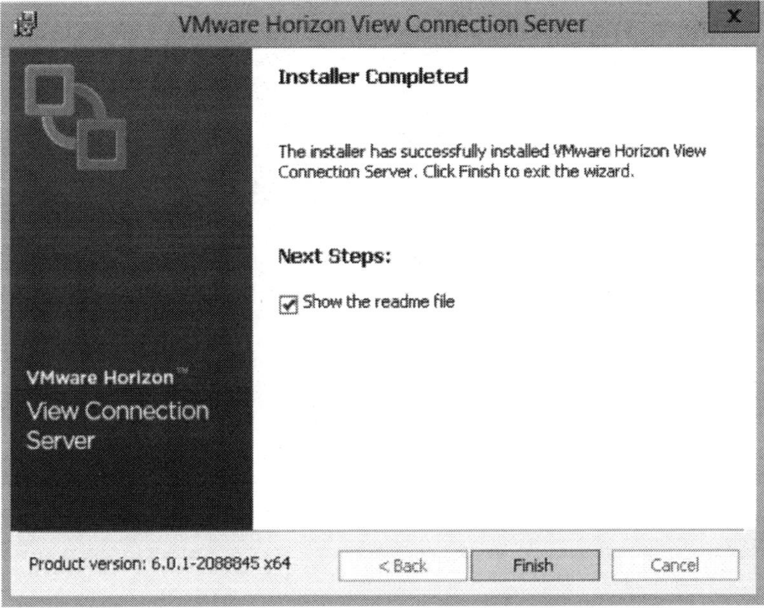

12. We are now going to reboot the View Connection Server and check whether the installation has been successful. Initially, we recommend that you check the log files mentioned earlier, view Windows services, and ensure all the View Services listed in the following screenshot have been registered and started as follows:

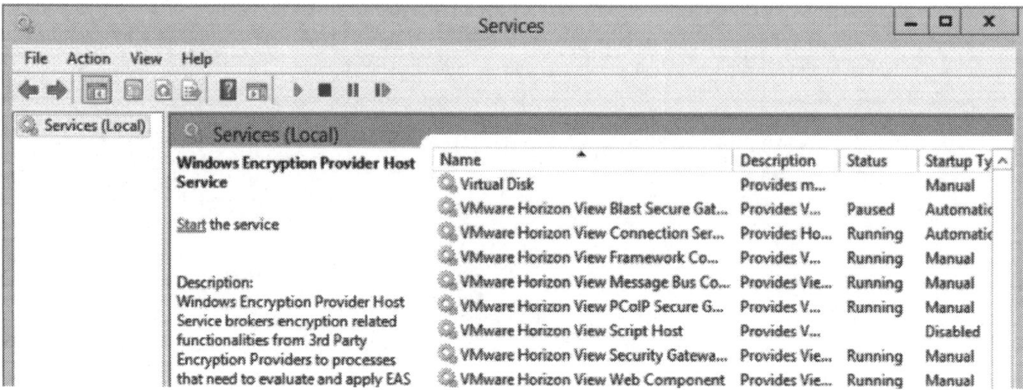

13. We should also be able to navigate to **View Administrator** by selecting the shortcut placed on the desktop or visiting `https://localhost/admin` in a web browser. Note, when visiting this address, Adobe Flash 10.1 or higher is required to proceed. Our advice at this point would be not to install Adobe Flash on this server but to continue the configuration on a workstation:

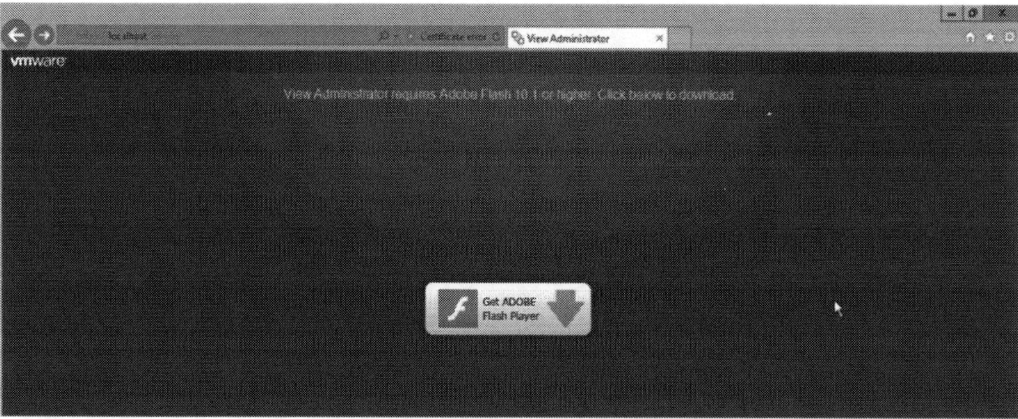

Initial configuration of the View Connection Server

You are now in a position to take the first few simple steps to get your Horizon View solution configured. From a workstation with Adobe Flash 10.1 or higher installed, you need to browse to your View Connection Server in a web browser to `https://{FQDN of View Connection Server}/admin`.

As you are yet to configure the SSL certificates, you need to create a security exception to allow you to browse to the HTTPS page with an unsecured certificate:

1. You need to log in to the **View Administrator** with a user account that you configured to be an administrator through the installation process:

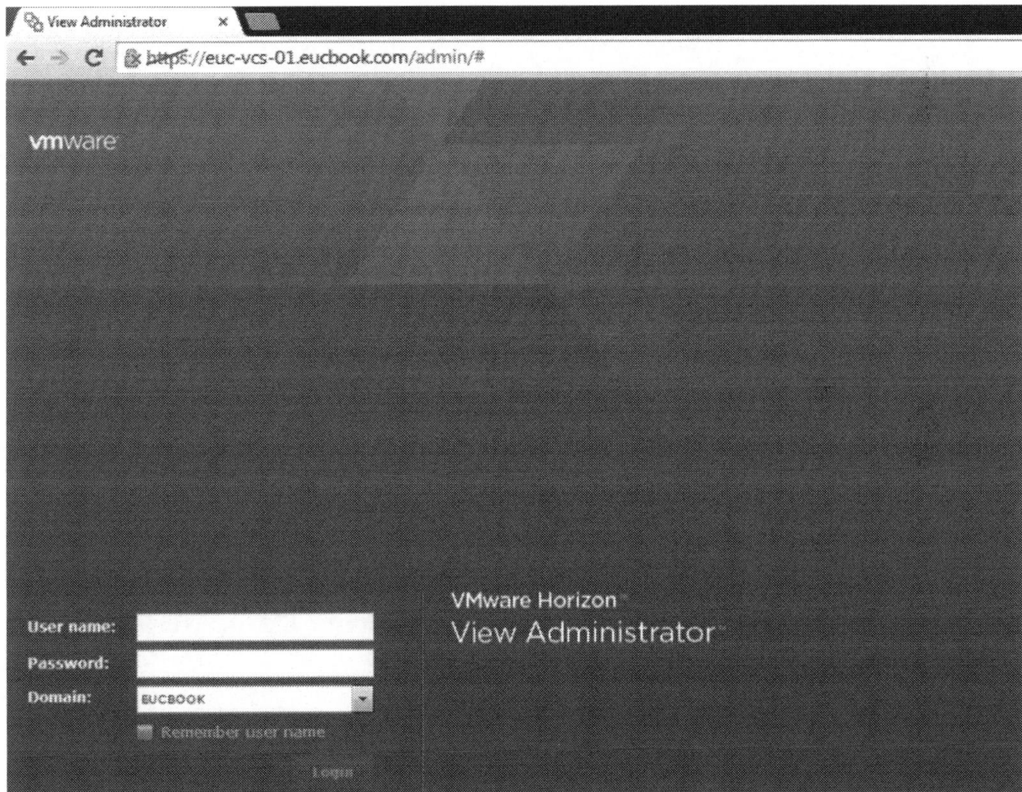

2. Now that we are in **View Administrator** for the first time, the first component to be configured is licensing. On the left-hand side of the screen, you will see many menus that can be expanded. Expand **View Configuration** and then select **Product Licensing and Usage** (**1**). Next, select **Edit License** (**2**). In the box that appears, you need to input your Horizon 6 license key:

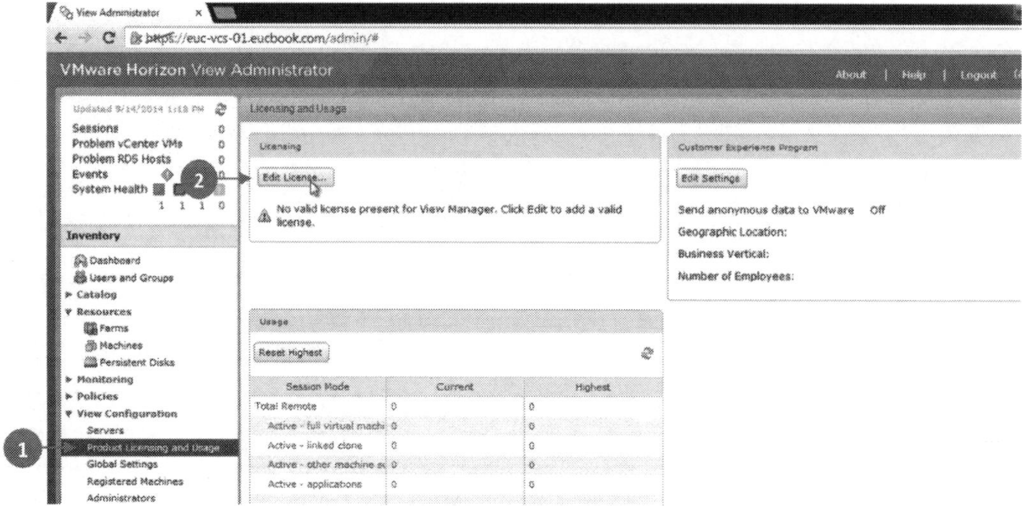

Once completed, you will see that under licensing, the relevant information is now complete. We have used a temporary key, and for this reason, we have an expiration date as well as a named user license model. Horizon View can be purchased in a concurrent or named user-licensing model. While you are on this screen, you can check your usage. This allows you to ensure you are within the remit of your purchased licenses and also allows you to have visibility of the usage so that you can preempt an upgrade before reaching the limits.

3. Finally, on the right-hand side, we can see the customer experience program registration information. Here, you can opt in or out, like the component we reviewed while installing the View Connection Server:

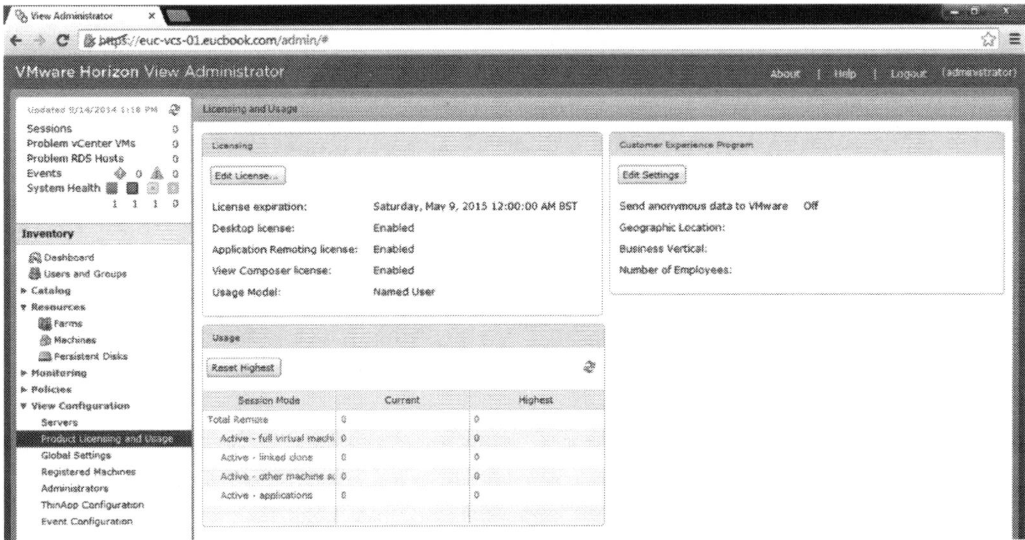

4. We now register our vCenter Server. This vCenter Server should be the one we are going to use to manage our desktops. In a larger environment with a block and pod architecture, we might have multiple View Connection Servers listed.
5. From the **View Configuration** menu, we select **Servers** (**1**). The first tab we see will be the **vCenter Servers** tab. From here select **Add...** (**2**):

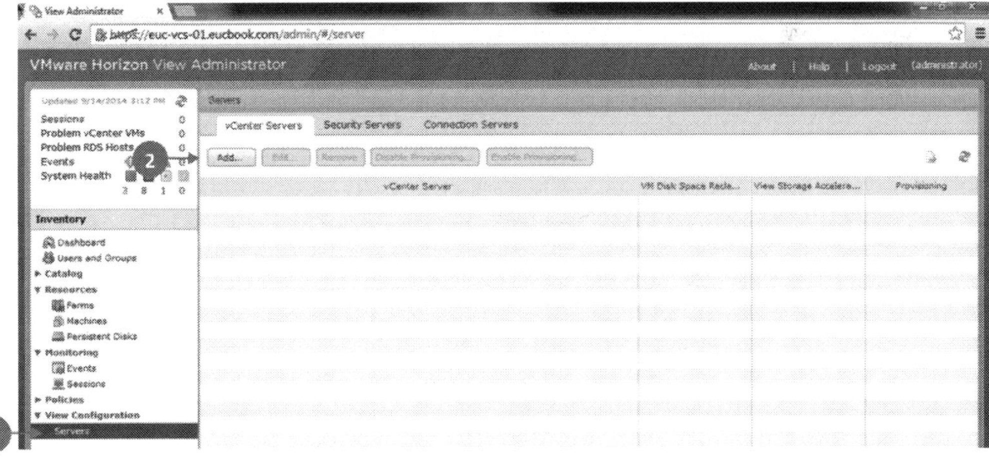

6. The **Add vCenter Server** wizard will open. We start by completing the information for connection to our vCenter. We will use the fully qualified domain name for our vCenter (**1**), and the **User name** (**2**) and **Password** (**3**) we created at the beginning of this chapter. For the time being, we will leave the **Advanced Settings** as is. These settings can be tweaked at a later date if you wish to customize your installation further. We are now able to progress with the install by clicking on **Next >** (**4**):

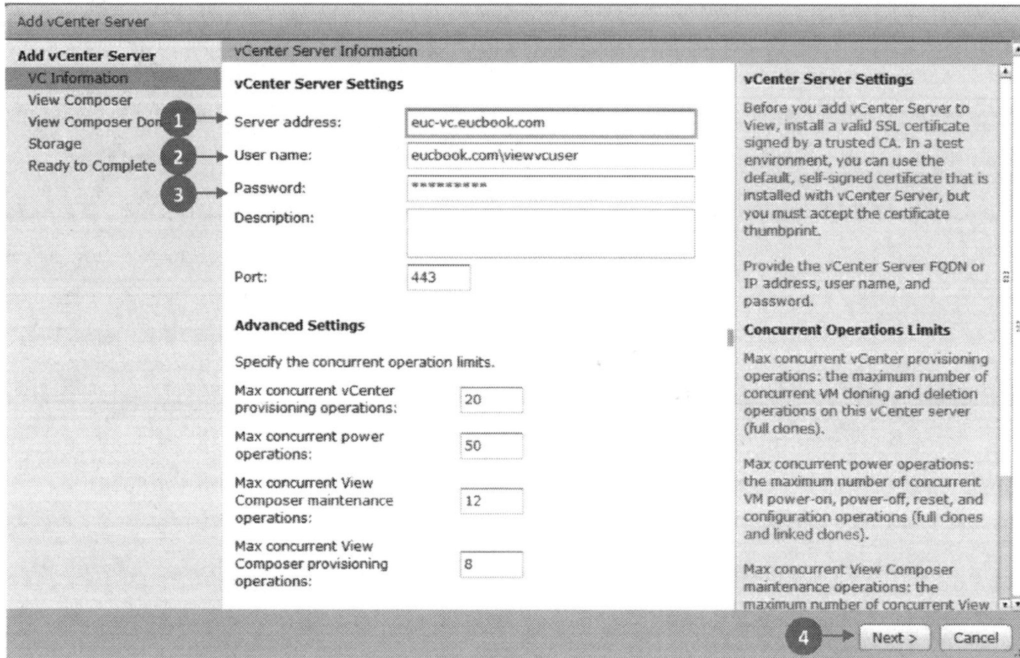

7. If your vCenter Server does not have a valid secure certificate, you will see the **Invalid Certificate Detected** dialog box. This will give you the opportunity to view the certificate using the **View Certificate...** option (**1**) and accept (**2**) it. In *Chapter 5, Securing Horizon View with SSL Certificates*, we will discuss installing a valid certificate on your vCenter Server. For the time being, click on **Accept**:

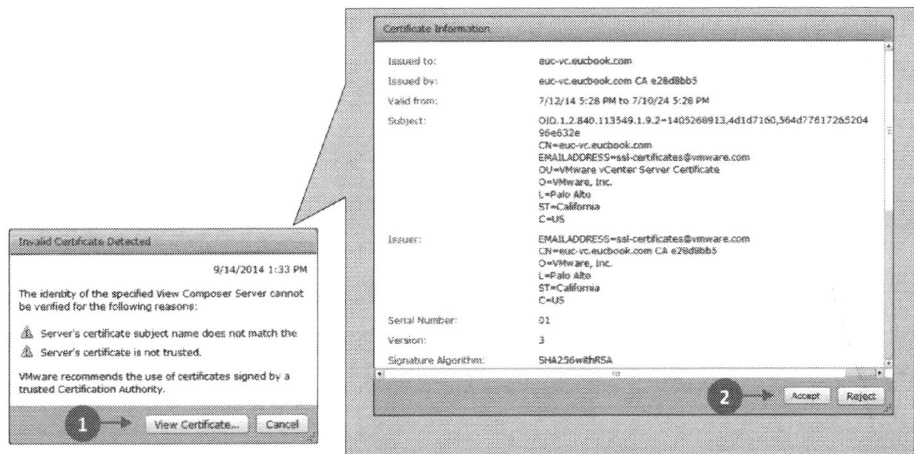

You now need to configure View Composer for use in conjunction with this vCenter Server. As we are using a vCenter Appliance, our Composer Server is installed on a separate Windows Server to that of our vCenter. Depending on scale, you may still wish to deploy View Composer onto a dedicated server.

8. First, you will need to select either **View Composer co-installed with vCenter Server** or **Standalone View Composer Server** (1), depending on your installation. If you are using a co-installed Composer Server, you can now continue by selecting **Next >** (5). If you are using a standalone Composer Server, prior to selecting **Next >** (5), you need to input the fully qualified domain name for your Composer Server in **Server address** field (2), the **User name** (3), and **Password** (4) that we configured at the beginning of this chapter, as well as the port to communicate upon:

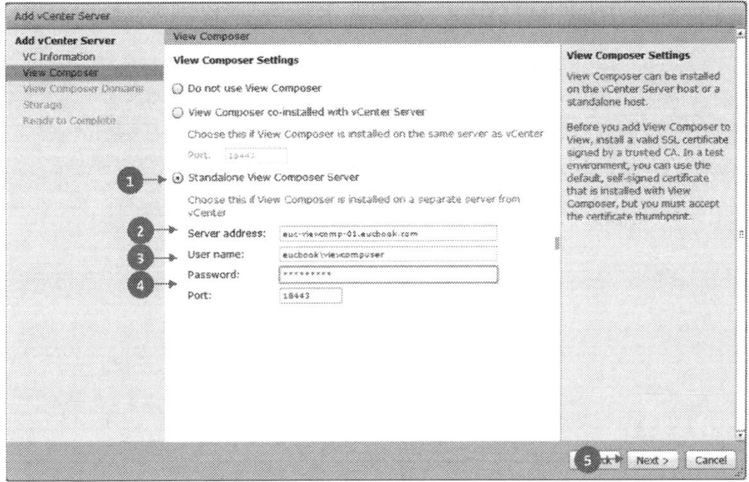

9. Again, if our View Composer Server is not using a valid SSL certificate, we need to select **View Certificate...** (**1**) and **Accept** (**2**) the self-signed certificate that is currently in use within the environment:

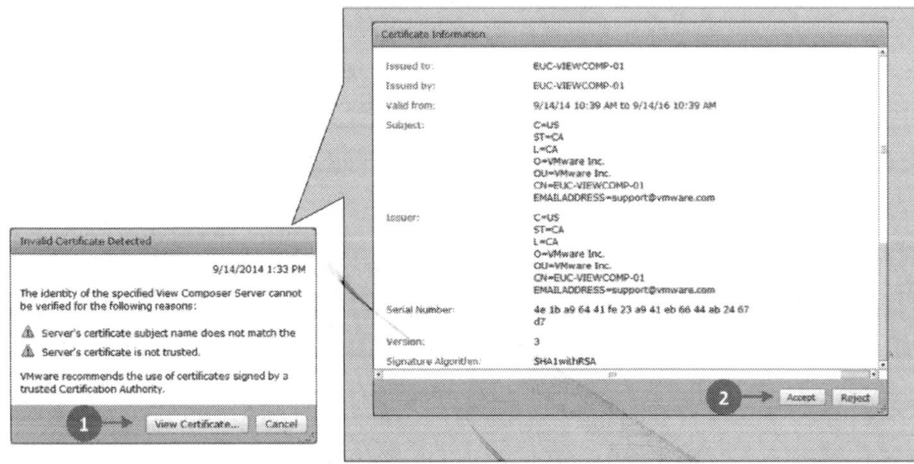

10. On the next screen, you configure the domain that you are going to use within your View environment in conjunction with **View Composer Domains**. In our example, we are only using one domain for our users' desktops. We will add this domain as shown in the following screenshot and move to the storage configuration:

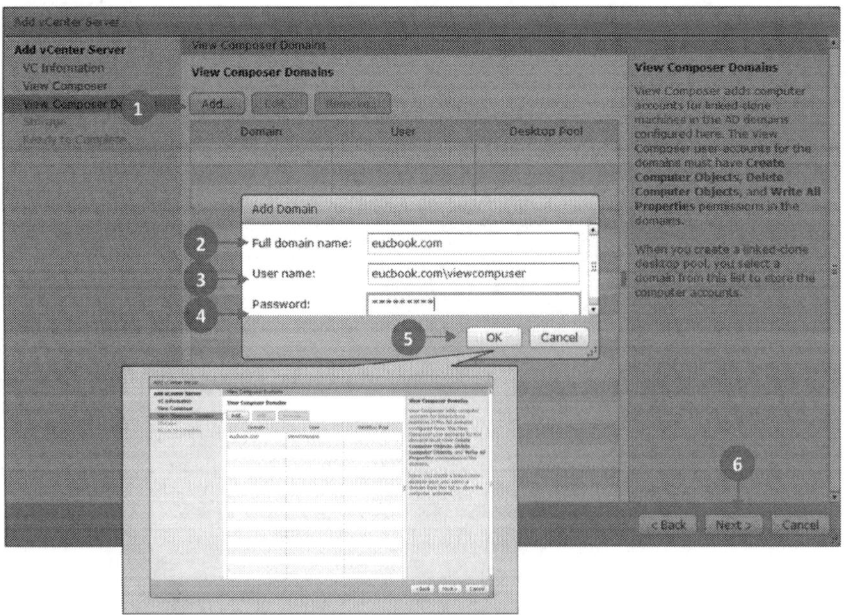

11. You are now going to configure the storage options for us in conjunction with Horizon View. As we can see in the following screenshot, there are two main elements for us to consider:
    - The first option is to configure whether we wish to reclaim VM disk space for our virtual desktops. If this is selected, our virtual machines will be configured with space-efficient disks, which will allow reclamation of unused space within each desktop.
    - The second option is to configure the View Storage Accelerator. This allows a specific amount of memory host to be utilized as a read cache to reduce the storage overheads on our shared or local storage used to run the virtual machines.

    By default, this will be 1 GB of memory per server; this can be increased to up to 2 GB per server, or alternatively, be configured differently on each host in our environment.

    The following screenshot shows our configuration for this screen of the wizard:

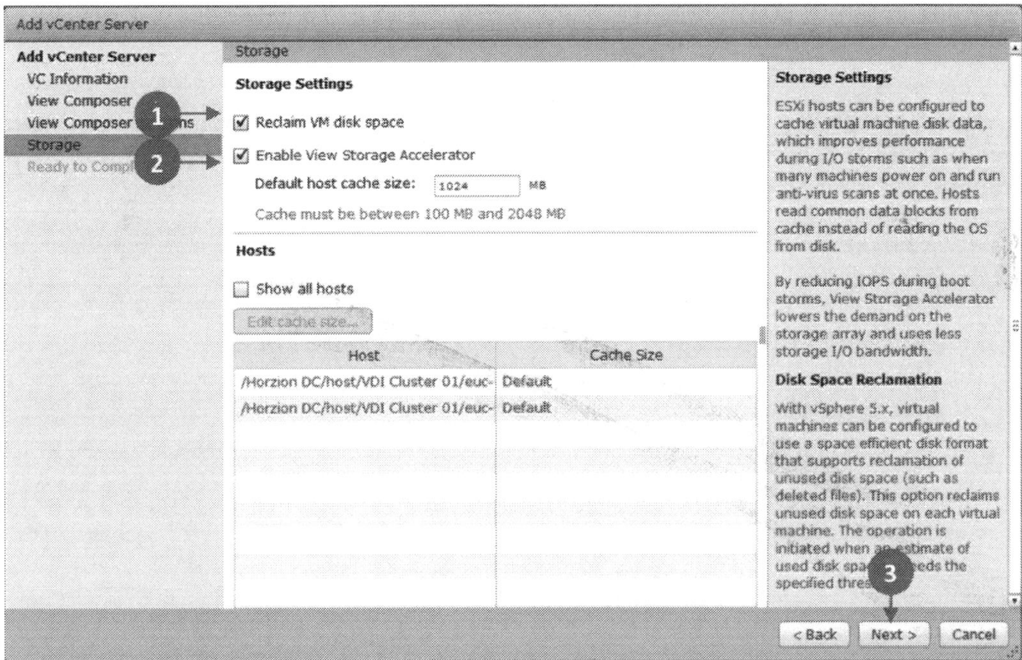

12. Once we have completed the **Add vCenter Server** wizard, we are taken back to the server configuration page. You should now be able to see your vCenter Server listed and the relevant boxes checked, based on the element you chose to configure as shown in the following screenshot:

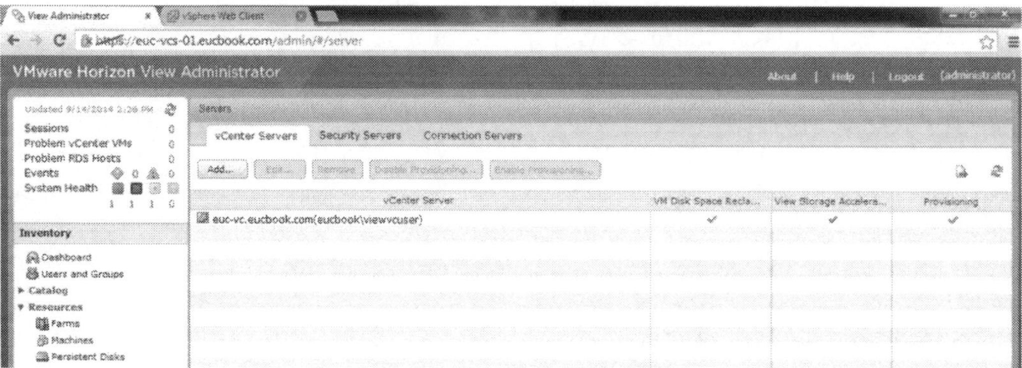

Creating and configuring the View Events database

You are now going to configure the View Events database for use within your environment. This will allow a full list of notifications to be collected to assist with troubleshooting issues within your environment. You will to need to configure a SQL database for use with the View Events:

1. Back in your SQL server, start by creating a new login in the SQL Server Management Studio. You need to configure the **Login name** (**1**) and **Password** (**2**) for SQL server authentication. Also, be sure to uncheck the **Enforce Password Policy**, **Enforce Password Expiration**, and **User must change password at next login** (**3**) options. For the time being, leave the **Default database** set to **master**:

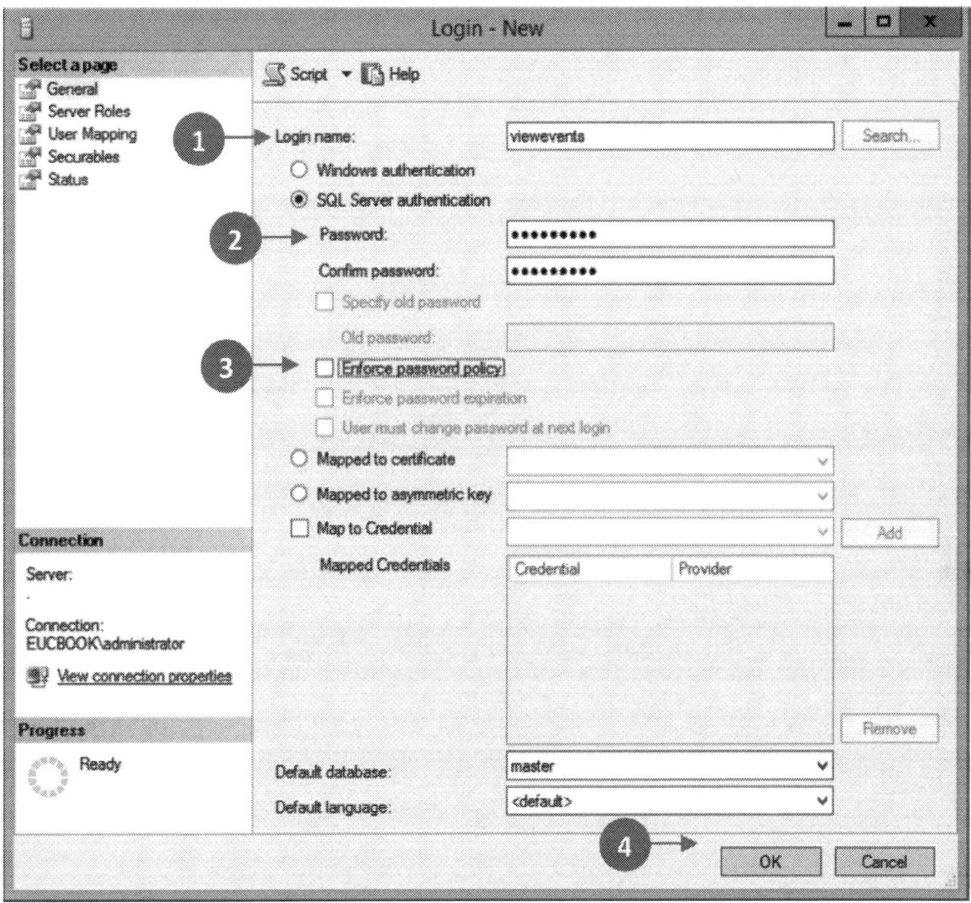

2. You now need to create a database for **viewevents**. Start by inputting a meaningful database name (**1**) for the database and then selecting the login we created earlier as the owner (**2**) as shown in the upcoming screenshot. Once again, work with your DBA to ensure you configure the database as per company guidelines and to ensure the recovery models and maintenance plans are configured.

3. Go back to the login you created and set your **viewevents** database as the default database for this user:

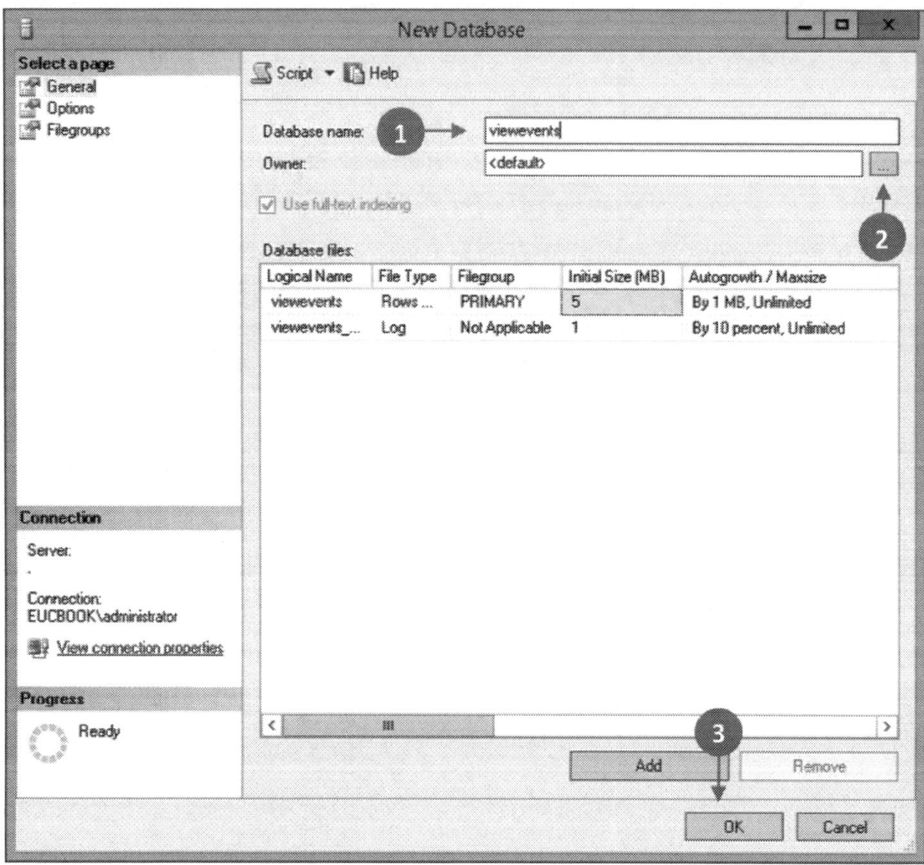

If you are making use of SQL Express for your **viewevents** database (we would only recommend this in a test environment and not production), you need to ensure TCP/IP communication is enabled.

4. This can be checked and changed from inside the **SQL Server Configuration Manager(Local)**, simply by expanding **SQL Server Network Configuration** **(1)** and **Protocols for MSSQLSERVER** **(2)** and then checking TCP-IP is enabled. If not, it can be enabled by right-clicking on **TCP/IP** and selecting **Enable** (3):

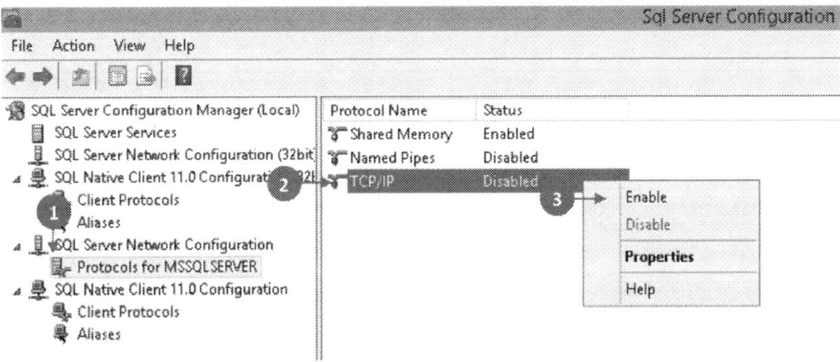

5. Back inside **View Administrator**, you will now need to configure the **Event Database**. Under **View Configuration**, select **Event Configuration** (**1**) and then select the **Edit** (**2**) button listed under the **Event Database** box.
6. You now need to input all of your SQL server details, including the **Database name**, **User name**, and **Password** into the **Edit Event Database** (**3**) dialog box prior to selecting **OK** (**4**).

> Note that you will also need to input a table prefix to be utilized; this could simply be a short name for a location or purpose. For example, if we have used prod in our environment, it is short for production. The table prefix allows you to use the same **Events Database** for multiple installations if required.

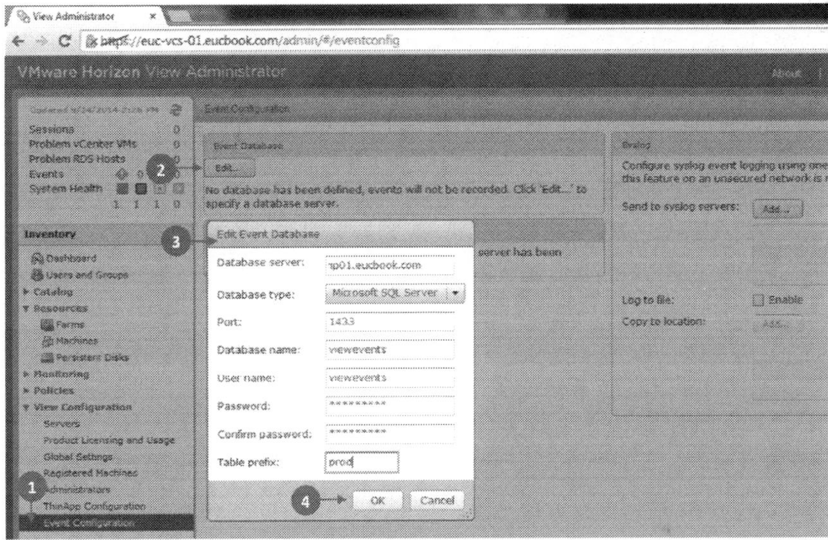

7. You now should be able to see the configuration for your **Event Database** listed. Also note that on this page, you can tune the configuration to retain events. You will also notice that you are able to configure a **Syslog** server. If you have a syslog server in use, we highly recommend you configure View to log in here as well, to allow you to capture and act upon issues as they occur:

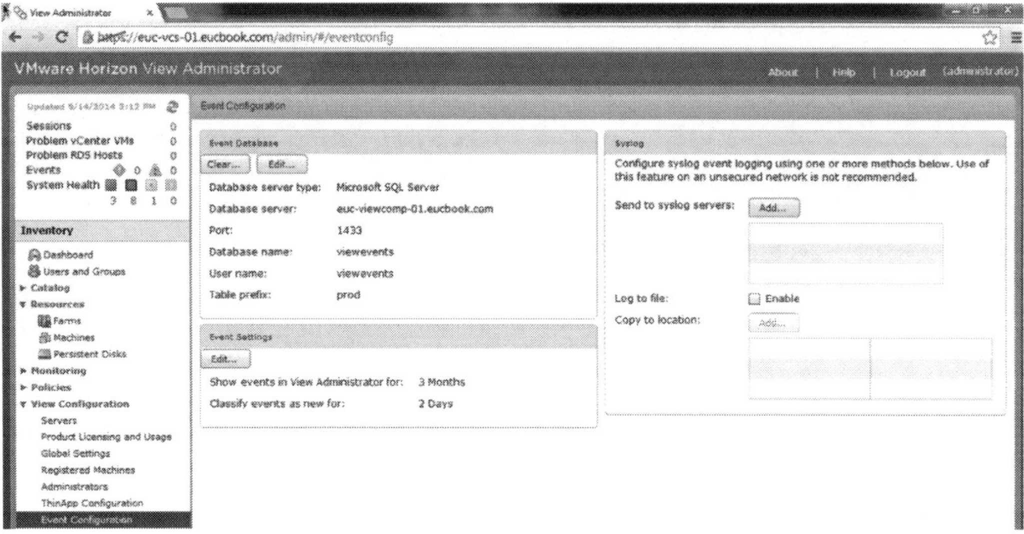

8. By navigating to **Monitoring** | **Events (1)** in the left-hand side menu, we can view the **Events** table. From here, you can see any events that have been logged, by using the top gray bar; we can also filter what is shown by time, word match, or criticality:

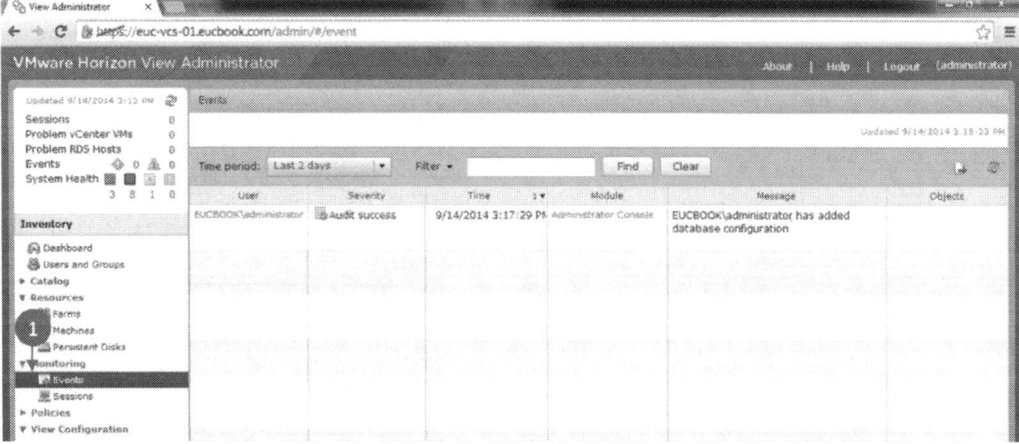

This concludes the initial configuration of our Horizon View environment. We are now going to move to installing a replica server and our first security server. We will be covering many other elements of configuration in this chapter and throughout the book.

Installing the replica server

You are now going to move on to deploy your second View Connection Server into your infrastructure. Additional View Connection Servers are referred to as **replica servers**. This is due to the nature in which View shares its configurations between multiple View Connection Servers using the ADAM database.

Additional Connection Servers are generally deployed for availability reasons, as discussed in the previous chapters. For test purposes, you could role out a single View Connection Server.

You need to roll out a further virtual machine from your template, to meet the requirements for View Connection Server; in our example, our virtual machine has been configured with a 10-GB RAM, 4 vCPUs, and a 60-GB hard disk. This machine needs to be given a static IP address and added to the AD domain.

Once your virtual machine is ready, you are able to install the Connection Server. From your files, once again the same are the first View Connection Server you are going to want to execute the `VMware-viewconnectionserver-x86_64-6.X.X-XXXXXXX.exe` file to start the installation. Following are the steps that need to be taken:

1. This time, when running through the wizard, you will want to install a **View Replica Server** (**1**). Once again, select **Install HTML Access**, if required for your installation, before proceeding by clicking **Next >** (**2**):

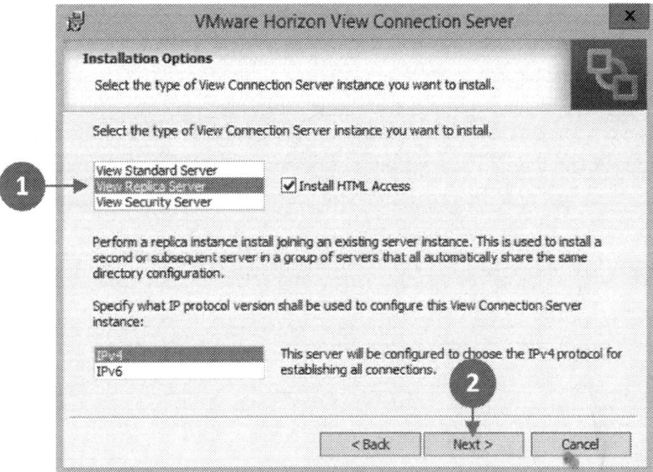

2. While selecting a replica server, you need to input the fully qualified domain name for the first View Connection Server that you implemented into the **Server** (**1**) input box as shown in the upcoming screenshot.
3. You can then proceed to the rest of the installation by selecting **Next** > (**2**), before completing the installation in the same manner as the first View Connection Server you installed:

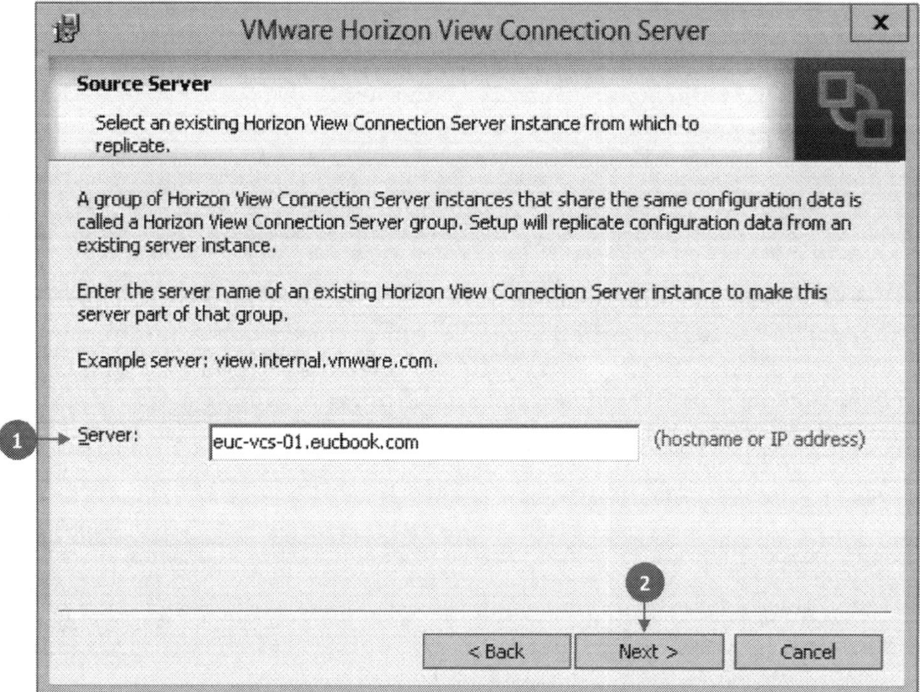

Once the installation is complete, once again, reboot the server, check the logs and services, and ensure you are able to access the **View Administrator** from the local server.

4. When accessing the **View Administrator** dialog box this time, you should browse to **View Configuration** and then to **Servers** (**1**) and then select the last tab labeled as **Connection Servers** (**2**). In this list, you should see the two View Connection Servers you have configured:

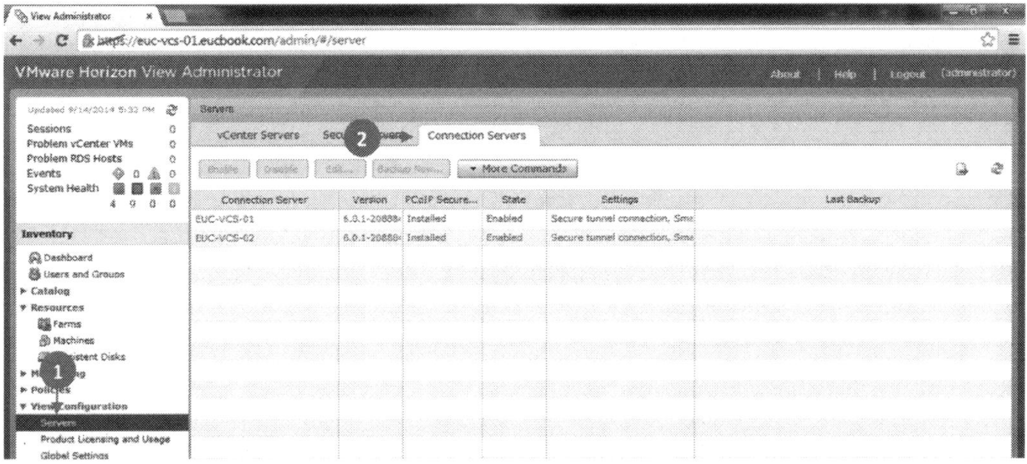

You have now configured your first replica server. Additional replica servers can be configured in the same manner.

Don't forget that Horizon View, as a standard, includes no method to load balance Connection Servers or security servers. As such, you should work with the relevant documentation from your load balancing manufacturer to configure your load balancers to work with your View Connection Servers as required; this allows users to be load balanced for availability and scale.

We have worked with F5 Networks and JetNexus in the past to load balance View Connection Server, but other vendors are supported as well. It is possible to use Microsoft Network Load Balancing, however, we would recommend this to be restricted to lab and smaller production environments only.

Installing the security server

You should now have an infrastructure that has vCenter configured ready for your VDI desktops, View Composer configured ready to be used in conjunction with Horizon View, and two or more View Connection Servers. We are now going to look at this process to roll out your first security server in your environment.

The first thing you need to do is configure your relevant View Connection Server to be able to accept the connection from the security server.

Don't forget that a security server has a one-to-one relationship with a Connection Server, if you wish to roll out a number of security servers, you will want to have multiple View Connection Servers.

We would also recommend that you have dedicated external View Connection Servers ready to pair with your security servers and separate View Connection Servers for internal connections. This will allow you to specify which users can access desktops from outside the organization by using the tagging functionality, which we will discuss later in this chapter and in *Chapter 7, Managing and Configuring Desktop Pools*:

1. To prepare your View Connection Server with a security server, we need to access the **View Administrator**. From the left-hand side menu, navigate to **View Configuration** | **Servers (1)** | **Connection Servers (2)** as shown in the upcoming screenshot.
2. Now, right-click on the relevant **View Connection Server (3)** and select **Specify Security Server Pairing Password... (4)**:

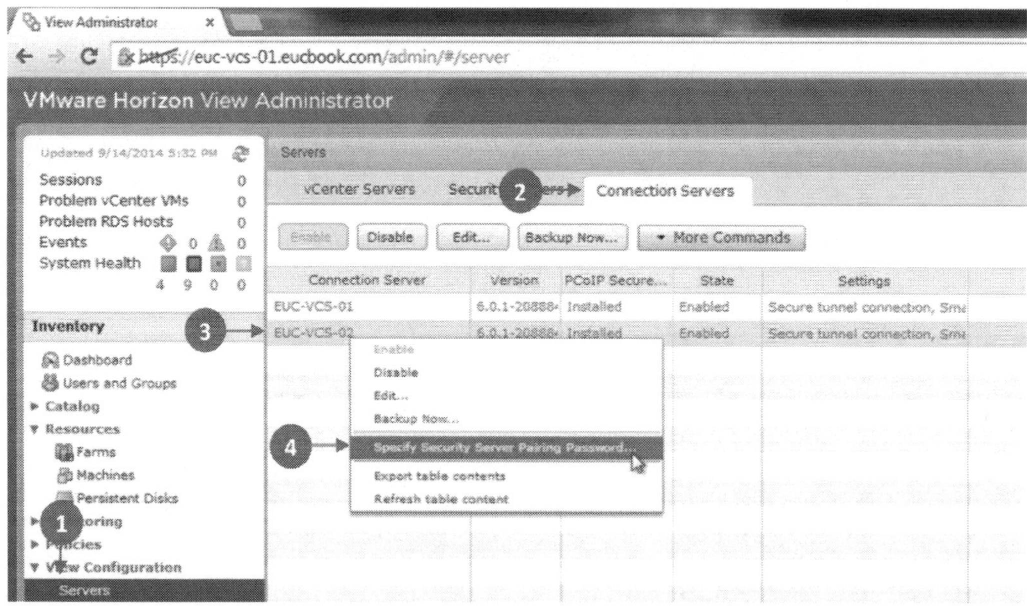

3. Input a password, which will be used to pair as well as a password timeout; the security server will only be able to pair with the View Connection Server during this timeframe. You are now ready to roll out your first security server:

4. Once again, you will need to roll out a further virtual machine from your template. This machine needs to meet the requirements for the View Security Server in your environment; in our example, our virtual machine has been configured with a 10-GB RAM, 4 vCPUs, and a 60-GB hard disk. This machine needs to be given a static IP address and should NOT be added to the AD domain. Keep in mind that the security server is designed to be added to your DMZ for security purposes.
5. Once your virtual machine is ready, you can install the security server. From your files, once again the same are the first View Connection Server you are going to want to execute the `VMware-viewconnectionserver-x86_64-6.X.X-XXXXXXX.exe` file to start the installation.

6. We will run through the installation just like we did for the View Connection Server, but this time we select the **View Security Server** (**1**) option from the menu before moving on, by selecting **Next >** (**2**):

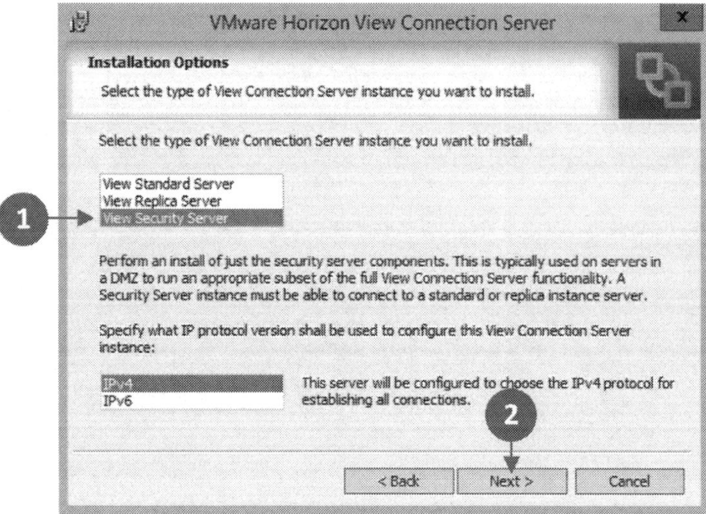

7. As you have now selected the **View Security Server** option, you need to enter specific information based on your configuration.
8. First of all, you need to input the fully qualified domain name for the View Connection Server, which you will pair the security server against, into the **Server** (**1**) input box before selecting **Next >** (**2**):

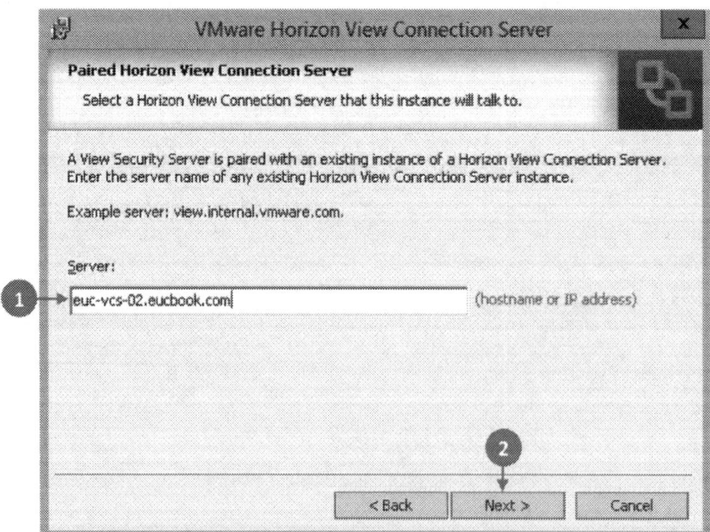

9. Next, we configure the network-specific details for your **View Security Server Configuration**; this includes the **External URL** (**1**) option, which users will use to connect to their desktops over the Internet, the **PCoIP External URL** (**2**) option (confusingly, this needs to be an IP address); in our example we have used an internal IP address, but in your environment, this needs to be the IP address that your users connect to their desktops to over the Internet. Finally, we need to complete the details for **Blast External URL** (**3**), which will be used for external HTML5-based connections. Once completed, we will continue with the installation by selecting **Next >** (**4**):

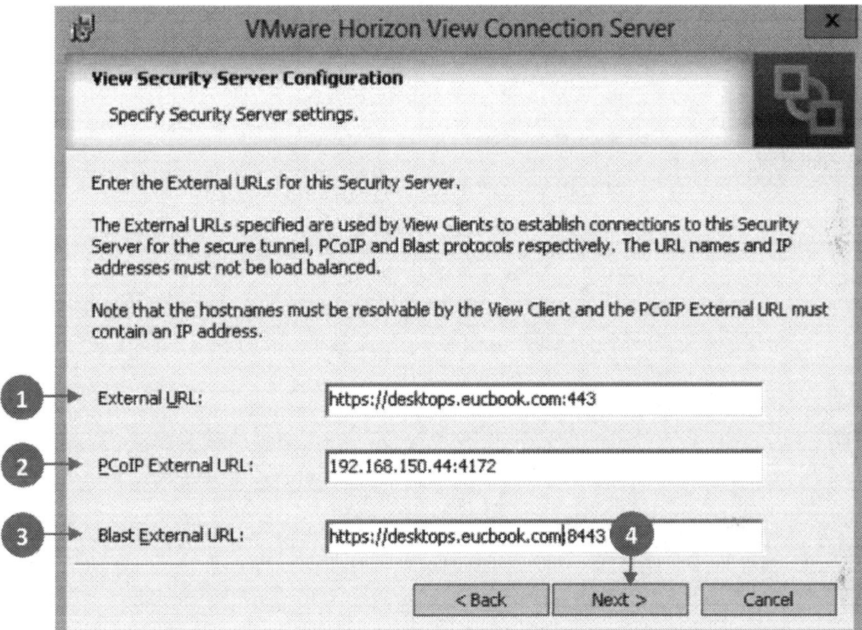

10. You will now continue through the wizard once again, either configuring Windows Firewall yourself, or allowing the wizard to configure it for you as recommended:

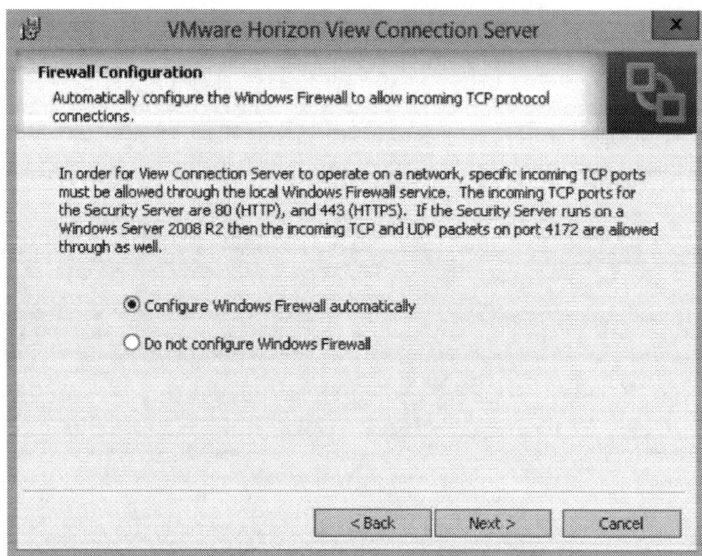

11. You will now finish the wizard and allow the installation to complete. Once the installation is complete, reboot the server and check the installation logs, as previously mentioned, and also the Windows services. On a security server, you can expect to see the services mentioned in the following screenshot:

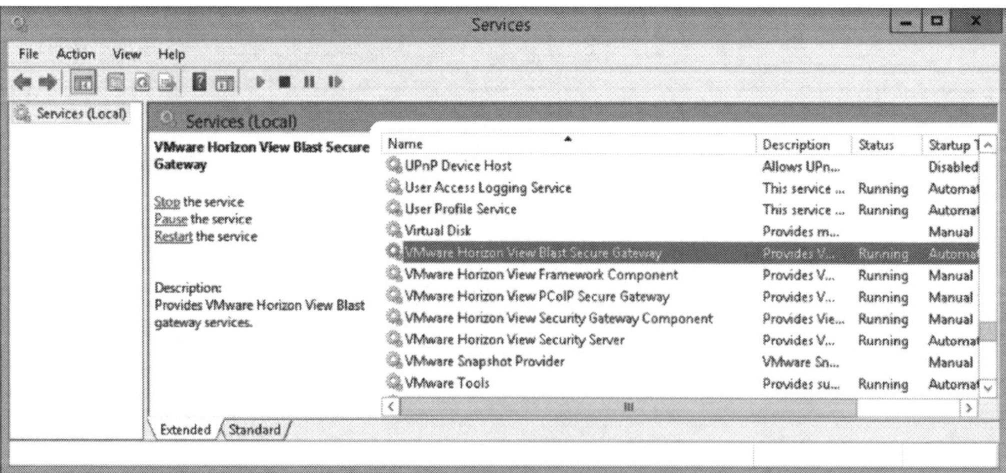

12. You are now also able to view the **Security Server** in **View Administrator** by browsing to **View Configuration** and selecting **Servers** (**1**) before selecting the **Security Servers** (**2**) tab:

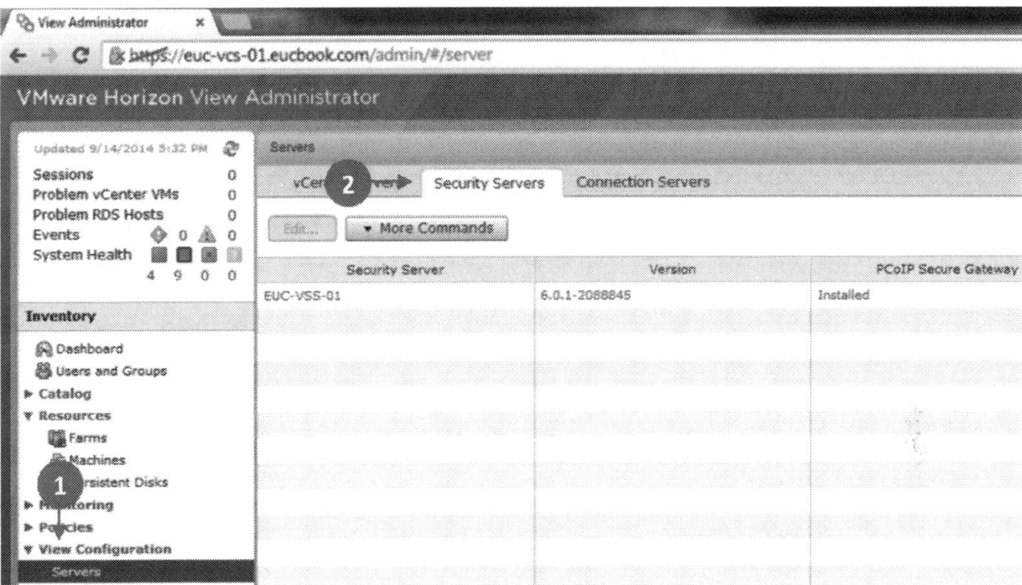

13. As mentioned earlier, we recommend installing security servers in conjunction with dedicated external View Connection Servers so you can limit access to the desktops from external connections by using the tagging functionality.

14. The first step in achieving this is by tagging our external Connection Servers. From inside the **View Administrator** navigate to **View Configurations** | **Servers** (**1**) | **Connection Servers** (**2**). Now select your external View Connection Servers one at a time and right-click and select **Edit** (**3**).

15. From here, you will need to choose a tag and tag all external Connection Servers with this tag (**4**); we have used the word **external** to tag these servers in our example:

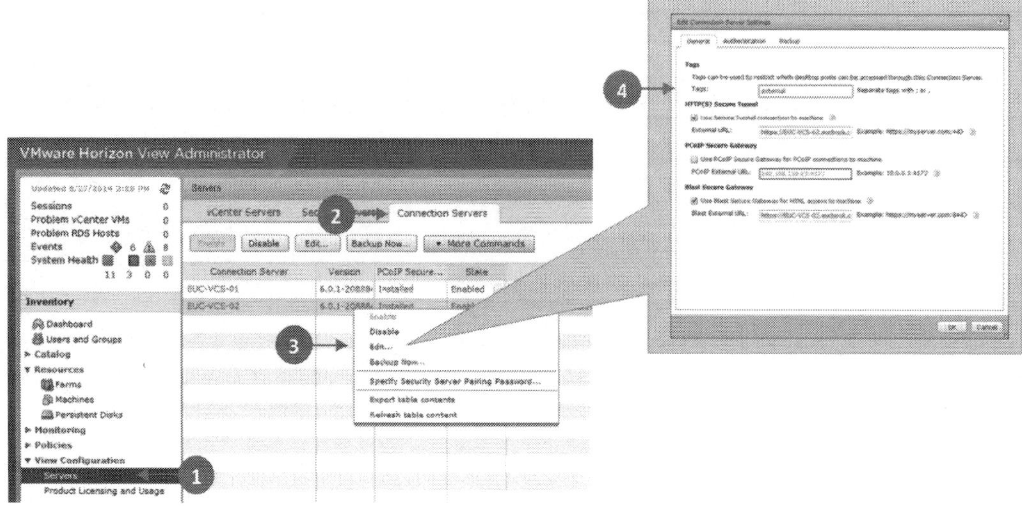

Configuring View for GPU-enabled virtual machines

In *Chapter 2, An Overview of Horizon View Architecture and its Components*, we discussed the ability of Horizon View virtual desktop machines to be configured to use hardware installed in the ESXi host server hosting those desktops.

As we said earlier, an advanced feature of Horizon View is the ability to use dedicated hardware installed in the ESXi host servers, configured with a PCI pass through so that the virtual desktop machine can see the hardware. In this section, we will perform the initial steps and install an NVIDIA GRID K2 GPU card into one of our host servers. Later on, in *Chapter 6, Building and Optimizing the Desktop Operating System*, we will create a virtual desktop machine image, which will have a dedicated assignment and access to the GPU resource using vDGA. This process is also the same for installing vGPU, however you will need vSphere 6 installed as the hypervisor to support this.

> vDGA requires a dedicated virtual machine assignment and, therefore, you will have a 1:1 mapping between the virtual desktop machine and GPU.

Configuring the ESXi host and vCenter Server

Before you build the virtual desktop machine, you need to have the graphics card physically installed into the ESXi host in preparation to build the new virtual desktop machine, which is configured to use the graphics cards.

In our example lab, we are using the NVIDIA GRID K2 card. These cards are available via the OEM route and come ready configured from the server vendors due to them requiring additional power connectors, cooling fans, and specific BIOS settings.

It's worth checking these before you start; just retrofitting the cards to an existing server might mean that they do not work. You will find the list of certified servers at `http://tinyurl.com/msdzu6b`.

With the hardware installed, log in to the vSphere web client, select the host into which the cards have been installed, and follow the listed steps:

1. Click the **Manage** tab (**1**) and then click on the **Settings** option (**2**), as shown in the following screenshot:

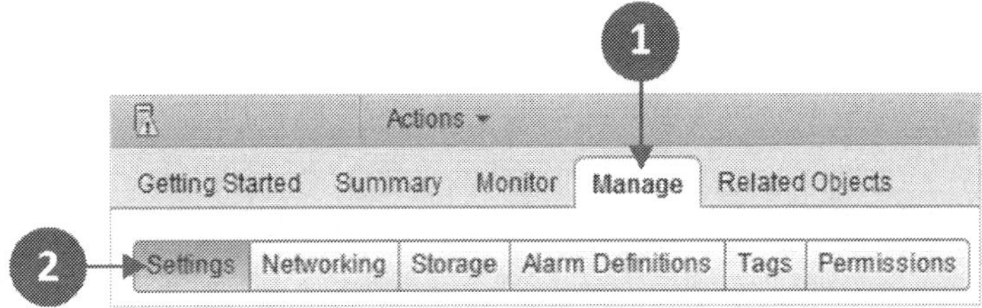

2. Expand the **Hardware** section (**3**) and click on **PCI Devices** (**4**). In the main screen, click on the pencil icon (**5**) to edit the settings, as shown in the following screenshot:

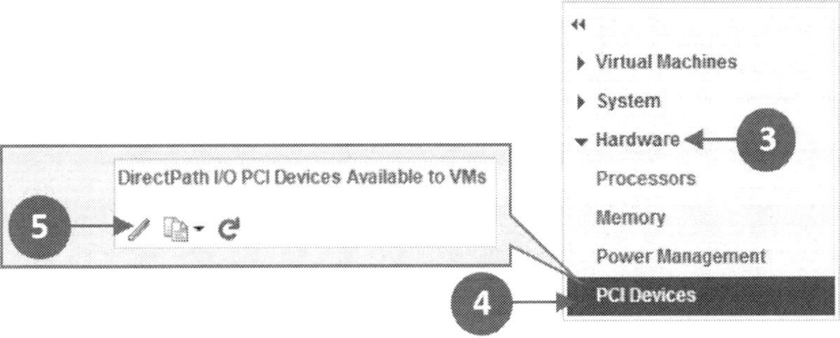

3. You will now see the following screenshot showing device availability:

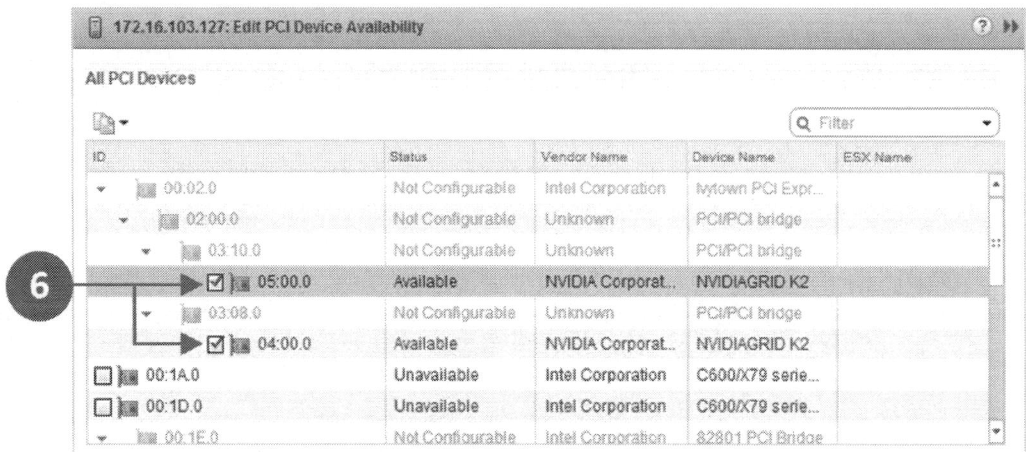

4. In our example, we have a server configured with two NVIDIA GRID K2 cards. Check the boxes for the two GPU cards (**6**), as shown in the previous screenshot, and click on **OK**.

We have now configured the ESXi host servers to use the NVIDIA GRID K2 GPU cards. We will build the virtual desktop machines to make use of these cards in *Chapter 6, Building and Optimizing the Desktop Operating System*.

Summary

In this chapter, we have walked you through configuring the key server components of your Horizon View Environment, including your View Composer Server, your first View Connection Server, your first replica server, and your first security server. We have discussed the initial configuration items that you will need to undertake, such as licensing your environment, connecting your vCenter and View Composer Servers, and configuring the View Security Server for external connections. We have also looked at the configuration items needed to prepare your environment for advanced graphics with NVidia GRID.

In *Chapter 5, Securing Horizon View with SSL Certificates*, we are going to configure SSL certificates across our environment to ensure it is secure.

5

Securing Horizon View with SSL Certificates

In this chapter, we will discuss the security aspect of VMware Horizon View 6. In particular, how we deliver secure communication not only with the end user client, but also the different infrastructure components in the data center. We will start with an overview of what a **Secure Sockets Layer** (**SSL**) certificate is and then learn how to create/issue a certificate before configuring Horizon View to use it.

Introducing SSL certificates

Let's start by defining SSL, SSL is an encryption technology developed by Netscape. It is used to create an encrypted connection between a web server and the web browser from where you will view the web pages. By using SSL, you can securely view the information sent to your browser, knowing that nobody else can access it.

SSL works by means of an SSL Certificate that is installed on a server and is used to identify you. So the question is, "How do you know whether you are using a secure connection to connect to the server?" If you have a secure connection, you will see a padlock icon in your browser, or the address bar will be colored green.

To ensure you have a secure connection, you can also access the site using `https://` in your browser rather than the usual `http://`.

SSL certificates are provided by **Certificate Authorities** (**CAs**).

What is a certificate authority?

A certificate authority is a service that issues digital certificates to organizations or people after validating them. Certification authorities keep detailed records of the certificates that have been issued and any other information that was used when the certificate was issued. These are regularly audited to ensure compliance.

You can obtain a certificate authority from different organizations, or you can create your own from a Root CA.

Why do I need SSL for Horizon View?

If you are transmitting sensitive information from a website to an endpoint device, you need to secure the information with SSL encryption; otherwise, data could be compromised.

As Horizon View is essentially like a web service to which end users connect from their endpoint device to the View Connection Server, you need to ensure that this connection is secured. Although, with View, no actual data is transmitted. The pixels from your virtual desktop machine are transmitted, and if a third-party intercepts this transmission, they could potentially see your screen.

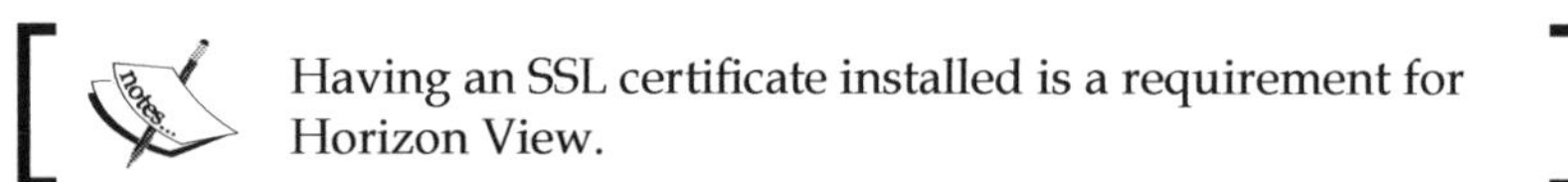

Having an SSL certificate installed is a requirement for Horizon View.

SSL certificates for Horizon View

By default, Horizon View comes with self-signed certificates that are fine for POC or a small-scale pilot, but for a production environment, you need to have proper certificates.

The use of certificates was first introduced with View 5.1, where they were used for these Horizon View components: the Connection Server, replica server, View Composer, and others. Each of these components needs to have a certificate installed along with the client device that is connecting.

In the following section of this chapter, we will briefly cover how to set up certificates by installing a Root CA in our example test environment to get you started with Horizon View. However, we strongly recommend that you engage with your security team to deploy the correct type of certificate for your organization/environment.

Installing a Root CA

In this section, we are going to walk through the steps to set up a server that will act as our Root CA. For our example lab, we will use a server named **HZN6-SQL.**:

1. On the **HZN6-SQL** server, launch the **Server Manager(HZN6-SQL.)** and perform the following steps to add the Root CA role.
2. Click on **Roles** (**1**) and right-click, and then click on **Add Roles** (**2**), as shown in the following screenshot:

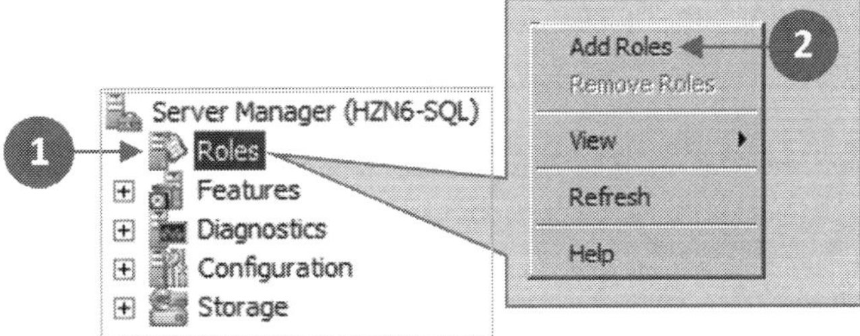

3. You will now see the **Before You Begin** page, as shown in the | following screenshot:

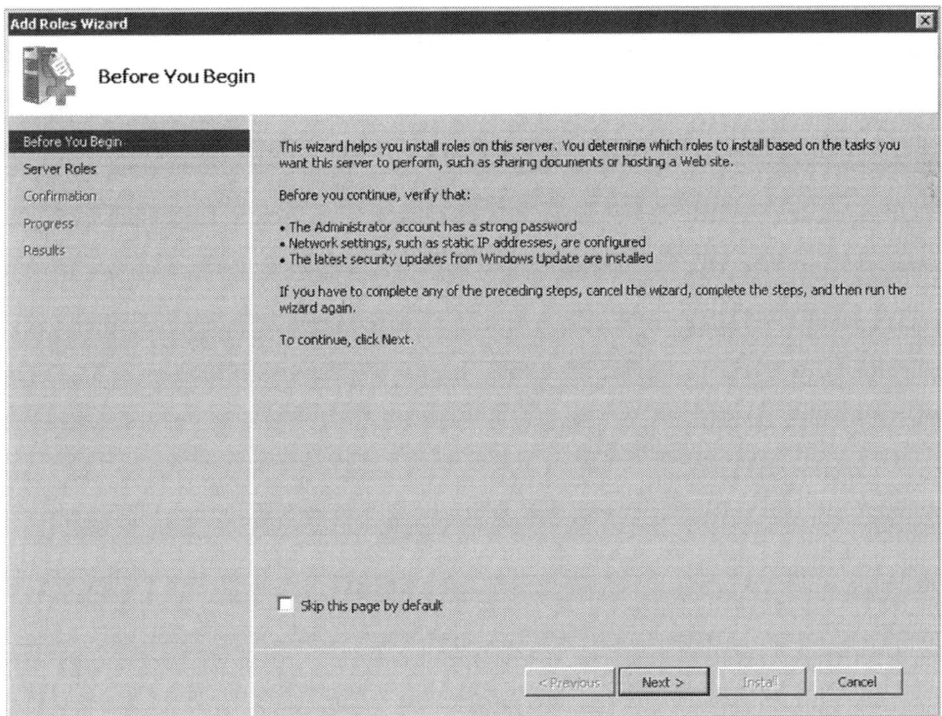

4. Click on **Next >** to continue.
5. Next, you will see the **Select Server Roles** configuration page.
6. In the **Roles** box, check the box for **Active Directory Certificate Services** (3), as shown in the following screenshot:

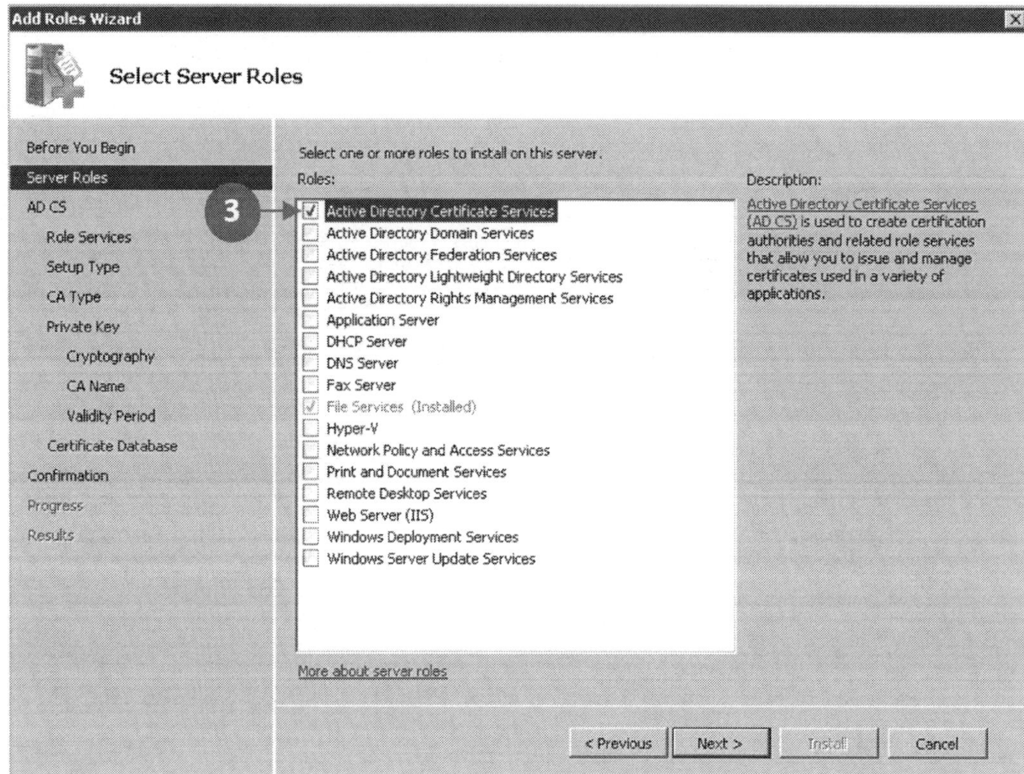

7. Click on **Next >** to continue.
8. On the **Introduction to Active Directory Certificate Services** page, as shown in the following screenshot, click on **Next >** to continue:

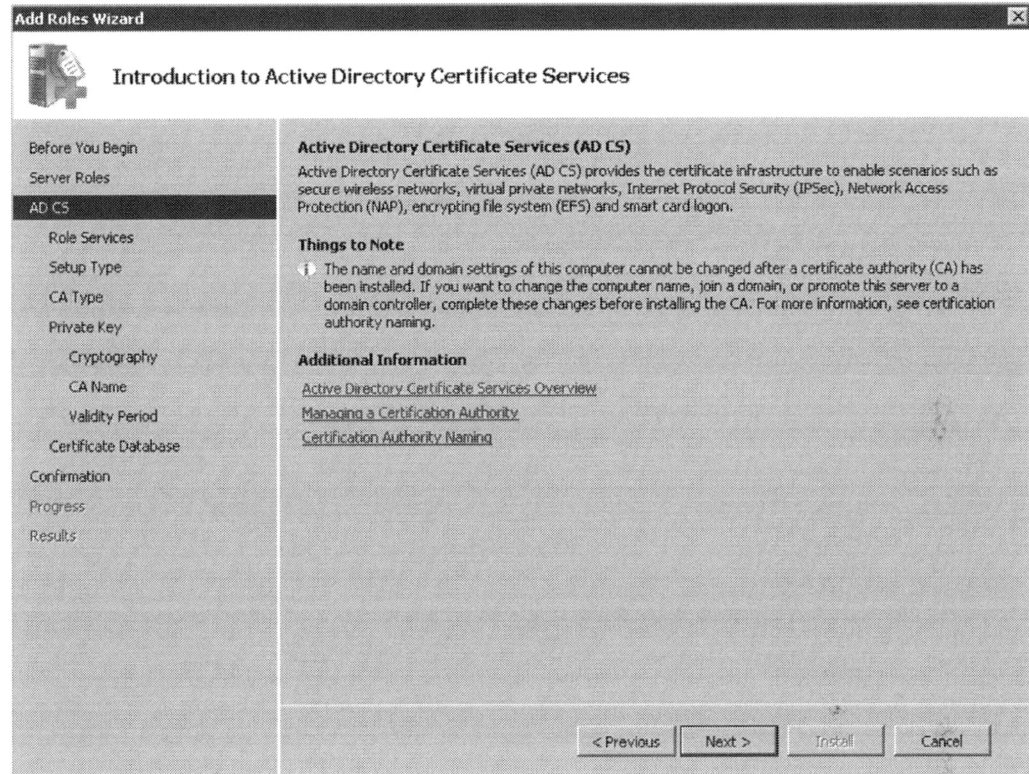

9. You will now see the **Select Role Services** page, as shown in the following screenshot. Check the box for **Certification Authority** (**4**) and click on **Next >**:

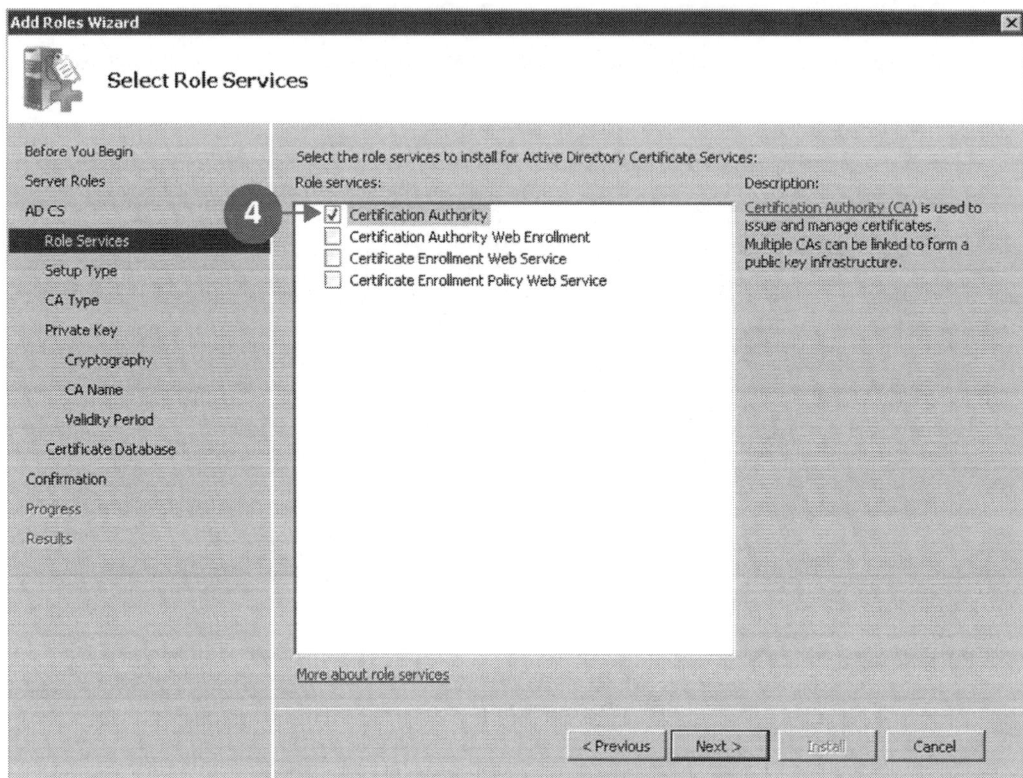

10. Next you will see the **Specify Setup Type** page, as shown in the following screenshot. Select the radio button for **Enterprise** (**5**) and then click on **Next >**:

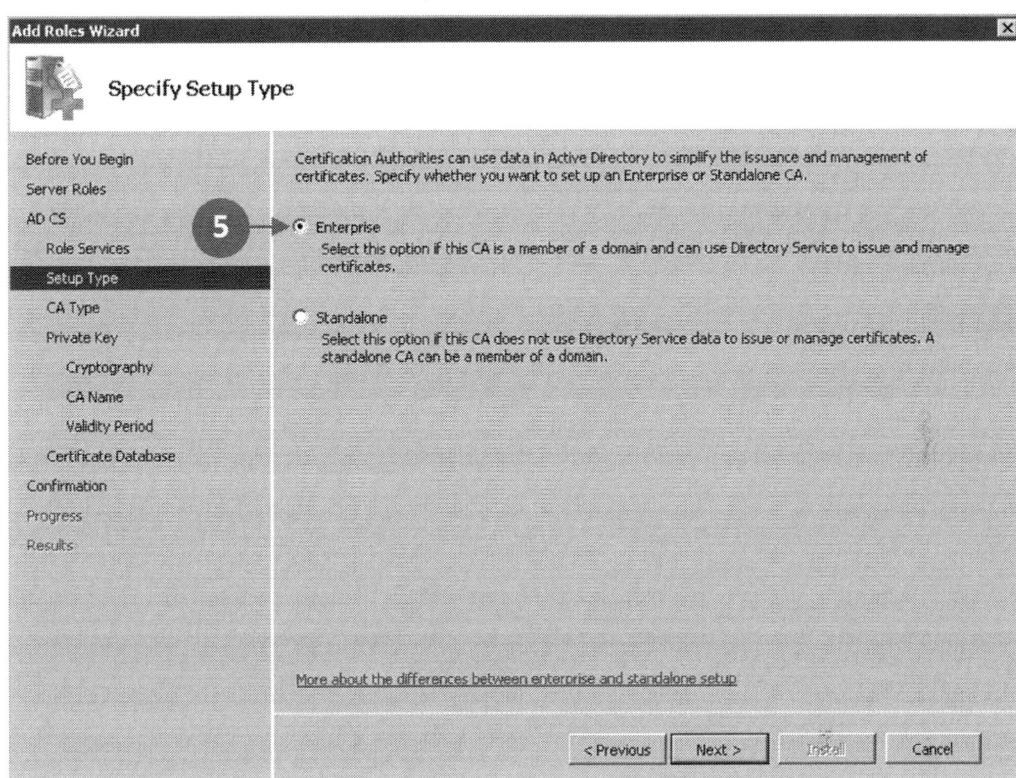

11. On the **Specify CA Type** page, select the radio button for **Root CA** (**6**), as shown in the following screenshot, and click on **Next >**:

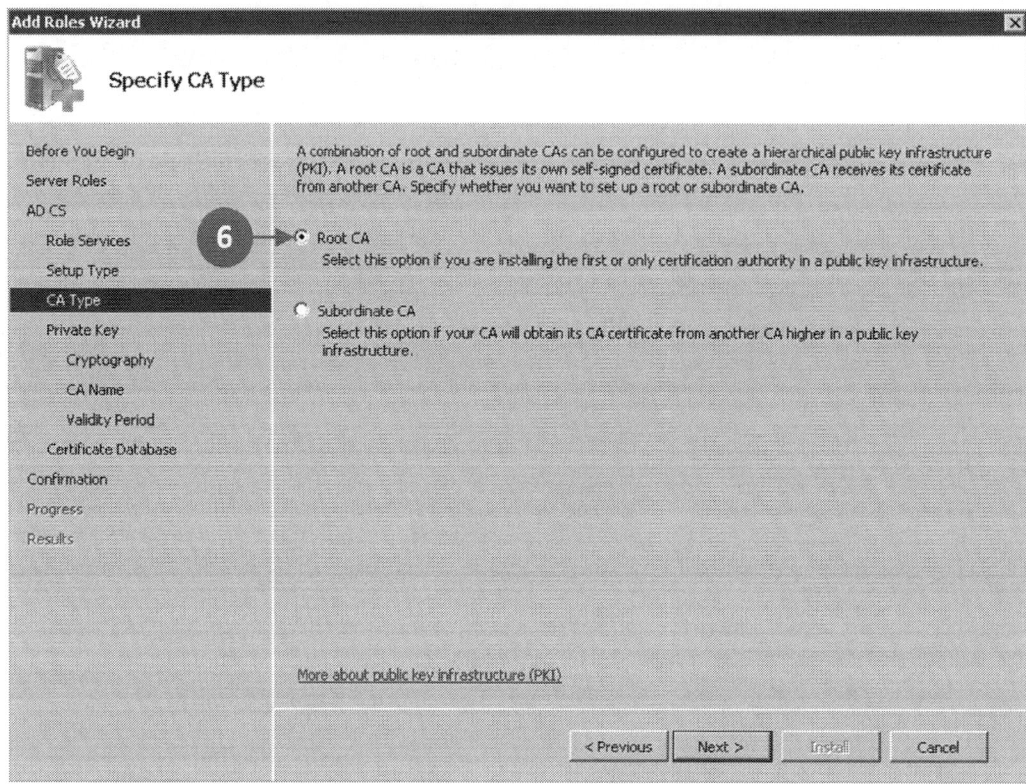

12. On the **Set Up Private Key** page, select the radio button for **Create a new private key** (7), as shown in the following screenshot, and click on **Next >**:

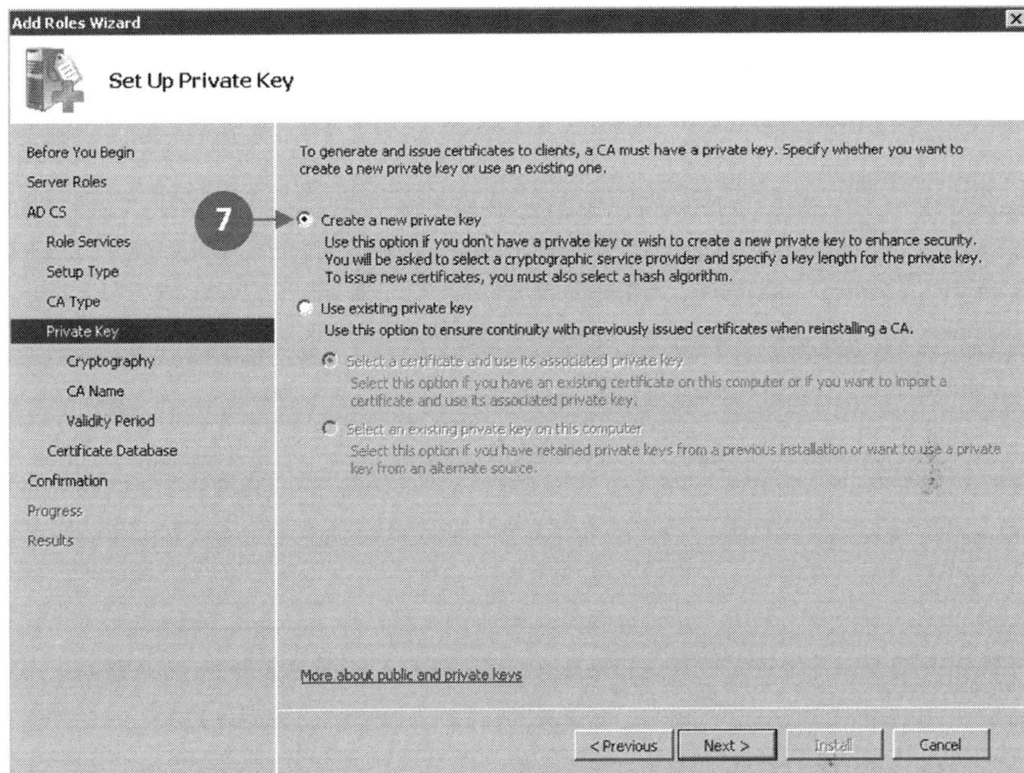

13. On the **Configure Cryptography for CA** page shown in the following screenshot, accept the defaults and click on **Next >**:

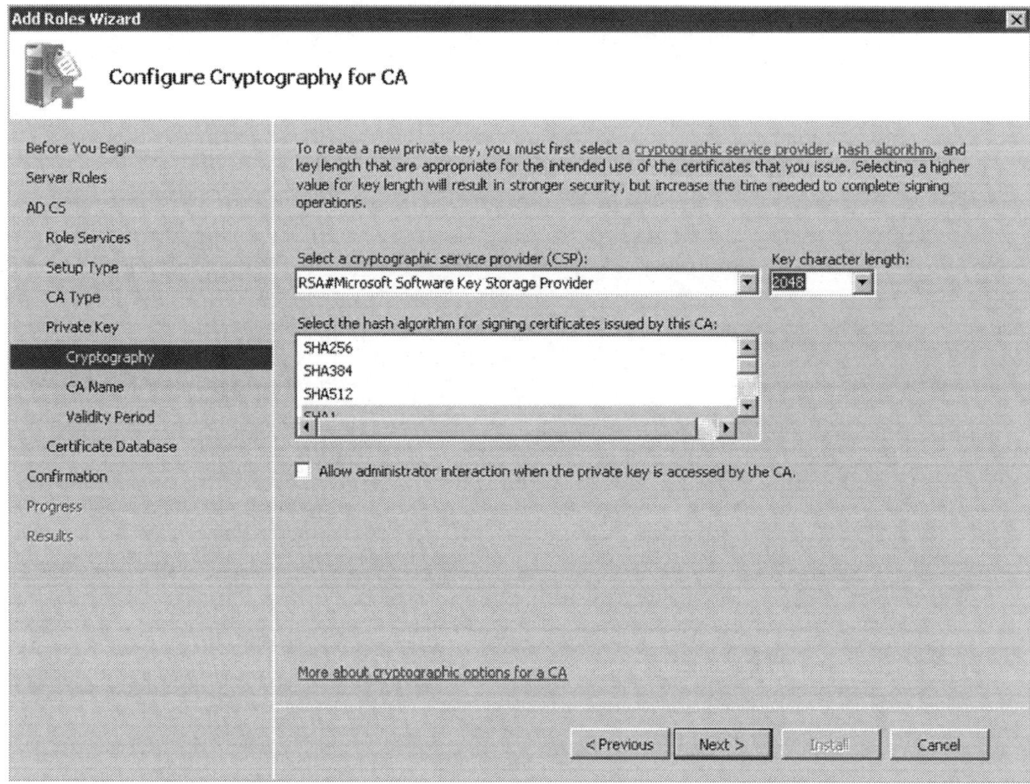

14. On the **Configure CA Name** page shown in the following screenshot, accept the defaults and then click on **Next >**:

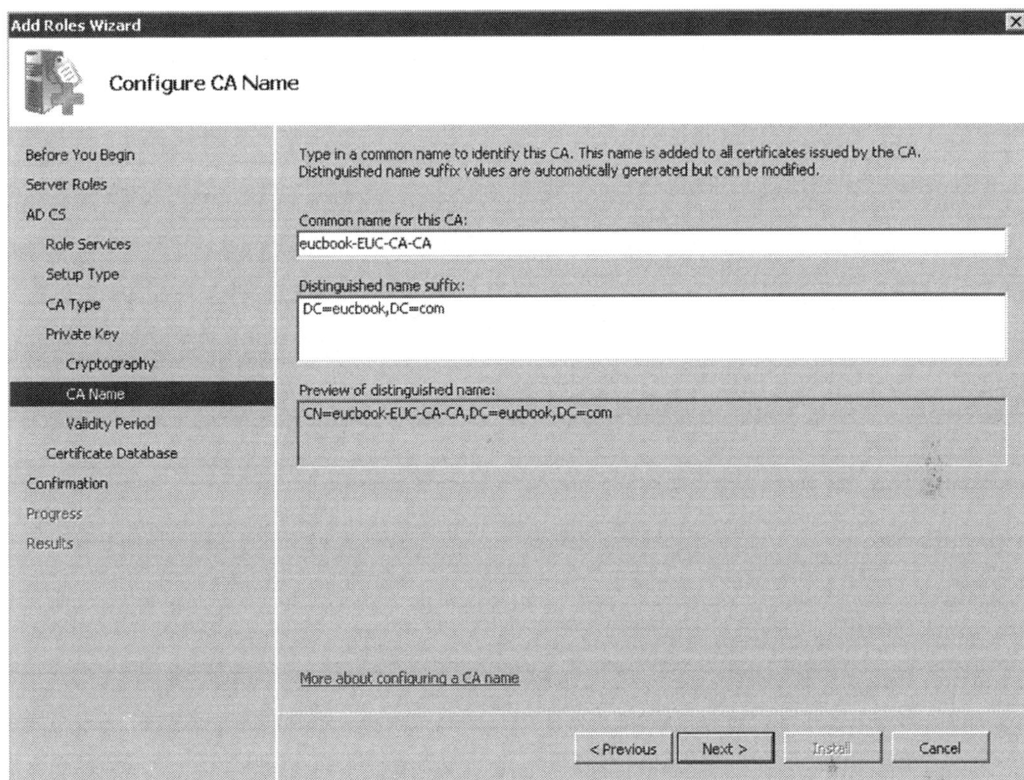

15. Next you will see the **Set Validity Period** page, as shown in the following screenshot. Set a time for which certificates from this Root CA are valid; we will leave the default value of **5 Years** (**8**). Click on **Next >**:

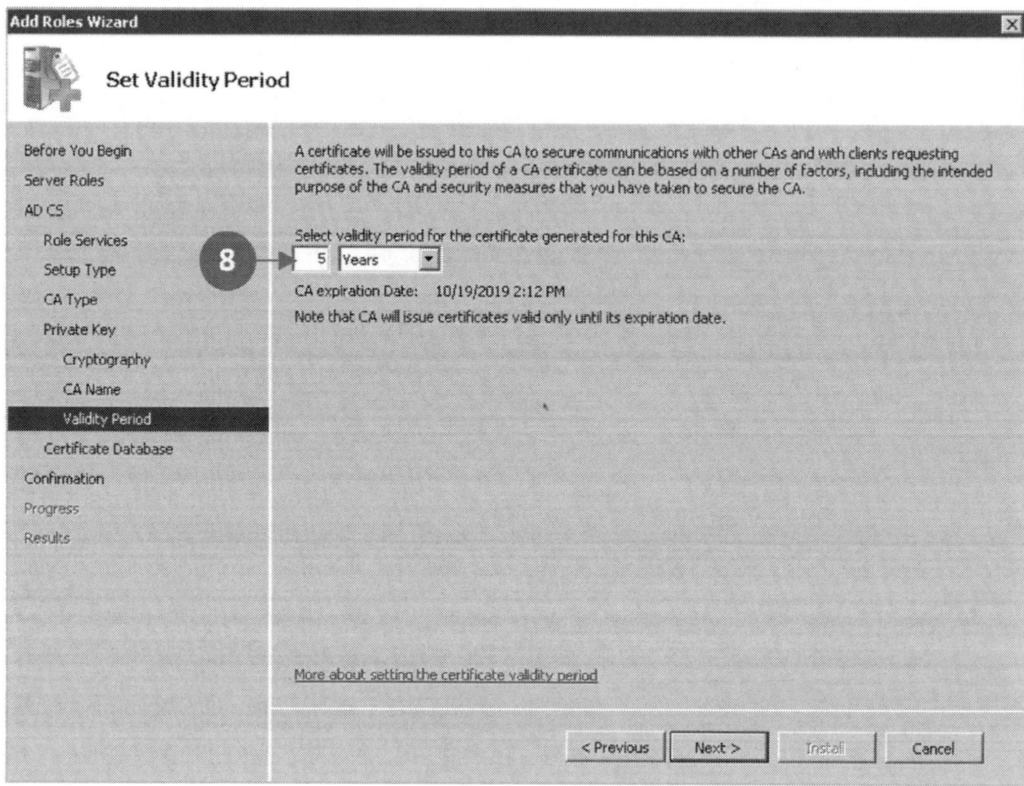

16. On the **Configure Certificate Database** page, accept the defaults and click on **Next >**:

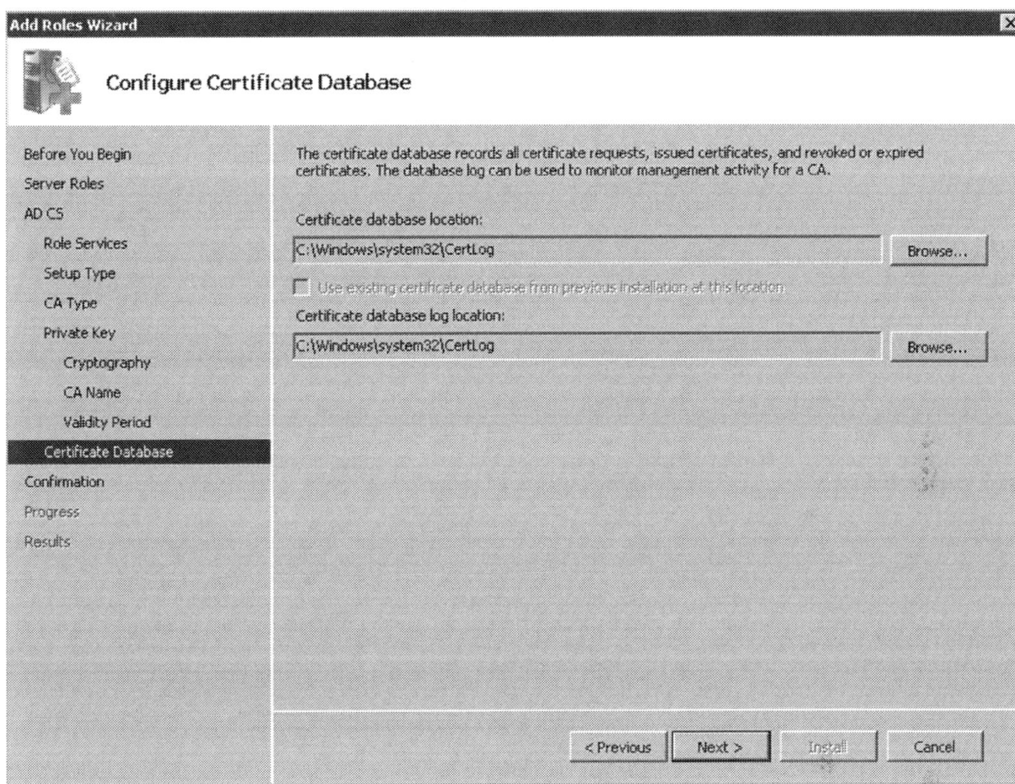

17. Finally, you will see the **Confirm Installation Selections** page, as shown in the following screenshot. Ensure that you have entered the configuration details correctly, and then click on **Install** to start the installation process:

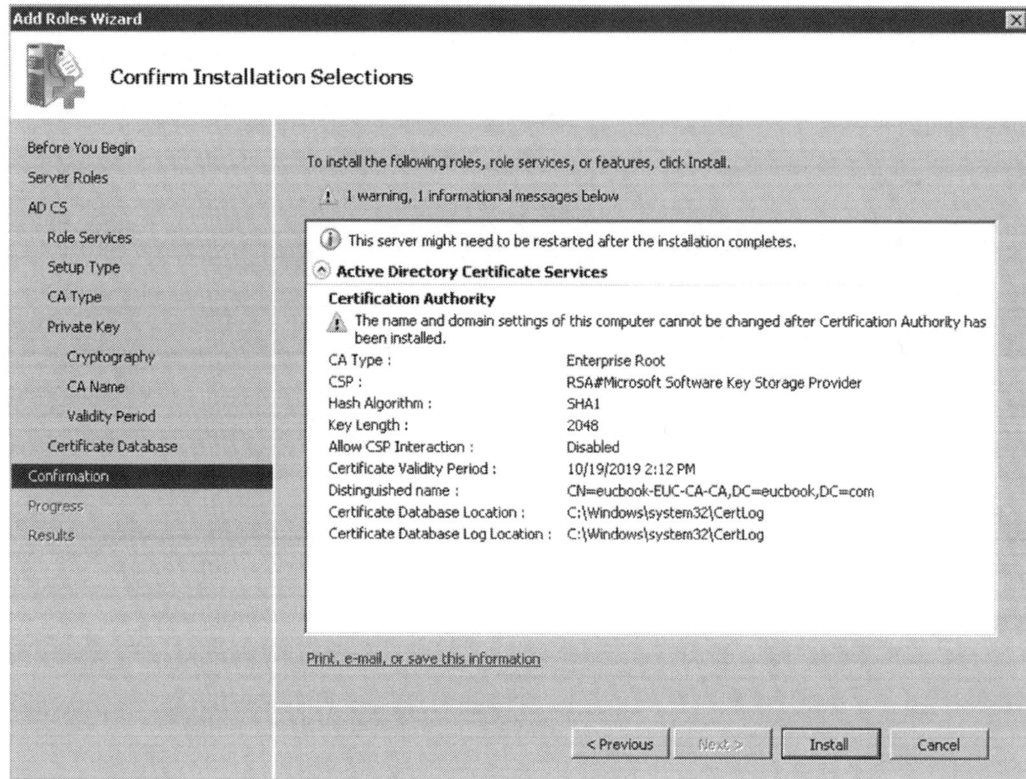

18. You should now have successfully installed the Root CA role onto the server, as shown in the following screenshot:

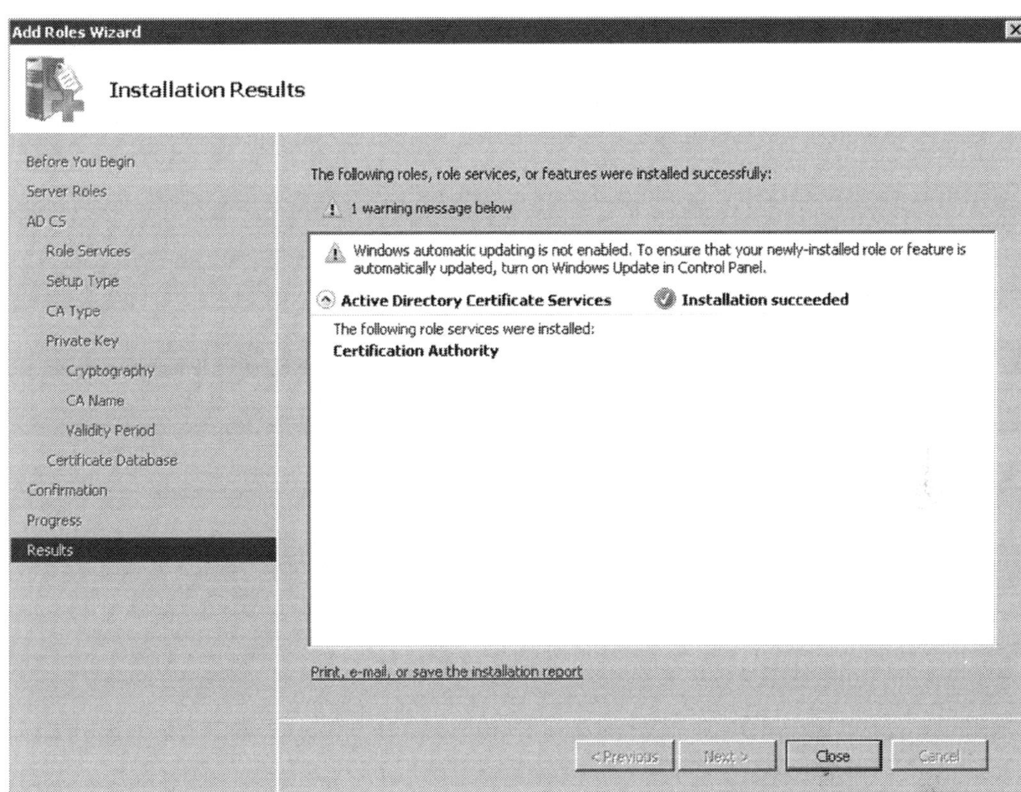

The warning with the yellow symbol just says that this server does not have the Windows automatic updating feature enabled.

Now that we have our certificate server set up and running, we can start configuring the Horizon View software components to use it. In this example, we will start by installing the certificate on the Horizon View Connection Server.

Installing a certificate on the View Connection Server

With our certificate server installed and configured, we are now going to install the certificate on the View Connection Server. On the server named **EUC-VCS01**, we are going to perform the following tasks:

1. Click on **Start** and then click on **Run...**.
2. In the **Run** dialog box, type `mmc` (**1**) to open Microsoft Management Console, as shown in the following screenshot. Then click on **Add/Remove Snap-in...** (**2**):

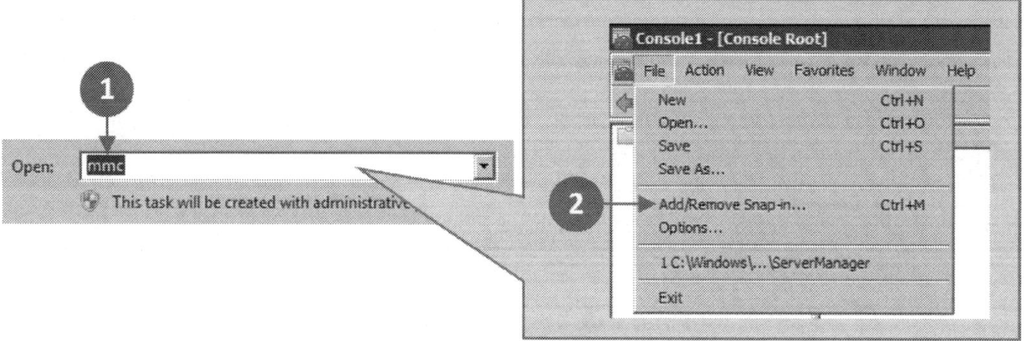

3. You will now see the **Add or Remove Snap-ins** page. Click on **Certificates** (**3**) from the **Available snap-ins** list and then click on **Add >** (**4**), as shown in the following screenshot:

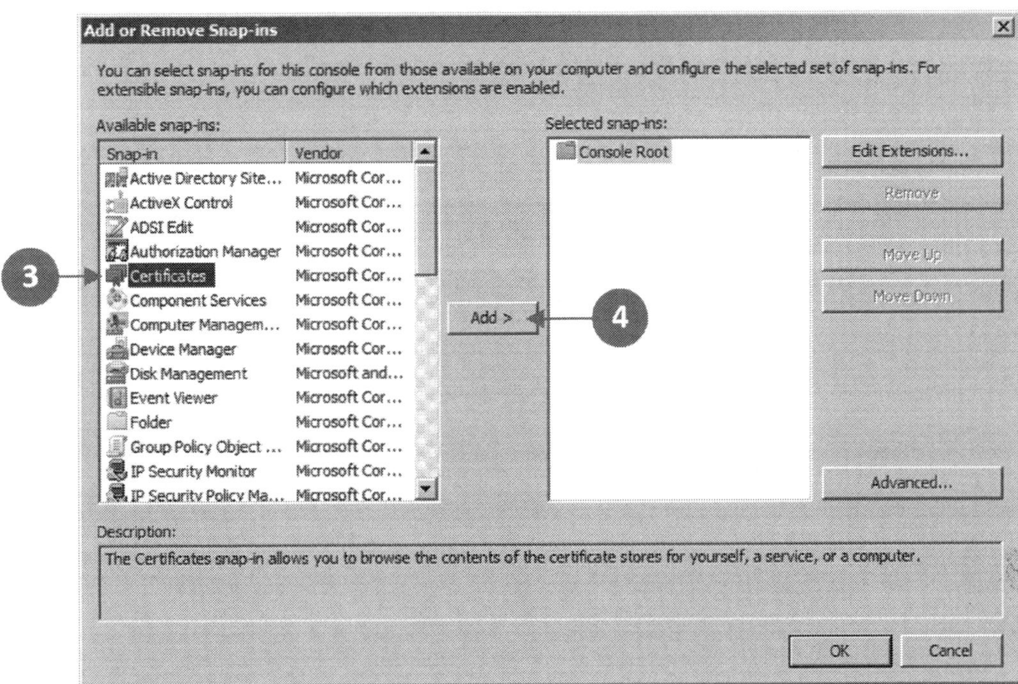

4. In the **Certificates snap-in** dialog box shown in the following screenshot, select the radio button for **Computer account** (**5**), and then click on **Next >**:

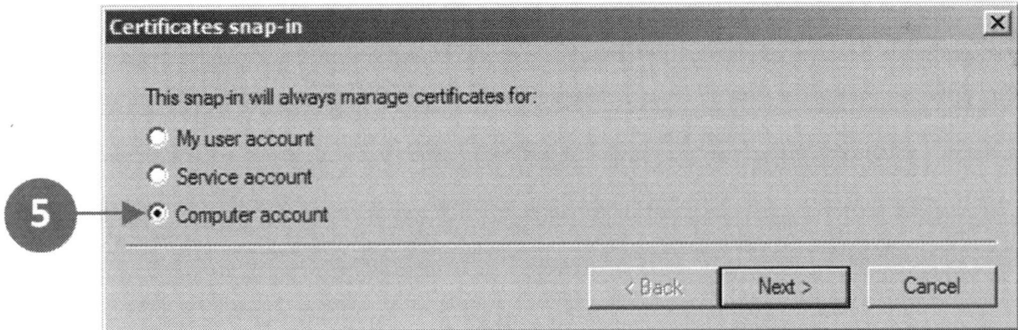

5. Select the radio button for **Local computer: (the computer this console is running on)** (6) from the **Select Computer** dialog box and then click on **Finish**, as shown in the following screenshot:

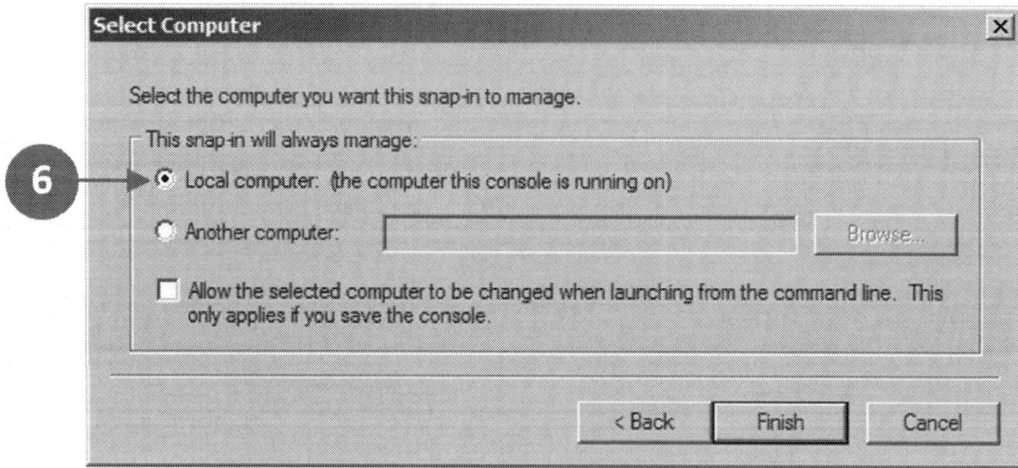

6. Finally, click on **OK** in the **Add or Remove Snap-ins** dialog box. You will now have the **Certificates (Local Computer)** option in your management console, as shown in the following screenshot:

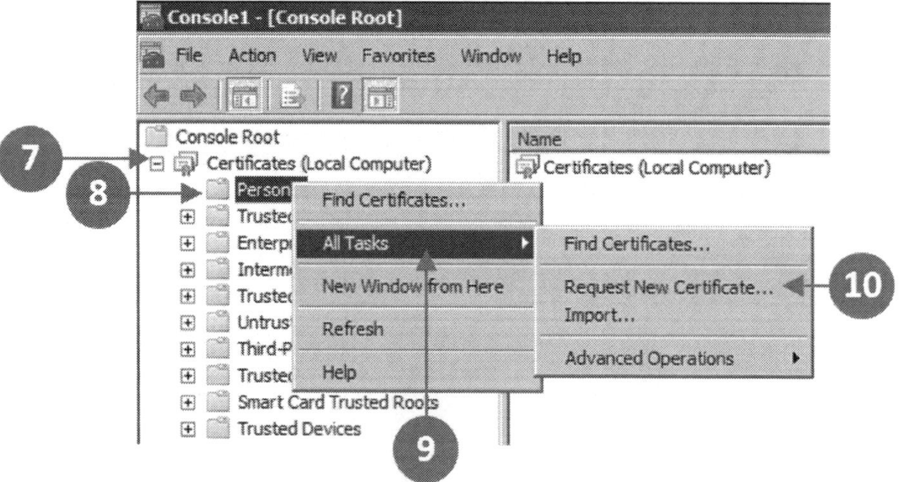

The next part of the process is to request a certificate from the Root CA.

7. Expand **Certificates (Local Computer)** (7), and then right-click on **Personal** (8). From the menu, navigate to **All Tasks** (9) | **Request New Certificate...** (10), as shown in the previous screenshot.
8. You will now see the **Before You Begin** section on **Certificate Enrollment** screen, as shown in the following screenshot:

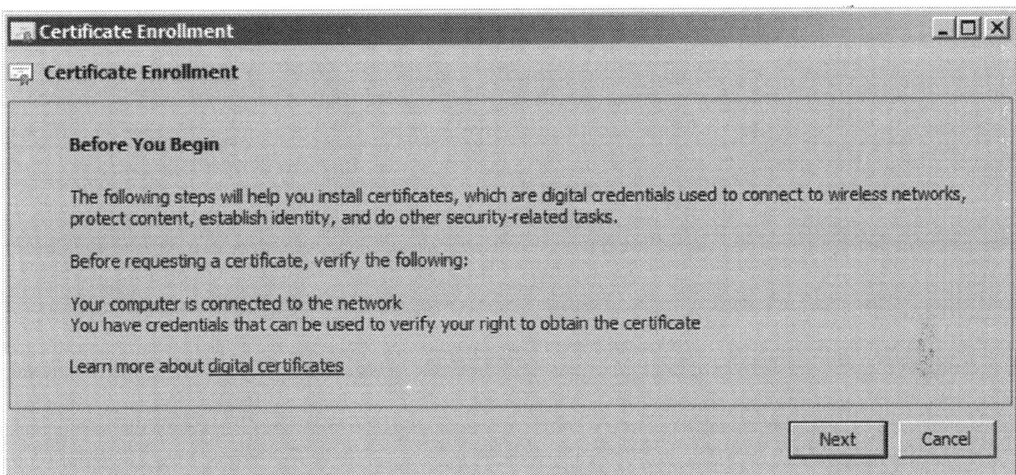

9. Click on **Next** to start the enrollment process.
10. In the **Certificate Enrollment** dialog box, click on **Active Directory Enrollment Policy** (11), as shown in the following screenshot, and then click on **Next**:

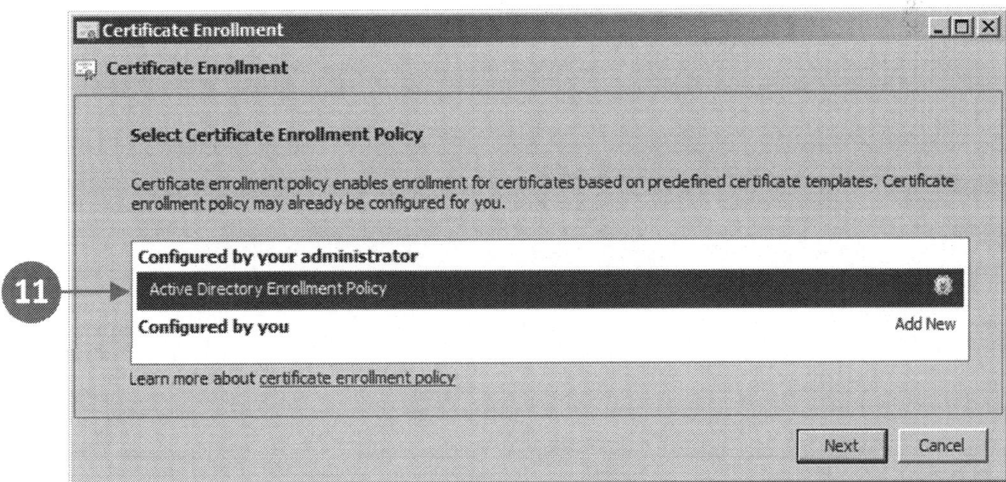

11. In the **Request Certificates** dialog box, check the box for **Computer**. We will use this policy template for our certificate. However, you can create your own template on the Root CA server.
12. Now click on the arrow next to **Details** (**13**), and then click on **Properties** (**14**) so that we can configure the properties of the certificate:

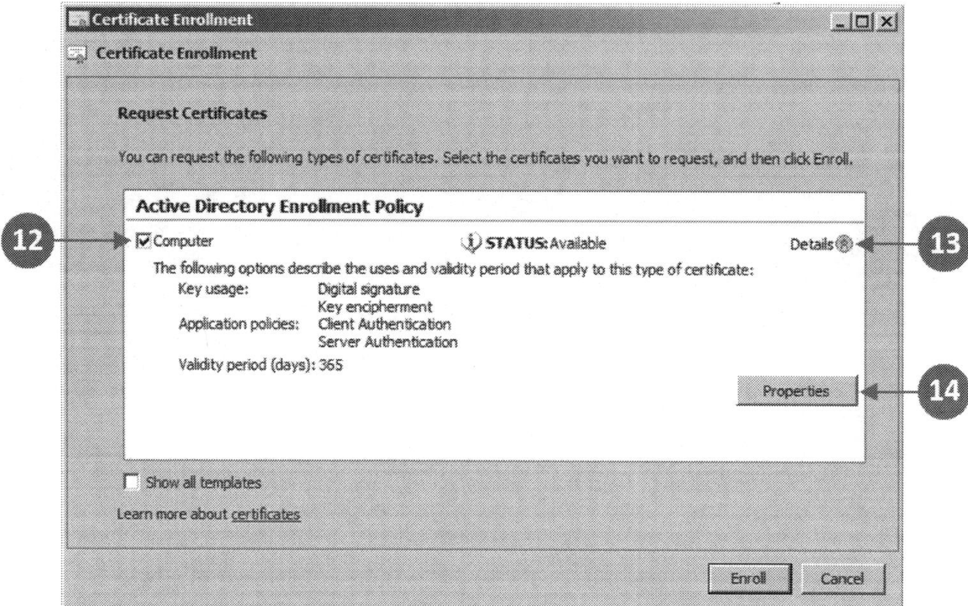

13. You will now see the **Certificate Properties** dialog box, where we will make a few configuration changes.
14. For the first part, click on the **General** (**15**) tab and type `vdm` as **Friendly name** (**16**), as shown in the following screenshot:

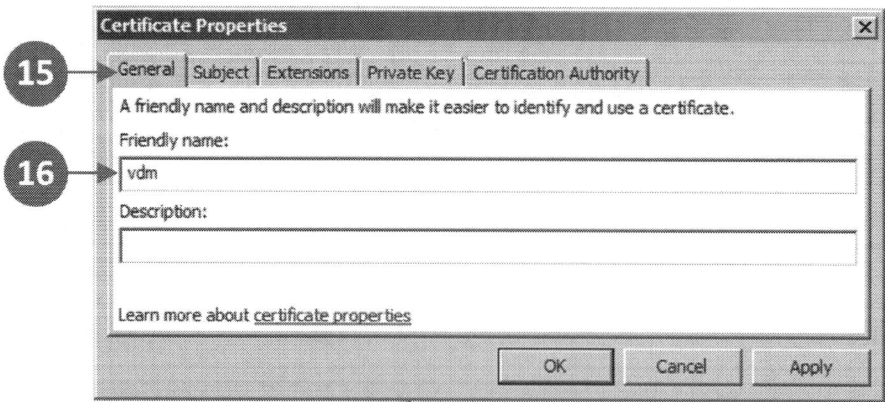

15. The second task to perform in the **Certificate Properties** dialog box is to configure the private key.
16. Click on the **Private Key** tab (**17**) and then expand the **Key options** section by clicking on the arrow next to it (**18**). Check the box for **Make private key exportable** (**19**), as shown in the following screenshot:

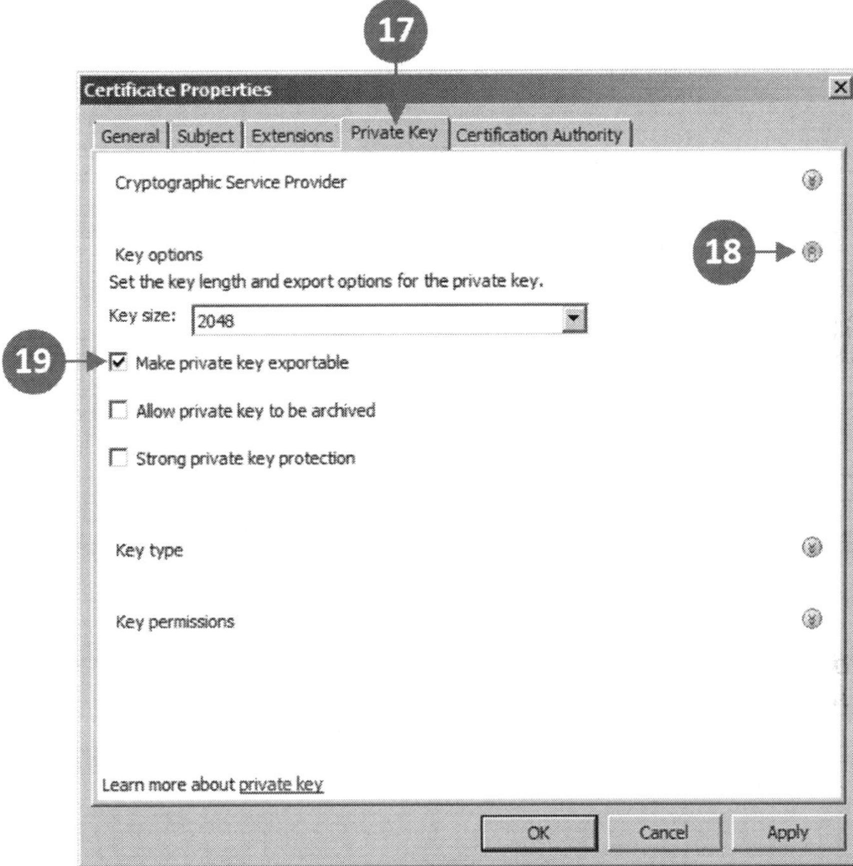

17. The final task to perform in the **Certificate Properties** dialog box is to configure the certification authority.

18. Click on the **Certification Authority** tab (**20**) and ensure you check the box next to the appropriate certificate server; in our example we select **eucbook-EUC-CA-CA** (**21**), as shown in the following screenshot:

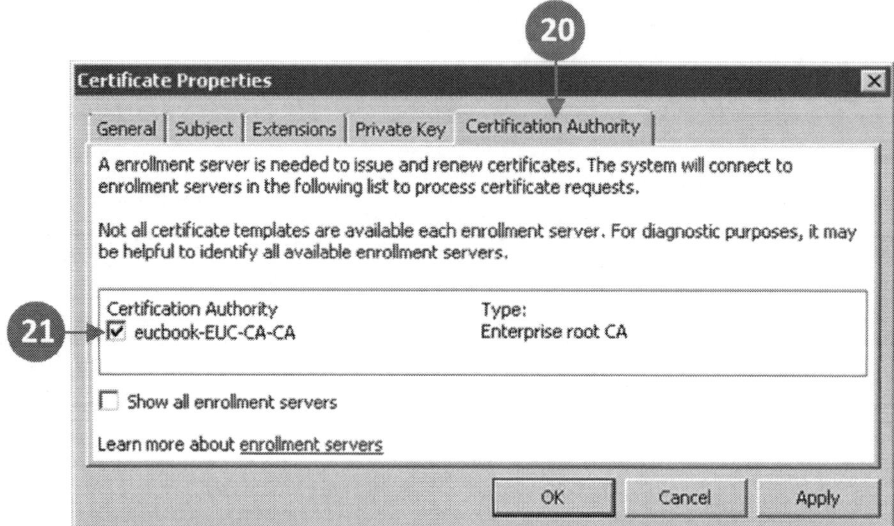

19. That's the final part of the configuration. Click on **Enroll** (**22**), as shown in the following screenshot:

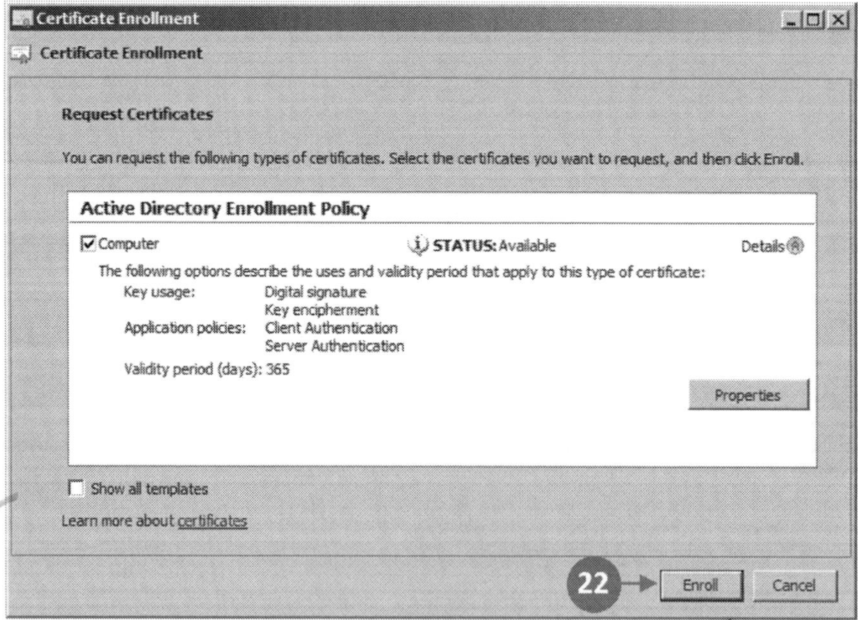

20. Once the task is completed successfully, you will see the following screenshot. Click on **Finish** to complete and close the certificate enrollment process:

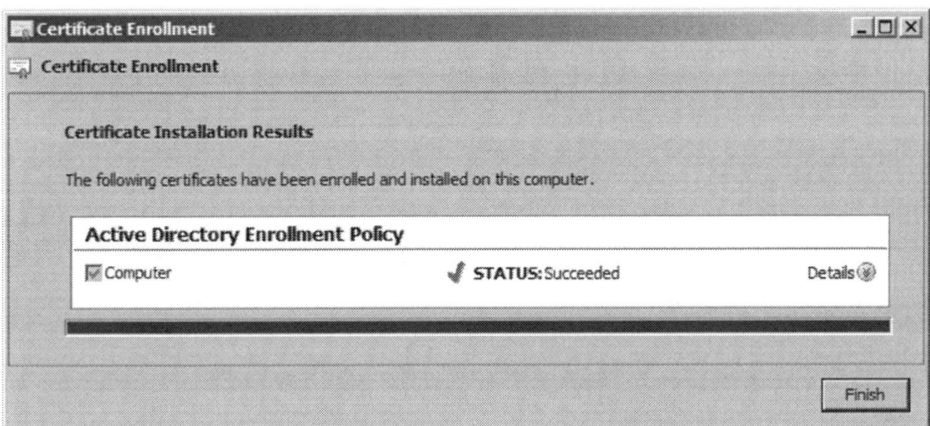

Don't forget that you need to complete the certificate enrollment process on all the Horizon View components.

In the next section, we will take a look at what to do now that we have our Root CA certificate server and the certificate is installed on out Connection Servers.

Post-certificate configuration tasks

Even though we have installed a certificate server and installed a valid certificate on our Connection Server, there are still a few things to configure. Following are the steps that illustrate the things yet to be configured:

1. If you try to connect to the Horizon View Administrator using your browser, you will still see an error, as shown in the following screenshot:

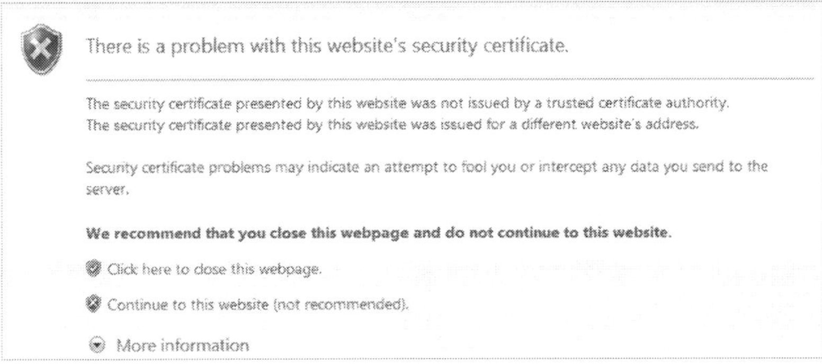

2. If you remember from the beginning of this chapter, we also discussed accessing web pages using `http://`, or `https://` for secure web pages. You will remember that, if your address bar in your browser is red, as shown in the following screenshot, then the connection is not secure and there are no certificates:

3. You can, of course, ignore these errors. Clicking on **Continue to this website (not recommended)** allows you to continue past the warning and log on to **View Administrator**.
4. However, when you log on, you will see that, in the **System Health** section of the **View Administrator**, there is also a red warning box.
5. Click on **Dashboard** (**1**). Then, click on the down arrow to expand the options for **View components** (**2**) and then **Connection Servers** (**3**). Now, click on the Connection Server you want to select (**4**); in our example, the Connection Server is **EUC-VCS01**.

   As far as View is concerned, as you can see, if you don't have a valid certificate installed, the health warning tells you that the connections will be untrusted.

6. The following screenshot shows the untrusted certificate for our View Connection Server **EUC-VCS01**:

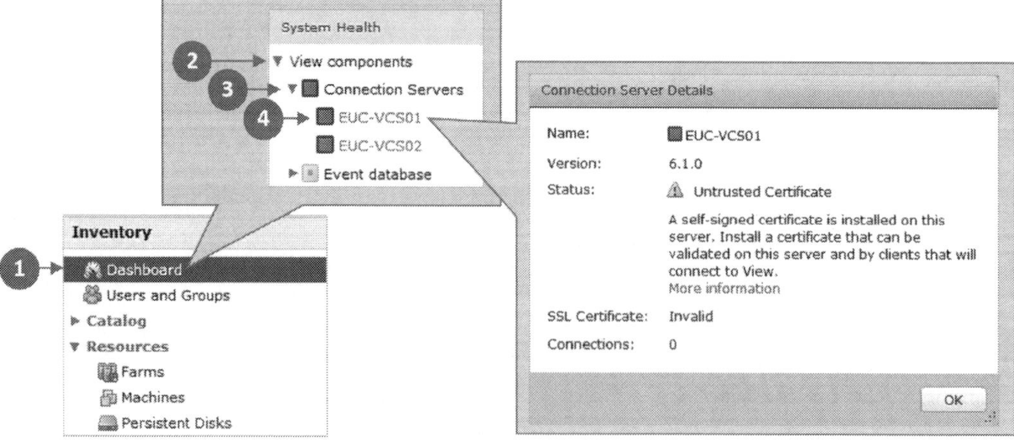

7. A user would see something like the following:

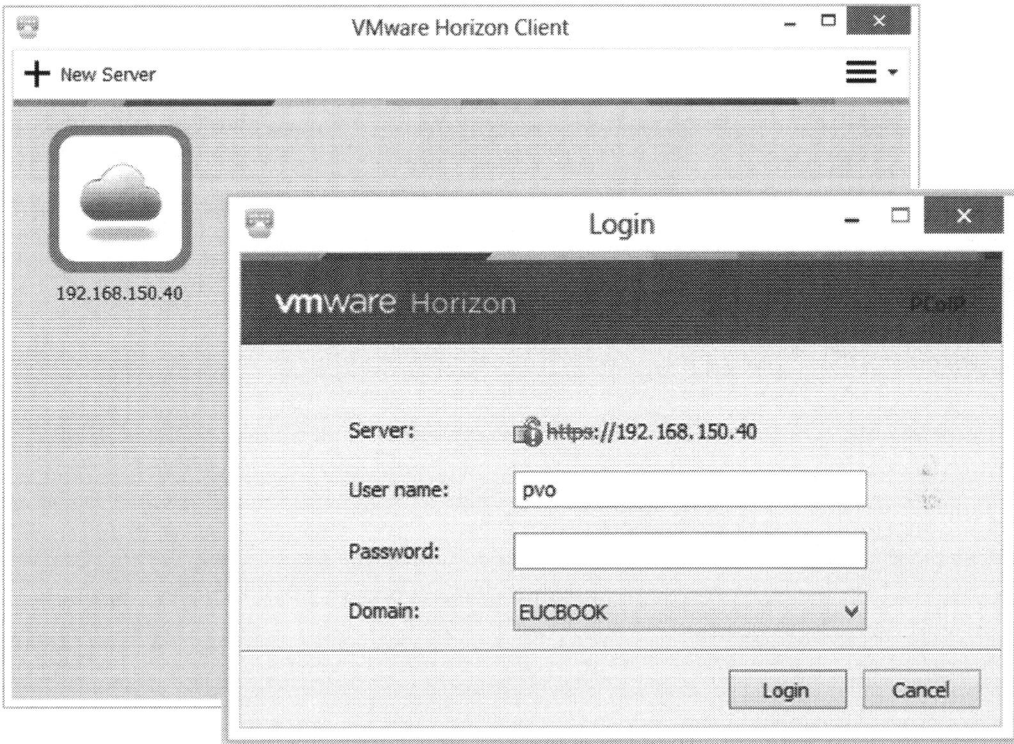

8. In order for View to pick up the recently installed certificate, you need to restart the View Connection Server service in Windows services.
9. Click on **Start** and then click on **Run....** In the **Run** dialog box, type `services.msc` to open the **Services** screen. Scroll down to **VMware Horizon View Connection Server**, as shown in the following screenshot:

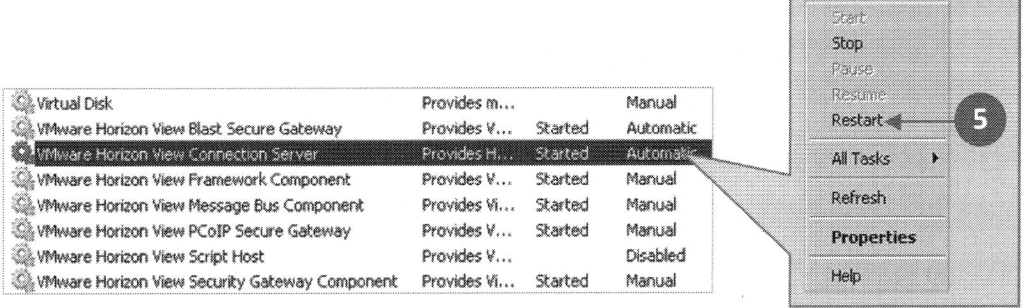

10. Right-click **VMware Horizon View Connection Server** and, from the menu, click on **Restart** (**5**). When the service restarts, close the **Services** screen. Repeat the same steps for all your View components.
11. Now, log back into the **View Administrator**. Click on **Connection Servers** (**6**), and then click on the **EUC-VCS01** Connection Server. You will now see that the SSL certificate is valid and the error boxes have changed from red to green.

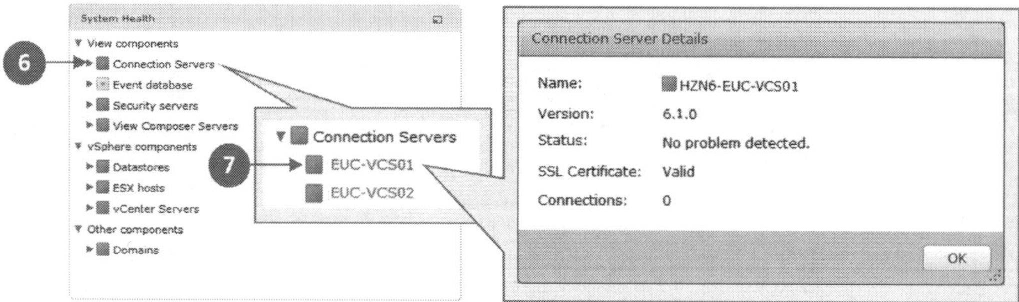

12. We have now finished configuring our certificate. Click on **OK** to close the dialog box for the **Connection Server Details** and then log out of the **View Administrator**.

Don't forget that you need to install the certificate on all of the Horizon View components, such as any replica servers, security servers, and View Composer servers.

Summary

In this chapter, we started off by describing what an SSL certificate is and why Horizon View uses them. We then went on to install and configure a Root CA server to provide certificates for the View components in our environment before installing them on the servers.

In the next chapter, we will turn our attention to virtual desktop machines and look at how we build and optimize the desktop operating system.

6

Building and Optimizing the Desktop Operating System

After building the Horizon View infrastructure and its components, in this chapter we will look at how to create and configure virtual desktop machines and then build a desktop operating system on them, configuring that operating system to run at its optimum performance levels.

The actual steps involved in building the core operating system are similar to the process of building a physical desktop machine. However, there are some additional tasks and software components that we need to install on the operating system to turn it into a virtual desktop machine fit for our Horizon View environment.

In the following screenshot, you will see an outline of the key steps in building the virtual desktop machine:

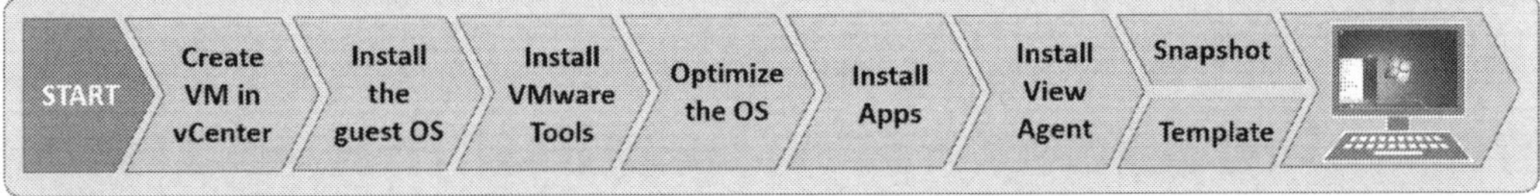

In the following sections of this chapter, we will cover each of these steps in more detail and also build two images along the way, using our example lab.

One virtual desktop machine will be a Windows 7 desktop, which will be configured with a floating desktop assignment, built using linked clones, and a second virtual desktop machine running Windows 8, which is configured with a dedicated assignment and built from a full clone.

In a physical desktop environment, there are a number of ways in which the operating system can be built and deployed. For example, you could use the **Microsoft Deployment Toolkit** (**MDT**) or maybe the **Microsoft System Center Configuration Manager** (**SCCM**). Both of these options can be used along with all the other tools available to build desktop images, including VMware's own Mirage product, of course. We will talk about VMware Mirage later in this book in *Chapter 14, Horizon 6 Advanced Edition*.

So, we just talked about a couple of options that you can use to build your desktop images, but let's just highlight the one that you should not use: a **physical-to-virtual tool** (**P2V**), which turns your physical image into a virtual one.

Best practice would be to build a new image from scratch as a virtual desktop image so that it's designed to be a virtual machine from day-one. You would potentially build a new image for a new hardware platform in any case.

There are a few reasons for not using your physical image to create your virtual desktop image. One of the reasons is the size of the image, which might become bloated with numerous patches being applied over the last year or so. We want our VDI image to be lean, and fresh as well, with just the most recent software installed.

Another reason is that there might be some hardware drivers or other hardware-based software elements within the image, probably a desktop management solution, such as Intel **Active Management Technology** (**AMT**), that relies on firmware and other components built into the chipset of the physical machine. As we are now using virtualized desktops, this type of hardware is not present and, therefore, we do not require it to be installed.

The worst case scenario is that having this type of solution installed will affect the performance of your virtual desktop machine.

Virtual desktop hardware requirements

Before we get on with the build process, we need to look at the specifications of the virtual desktop machine from a hardware perspective and what we need to configure it. The following screenshot lists the requirements for you:

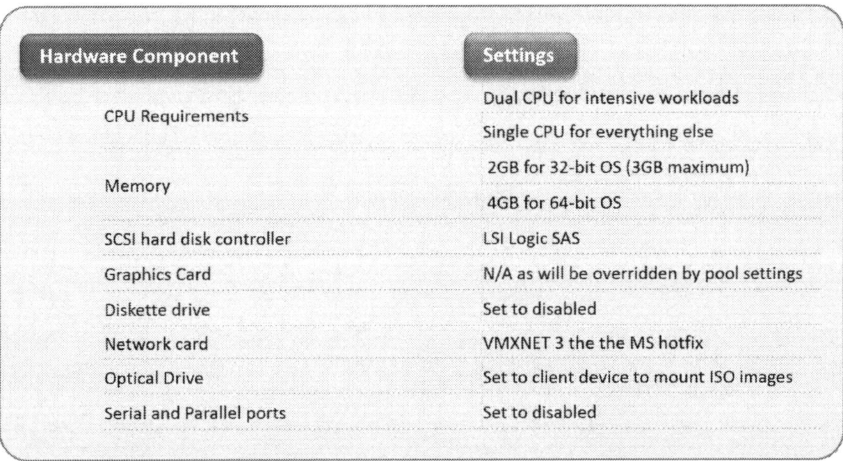

Hardware Component	Settings
CPU Requirements	Dual CPU for intensive workloads
	Single CPU for everything else
Memory	2GB for 32-bit OS (3GB maximum)
	4GB for 64-bit OS
SCSI hard disk controller	LSI Logic SAS
Graphics Card	N/A as will be overridden by pool settings
Diskette drive	Set to disabled
Network card	VMXNET 3 the the MS hotfix
Optical Drive	Set to client device to mount ISO images
Serial and Parallel ports	Set to disabled

You should be able to work out the requirements for your environment by using your assessment data captured at the start of the project. The one thing to bear in mind is that you can quite easily change the configuration should you need to.

Another important factor when configuring the size of the hardware is not to fall into the trap of over-sizing your virtual desktop machines. For example, if you only need one CPU, then only give the virtual desktop machine one CPU. As previously mentioned, this is why your assessment data is critical.

The virtual desktop machine should be configured using the guidelines for the hardware specifications outlined in the previous table.

Creating a Windows 7 virtual desktop machine

In this section, we will build a virtual desktop machine with Windows 7 as the operating system. We will follow the steps outlined at the beginning of this chapter to optimize and prepare the image to be used as a floating-assigned, linked-clone virtual desktop machine.

Creating the virtual desktop machine container

The first thing we need to do is build and configure the actual virtual desktop machine on our vCenter Server. This will define the virtual hardware configuration. To define the configuration, follow these steps:

1. Open a browser and log in to the vSphere Web Client, as shown in the following screenshot:

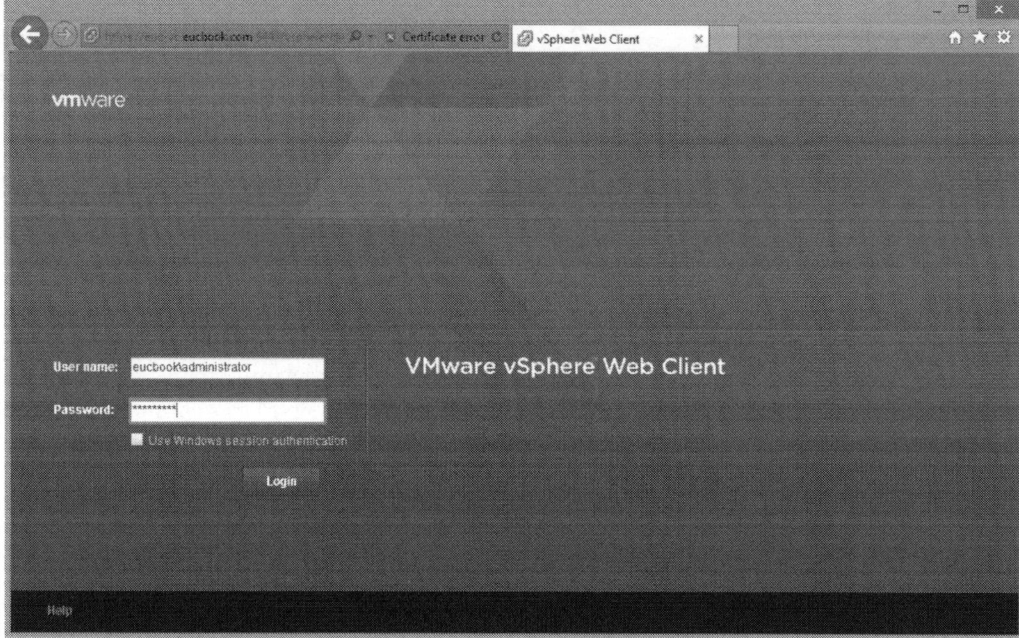

2. From the home page, navigate to the ESXi host server on which we are going to create this virtual desktop machine.
3. From the **Home** tab, click on **Hosts and Clusters** (**1**), shown in the following screenshot. Navigate to **Horizon DC** | **VDI Cluster 01**.
4. Highlight the host server; in our example lab, we will select the host server **euc-host2.eucbook.com** (**2**). Right-click on the host server and then select the option for **New Virtual Machine...** (**3**):

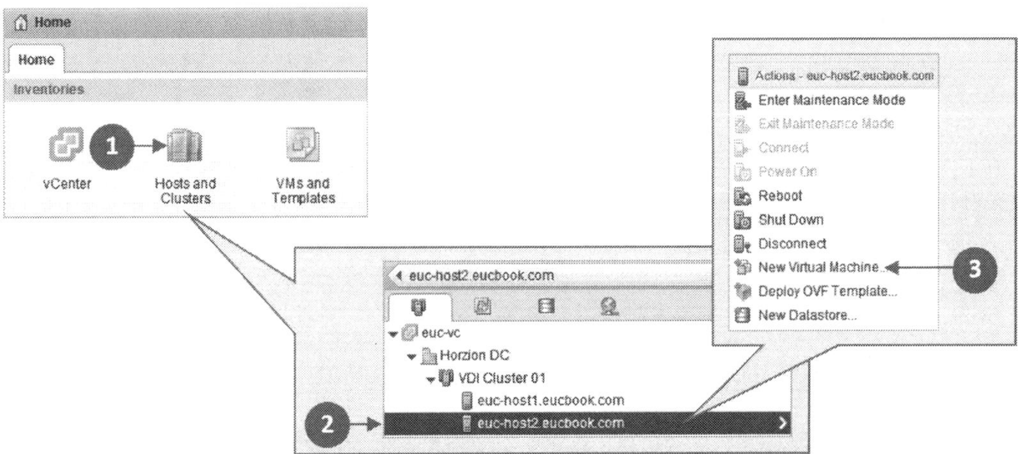

5. The **New Virtual Machine** configuration window now opens, as shown in the following screenshot. Click on **Create a new virtual machine** (**4**):

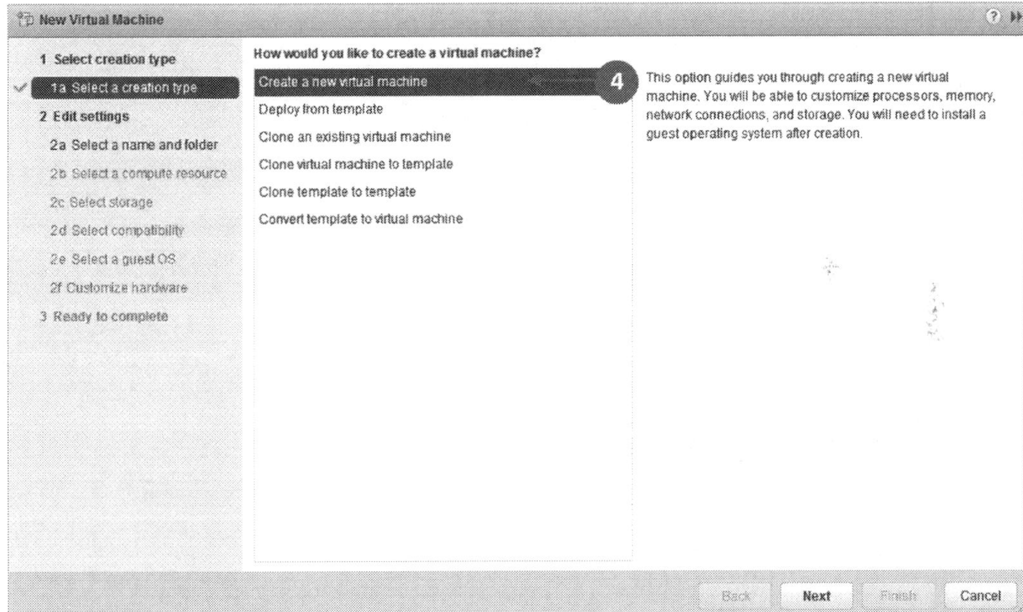

6. Click on **Next** to move to the next configuration screen.
7. On the first part of the **Edit Settings** configuration page, the first thing we need to do is enter a name for the new virtual desktop machine.

8. For our example lab, we will call our virtual desktop machine `Windows 7 Gold Image`, so enter this in the **Enter a name for the virtual machine** box (**5**).
9. Next, select the data center or folder where this virtual desktop machine is to be created. In our example, we will create it in our data center, so select **Horizon DC** (**6**):

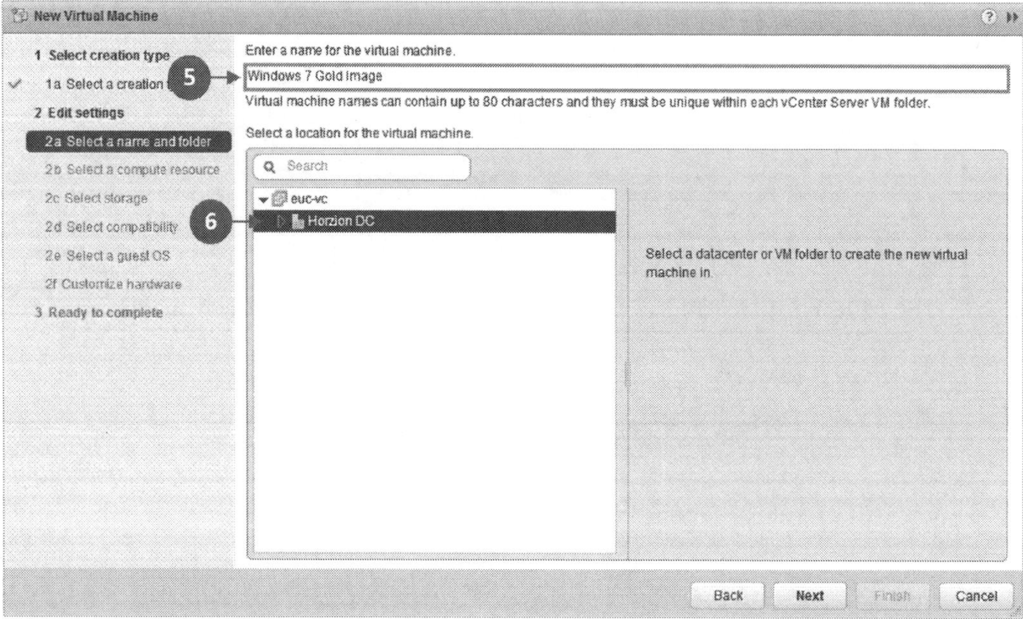

10. Click on **Next** to move to the next configuration screen.
11. On the **Select a compute resource** page, we need to select where this virtual desktop machine will run.

As this is going to be our gold/master image or parent virtual desktop machine, it probably is not as important with regard to the location when compared to the live production virtual desktop machines.

12. From the options, expand the **Horizon DC** data center and then **VDI Cluster 01**. Select the host server **euc-host2.eucbook.com** (7), as shown in the following screenshot:

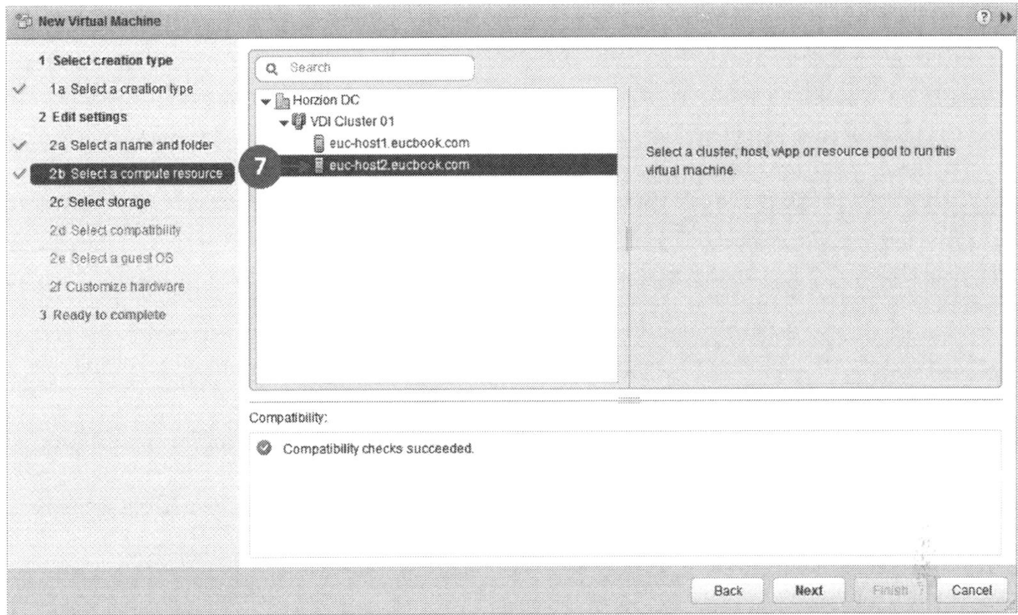

13. Click on **Next** to move to the next configuration screen.
14. On the **Select storage** configuration page shown in the following screenshot, we will choose where our virtual desktop machine will be stored:

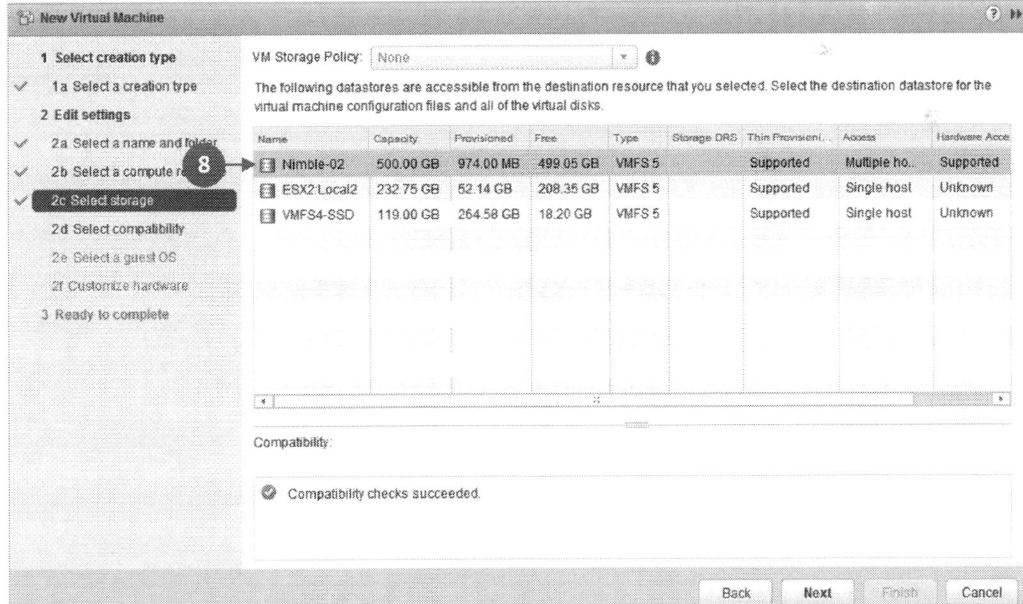

As you can see, we have three different data stores available to us. Two are using local server storage and the third is a Nimble storage array.

15. In our example, we will use the Nimble storage array as it has the highest storage capacity; also, it has the ability to use **vstorage APIs for Array Integration** (**VAAI**) to provide better performance. Click on **Nimble-02** (**8**) to select it as the data store.
16. Click on **Next** to move to the next configuration screen.
17. The next configuration page is **Select Compatibility**. This is where we will choose the virtual machine version for our virtual desktop machine. As the page says, for the best performance we must use Version 10, which means using vSphere 5.5 as our hosting platform.

    If you choose hardware version 9 and greater, remember that you will need to manage this virtual desktop machine by using the vSphere Web Client and not the old console.

18. From the drop-down menu (**9**), select **ESXi 5.5 and later** (**10**), as shown in the following screenshot:

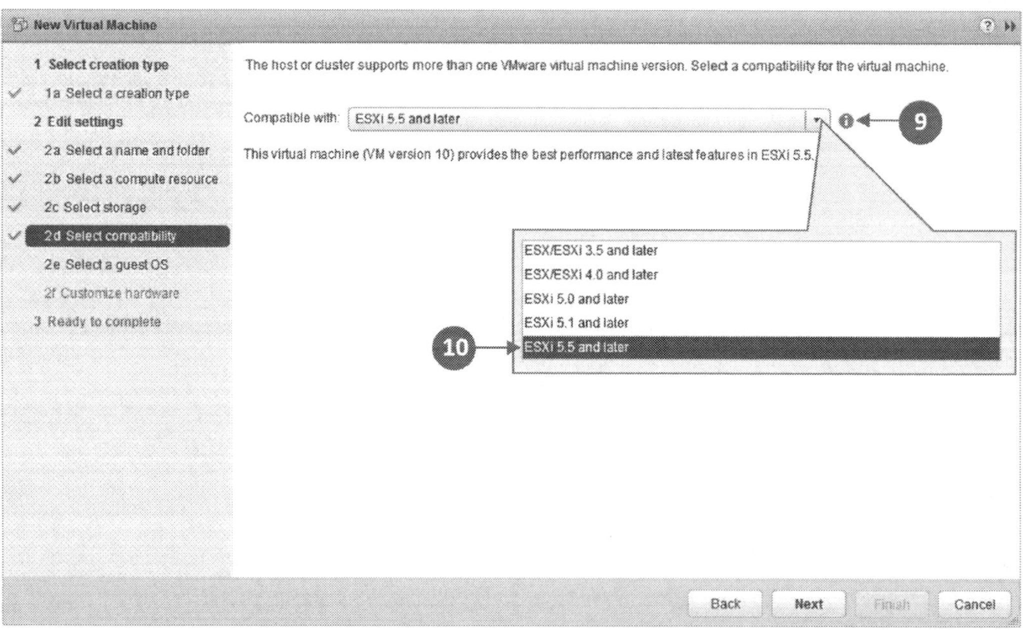

19. Click on **Next** to move to the next configuration screen.
20. The next step is to choose the operating system for our virtual desktop machine from **Select a guest OS**. For this example, and for our first virtual desktop machine, we will build a Windows 7 64-bit image.
21. From the **Guest OS Family** drop-down menu (**11**), click on the arrow to expand the options and select **Windows**. Then, from the **Guest OS Version** drop-down menu (**12**), click on the arrow to expand the options and select **Microsoft Windows 7 (64-bit)**. The guest OS selection also determines which drivers are installed when VMware Tools is installed, as shown in the following screenshot:

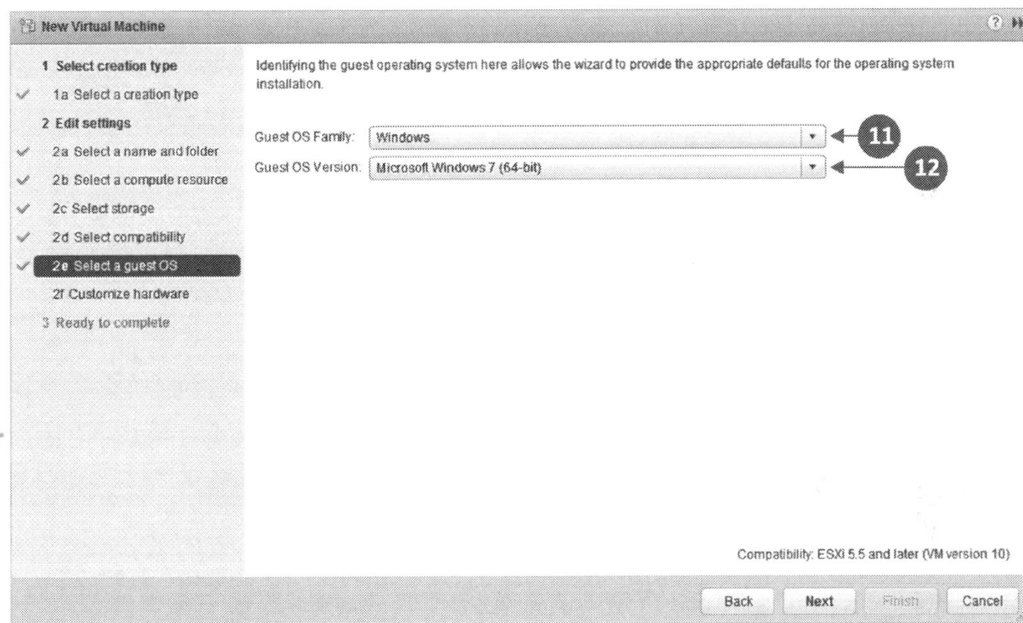

22. Click on **Next** to move to the next configuration screen.

23. On the next page, we will configure the virtual hardware specification for our virtual desktop machine. The following screenshot highlights the recommended virtual hardware configuration for our virtual desktop machine. However, you might need to change this based on the use case and application requirements. Given that we are talking about virtual hardware now, it's easy to change the configuration, should you need to:

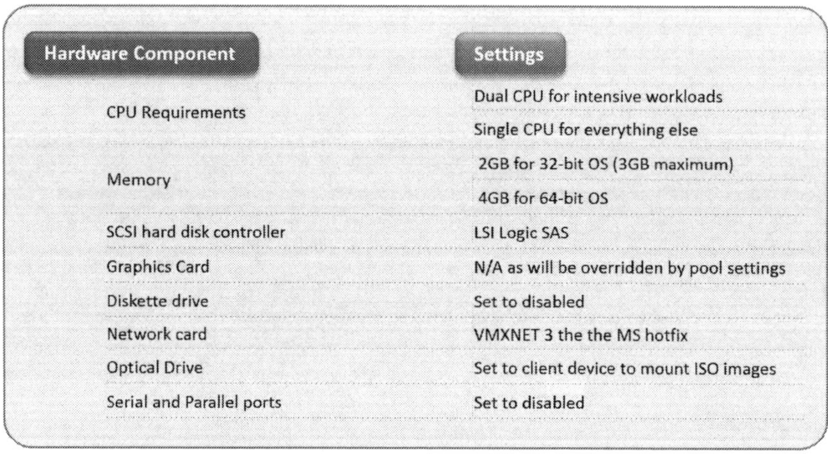

Hardware Component	Settings
CPU Requirements	Dual CPU for intensive workloads
	Single CPU for everything else
Memory	2GB for 32-bit OS (3GB maximum)
	4GB for 64-bit OS
SCSI hard disk controller	LSI Logic SAS
Graphics Card	N/A as will be overridden by pool settings
Diskette drive	Set to disabled
Network card	VMXNET 3 the the MS hotfix
Optical Drive	Set to client device to mount ISO images
Serial and Parallel ports	Set to disabled

24. We will now build our virtual hardware configuration for our virtual desktop machine:

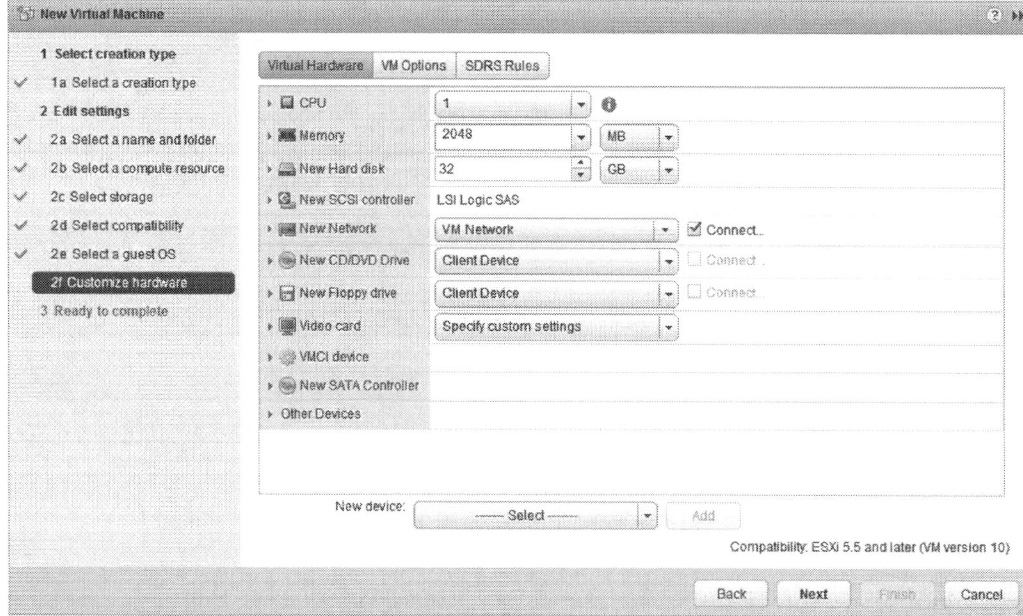

25. Your configuration page should look something like the preceding screenshot. We have left most of the options at their default settings, but you might want to change the hardware specifications to suit your application requirements and connect the virtual desktop machine to a network appropriate for your environment. Before we move on to the next configuration page, we need to configure some other options, so click on **VM Options** (**13**), as shown in the following screenshot:

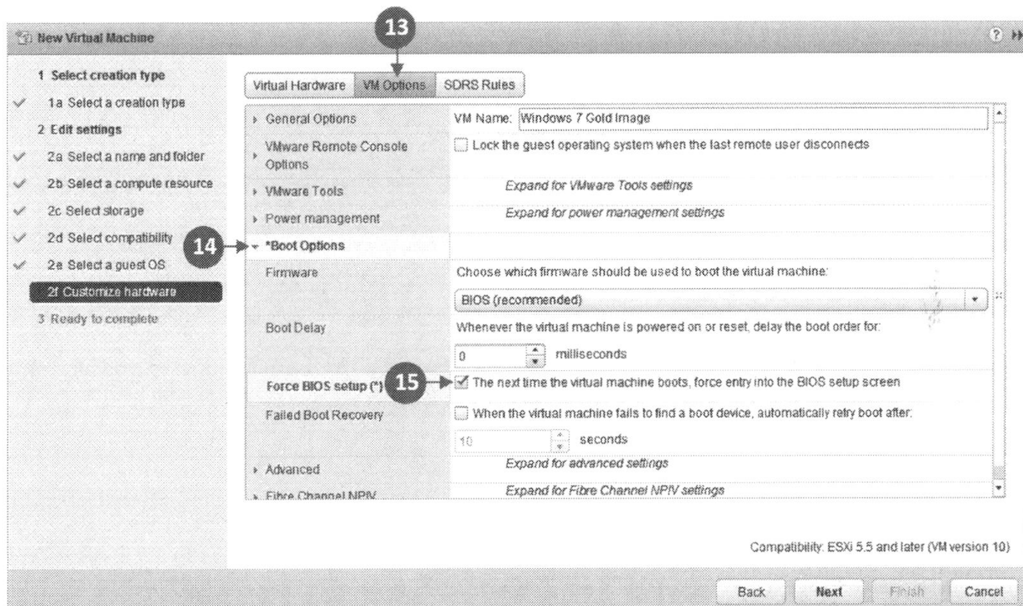

26. We need to change one of the boot options. Expand the arrow for **Boot Options** (**14**), and then check the tick box in the **Force BIOS Setup(*)** option for **The next time the virtual machine boots, force entry into the BIOS setup screen** so that, the next time the virtual desktop machine powers on and boots, it goes straight into the BIOS. You could, of course, open a console to the virtual desktop machine and press the *F2* key as it boots. However, that can flash past so quickly you might miss it, so the former option is easier.

    The reason we need to select this option is because we need to change some of the configuration settings so that this virtual desktop machine behaves as a virtual machine rather than a physical desktop PC. We will cover this a bit later when we power on the newly created virtual desktop machine for the first time.

27. Click on **Next** to move to the next configuration screen.

28. You should now see the **Ready to complete** page, which summarizes all the settings and configuration details we have just selected and should look something like the following screenshot:

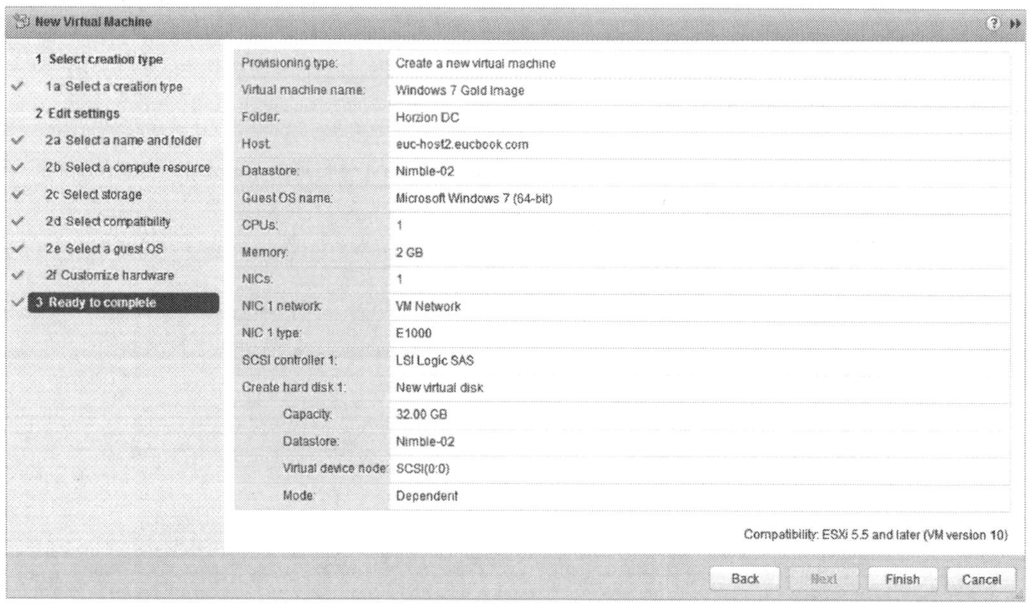

29. Once you have reviewed all the configuration details and are happy that they are all correct, click on **Finish** to build the virtual desktop machine. If you need to change something, then click on **Back** to return to the section that you need to change.

30. With the virtual desktop machine now built and configured, it's time to power it on and continue the build process. Navigate to the virtual desktop machine in the inventory. You should see an entry called **Windows 7 Gold Image** (**16**). Click on it to highlight it and then right-click. From the menu options, click on **Power On** (**17**), as shown in the following screenshot:

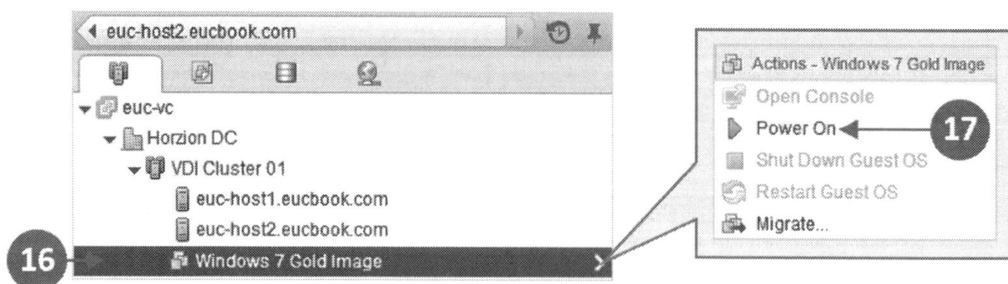

The virtual desktop machine will now power on and boot into the BIOS setup screen, as that's what we configured to happen on the next boot. Any subsequent boot ups will boot as normal into the operating system once it's installed. In the next section, we will make the configuration changes to the machine BIOS.

Updating the virtual desktop machine BIOS

With the virtual desktop machine now booting up, we need to launch a console session to it so that we can perform the configuration steps, which are as follows:

1. Highlight the **Windows 7 Gold Image** virtual desktop machine in the **Inventory** section and then highlight the main page section. Click on the **Summary** tab (**1**), as shown in the following screenshot:

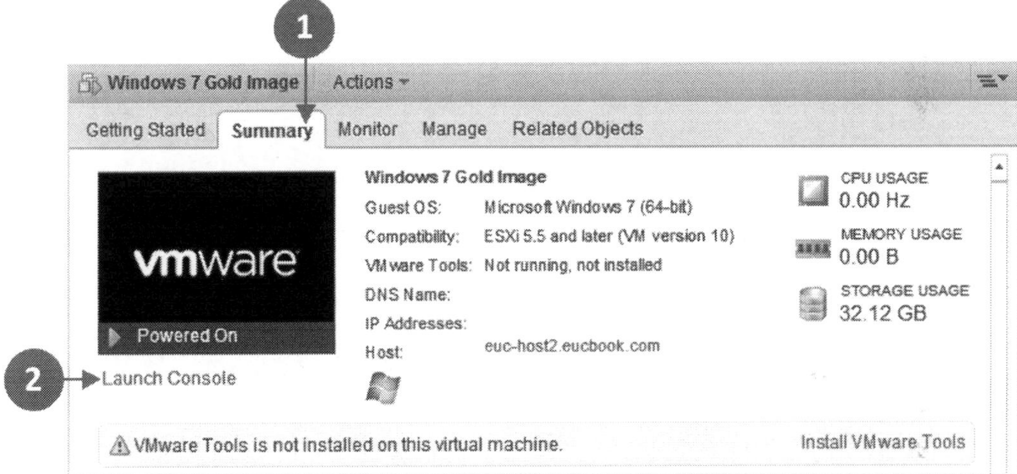

2. Now click on **Launch Console** (**2**) to open the console as another browser window.
3. If you get an error message displaying a warning about the website's security certificate, just click on **Continue**. You will now see the BIOS setup screen of the virtual desktop machine.

4. The first thing we need to do is disable the floppy drive. On the **Main** section of the BIOS screen, use the cursors keys to move to the **Legacy Diskette A:** (**3**) option and then press *Enter*. You will now see a box popup displaying some options, as shown in the following screenshot:

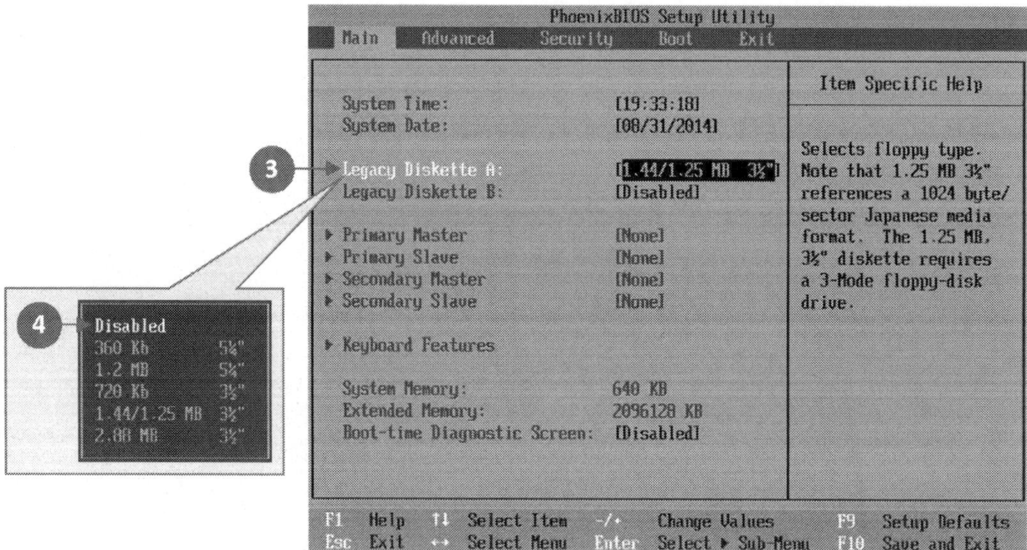

5. Use the cursor keys to highlight the **Disabled** option (**4**) and then press *Enter*. Next, we need to move to the advanced section of the BIOS setup. To do this, press the right arrow cursor to move across the tabs along the top, until **Advanced** is highlighted (**5**), as shown in the following screenshot:

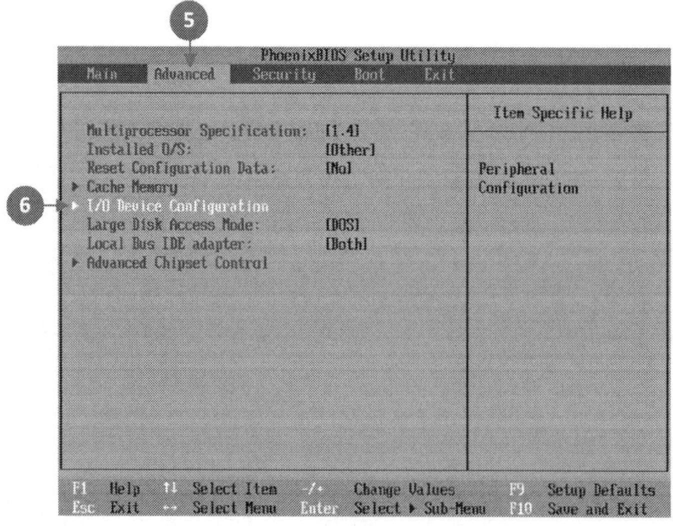

6. Now use the down arrow cursor to move down to the option for **I/O Device Configuration** (6) and press *Enter*. You will now see the following configuration screen.

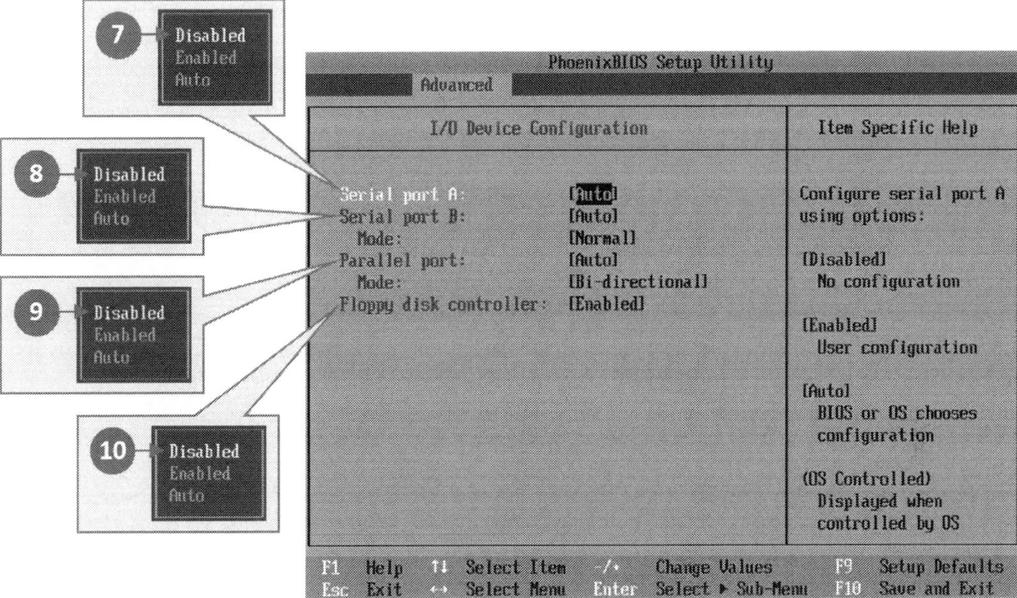

7. Move the cursor to **Serial port A:**, press *Enter*, select the option for **Disabled** (7), and press *Enter* again. Follow the same procedure to disable **Serial port B:** (8), **Parallel port:** (9), and the **Floppy disk controller:** (10).
8. Once you have completed these changes, press the *F10* key to save and exit. Confirm the configuration changes by selecting **Yes** (11), and then pressing *Enter*:

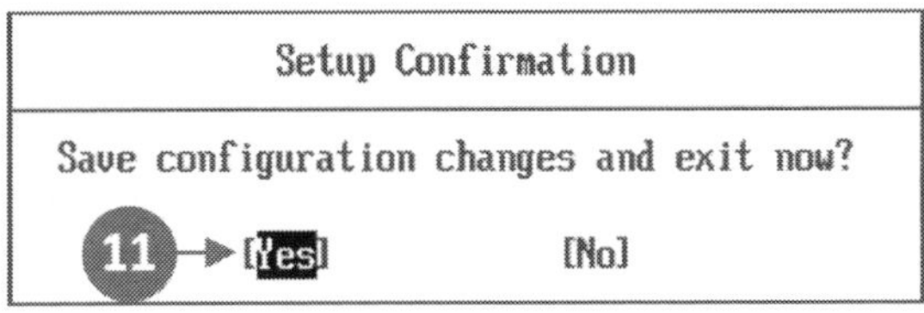

The BIOS changes are now saved and the virtual desktop machine is rebooted.

Operating system installation options

There are a couple of options you can use in order to build your virtual desktop machine's operating system. The first option is to use something such as MDT or SCCM, but we will use a different option, which is to build the image manually by using the installation media.

The other option, of course, is to use VMware Mirage, if you plan to use full-clone virtual desktop machines. We will cover VMware Mirage in *Chapter 14, Horizon 6 Advanced Edition*.

For this environment, we will build a Windows 7 desktop from scratch using the ISO installation media. This process is no different from building any other virtual machine on vSphere; thus, we will just briefly cover this, to serve as a quick reminder for those already familiar with working on the vSphere platform, and in enough detail, so that those that are new to the technology can quickly get their first virtual desktop machine image built.

Installing the guest operating system

The first thing we need to do in order to start the installation of the guest operating system is to attach the installation media to the virtual desktop machine:

1. From the vSphere Web Client, highlight the **Windows 7 Gold Image** virtual desktop machine in the **Inventory** section. Click on the **Summary** tab and then, in the **VM Hardware** section, click on the down arrow next to the entry for **CD/DVD drive 1** (**1**):

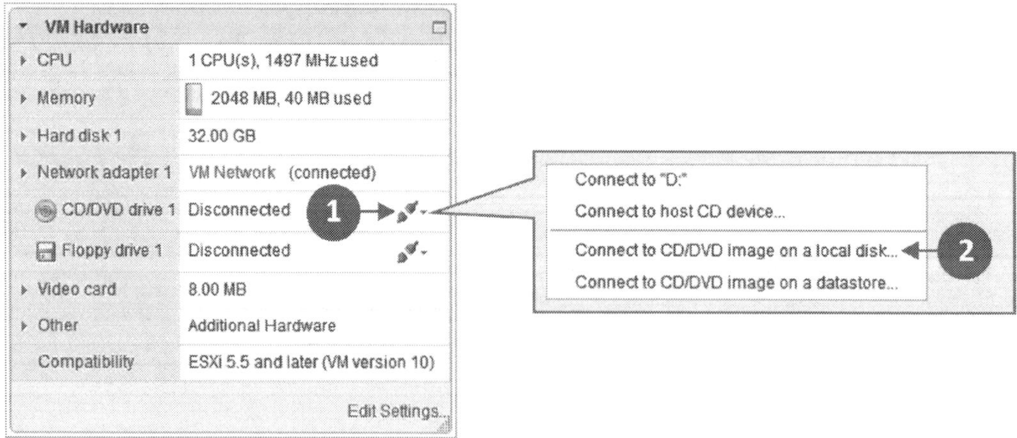

2. From the menu that pops up, select **Connect to CD/DVD image on a local disk... (2)**, as shown in the previous screenshot. We connect to the Windows 7 ISO image that is stored on our shared software folder.
3. You will see a warning box pop up and warn you that the VMware Client Integration Plug-in is going to access your operating system. Click on **Allow (3)** so that we can connect to our shared folder, as shown in the following screenshot:

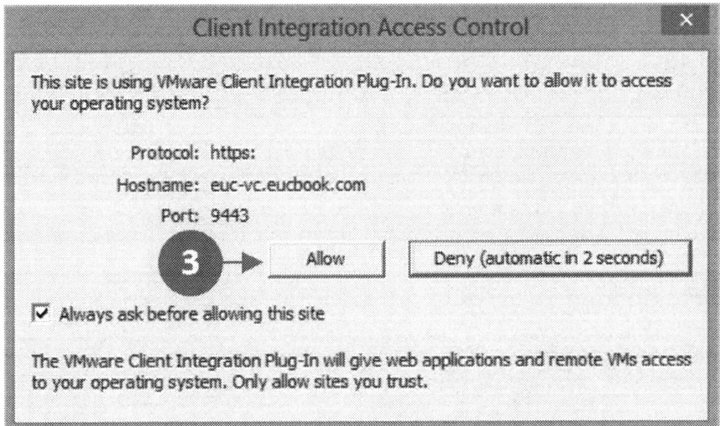

> You only have a few seconds to click on **Allow**, otherwise you will have to try the connection process again. If you are happy to allow this in the future, then it's worth unchecking the box for **Always ask before allowing this site**.

4. The **Open** dialog box now appears, allowing you to browse to the location of the ISO image for the guest operating system. In our example lab, we have a shared folder for software, so we will enter the path to that shared folder in the **File name** field first.

5. Browse to the ISO and highlight it (**4**), as shown in the following screenshot, and then click on **Open**:

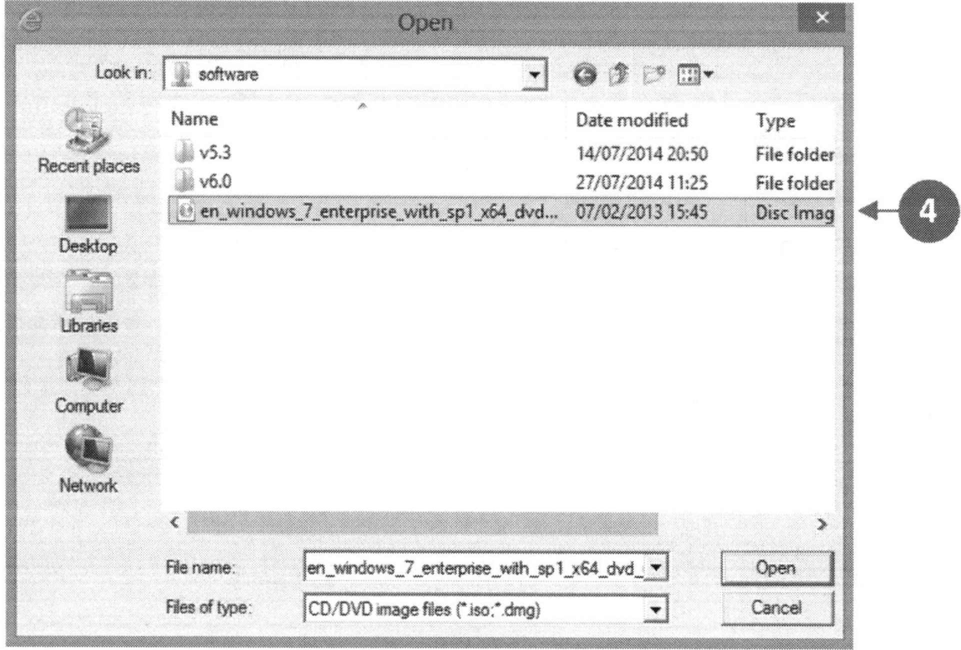

6. In our example lab, we will install Windows 7 as the first virtual desktop machine parent image; so the filename is `en_windows_7_enterprise_with_sp1_dvd`. We have now attached this ISO to our virtual desktop machine, ready to boot up and start the installation process.
7. As we still have a console open to the virtual desktop machine (open one if you have closed it), switch back to it and click on **Send Ctrl-Alt-Delete** (**5**) to reboot:

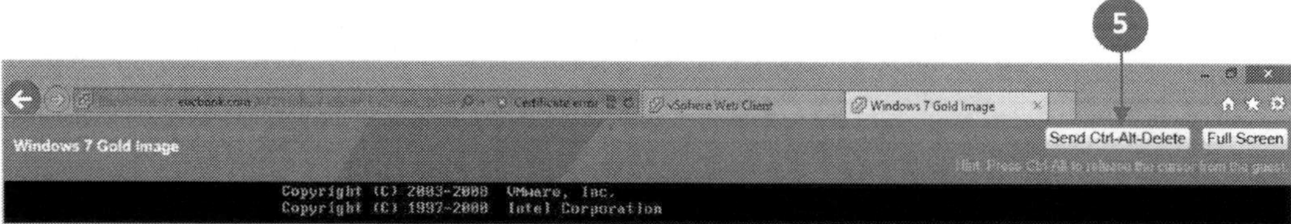

8. The virtual desktop machine reboots and starts to boot from the ISO image, loading the Windows installer, as shown in the following screenshot:

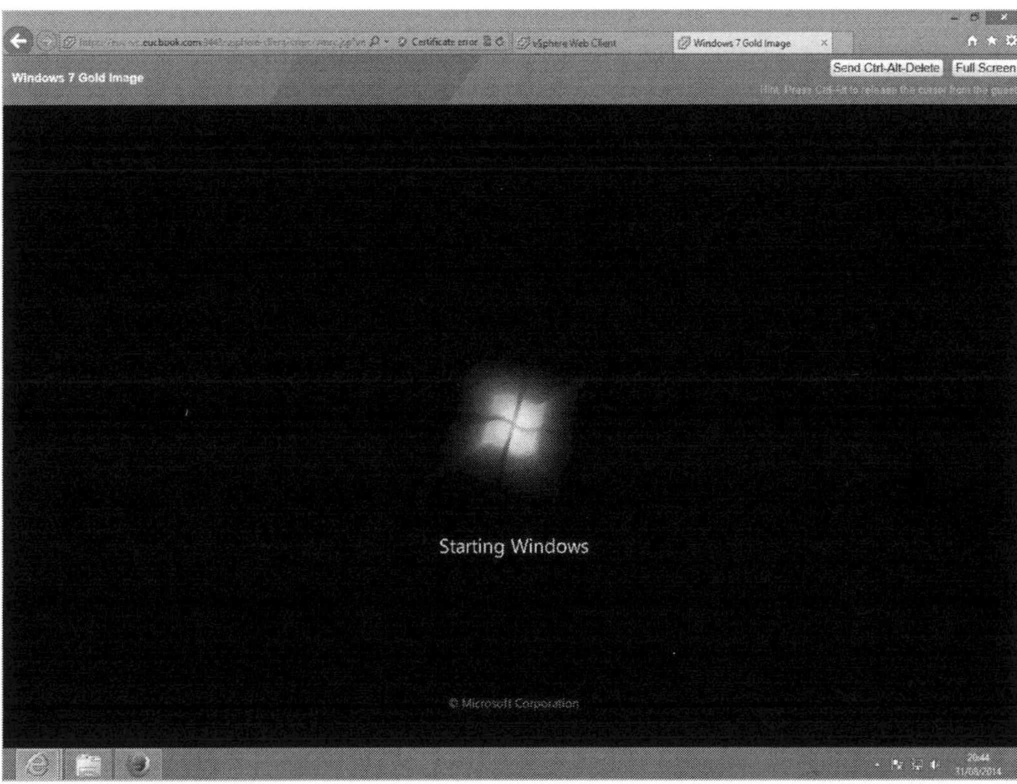

We won't cover how to install Windows 7, so carry on with a base install; once it has been completed, make sure you apply any updates and patches and then join the virtual desktop machine to the domain.

> The reason we want to join the virtual desktop machine to the domain, even though this machine is effectively the template, is so that all the software components, DLL files, and so on that are needed on the machine for it to be domain joined are present. Otherwise, when you create the linked clones from this parent image and try to join them to the domain, they will ask for the installation media.

Once you are happy that the parent image has been patched and is joined to the domain, we can start installing some of the VMware-specific virtual machine tools and View components, starting with VMware Tools.

Installing VMware Tools

VMware Tools are installed to enhance the usability of the virtual desktop machine. It installs VMware-specific device drivers that allow it to run as a virtual desktop machine, replacing the physical hardware equivalents. The installation of VMware Tools is initiated from the vSphere Web Client:

1. As we did in the previous section, highlight the **Windows 7 Gold Image** virtual desktop machine in the **Inventory** section and click on the **Summary** tab (**1**). Click on **Install VMware Tools** (**2**), as shown in the following screenshot:

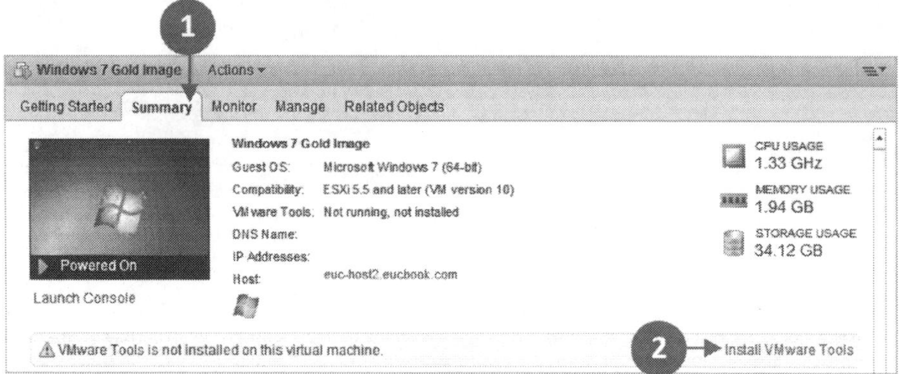

2. The following dialog box will pop up. Initiating the installation from the vSphere Web Client effectively mounts the VMware Tools installation media as a virtual CD drive on the virtual desktop machine:

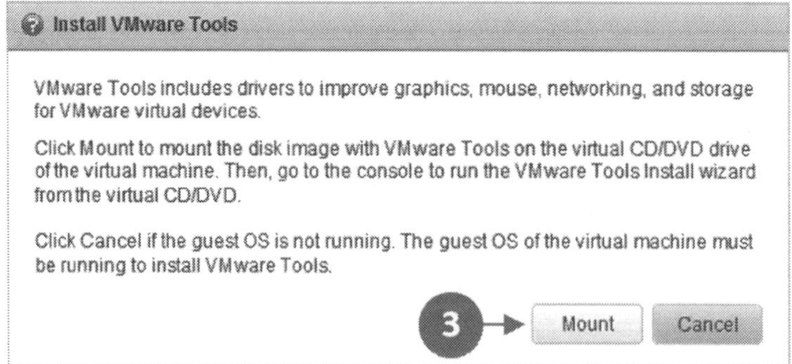

3. Click on **Mount** (**3**) to mount the installation media, as shown in the preceding screenshot.
4. Now switch back to the console view of the virtual desktop machine.

5. You will see from the following dialog box that the **AutoPlay** feature has kicked in, showing a DVD drive containing the installation program:

6. Click on **Run setup64.exe** (**4**). The VMware Tools installation program launches.
7. If you see the **User Account Control** box pop up warning you about making changes to the computer, ignore it by clicking on **Yes**. You will now see the **Welcome to the installation wizard for VMware Tools** dialog box, as shown in the following screenshot:

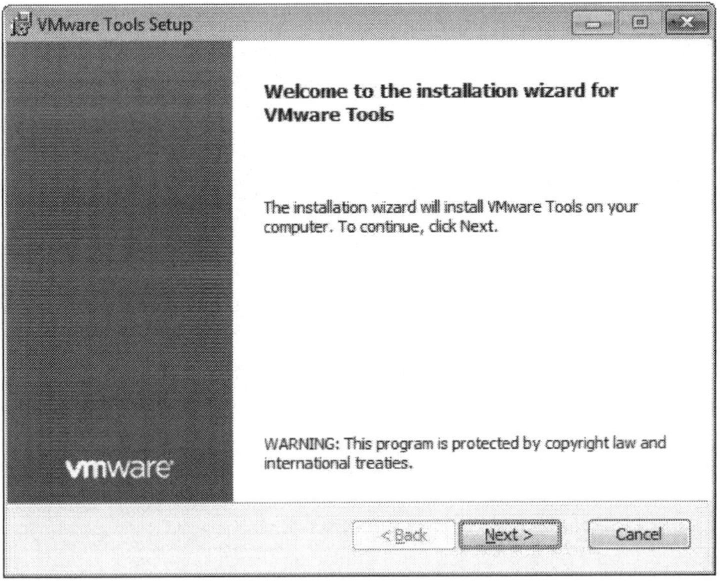

8. Click on **Next >** to continue.
9. In the next dialog box, we will choose the type of setup we want to perform. In our example, click on the radio button for **Custom** (**5**), as we are going to go through the different options in a bit more detail rather than look at a typical installation:

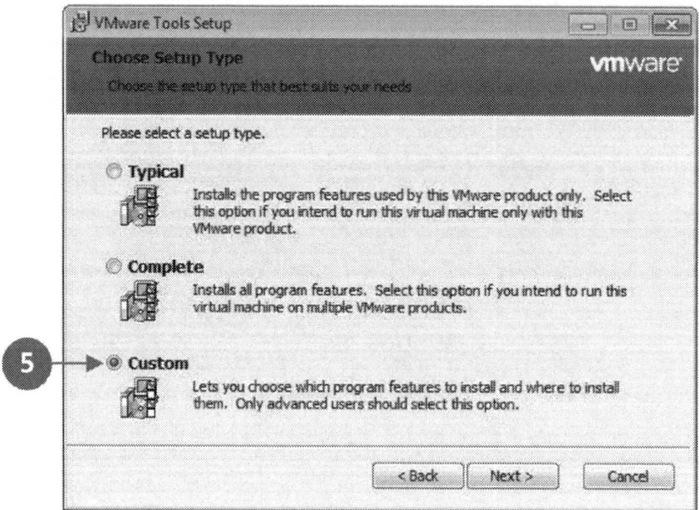

10. Click on **Next >** to continue.
11. You will now see the **Custom Setup** dialog box, as shown in the following screenshot:

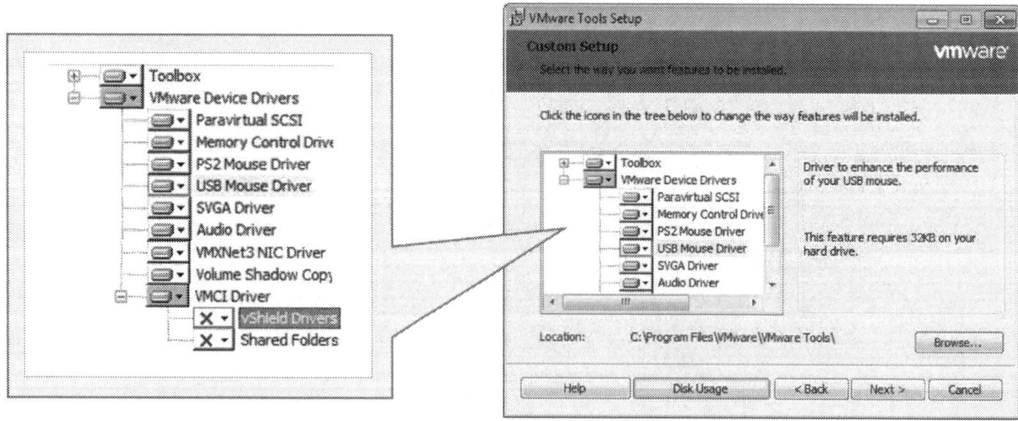

12. VMware Tools will install the following VMware device drivers:
    - **Paravirtual SCSI**: This is for PVSCSI adapters to enhance the performance of virtualized applications.
    - **Memory Control Driver**: This allows memory management of the virtual desktop machine when running on an ESXi host.
    - **PS2/USB Mouse Driver**: This virtual mouse driver improves the performance of the mouse in a virtual desktop machine.
    - **SVGA Driver**: This enables 32-bit displays, high resolution, and faster graphics performance. It installs a virtual SVGA driver that replaces the standard VGA driver. On Windows Vista or later versions, the VMware SVGA 3D (Microsoft - WDDM) driver is also installed, adding support for Windows Aero.
    - **Audio Driver**: This is required for all 64-bit guest operating systems to enable sound capabilities.
    - **VMXNET3 NIC Driver**: This improves network performance and is recommended for virtual desktop machines.
    - **Volume Shadow Copy**: This allows taking backup copies or snapshots of the virtual desktop machine.
    - **VMCI Driver**: This allows faster communication between virtual machines.
    - **vShield Drivers**: This installs the agent to use AV offload scanning.
    - **Unity Touch**: This allows you to use an iPad or Android tablet to connect to the virtual desktop machine and provides an extra level of control and interaction.
13. Other options in this dialog box allow you to change where VMware Tools are installed, and to check the disk space requirements so that you can check the amount of disk space that VMware Tools need to install your chosen options.
14. When you are happy with the selection of features to be installed, click on **Next >** to continue.

15. VMware Tools are now ready to install. Click on **Install** to start the process, as shown in the following screenshot:

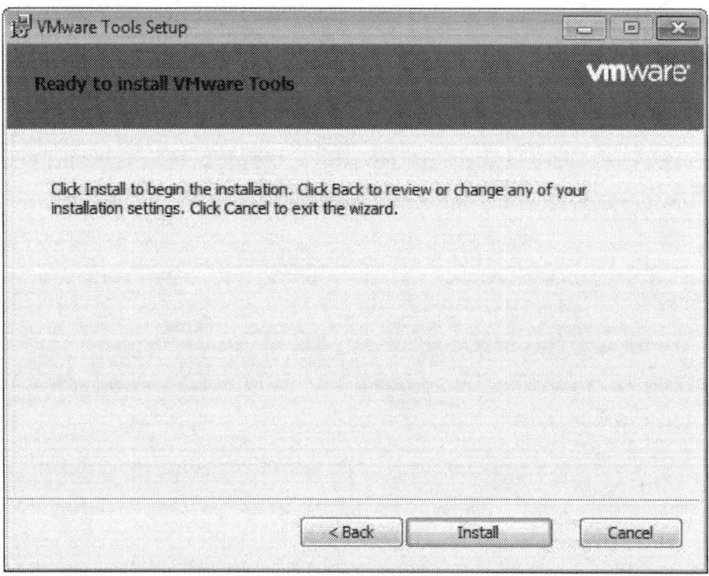

16. Once competed, you will see the **Completed the VMware Tools Setup Wizard** dialog box. Click on **Finish** to complete the installation process, as shown in the following screenshot:

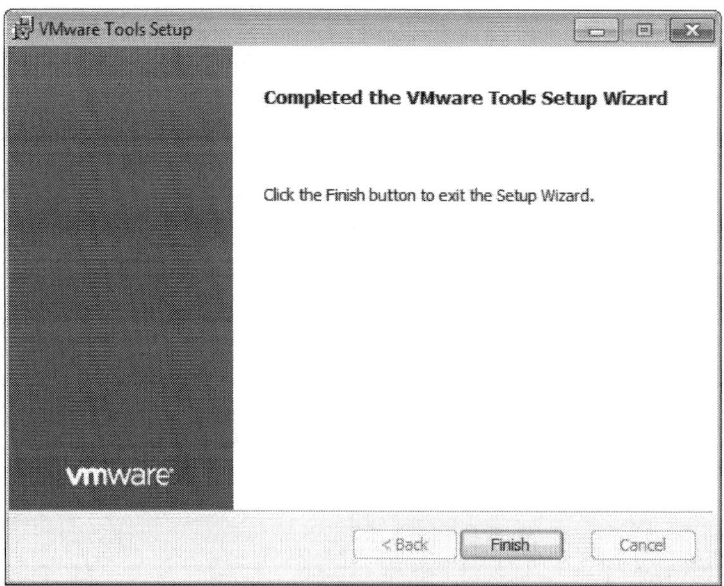

17. To start the VMware Tools service, you will need to reboot the virtual desktop machine. From the following dialog box, click **Yes** to reboot.

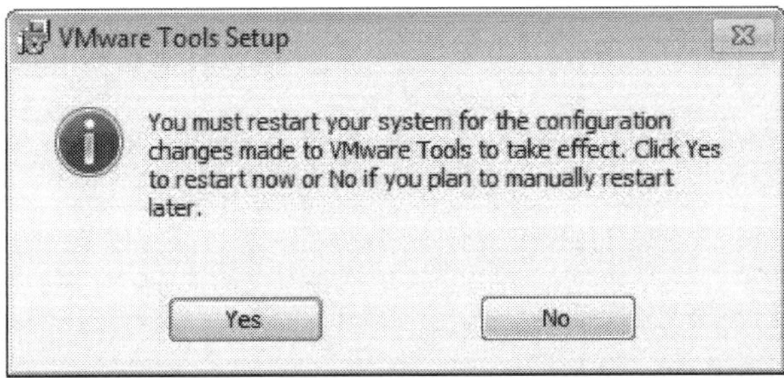

18. Once the virtual desktop machine has restarted, check that VMware Tools are running by clicking on the taskbar and checking for the **vm** icon (**6**) as shown in the following screenshot:

You should now have successfully installed VMware Tools. The next step of the process is to install any core applications that you want to include as part of the parent image.

Installing applications for the parent image

The next stage of the process is to install any applications that you want as part of your parent image. These are typically applications that will be used by every user in your organization. You may also deliver applications using another technology, such as ThinApp, so that you can manage updates that way rather than using the parent image.

In our example, we will install Adobe Reader, as shown in the following screenshot:

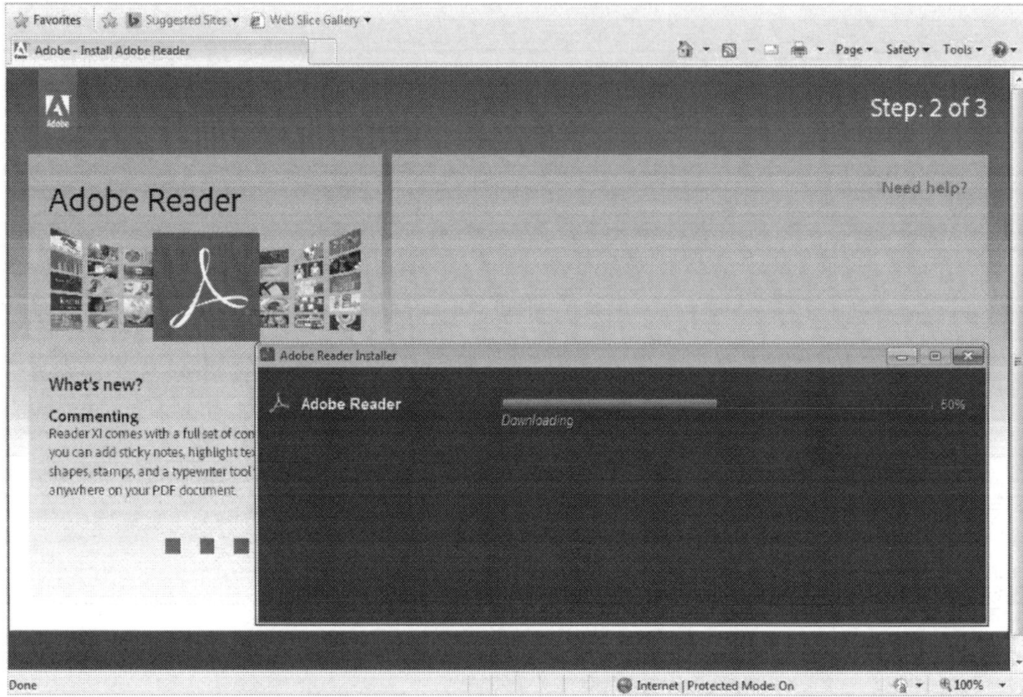

Once you have installed all your applications and any other software components, you will install the Horizon View Agent.

Installing the Horizon View Agent

The Horizon View Agent is installed on a virtual desktop machine and is used for communication between the Horizon View Client and the virtual desktop machine. It also adds components for things such as USB redirection and View Persona Management. We will cover these different components in more detail in this section as we install the agent:

1. From the desktop of the virtual desktop machine, navigate to the installation file for the View Agent. In our example lab, the software is in our shared folder.

2. Find the View Agent software and launch the installation program (**1**). As our virtual desktop machine is the 64-bit version of Windows 7, we will use the 64-bit installer, as shown in the following screenshot:

Name	Date modified	Type	Size
VMware-viewconnectionserver-x86_64-6.1.0-2509221	3/18/2015 1:53 PM	Application	175,837 KB
VMware-viewcomposer-6.1.0-2506641	3/18/2015 1:57 PM	Application	32,084 KB
(1) VMware-viewagent-x86_64-6.1.0-2509441	3/18/2015 1:56 PM	Application	161,800 KB
VMware-viewagent-direct-connection-x86_64-6.1.0-2509221	3/18/2015 1:57 PM	Application	15,144 KB
VMware-viewagent-direct-connection-6.1.0-2509221	3/18/2015 1:57 PM	Application	13,719 KB
VMware-viewagent-6.1.0-2509441	3/18/2015 1:54 PM	Application	122,825 KB
VMware-personamanagement-x86_64-6.1.0-2509221	3/18/2015 1:56 PM	Application	18,387 KB
VMware-personamanagement-6.1.0-2509221	3/18/2015 1:56 PM	Application	12,478 KB
VMware-Horizon-View-HTML-Access-2.6.0-2329873	3/18/2015 1:58 PM	Compressed (zipp...	1,869 KB
VMware-Horizon-View-Extras-Bundle-3.3.0-2491779	3/18/2015 1:57 PM	Compressed (zipp...	2,694 KB

3. The name of the file we are launching is `VMware-viewagent-x86_64-6.1.0-2509441`. The number at the end of the filename refers to the build number and varies, depending on what build you use. Once launched, you will see the following screenshot:

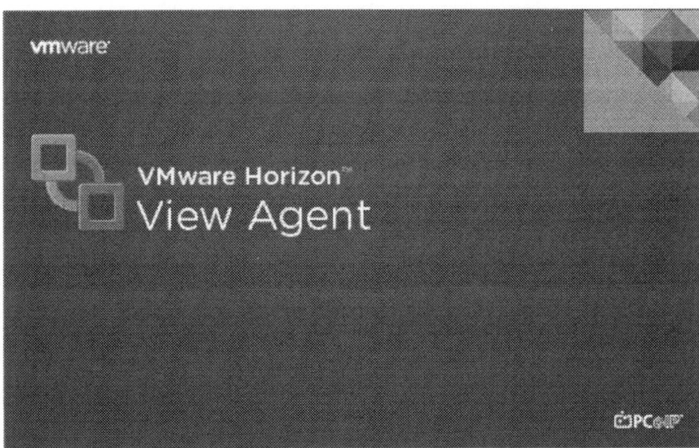

4. Next you will see the **Welcome to the Installation Wizard for VMware Horizon View Agent** page.

5. Click on **Next >** to continue:

6. The **License Agreement** page is shown next. Click on the radio button for **I accept the terms in the license agreement** (2).
7. Click on **Next >** to continue, as shown in the following screenshot:

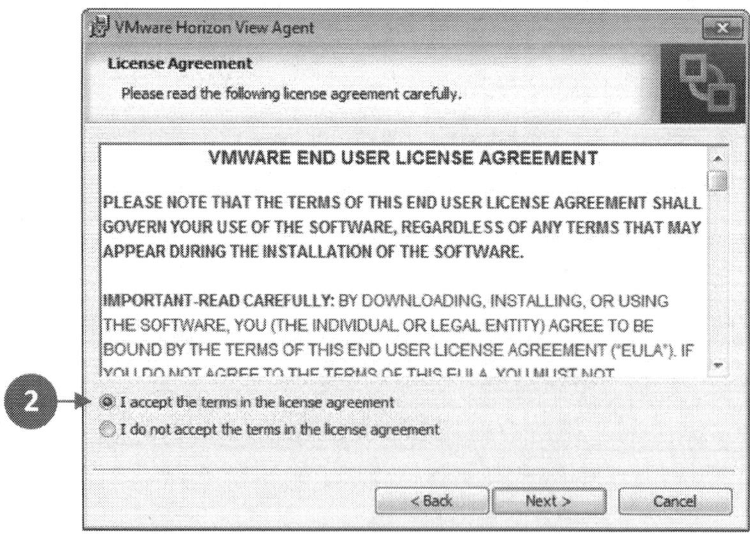

8. On the **Custom Setup** page, you can choose the features and functions you want to install. These features are all installed by default, but you might want to review some of them and deselect them from the installation process as you might not want to use some features. You can always install them again later if need be:

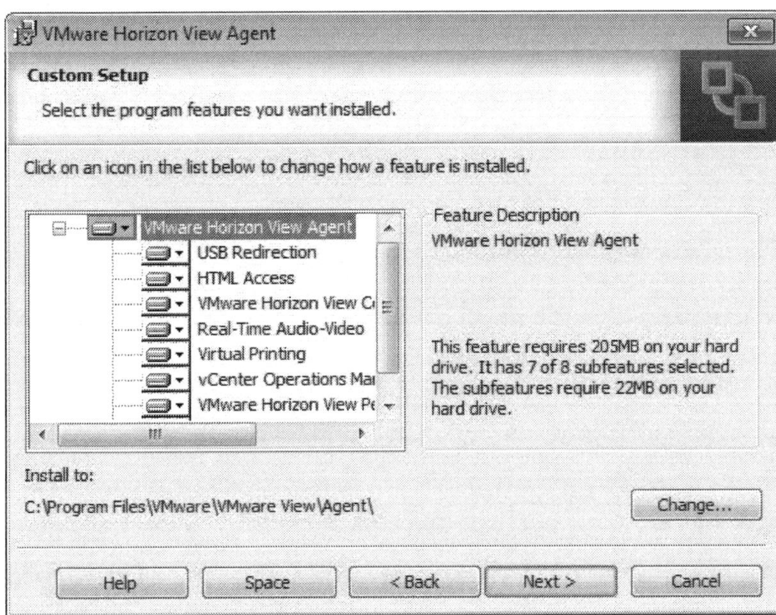

9. You can choose to install the following features:
   - **USB Redirection**: This allows a USB device to be plugged into the end point device and then redirect the USB traffic to the virtual desktop machine
   - **HTML Access**: This allows the virtual desktop machine to be accessed using an HTML-enabled browser
   - **VMware Horizon View Composer Agent**: This allows the virtual desktop machine to be run as a linked clone desktop
   - **Real-Time Audio-Video**: This allows you to redirect locally connected audio and video devices (such as USB webcams) to your virtual desktop machine
   - **Virtual Printing**: This allows users to print to printers without the need to install print drivers

- **vCenter Operations Manager Agent**: This allows the virtual desktop machine to be monitored by vCenter Operations Manager for Horizon View
- **VMware Horizon View Persona Management**: This synchronizes a user's profile from the virtual desktop machine to a repository on a central server, meaning that a profile can be delivered to a floating assigned desktop to personalize it for that user so that they can access their profile
- **PCoIP Smartcard**: This allows users to use a smartcard for authentication; it is not installed by default

10. When you are happy with the features you have chosen to install, click on **Next >** to continue.
11. On the next screen, you will see the **Remote Desktop Protocol Configuration** option dialog box. You need remote desktop support enabled for the View Agent to work. You could always enable this using a Group Policy.
12. Click on the radio button for **Enable the Remote Desktop capability on this computer** (3), as shown in the following screenshot:

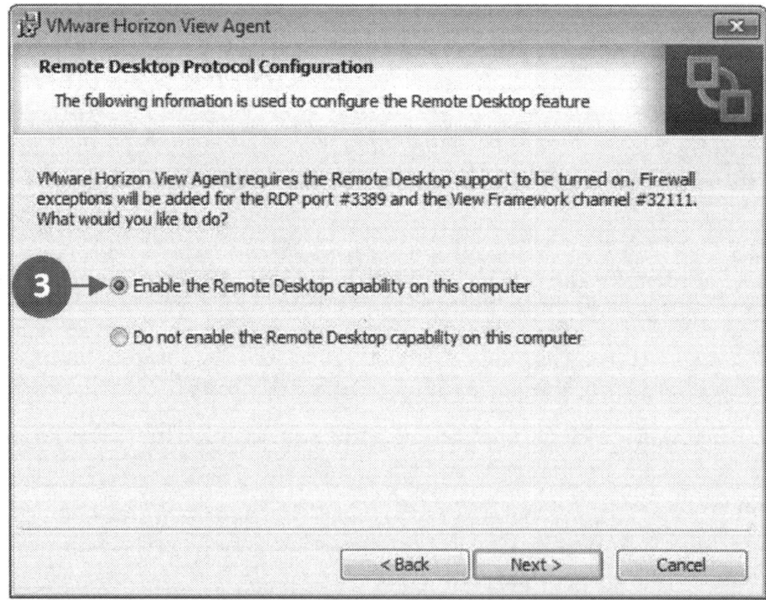

13. Click on **Next >** to continue.

14. You will now see the **Ready to Install the Program** page. Click on **Install** to start the installation, as shown in the following screenshot:

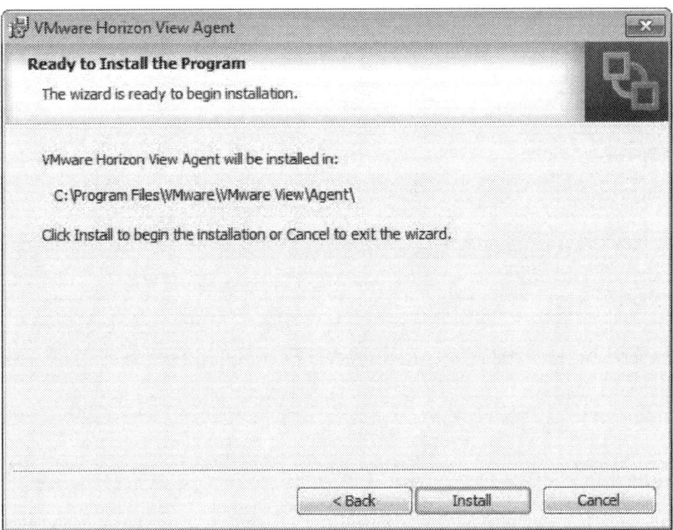

15. The Horizon View Agent is now installed.
16. When you see the **Installer Completed** page, as shown in the following screenshot, click on **Finish**:

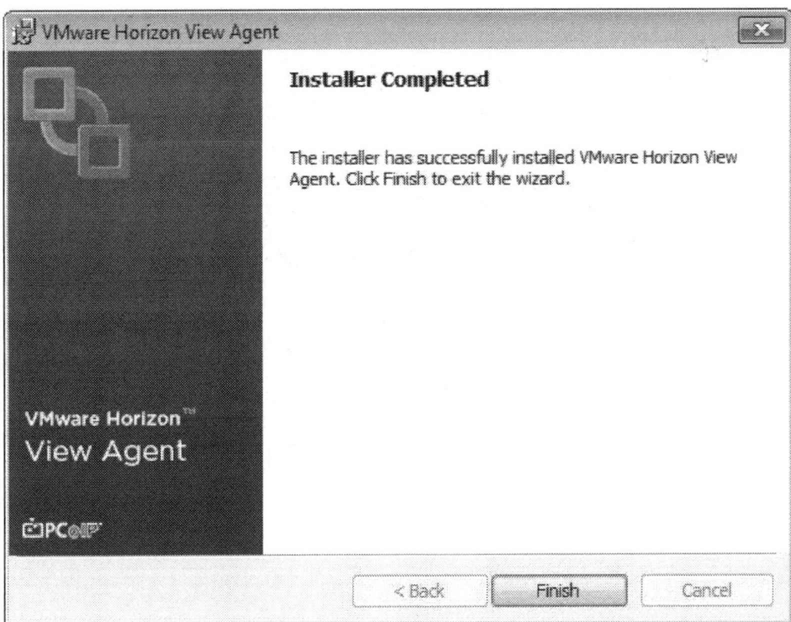

17. You will then be prompted to reboot the virtual desktop machine. Click on **Yes** to reboot:

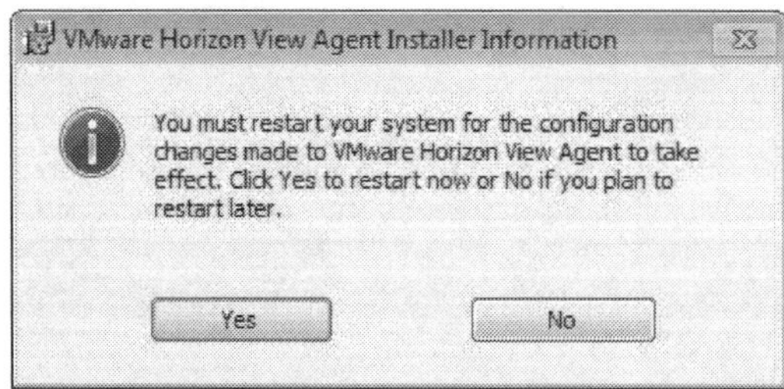

You should now have successfully installed the Horizon View Agent. In the next section, we will start optimizing the parent image to run as a virtual desktop machine.

Optimizing the guest operating system

There are various tools and manual processes to optimize the virtual desktop operating systems. In this chapter, we will cover two of these. The first one we will look at is the manual, script-based process, and the second is one of the many automated tools available that uses a GUI-driven console.

Using the VMware optimization script

The VMware optimization script is part of the VMware View Optimization Guide for Windows 7 and 8, downloadable from the VMware website at `http://www.vmware.com/resources/techresources/10157`.

The guide itself explains the steps required to optimize the guest operating system but, more importantly, it also comes with a number of prebuilt scripts that can be found as attachments to the PDF document. These scripts are referred to as `commands.bat` files, with each of the four versions designed for slightly different guest operating systems, and with or without support for View Persona Management.

The four different versions are for the following operating systems:

- Windows 7
- Windows 8
- Windows 7 with View Persona Management support
- Windows 8 with View Persona Management support

So let's download the four scripts and then select the one that reflects our environment:

1. Once downloaded, open the document in Adobe Reader and save the embedded files. To do this, click on the paperclip icon (**1**) to show the documents that are attached in the PDF, as shown in the following screenshot:

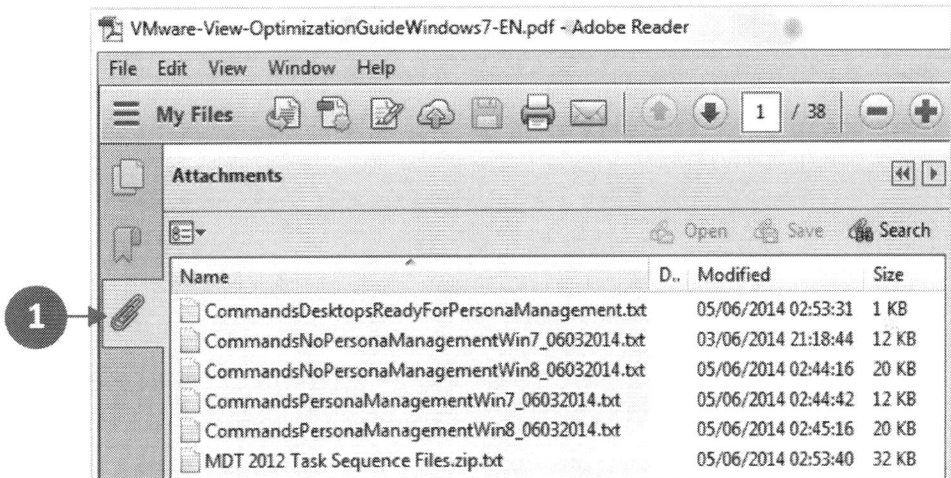

2. As we are building a Windows 7 parent image that has support for View Persona Management, this is the script we are going to use. For this example, click and highlight `CommandsPersonaManagementWin7_06032014.txt`.
3. Right-click on the file and then click on **Save Attachment**. In this example, we will save the files to the shared software folder so that we can use them later on. If you want to save the other files as well, then repeat this process for all of the attached files until all of them are saved in the shared folder. Now switch back to the console of the virtual desktop machine.

   Before we can run the optimization file script that we just downloaded, we first need to turn it into a `.bat` batch file rather than a `.txt` file. As you are aware, it's not just a case of renaming it and changing the file extension.

4. Open the file using WordPad. From the Windows Explorer window, click to highlight the filename (**2**), and then right-click. From the menu, click on **Open with** (**3**) and then choose **WordPad** (**4**), as shown in the following screenshot. You can use **Notepad**, but beware that Notepad can introduce additional characters, such as spaces, that might corrupt the file:

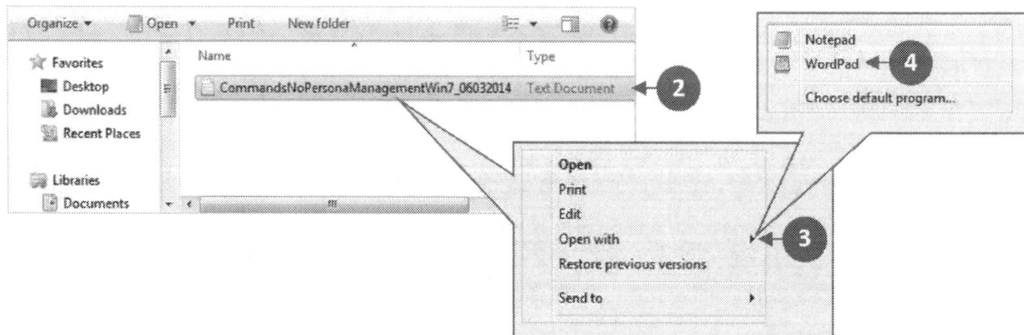

5. At this stage, with the text file open, you could edit the script and make some changes to it if there is something specific that you want to change to suit your environment. In our example lab, we are going to keep the default customization options.
6. In WordPad, click on the down arrow at the top-left corner (**5**), click on **Save as** (**6**), and finally, click on **Other formats** (**7**), as shown in the following screenshots:

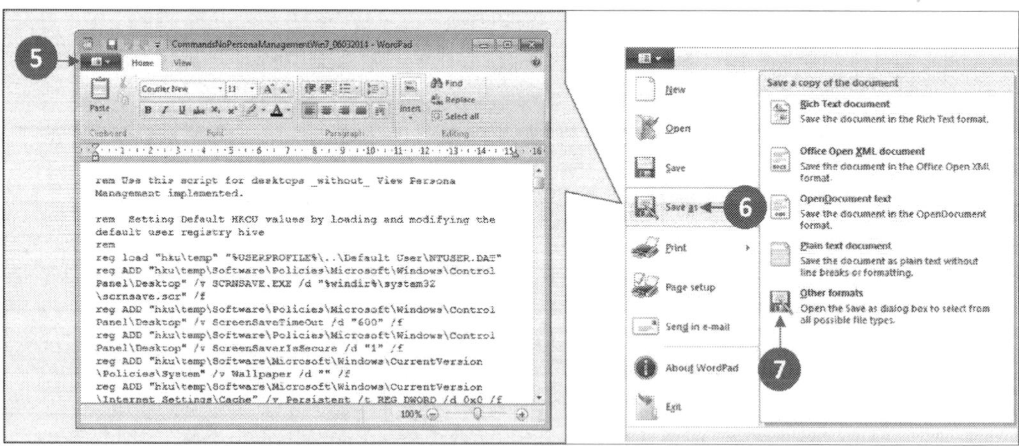

7. In the **Save As** dialog box, type `"commands.bat"` (**5**), ensuring that you use quotes around the filename, as shown in the following screenshot:

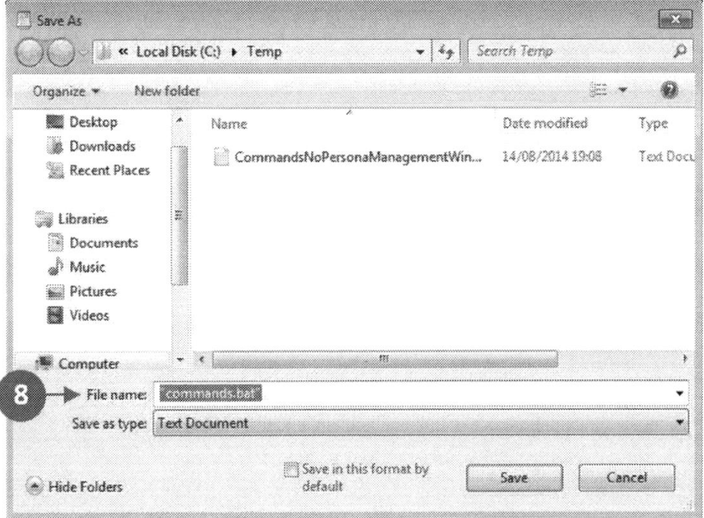

8. Click on **Save** to save the file and create the `commands.bat` script.
9. You should now see that the file has not only been saved, but is also now a `.bat` file **(9)** that we can run to execute the optimization script:

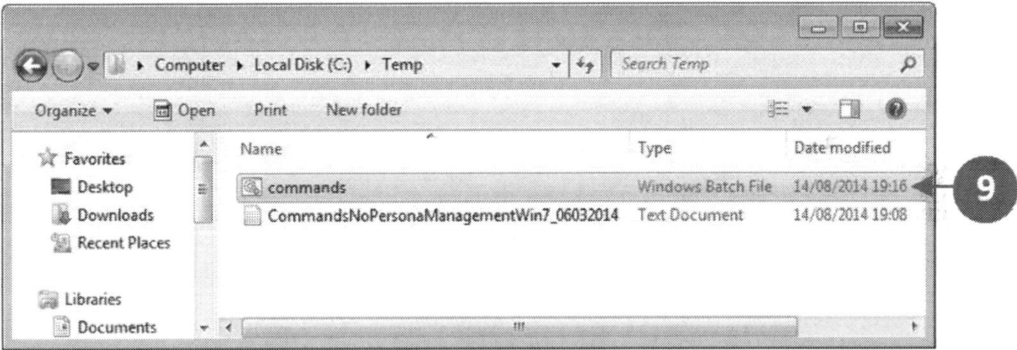

10. Close WordPad. We can now run our newly created script from the command line. In order to run the script correctly, you need to make sure you run it with administrative privileges. You might already be logged in as an administrator but, just to be certain, we will run with the **Run as administrator** option.

11. Navigate to **Start** | **All Program** | **Accessories**, and then highlight **Command Prompt** (**10**). Right-click on **Command Prompt** and then choose **Run as administrator** (**11**) from the menu, as shown in the following screenshot:

12. In the **Command Prompt** window, type `commands.bat` (**12**) and press *Enter*, as shown in the following screenshot:

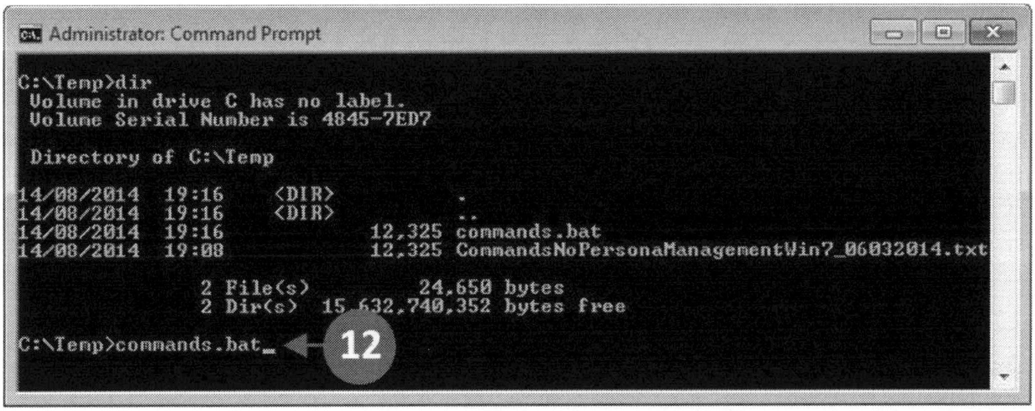

```
Administrator: Command Prompt
C:\Temp>dir
 Volume in drive C has no label.
 Volume Serial Number is 4845-7ED7

 Directory of C:\Temp

14/08/2014  19:16    <DIR>          .
14/08/2014  19:16    <DIR>          ..
14/08/2014  19:16            12,325 commands.bat
14/08/2014  19:08            12,325 CommandsNoPersonaManagementWin7_06032014.txt
               2 File(s)         24,650 bytes
               2 Dir(s)  15,632,740,352 bytes free

C:\Temp>commands.bat_
```

12

13. The script will now run and might take a few minutes to complete. Once it is completed, scroll back through the window and check to make sure nothing failed or that there weren't any errors. When you are happy that it has run correctly, type `exit` and press *Enter*.

Using the VMware optimization tool

The other option to optimize the virtual desktop machine is to use a GUI-based tool. In our example lab, we will use a VMware version available from the VMware fling website.

A fling, in VMware terms, is a free piece of software for people to try out and give feedback to VMware. Often, these products make it into production as products in their own right or they form part of a new feature of an existing product. The only thing to bear in mind, should you choose to use them in your production environment, is that these product flings don't have any official support.

Download the tool and save it in the shared folder. You can download the tool at `https://labs.vmware.com/flings/vmware-os-optimization-tool`. Once downloaded, save it in the shared software folder. Now, let's take a few minutes just to see how this tool works.

VMware OS Optimization Tool is an application that you can execute on the virtual desktop machine you are optimizing. It also has the ability to analyze and optimize remote systems.

From the Windows 7 virtual desktop machine we are using to create our parent image, navigate to the shared software folder, locate the application, and launch it. You will see the following screenshot:

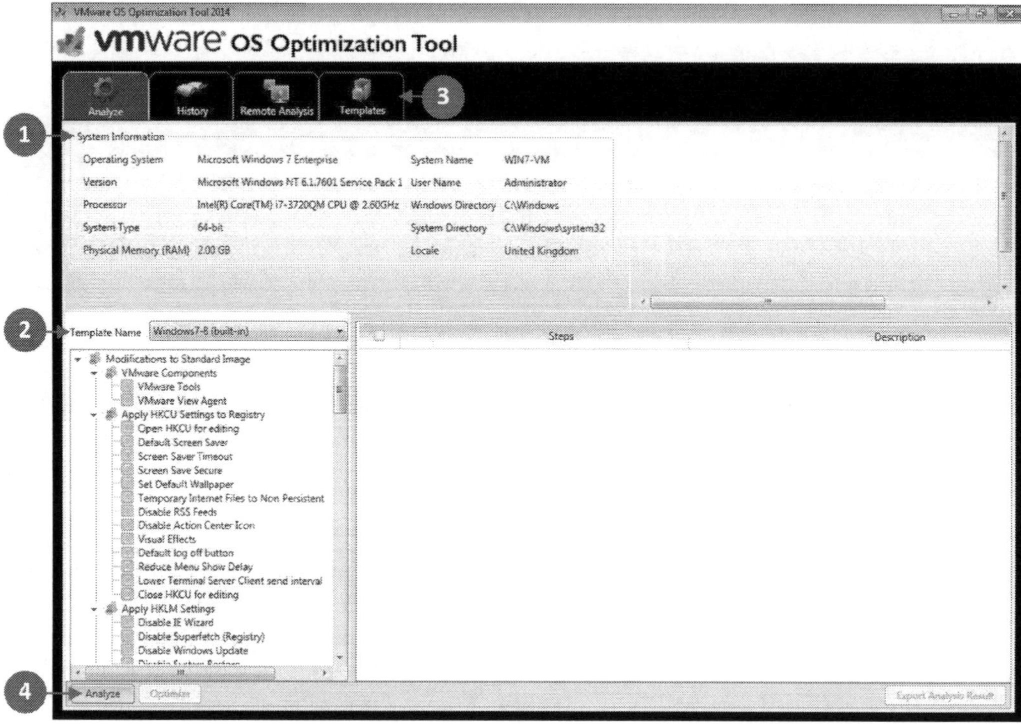

At the top of the screen (**1**), you can see the details of the virtual desktop machine's operating system and hardware configuration.

The next section (**2**) is where you choose the template you want to use for the optimization. You have the ability to create new templates using this tool by clicking on the **Templates** tab (**3**).

To start the process, the tool firstly analyzes the differences between the current virtual machine state and the optimizations contained in the template. Click on **Analyze** (**4**) to start the process.

The tool will run the analysis and then come back with a report showing the components that need to be optimized. At this stage, you can select or deselect options before you actually run the optimization. Scroll through the analysis results to understand what is going to be changed:

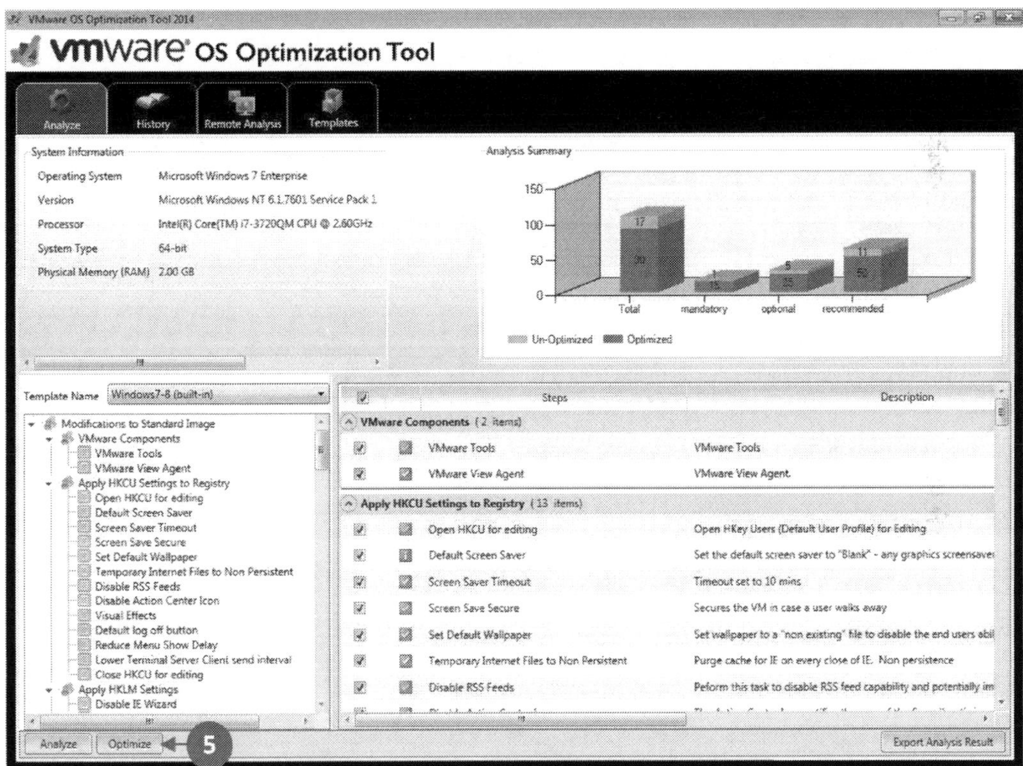

When you are happy, click on **Optimize** (5) to start the optimization process. The image will now be optimized as per the settings and configuration details contained in the template that you chose. Click on the **Optimize** tab (6) and you can see the results of what has been changed during the optimization:

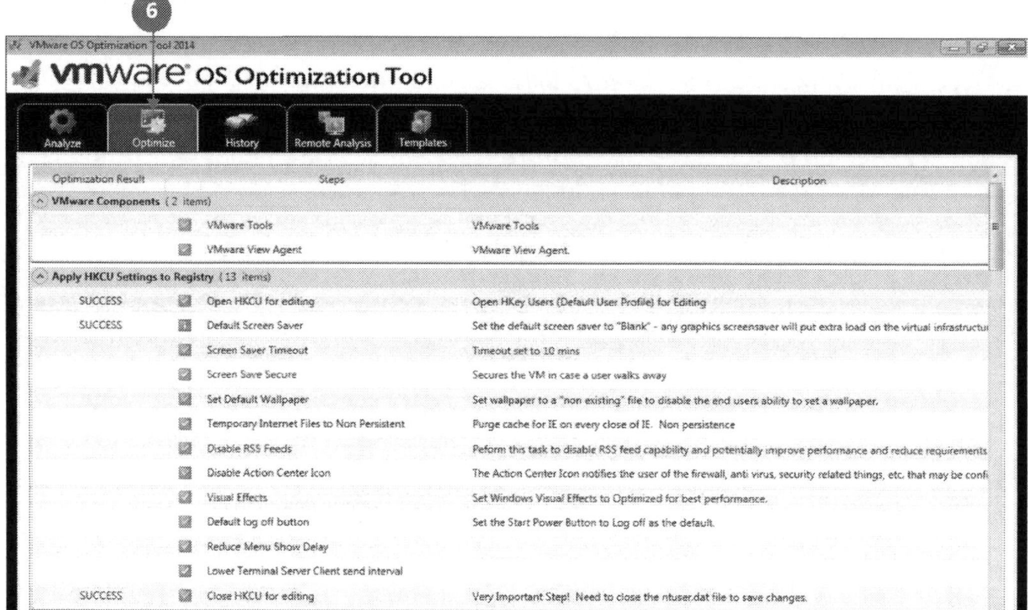

Once completed, exit the tool. In the next section, we will look at what's next for our virtual desktop machine.

Post-optimization tasks

One of the final things to do is to release the IP address if you have been using DHCP so that, when the new virtual desktop machines are created from this parent image, they don't have an IP address and, therefore, will obtain a new IP address.

Open the command prompt window and type `ipconfig /release`, as shown in the following screenshot:

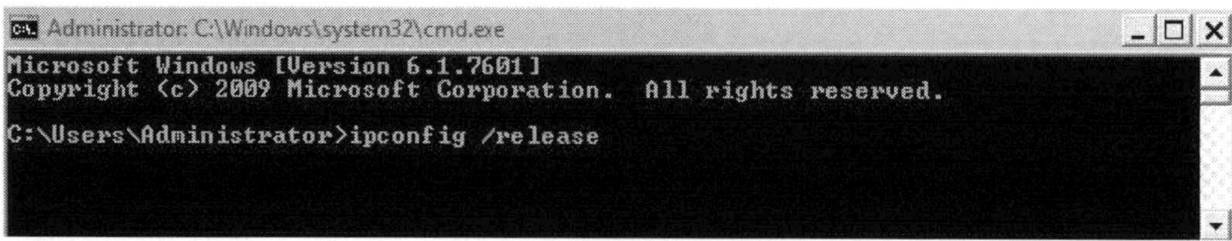

Before shutting down the virtual desktop machine and completing the build, there are just a few housekeeping tasks to perform.

Don't forget to tidy up behind you. For example, empty the Recycle Bin and delete any browser history or temporary files. Basically, delete everything that is not part of that parent image; once you are happy that the image is optimized to your requirements, you can shut down the virtual desktop machine.

We will prepare the parent image for delivery later in this chapter.

Creating a Windows 8.1 virtual desktop machine

For our example lab, we will repeat the build and optimization process to build a second parent image but, this time, we are going to build a Windows 8 virtual desktop machine. In the next section, we will repeat the process described in the previous section and build a Windows 8.1 virtual desktop machine.

Just as a reminder, the process is shown in the following image:

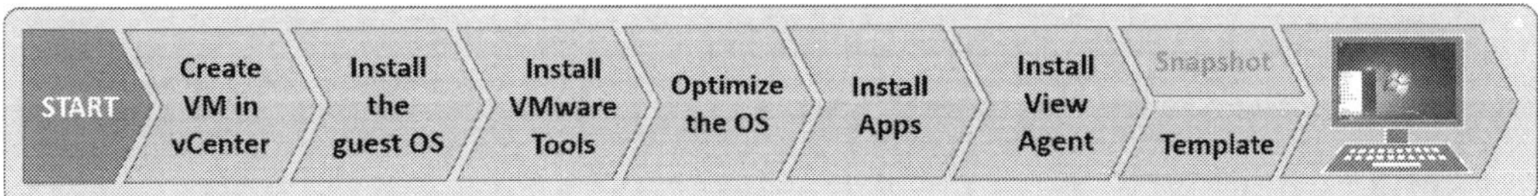

Once built, this Windows 8.1 parent image is converted to a template that will then be used to create full clone, dedicated virtual desktop machines.

Rather than go through every step again screenshot by screenshot, we will list the steps we followed when creating the Windows 7 parent image and then just show the screenshots to highlight the differences. You can refer to the previous section to get more details.

Creating the virtual desktop machine container

As done earlier, the first thing we need to do is create the virtual desktop machine:

1. From the **Home** tab, click on **Hosts and Clusters** (**1**). Expand the **Horizon DC** data center and go to **VDI Cluster 01**. Highlight the host server; in our example lab; we are going to select the host server `euc-host2.eucbook.com` (**2**).
2. Right-click on the host server and then select the **New Virtual Machine...** (**3**) option:

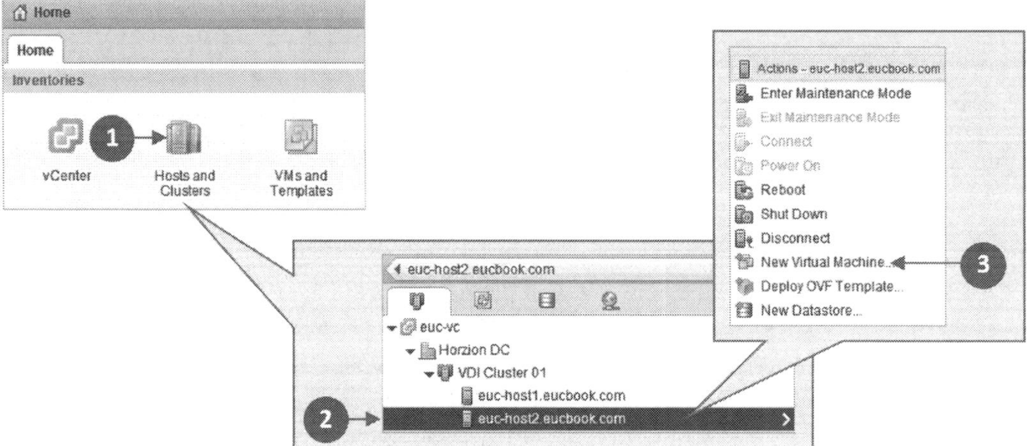

3. The **New Virtual Machine** configuration window now opens. Click on **Create a new virtual machine**.
4. Click on **Next** to move to the next configuration screen.
5. On the first part of the **Edit Settings** configuration page, the first thing we need to do is enter a name for the new virtual desktop machine.
6. For our example lab, we will call our virtual desktop machine `Windows 8 Gold Image`. Enter this, as shown in the following screenshot, in the **Enter a name for the virtual machine** box (**4**).

7. Next select the data center or folder where this virtual desktop machine is to be created. In our example, we will create it in our data center, so click on **Horizon DC** (**5**):

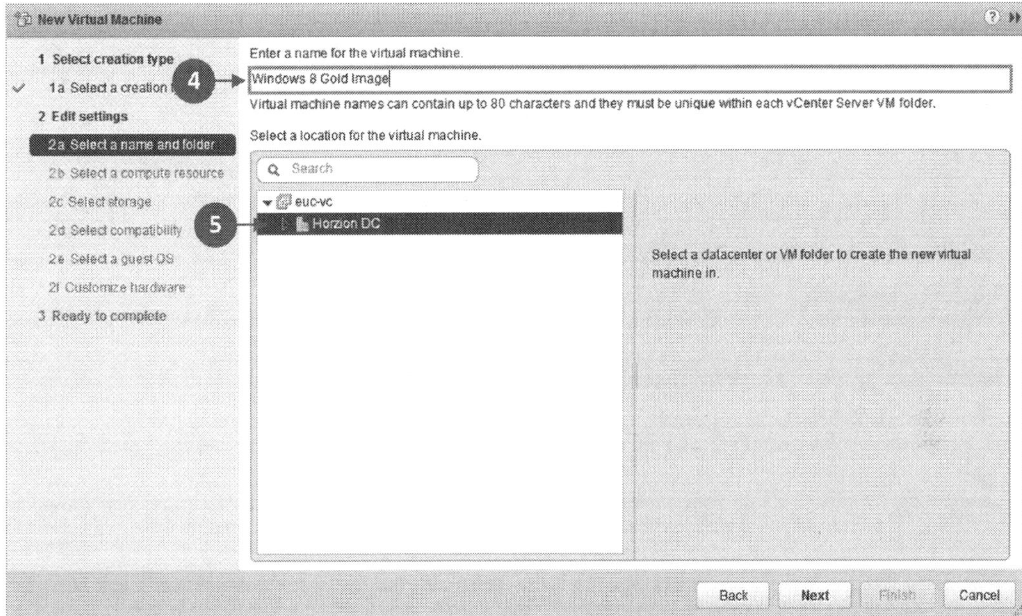

8. Click on **Next** to move to the next configuration screen.
9. On the **Select a compute resource** page, expand the **Horizon DC** data center and then go to **VDI Cluster 01**. Select the **euc-host2.eucbook.com** host server.
10. Click on **Next** to move to the next configuration screen.
11. On the **Select Storage configuration** page shown in the following screenshot, we will choose where our virtual desktop machine is going to be stored. Click on **Nimble-02** to select it as the data store.
12. Click on **Next** to move to the next configuration screen.
13. The next configuration page is **Select Compatibility**. From the drop-down menu, select **ESXi 5.5 and later**.
14. Click on **Next** to move to the next configuration screen.

15. In the next configuration step, **Select a guest OS**; we will build a Windows 8 64-bit image. From the **Guest OS Family** drop-down menu, select **Windows** (**6**), and then, from the **Guest OS Version** drop-down menu, select **Microsoft Windows 8 (64-bit)** (**7**), as shown in the following screenshot:

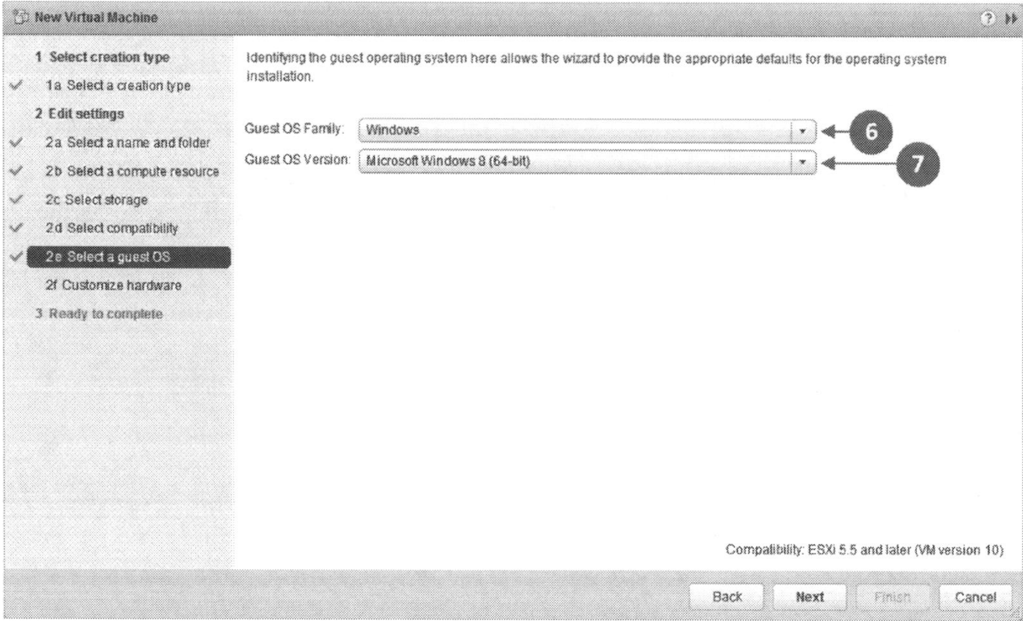

16. Click on **Next** to move to the next configuration screen.
17. On the **Customize hardware** configuration page, accept the default configuration and then click the **VM Options** tab. As with the Windows 7 build, we need to check the box for **Force BIOS Setup(*)** so that, on the first boot, the virtual desktop machine boots into the BIOS setup screen.
18. Click on **Next** to move to the next configuration screen.
19. On the **Ready to Complete** page, review all the configuration details you have entered and, when you are happy that they are all correct, click on **Finish** to build the virtual desktop machine. We should now have our second virtual desktop machine built, ready for the next steps.

Updating the virtual desktop machine BIOS

As we did with the Windows 7 virtual desktop machine, we need to power on the newly created Windows 8.1 virtual desktop machine and make some configuration changes to the BIOS.

Make exactly the same changes as made previously and disable floppy drives, serial ports, and parallel ports.

Installing the guest operating system

With the BIOS updated, we can now install the guest operating system. Connect a virtual CD/DVD drive to the virtual desktop machine and, this time, navigate to the Windows 8.1 installation media, as shown in the following screenshot:

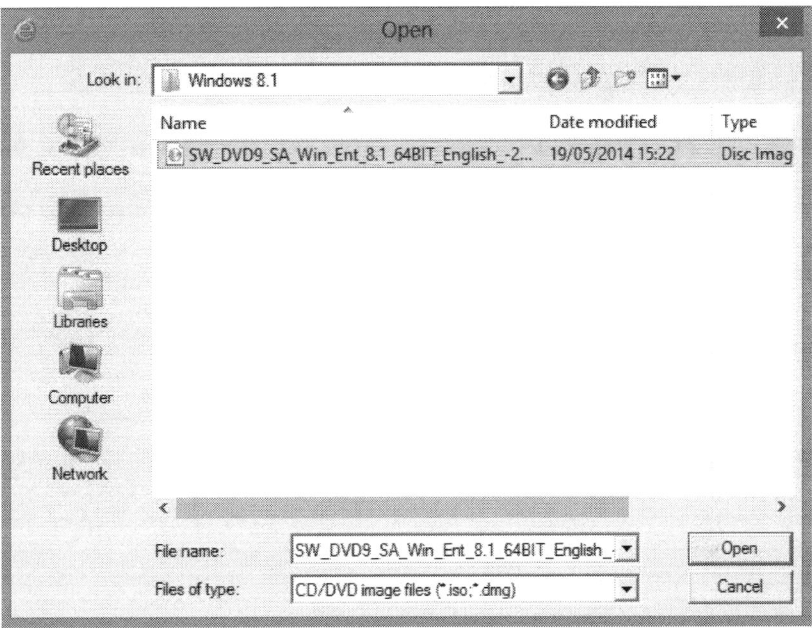

Follow the Windows 8.1 installation steps until you have built the operating system. Once built, apply any updates and patches and then also join the virtual desktop machine to the domain.

Installing VMware Tools

The next step is to install VMware Tools. Follow the steps outlined during the Windows 7 virtual desktop machine build, using the same details.

Installing applications for the parent image

The next step is to install any applications that will form a part of the parent image.

Installing the Horizon View Agent

Now we can install the Horizon View Agent. The installation process is again no different from the one we worked through during our Windows 7 build, so please refer to the previous section for more details.

Optimizing the guest operating system

Again, you can use either of the two methods of optimization that we described in the Windows 7 section of this chapter.

If you are going to use the manual script version of optimization, then we already have the optimization scripts downloaded into our shared folder; so navigate to this folder. This time, however, we will use a different version to reflect not only the different operating systems, but also the different assignments, as this virtual desktop machine is going to be dedicated to an end user.

In this example, we will use `CommandsNoPersonaManagementWin8_06032014.txt` to create our `commands.bat` file.

Once the file has been created, you need to run the script in exactly the same way as we did previously.

Post-optimization tasks

Now that we have completed all the build tasks, all that remains is releasing the IP address and then clearing up any temporary files, browser histories, and so on. Once we have finished these, power off the virtual desktop machine, which is ready for us to prepare the image as our virtual desktop machine template.

Creating a GPU-enabled virtual desktop machine

We are going to create one last virtual desktop machine. In this section, we are going to build a second Windows 7 virtual desktop machine for use with a dedicated hardware-based NVIDIA GPU card. As we discussed previously, there are two models for delivering high-end graphics. For this example, we will set up a virtual desktop machine to use vDGA.

Creating the virtual desktop machine container

The first step, as with the build process we have covered previously for Windows 7, is to build the virtual machine itself. We will follow the steps, as previously described in this chapter, to build a Windows 7 virtual desktop machine, up to the point where we configure the virtual hardware, as we need to add in the GPU card at this point.

[To make use of this feature, the hardware version of this virtual desktop machine should be Version 9 or higher. One point to highlight is that you will now need to manage the virtual desktop machine using the vSphere Web Client.]

Follow the steps to build a Windows 7 machine as described in the previous section, *Creating a Windows 7 Virtual Desktop Machine*, until you get to the **Customize Hardware** section. In the **2f Customize Hardware** section, under the **Virtual Hardware** tab, click on the drop-down arrow (**1**) for new device, and, from the list of options, click on **PCI Device** (**2**). Click on **Add** (**3**) to add the new device:

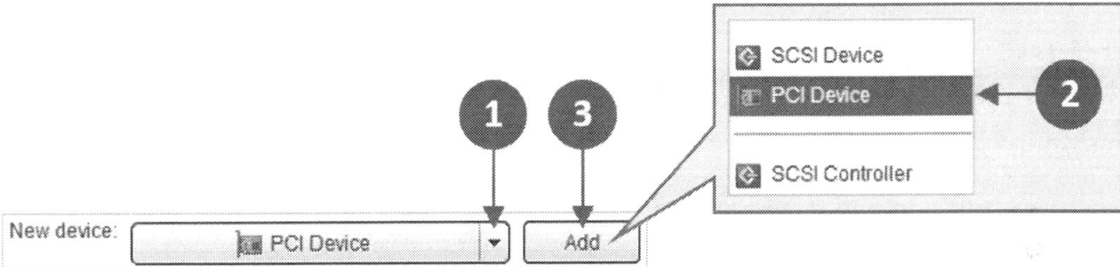

You will now see the following dialog box. Select one of the two NVIDIA cards from the drop-down box. It's also worth noting the warning information around some of the operations that are not available on the virtual desktop machine:

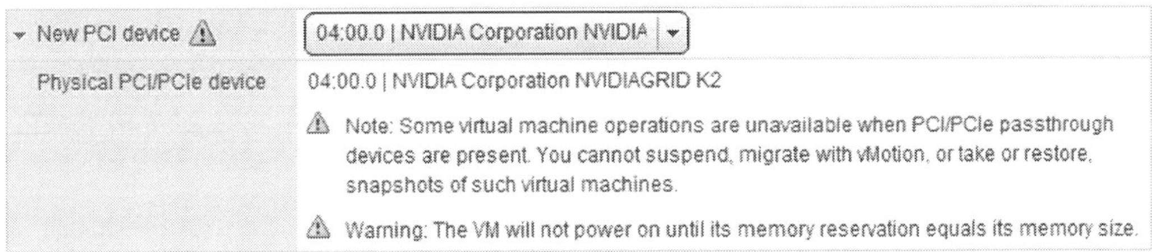

With the additional hardware now added, and the NVIDIA card added (**4**) in the **Virtual Hardware** section, the final task is to tick the box for **Reserve all guest memory (All locked)**, (**5**) as shown in the following screenshot:

If you do not configure memory reservation, then the virtual desktop machine will fail to power on, as it can't guarantee that the memory will be available.

You will also need to follow these steps for each vDGA-enabled virtual desktop machine you want to create and build. You need to do this because, being a 1:1 assignment, each machine has its own dedicated GPU memory address.

The final step in the building of the virtual desktop machine process is to add an entry to the **virtual machine configuration file** (**VMX file**). This is only a requirement if your virtual desktop machine has more than 2 GB of memory configured. This is a limitation of the 32-bit hardware and 32-bit operating systems that causes a PC to appear to have less memory available than is actually installed.

There is an amount of system memory that is hidden and unavailable that varies depending on the chipset, BIOS, physical memory installed, the amount of video RAM installed on the graphics cards, and the number and type of PCI cards configured. More than 1 GB of the 32-bit system memory can be unavailable when 4 GB of physical memory and multiple 3D cards with large amounts of video memory are installed.

Edit the VMX file and add the line `pciHole.start = "2048"`, as shown in the following screenshot:

```
pciHole.start = "2048"
pciPassthru0.present = "TRUE"
pciPassthru0.deviceId = "11bf"
pciPassthru0.vendorId = "10de"
pciPassthru0.systemId = "51baead3-61b2-2958-6a0d-90b11c18c094"
pciPassthru0.id = "07:00.0"
pciPassthru0.pciSlotNumber = "192"
```

With these steps complete, follow the steps to update the BIOS before moving on to installing the guest operating system.

Installing the operating system for GPU-enabled desktops

In our example, we are going to build a Windows 7 virtual desktop machine for our high-end graphics. To install the operating system, follow the steps described in the *Installing the guest operating system* section under the *Creating a Windows 7 Virtual Desktop Machine* section of this chapter, but with one difference.

After you have installed the Horizon View Agent, you need to install the NVIDIA drivers on the virtual desktop machine. The drivers can be downloaded at `http://tinyurl.com/mzf2b33`.

When you install the NVIDIA driver software, make sure you select all the components to be installed and don't use the express option. Express will miss out some of the key components to run in a virtual desktop machine.

Once you have the drivers installed, complete the operating system setup by installing any additional applications and then performing the optimization steps. It's probably worth checking that the graphics card has been installed correctly, by checking the device manager of the virtual desktop machine, as shown in the following screenshot:

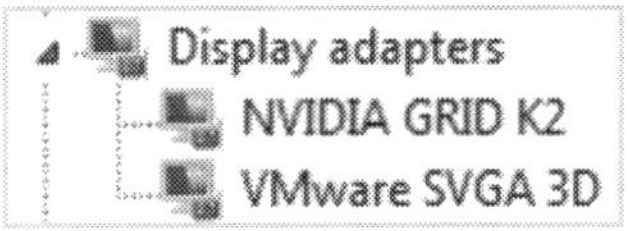

You should now have a GPU-enabled virtual desktop image ready to be prepared for delivery to end users, which we will cover in the next sections of this chapter.

Due to the nature of these virtual desktop machines, the best way to deploy additional machines will be by cloning the virtual desktop machines and then making sure that each one is assigned to its own GPU resource.

Completing the GPU-enabled desktop build

With the operating system now built and the NVIDIA components installed, we can follow the remaining tasks to complete our build. These are all covered in the previous section and are listed as follows:

- Installing VMware Tools
- Installing applications for the parent image
- Installing the Horizon View Agent
- Optimizing the guest operating system
- Post-optimization tasks

With these tasks complete and with our three virtual desktop machines built and ready, in the next section we are going to perform one last task to prepare them to be used to create virtual desktop machines for your end users.

Preparing virtual desktops for delivery

Now that we have three fully optimized virtual desktop machine parent images that can be used by Horizon View, the next stage of the process is to prepare them for delivery to the end users.

There are two different ways in which a desktop needs to be prepared, depending on whether you are using a full clone desktop or a linked clone desktop.

Pool design – a quick recap

We will cover creating desktop pools in *Chapter 7, Managing and Configuring Desktop Pools*, but just as a quick recap around pool design. You will typically have a desktop pool for each type of virtual desktop machine you want to deliver, probably by use case or department. In this chapter, we have built three different types of virtual desktop machines:

- **Windows 7**: This is to be used as a floating assignment, linked clone desktop

- **Windows 8**: This is to be used as a dedicated, full clone desktop
- **Windows 7**: This is to be used as a dedicated, full clone with hardware-enabled GPU

As we have both linked clone and full clone desktops, the preparation method for each is different. We will cover this in the next sections.

Creating a snapshot for linked clones

For our Windows 7 floating, linked clone virtual desktop machine, we will need to take a snapshot of the virtual desktop machine using vCenter and the vSphere Web Client. Once you have taken the snapshot, it can then be used by the View Administrator to create a new desktop pool for virtual desktop machines using linked clones. It will be used to create the replica in View Composer:

1. Log in to the vSphere Web Client and navigate to the **Windows 7 Gold Image** virtual desktop machine (**1**), ensuring that it's powered off.
2. Right-click and select **Take Snapshot...** (**2**), as shown in the following screenshot:

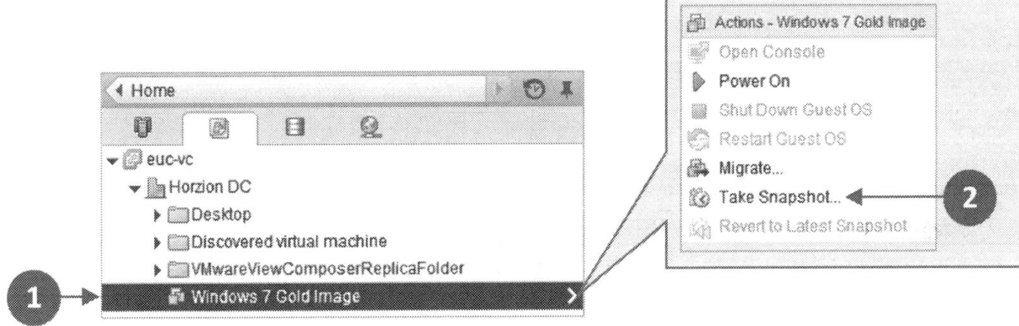

3. You will now see the **Take VM Snapshot for Windows 7 Gold Image** dialog box. Type in a name for this snapshot in the **Name** box (**3**) and a description in the **Description** box (**4**):

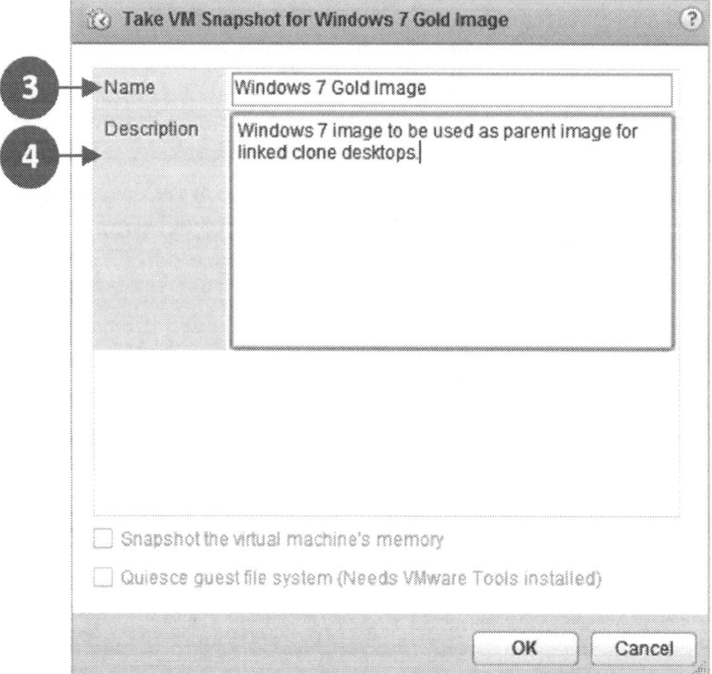

4. Click on **OK** when you are ready to create the snapshot.
5. To check that the snapshot has been taken, navigate to the snapshot manager.
6. To do this, from the vSphere Web Client, highlight the **Windows 7 Gold Image** virtual desktop machine.
7. Now click on **All vCenter Actions**, then Snapshots, and finally, select **Manage Snapshots...**.
8. You will now see the **Manage VM Snapshots for Windows 7 Gold Image** dialog box, where you will be able to see the snapshot that we have just taken, as shown in the following screenshot:

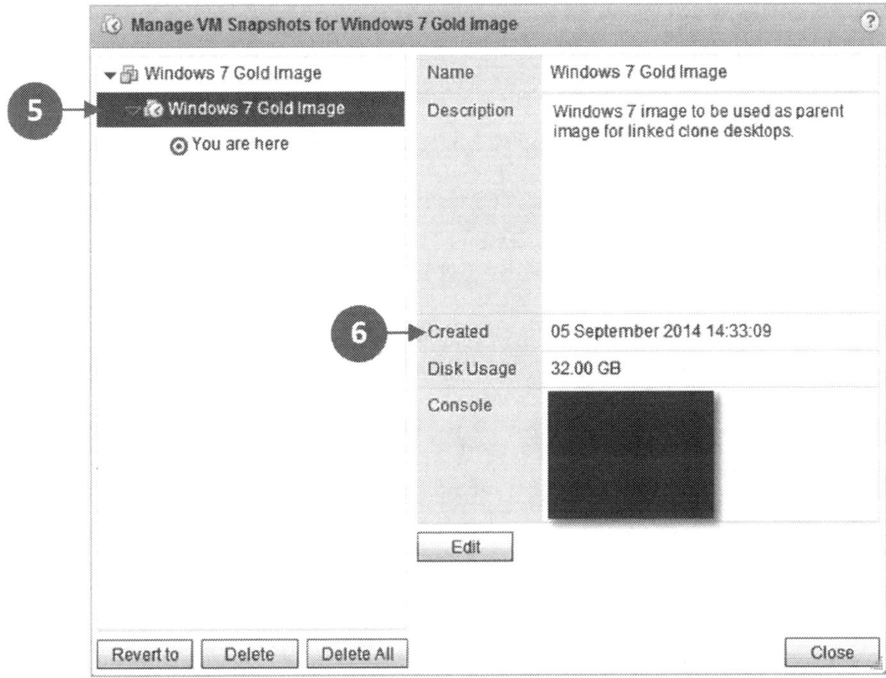

9. You will now be able to see how many snapshots have been taken (**5**) and also when they were created (**6**).
10. Click on **Close** to close the snapshot manager.

We now have a snapshot that we can work from. We will see how this snapshot is used to deliver the linked clone virtual desktop machines in *Chapter 7, Managing and Configuring Desktop Pools*.

Creating a template for full clones

For our Windows 8.1 and Windows 7 GPU-enabled virtual desktop machines, we are going to perform the tasks described in this section. To use these virtual desktop machines as parent virtual desktop machines for full clone desktops, we will firstly need to convert them into a virtual machine template, using vCenter and the vSphere Web Client. Once that's completed, we can use the View Administrator to create new desktop pools (one for Windows 8 and one for Windows 7 GPU), based on the virtual desktop machines using these templates for each desktop pool.

In our example lab, we will use the Windows 8 image because, in the next chapter, we will create a full clone, dedicated desktop pool based on that image. The process for the Windows 7 GPU-enabled virtual desktop machine is exactly the same at this point. However, the pool configuration will be different, as we will see in *Chapter 7, Managing and Configuring Desktop Pools*.

Log in to the vSphere Web Client. Navigate to the **Windows 8 Gold Image** virtual desktop machine (**1**) and right-click. Then, from the menu, click on **Clone to Template...** (**2**). This is shown in the following screenshot:

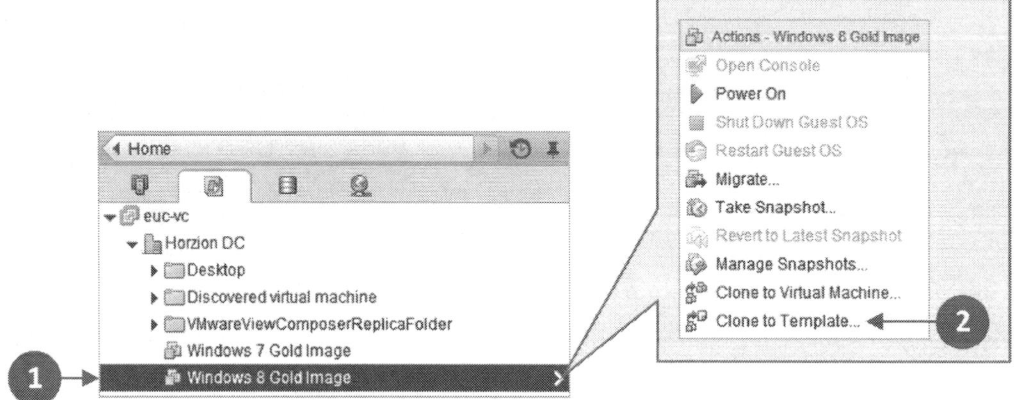

You could also select the **Convert to Template** option, which turns the parent image into a template. However, it's easier if you leave the original virtual desktop machine in place so that you can go back and update it before creating additional clones.

We will see how this template is used to deliver the virtual desktop machines in *Chapter 7, Managing and Configuring Desktop Pools*.

Summary

In this chapter, we have built three virtual desktop machine images that will act as our parent images. We installed the guest operating systems, optimized them to run as Horizon View virtual desktop machines, and then prepared them to be delivered to the end users.

In the next chapter, we will configure the View Administrator and create our desktop pools, ready to deliver our virtual desktop machines to our end users, which will allow them to connect and start using the virtual desktop machines we have just built.

7

Managing and Configuring Desktop Pools

After preparing our desktop images to be used by our View pools in the previous chapter, we will now look at how to create and manage our desktop pools within Horizon View. In *Chapter 2, An Overview of Horizon View Architecture and its Components*, and *Chapter 3, Design and Deployment Considerations*, we spoke about the use cases for the different types of desktop pools within View. To reiterate, the types of pools we have available are as follows:

- Automated desktop pool
- Manual desktop pool
- RDS desktop pool

An automated pool is a collection of desktops that are automatically created from a snapshot or a virtual machine template by Horizon View within your virtual infrastructure. Desktops within an automated pool may be created on demand or in advance. They can also be deleted or refreshed on log off. Automated pools are generally the most widely used pools within Horizon View deployments, as they allow great flexibility for administration.

A manual desktop pool provides access to an existing desktop, whether it is virtual or physical, as long as it has the View Agent installed on it. We generally use manual pools as a niche use case due to the administrative overhead. Also, we would generally use an image management tool, such has Horizon Mirage or SCCM, with these machines to simplify management as far as possible.

Finally, an RDS pool is a great way of offering high levels of consolidation for task workers within your Horizon View environment. An example of where an RDS desktop might be suitable would be call centers, where the user is using one or two simple applications. We will cover RDS desktops in *Chapter 10, Delivering Remote Applications with Horizon Advanced.*

Automated desktop pools

As automated desktop pools will be the largest use case within our Horizon View environment, we will start by looking at how to create and manage them.

As we start running through the relevant wizards to create our first desktop pool, we will be asked a number of questions that will further define how our users will use the desktop pool. The first of these questions is, "How is the desktop going to be assigned to the users?"

We will get two dedicated choices, with/without automatic assignment and with/without floating. Dedicated desktops are generally used due to something being stored or configured within the user's desktop that is important for that user, or due to application-specific nuances (for example, a requirement or licensing restriction that a specific Mac address must be used). This means that, every time they want to connect to a desktop and use it, they will always be given the same desktop. With a dedicated desktop, you can further include a persistent disk to hold all the changes that happen to the desktop while the user is using it; thus, if we need to refresh or recompose the desktop, the user won't lose the customizations or data that are important to them. However, we need to keep in mind that there is no easy way to back up the persistent disks and, as such, we might decide to use Horizon Mirage to protect and update these desktops. This means that, when we go further through the wizard, we need to ensure we choose full clone rather than linked clone for these desktops.

Floating desktops mean every time the user connects to the desktop pool, they will be randomly assigned a desktop from the pool. With this configuration, it generally offers the greatest freedom for the administrator to be able to maintain and update the desktops using Horizon View. However, we need to ensure the user's data and customizations are layered to the desktop using View Persona Management or other technology.

We will also need to decide whether we will use linked clone desktops, utilizing the View Composer technology discussed in *Chapter 2, An Overview of Horizon View Architecture and its Components*, or full clones. The main benefits of using the linked clone technology is the speed of deployment for the desktops and the space savings available. However, we need to be mindful of the interoperability of linked clones with other technology such as Horizon Mirage.

Dedicated desktops

We will now move through the wizards to create our first desktop pool from one of the desktop images we created in an earlier chapter, perform the following steps:

1. Inside the **Horizon View Administrator** page, you need to navigate to **Catalog** (1) | **Desktop Pools** (2) | **Add** (3):

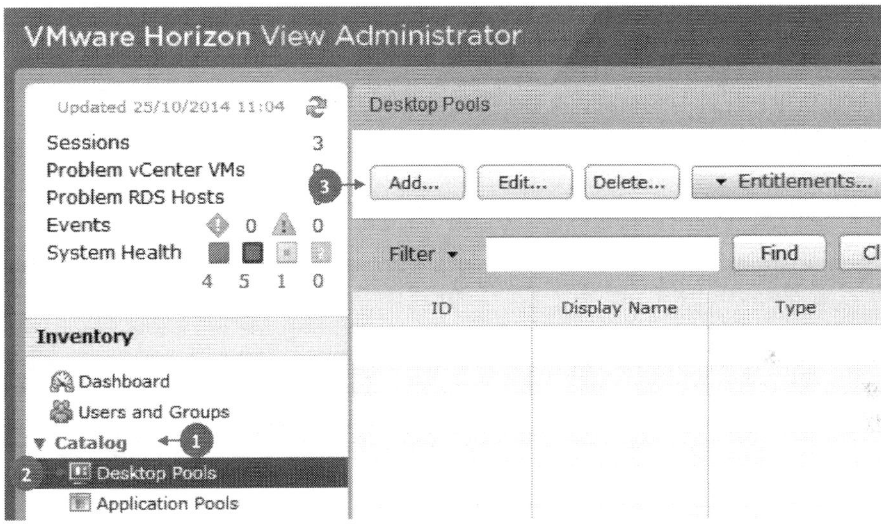

2. You will now see the **Add Desktop Pool** wizard appear on screen. Select **Automated Desktop Pool** (**1**) and then click on **Next** (**2**). When selecting the various types of desktop pool that are available, the description on the right-hand side will change, reminding you of the differences between types, as shown in the following screenshot:

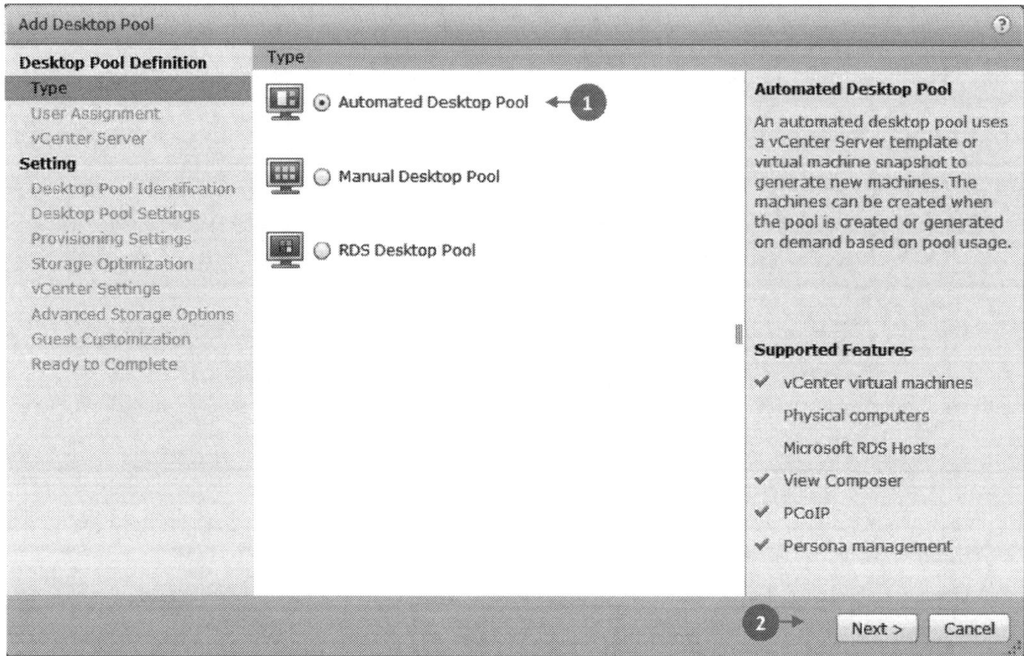

3. You will now need to select **Dedicated** (**1**) from the **User Assignment** page of the wizard. The **Enable automatic assignment** (**2**) option will already be selected on screen. This means the desktops will be assigned to the users on a first-come-first-serve basis. If for some reason you need to ensure a user is assigned a specific desktop, then you will need to un-tick this box. Finally, click on **Next** (**3**):

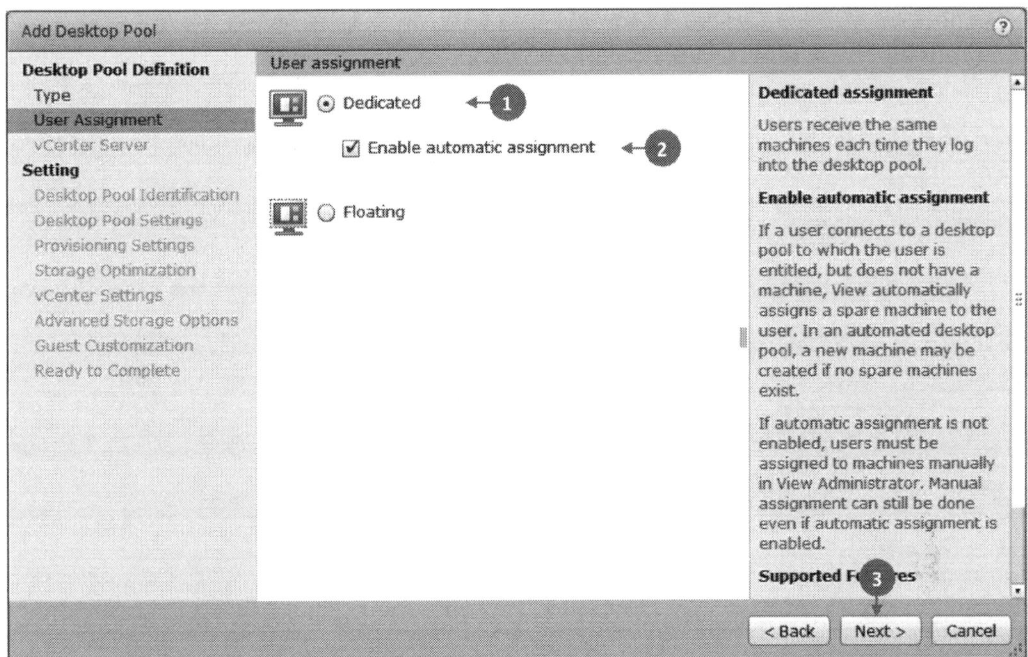

4. You will now have the option to configure your desktop pool as either **Full virtual machines** or **View Composer linked clones**. For this first pool, we will select **View Composer linked clones**. We need to keep in mind that linked clones are not compatible with Horizon Mirage, so if we want to use these two technologies in conjunction with each other, then we need to select full clone virtual machines.

5. Once we select **View Composer linked clones** (**1**), we need to select the relevant vCenter Server (**2**) and finally click on **Next >** (**3**):

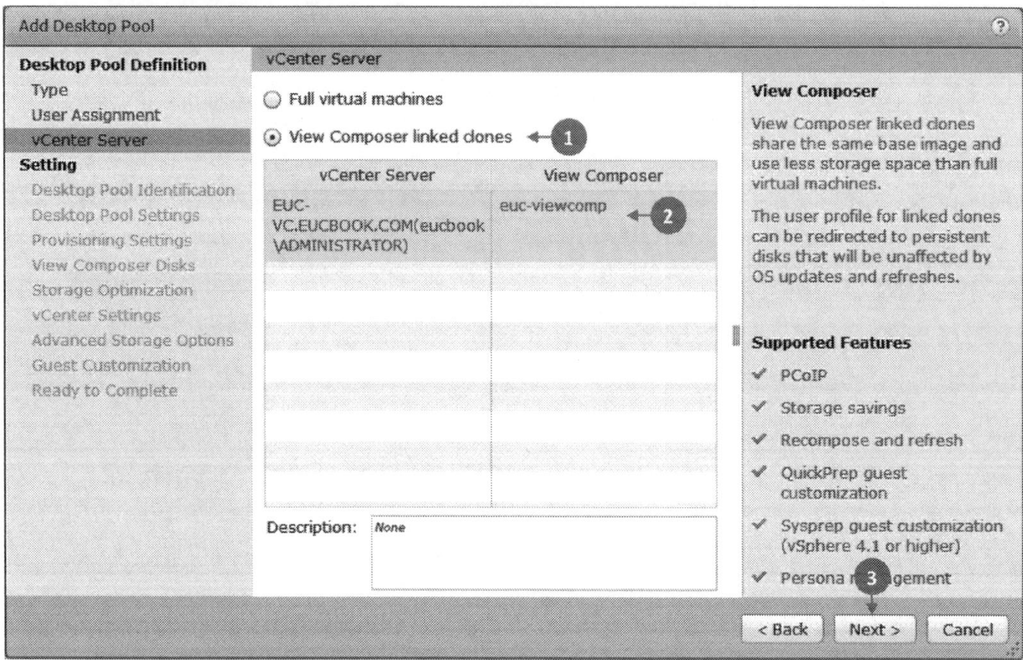

6. On the **Desktop Pool Identification** screen, you start configuring how your desktop will look to the users and be known to administrators. Under the **ID** (**1**) option, we need to configure a unique ID by which the desktop pool will be known to administrators. **Display name** (**2**) depicts how the desktop will be depicted to the end user, and **Description** (**3**) should contain a meaningful description of the desktop pool. Once this is complete, click on **Next >** (**4**):

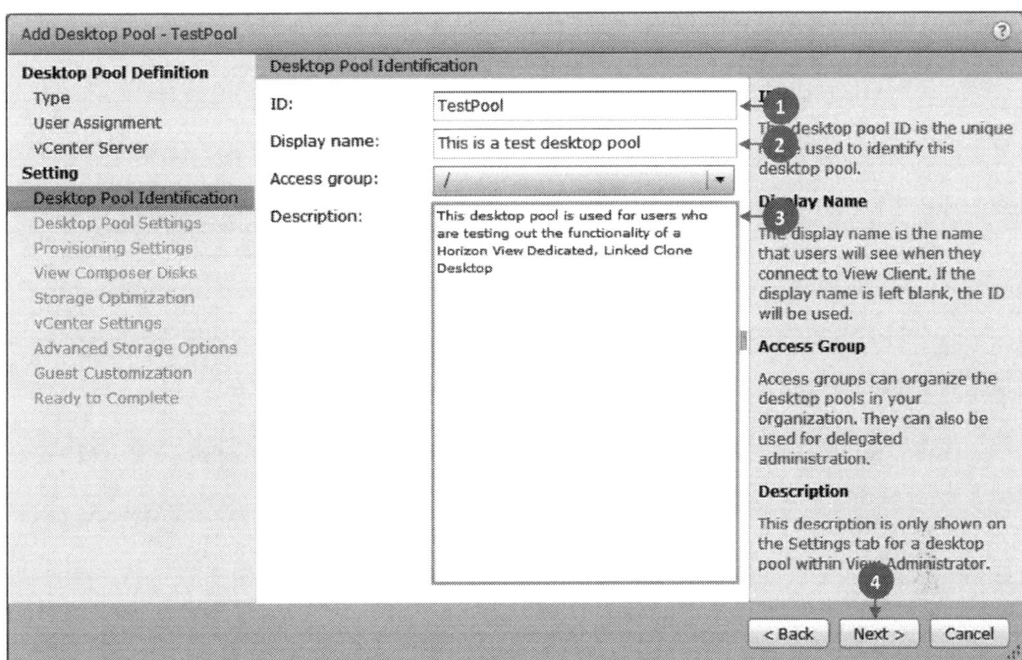

7. As you can now see from the upcoming screenshot, in the **Desktop Pool Settings** page we start configuring the settings that will define the way the desktop acts for users before they connect, while they use it, and finally, once they disconnect it.

8. Under **General**, we have **State** (**1**) and **Connection Server restrictions** (**2**). **State** defines whether the pool should be **Enabled** or **Disabled** when it is first created. If a desktop pool is enabled and entitled to users when it is created, the desktops will be provisioned and made available for the users to connect to. If you set **State** to **Disabled**, provisioning will not happen and the desktop will not be made available. You might wish to set **State** to **Disabled** if you are pre-configuring a new pool for users. With **Connection Server restrictions**, we are able to select tags associated with our Connection Servers to restrict where the users can connect from—for example, from inside or outside the company, as we have previously discussed:

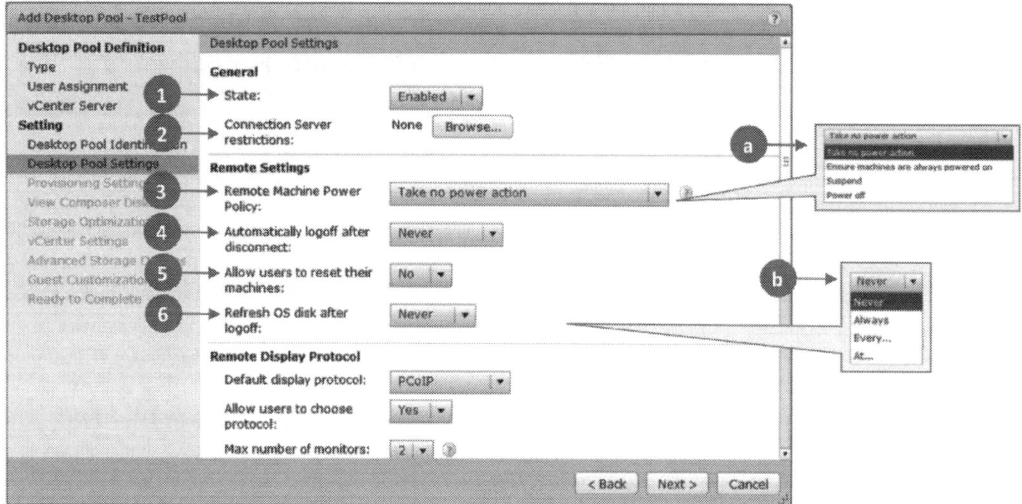

9. Under **Remote Settings**, we configure how the virtual desktops will behave in a number of situations and how the user is able to interact with their desktop.

10. The **Remote Machine Power Policy** option (**3**) depicts how the desktop behaves with regard to its state after maintenance operations and when a user disconnects. With **Take no power action** selected, the desktop will remain in the last state it was left in. For example, if the desktop was left powered on, it will remain powered on. With the **Ensure machines are always powered on** option, the desktop will always be restored to a powered on status after being shut down by an end user or an administrative task. The other options here follow a similar logic.

    The most important thing is to understand your use case and choose the correct options as appropriate. For example, if you have 200 users, all planning on logging in within a 10-minute window at 9:00 AM and the desktops are powered off or suspended, then this could cause some delay and a large performance spike while the desktops are resumed or powered on. Alternatively, if you are using a dedicated desktop model with a shift-based work pattern and choose to leave the desktops always powered on, this could cause your environment to be over allocated terms of resources.

11. With **Automatically logoff after disconnect** (**4**), we are selecting the option where a user simply disconnects from their desktop and doesn't choose to log off. We have three options, **Immediately**, **Never**, or **After**. With the **After** setting, we can choose after how many minutes the desktop will log off. Again, how you configure this setting will very much depend on how your users will use the desktop. Very rarely do we choose to log off the desktop immediately. In case the user has only temporarily disconnected from their desktop or been disconnected, we should give them at least a 5-10 minute cooling off period to stop this.

12. **Allow users to reset their machines** (**5**) is self-explanatory. If this option is set to **Yes**, it means that the users are able to use a reset button, either in the front of their thin client or from a menu in the software client, to hard-reset the VDI desktop. This can be useful to allow the end users to perform troubleshooting steps without the assistance of IT. However, it can also cause some confusion when the end user believes they are simply resetting the thin client but instead reset their desktop, resulting in loss of work.

13. The **Refresh OS disk after logoff** option (**6**) sets how the desktop behaves when a user has disconnected. We have four options to select from, **Never**, **Always**, **Every**, or **At**. With **Never**, the operating system disk will never be refreshed automatically; this will result in the linked clone growing over time, especially if a persistent disk and/or a disposable disk isn't configured in the later stages of this wizard. By refreshing the OS disk, the disk is refreshed to a snapshot that is taken when the desktop is originally created. Without a persistent disk, redirected profiles, and so on, all user settings/data will be lost. With the setting set to **Always**, the desktop will be refreshed every time the user logs off. With **Every**, we can set the number of days after which the desktop will be refreshed. Lastly, with **At**, we can set at what percentage of OS disk utilization the desktop will be refreshed. Again, how you configure this setting will depend greatly on your use cases and configuration:

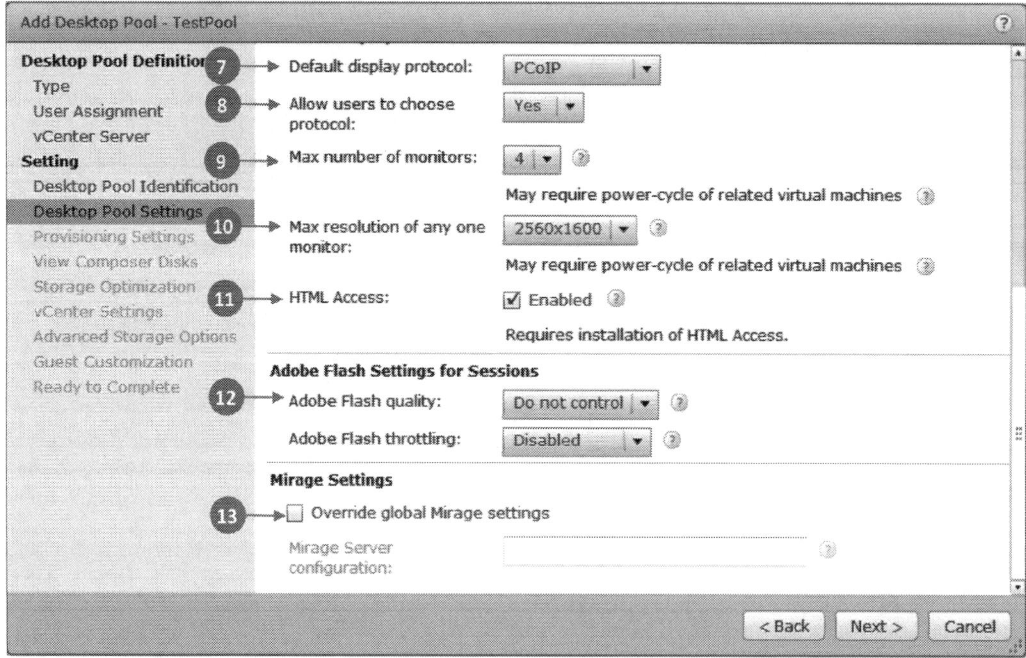

14. As you continue through the **Desktop Pool Settings** page, you will configure the **Remote Desktop Protocol**. Within this area, we can select what is going to be the **Default display protocol** (7), we get an option of **PCoIP** or **RDP**, and we can also select whether to **Allow users to choose protocol** (8). Usually, we choose PCoIP as our default protocol, unless there is a specific use case that determines where RDP must be used—for example, where more than four screens are required or where a user will always be connected behind a very strict outbound firewall. The same would apply if you wish the user to be able to select a different protocol.
15. You can select the **Max number of monitors** (9) a user can use and what the **Max resolution of any one monitor** (10) is going to be. By selecting more monitors and/or higher resolutions, more video memory will be required and, potentially, more CPU resource will be consumed when an end user connects from a source that utilizes the resolutions or multiple monitors. However, with modern servers, the difference may be limited under normal circumstances. So it is often easiest to select four monitors and the highest resolution.
16. By enabling **HTML Access** (11), users will be able to connect to their desktops using HTML 5 from the Horizon View portal. This can be useful when users connect from home or other devices, where it is not possible to install the relevant client—for example, from an Internet café (do they still exist?!) or Chromebooks.
17. The final options on this screen are to control **Adobe Flash quality** (12) and whether we should choose to **Override global Mirage settings** for configuration of the Mirage Server (13).
18. On the **Provisioning Settings** screen, we configure how View should automatically provision the desktops for our desktop pool. In the **Basic** setting (1), we will choose whether provisioning is enabled or not, and what should happen if there is an error during provisioning.
19. Under the **Virtual Machine Naming** section (2), we can choose whether we wish to **Specify names manually** or **Use a naming pattern**. It is usual to use a naming pattern, unless there is some reason your desktops need unique noncontiguous names. While using the naming pattern, you are able to specify how many digits the unique number should be or where the unique number is to be appended in the name. This can be done simply by using `{n}` in the name to set the location, or by adding `{n:fixed=2}` for two digits, `{n:fixed=3}` for three, and so on. This will ensure the desktops appear in numerical order in. Use normal text or insert obj type the vSphere Client when created.

20. You are going to configure the **Desktop Pool Sizing** option (**3**) that sets the **Max number of machines** option in the pool, the **Number of spare (powered on) machines** that should be waiting for users to connect to, and the **Minimum number of ready (provisioned) machines during View Composer maintenance operations**. How you configure these options is going to be critical to the success of the pool within your View Solution. We need to ensure there are enough desktops provisioned and available for the users they are required to connect to. We also need to ensure that we are able to meet user demand during maintenance operations.
21. Besides the settings shown in the following screenshot, we also need to configure whether these desktops should be provisioned upfront or on-demand. This can be an area that can often cause issue. If you are going to provision all the desktops upfront, we need to ensure that we do this at a time when the increase in performance is not going to have a knock-on effect for end users. If we choose to provision on-demand, we need to ensure there are enough desktops ready to meet user demand without causing long delays.

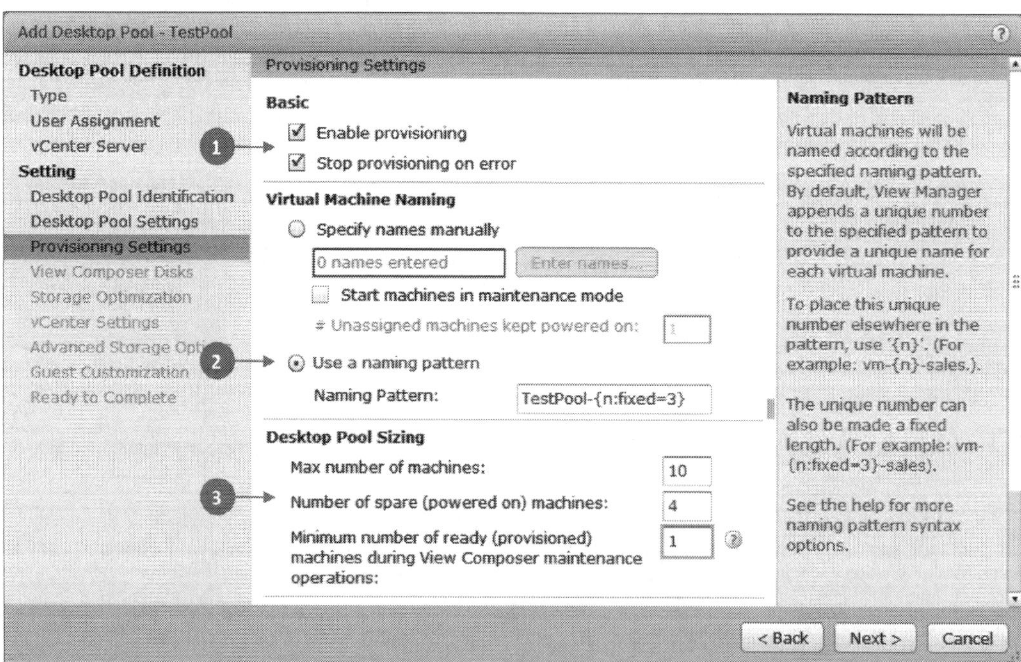

22. On the **View Composer Disks** screen, you can configure **Persistent Disk** and/or **Disposable File Redirection**. Careful consideration needs to be made as to whether you need to utilize these within your pool architecture or not. With a persistent disk, the Windows profile will be redirected to a dedicated disk that will be kept even if the OS disk is refreshed. This can be a great way to protect user configuration. However, you might also wish to investigate whether View Persona Management can offer you similar benefits without the complexity. The disposable disk contains all page and temporary files and is refreshed after every desktop reboot. This can be a great way to reduce the size of the linked clone between desktop refreshes. When configuring either of these, ensure you set the sizes appropriately for your use cases. Usually, a POC or desktop assessment will help you understand how large these need to be. Items such as whether an Outlook local cache is being used can effect the size of the persistent disk dramatically.

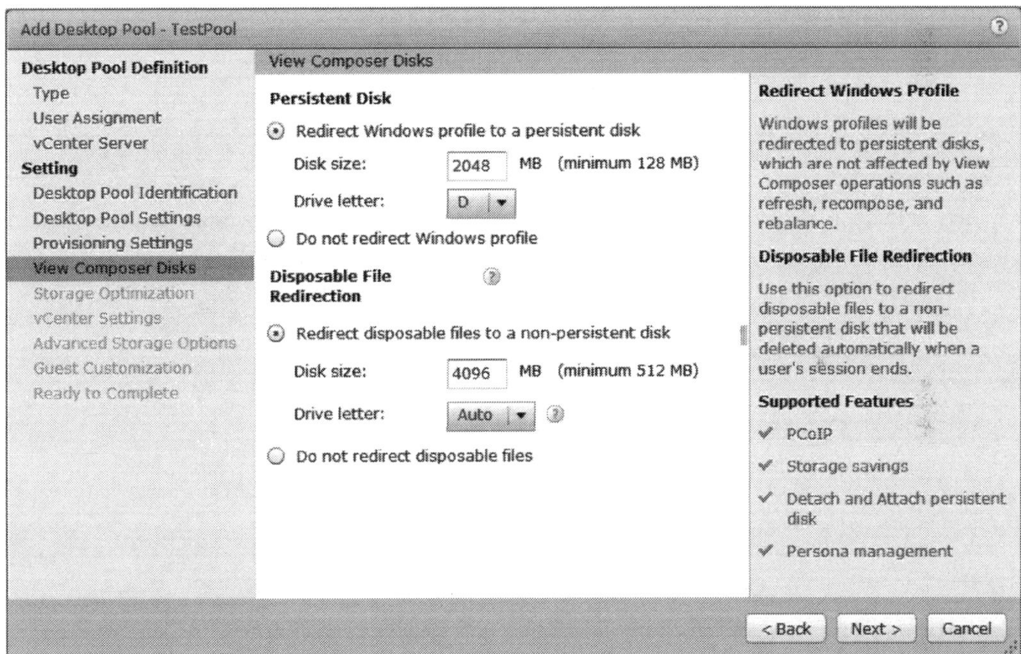

23. On the **Storage Optimization** screen, we are able to configure advanced options with regard to storage management. On this screen, we are able to configure the use of VMware Virtual SAN or, alternatively, the location of the various disks that we have selected to use within our desktop pool. Depending on our storage design, we might wish to place replica images on SSD storage and OS disks on a different tier of storage. In our environment, we are using a Nimble hybrid array, meaning the performance is equal across the array. Hence, we have no reason to place the replica on a different disk to the OS. However, we could choose to place the persistent disks on a different volume to allow a data protection policy to be put in place to protect the data on the persistent disks:

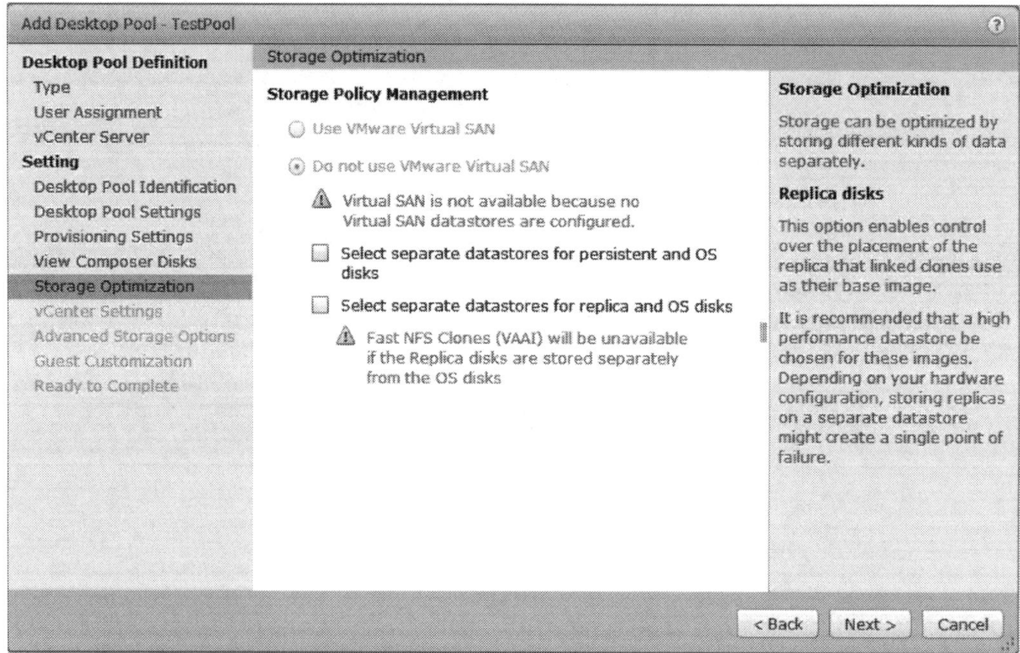

24. You are now in a position to select the VM and the snapshot that you have created, ready for your desktop pool, and also to configure where your linked clone desktops will be stored and run within your virtual infrastructure.

25. On the **vCenter Settings** screen, you will first need to select the **Parent VM** option (**1**). When you select **Browse** option, you will see the **Select Parent VM** (**a**) screen appear. From here you can select any valid VM. These will be VMs that contain snapshots and have the Horizon View Agent installed within them. The VMs that will be filtered from the View by default are Virtual Machines running on ESX/ESXi hosts older than 4.0, VMs that don't have a snapshot, VMs with unsupported guest OS, VMs already used by another desktop pool, and View Composer Replicas. It is possible to add these VMs to the View by pressing the **Show all partner VMs** button. However, if they are not compatible, you will not be able to select them.
26. You will now move through the wizard, selecting the relevant **Snapshot** (**2**) to be used to create your linked clone pool, the folder location (**3**) where the VM will be stored, the host or cluster where your desktop pool is to run from (**4**), and the resource pool (**5**).
27. Once these are selected, you are in a position to select where your VM will be stored. The configuration you have chosen will depend on how many datastores you need to configure. In the following example, we will configure the OS disk datastore, persistent disk datastore, and replica disk datastore. As we are using accelerated Nimble Storage, we have no real reason to place these on separate datastores to enhance performance. However, we will choose to place the persistent disks on a datastore that has a snapshot and replication policy for data security:

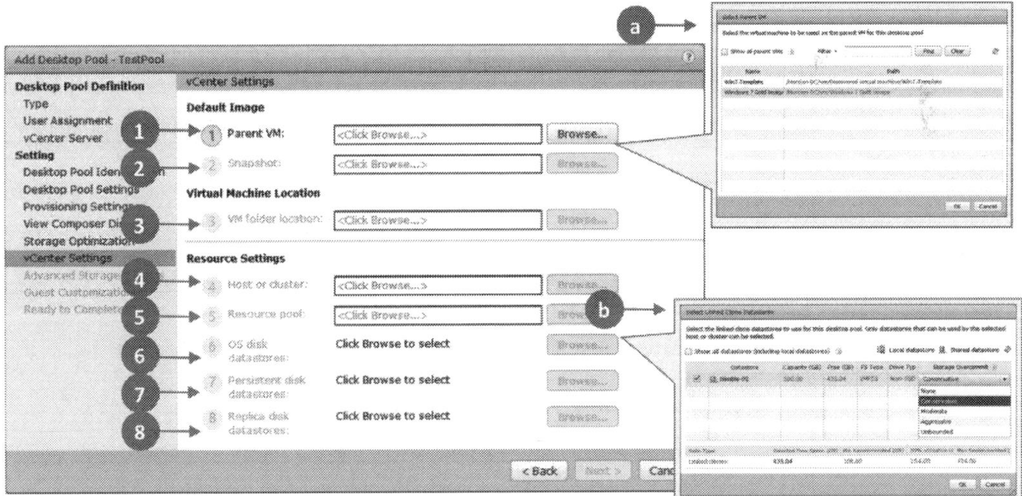

28. As you can see in the preceding screenshot, when you choose **Browse** option next to the datastore configurations, you will be given a filtered view of the recommended datastores. Local storage will be hidden from View due to the inability to offer HA to local storage. If you are using storage, for instance, a Fusion I/O card, you will need to select the **Show all datastores (including local datastores)** option, as shown in the following screenshot. You will also have to select the level up to which you wish to overcommit the datastores with your linked clone desktops. The overcommit level represents the multiplier that, when applied to the capacity of the full desktop, gives you the amount you wish to allow in the datastore. **Conservative** will allow you four times, **Moderate** will allow you seven, and **Aggressive** will allow you 14. For example, if the size of your full desktop was 10 GB and you had a 100 GB datastore, **None** would allow you to provision approximately 10 desktops, **Conservative** would allow you 40, **Moderate** would allow 70, **Aggressive** would allow 150, and **Unbounded** would have no restriction. You need to be careful with choosing how you are going to configure this setting, and the only way to judge is to monitor linked clone growth during the POC:

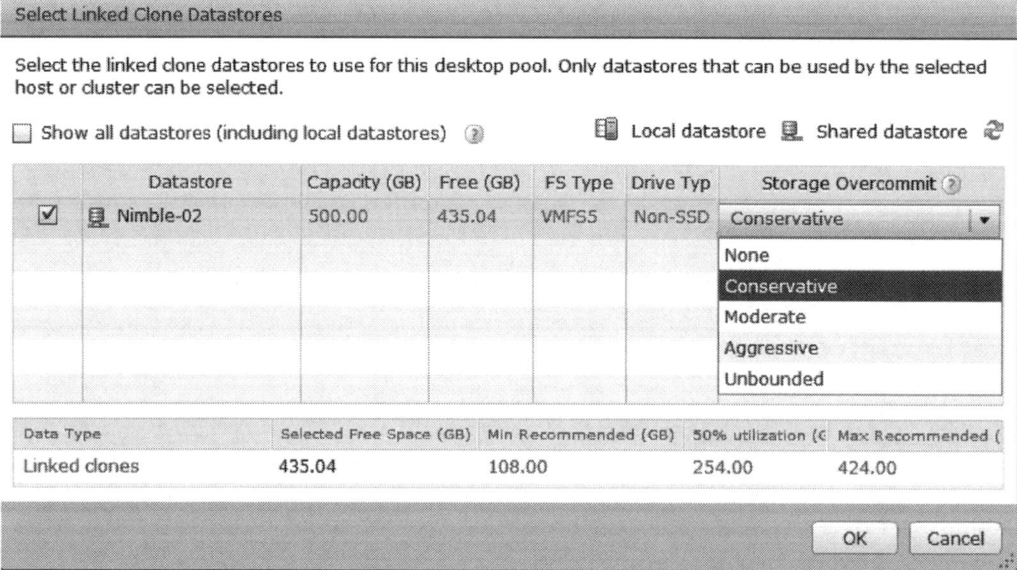

29. You will now move on to the **Advanced Storage Configuration** page. On block-based storage, you will only be configuring the advanced settings for the View Storage Accelerator. With NFS storage, you can configure VAAI API offloading of the linked clones to the storage device. When it comes to the View Storage Accelerator, you will configure whether it is used with the OS disks only, or OS disks and persistent disks. As the View Storage Accelerator provides read-only performance, it will benefit read-intensive disks the most, such as OS disks. However, it does depend on your workload. We are also able to configure the blackout times for cache regeneration and space reclamation. We should set this to ensure that these operations won't be scheduled during working hours and ensure users are not affected:

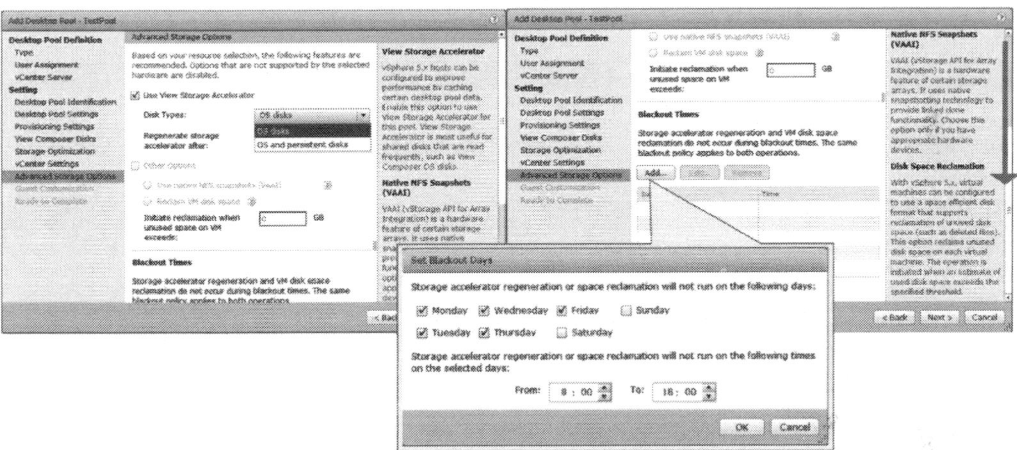

30. You will now reach the **Guest Customization** page. Here, we will configure how our desktops are going to be uniquely customized in terms of the hostname added to your domain. We have two choices, QuickPrep or Sysprep. QuickPrep will allow you to prepare your desktops in a quicker fashion than Sysprep; however, no unique SID will be created. Sysprep will create a new SID but will take longer for each desktop to prepare. Which one you choose to use will depend on your use cases. It is recommended that you test your configuration during the POC:

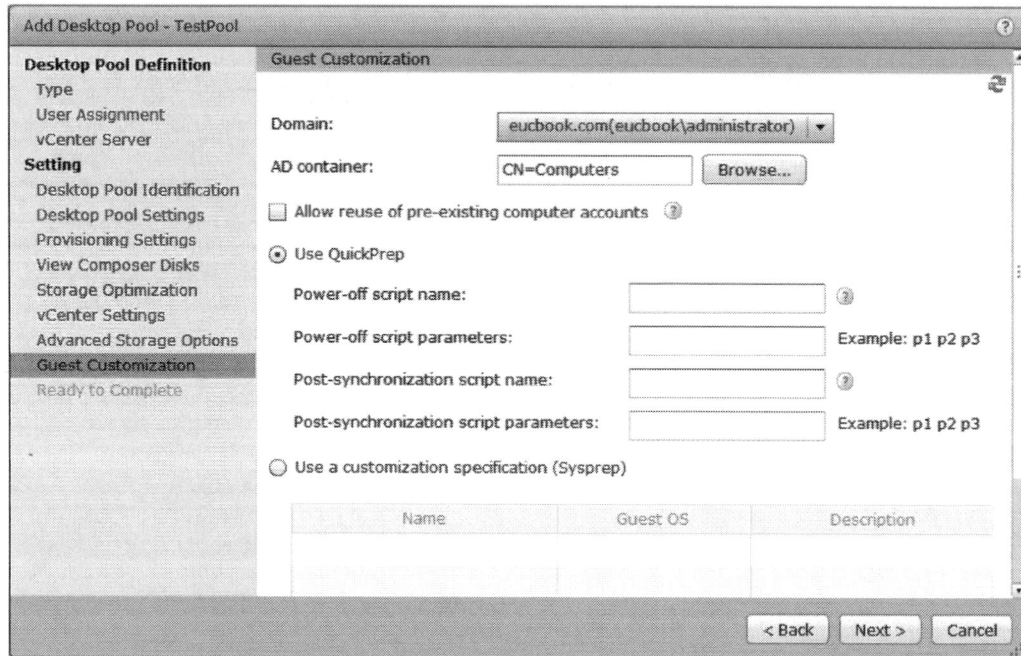

We are now ready to finalize the wizard, by reviewing our selections; we will need to entitle our users by either selecting the **Entitles users after this wizard finishes** selection box at the top right of the screen or through the View Administrator after the wizard closes:

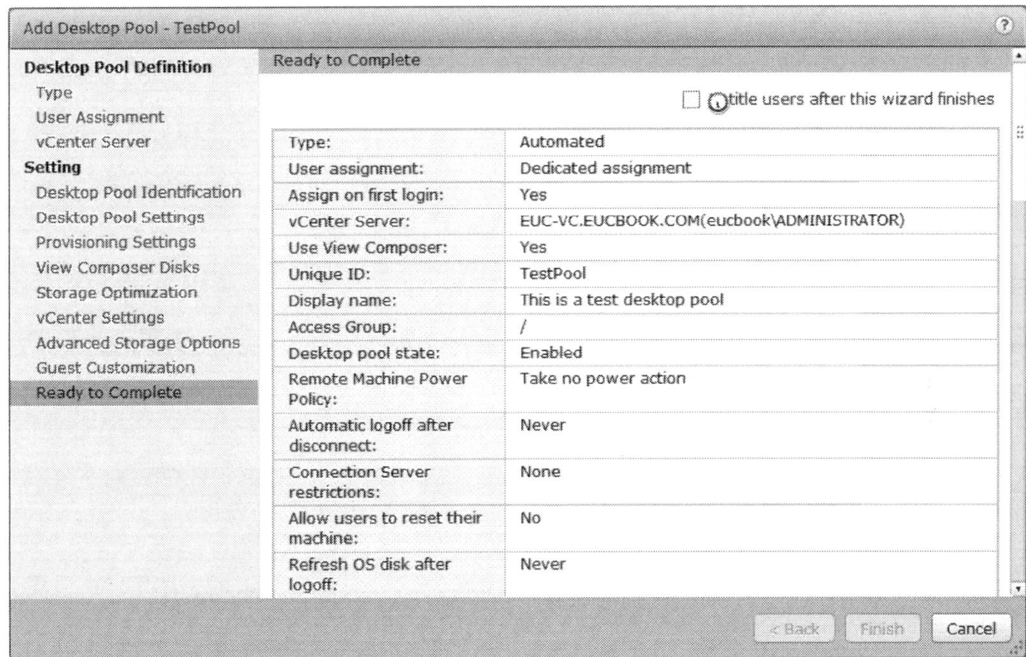

Floating desktops

The process to create a floating automated desktop pool is much the same as the dedicated pool procedure shown in the previous section. However, there will be no option to configure a persistent disk during this process.

Automated full virtual machines

Again, the process to create an automated full virtual machine pool is very similar to the method shown earlier for a dedicated linked clone. However, we need to select a virtual machine template on the **vCenter Settings** screen instead of a virtual machine snapshot:

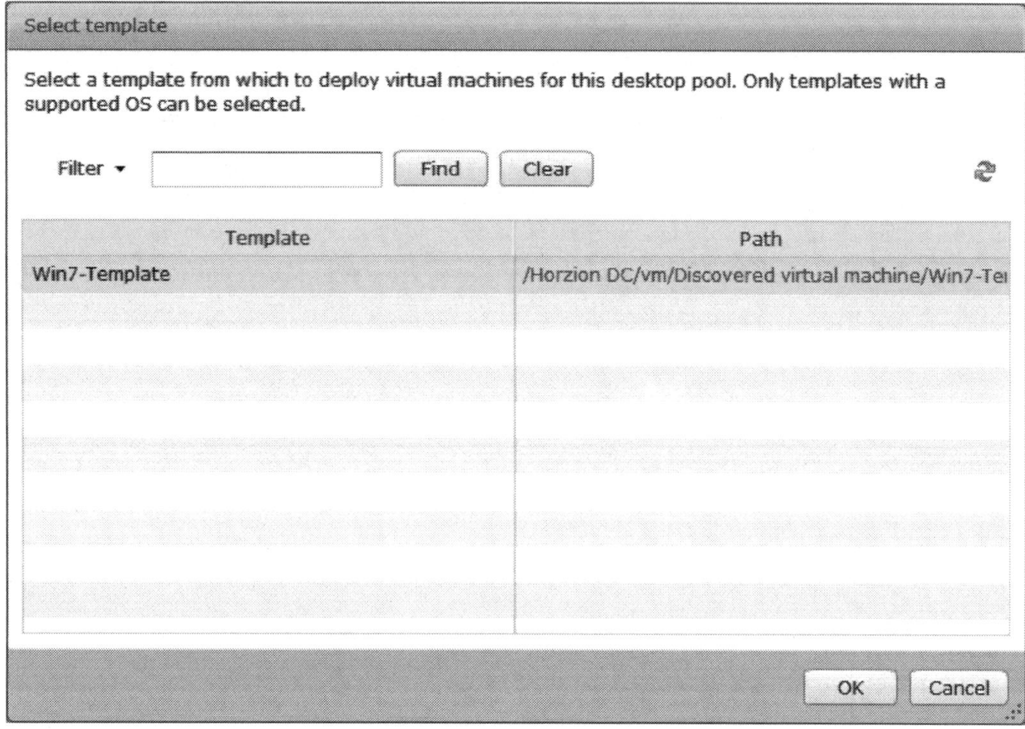

Manual desktops

It is also possible to configure manual desktop pools made up of pre-created virtual or physical machines. The wizards to create these machines are very similar to the process shown earlier, with a number of key differences. Perform the following steps:

1. When starting the **Add Desktop Pool** wizard, select the **Manual Desktop Pool** option:

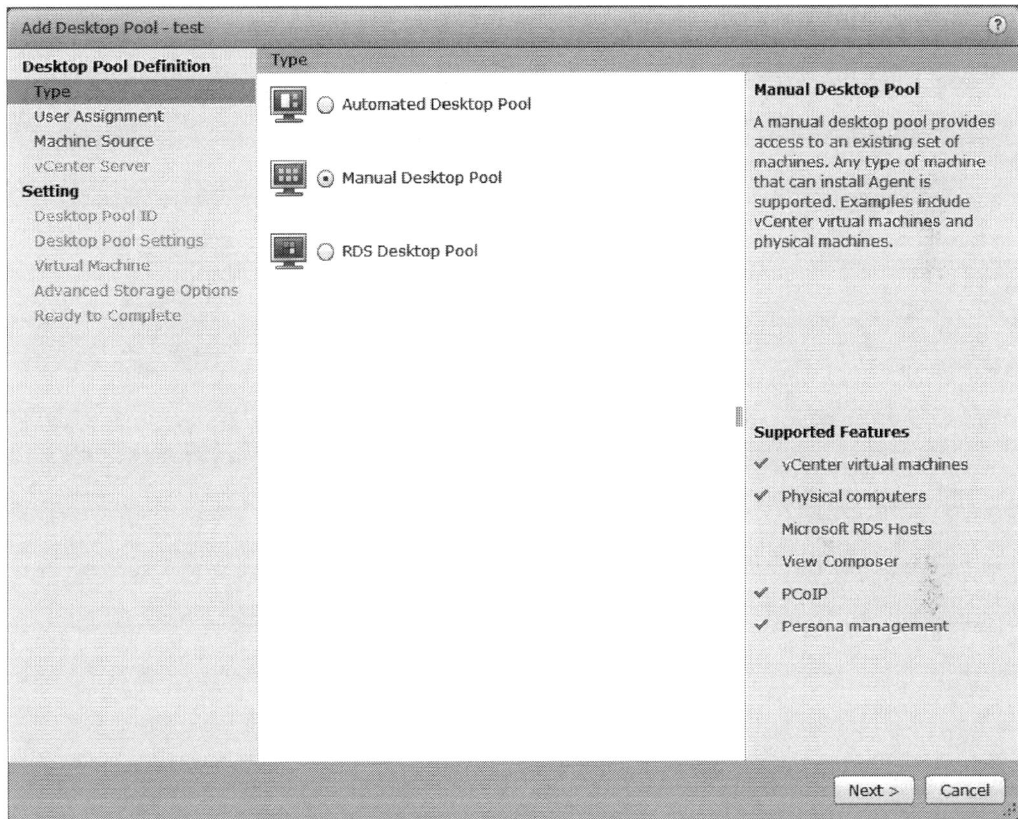

2. As you progress through the wizard, you will get the options to create a dedicated or floating pool prior to selecting the machine source. As mentioned previously, this can be a virtual or physical machine, but it should have the Horizon View Agent pre-installed:

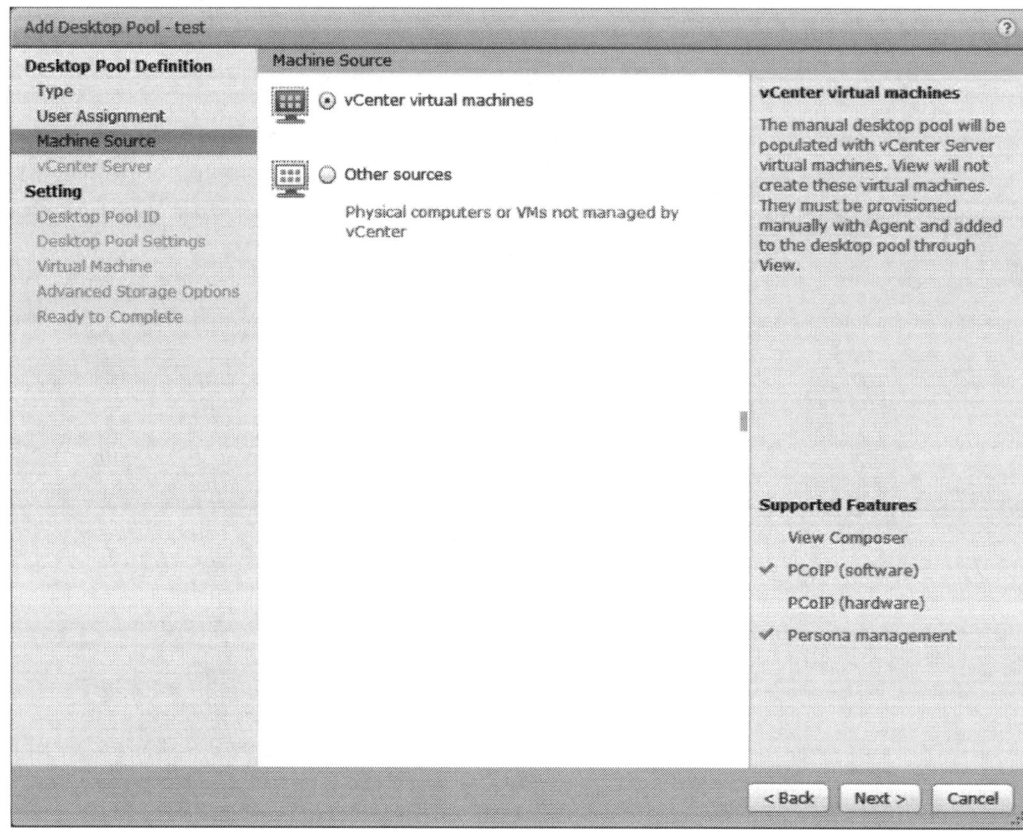

3. If you select a vCenter virtual machine, you will need to select the vCenter that has the VMs and is registered on the **vCenter Server** page:

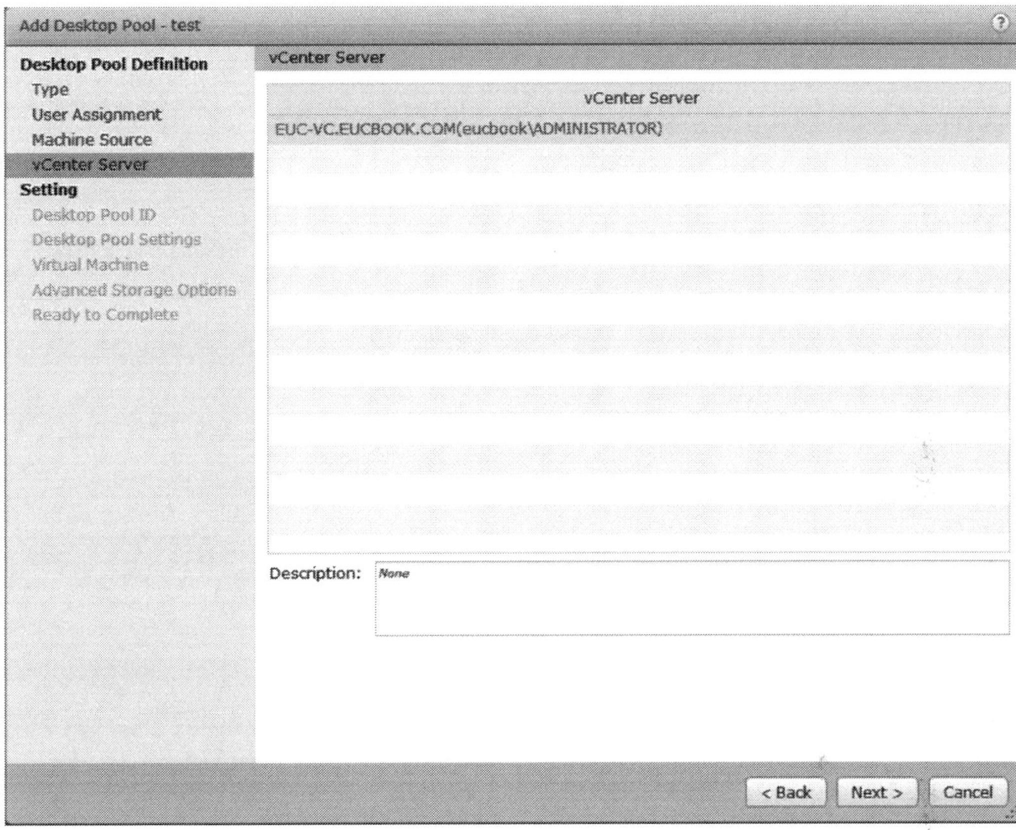

You will then configure the pool settings, as you have previously seen in the *Automated desktop pools* section, before moving on to select your desktop sources—in the given example we have selected the following virtual machine:

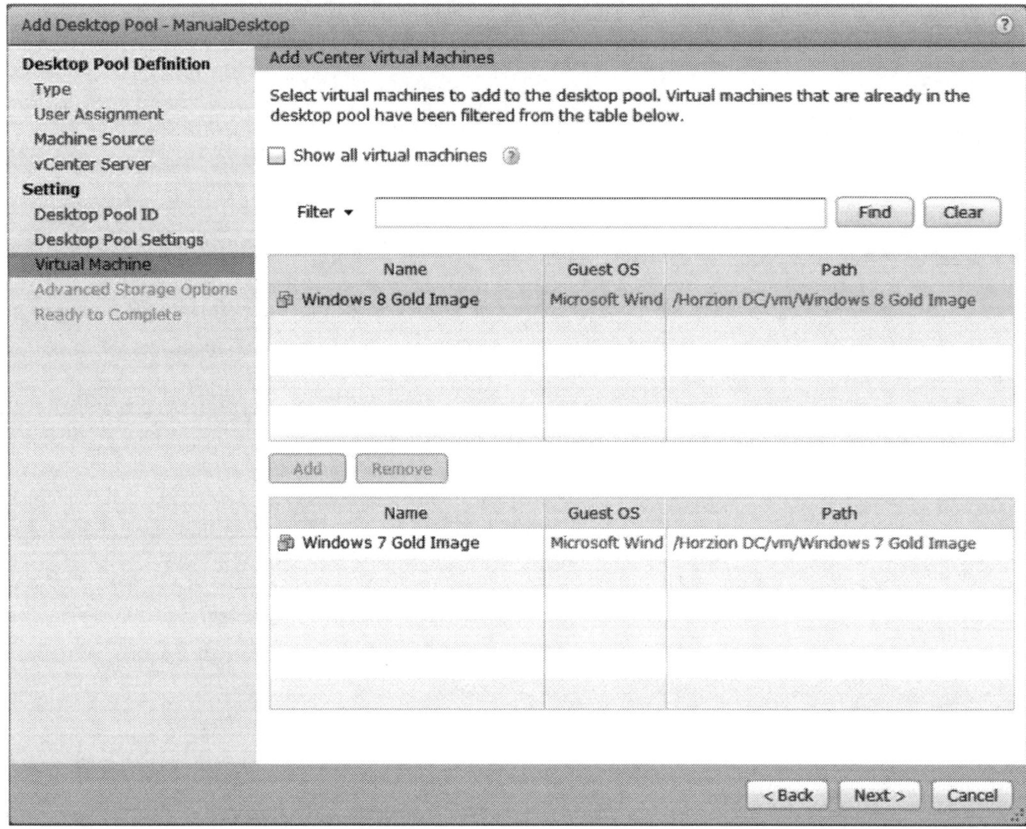

You will then complete the wizard in the same manner as the automated desktop pool prior to entitling your users.

Entitling users

The process of entitling your users is a very simple one. You can start the wizard in a number of different manners. Inside the **Horizon View Administrator** dialog box, expand **Catalog** on the left-hand-side menu bar. Here, select **Desktop Pools** (**1**). Then, select the chosen desktop pool and either right-click on the desktop (**2**) and choose **Add entitlement...** (3), or choose **Entitlements...** from the top menu bar:

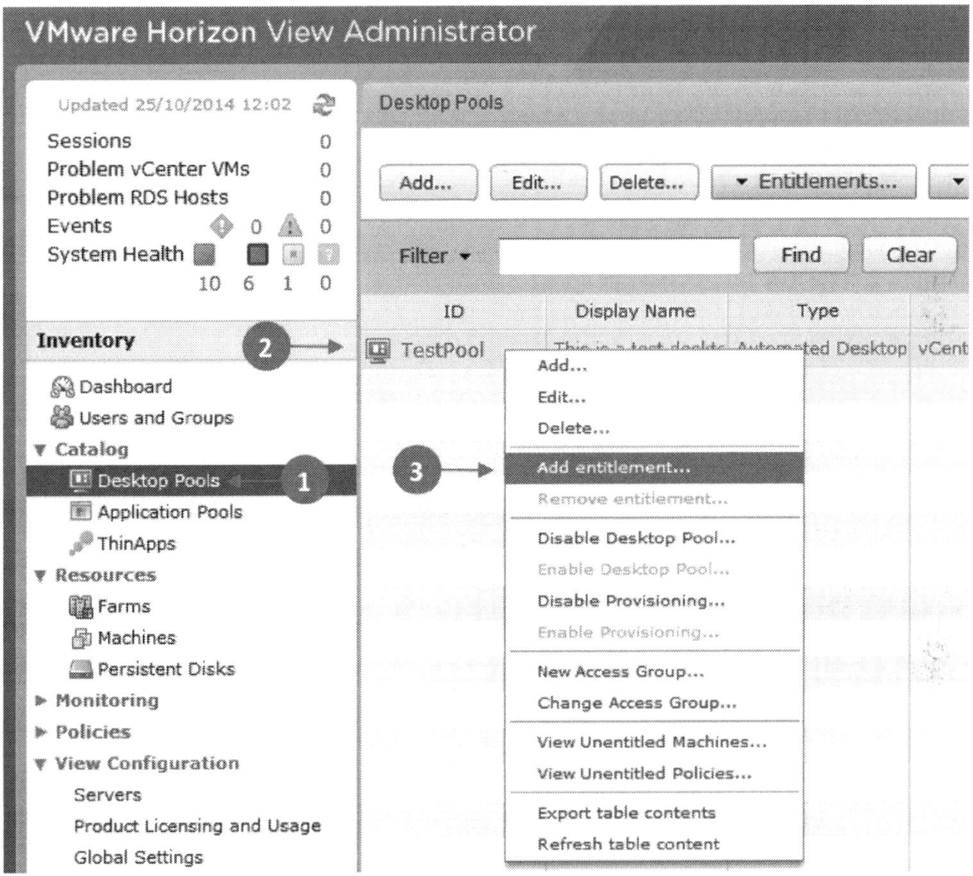

When the **Add Entitlements** wizard is displayed, you can select individual users or security groups to entitle with access to the desktop pool. Where possible, we recommend that you align the access of your desktop with security groups to allow simplified administration:

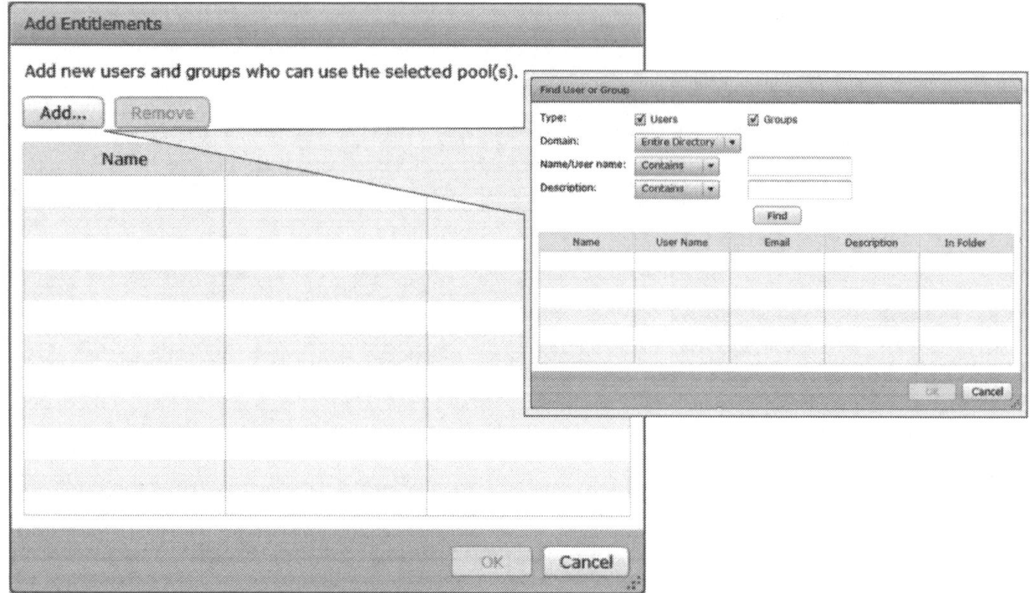

Pool management

With an automated desktop pool, once you create and entitle your desktop pool, your desktops will be created, first by creating the replica and then by creating the linked clones. You will be able to see the progress of this process inside the vSphere Client and also from inside the Horizon View Administrator.

Inside the **Horizon View Administrator** dialog box, select **Catalog** from the left-hand side menu bar. From here, select **Desktop Pools**. Then select the name of the desktop pool you wish to examine, by clicking on it and then selecting the **Inventory** tab; as shown in the following screenshot:

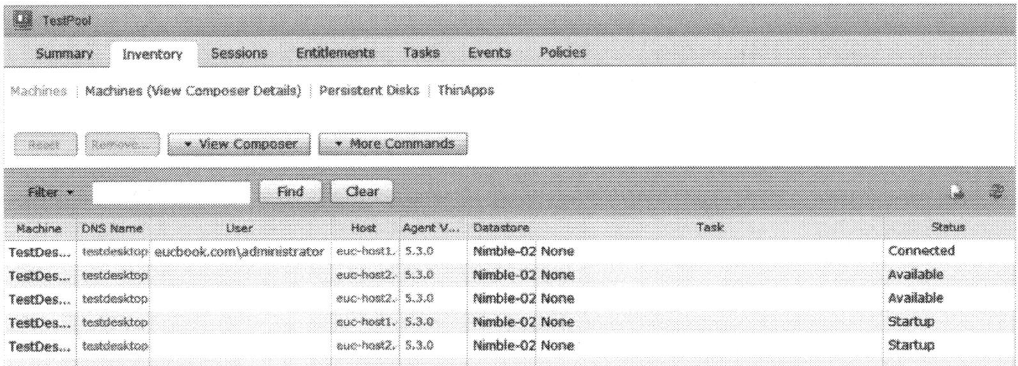

Here you will see the names of the desktops, including the VM name and the DNS name, the name of any connected or dedicated users, the hosts on which they reside, the agent version, and the datastore they reside on. You will also see any tasks and the current status.

We can see different statuses in the preceding screenshot. In total, there are 24 different statuses that you might see for vCenter-managed virtual machines. You can see a breakdown of all the statuses taken from the Horizon View documentation:

Status	Description
Provisioning	The virtual machine is being provisioned.
Customizing	The virtual machine in an automated pool is being customized.
Deleting	The virtual machine is marked for deletion. View will delete the virtual machines soon.
Waiting for Agent	View Connection Server is waiting to establish communication with View Agent on a virtual machine in a manual pool.
Maintenance mode	The virtual machine is in maintenance mode. Users cannot log in or use the virtual machine.
Startup	View Agent has started on the virtual machine but other required services, such as the display protocol, are yet to start. For example, View Agent cannot establish an RDP connection with client computers until RDP has started. The View Agent startup period allows other processes, such as protocol services, to start up as well.

Status	Description
Agent disabled	This state can occur in two cases. First, in a desktop pool with the **Delete or refresh machine on logoff** or **Delete machine after logoff** setting enabled, a desktop session is logged out. However, the virtual machine is not yet refreshed or deleted. Secondly, View Connection Server disables View Agent just before sending a request to power off the virtual machine. This state ensures that a new desktop session cannot be started on the virtual machine.
Agent unreachable	View Connection Server cannot establish communication with View Agent on a virtual machine.
Invalid IP	The subnet mask registry setting is configured on the virtual machine. No active network adapters have an IP address within the configured range.
Agent needs reboot	A View component was upgraded, and the virtual machine must be restarted to allow View Agent to operate with the upgraded component.
Protocol failure	A display protocol did not start before the View Agent startup period expired. View Administrator can display machines in a Protocol failure state when one protocol failed but other protocols started successfully. For example, the Protocol failure state might be displayed when HTML Access failed but PCoIP and RDP are working. In this case, the machines are available and Horizon Client devices can access them through PCoIP or RDP.
Domain failure	The virtual machine encountered a problem reaching the domain. The domain server was not accessible or the domain authentication failed.
Already used	In a desktop pool with the **Delete or refresh machine on logoff** or **Delete machine after logoff** setting enabled, there is no session on the virtual machine, but the session was not logged off. This condition might occur if a virtual machine shuts down unexpectedly or the user resets the machine during a session. By default, when a virtual machine is in this state, View prevents any other Horizon Client devices from accessing the desktop.

Status	Description
Configuration error	The display protocol, for example, RDP or PCoIP, is not enabled.
Provisioning error	An error occurred during provisioning.
Error	An unknown error occurred in the virtual machine.
Unassigned user connected	A user other than the assigned user is logged in to a virtual machine in a dedicated pool. For example, this state can occur if an administrator starts vSphere Client, opens a console on the virtual machine, and logs in.
Unassigned user disconnected	A user other than the assigned user is logged in and disconnected from a virtual machine in a dedicated assignment pool.
Unknown	The virtual machine is in an unknown state.
Provisioned	The virtual machine is powered off or suspended.
Available	The virtual machine is powered on and ready for a connection. In a dedicated pool, the virtual machine is assigned to a user and will start when the user logs in.
Connected	The virtual machine is in a session and has a remote connection to the Horizon Client device.
Disconnected	The virtual machine is in a session, but it is disconnected from the Horizon Client device.
In progress	The virtual machine is in a transitional state during a maintenance operation.

By right-clicking on any desktop, we are able to undertake any of a number of tasks on that given desktop. The **Reset** option will complete a hard reset on the desktop and could be used in the case of a system lockup. **Remove...** will delete the desktop. **Refresh...**, **Recompose...**, and **Rebalance...** have been described in *Chapter 2, An Overview of Horizon View Architecture and its Components*, and can be completed here on an individual desktop basis. **Cancel task...** will cancel any outstanding task on the individual virtual machine. **Assign User...** can be used to allocate a desktop to a specific user; **Unassign User...** will remove this allocation. **Enter Maintenance Mode...** will place the desktop in a state where users cannot be allocated to the desktop or connect to it while maintenance is carried out. **Exit Maintenance Mode...** will return the desktop to the pool.

Disconnect Session... will disconnect the currently connected user from the pool without logging them off, whereas **Logoff Session...** will log the user off. We are finally able to use **Send Message...** to send a message to any given user:

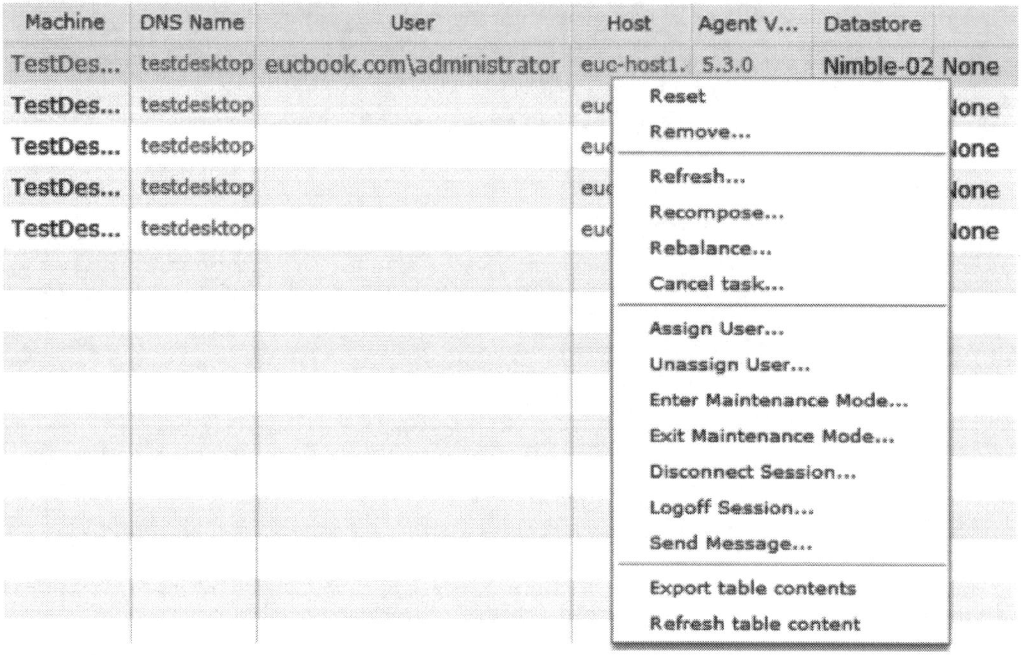

Recomposing a pool

You might wish to recompose a pool to update the operating systems or applications held within it or alternatively, to add further applications. We always recommend having test pools available for you to test updates prior to seeding these updates to end users.

We will recompose your desktop pool from inside the **Horizon View Administrator** interface. You will need to expand **Catalog** (**1**), on the left-hand side, before selecting **Desktop Pools** (**2**). Within the **Summary** tab of your chosen desktop, select **View Composer** (**3**) before selecting **Recompose** (**4**):

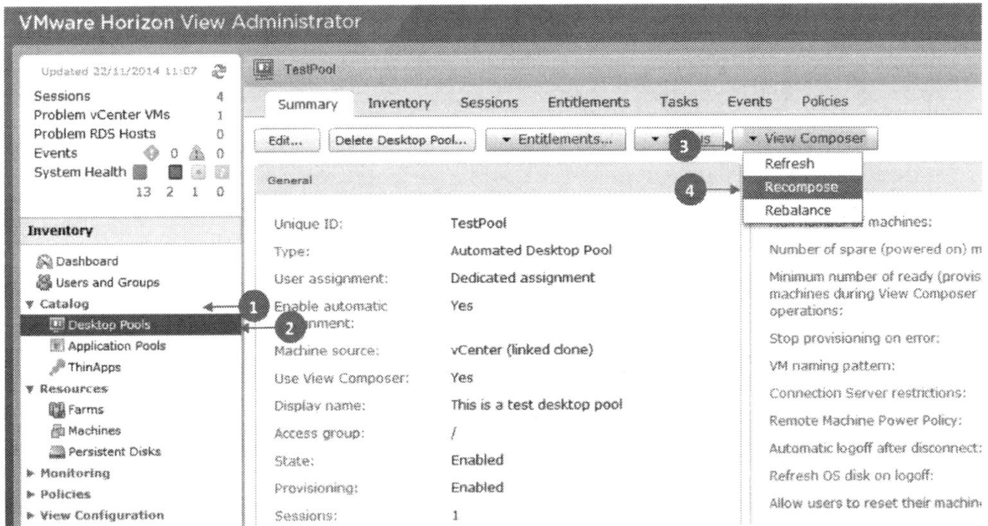

You will now see the **Recompose** wizard appear. Here, you are either able to change the parent VM as a whole, or, more likely, simply the snapshot it is recomposed from. Start by selecting the new snapshot that you have created inside vSphere for your Parent VM (**1**)—see the following screenshot. Also, ensure the **Change the default image for new machines** option is selected. You are now able to continue through the wizard by clicking on **Next >** (**2**):

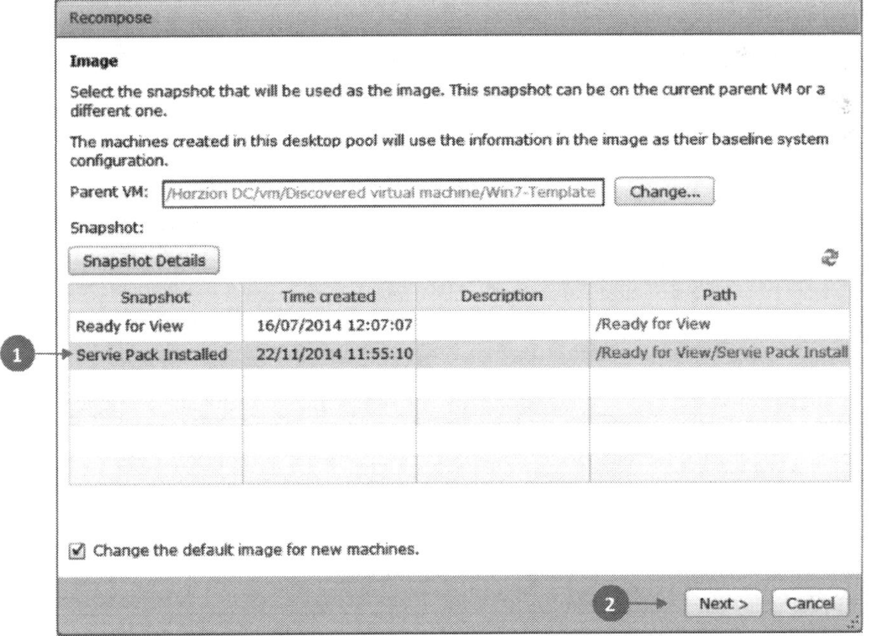

You will now configure the settings for how and when the pool will start recomposing. Initially, you will start by scheduling the time (**1**) you wish the recompose to start. You will need to take into consideration the effect this might have on the storage hosts, so you might wish to schedule this at a quieter time or out-of-hours. You will then need to select the option that will dictate how users utilizing the desktops will be managed; this can either be **Force users to log off** (**2**) or **Wait for users to log off** (**3**). We should also select the **Stop at first error** checkbox, to set what we wish to happen if an error occurs. The final options within this screen are there only for informational reasons and show what will be displayed to the users if they are forced to log off (**5**). These can be customized in the global settings area within the **Horizon View Administrator** dialog box:

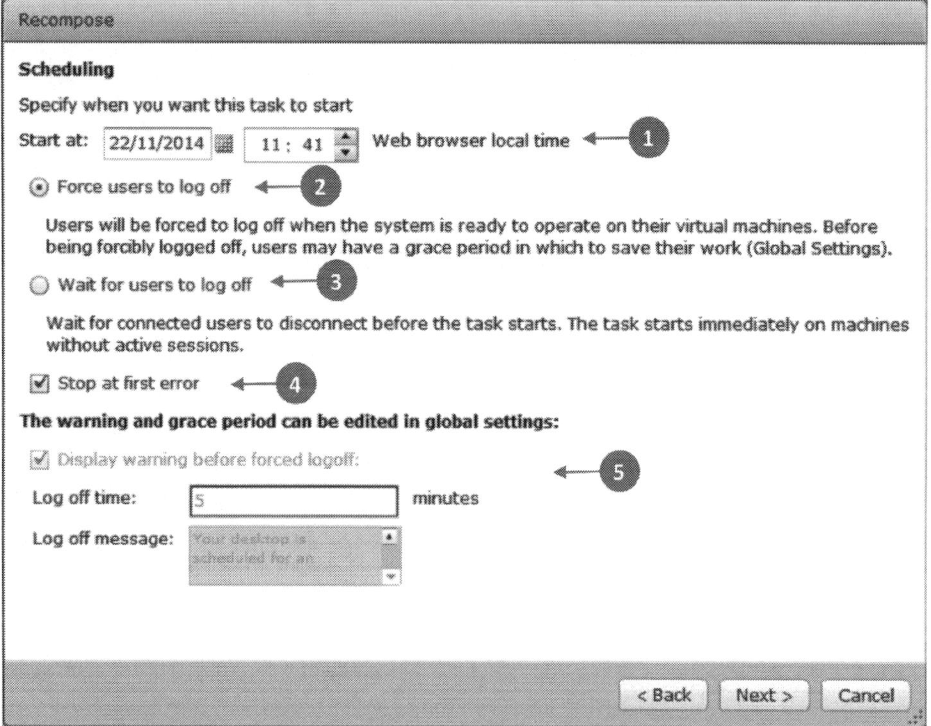

The final screen will confirm your selection prior to you selecting **Finish** to start the recompose process. First, the replica VM will be updated prior to the desktops being recomposed. Once all desktops have been recomposed and are utilizing the new replica, the old replica will then be deleted:

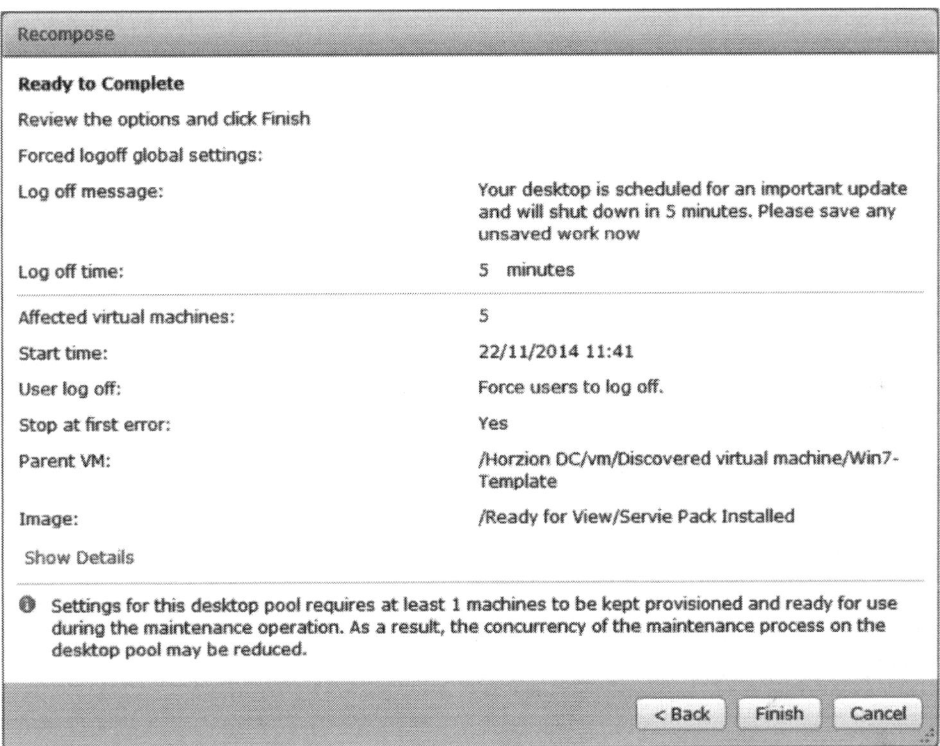

Managing persistent disks

As previously discussed, a persistent disk can be configured on a dedicated virtual hard disk per user, which will allow you to preserve user data and settings between recompose operations and more. There are a number of tasks that can be undertaken with regard to persistent disk management.

We are able to detach the virtual disk from a dedicated desktop. This probably needs to be done as the user is leaving the company, and so the desktop is no longer needed but the data needs to be kept. It could also be because there is an issue with the desktop and you need to recreate it afresh without losing the user's data. Perform the following steps for this:

1. Inside the **Horizon View Administrator**, you need to expand the **Catalog** option (**1**) and then select **Desktop Pools** (**2**). You will then select the relevant desktop pool (**3**). Once on the **Summary** page for the desktop pool, select the **Inventory** tab (**4**) before selecting **Persistent Disks** (**5**). Here you can see a list of all the VMs, the assigned users, and the related persistent disks. Select the disk (**6**) you wish to detach and then click on the **Detach...** button (**7**). Depending on the reason to detach the disk, you might wish to keep the detached disk in the current datastore (**8**). Alternatively, select another datastore just as an archive tier of storage. Finally, select **OK**. Assuming the user isn't currently connected to the desktop, the persistent disk will be archived and then the VM will be deleted:

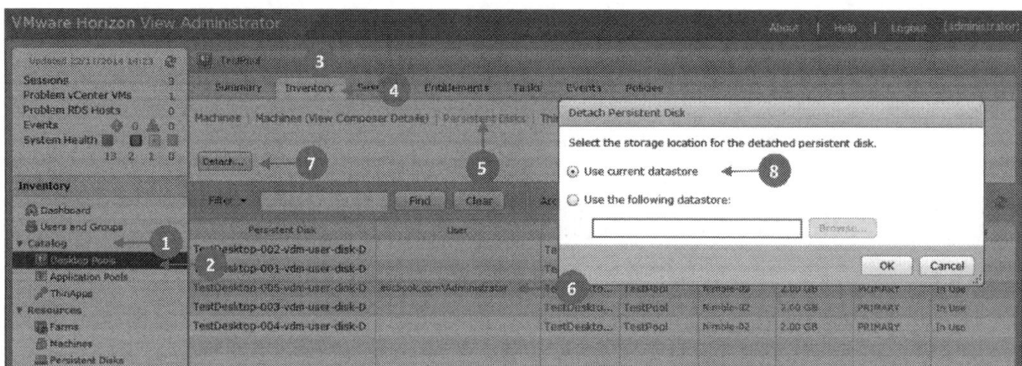

2. You can view all the detached disks inside the **Horizon View Administrator** dialog box by navigating to **Resources** | **Persistent Disks** | **Detached**. Here, you are able to reattach the disk to a desktop, assuming the desktop has been reassigned to the user. Change who the disk is assigned to by editing the owner, deleting the disk permanently, or recreating a machine with the disk attached to it:

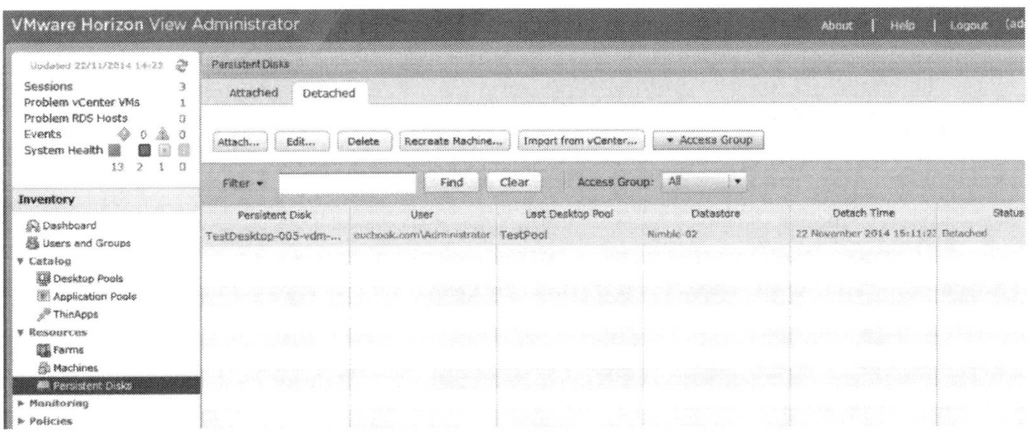

3. In the following example, we will edit the ownership of the disk to a different user. We select the disk to be edited, right-click on it, and select **Edit....** From here, we simply browse the AD to select a user before reattaching the disk as needed or recreating the VM:

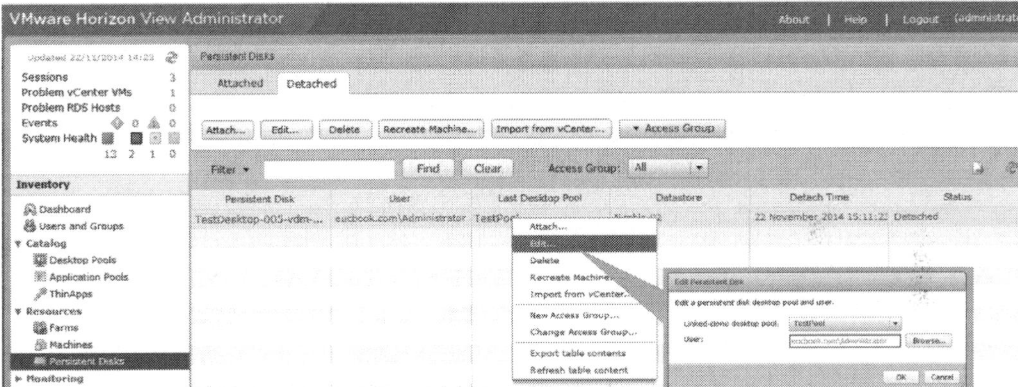

4. From the persistent disks view, we are also able to import disks from a vCenter Server. In the following example, we are going to assume there has been an issue with the user's persistent disk, possibly a corruption or accidental deletion of the whole disk or files held within it. Our persistent disks are being held on a dedicated disk on our **Nimble Storage Array** and we have configured regular snapshotting for data protection. We will start by connecting to our storage array, selecting the relevant volume (**1**), and choosing the snapshot we wish to recover from (**2**) prior to cloning it to a new volume instantly (**3**):

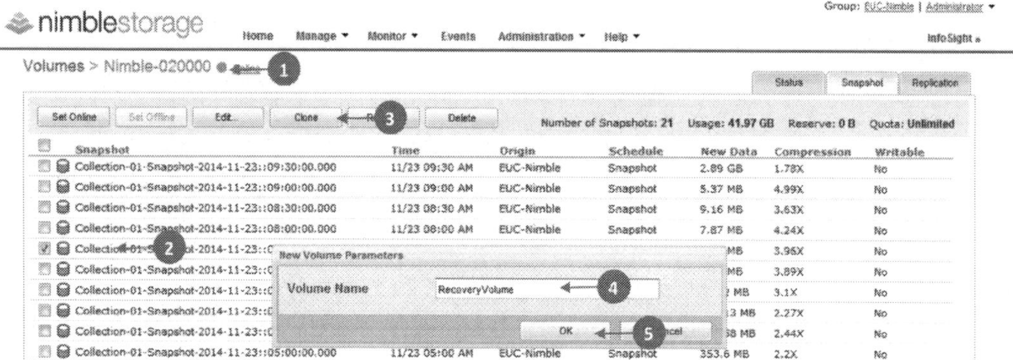

5. You then need to follow a process to restore the persistent disks, from the cloned volume or other sources, to the datastore where our persistent disks reside and delete any clones used for restoration. You will now use the View Administrator to import the persistent disk. From the **Persistent Disks** view, under **Resources** on the left-hand-side menu, choose the **Detached** (**1**) tab and select **Import from vCenter** (**2**)—see the following screenshot. Here, you need to select the relevant vCenter, datacenter, linked clone desktop pool, and the persistent disk file and user:

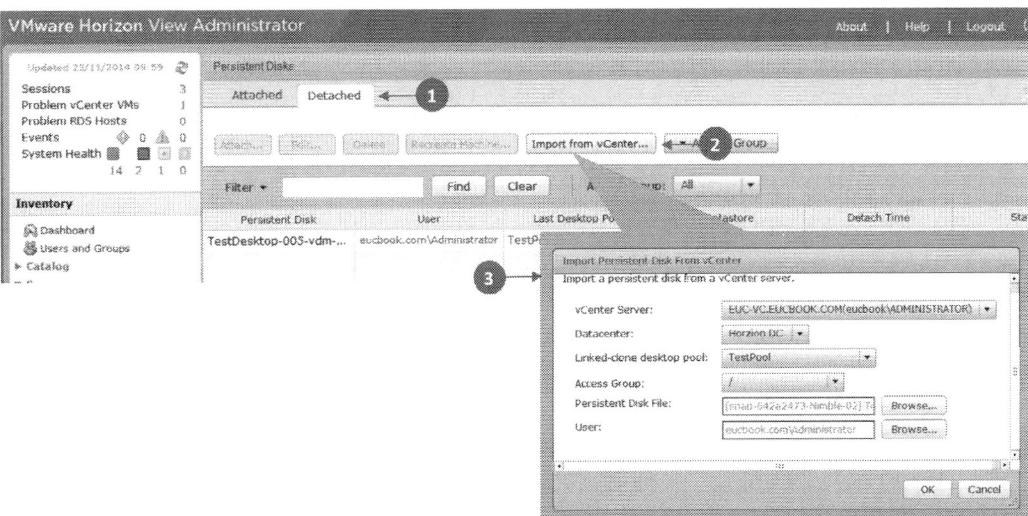

You will now see that the persistent disk has been registered in the **Detached** disks view and you can recreate the machine from here:

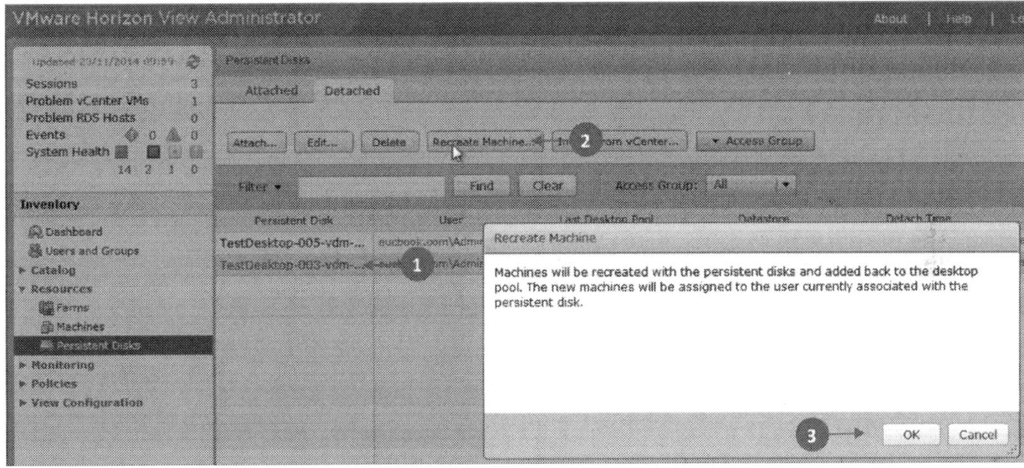

Creating a desktop pool for high-end graphics

In the previous sections, we covered creating desktop pools for different use cases, with a desktop pool for each type.

Another use case to create a desktop pool is when you have a specific hardware requirement for the virtual desktop machine, such as a high-end graphics card to take advantage of either vGPU, vSGA, or vDGA. We have previously covered the building of a virtual desktop machine that is GPU-enabled. In this section, we will build a desktop pool specifically for this virtual desktop machine.

To create the desktop pool, follow these steps:

1. From the **Inventory** section, click on **Desktop Pools** and then click on **Add...**.
2. Select the radio button for **Manual Desktop Pool** from the pool type menu. Click on **Next >** to continue.
3. On the **User Assignment** page, select the radio button for **Dedicated** and make sure that the box for **Enable automatic assignment** is not ticked, Click on **Next >** to continue.
4. Select the radio button for **vCenter virtual machines** on the **Machine Source** configuration page. This means the virtual desktop machines will be listed from the vCenter Server. Click on **Next >** to continue.
5. On the **vCenter Server** page, select the vCenter Server that manages the hosts and virtual desktop machines you want to use.
6. Enter the details for **Desktop Pool ID** on the next configuration page. In this example, we will name the pool `vDGA_Desktops` and enter the display name `Windows 7 vDGA`. Click on **Next >** to continue.
7. You will now see the **Desktop Pool Settings** configuration page, as shown in the upcoming screenshot. Most of the settings are the same as the ones we set for the previous pools. However, we need to change some settings in the **Remote Display Protocol** section.
8. Ensure that **Default display protocol** is set to **PCoIP** (**1**). To allow View to make use of the advanced graphics settings, you need to make sure that you set the **Allow users to choose protocol** option to **No** (**2**). The reason being, these features only work with PCoIP. If you leave the option set to **Yes**, then the **3D Renderer** section will remain grayed out and you won't be able to select the option for **Automatic** (**3**):

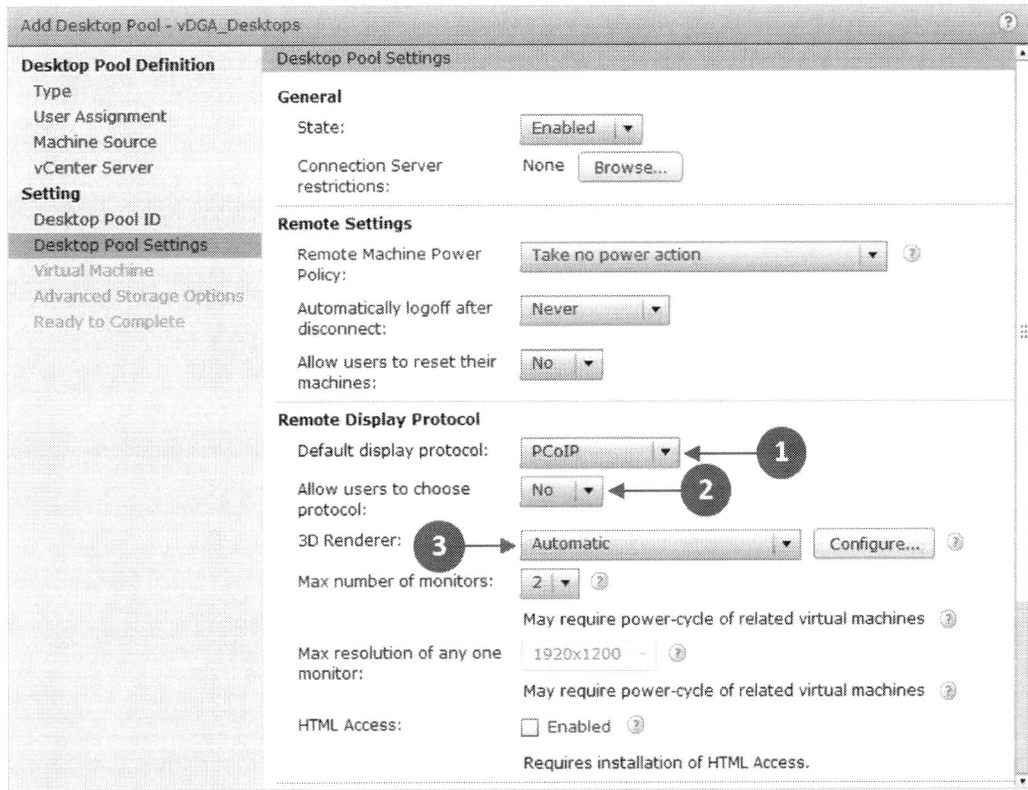

9. There are four different options for the **3D Renderer**:
    - **Automatic**: ESX reserves GPU resources on a first come, first served basis and, if they can't be fulfilled, will revert to software rendering.
    - **Software**: ESX uses software rendering only.
    - **Hardware**: Like **Automatic**, ESX reserves GPU resources on a first come, first served basis. If they can't be fulfilled, then the virtual desktop machine will not power on.

10. **Disabled**: This does not configure 3D rendering.

    The other option you have is to configure the amount of video memory allocated to that virtual desktop machine. Click on **Configure...** next to the **3D Renderer** option. You can adjust the slider bar to configure from **64 MB** to to **512 MB** OS VRAM:

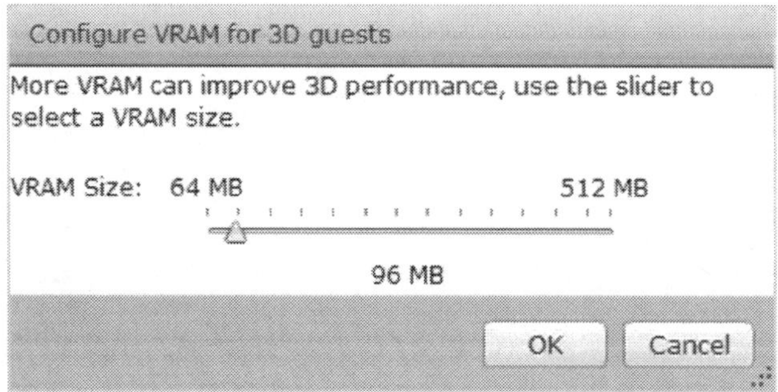

11. On the **Virtual Machine settings** configuration page, under **Add vCenter Virtual Machines**, search for the virtual desktop machines you want to add to this desktop pool. You can either tick the box to show all virtual machines or use the **Filter** option to search for specific machines. Select each of the machines you want to add to the pool and then click on **Add**.
12. On the **Advanced Storage Options**, tick the box for **Use View Storage Accelerator** and click on **Next >** to continue.

Finally, you will see the **Ready to Complete** page. Check the settings and click on **Finish** when you are happy to continue.

You should now have a manual desktop pool created in the View Administrator, which contains your dedicated, GPU-enabled virtual desktop machines. There is one final thing you need to configure. However, you can only do that by connecting to the virtual desktops using View.

Once you have connected to the virtual desktop machine, open a command prompt window and navigate to the directory: `C:\program files\common files\VMware\Teradici PCOIP Server\`.

From that directory, run the following command:

```
Montereyenable.exe - enable
```

This enables the NVIDIA APIs. Reboot the virtual desktop machine when complete. You should now have a working, GPU-enabled virtual desktop machine that you can start entitling to users. To do this, follow the steps that we described in the *Entitling users* section of this chapter.

If you want to make sure that the virtual desktop machine is using vDGA and the NVIDIA graphics card, click on the **Start** button and then **Run**. In the **Run** dialog box, type the command `dxdiag` and click on **OK**. The **DirectX Diagnostic Tool** will launch. Click on the **Display** tab at the top; you will see something similar to the following screenshot:

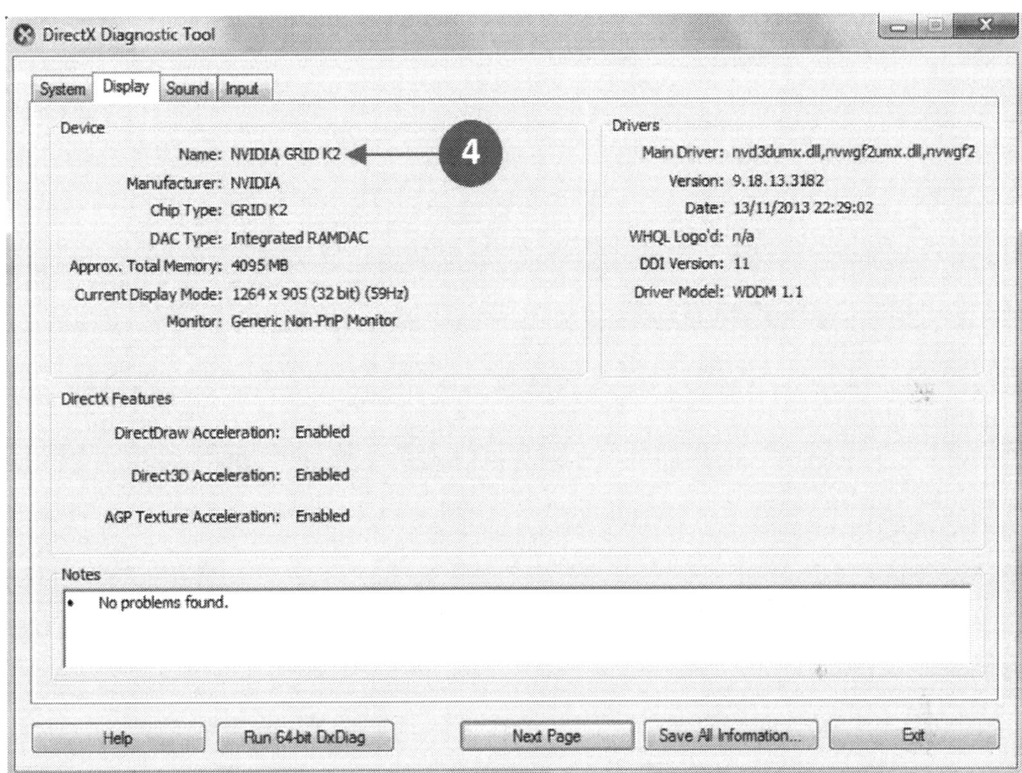

You can see that the graphics card in use is **NVIDIA GRID K2** (**4**).

One thing to note is that vDGA will not work when opening a console session to the virtual desktop machine from the vSphere Web Client. You won't see anything displayed in the console. You will need to use RDP to connect or connect View itself.

Summary

In this chapter, we have configured the Horizon View Administrator to deliver our virtual desktop machines. We have built and configured different desktop pools to match our different use cases, including a dedicated pool for our high-end graphics users.

In the next chapter, we will look at client options to connect to the virtual desktop machines within the desktop pools that we have just configured.

8

Fine-tuning the End User Experience

So, now we have built our Horizon View infrastructure, deployed and optimized our virtual desktop operating system, and configured our user entitlements by means of creating Horizon View desktop pools. This means end users now have access to their virtual desktop machines.

In this chapter, we will look at how to fine-tune the end user experience, by which we mean how the desktop will perform and the features that will be made available to the users.

We have already talked about optimizing the virtual desktop operating system and how we tune the OS so that it behaves as a virtual desktop machine. However, now we will talk about fine-tuning and configuring the delivery protocol, as well as enabling and disabling certain functionalities relating to how the user interacts with their virtual desktop machine. By this we mean configuring things, such as whether or not you can cut-and-paste text between the end point device running the client and the virtual desktop machine.

Configuring AD

The behavior of a virtual desktop machine and how a user interacts with it is governed by an AD policy. As we mentioned previously, this policy configures things such as a graphics experience and cut-and-paste options, to name but a few.

To make life easier, the templates for these policies have already been created and are part of the Horizon View software that we downloaded as part of the software downloads in *Chapter 4, Installing and Configuring Horizon View*, and can be found in the ZIP file named `VMware-Horizon-View-Extras-Bundle-3.3.0-2491779`.

If you unzip this file, you will see that it contains 13 **Administrative Template (ADM)** files, as shown in the following screenshot:

Name	Type	Size
en-US	File folder	
ThinPrint	File folder	
pcoip.adm	ADM File	63 KB
pcoip.client.adm	ADM File	31 KB
vdm_agent.adm	ADM File	23 KB
vdm_agent_rtav.adm	ADM File	3 KB
vdm_agent_scanner.adm	ADM File	11 KB
vdm_blast.adm	ADM File	8 KB
vdm_client.adm	ADM File	46 KB
vdm_common.adm	ADM File	10 KB
vdm_server.adm	ADM File	2 KB
view_agent_direct_connection.adm	ADM File	12 KB
ViewPM.adm	ADM File	41 KB
vmware_rdsh.admx	ADMX File	16 KB
vmware_rdsh_server.admx	ADMX File	5 KB

In the next section, we will look at the OU requirements for the deployment of virtual desktop machines and the things we need in place to configure and tune our environment.

Creating an organizational unit

The first thing we need to do is create an **organizational unit (OU)** for our virtual desktop machines. It's best practice to have a separate OU for virtual desktop machines so as to ensure we don't apply the wrong policies to them, for example, those used for your physical machines, which could potentially contain components that might impact performance, and vice versa. We don't want to apply VDI-based policies to the physical desktop estate.

Depending on your own environment, you might want to create an OU for different use cases. For example, you might want a different OU for each department within your organization. This would then allow you to apply different VDI-based policies to each OU. For example, a particular department might use high-end graphics, which would mean that PCoIP will be configured to deliver a richer experience more than that of a standard office user. It could also be a policy specific to LAN users, where the policy governs the behavior based on the bandwidth.

Creating Group Policy Objects for Horizon View

Now that we have an OU created for our virtual desktop machines, we can create **Group Policy Objects** (**GPO**) to link to the OU. In our example lab, we'll call this policy Horizon View Virtual Desktop Policy:

1. Press the Windows key and then, from the **Start** menu options, click on **Administrative Tools**:

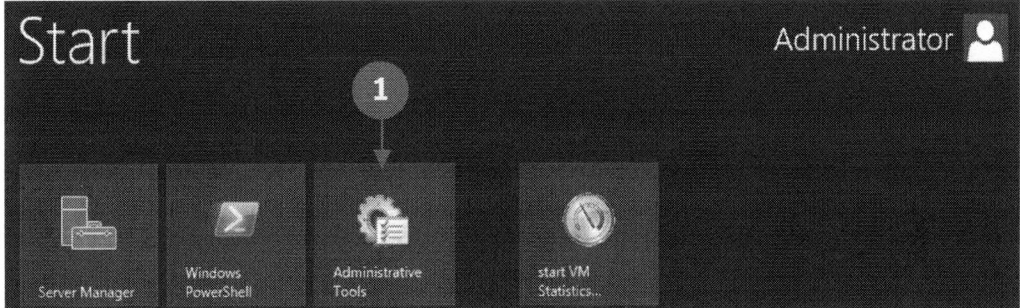

2. You will now have the **Administrative Tools** options displayed, as shown in the following screenshot. Click on **Group Policy Management** (**2**):

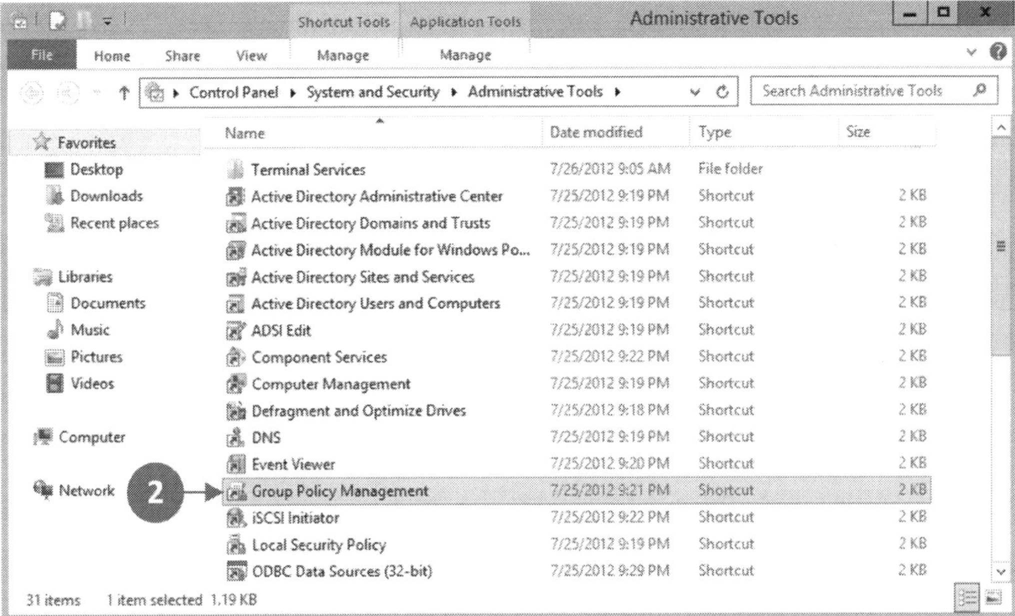

3. The **Group Policy Management** configuration page is now displayed:

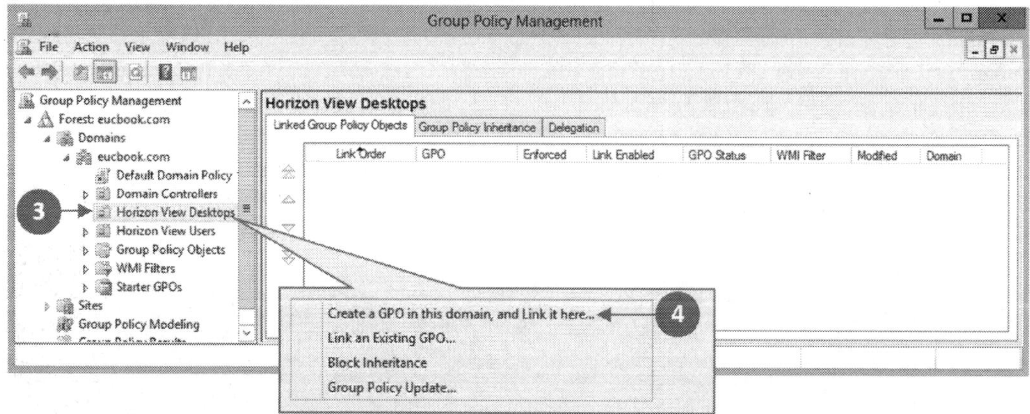

4. Navigate to **Forest: eucbook.com** | **Domains** | **eucbook.com** | **Horizon View Desktops OU** (**3**) that we created previously. We will create and link the policy to this OU.
5. Right-click on **Horizon View Desktops OU** and then select **Create a GPO in this domain, and link it here...** (**4**).
6. You will now see the **New GPO** dialog box as shown in the following screenshot:

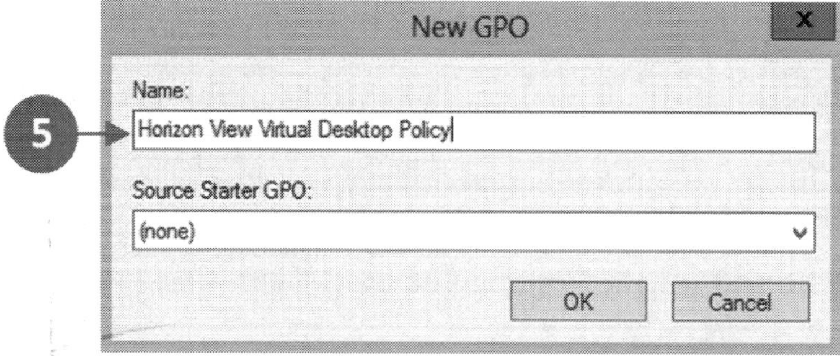

7. Type in the name for the new policy in the **Name:** box (**4**). As we mentioned previously, we will call this policy `Horizon View Virtual Desktop Policy`.
8. Click on **OK** once you have entered the name for the GPO. You will return to the **Group Policy Management** configuration page with the newly created policy displayed. In the next section, we will add the Horizon View ADM templates to the policy.

Importing and applying Horizon View ADM templates

Now that we have created a policy, the next step is to edit it and add the ADM templates so that we can start configuring the policy options:

1. From the **Group Policy Management** configuration page, highlight the policy (**6**) and then right-click on it. From the menu options, click on **Edit** (**7**):

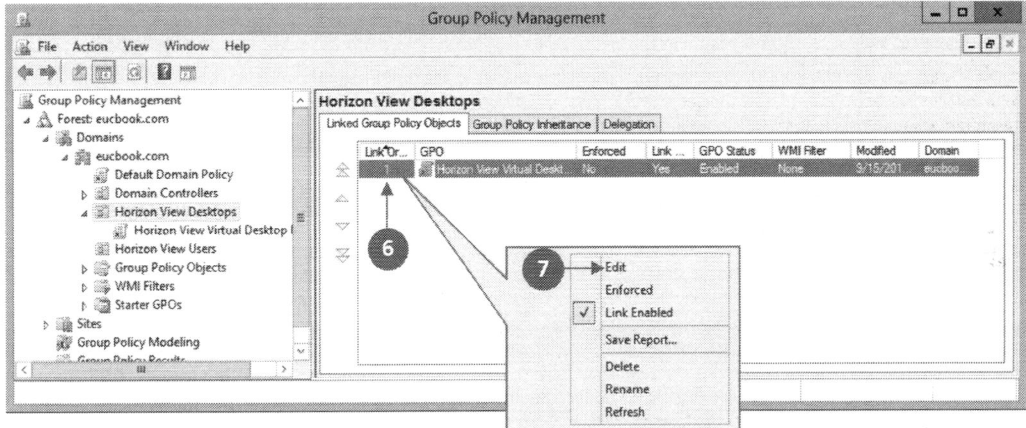

2. You will now see the **Group Policy Management Editor** dialog box, as shown in the following screenshot:

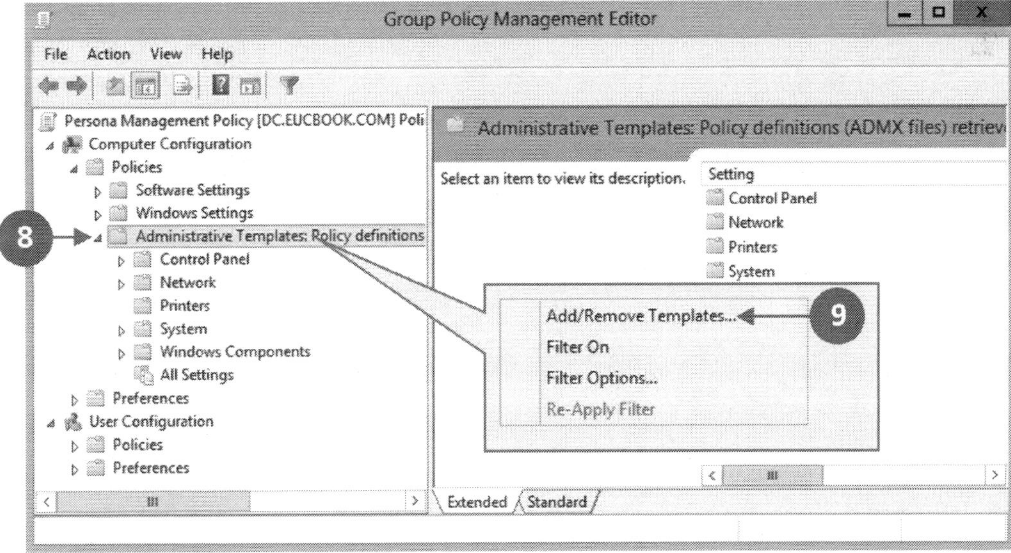

3. Navigate to **Computer Configuration | Policies | Administrative Templates: Policy definitions** (**6**) and right-click.
4. From the menu options, click on **Add/Remove Templates...** (**8**).
5. You will now see the **Add/Remove Templates** dialog box, as shown in the following screenshot. Click on **Add...** (**9**) to add new ADM templates:

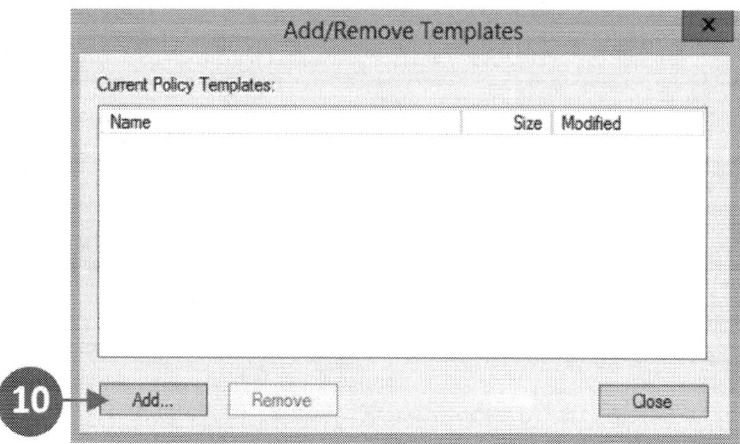

6. You will now see a Windows-Explorer-type dialog box from where you can choose the templates to be added, as shown in the following screenshot:

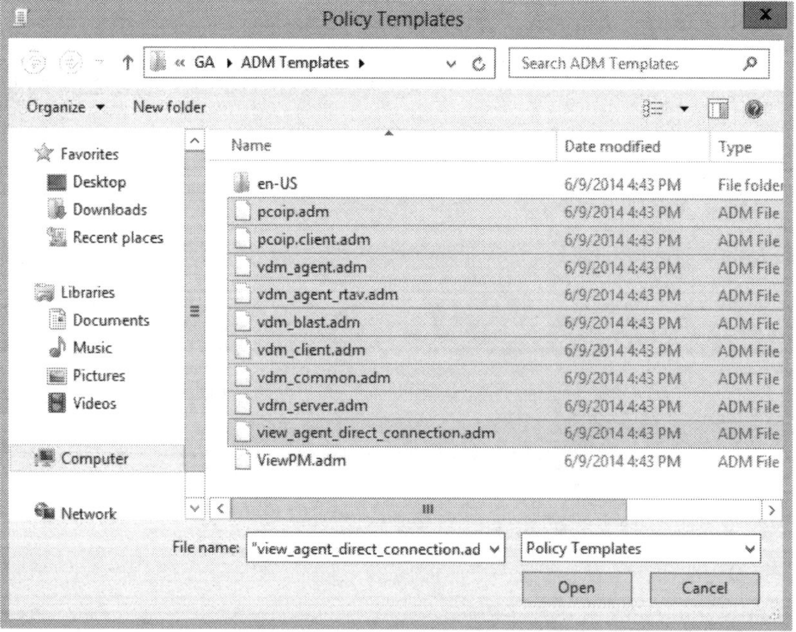

7. Navigate to the location where you have saved the ADM template files. In our example, we have saved them in the shared software folder on the file server. Once located, select all the `.adm` files with the exception of the `ViewPM.adm` template. We will cover this template in *Chapter 9, Managing User Profiles with View Persona Management*, as this policy template provides options to manage user profiles.
8. Once selected, click on **Open**. You will now see the templates that will be added in the **Add/Remove Templates** box, as shown in the following screenshot:

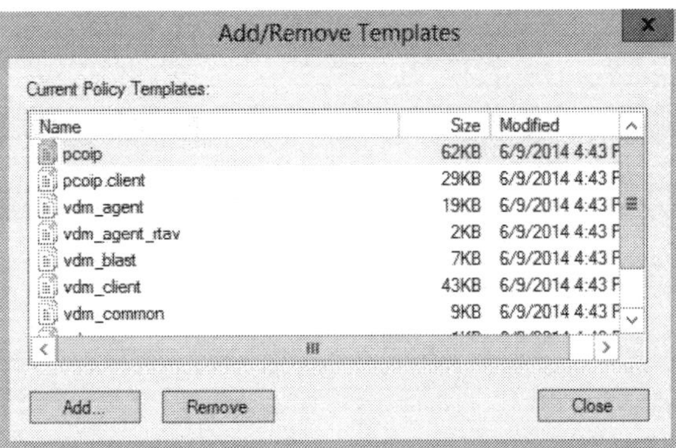

9. Click on **Close** when you have selected all the templates and return to the **Group Policy Management Editor** screen. We can now check the templates that have been added, as shown in the following screenshot:

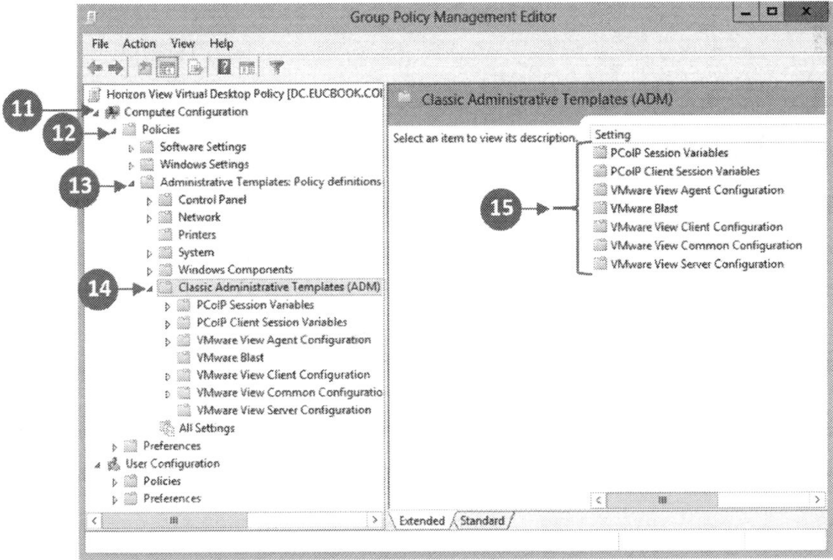

10. Navigate to **Horizon View Virtual Desktop Policy [DC.EUCBOOK.COM] | Computer Configuration (11) | Policies (12) | Administrative Templates: Policy definitions (13) | Classic Administrative Templates (ADM) (14)**.
11. On the right-hand side of the screen (**15**), you will see all the different policy categories.

In our example, we will add all the templates to one policy just to illustrate the various options. In your environment, and depending on your design, you might want to create different policies and apply different templates to different polices. As we have previously mentioned, this is probably on a departmental basis or for different use cases. This is the recommended approach, as it makes troubleshooting far easier.

In the next section, we will complete one final configuration task and configure the loopback policy.

Enabling the loopback policy

In a VDI model, and particularly with floating desktop assignments, we have multiple users accessing the same desktop, so that any configuration changes that a user makes to one of the virtual desktop machines applies to all of the users that use that machine. Then, we need to enable the loopback processing feature. This is particularly important if you are using virtual desktop machines in a kiosk-type environment. To configure loop-back mode, complete the following steps:

1. From the **Group Policy Management Editor** screen, navigate to **Computer Configuration | Policies (1) | Administrative Templates: Policy definitions (ADMX files) (2) | System (3)**.
2. Highlight **Group Policy (4)**. You will see the policy options listed on the right-hand side.
3. Scroll down to **Configure user Group Policy loopback processing mode** (5) and select it, as shown in the following screenshot:

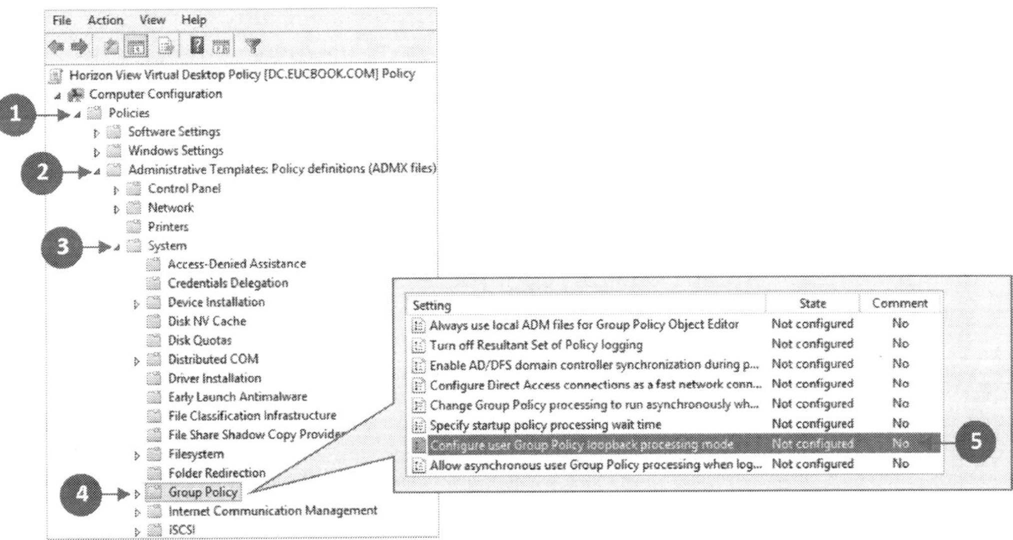

4. Right-click and select **Edit** in the loopback policy to change the setting. The following dialog box appears:

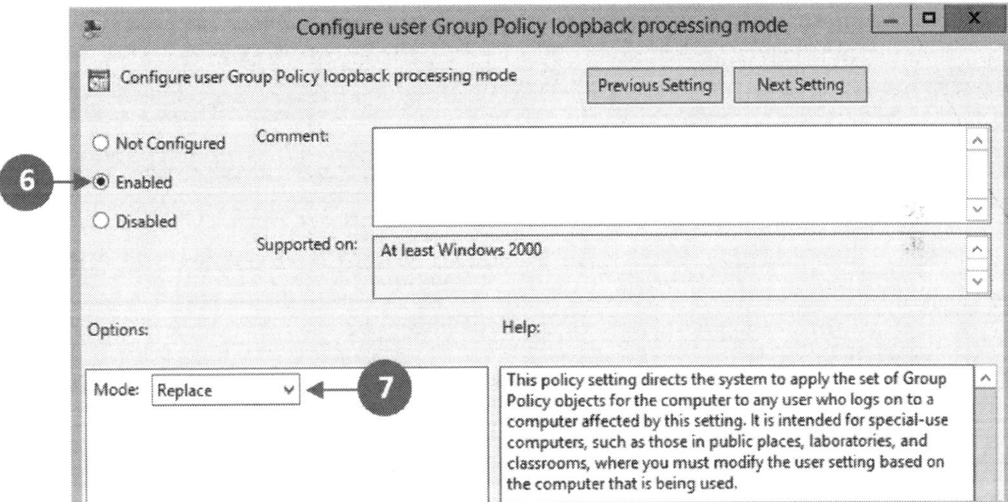

5. Click on the radio button for **Enabled** (6) to turn the policy on. You then have the option to configure the operation mode (7).

6. With the **Replace** option, the user policy applied is just the one that is associated with the computer. Any other user policies are ignored. Choosing the **Merge** option means the policies applied are both, user-and computer-related, where the computer policies win in the event of a conflict.

Configuring policy settings

In this section, we will walk through all the different configurable policy options from the templates we added, starting with the PCoIP Session Variable policies.

For the first few policies, we will go into a bit more detail on how to enable and configure the policy. However, as there are so many policies to cover, for the rest, we will briefly cover what the policy is used for and any configuration options available. For the policies that are simply enabled or disabled, we will just cover what they do.

PCoIP Session Variables

In this section, we will walk through the policy configuration options for the PCoIP protocol and how we can configure the best user experience:

1. From the **Group Policy Management Editor** screen, navigate to **Classic Administrative Templates (ADM)** | **PCoIP Session Variables** (**1**):

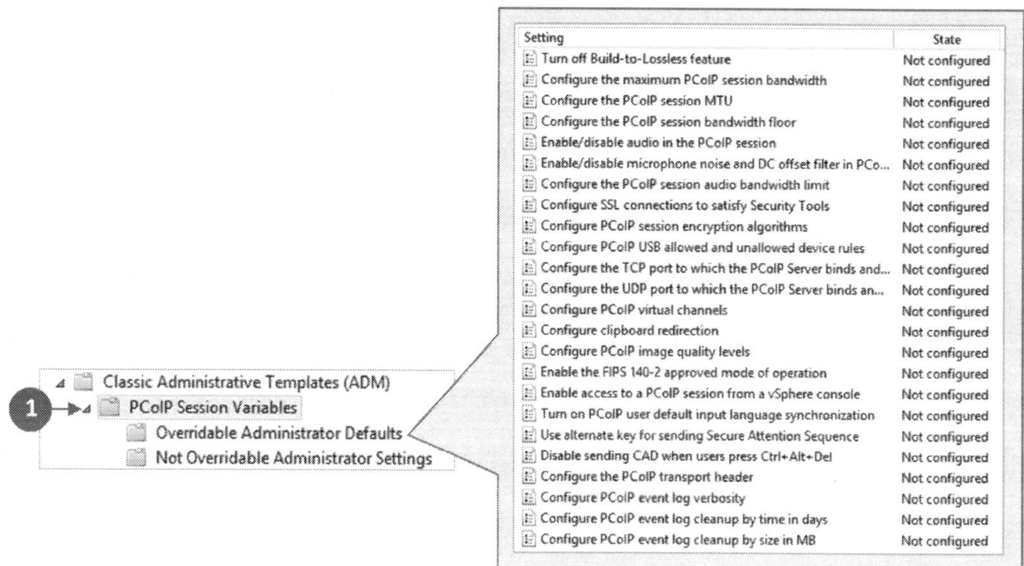

2. Select **Overridable Administrator Defaults** to show the configurable policy options (the **Not Overridable Administrator Settings** are identical). Double-click the first option, **Turn off Build-to-Lossless feature**.

[One thing to quickly highlight for anyone who has used previous versions of View. Before View 6, the default option for PCoIP build-to-lossless was enabled, meaning you needed more bandwidth for that level of image detail. In View 6, the default option is for build-to-lossless to be disabled.]

You will now see the configuration dialog box, and the first thing to do is to set the policy to **Enabled** (**2**).

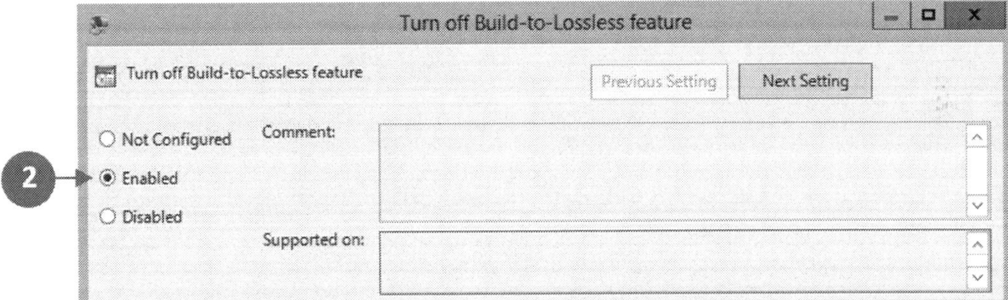

3. Once enabled, click on **Next Setting** to go to the next policy.
4. On the next policy, **Configure the maximum PCoIP session bandwidth**, we can enter a figure in kilobits for the maximum session bandwidth (**3**):

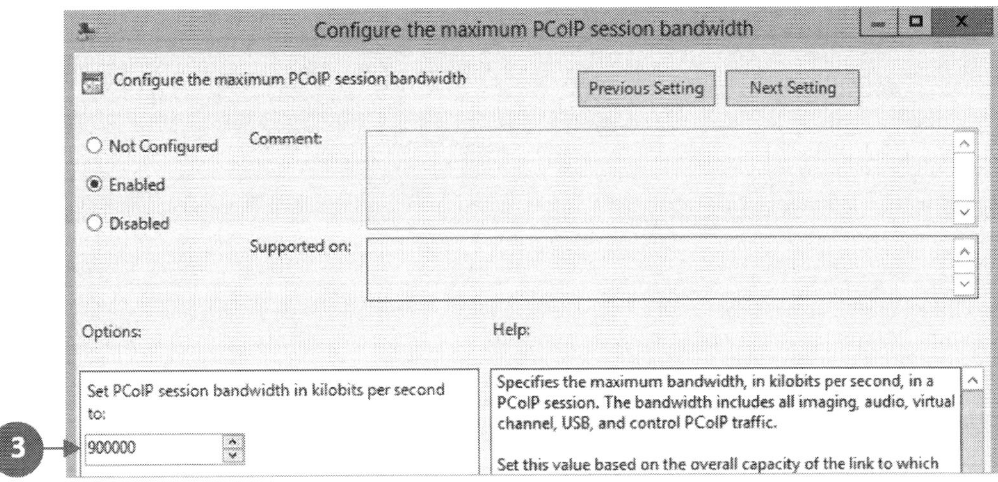

5. Click on **Next Setting** to go to the next policy.
6. On the **Configure the PCoIP session MTU** page, you can enter an MTU size for the PCoIP packets (**4**):

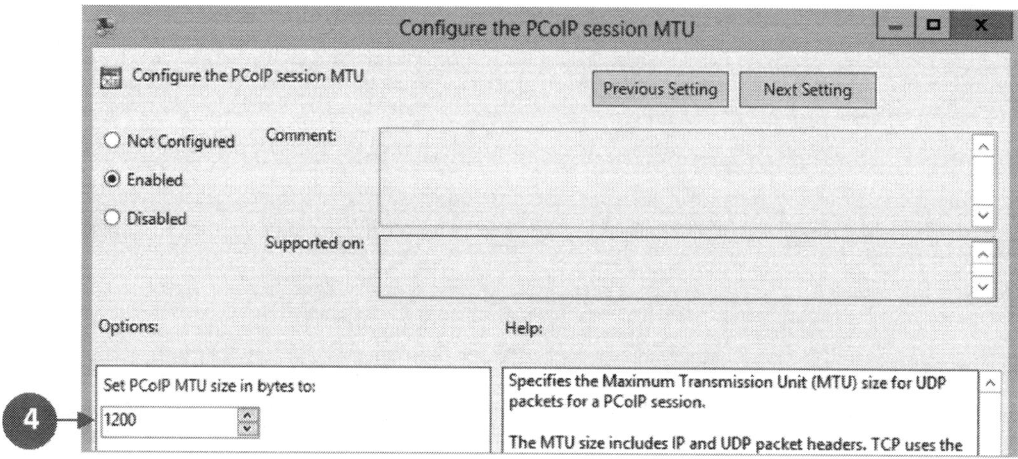

7. Click on **Next Setting** to go to the next policy:

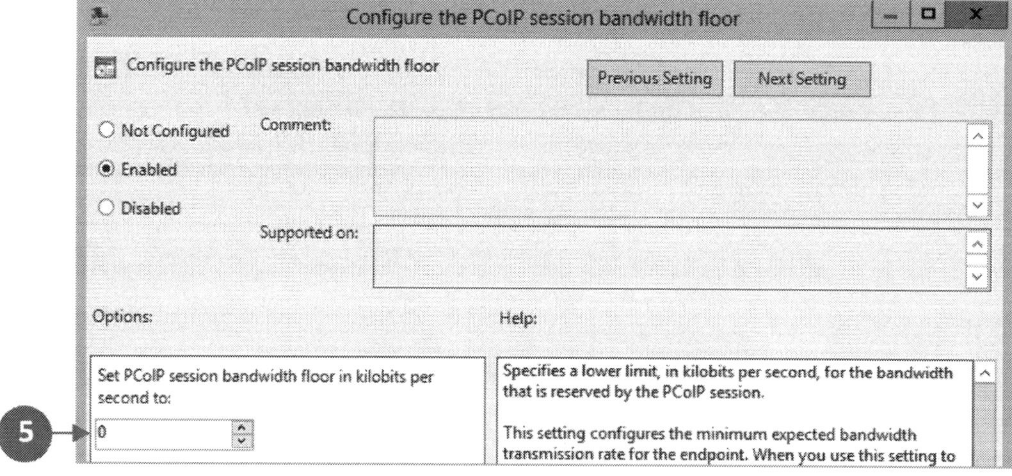

8. On the **Configure the PCoIP session bandwidth floor** page, you can enter a lower limit in kilobits (**5**); this is reserved for use by the PCoIP session.
9. Click on **Next Setting** to go to the next policy.
10. The next two policy settings are simply enable or disable options, and they have no settings that you can configure specific values for. The settings are as follows:
    - **Enable/disable audio in the PCoIP session**
    - **Enable/disable microphone noise and DC offset filter in PCoIP**
11. The **Configure the PCoIP session audio bandwidth limit** policy shown in the following screenshot allows you to set a limit on the amount of bandwidth that is used for the PCoIP audio stream. Enter a figure in kilobits (**6**):

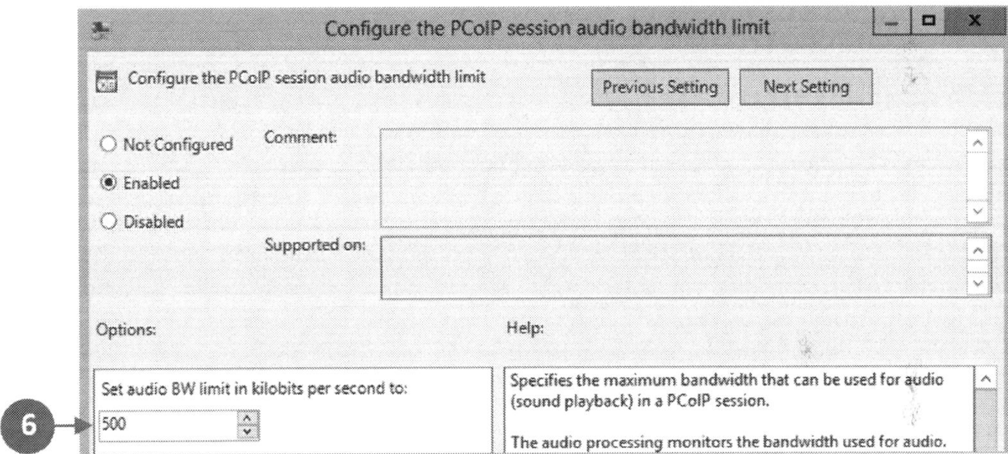

12. Click on **Next Setting** to go to the next policy.

13. On the **Configure SSL connections to satisfy Security Tools** policy, shown in the following screenshot, you can control how the SSL connection behaves:

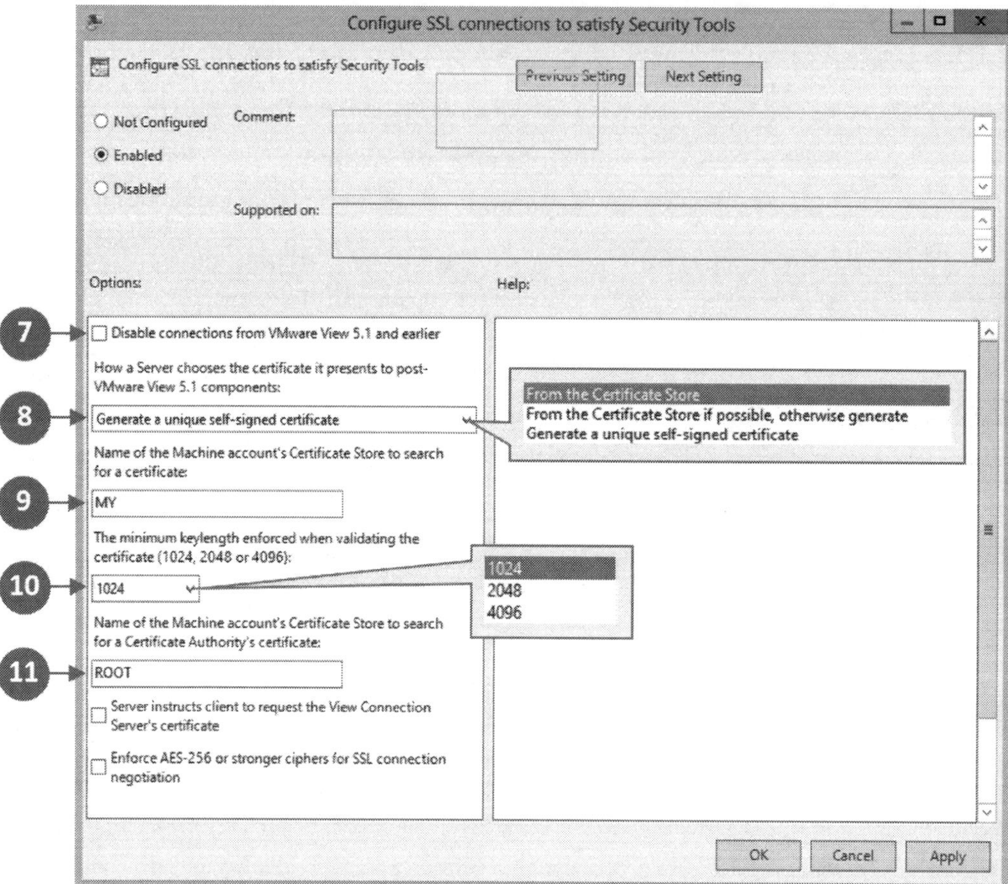

14. If you tick the box for **Disable connections from VMware View 5.1 and earlier** (7), you can prevent connections from previous versions of View. You can choose how the certificate is presented (8) and the name of the machine account used to search for the certificate (9).
15. You can then choose the minimum key length (10) and the name of the certificate store to search for the CA certificate (11).
16. Click on **Next Setting** to go to the next policy:

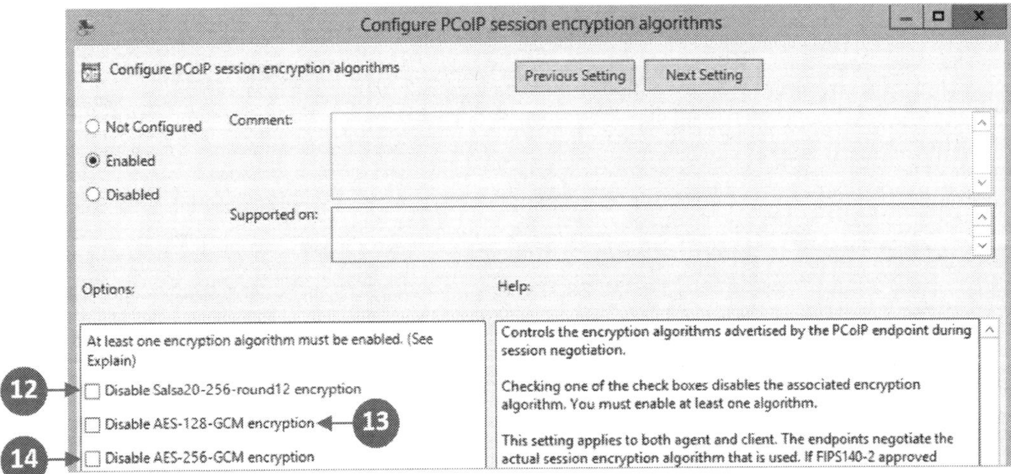

17. The next policy is **Configure PCoIP session encryption algorithms**. Check the relevant box/boxes to disable that articular encryption algorithm.
18. Click on **Next Setting** to go to the next policy.
19. On the **Configure PCoIP USB allowed and unallowed device rules** policy page, you can define which USB devices are allowed, by adding them to the authorization table (**15**), and define those that are not allowed by adding them to unauthorization table (**16**):

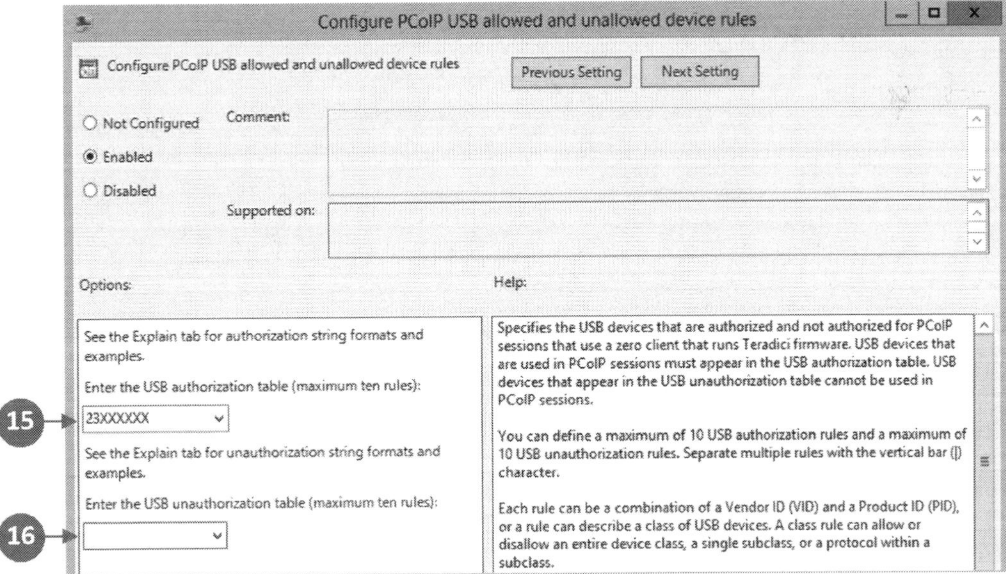

20. Click on **Next Setting** to go to the next policy:

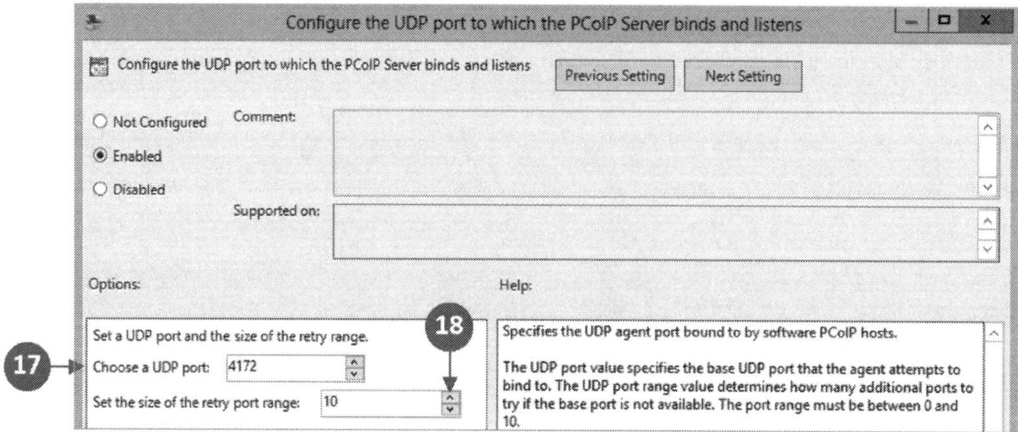

21. This **Configure the UDP port to which the PCoIP Server binds and listens** policy allows you to change the PCoIP port from the default port **4172**.

    If you change this, make sure it's reflected in your View configuration, as this will most likely use the default port 4172.

22. Click on **Next Setting** to go to the next policy.
23. The next policy allows you to **Configure PCoIP virtual channels**, as shown in the following screenshot. By default, all virtual channels are enabled. For example, clipboard redirection will be implemented as a virtual channel:

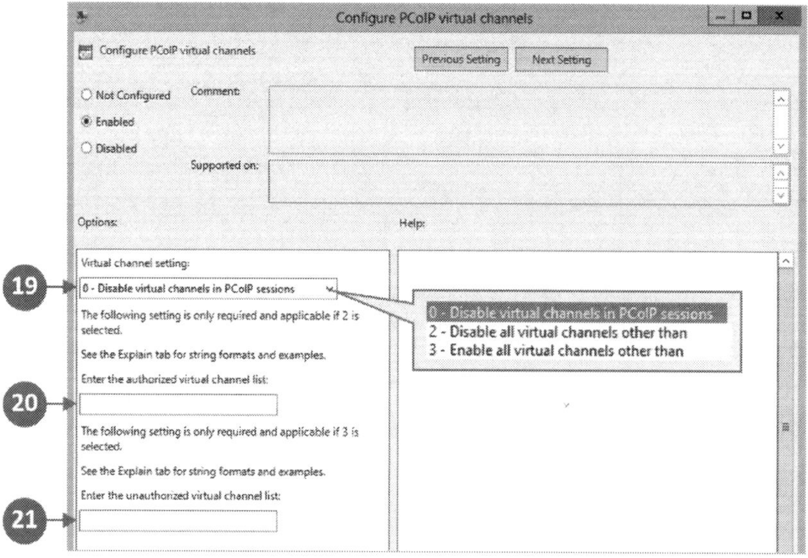

24. Click on **Next Setting** to go to the next policy:

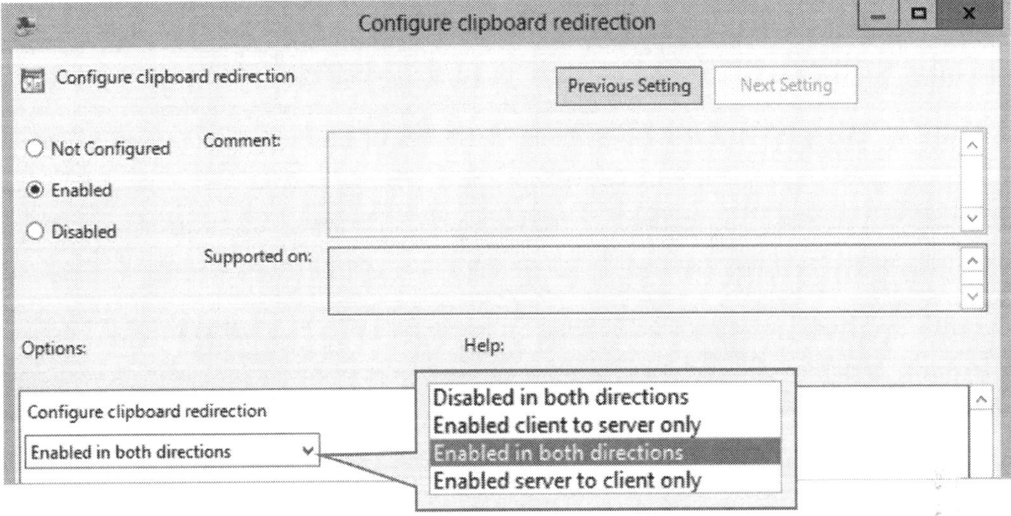

25. The **Configure clipboard redirection** policy allows you to control the cut-and-paste function of the virtual desktop machine. You can configure the policy from the drop-down menu options (**22**) as follows:
    - **Disabled in both directions**
    - **Enabled agent to client only (from virtual desktop to end point device)**
    - **Enabled client to agent only (from end point device to virtual desktop)**
    - **Enabled in both directions**
26. Click on **Next Setting** to go to the next policy.

27. The next policy allows you to **Configure PCoIP image quality levels**, as shown in the following screenshot:

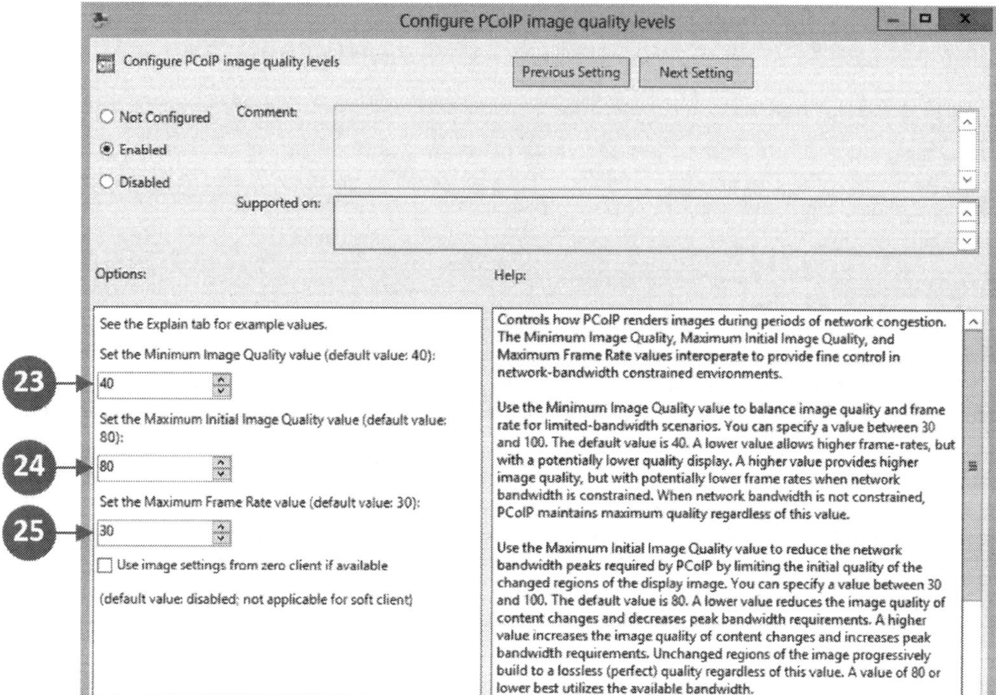

This policy is important and should be used in conjunction with end user acceptance testing. This policy should also be applied to groups of users based on their individual use case. For example, high-end graphics users require a higher setting, whereas standard office workers don't need high-end image quality.

Who you apply this policy to will also depend on the network location, as giving someone high-end image quality on a poor network connection could impact other users and services on that network. This is where your infrastructure design becomes critical.

28. Click on **Next Setting** to go to the next policy.
29. The next three policy settings are simply enable or disable options, and they have no settings that you can configure specific values for. The settings are as follows:
    - **Enable the FIPS 140-2 approved mode of operation**
    - **Enable access to a PCoIP session from a vSphere console**
    - **Turn on PCoIP user default input language synchronization**
30. The next policy is **Use alternate key for sending Secure Attention Sequence**. Enabling this policy allows you to specify an alternative key to be used instead of the *Insert* key. You can select the key from the drop-down menu.
31. Click on **Next Setting** to go to the next policy.
32. The next policy is **Disable sending CAD when users press Ctrl+Alt+Del**. This policy is simply an enable or disable option and has no configurable settings.
33. Click on **Next Setting** to go to the next policy.
34. The **Configure the PCoIP transport header** policy allows you to set whether the transport header for PCoIP is sent as high, low, medium, or undefined priority:

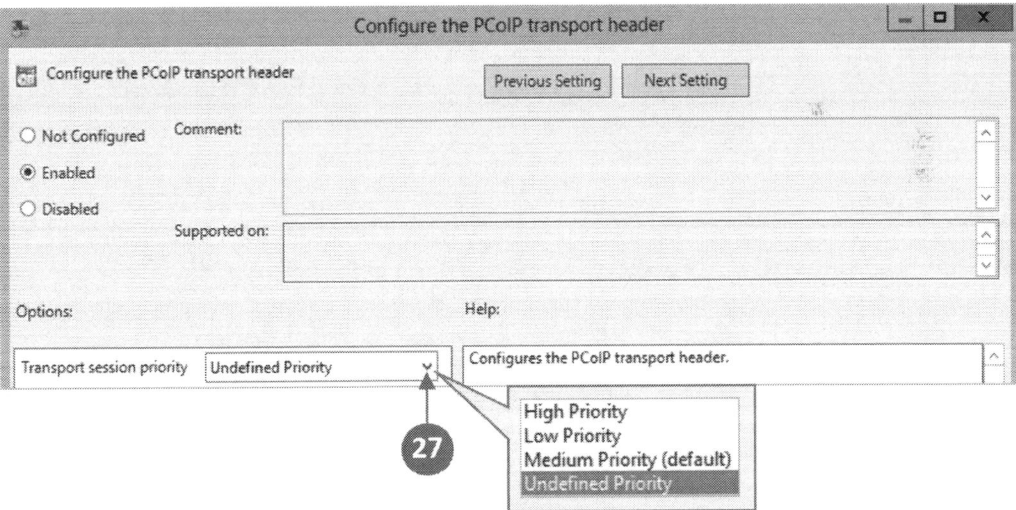

35. Click on **Next Setting** to go to the next policy.
36. Enter a value in the **Configure PCoIP event log verbosity** policy:

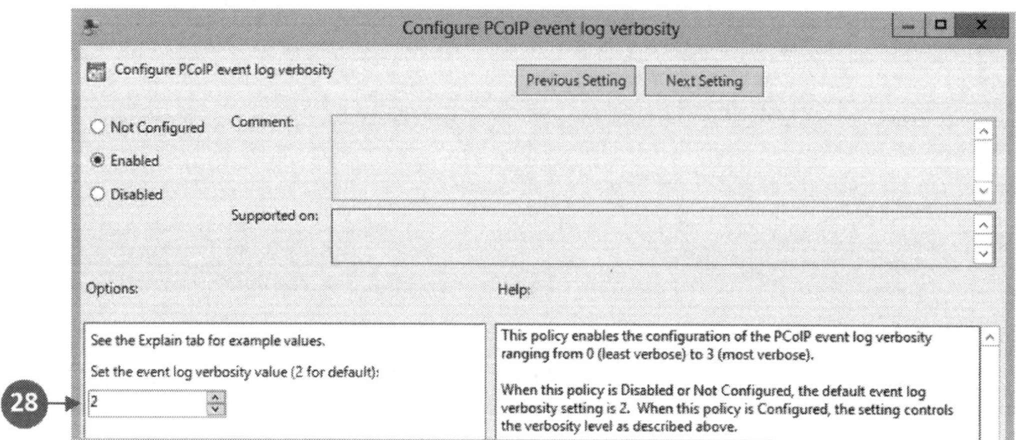

37. Click on **Next Setting** to go to the next policy.
38. The **Configure PCoIP event log cleanup by time in days** policy allows you set a time at which the PCoIP event log is cleaned up. The default is seven days (**29**):

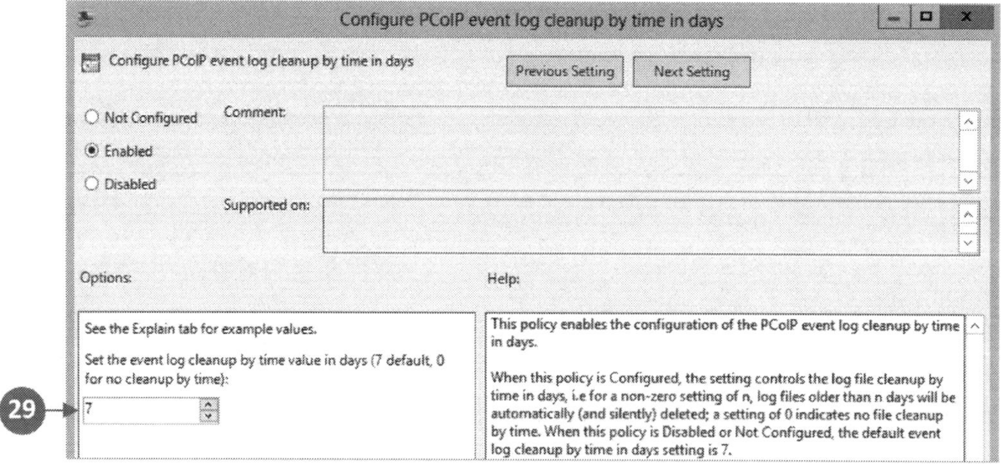

39. Click on **Next Setting** to go to the next policy.
40. The final policy is **Configure PCoIP event log cleanup by size in MB**, which allows you to set a size for the logfile. The default size is **100** MB (**30**). If the logfiles grow bigger than the set size, it will be deleted:

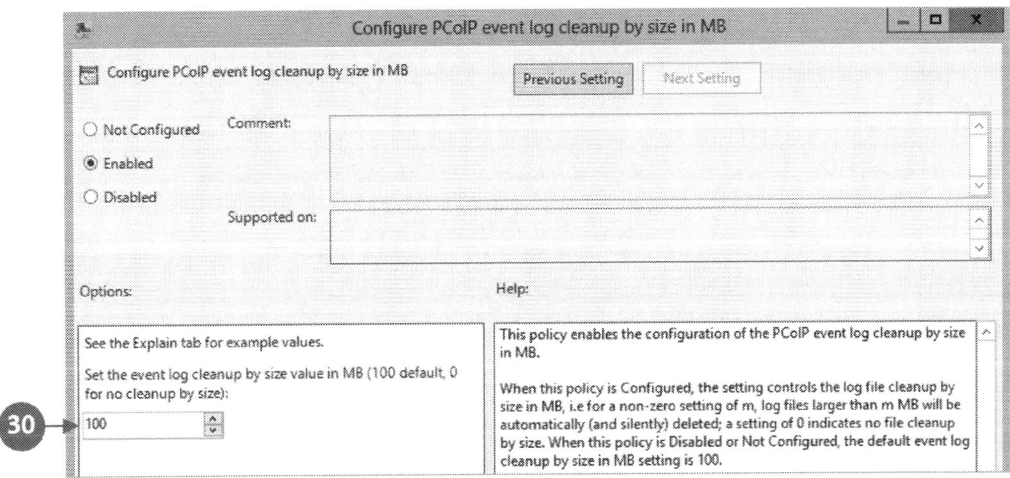

Next, we will take a look at the PCoIP policy settings for the client session.

PCoIP Client Session Variables

The next set of policy settings is for the client PCoIP session, and therefore, consist of many of the same policy settings that we covered in the previous section. The following screenshot shows the configurable policies:

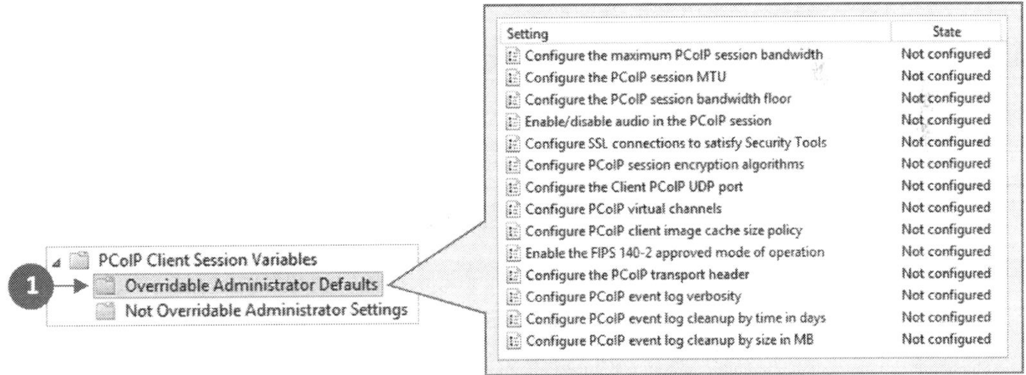

Rather than cover all the same policies again, please refer to the previous section for the configurable policy options and details of setting each of them. As stated earlier, the **Not Overridable Administrator Settings** are identical to the **Overridable Administrator Defaults**.

In the next section, we will take a look at the policy options for the View Agent.

VMware View Agent Configuration

The next set of policy options allows you to configure the View Agent. The following screenshot outlines all the available configuration options in detail:

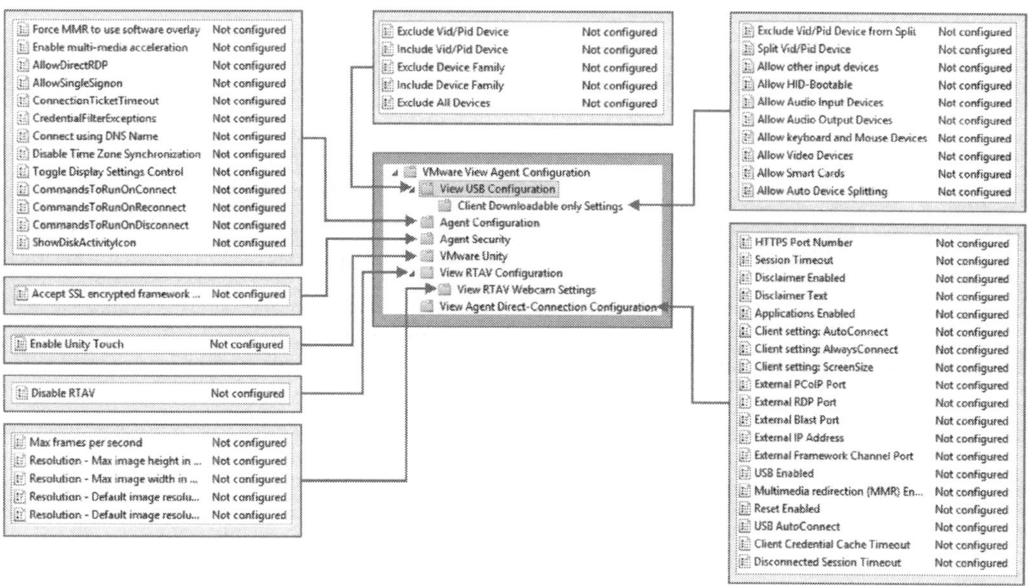

In the following sections, we will run through the configuration details and explain what each one is designed to deliver:

1. Click on the **VMware View Agent Configuration** option from the configuration window to the left. In the right-hand side window pane, you will see the options for this policy.
2. Double-click on **Recursive Enumeration of Trusted Domains**. This policy is either enabled or disabled, and there are no other configurable settings.
3. By default, this policy is enabled. Its job is to check whether every domain trusted by the domain in which the server resides is enumerated so that a chain of trust can be put in place. Each of the domains trusted by each trusted domain is also enumerated, meaning it effectively flows down through your environment until all domains are captured.
4. The list of trusted domains is used by Connection Server so that it knows about all the domains that can be used by the end user.
5. Click on **Apply** to complete the configuration for these policies.

Let's now look at the other policy headings within agent configuration, starting with the USB configuration options.

View USB Configuration

The next set of policies configure the behavior of USB devices:

1. Click on the **VMware View Agent Configuration** option from the configuration window to the left. Then click on **View USB Configuration**. From the right-hand side window pane, double-click on the first policy, **Exclude Vid/Pid Device**. You will see the dialog box shown in the following screenshot:

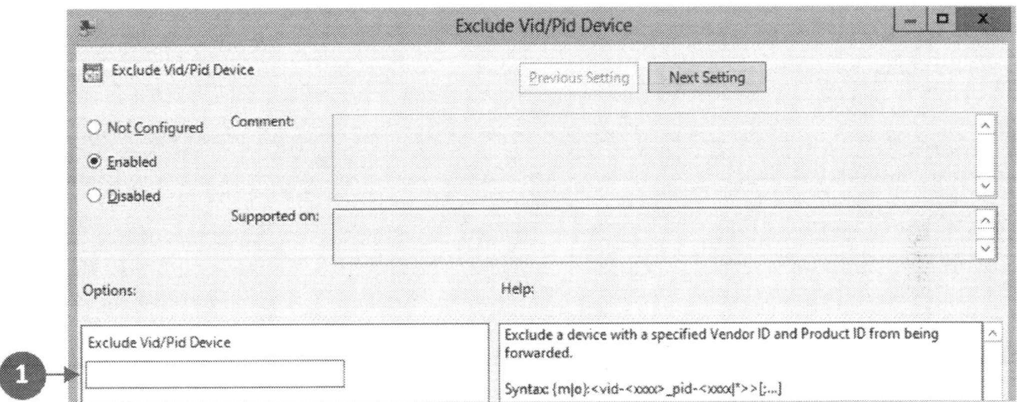

2. This policy allows you to exclude a device USB device from being connected to your virtual desktop machine. It does this when you enter the **Vendor ID (Vid)** and **Product ID (Pid)** of the device in the **Exclude Vid/Pid Device** box (**1**).
3. Apart from entering the ID of the product, there are two other options you can use in the command. Adding `m` to the command configures the client setting to merge with the agent setting, and adding `o` allows the agent setting to override the client setting. A sample command is as follows:

   ```
   o:vid-1058_pid-07a8
   ```

   The device in the given example is for a Western Digital My Passport 1 TB external USB hard drive, which we have excluded, and set the agent to override the client.

> You can find the Vendor ID and Product ID of a device by looking at its properties in Windows Device Manager. Click on the **Details** tab, and then, from the drop-down menu, select the **Hardware Ids** option.

4. Click **Next Setting** to move to the next policy setting.
5. The next setting is the **Include Vid/Pid Device** option. This is the opposite of the previous exclude setting. With this setting, we can specify a device that we want to allow to be connected to our virtual desktop machine:

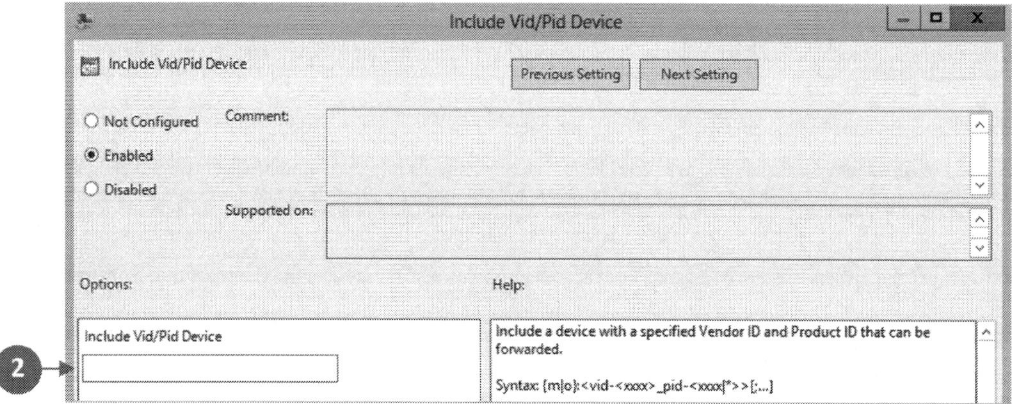

6. As with the command option in the exclude setting, enter the device details in the **Include Vid/Pid Device** box (**2**), as shown in the previous screenshot.
7. Click on **Next Setting** to move to the next policy setting.
8. The next setting is the **Exclude Device Family** option that allows you to exclude a specific family or type of device. For example, with this setting, we can specify that we don't want to allow any storage device to be connected to our virtual desktop machine. The configuration dialog box is shown in the following screenshot:

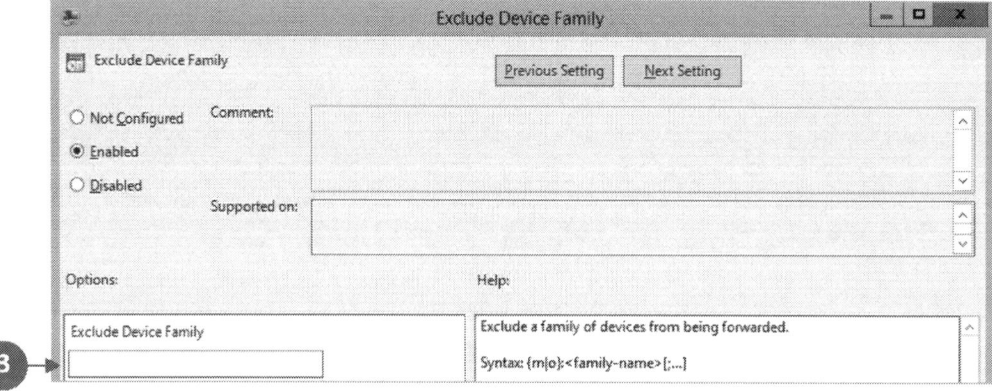

9. Enter the device family details in the **Exclude Device Family** box (**3**), as shown in the previous screenshot. You also have the **Merge** and **Override** options.
10. Click on **Next Setting** to move to the next policy setting.
11. The next setting is the **Include Device Family** option, which is the opposite of the previous setting. This allows you to include a specific family of devices. For example, with this setting, we can specify that we want to allow any storage device to be connected to your virtual desktop machine.
12. As done earlier, enter the device family details in the **Include Device Family** box.
13. Click on **Next Setting** to move to the next policy setting.
14. The last policy setting in this section is the **Exclude All Devices** option. As the name suggests, enabling this policy will exclude all devices from being connected from the end users client device to the virtual desktop machine, unless they are included in one of the include policies.
15. This setting is disabled by default, meaning all devices that are allowed can be used, unless specifically included by one of the previous exclude settings.
16. Click on **Apply** to complete the configuration.

Client-downloadable settings

The next set of policies we will configure are the behavior of USB devices on the client device and are based on the agent configuration. The agent does not enforce these policies. Instead, its job is to pass the information to the client for the client to decide how the policy should be enforced and how the USB devices behave, by performing the following steps:

1. Click on the **VMware View Agent Configuration** option from the configuration window on the left-hand side. Navigate to **View USB Configuration | Client Downloadable on Settings**.

2. Double-click on **Exclude Vid/Pid Device from Split**, as shown in the following screenshot:

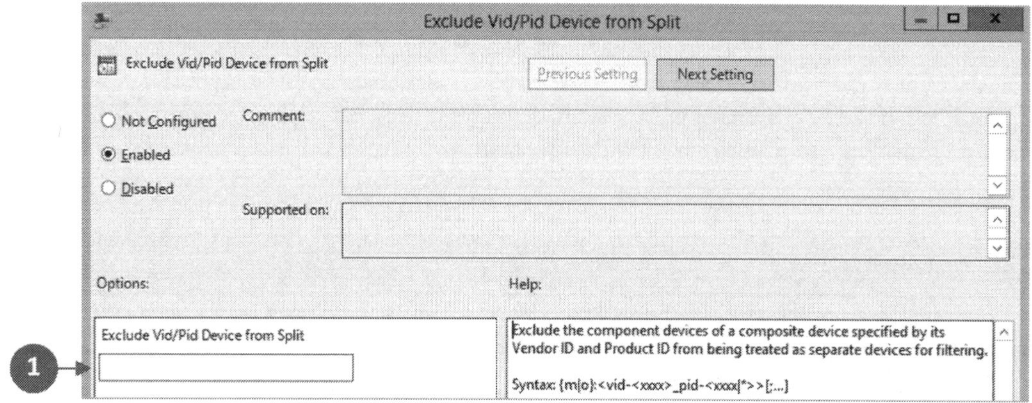

By enabling this policy, you can exclude the component devices of a particular USB device from being treated as separate devices for device filtering. As we did with the previous USB policy configuration, in the **Exclude Vid/Pid Device from Split** box (**1**), enter the device details.

We covered some details about device filtering in *Chapter 2, An Overview of Horizon View Architecture and Components*.

3. Click on **Next Setting** to move to the next policy setting.
4. In the next policy setting, shown in the following screenshot, we can configure component devices of a composite USB as separate devices for filtering:

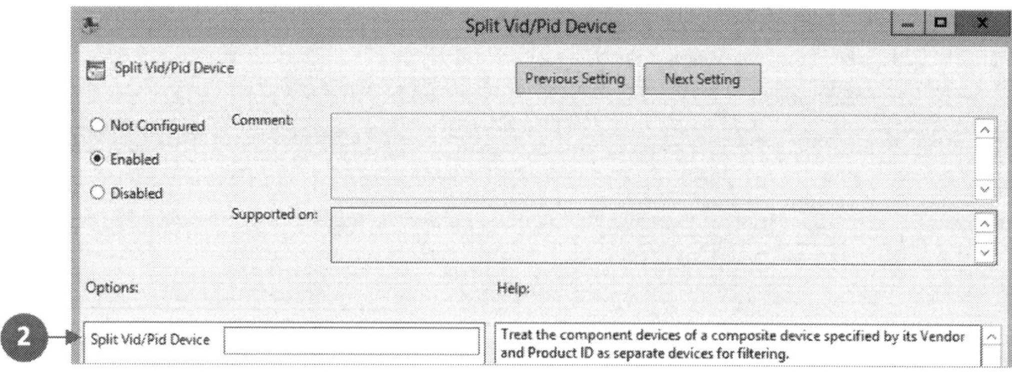

5. Enter the device details in the **Split Vid/Pid Device** box (**2**). There is an additional command you can enter to exclude components from redirection by specifying their interface number in decimal including any leading zero. So, if we go back to our previous example, we might enter a command as: `o:vid-1058_pid-07a8(exintf:001)`. In this example, we specify that the agent setting will override the client setting. We also exclude the component that uses interface 001.
6. Click on **Next Setting** to move to the next policy setting.
7. The next eight policy settings are all configured in the same way, either enabled or disabled. These policies are for the following settings:
    - **Allow other input devices**
    - **Allow HID-Bootable**
    - **Allow Audio Input Devices**
    - **Allow Audio Output Devices**
    - **Allow Keyboard and Mouse Devices**
    - **Allow Video Devices**
    - **Allow Smart Cards**
    - **Allow Auto Device Splitting**
8. Click on **Next Setting** after each policy screen, to move to the next policy setting.
9. The next policy is **Allow Auto Device Splitting**, as shown in the following screenshot:

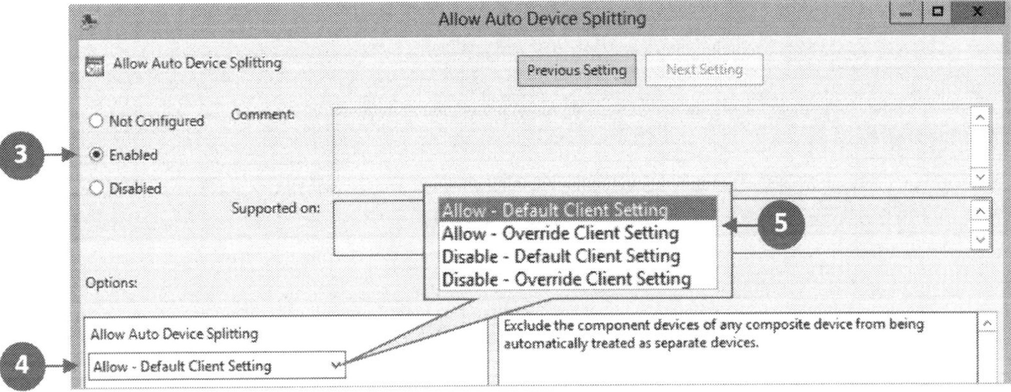

10. Click on the arrow on the drop-down menu (**4**). Select one of the four options (**5**), which include allowing the default client settings, overriding the default client settings, disabling the default client settings, or override the default client settings.
11. As this is the last policy in this group, click on **Apply** to complete the configuration.

In the next section, we will look at agent configuration.

Agent Configuration

In this section, we will cover the details of the agent configuration policy settings and how that policy configures things such as authentication and environmental settings in the agent:

1. Click on the **VMware View Agent Configuration** option from the configuration window to the left. Then, click on **Agent Configuration**. Double-click on **Force MMR to use software overlay**. This policy is either enabled or disabled and there are no other configurable options to choose.

   By default, the **Multi Media Redirection** (**MMR**) feature will try and use hardware overlay to playback video for better performance. If you have a configuration that uses multiple displays, then hardware overlay will only use one of those displays; typically, the display that was used to start Windows Media Player in the first place. If you then drag Windows Media Player to one of the other screens, then that video just shows as a black box. By enabling this policy, by clicking the radio button for **Enabled**, you can force MMR to use a software-based overlay rather than a hardware-based one, allowing it to work on all of your displays.
2. Click on **Next Setting** to move to the next policy setting.
3. In the next policy setting, we can configure multi media acceleration. This policy is simply enabled or disabled. With this policy, you can configure MMR to be enabled on the agent. MMR sends multimedia data from specific codecs on the virtual desktop machine (through a TCP socket) to the client running on the end point device. The sent data is decoded on the client and then played.

> MMR will only work if the end point device running the client is able to support the overlay function that MMR uses and if the end point client device has the resources to run the decoding process. This is where choosing the correct client device becomes important in this use case. For example, a zero client would not be able to support this feature.

4. Click on **Next Setting** to move to the next policy setting.
5. In the **AllowDirectRDP** policy, you can configure whether or not non-View based clients are allowed to connect directly to a virtual desktop machine using the RDP protocol. By clicking the radio button for **Enabled**, you can connect using RDP. This is the default setting. Disabling this feature means that only View connections from the client and the View web page will be allowed.
6. Click on **Next Setting** to move to the next policy setting.
7. The next setting, **AllowSingleSignon**, allows you to configure Single Sign On to the virtual desktop machine, and again, is simply either enabled or disabled. Clicking on the radio button for **Enabled** means when a user enters their credentials in the View Client or the View web page portal, they will automatically be authenticated onto their virtual desktop machine. If you disable this feature, the user will be prompted to enter their credentials again once the connection to their virtual desktop machine has been made.

   To enable this policy setting, you need to make sure that the Secure Authentication component of the agent is installed on the desktop and is enabled by default.
8. Click on **Next Setting** to move to the next policy setting.
9. The **ConnectionTicketTimeout** policy allows you to set the time (in seconds) for which the View connection ticket is valid. The connection ticket is used by View clients while connecting to View Agent, and it is also used for verification and Single Sign On:

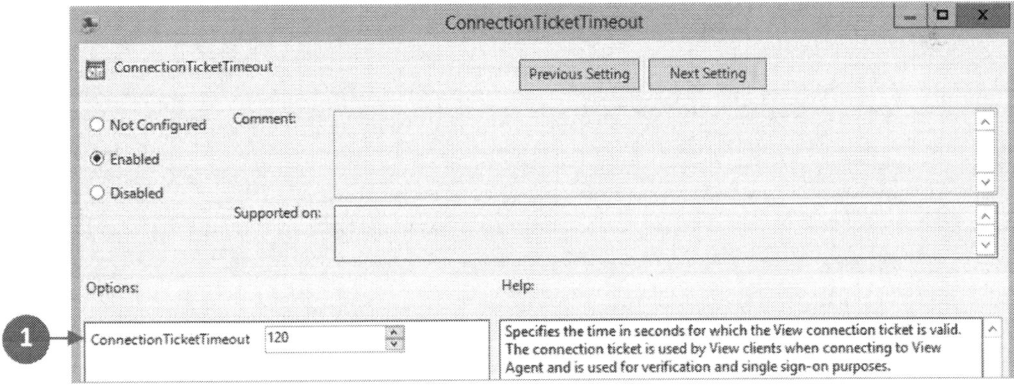

10. Enter a value in the **ConnectionTicketTimeout** box (**1**). The default setting is 900 seconds.

11. Click on **Next Setting** to move to the next policy setting.
12. In the **CredentialFilterExceptions** policy, you can enter specific executable files that are not allowed to load the agent CredentialFilter. Filenames must not include a path or suffix. Enter the details in the **CredentialFilterExceptions** box (**2**), as shown in the following screenshot:

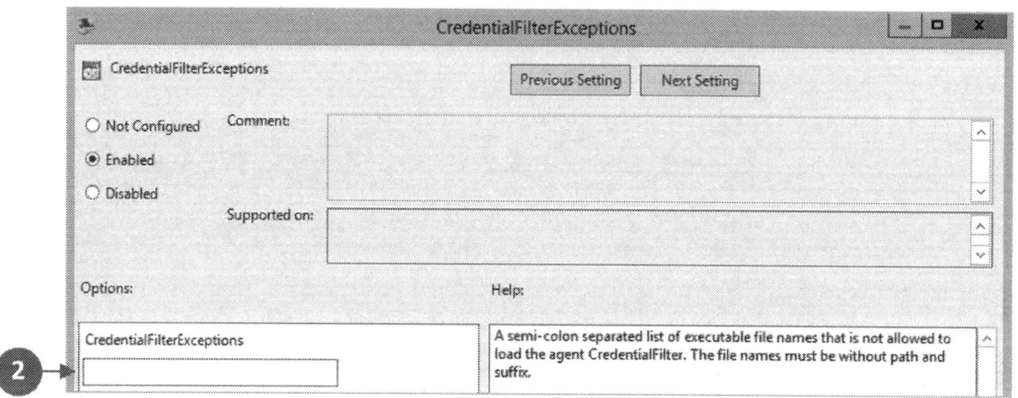

13. Click on **Next Setting** to move to the next policy setting.
14. The next three settings are simply enabled or disabled, and they have no configurable options. These policies are for the following settings:
    - **Connect using DNS Name**: This allows connection using the DNS name of the Connection Server
    - **Disable Time Zone Synchronization**: This determines whether the time zone of the View desktop is synchronized with that of the connected client
    - **Toggle Display Settings Control**: This allows you to disable the Settings page on the Display Control Panel when a View Client is connected over PCoIP
15. After these three settings, click on **Next Setting** to move to the next policy setting.
16. In the following screenshot, we show two separate polices, namely **CommandsToRunOnDisconnect** and **CommandsToRunOnConnect**:

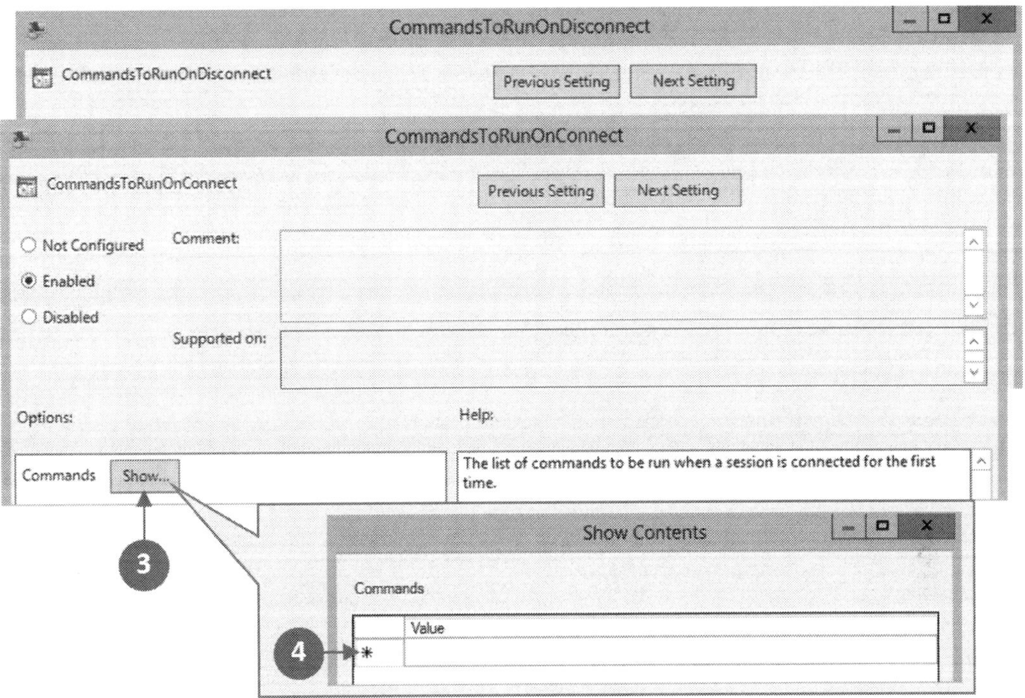

17. In this policy, you can enter commands that you want to run whenever the client connects or disconnects. To configure and add the command, click on **Show...** (**3**), and then enter the command to run in the * box (**4**). This is the same for both options.
18. Click on **Next Setting** to move to the next policy setting.
19. The final option is **ShowDiskActivityIcon**, which is either enabled or disabled. It simply shows a disk activity icon in the system tray.
20. Click on **Apply** to complete the configuration.

Agent security

In this section, there is just the one policy setting, **Accept SSL encrypted framework channel**, as shown in the following screenshot:

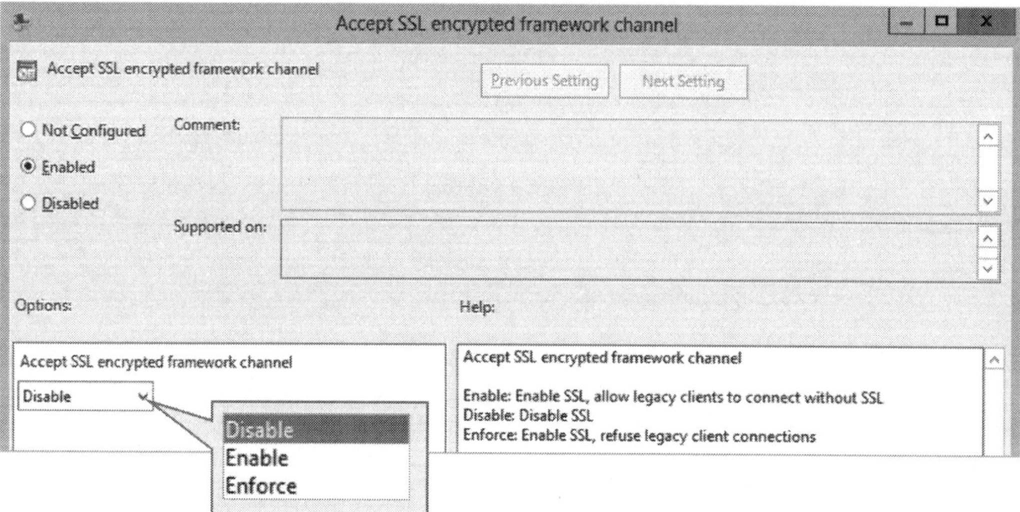

You have three options from the drop-down menu to accept SSL:

- **Enable**: This enables SSL and allows legacy clients to connect without SSL
- **Disable**: This disables SSL completely
- **Enforce**: This enables SSL but refuses connections from legacy clients

Click on **Apply** to complete the configuration.

Unity Touch and Hosted Apps

From **Group Policy Management Editor**, click on the **VMware Unity** option. In this policy, there are two options. The first one is the **Enable Unity Touch** feature for users who access their virtual desktop machine from a tablet device. This policy can be enabled or disabled, so there is nothing to configure. By default, this policy is enabled.

The second option is the **Enable system tray redirection for Hosted Apps** feature. This policy can simply be enabled or disabled, so there is nothing else to configure. When enabled, this policy determines whether the system tray should be redirected when using View remote apps.

Click on **Apply** to complete the configuration.

View Real-time Audio Video configuration

From the **Group Policy Management Editor**, click on the **View RTAV Configuration** option. There is just one policy option for **Disable RTAV** under this section. By enabling this policy, you will disable the RTAV feature.

Click on **Apply** to complete the configuration. Then, from **Group Policy Management Editor**, click on **View RTAV Webcam Settings**. In the next section, we will cover the settings for RTAV.

View RTAV Webcam Settings

In the previous policy, you either enabled or disabled RTAV. If you enabled it, you now have some additional configuration options, they are:

1. To configure these options, from the **Group Policy Management Editor**, under **View RTAV Webcam Settings**, double-click on the first policy, **Max frames per second**, you will get a screen similar to the one shown in the following screenshot:

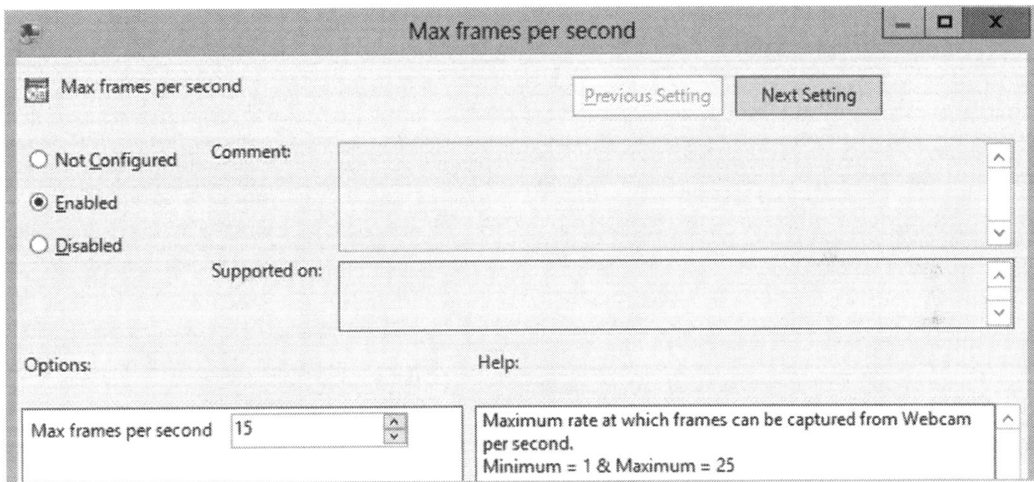

   In this policy, you can set the frame rate for RTAV.

2. Click on **Next Setting** to move to the next policy setting.

3. The next policy settings are **Resolution – Max image height in pixels** and **Resolution – Max image width in pixels**. These settings allow you to set the maximum image height and width for an image that is captured using a webcam. Enter a value in the box for both screens, as shown in the following screenshots:

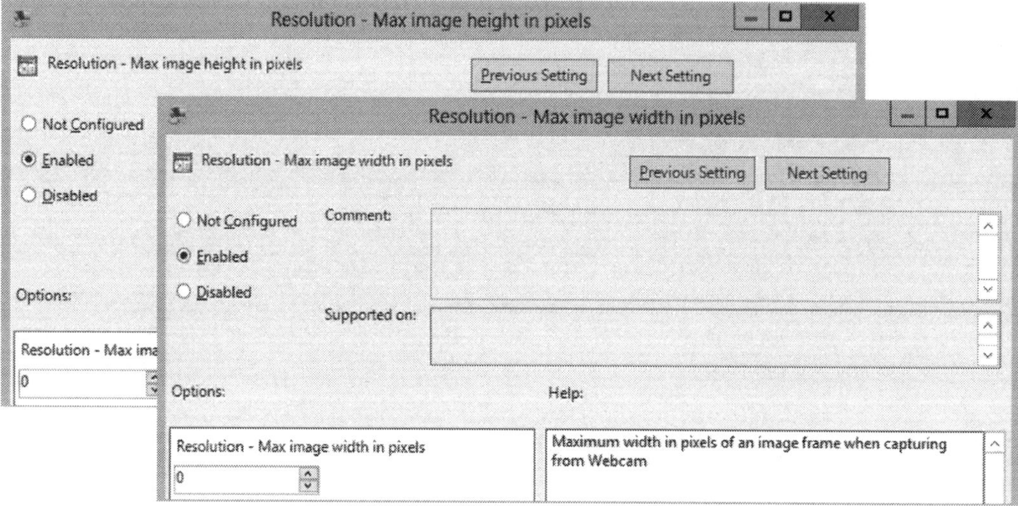

4. Click on **Next Setting** to move to the next policy setting.
5. The final two policy settings are **Resolution – Default image resolution height in pixels** and **Resolution – Default image resolution width in pixels**. These settings allow you to set the default image resolution height and width for an image. Enter a value in the box for both screens, as shown in the following screenshots:

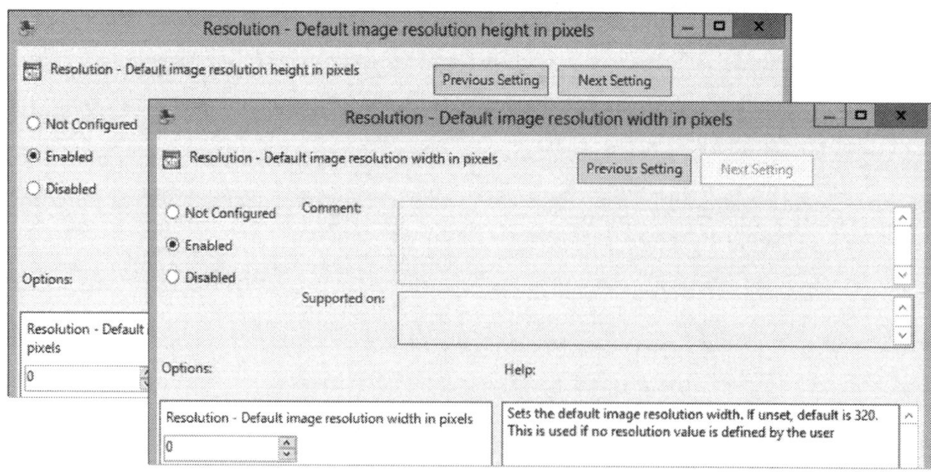

6. Click on **Apply** to complete the configuration.

In the next section, we will cover the policy options for View Agent Direct Connect.

Scanner Redirection

A new option to redirect scanners was introduced with Horizon View 6. This allows you to control the behavior of a scanner on a virtual desktop machine. Perform the following steps:

1. From the **Group Policy Management Editor**, click on the **Scanner Redirection** option.
2. There are four policy settings in total. The first three are simply enable or disable options, and they have no settings that you can configure specific values for. These policies are as follows:
    - **Disable functionality**: This enables or disables scanner redirection.
    - **Lock Config**: This locks the settings interface, so users cannot change the scanner configuration.
    - **Hide Webcam**: Webcams can be used as virtual scanners when redirected using the View Agent. This option prevents this webcam from appearing as an option in the scanner selection menu.
3. The fourth option is to configure the **Default Scanner**, as shown in the following screenshot:

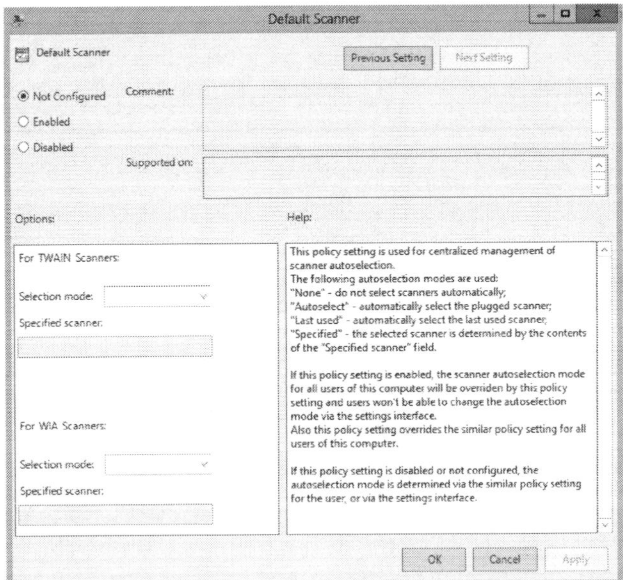

4. In this policy, you can configure options either for a TWAIN scanner or a WIA scanner. You have the following options to set how the scanner is selected:
   - **None**: This does not select any scanner automatically
   - **Autoselect**: This automatically connects the scanner currently plugged into the end point device
   - **Last used**: This selects the last scanner that you connected
   - **Specified**: If you select this option, then you also need to add the scanner details in the **Specified scanner** box
5. Click on **Apply** to complete the configuration.

View Agent Direct-Connection Configuration

To configure these options, from the **Group Policy Management Editor**, under **View Agent Direct-Connection Configuration**, we perform the following steps:

1. Double-click on the first policy, **HTTPS Port Number** and a screen similar to the following screenshot will be displayed:

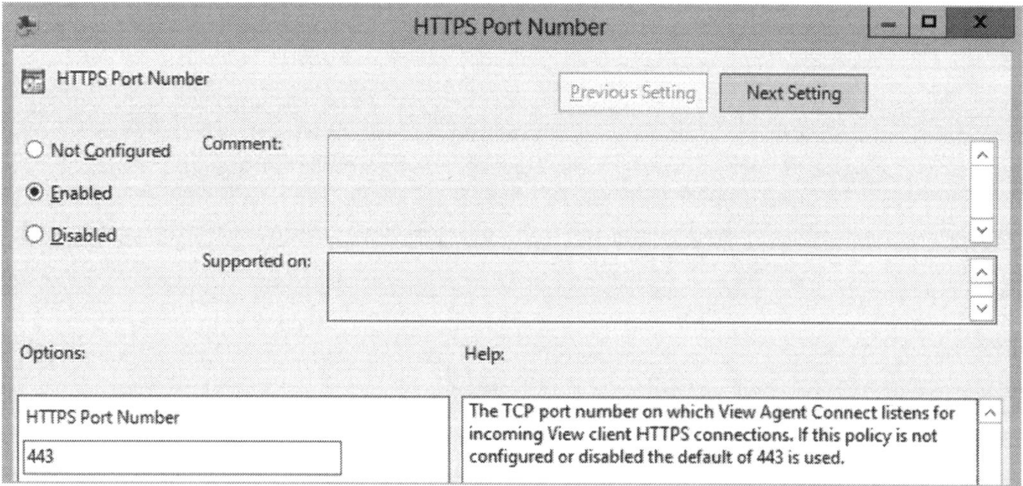

2. Enter a port number for the TCP port that the View should listen to for incoming connections from the View Client.
3. Click on **Next Setting** to move to the next policy setting.
4. In the **Session Timeout** policy, enter a time for the user to keep the session open after logging in, as shown in the following screenshot:

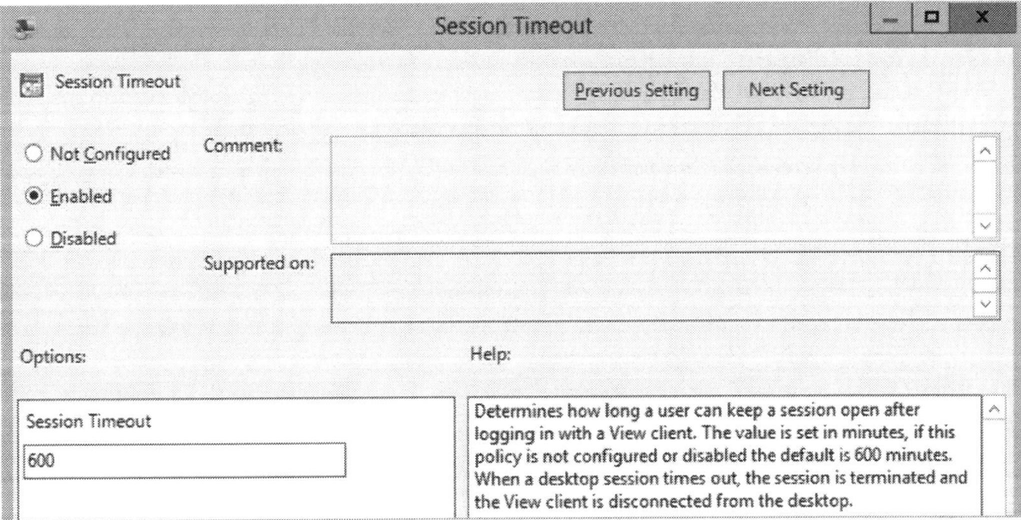

5. Click on **Next Setting** to move to the next policy setting.
6. The next policy is the **Disclaimer Enabled** policy to enable or disable the disclaimer screen, with no configuration options.
7. Click on **Next Setting** to move to the next policy setting.
8. You will now have the option of the **Disclaimer Text** policy, to enter the text you want displayed to the end users when they log in.
9. Enter the text in the **Disclaimer Text** box, as shown in the following screenshot:

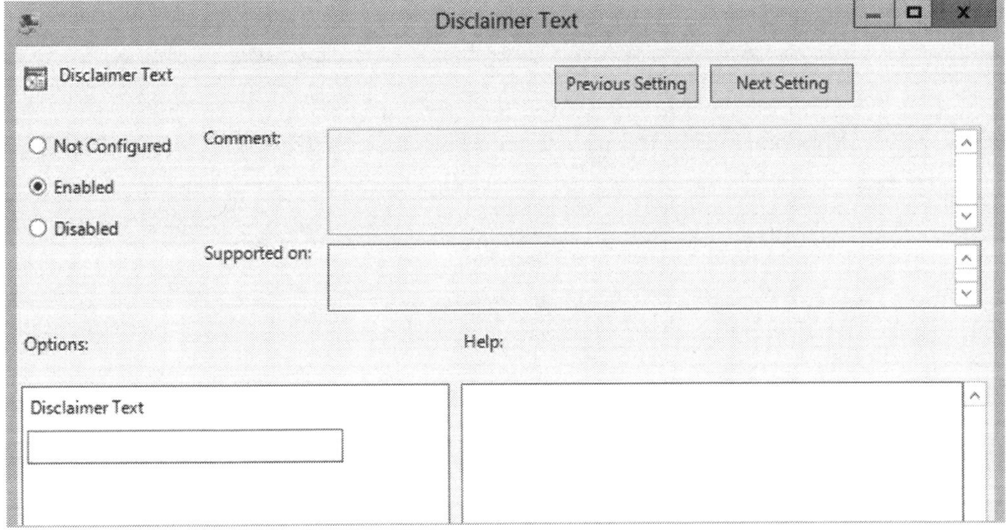

10. Click on **Next Setting** to move to the next policy setting.
11. The next three policy settings are for the following options. These are simply enable or disable options, and have no settings that you can configure specific values for. The settings are as follows:
    - **Applications Enabled**
    - **Client setting: AutoConnect**
    - **Client setting: AlwaysConnect**
12. Click on **Next Setting** to move to the next policy setting once you have configured the three policies.
13. The next policy setting is **Client setting: ScreenSize**, as shown in the following screenshot. Enter a value for the screen size. This policy will override any client settings:

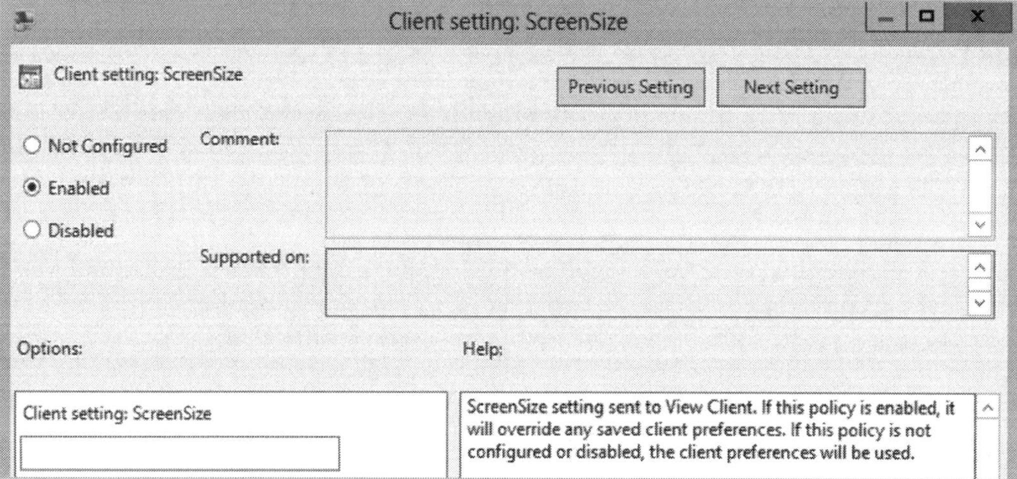

14. Click on **Next Setting** to move to the next policy setting.
15. In the next two policy settings, you can set external port numbers. The first is for **External PCoIP Port** and the other for **External RDP Port,** as shown in the following screenshots:

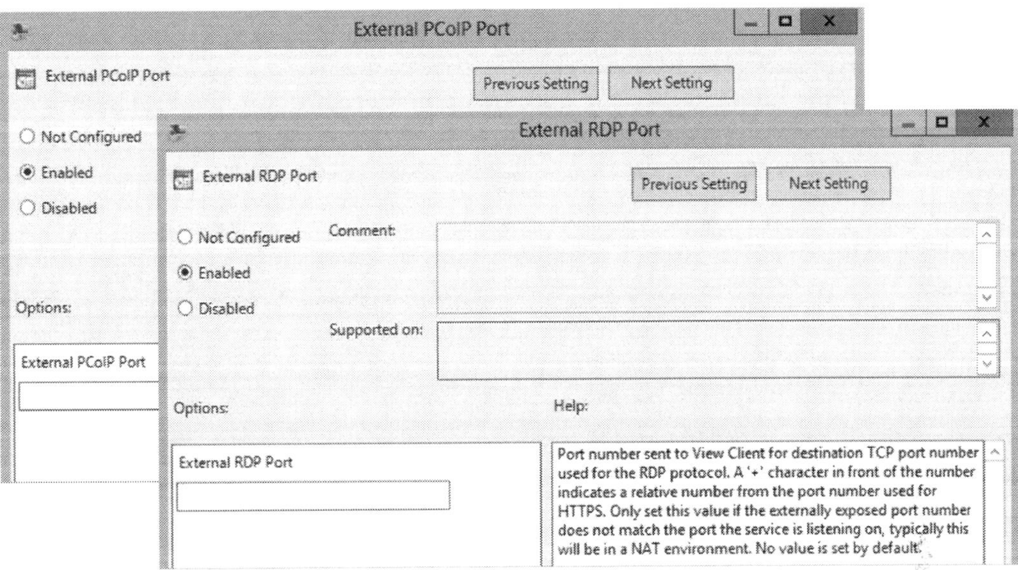

16. Enter the port numbers into the respective configuration boxes and click on **Next Setting** to move to the next policy setting.
17. The next policy is **External Blast Port**. Enter a port number in the box, as shown in the following screenshot:

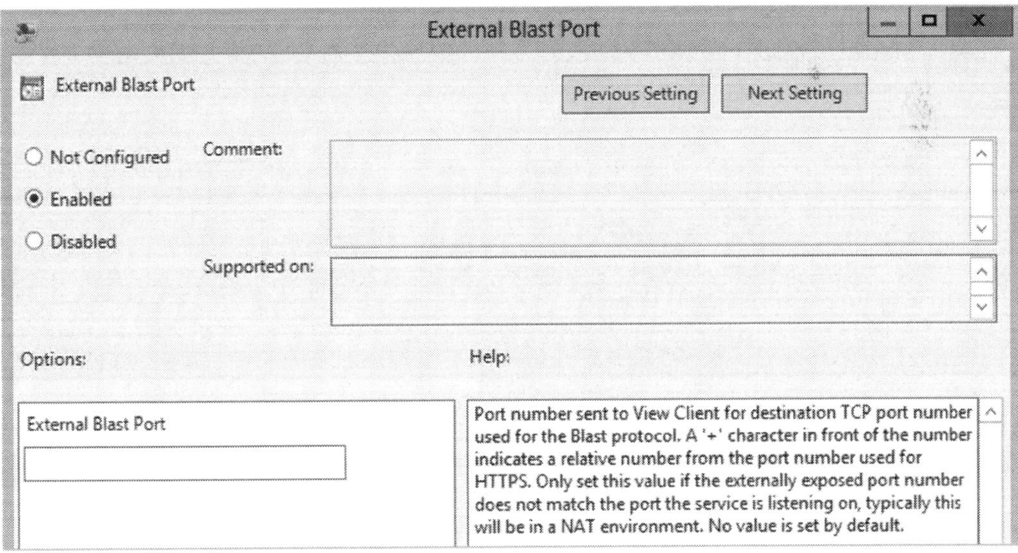

18. Click on **Next Setting** to move to the next policy setting.
19. In the **External IP Address** policy setting, you can enter an IP address for an external address when the address doesn't match the virtual desktop machines. This is typically used in an environment where you use NAT. Enter an IP address in the box, as shown in the following screenshot:

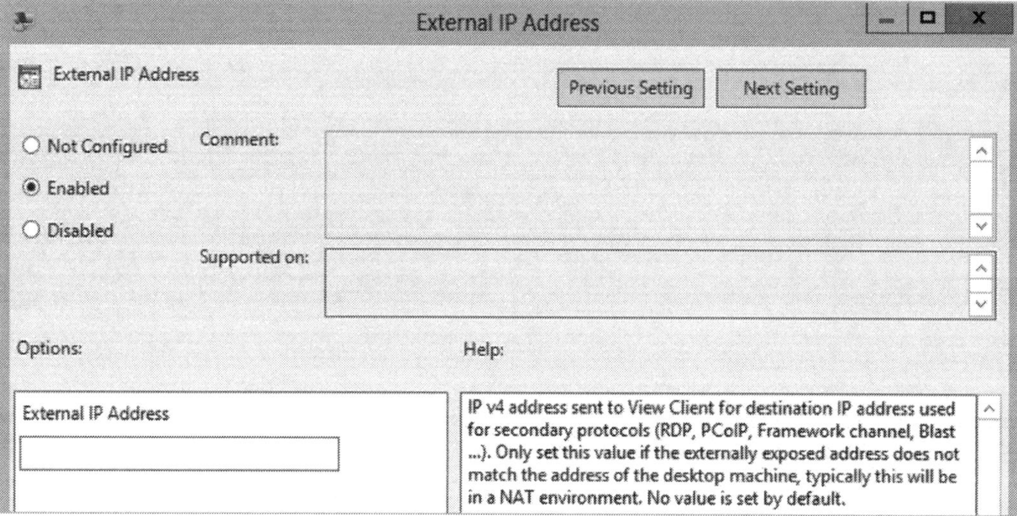

20. Click on **Next Setting** to move to the next policy setting.
21. The next policy is **External Framework Channel Port**. It is only required if the externally exposed port number does not match the port the service is listening on.
22. Enter an external framework channel port in the box, as shown in the following screenshot:

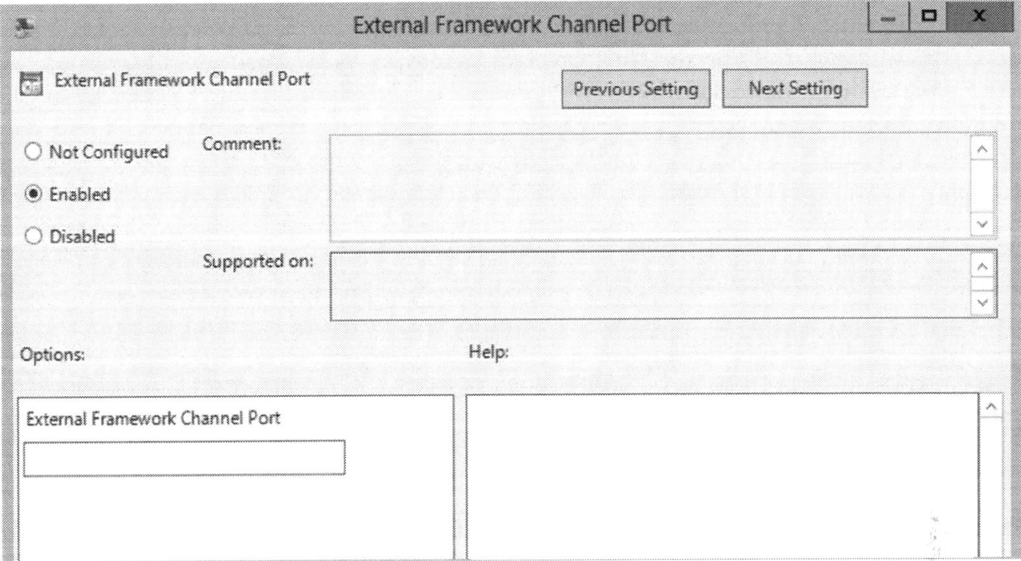

23. Click on **Next Setting** to move to the next policy setting.
24. The next four policy settings are simply enable or disable options, and they have no settings that you can configure specific values for. The settings are as follows:
    - **USB Enabled**: This allows USB redirection
    - **Multimedia redirection (MMR) Enabled**: This allows MMR

> Please note that MMR does not work correctly if the client system's video display hardware does not have overlay support, and is supported for XP and Vista desktop sources.

    - **Reset Enabled**: This allows the client to perform an operating-system-level reboot
    - **USB AutoConnect**: This connects USB devices to the desktop when they are plugged in

25. Click on **Next Setting** to move to the next policy setting.
26. With the **Client Credential Cache Timeout** policy, you can set a time until when a user should use a saved password. The default setting is not to save passwords.
27. Click on **Next Setting** to move to the next policy setting.
28. In the **Disconnected Session Timeout** policy, you can set a length of time for which the session is kept active if the client is not connected. The default setting is 10 hours.
29. Click on **Apply** to complete the configuration.

In the next section, we will cover the policy options for VMware Blast.

VMware Blast

In the next policy settings, we will configure settings for when users connect to their virtual desktop machine using Blast. The different options are shown in the following screenshot:

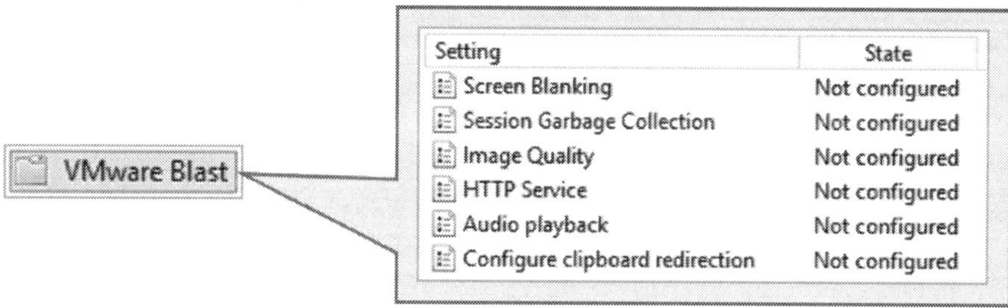

To configure these options, we go to **Group Policy Management Editor** and follow these steps:

1. Double-click on the first policy, **Screen Blanking**, as shown in the following screenshot. Enabling this policy clears the screen of the virtual desktop machine to which the client is connected:

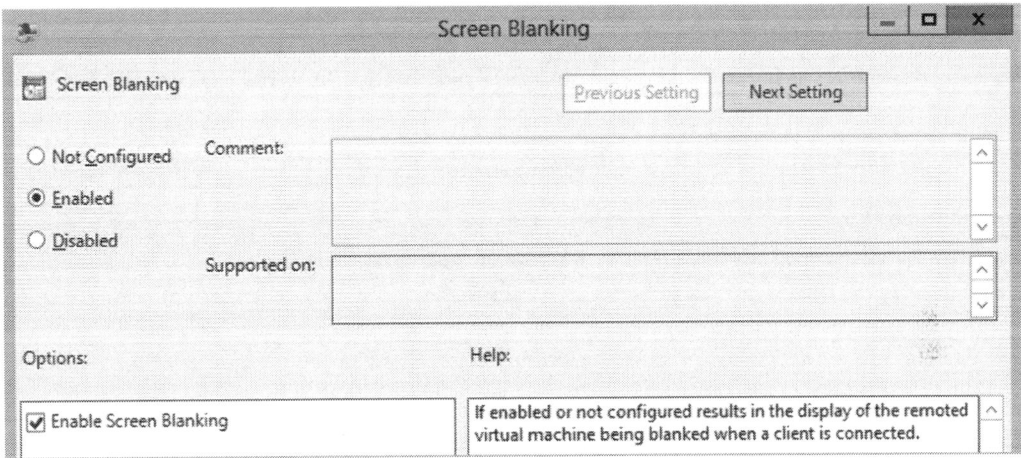

2. Click on **Next Setting** to move to the next policy setting.
3. The **Session Garbage Collection** policy allows you to configure the interval at which the garbage collector runs. The threshold setting determines the age that an abandoned session must reach before it gets deleted:

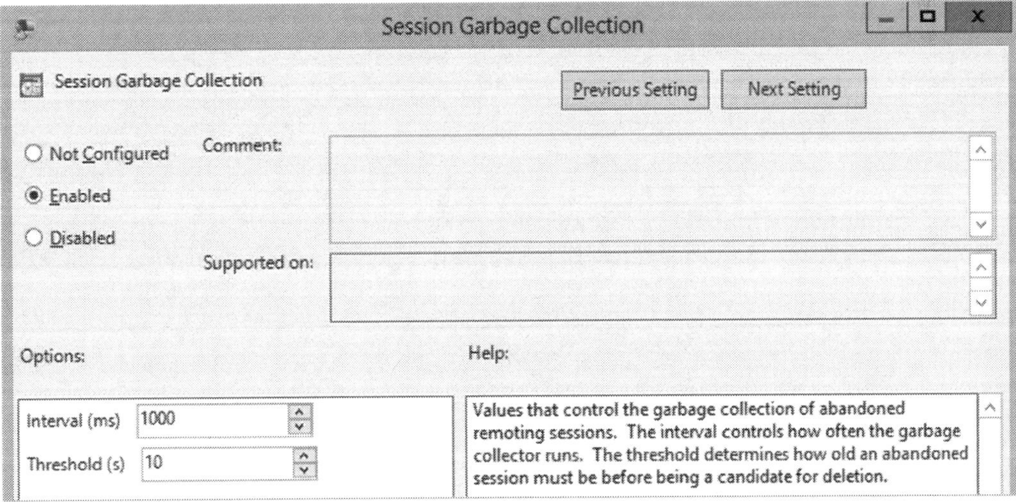

4. Click on **Next Setting** to move to the next policy setting.
5. In the **Image Quality** policy, you can control the image quality of the remote display. There are two profiles, low and high. The low profile is used when areas of the screen change often; for example, when scrolling. The high quality profile is used to refine regions of the screen that change less, resulting in a better final image. The options are shown in the following screenshot:

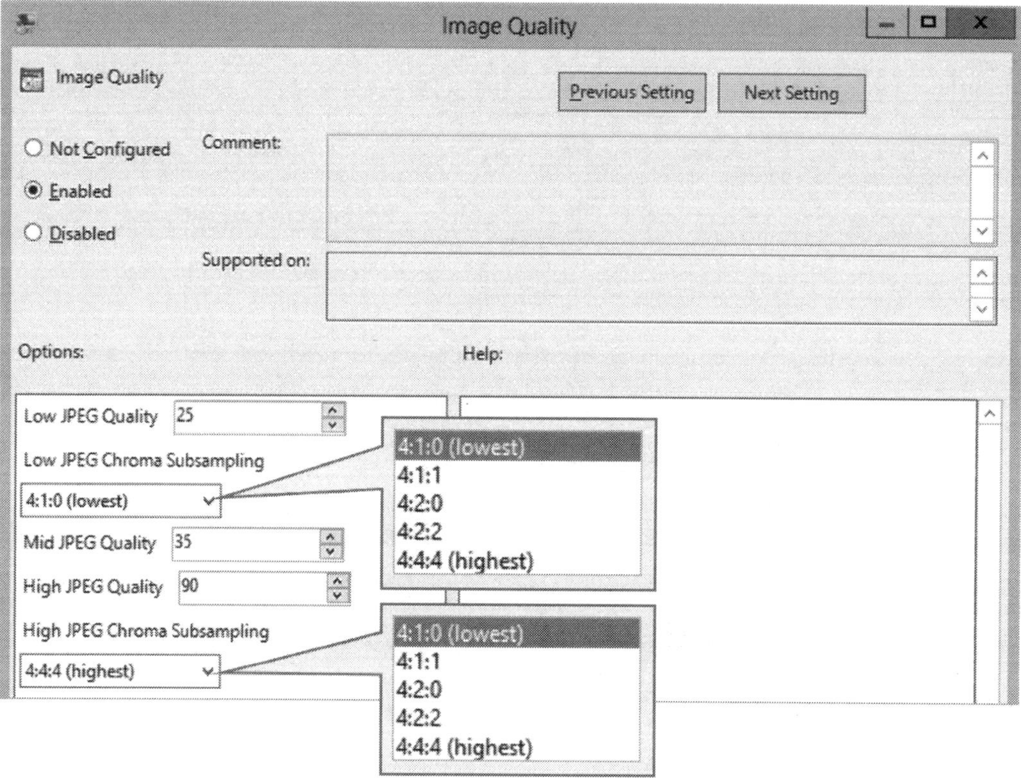

6. Click on **Next Setting** to move to the next policy setting.
7. In the **HTTP Service** policy, you can set the port for secured HTTPS traffic. Enter the port number in the box, as shown in the following screenshot:

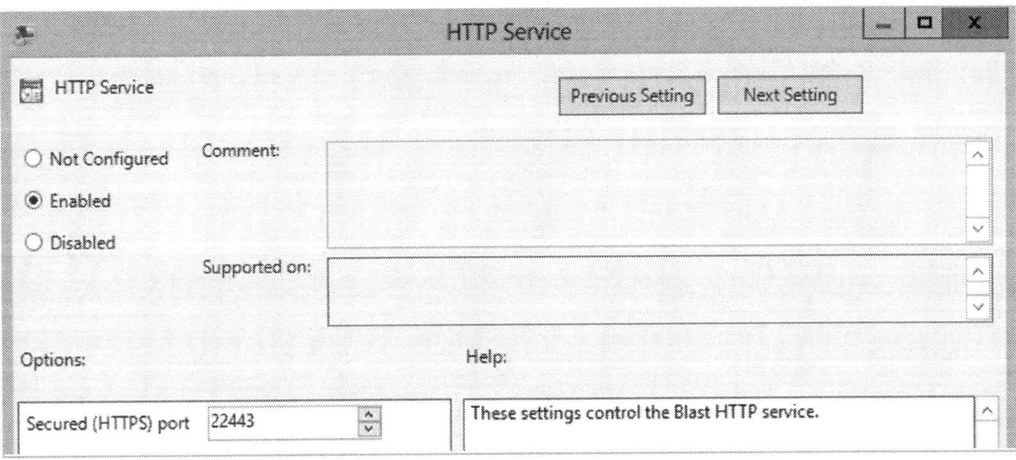

8. Click on **Next Setting** to move to the next policy setting.
9. The **Audio Playback** policy allows you to either enable or disable the audio playback for the session. By default, it is enabled.
10. Click on **Next Setting** to move to the next policy setting.
11. The **Configure clipboard redirection** policy allows you to control the cut-and-paste function of the virtual desktop machine, as shown in the following screenshot:

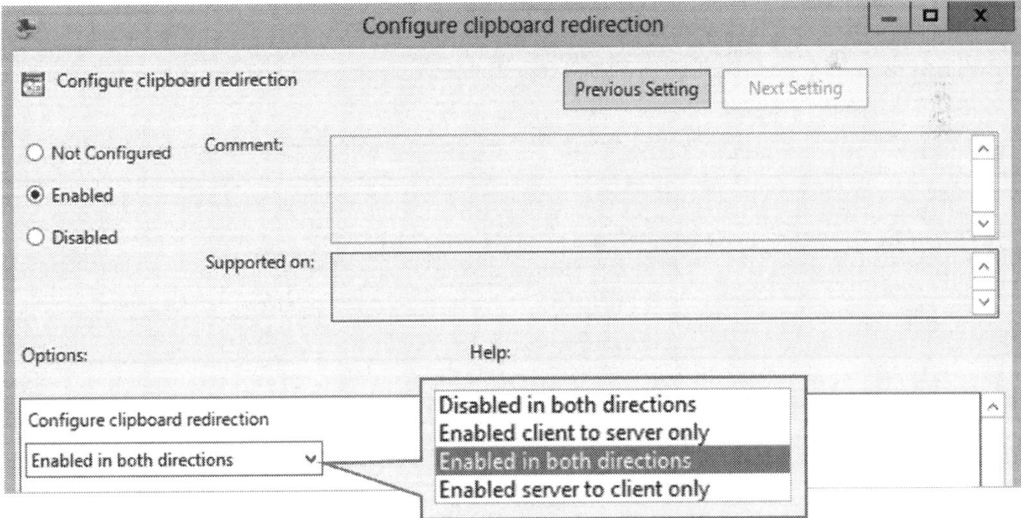

12. You can configure the policy from the drop-down menu options for the following settings:
    - **Disabled in both directions**
    - **Enabled client to server** (from the virtual desktop to the end point device)
    - **Enabled in both directions**
    - **Enabled server to client only** (from the end point device to virtual desktop)
13. Click on **Apply** to complete the configuration.

In the next section, we will configure the policy settings for View Client.

VMware View Client Configuration

In this section, we will look at the policy configuration options for View Client. The options are shown in the following screenshot:

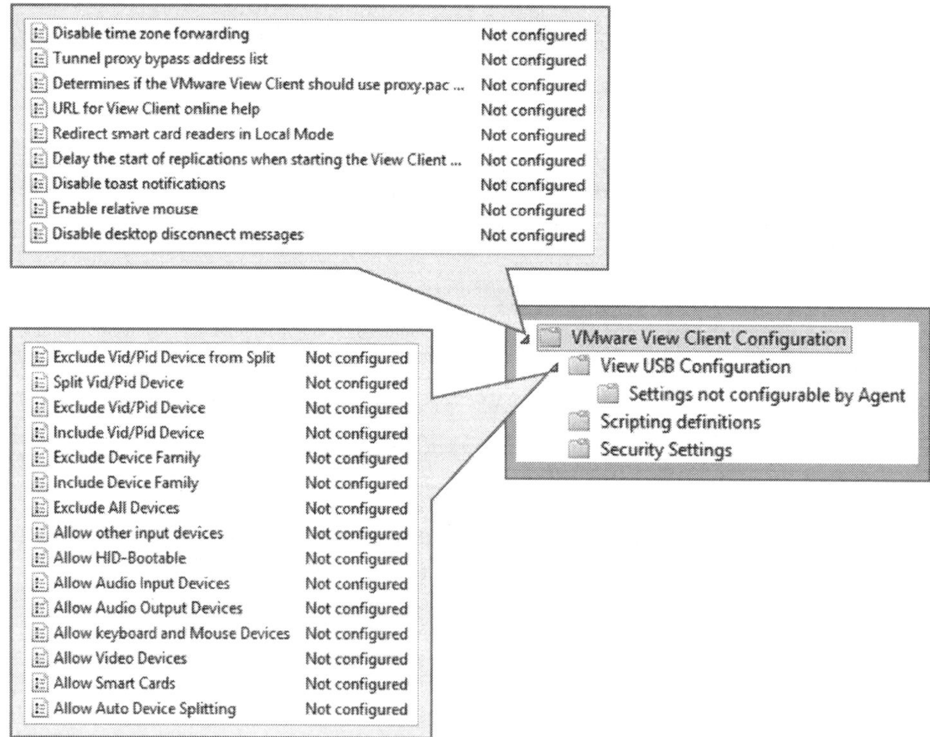

However there are some more options, please have a look at those in the following screenshot:

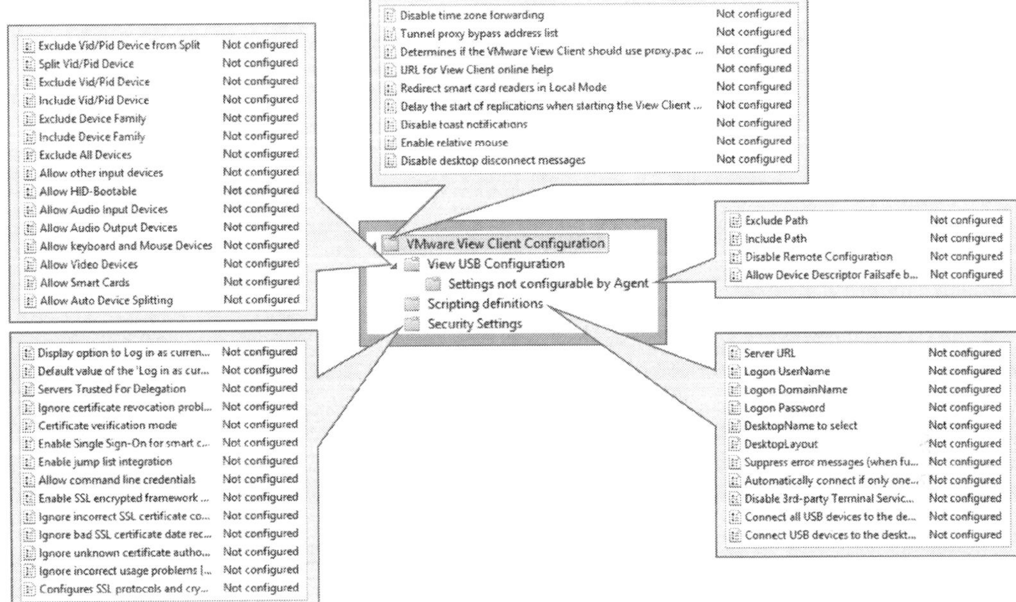

To configure these options, go to **Group Policy Management Editor** and follow these steps:

1. Click on **VMware View Client Configuration** and then double-click on the first policy, **Disable time zone forwarding**.
2. This policy is simply enabled or disabled, and there are no configurable options.
3. Click on **Next Setting** to move to the next policy setting.

4. The **Tunnel proxy bypass address list** option, shown in the previous screenshot, allows you to configure a tunnel proxy bypass list:

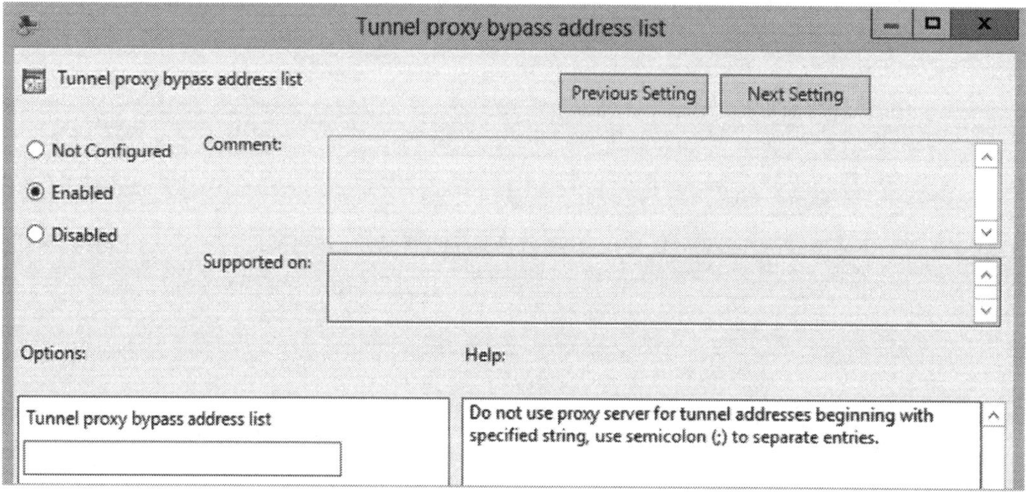

5. Click on **Next Setting** to move to the next policy setting.
6. The next policy determines if the VMware View Client should use `proxy.pac`. This is for View 4.x client versions and earlier, so you can ignore this policy as we are using the latest version.
7. Click on **Next Setting** to move to the next policy setting.
8. In the **URL for View Client online help** policy, you can specify an alternative address for help pages, as shown in the following screenshot:

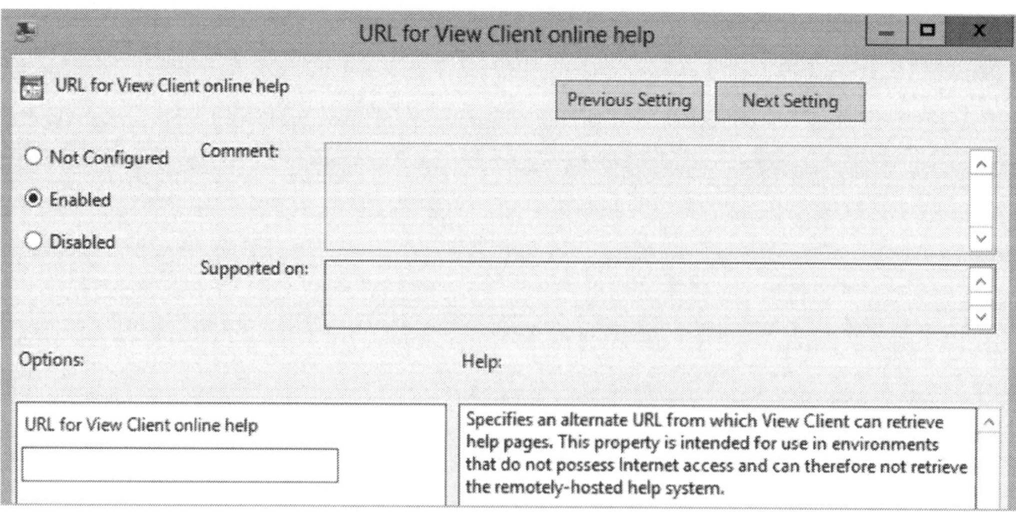

9. Click on **Next Setting** to move to the next policy setting.
10. The next two policies, **Redirect smart card readers in Local Mode** and **Delay the start of replications when starting the View Client with Local Mode**, are no longer required, given that local mode no longer exists in Horizon View 6.
11. Click on **Next Setting** to move to the next policy setting.
12. In the **Disable toast notifications** policy, you simply enable or disable this policy. This setting disables the toast notifications from the View Client. Enable this setting if you do not want the user to see toast notifications pop up in the corner of their screen.
13. Click on **Next Setting** to move to the next policy setting.
14. You will now see the **Enable relative mouse** policy, which is again simply a policy that you can either enable or disable.
15. This setting enables relative mouse from the View Client for PCoIP desktops. Enable this setting if you want the user to use relative mouse mode with PCoIP desktops always. Relative mouse mode improves mouse behavior for certain graphics, applications, and games. If the remote desktop does not support relative mouse, then this setting will not be used.
16. Click on **Next Setting** to move to the next policy setting.
17. The final policy option is **Disable desktop disconnect messages**, and is either enabled or disabled. It configures whether or not messages that are usually shown when the desktop is disconnected should be disabled.
18. Click on **Apply** to complete the configuration.

In the next section, we will configure the policy settings for VMware View USB configuration.

VMware View USB Configuration

The View USB configuration for the View Client contains exactly the same policy options as the View Agent configuration for USB section that we covered previously in this chapter, but now these apply to the client.

For example, these policy options that are applied to the client machine could be used for split settings, where you need to direct View to split a device's functions between client and virtual desktop machines. In such cases, client settings don't need to be configured on every client; instead, they can be configured using a GPO, which is then applied to the desktop pool.

When the end user logs in to their virtual desktop machine, the client configuration is downloaded to the client machine and applied only to the client and not to the agent running on the virtual desktop machine.

Rather than repeating every policy option again, please refer to the respective sections for the policy details. The following diagram shows the policy options:

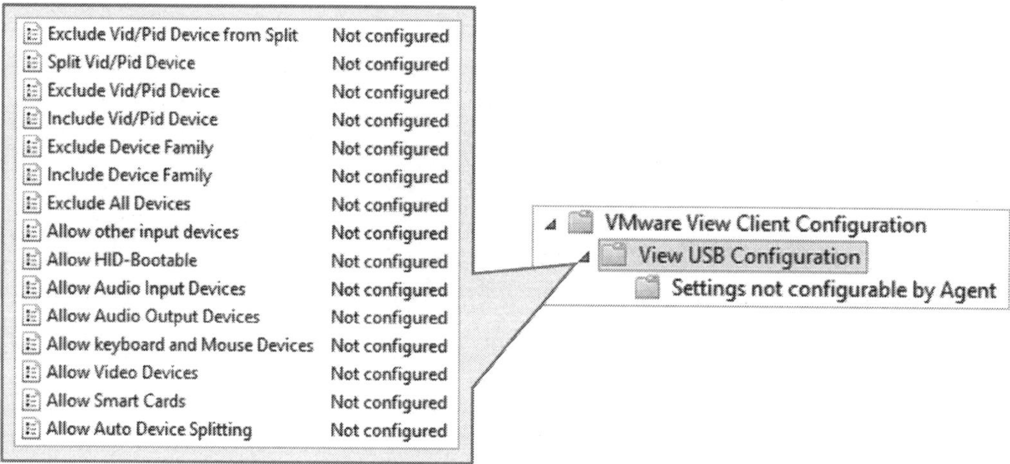

There are a few policy settings that are not configurable by the agent, which we will cover in the next section.

Settings not configurable by Agent

To configure these options, from the **Group Policy Management Editor** we will follow these steps:

1. Click on **VMware View Client Configuration** and then **Settings not configurable by Agent**. Double-click on the first policy, **Exclude Path**.
2. The **Exclude Path** and **Include Path** policy settings are shown together in the following screenshots:

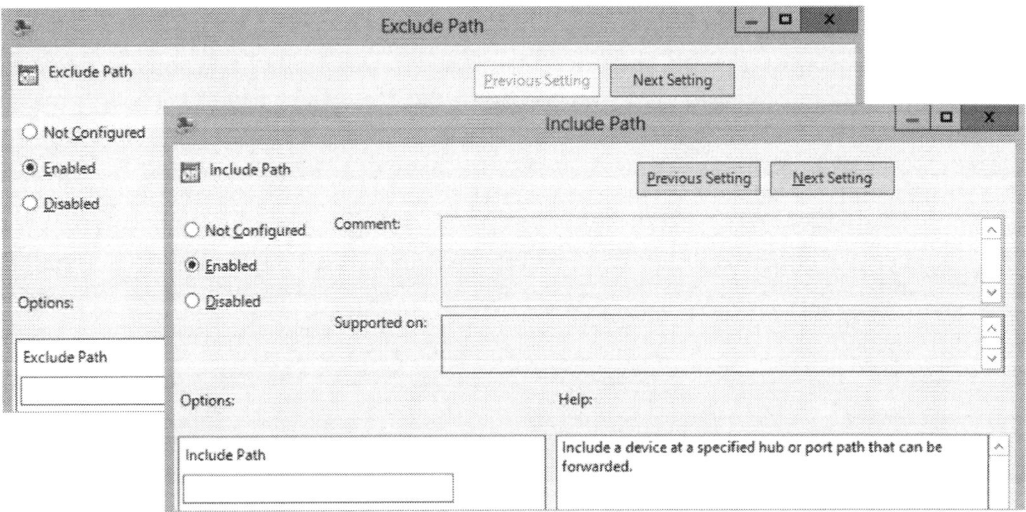

This policy allows you to either exclude or include a device at a specified hub or port path from being forwarded.

3. Click on **Next Setting** to move to the next policy setting.
4. The next two policy settings are simply enable or disable options, and have no settings that you can configure specific values for. The settings are as follows:
    - **Disable Remote Configuration**
    - **Allow Device Descriptor Failsafe behavior**
5. Click on **Apply** to complete the configuration for these policies. In the next section, we will look at policy options for script definitions.

Scripting definitions

In the next set of policies, we will look at scripting definitions. To configure these options from the **Group Policy Management Editor**, we will follow these steps:

1. Click on **VMware View Client Configuration** and then click on **Scripting definitions**. Double-click on the first policy, **Server URL**. By enabling this policy, you enter a URL for the Connection Server that is used by the client when the end user logs in. Type in the server URL in the box, as shown in the following screenshot:

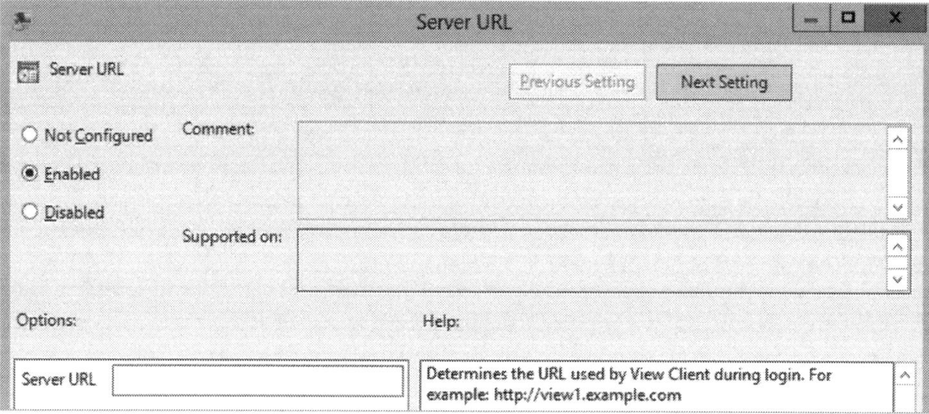

2. Click on **Next Setting** to move to the next policy setting.
3. In the **Logon UserName** policy setting, enter a username for the client to use during the login process. Enter the name in the box, as shown in the following screenshot:

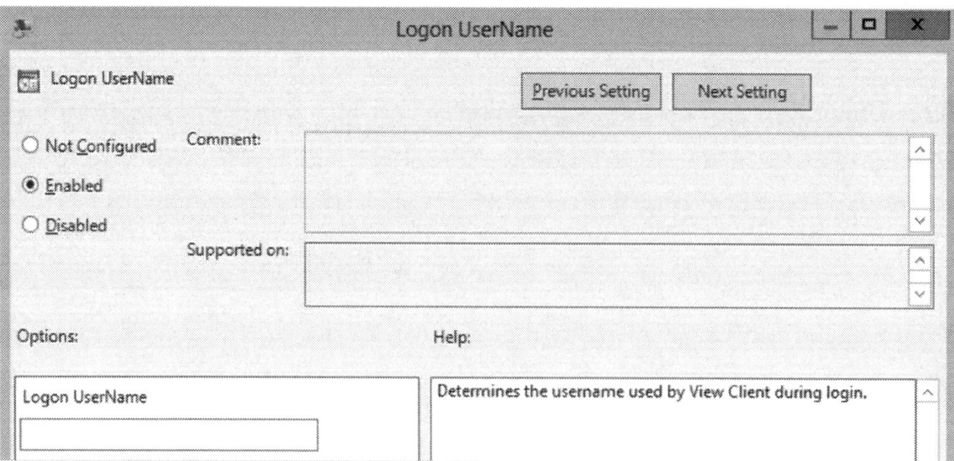

4. Click on **Next Setting** to move to the next policy setting.
5. In the **Logon DomainName** policy setting, enter a domain name for the client to use during the login process. Enter the name in the box, as shown in the following screenshot:

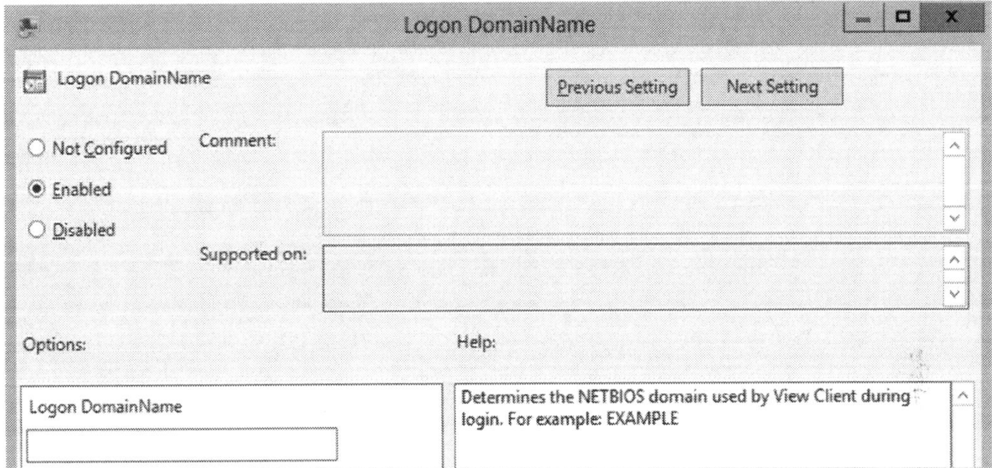

6. Click on **Next Setting** to move to the next policy setting.
7. In the **Logon Password** policy setting, enter a password for the client to use during the login process. Enter the password in the box, as shown in the following screenshot. Beware that this password is stored in AD as plain text:

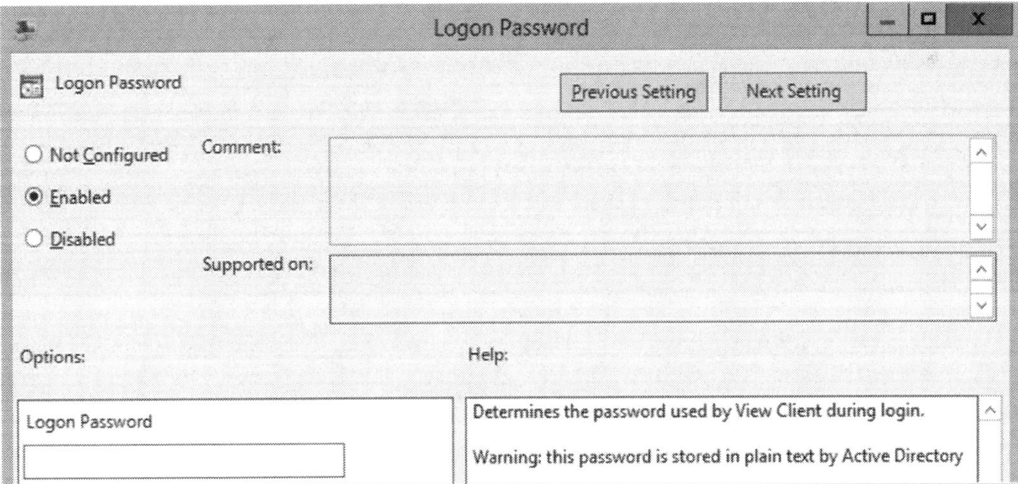

8. Click on **Next Setting** to move to the next policy setting.
9. In the **DesktopName to select** policy setting, you can enter the name of the default desktop that you want the user to use during the login process. Enter the name in the box, as shown in the following screenshot:

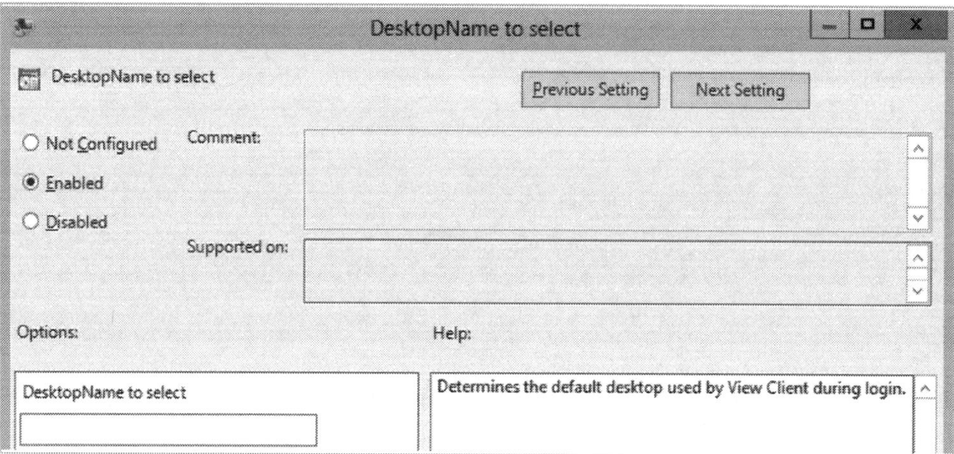

10. Click on **Next Setting** to move to the next policy setting.
11. In the **DesktopLayout** policy setting, you can choose how the desktop is displayed to the user when they connect. You can choose **Full Screen**, **Multimonitor**, **Window - Large**, or **Window - Small**. Choose one from the drop-down menu, as shown in the following screenshot:

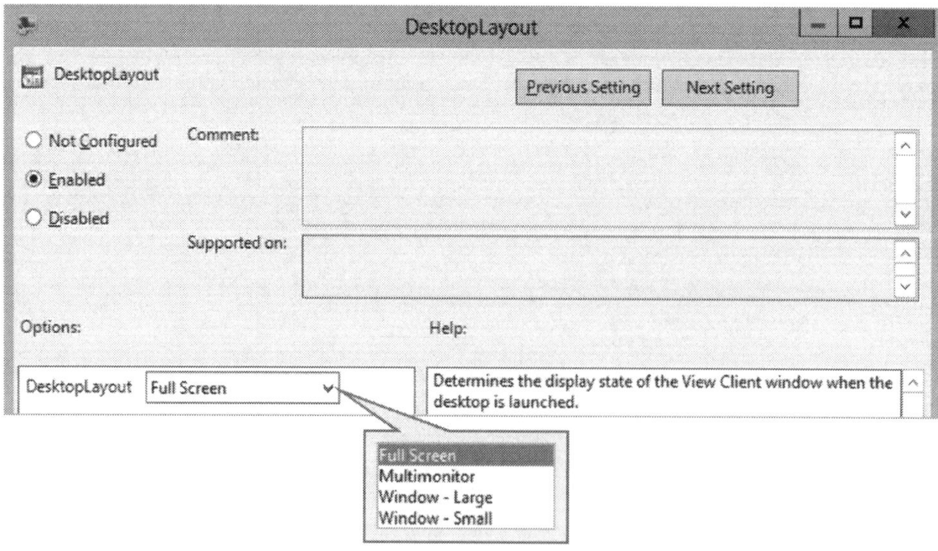

12. Click on **Next Setting** to move to the next policy setting.
13. The next five policy settings are are simply enable or disable options, and have no settings that you can configure specific values for. The policies are as follows:
    - **Suppress error messages (when fully scripted only)**
    - **Automatically connect if only one launch item is entitled**
    - **Disable 3rd-party Terminal Services plugins**
    - **Connect all USB devices to the desktop on launch**
    - **Connect USB devices to the desktop when they are plugged in**
14. Click on **Apply** to complete the configuration for these policies. In the next section, we will look at the policy options for security settings.

Security settings

In the next set of policies, we will look at security settings. To configure these options, from the **Group Policy Management Editor**, we will follow these steps:

1. Click on **VMware View Client Configuration** and then click on **Security Settings**. Double-click on the first policy. The first two policies in this section, listed as follows, can be set either to be enabled or disabled:
    - **Display option to Log in as current user**: This allows you to automatically check a box and log in as the currently logged in user and also enter your credentials if they are different for your virtual desktop machine
    - **Default value of the 'Log in as current user' checkbox**: This allows you to have this checkbox automatically checked so that users are forced to log in as the current user
2. Click on **Next Setting** to move to the next policy setting.

3. In the **Server Trusted For Delegation** policy, you can add the details for Connection Servers that are allowed to have credentials delegated to them. To add the server details, click on **Show...** and then enter the details, as shown in the following screenshot:

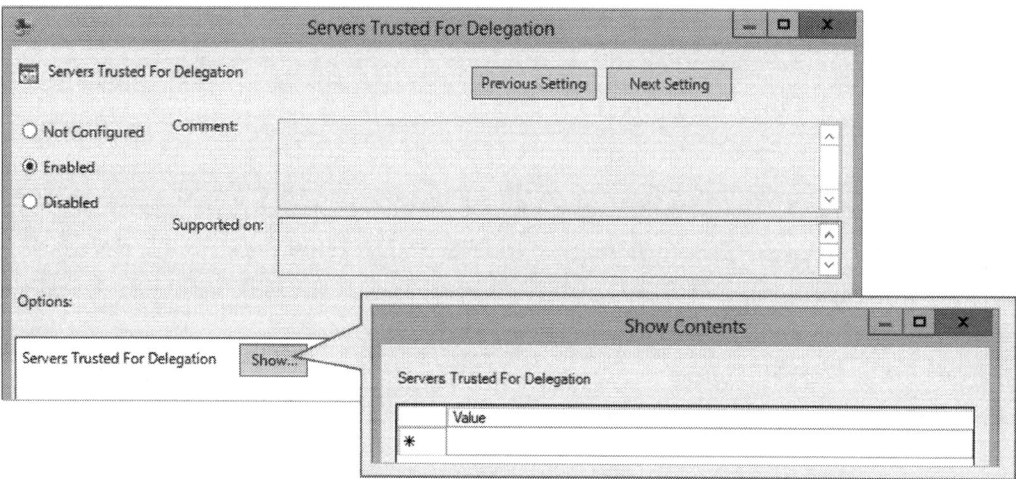

4. Click on **Next Setting** to move to the next policy setting.
5. In the **Certificate verification mode** policy, you can configure how the client checks the certificate. From the drop-down menu, you can choose from the following three verification mode options:
   - **Full Security**: This reports all certificate errors to the user and they are not allowed to connect to the server
   - **No Security**: This does not perform certificate verification
   - **Warn But Allow**: This is the default option, where the user is warned but allowed to proceed if the server certificate is self-signed

These options are shown in the following screenshot:

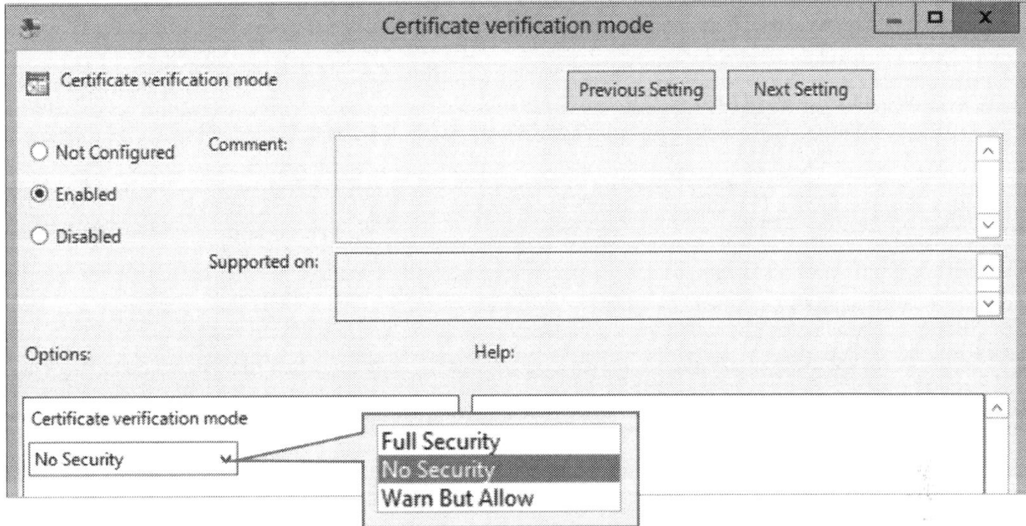

6. Click on **Next Setting** to move to the next policy setting.
7. The next three policy settings are simply enable or disable options, and have no settings that you can configure specific values for. The settings are as follows:
    - **Enable Single Sign-On for smart card authentication**: This requires the View Client to store the encrypted smart card PIN in memory momentarily, before submitting it to the View Connection Server
    - **Enable jump list integration**: This adds a jump list to the View Client icon in the taskbar on Windows 7 and later; it allows users to easily connect to recent View Connection Servers and remote desktops
    - **Allow command line credentials**: This allows a password or PIN to be provided via command-line parameters
8. Click on **Next Setting** to move to the next policy setting.

9. You will now see the **Enable SSL encrypted framework channel** policy, where you can configure how SSL encryption is handled. In the drop-down menu, you can choose from the following three options:
    - **Enable**: This enables SSL and allows fall-back to desktops with no SSL support
    - **Disable**: This disables SSL altogether
    - **Enforce**: This will actively refuse to connect to desktops that have no SSL support

   These options are shown in the following screenshot:

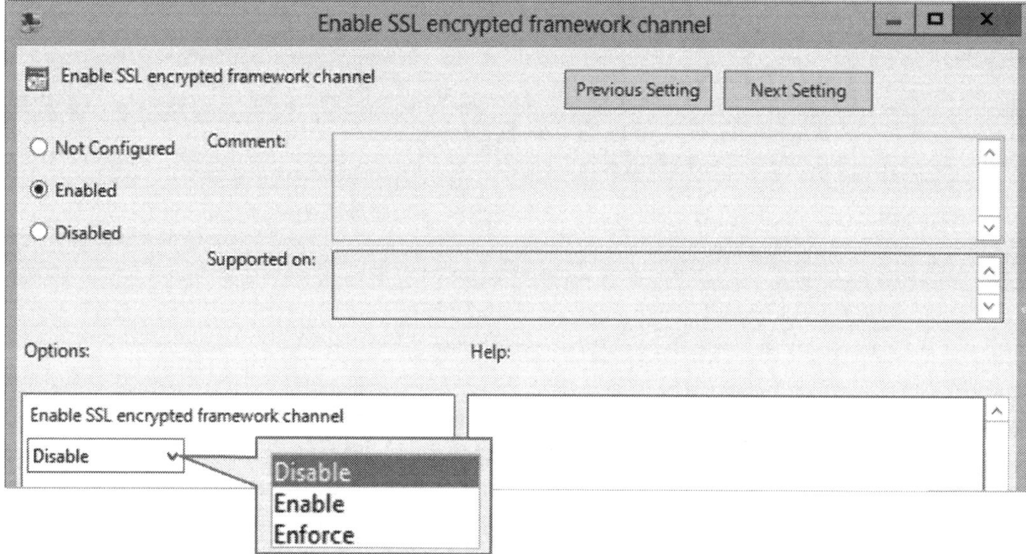

10. Click on **Next Setting** to move to the next policy setting.
11. The next four policy settings are simply enable or disable options, and they have no settings that you can configure specific values for. These policies are also for View Client versions 4.x and earlier. They are as follows:
    - **Ignore incorrect SSL certificate common name (hostname field)**
    - **Ignore bad SSL certificate date received from the server**
    - **Ignore unknown certificate authority problems**
    - **Ignore incorrect usage problems**
12. Click on **Next Setting** to move to the next policy setting.

13. In the **Configures SSL protocols and cryptographic algorithms** policy, you can configure a cipher list to restrict the use of certain cryptographic algorithms and protocols before establishing an encrypted SSL connection. The list is made up of at least one cipher string. Cipher strings are case-sensitive. An example is shown in the following screenshot:

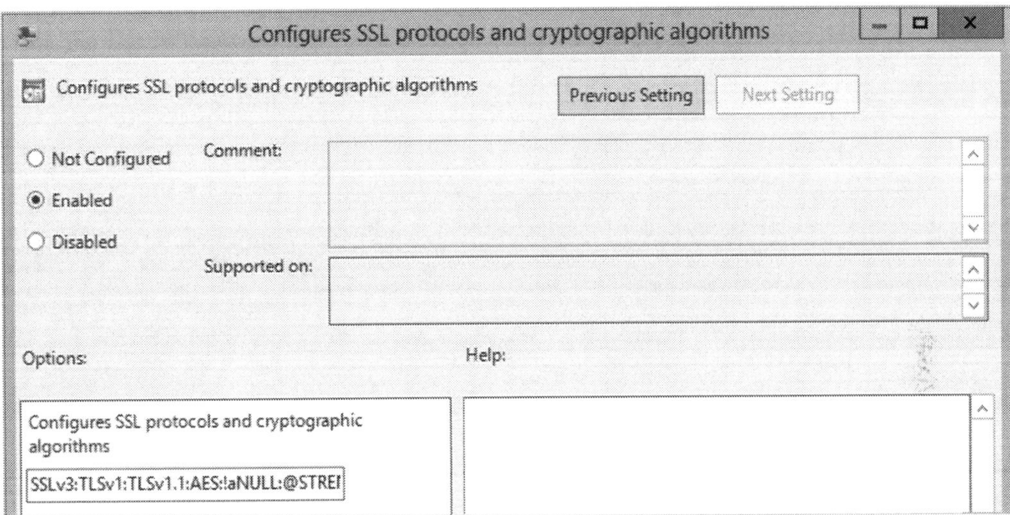

14. Click on **Apply** to complete the configuration for these policies. In the next section, we will look at the policy options for Common Configuration.

VMware View Common Configuration

The final set of policies are for common configuration options. They are categorized as shown in the following screenshot:

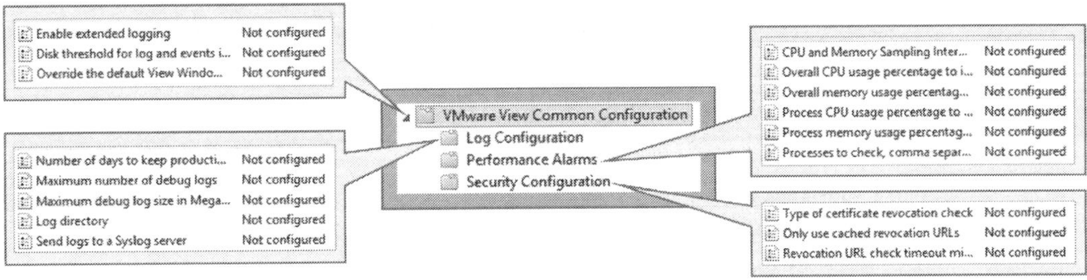

Let's now look at each individual policy setting. To configure these options, from the **Group Policy Management Editor**, we will follow these steps:

1. Click on **VMware View Common Configuration**. Double-click on the first policy, **Enable extended logging**. This policy is either enabled or disabled.
2. Click on **Next Setting** to move to the next policy setting.
3. Next is the **Disk threshold for log and events in Megabytes** policy. This policy allows you to configure a minimum amount of disk space available to store logfiles and event information. Once the threshold is reached, logging stops. Enter a value (in MB) in the box, as shown in the following screenshot:

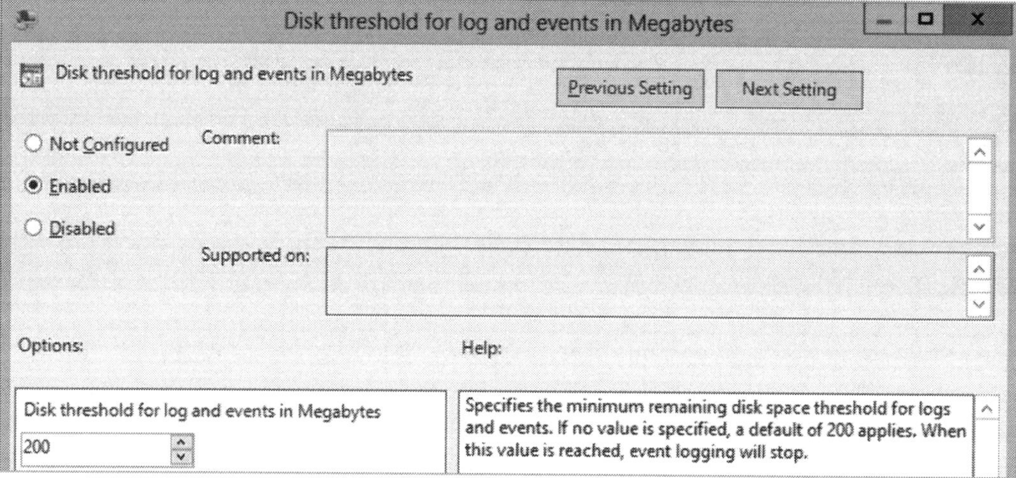

4. Click on **Next Setting** to move to the next policy setting.
5. The next policy is **Override the default View Windows event generation**. There are three different configurable options, which are as follows:
    - **0**: This produces event log entries only for view events (no event log entries are generated for log messages).
    - **1**: This produces event log entries in View 4.5 (and earlier) compatibility mode. Event log entries are not produced for standard View events. Event log entries are based solely on the logfile text.
    - **2**: This produces event log entries in View 4.5 (and earlier) compatibility mode, with view events also being included.

    Enter a value in the box, as shown in the following screenshot:

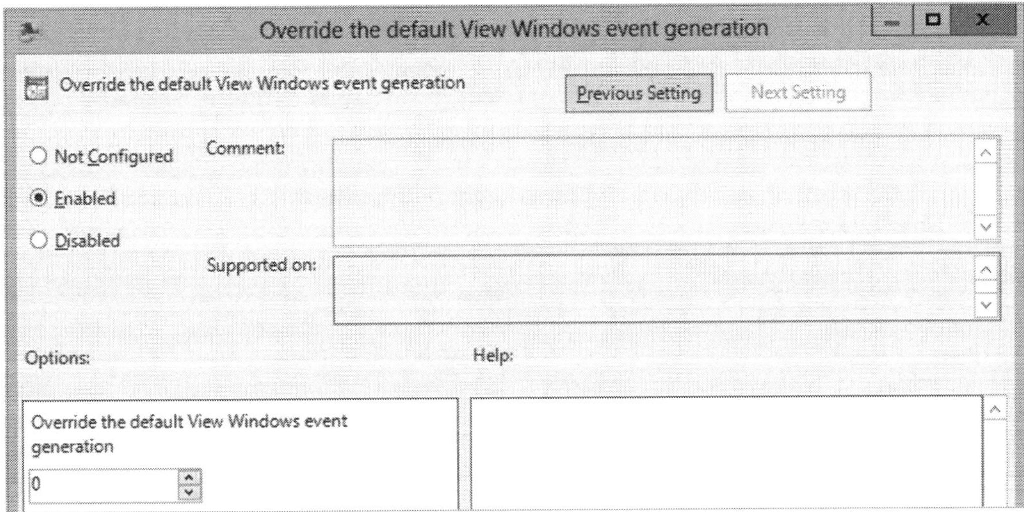

6. Click on **Apply** to complete the configuration for these policies. In the next section, we will look at the policy options for log configuration.

Log Configuration

To configure these options, from the **Group Policy Management Editor**, we will follow these steps:

1. Click on **VMware View Common Configuration**, and then click on **Log Configuration**. Double-click on the first policy, **Number of days to keep production logs**. Enter the number of days you want to keep the logfiles for, as shown in the following screenshot:

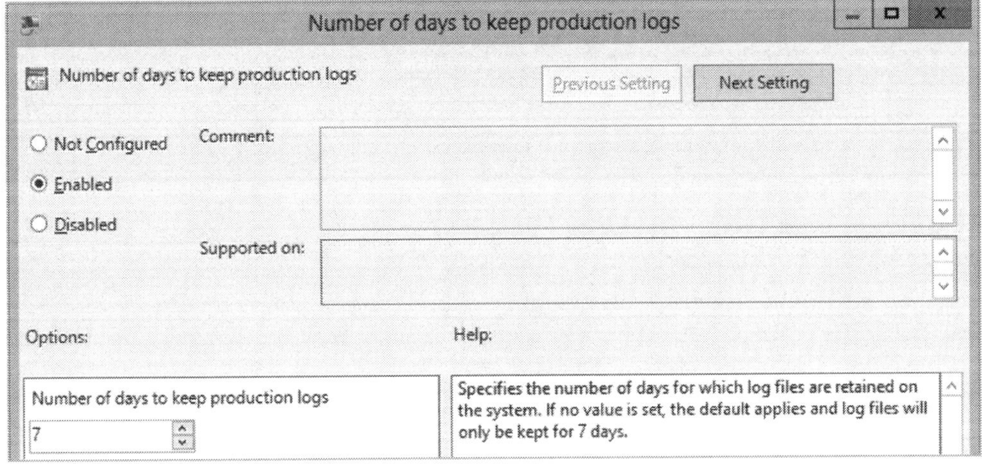

2. Click on **Next Setting** to move to the next policy setting.
3. In the **Maximum number of debug logs** policy, enter a value for the number of logfiles you want to keep. When a file gets to its maximum size, then another logfile is created up to the number you have configured to keep. Any new logs created after this point means the oldest file gets deleted. Enter the number of logfiles you want to keep the logfiles for, as shown in the following screenshot:

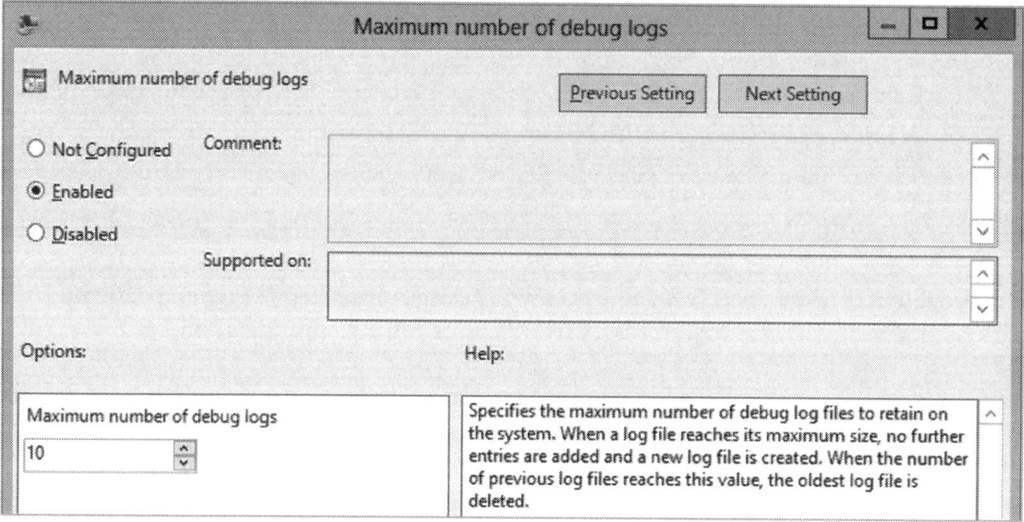

4. Click on **Next Setting** to move to the next policy setting.
5. In the **Maximum debug log size in Megabytes** policy, enter the size you want as the maximum logfile size. Enter the size (in MB) of the debug logfiles in the box, as shown in the following screenshot:

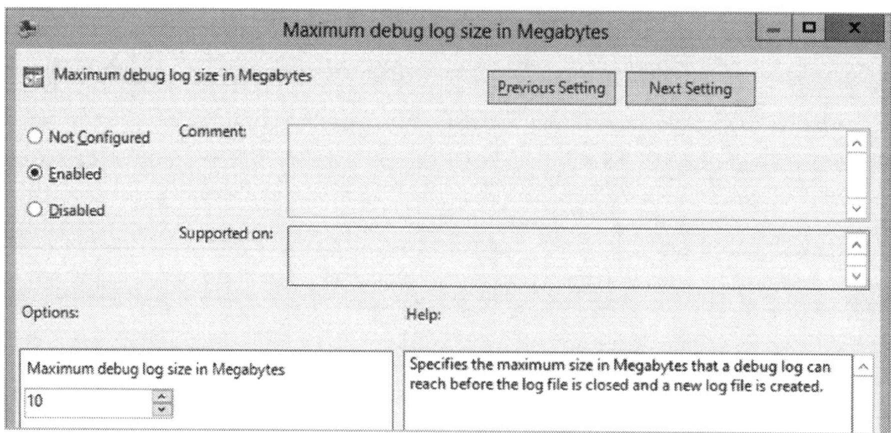

6. Click on **Next Setting** to move to the next policy setting.
7. In the **Log directory** policy, you can enter your own directory to store the logfiles. Enter a directory in the box, as shown in the following screenshot:

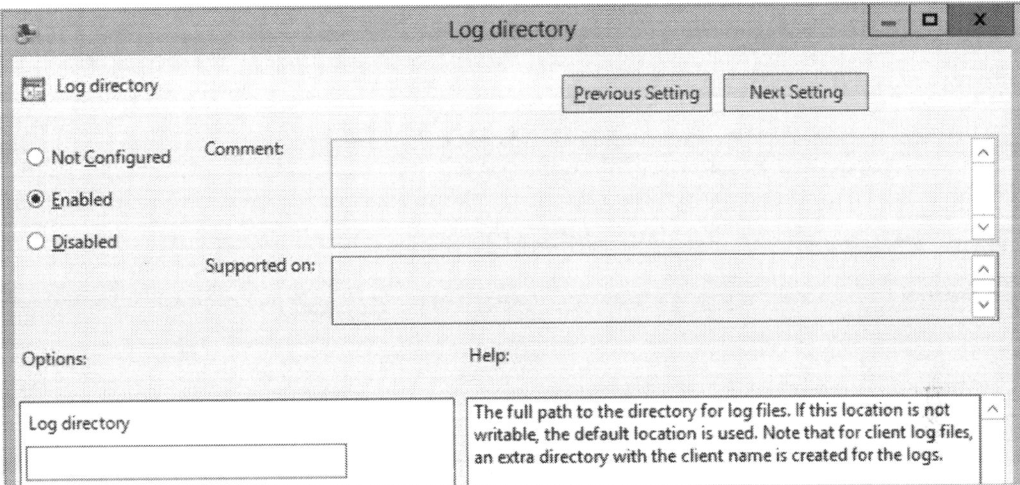

8. Click on **Next Setting** to move to the next policy setting.
9. In the **Send logs to a Syslog server** policy, you can enter the details of a Syslog server to send the server logs to. Enter the details of the server in the box, such as `VMware LogInsight Server`, as shown in the following screenshot:

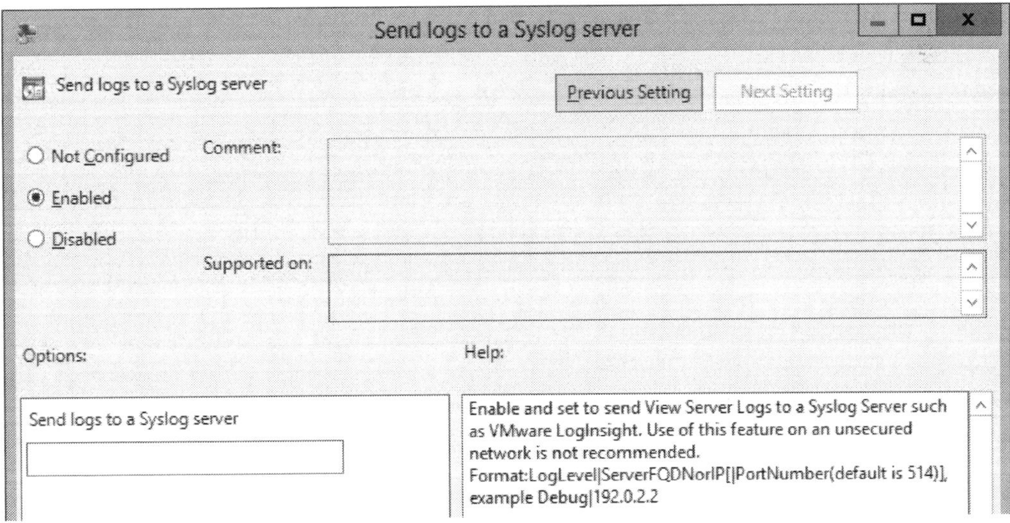

10. Click on **Apply** to complete the configuration for these policies. In the next section, we will look at policy options for performance alarms.

Performance alarms

To configure these options, from the **Group Policy Management Editor**, we will follow these steps:

1. Click on **VMware View Common Configuration** and then click on **Performance Alarms**. Double-click on the first policy, **CPU and Memory Sampling Interval in Seconds**. Enter the number of seconds after which you want to check CPU and memory, as shown in the following screenshot:

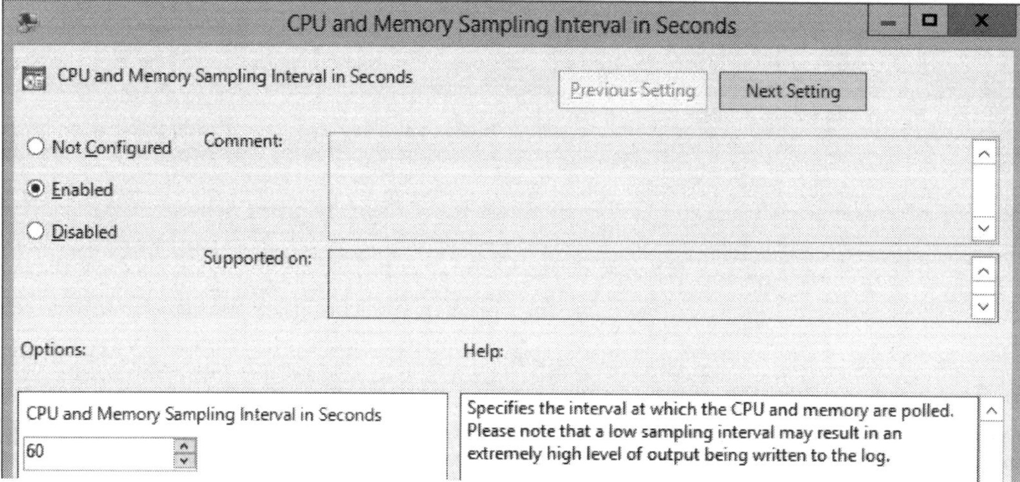

2. Click on **Next Setting** to move to the next policy setting.
3. The next two policies are **Overall CPU usage percentage to issue log info** and **Overall Memory usage percentage to issue log info**, where you can set a percentage value for when the CPU and memory usage start getting logged respectively. Enter the percentage in the boxes for the CPU and then the memory policy, as shown in the following screenshots:

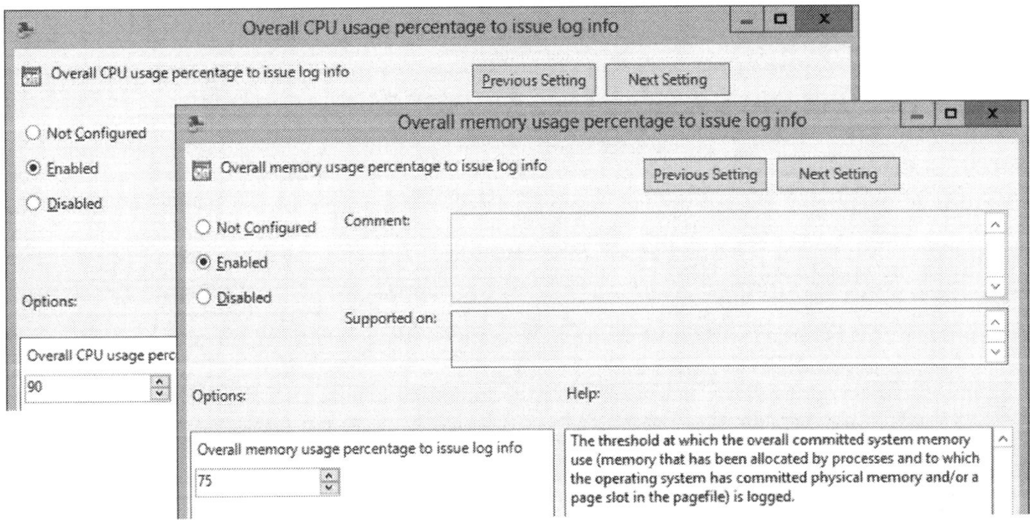

4. Click on **Next Setting** when you have configured the policies, to move to the next policy setting.
5. The next two policies are **Process CPU usage percentage to issue log info** and **Process Memory usage percentage to issue log info**, where you can set a percentage value for when the CPU and memory usage for an individual process start getting logged respectively. Enter the percentage in the boxes for the CPU and then the memory policy, as shown in the following screenshots:

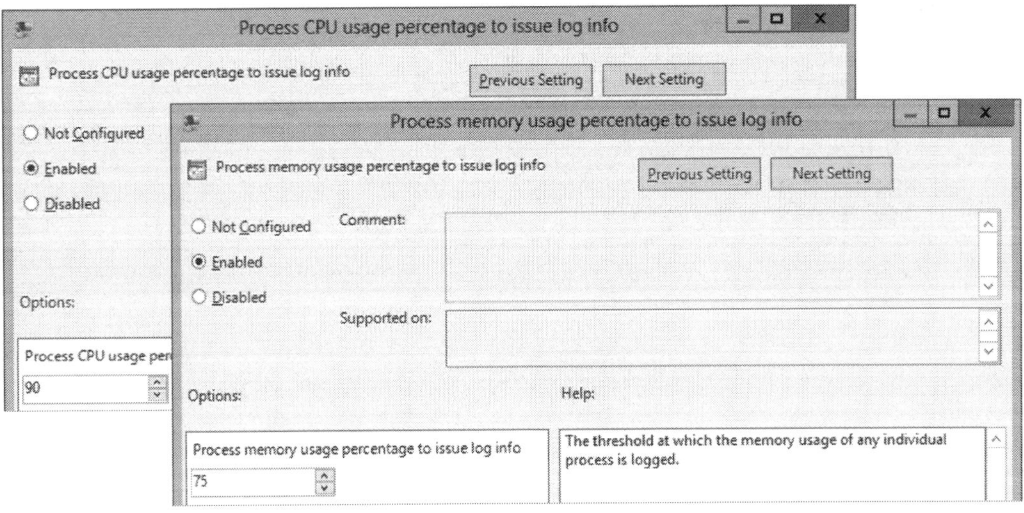

6. Click on **Next Setting** when you have configured the policies, to move to the next policy setting.
7. In the **Processes to check, comma separated name list allowing wild cards and exclusion** policy, you can create a list of queries that correspond to the name of the processes you want examined. In order to filter the list, you can use wildcards in each query:
   - **(*)**: This indicates processes that match zero or more characters
   - **(?)**: This matches exactly one character
   - **(!)**: This can be used as a prefix to a query, in order to exclude any results from the query

   Enter the query in the box, as shown in the following screenshot:

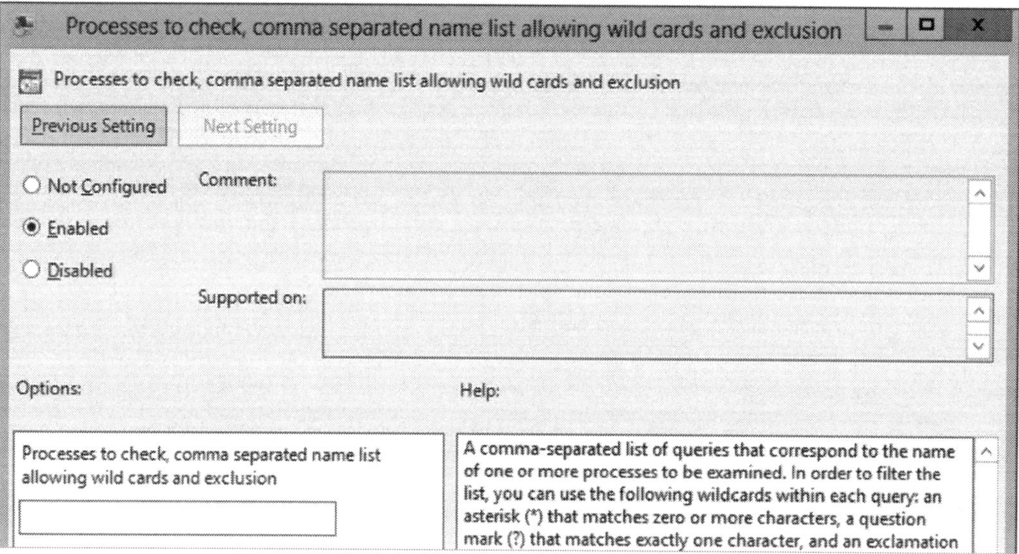

8. Click on **Apply** to complete the configuration for these policies.

In the next section, we will look at the policy options for security configuration.

Security Configuration

To configure these options, from the **Group Policy Management Editor**, we will follow these steps:

1. Click on **VMware View Common Configuration** and then on **Security Configuration**. Double-click on the first policy, **Type of certificate revocation check**. In this policy, you can configure what type of revocation check is performed on the SSL certificate. From the drop-down menu, choose one of the following options:
    - **EndCertificateOnly**
    - **None**
    - **WholeChain**
    - **WholeChainButRoot**

   These options are shown in the following screenshot:

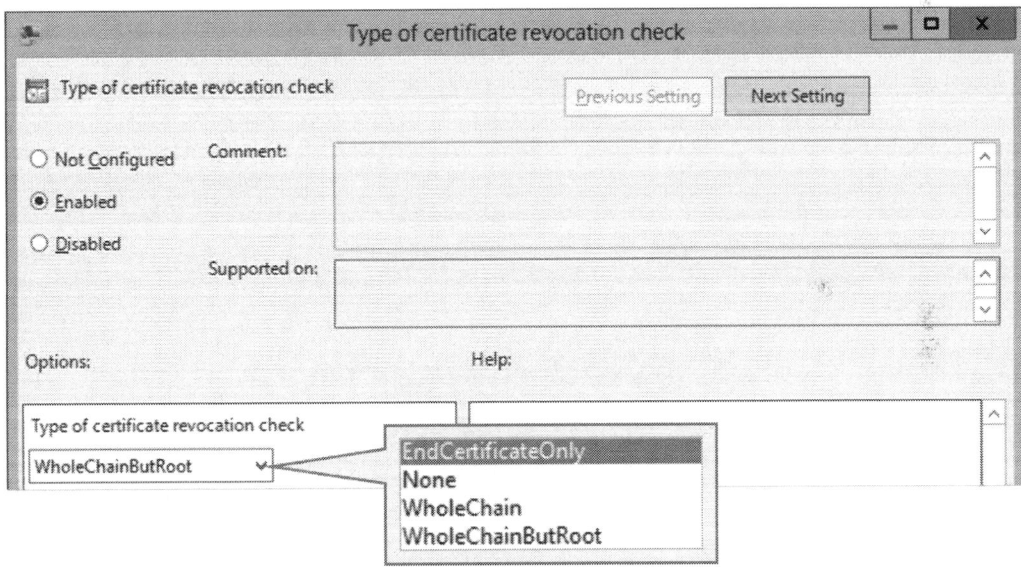

2. Click on **Next Setting** to move to the next policy setting.

In the next policy, **Only use cached revocation URLs**, the options are either to enable or disable the policy. There are no other configurable options.

3. Click on **Next Setting** to move to the next policy setting.

   The final policy setting in this section is **Revocation URL check timeout milliseconds**, where you can set a time in milliseconds for the check to take place. Enter the time in the box, as shown in the following screenshot:

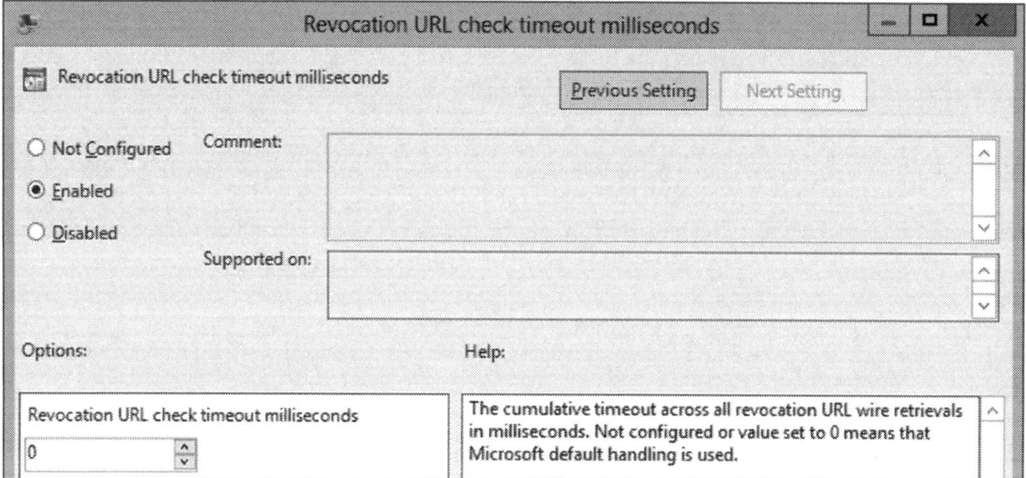

4. Click on **Apply** to complete the configuration for these policies. In the next section, we will look at the policy option for View Server.

VMware View Server Configuration

The final policy is to configure View Server, and there is only one option to configure, as shown in the following screenshot:

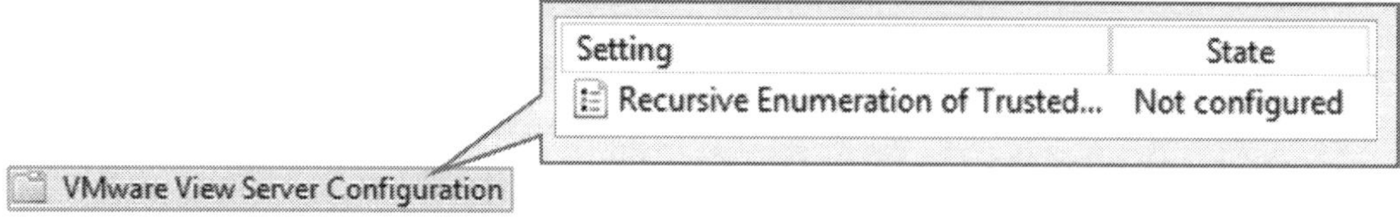

To configure this option, from the **Group Policy Management Editor**, follow these steps:

1. Click on **VMware View Server Configuration**.
2. Double-click on the **Recursive Enumeration of Trusted Domains** policy. This policy can simply be set to either enable or disable, and there are no other configurable options.

   Enabling this policy determines whether or not every domain, trusted by the domain in which the server resides, is enumerated. In order to establish a complete chain of trust, the domains trusted by each trusted domain are also enumerated. So, the process continues until all the trusted domains have been discovered. View Connection Server then uses this information to make sure all trusted domains are available to the client when they log in.

   We have now gone through the various policy and configuration options. In the next section, we will take a brief look at how we can tune the protocol dynamically on virtual desktop machines.

PCoIP tuning tool

The final thing we will cover in this chapter is how we can dynamically tune the virtual desktop machines using the PCoIP tuning tool. You can download this tool from `http://tinyurl.com/ocqxykn`.

One of the things that this tuning tool enables is the ability to change things on the fly rather than manually editing policies, and as you can see from the number of policies, there are a large number of configurable options.

Once you have the tool downloaded, launch it on the virtual desktop machine you want to tune. It's probably worthwhile to do this on your parent image, and with an end user, so that you can not only get their feedback, but also get their buy-in to the solution.

With the tool launched, you will see that there are a number of options to choose from:

- **Activate Profile**
- **Manage Profiles**
- **Clear Profile Settings**
- **Show Session Stats**
- **Show Session Health**

These options are shown in the following screenshot:

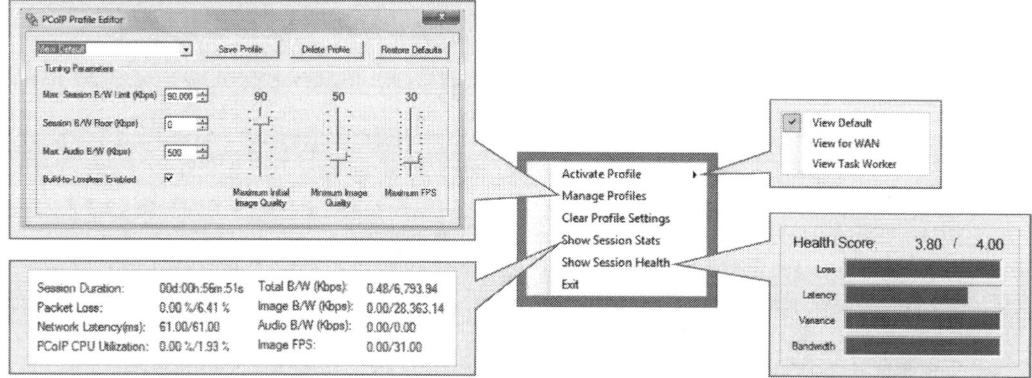

In the following sections, we will briefly cover what each option configures.

Activating the profile

The **Activate Profile** setting allows you to activate one of the preset profiles. Each profile is based on a different use case, and there are three already built to choose from. One for a default user, one for a WAN-based user, and the final one for a task worker.

By selecting one of the present profiles, the settings for things such as session bandwidth, image quality, or frame rate will be updated and changed to a setting that matches this particular use case.

To activate a profile, you need to reboot the virtual desktop machine.

Managing profiles

The **Manage Profiles** option allows you to adjust the settings of a particular profile. You can dynamically change image quality, frames per second, band width, and switch on build-to-lossless. You can choose from the prebuilt profiles or create a new one and then save it.

Clearing profile settings

The **Clear Profile Settings** is will clear the profile settings and restore them to defaults.

Showing session statistics

The **Show Session Stats** option shows you real-time usage statistics for things such as bandwidth, frames per second, latency, and CPU utilization, allowing you to understand what a particular virtual desktop machine is consuming. By clicking this option, you effectively switch it on. It then appears on the desktop so you can monitor it.

Showing health of the session

As with the **Show Session Stats** option, by clicking on this option you effectively switch it on and it then appears on the desktop. It gives you a health score for the PCoIP session so as to give you an indication of where there might be a problem. For example, the latency score might be low, indicating a higher latency between the client and the virtual desktop machine.

For a more in-depth overview of performance, capacity planning, and troubleshooting, it's worth installing vCenter Operations for Horizon View. We will cover more of this in *Chapter 15, Introduction to App Volumes*.

Summary

In this chapter, we looked at how to start fine-tuning the performance and experience of the end user's session with their virtual desktop machine.

We have covered how to prepare AD with Horizon View-specific policies and administrative templates to define how the virtual desktop machine behaves and also the experience for the end user.

We then walked through each policy setting, explaining what it does and the options you can configure.

Finally, we looked at one of the many tools available to help in the tuning process.

In the next chapter, we will look at how we manage user profiles in a Horizon View environment using View Persona Management.

9

Managing User Profiles with View Persona Management

One of the topics we touched on earlier in this book was the need to manage user profiles when deploying a virtual desktop environment, particularly with regard to using a floating desktop assignment, where the desktop doesn't belong to any of the users. Therefore, it contains none of their personal information or settings.

There are a number of third-party tools available to manage user profiles. However, in this chapter, we will discuss the VMware version that ships as part of the Horizon View product known as View Persona Management.

VMware View Persona Management allows you to configure user profiles that are dynamically synchronized with a central profile repository, stored on a server in the data center. By using View Persona, you can give users access to their own personalized desktop, irrespective of which virtual desktop machine they log in to.

Before we get into the details and the configuration steps required to get Persona Management up and running, let's briefly discuss what we mean by a user profile, how View Persona Management works, and the benefits of using a tool to manage the profile.

Defining a user profile

A user profile is a collection of settings that makes the computer look and work the way the end user wants it to. It contains their settings for desktop backgrounds, screensavers, data files, configuration settings, and other features that are user specific. User profiles ensure that the desktop a user logs in on contains their own personal preferences.

A user profile includes the following information:

- User-generated information
- User-specific data and desktop settings
- Application data and settings
- Windows Registry entries that are configured by applications

If you are deploying ThinApp virtualized applications to the desktop, the ThinApp sandbox can also be included within the user profile and, as such, be roamed with it. We will cover more on ThinApp later in this book.

A user profile is different from a user account, which is what you use to log on to the Windows desktop. Each user account has at least one user profile associated with it.

Why do we need profile management?

As we discussed back in *Chapter 2, An Overview of Horizon View Architecture and Components*, the key reason you would want to deploy Persona Management is to move the end users away from having persistent desktops and get them to use nonpersistent desktops or floating/stateless desktops. This will ultimately save management costs as well as reduce infrastructure, as you can now look at concurrent user connections rather than having to deploy a virtual desktop machine for every user in your organization.

View Persona Management features

With Persona Management, you can configure user profiles to be dynamically synchronized with the central repository. The user data and information is downloaded when the user requests it. It also provides the following features:

- Delivers end users access to a personalized desktop experience whenever they log in to a desktop, no matter which virtual desktop machine is assigned to them. Persona Management operates independent of the virtual desktop machine.
- Expands the functionality and improves the performance of Windows roaming profiles.

- Has centralized configuration using the View Administrator.
- Is configured via Group Policy.
- Requires less IOPS than a Windows roaming profiles deployment.
- Can store files on any CIFS share.
- Supports full clone and linked clone virtual desktop machines.
- Complies with security policies as the end user still owns the files and folders.
- Integrates with existing Windows roaming profile deployments.

Understanding how Persona Management works

The question that typically gets asked is, "How does Persona Management differ from other profile management tools, specifically Windows roaming profiles?"

When the end user logs in to their virtual desktop machine, View will only download the files that Windows requires in order to run. One of the tricks here is that Persona Management lets Windows think that it has downloaded the user's profile, and so, Windows continues with the login process, thus speeding up login times.

What actually happens is that, the profile folder on the virtual desktop machine appears to the end user as if all of their files and data have been downloaded and are present. In reality, the files and data only get downloaded when the user requests them or when they launch an application that requires additional files and data.

If some of these files are larger than normal files, then there is the option to preload certain types of files to help improve the performance.

When the user uses their desktop normally, Persona Management periodically copies any recently changed files or data that have been changed on their virtual desktop machine. It then copies those files and data to the central repository. By default, this replication interval is set to happen every 10 minutes, but you can configure it to a time interval that is more suited to your environment. This is a key feature, as you reduce data loss inside the VDI environment when compared to physical desktops, or when using roaming profiles. Once the end user has completed their work and they log out of their virtual desktop machine, Persona Management will only copy files and data that have been updated since the last replication occurred. These file and data changes are then uploaded to the central repository. This is shown in the following screenshot:

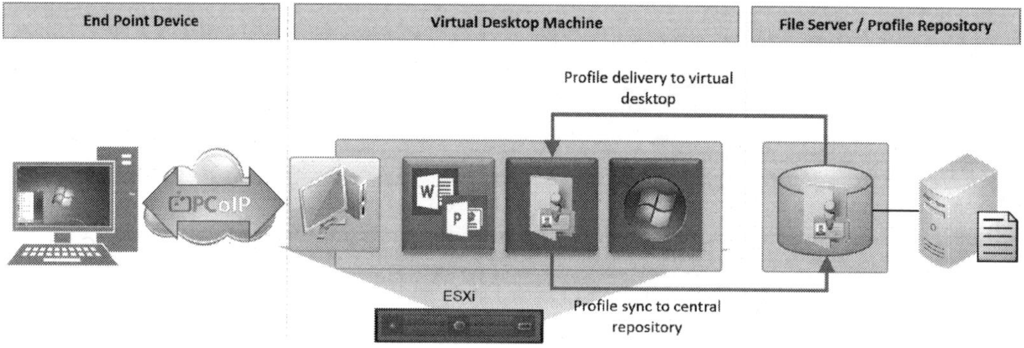

Next, we will quickly talk about how Microsoft roaming profiles fits with Persona Management.

Persona Management and roaming profiles

If View Persona Management is enabled, you cannot manage a Horizon View user's profile by using Windows roaming profiles at the same time. You can, however, choose other files and folders that could be managed using Windows roaming profiles. For example, you might want to do this if you are already using Folder Redirection.

To do this, you need to specify a list of files and folders that you want Windows roaming profiles to manage. When the end user logs in to their virtual desktop machine, these files and folders are retrieved from the central repository and then copied back to the central repository when they log out. The point to note here is that all the files and folders are copied, whereas while using Persona Management, they are only copied in demand and, therefore, there is no replication interval.

Configuring View Persona Management

Now that we have explained what View Persona Management is and how it works, we are now going to configure our environment to make use of this feature.

Configuring a user profile repository

First, we need to create a shared folder that will be used to store the user profiles. This folder will be located on a file server that has enough storage capacity to store the profiles. Perform the following steps:

1. In our example lab, we will create this folder on our domain controller, as shown in the following screenshot:

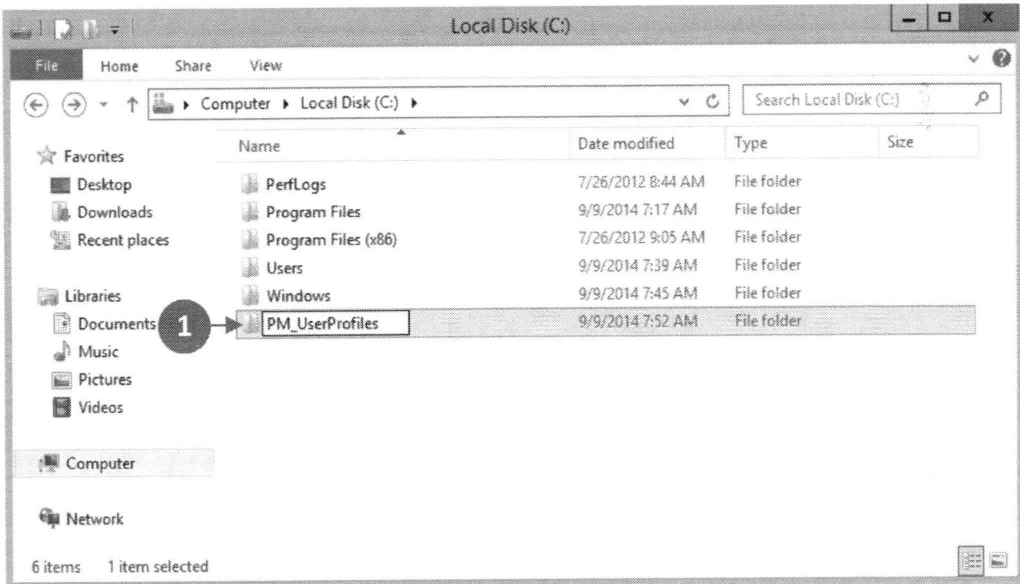

In our example lab, we have created a folder called `PM_UserProfiles` **(1)**.

2. The next step is to share the newly created folder so that all the users have access to it as this is where their profiles will be stored. To do this, right-click on the folder and then click on **Share with** (2) from the menu. Then, select the **Specific people...** (3) option, as shown in the following screenshot:

3. You will then see the **File Sharing** dialog box, as shown in the following screenshot:

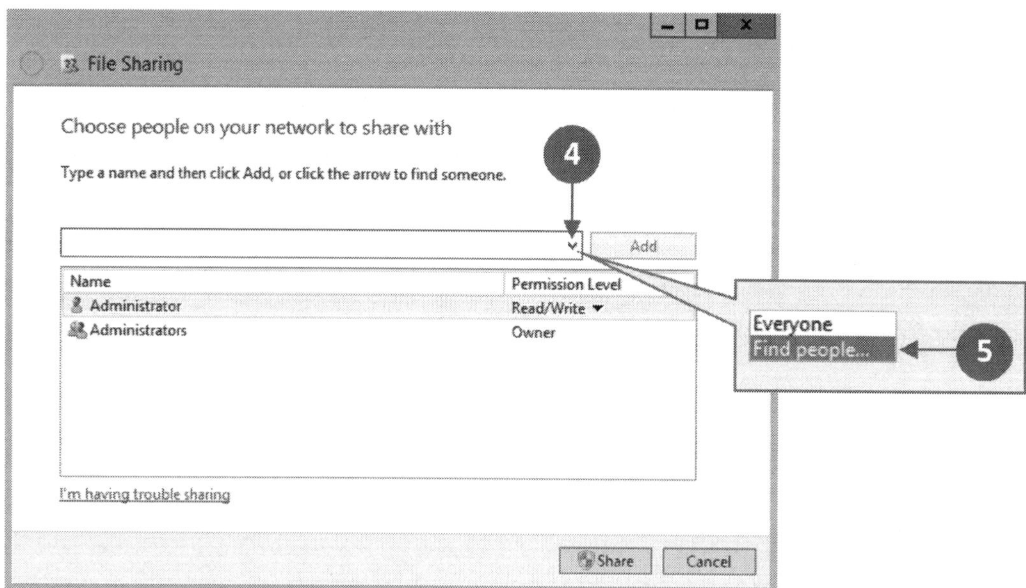

You can either type the username or group name directly into the box. In our example, we look up a user group.

4. Click the down arrow (**4**) and then from the menu options click **Find people...** (**5**). You will now see the **Select Users or Groups** dialog box as shown in the following screenshot:

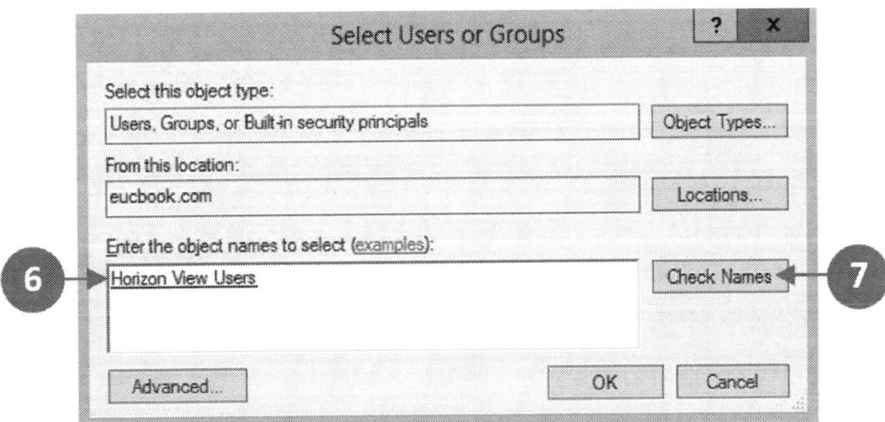

5. In our example, we will look for the Horizon View Users group. Type this into the **Enter the object names to select (examples):** box (**6**). Then, click on **Check Names** (**7**), as shown in the previous screenshot. If you successfully find the user, then it will be underlined as shown in the previous screenshot.
6. Click on **OK** when you have added the example user, or repeat the process to add any other additional users. You will then return to the **File Sharing** dialog box, as shown in the following screenshot:

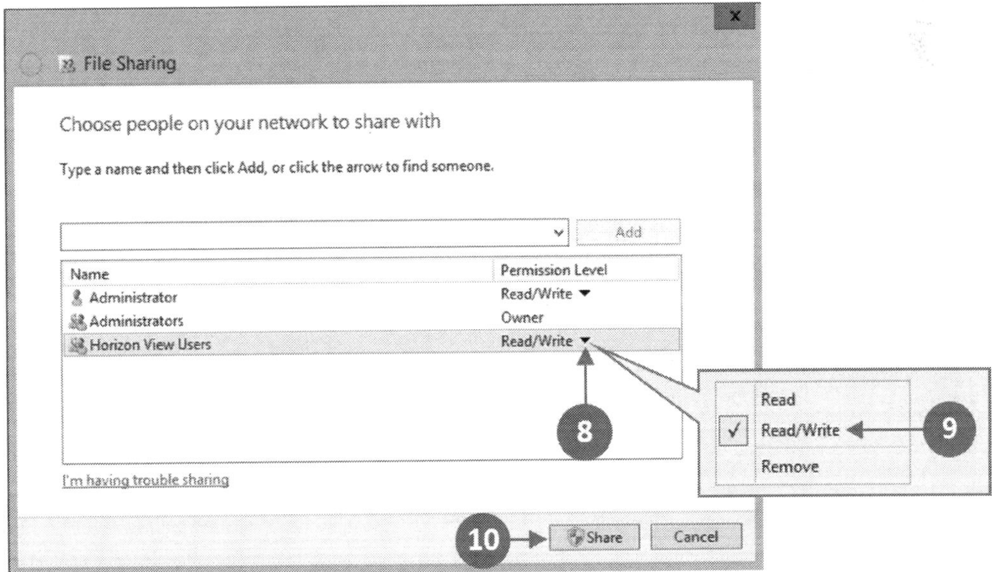

7. The final step is to set the **Permission Level** for the users or groups we just added. In our example, we will set the permission levels for the user.
8. Click on the Horizon View Users group, and then click on the down arrow to change the setting (**8**). From the menu, select **Read/Write** (**9**).
9. Once you have set the permission level, click on **Share** (**10**) to share the folder.
10. The next dialog box shows the newly shared folder and, more importantly, the path to that folder. In our example, the path is `\\DC\PM_UserProfiles` (**11**), as shown in the following screenshot:

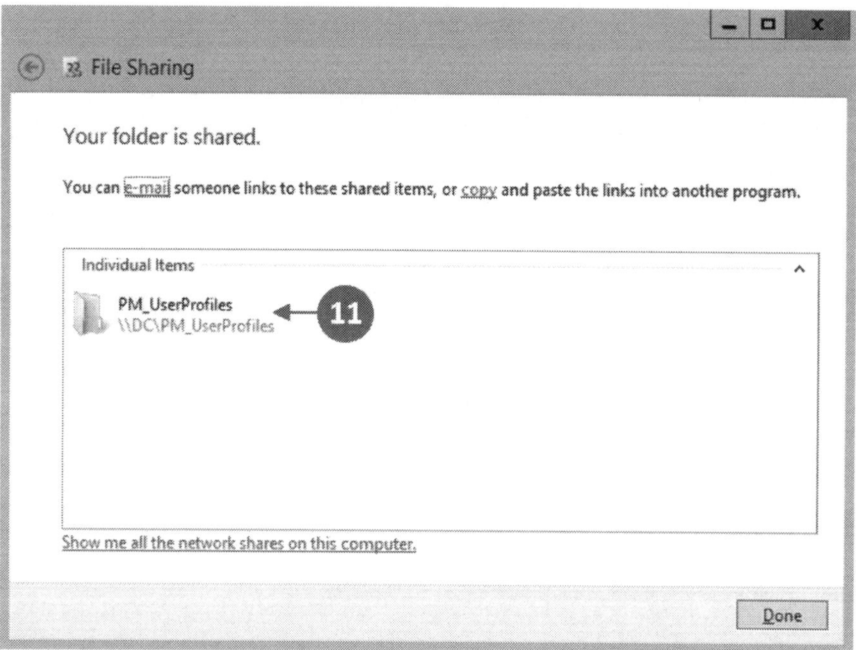

11. Click on **Done** when you have finished setting up the shared folder.

> If you are using Windows Server 2008, there is another step in the folder sharing process to set the folder permissions, as Windows Server 2008 does not add the permissions for all the users in this group. You need to go into the properties of the shared folder and click on the **Sharing** tab and then on the **Advanced Sharing** button.
>
> Tick on the box for **Share this folder** and then click on the **Permissions** button. Then, you need to add the group you want to share the folder with, and then tick the box to give the group the permission for **Full Control**.

You should now have a shared folder set up ready to store the user profiles. The next step is to add the Persona Management policy to our virtual desktop machines.

Installing the ADM template on the virtual desktop

In this section, we will add the Persona Management Group Policy template to the virtual desktop machines. In this example, we will add the GPO to the virtual desktop machine that we are using as our Windows 7 parent image because this image will be used to build our floating, linked clone desktops.

This means when we deploy the virtual desktop machines, the Persona Management settings will already be in place. You would also do this for any other parent images where you want to use Persona Management.

The first step is to power on the Windows 7 parent image virtual desktop machine that we built in *Chapter 6, Building and Optimizing the Desktop Operating System*, and then open a console window to it.

Adding Persona Management is an additional step, and as we are going to add this to our existing parent image, we need to make sure that we take a new snapshot (for linked clones) or create a new template (for full clones) when we have completed the configuration steps.

Adding the ADM template

Here are the steps that we need to perform:

1. From the Windows desktop, click on **Start** and then on **Run**. In the **Run** dialog box, type the command `gpedit.msc` and click on **OK**. This is shown in the following screenshot:

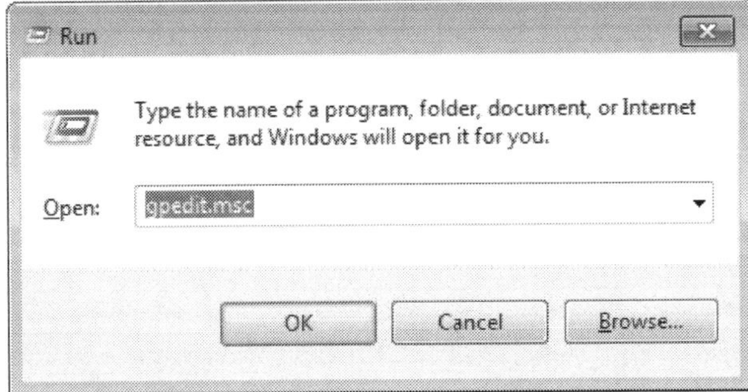

2. Click on **OK** to launch the **Local Group Policy Editor** page. Navigate to **Local Computer Policy | Computer Configuration | Administrative Templates (1)**.
3. Right-click on **Administrative Templates**, and from the menu, click on the option for **Add/Remove Templates... (2)**, as shown in the following screenshot:

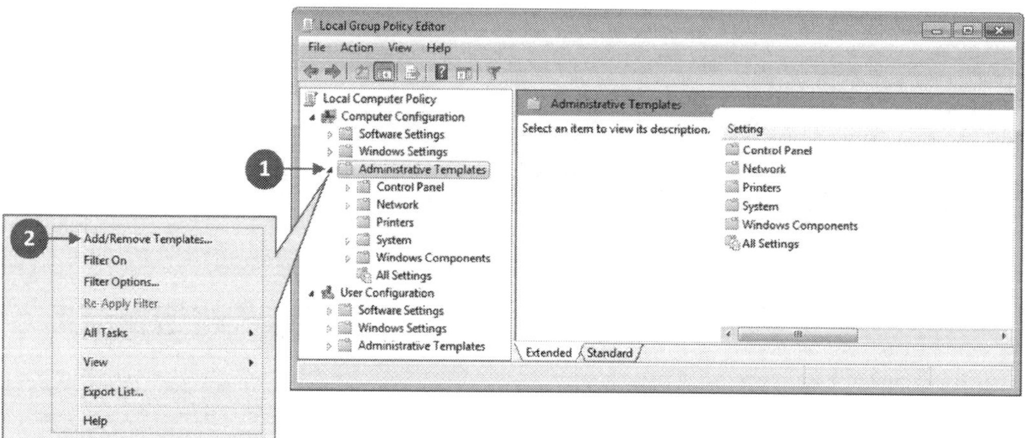

4. You will now see the **Add/Remove Templates** dialog box, as shown in the following screenshot:

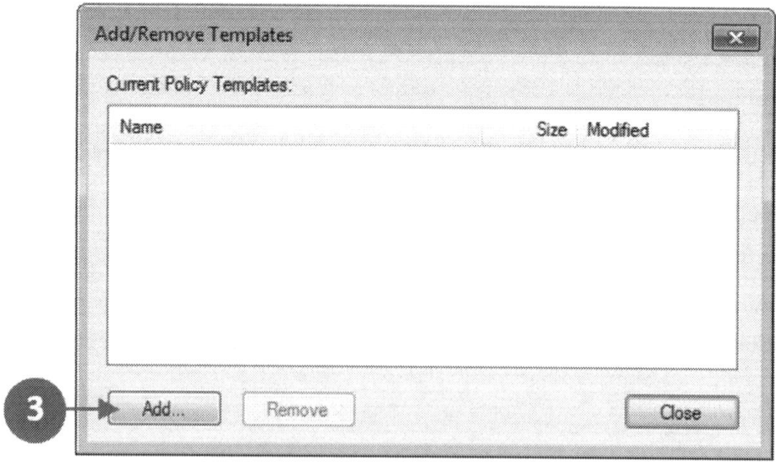

5. Click on **Add... (3)** to add a new ADM template. A Windows Explorer box will open so that you can browse and find the required template:

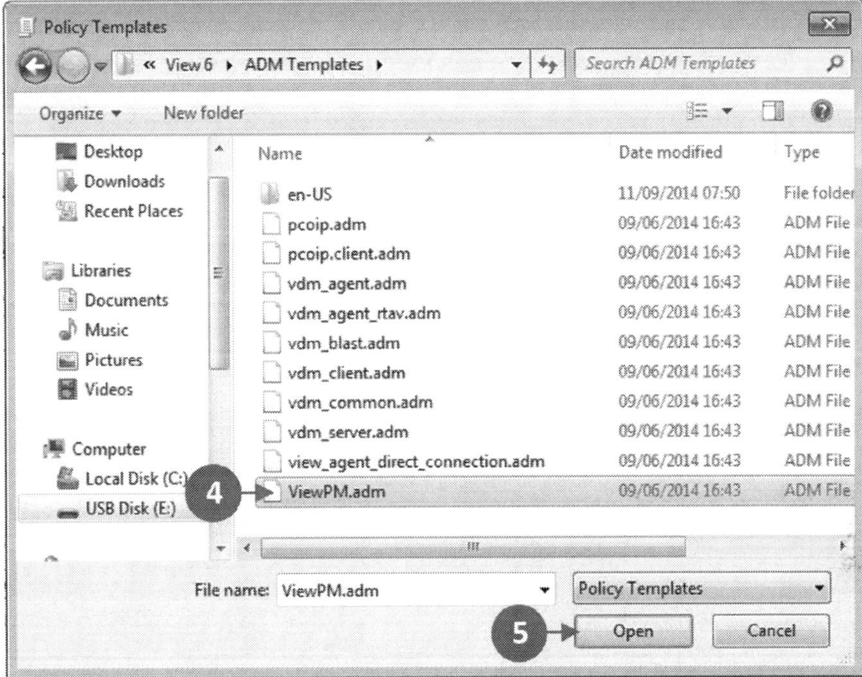

We have copied all of the View ADM templates into our shared software folder on the fileserver. So, in our example, we will browse to file share and click on the template named `ViewPM.adm` (**4**). Then click on **Open** (**5**), as shown in the previous screenshot.

6. You will now see that the template is listed in the **Add/Remove Templates** dialog box (**6**), as shown in the following screenshot:

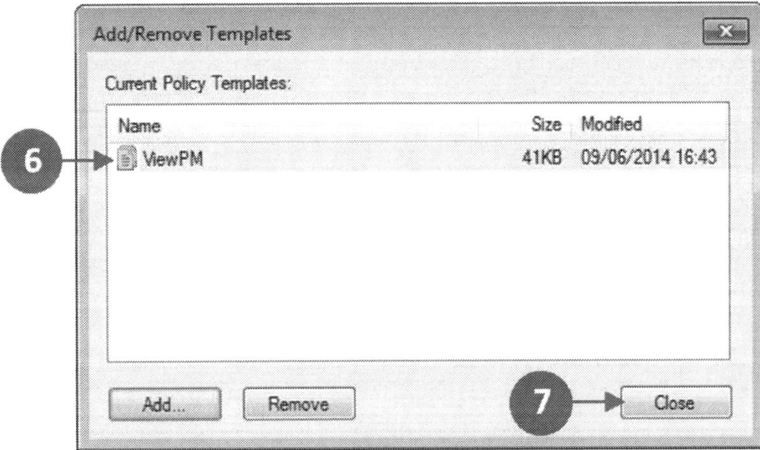

7. Click on **Close** (7) to complete the task of adding the template.
8. You will now go back to the **Local Group Policy Editor** screen, as shown in the following screenshot. We will check to make sure that the template has been added. You will now see that there is an entry for **Classic Administrative Templates (ADM)** (8):

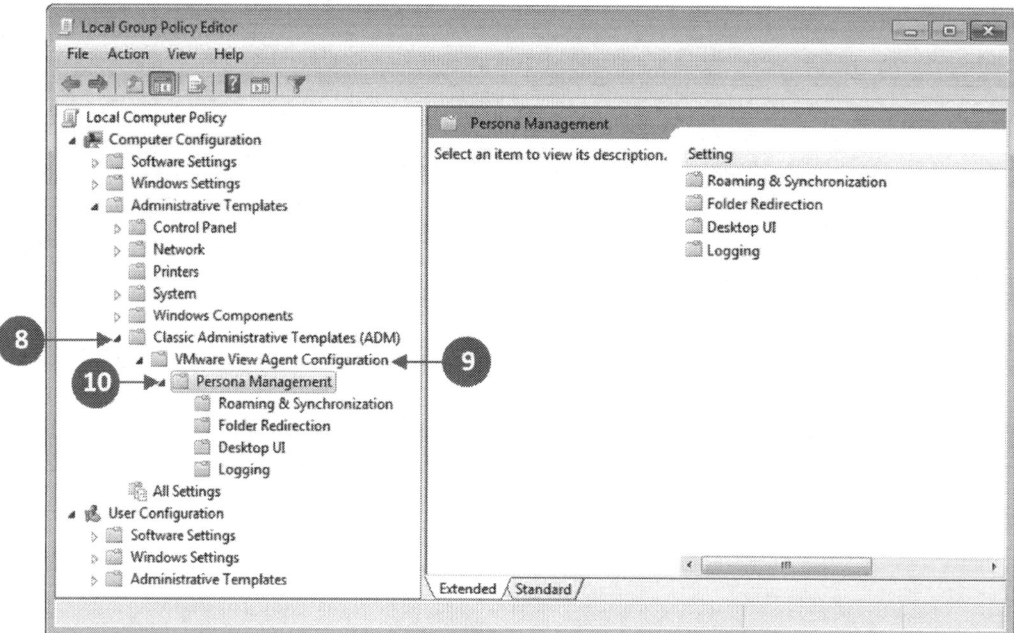

9. Here, navigate to **VMware View Agent Configuration** (9) | **Persona Management** (10). You will see the four sections for the different configuration options for Persona Management, which are as follows:
   - **Roaming & Synchronization**
   - **Folder Redirection**
   - **Desktop UI**
   - **Logging**

In the next section, we will walk through configuring these options.

Configuring Persona Management on the virtual desktop

In this section, we will cover the four Persona Management configuration options in more detail and show how to configure some of the policies.

Roaming & Synchronization

Under this category heading, the policies are all about how files, folders, and user profiles are handled. We will walk through each one and explain what it does, starting with **Manage user persona**:

1. Click on **Roaming & Synchronization** in the **Local Computer Policy** pane. Then, from the options in the pane to the right, double-click on **Manage user persona**. By default, the policy is disabled, meaning, Persona Management is effectively switched off.
2. Click on the radio button for **Enabled** (**1**). The second option is the **Profile upload interval (in minutes):** (**2**), which determines the frequency of upload. By default, it is set to 10 minutes, but you can change this based on certain criteria, for example, your network bandwidth:

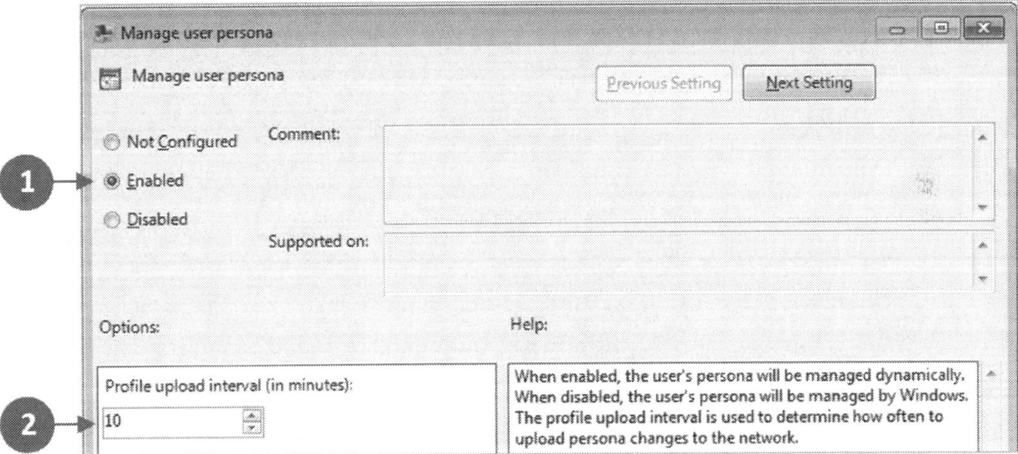

3. Click on **Next Setting** to configure the next policy.
4. The next configuration option is for **Persona repository location**. This configures the folder in which the user's profile and data will be stored. In the previous section, *Configuring a user profile repository*, we configured a shared folder for this specific task. Now, we will configure Persona Management to use it.
5. First, click on the radio button for **Enabled** (**3**) and then under the **Share path:** box, type the location to the shared folder. In our example, the path to the share is `\\DC\PM_UserProfiles` (**4**), as shown in the following screenshot. If you enable the location feature and do not enter a path, it will default to the profile path that AD uses. You can also tick the box to override AD paths if you had them configured previously:

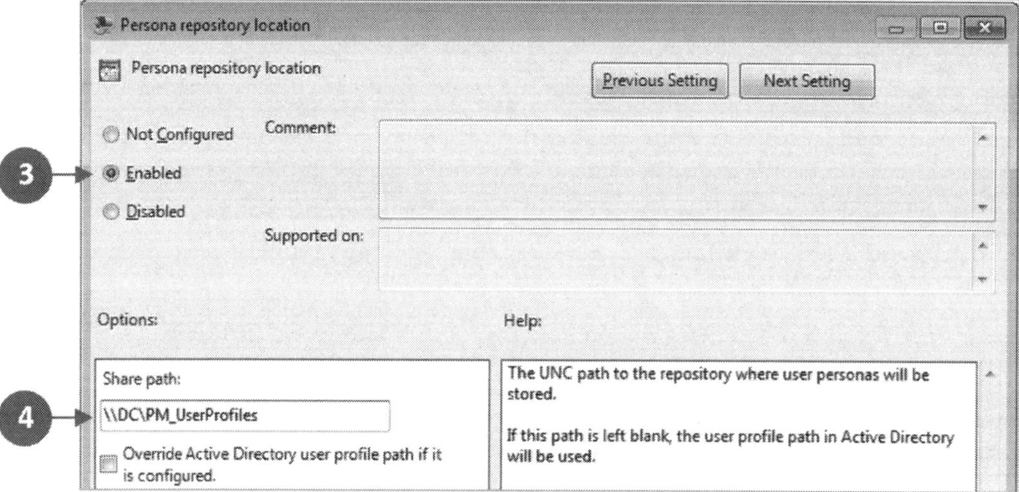

6. Click on **Next Setting** to configure the next policy.
7. The next configuration option is **Remove local persona at log off**, as shown in the following screenshot. Clicking on the radio button for **Enabled** (**5**) means that when a user logs off, their profile will be deleted from that virtual desktop machine. This is a useful feature when using linked clones, as users get allocated different desktops:

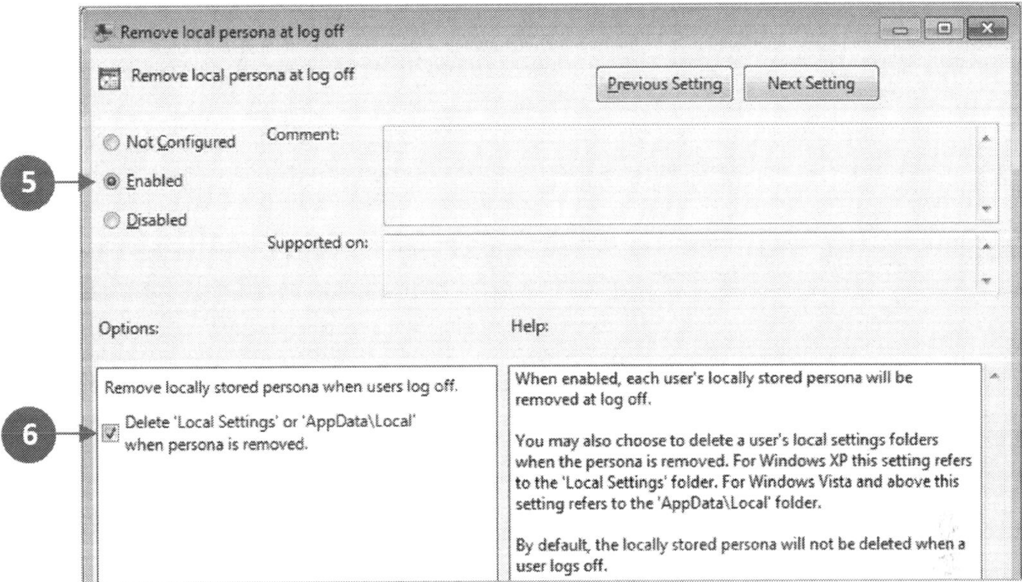

8. The other option on this page is to delete any local setting that might get stored. Check the tick box (**6**) to enable this feature.
9. Click on **Next Setting** to configure the next policy.
10. Next, with the **Roam local settings folders** page, we can choose whether or not to allow the user's folder to follow them through their profile data.
11. Click on **Enabled** (**7**) to switch this option on, as shown in the following screenshot:

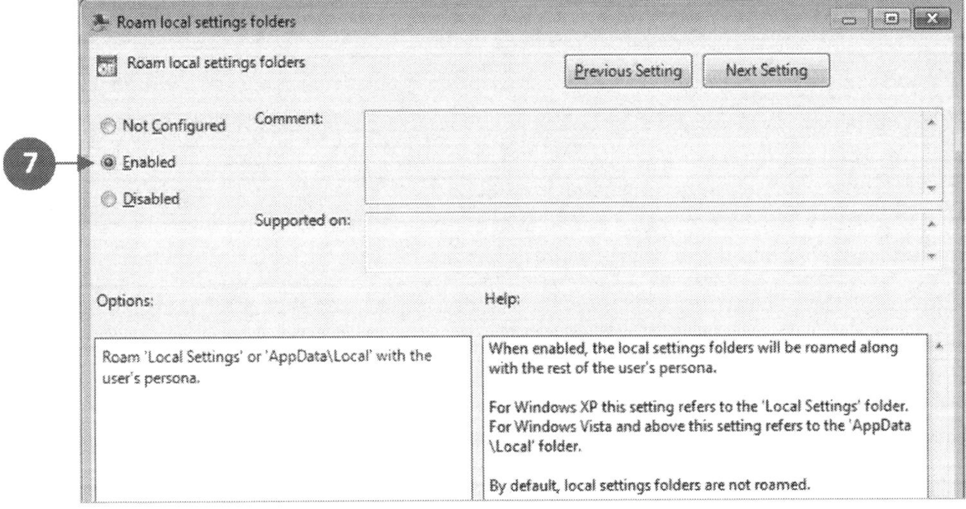

12. Click on **Next Setting** to configure the next policy.
13. On the next configuration page, **Files and folders to preload**, we can choose which folders get loaded upfront.

    If you remember how Persona Management works, folders and data only get loaded to the virtual desktop machine when the user requests them. The preload option means we can choose a set of files and folders that automatically get loaded onto the virtual desktop machine at login time rather than on demand.

    You might want to do this if there are specific folders that you know a particular user is always going to need. It might be a company-wide folder, which everyone uses, that makes it quicker if it gets loaded at login rather than everyone requesting it at once. Choosing this option might mean it would take longer for the login process while the files and folders complete the preload download.

14. To configure this option, click on **Enabled** (**8**), as shown in the following screenshot:

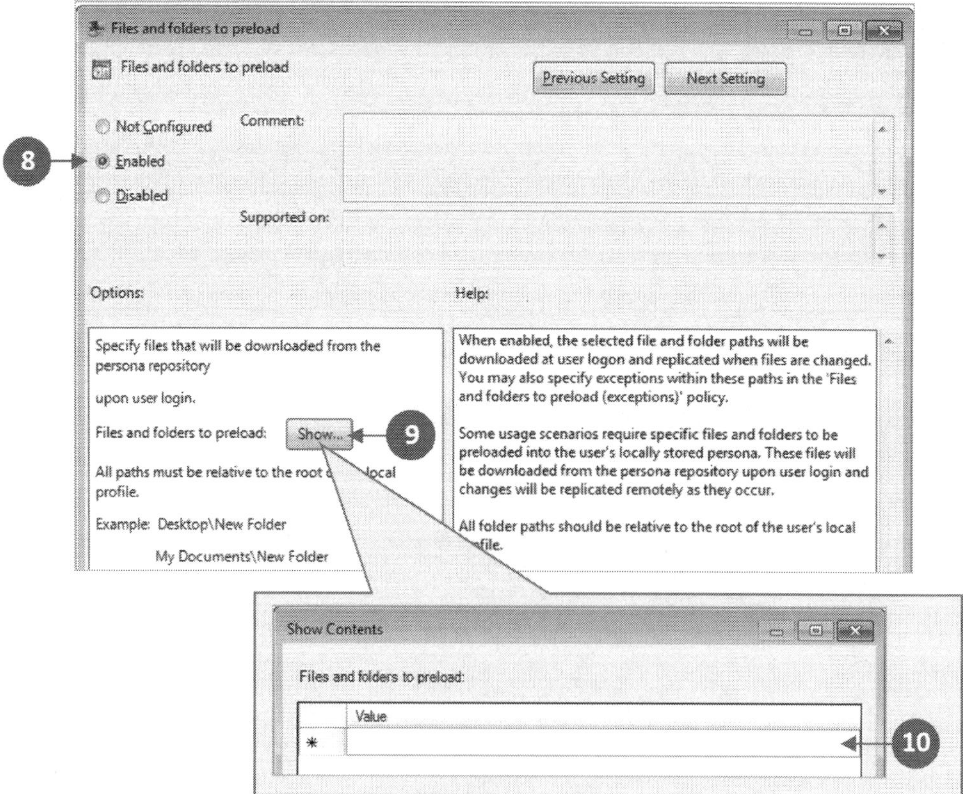

15. Then, click on **Show...** (**9**). The **Show Contents** dialog box appears. In this box, type the names of the files folder that you want to preload (**10**).
16. Click on **Next Setting** to configure the next policy.
17. The next option, **Files and folders to preload (exceptions)**, allows you to configure any exceptions to the previous policy you have just configured. The exception means it won't be preloaded. For example, you might need to preload a folder (as configured on the previous configuration page), but there are specific files in this folder that you don't want to preload; probably because they are too big or aren't used that often.
18. Click on **Enabled** (**11**), as shown in the following screenshot. As done previously, click on **Show...** (**12**) to open the dialog box where you can enter the files and folders that you don't want to preload:

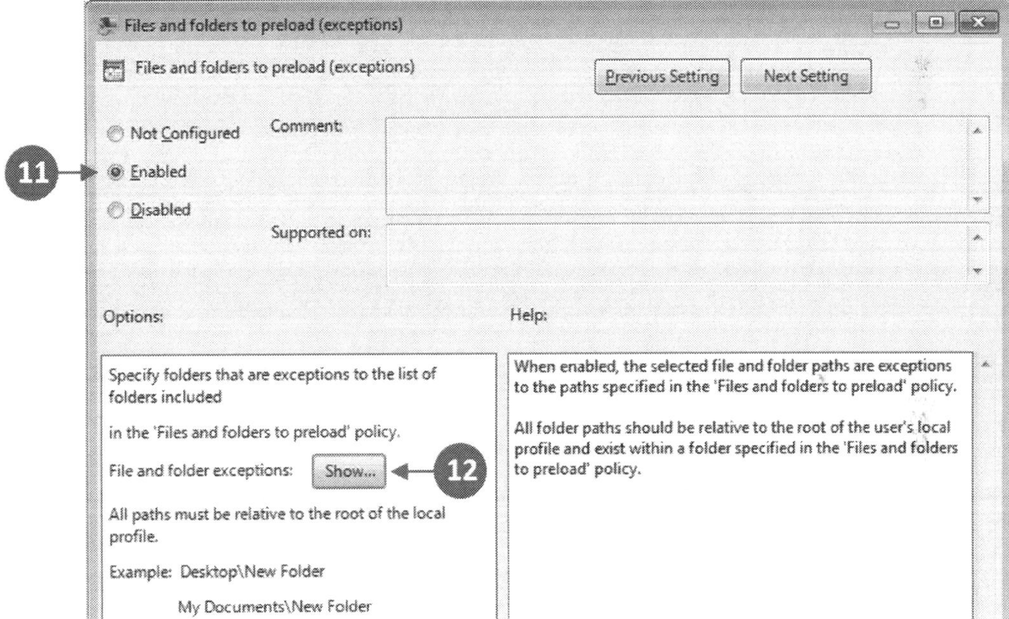

19. Click on **Next Setting** to configure the next policy.
20. The **Windows roaming profiles synchronization** option allows you to use the standard Windows technology. This means profiles are only synchronized at login and logoff times rather than at specific time intervals.

21. Click on **Enabled (13)** to switch this policy on, as shown here:

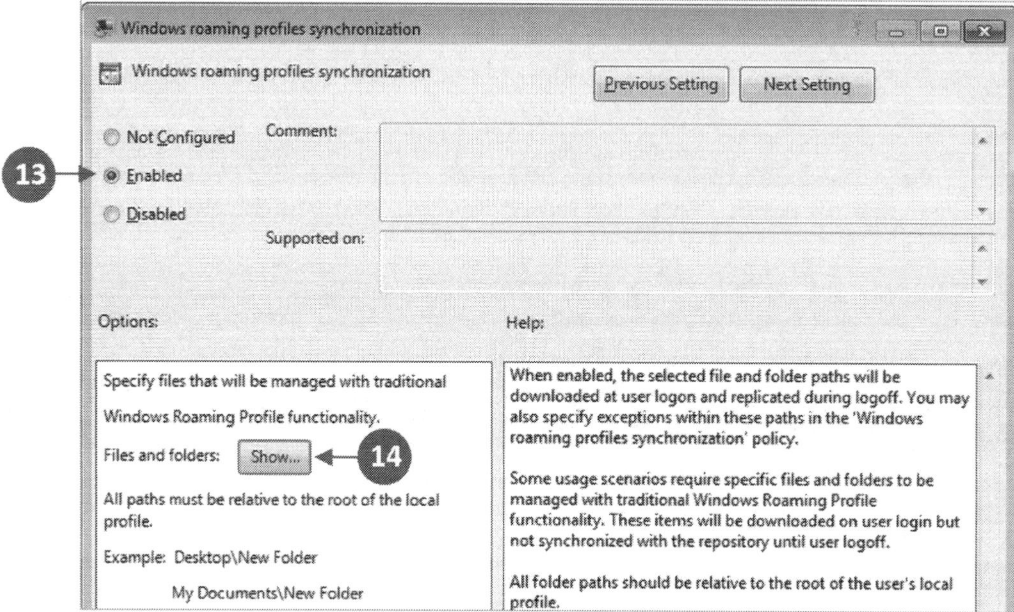

22. To configure specific files or folders that you want managed by the standard Windows roaming profiles, click on **Show... (14)**. Then, in the **Show Contents** dialog box, type the names of the files or folders.
23. Click on **Next Setting** to configure the next policy. On the **Windows roaming profiles synchronization (exceptions)** page, you can configure specific files and folders that do not get synchronized.
24. Click on **Enabled (15)** to switch this policy on and then click on **Show... (16)** to open the **Show Contents** dialog box. Type the names of the files and folders for the exception:

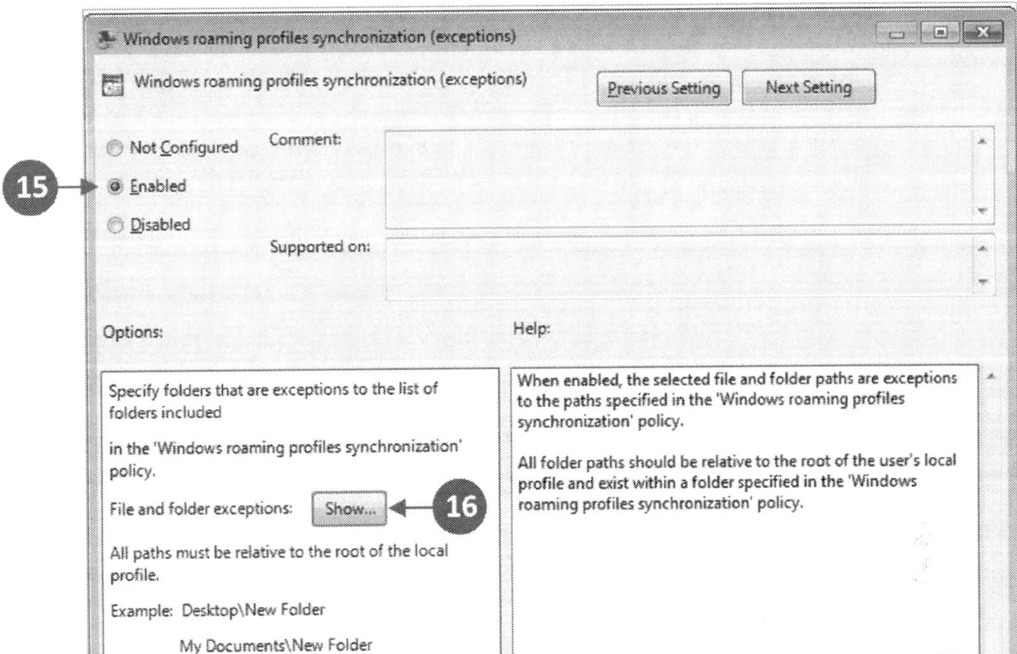

25. Click on **Next Setting** to configure the next policy. The next option is to configure **Files and folders excluded from roaming**:

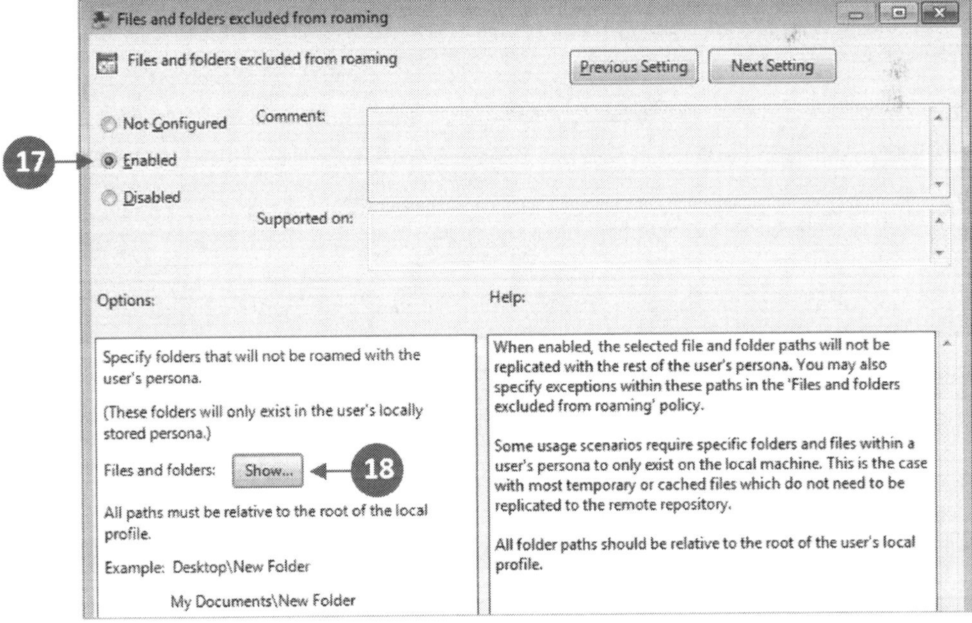

26. This option allows you to configure the files and folders that you don't want synchronized as part of a user's profile. For example, any temporary files need to be excluded. To use this policy, click on **Enabled** (**17**). Then, click on **Show...** (**18**) to open the **Show Contents** dialog box. Type the names of the files and folders for the exception. This is shown in the previous screenshot.
27. Click on **Next Setting** to configure the next policy. In the next configuration, **Files and folders excluded from roaming (exceptions)**, you can configure any exceptions to the policy we previously created.
28. Click on **Enabled** (**19**) to switch this policy on. Next, click on **Show...** (**20**) to open the **Show Contents** dialog box. Type the names of the files and folders for the exception, as shown in the following screenshot:

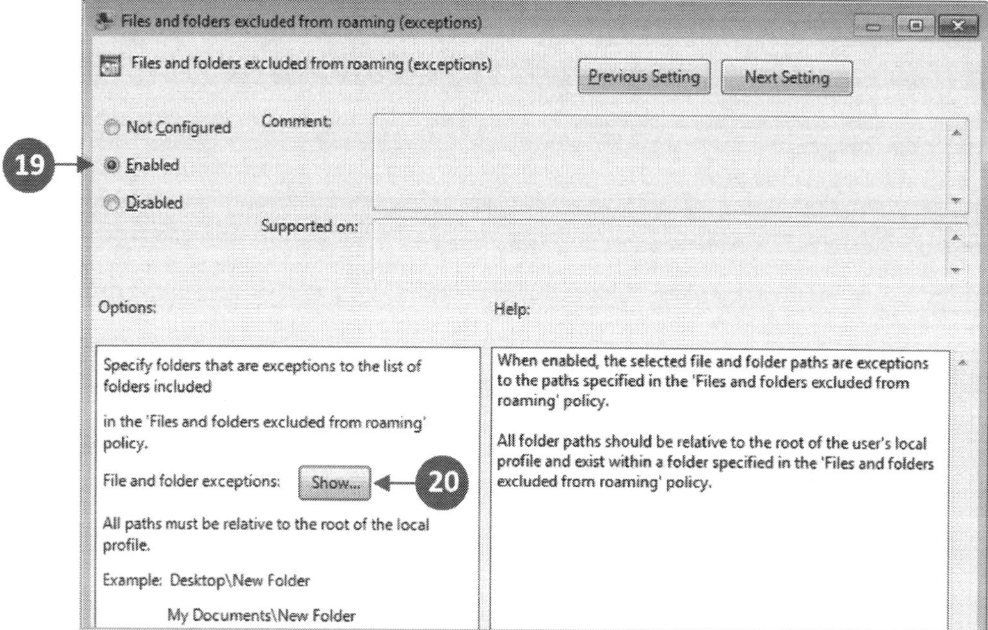

29. Click on **Next Setting** to configure the next policy. The next option is not for a virtual desktop environment; it is for a laptop computer. You might well ask, "Then why is it part of a virtual desktop Persona Management solution?" Good question. The answer is, because Persona Management can also be used on physical desktops and laptop computers. We will cover this later in this chapter. The following screenshot shows the next option, which is, **Enable background download for laptops**:

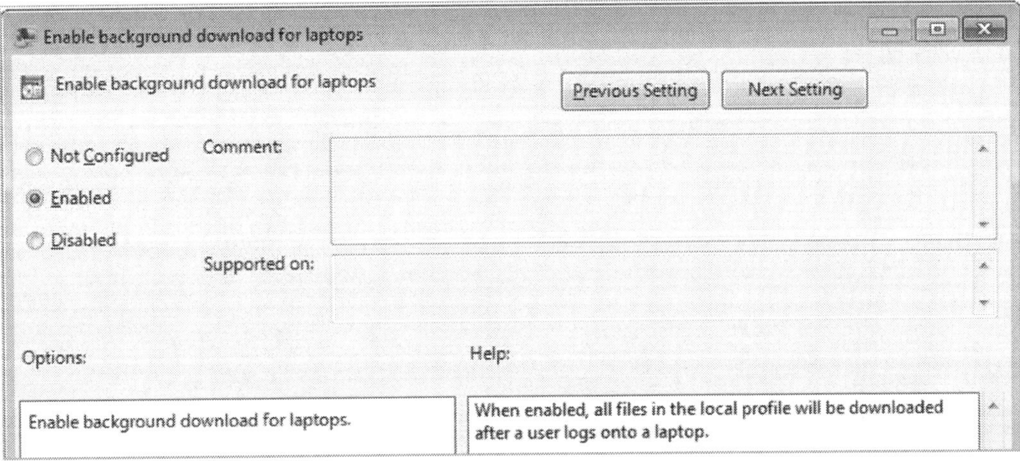

30. For now, we will just skip this policy setting. So click on **Next Setting** to configure the next policy.
31. The next option is to configure the **Folders to background download** option. This allows you to select folders that get downloaded in the background once you have logged in. This basically means that a user will not have to wait for things, such as large files, to download, or preload when they launch an application. So, while usually a user would have to wait for files to preload, with this option, the folders download in the background, allowing the login process to continue:

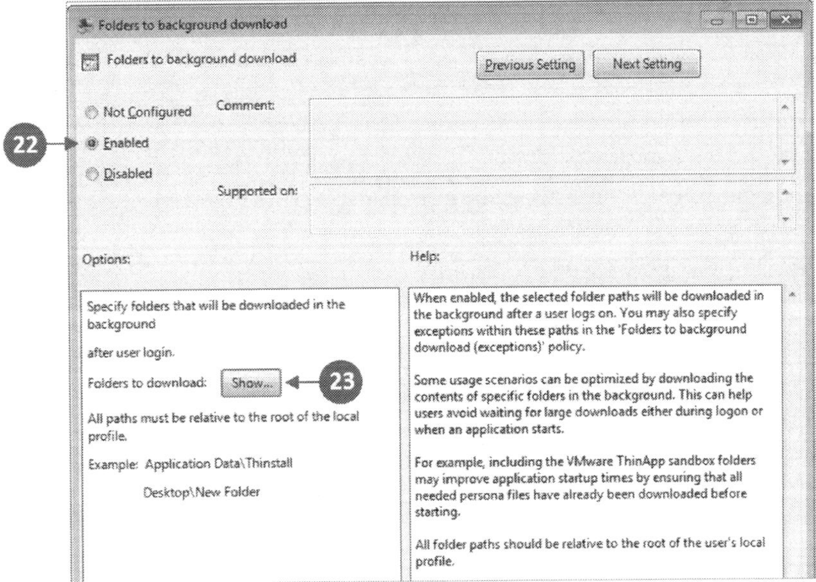

32. Click on **Enabled** (**22**) to switch this policy on and then click on **Show...** (**23**) to open the **Show Contents** dialog box. Type in the files or folders for the exception, as shown in the previous screenshot.
33. Click on **Next Setting** to configure the next policy.
34. The next option is to configure the **Folders to background download (exceptions)** option. As with the previous exception policies, this allows you to configure files and folders within the folder being downloaded, to be ignored. This is shown in the following screenshot:

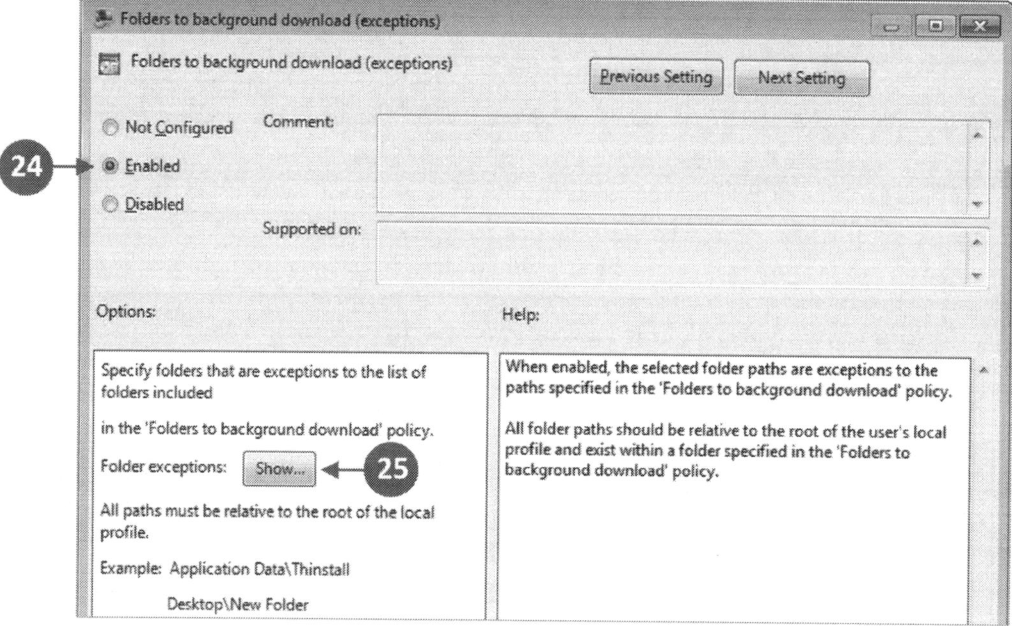

35. Click on **Enabled** (**24**) to switch this policy on. Then, click on **Show...** (**25**) to open the **Show Contents** dialog box and type in the names of the files and folders for the exception.
36. Click on **Next Setting** to configure the next policy.
37. In the **Excluded Processes** option, shown in the following screenshot, you can configure Persona Management to ignore any I/O generated by particular processes, such as antivirus applications or other applications that generate I/O files, which you would not want to synchronize as part of the user profile:

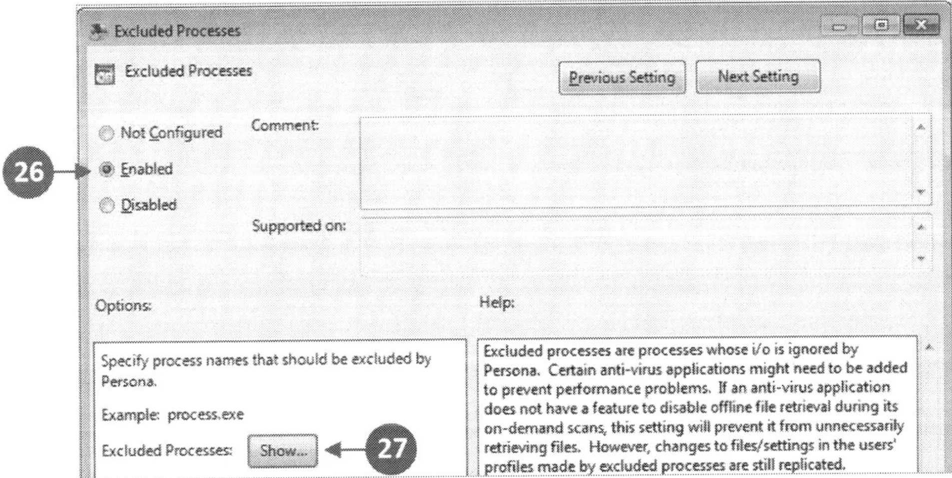

38. Click on **Enabled** (**26**) to switch this policy on and then click on **Show...** (**27**) to open the **Show Contents** dialog box. Type in the names of the processes that you want to exclude.
39. Click on **Next Setting** to configure the next policy.
40. The final policy in this section is to configure whether or not you want to delete any files that are created by the **Common Log File System** (**CLFS**). CLFS is part of the Windows OS and is used to create transaction logs and metadata used to access log data. This gets stored in the **Users** folder on the C drive of the machine along with user-level registry information so that we can manage this with Persona Management:

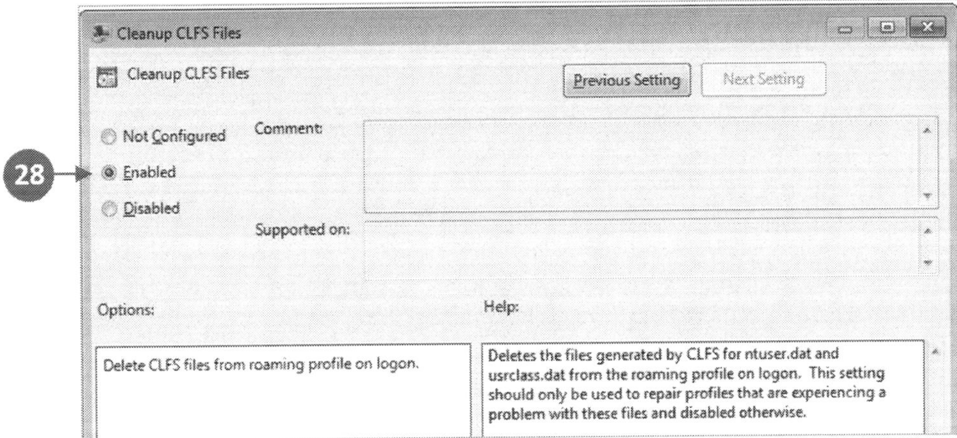

41. Click on **Enabled** (**28**) to switch this policy on.

We have now covered in detail the Persona Management policy settings that fall under the heading of Roaming & Synchronization. In the next section, we will take a look at the specific Folder Redirection options.

Folder Redirection

With Folder Redirection, you can specify which folders get synchronized to the central repository on the fileserver. This data is stored directly on the network share during the user session.

One of the use cases for Folder Redirection is for high availability and backup. In this example, you will configure the folders that contain critical data so that they are regularly synchronized with the central repository.

When you configure the folders to redirect, you can decide which particular folders get redirected and which ones remain local to the virtual desktop machine.

You can also choose to redirect different folders to different shared folders.

The following screenshot shows a list of all the folders for which you are able to configure a Folder Redirection policy:

Setting	State
Add the administrators group to redirected folders	Not configured
Files and folders excluded from Folder Redirection	Not configured
Files and folders excluded from Folder Redirection (exceptio...	Not configured
Application Data (Roaming)	Not configured
Contacts	Not configured
Cookies	Not configured
Desktop	Not configured
Downloads	Not configured
Favorites	Not configured
History	Not configured
Links	Not configured
My Documents	Not configured
My Music	Not configured
My Pictures	Not configured
My Videos	Not configured
Network Neighborhood	Not configured
Printer Neighborhood	Not configured
Recent Items	Not configured
Saved Games	Not configured
Searches	Not configured
Send To	Not configured
Start Menu	Not configured
Startup Items	Not configured
Templates	Not configured
Temporary Internet Files	Not configured

As you can see, there are a number of folder options you can configure. We are not going to go through all of them and show the configuration for each one, as the process is identical for each one, but we will cover one just to show what the process is.

In our example, we will redirect the **Downloads** folder, as shown in the following screenshot. So, double-click on the entry for **Downloads**. The configuration box will appear, as shown in the following screenshot:

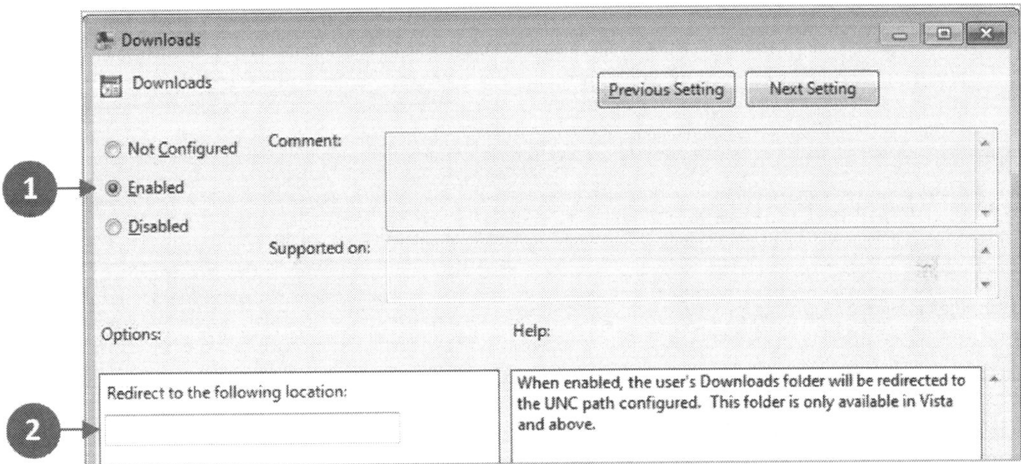

Click on **Enabled** (**1**) to switch this policy on. We now need to enter the path to which we want to redirect the folder (**2**). Here, we will enter the path to the shared folder we configured earlier, but we will add an entry to the end of the path so that we create and redirect folders to a unique folder for each user. To do this, we will use the `%username%` variable.

For our example lab, we will type `\\DC\PM_UserProfiles\%username%` to create a folder for each user.

We will then repeat this process for any other folders that we want to redirect. As we mentioned in the previous section, you could actually set up multiple shared folders and configure different folders to be redirected to different repositories.

Desktop UI

In the third category of our four Persona Management categories, namely the Desktop UI option, we can configure what a user sees when Persona Management is running and performing its tasks, by hiding icons and progress bars. These options are shown in the following screenshot:

Setting	State
Hide local offline file icon	Not configured
Show critical errors to users via tray icon alerts	Not configured
Show progress when downloading large files	Not configured

There are three options that we can configure:

- **Hide local offline file icon**: This simply hides the tray icon from the user
- **Show critical errors to users via tray icon alerts**: This will pop up an alert if the synchronization process fails
- **Show progress when downloading large files**: This displays a progress bar when a large file is downloaded

The configuration options for the first two of these policies is simply to enable or disable them in the same way as for all the other polices covered in this chapter.

However, in addition to these options, the **Show progress when downloading large files** policy has an additional configuration option, which we will take a closer look at.

This additional option allows you to configure a minimum file size for when the progress bar should be displayed. For example, if I set this option to 100 MB and I download an 80 MB file, then the progress bar will not be displayed. However, if I download a 120 MB file, then I will see the progress bar.

Here's another example. I download a 50 MB file and a 60 MB file at the same time. Individually, they would not be displayed on the progress bar. However, the sum of both files would mean I was over the minimum limit of 100 MB that I set, and so, I would see the progress bar, meaning that this setting will use the total sum of the file size being downloaded.

To configure the minimum size, enter a value into the **Minimum file size to show progress window (MB)** (**1**), as shown in the following screenshot:

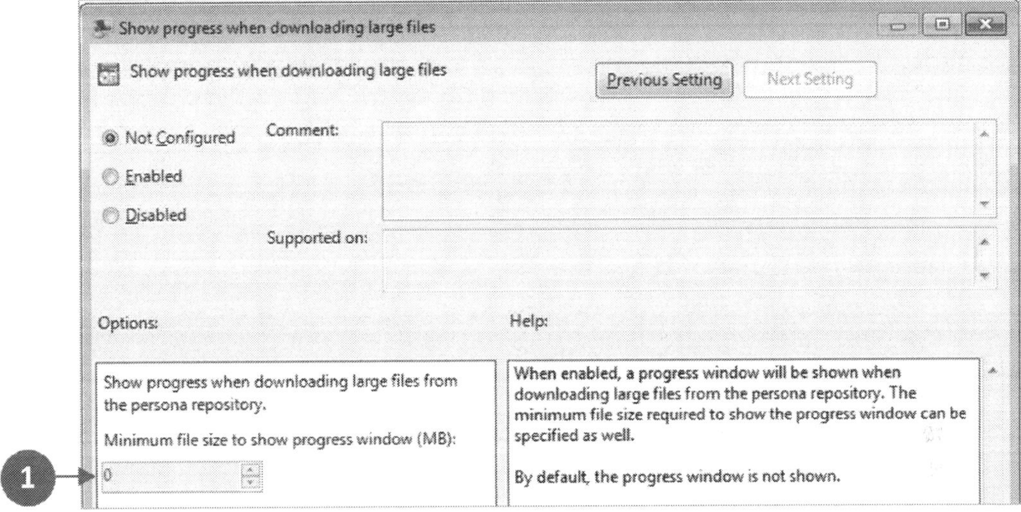

The next option we are going to look at is the Logging policy.

Logging

With the Logging Group Policy setting, you can configure the name, location, and the behavior of the logfiles that get generated for Persona Management. There are six configurable options, as shown in the following screenshot:

Setting	State
Debug flags	Not configured
Log History Depth	Not configured
Logging destination	Not configured
Logging filename	Not configured
Logging flags	Not configured
Upload log to network	Not configured

Let's take a look at the configurable options in each policy:

1. Double-click on **Debug flags**. You will now see the **Debug flags** policy configuration box.
2. Click on **Enabled (1)** to switch this policy on. Choose the type of debug report you want to generate. You can choose from the following three options:
    - **Debug error messages.**
    - **Debug information messages.**
    - **Debug port messages.**

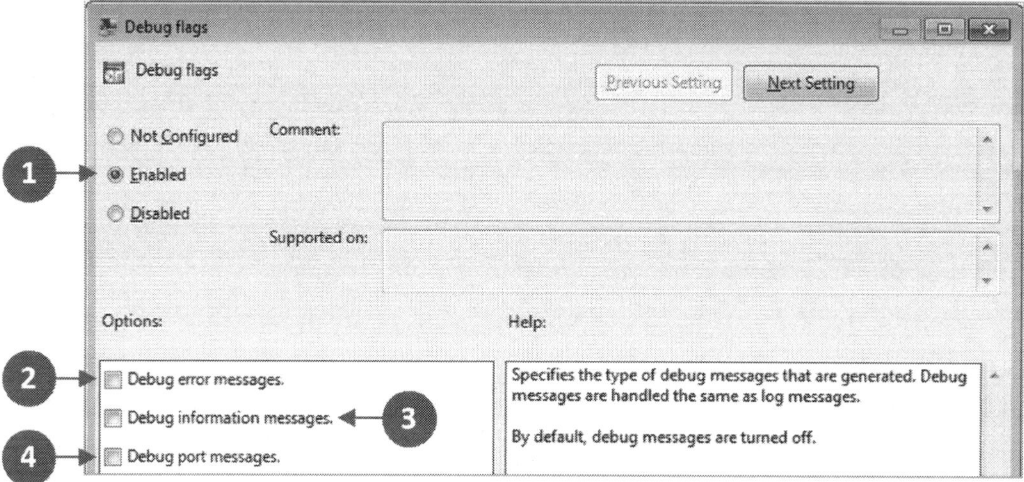

3. Click on **Next Setting** to configure the next policy, as shown here:

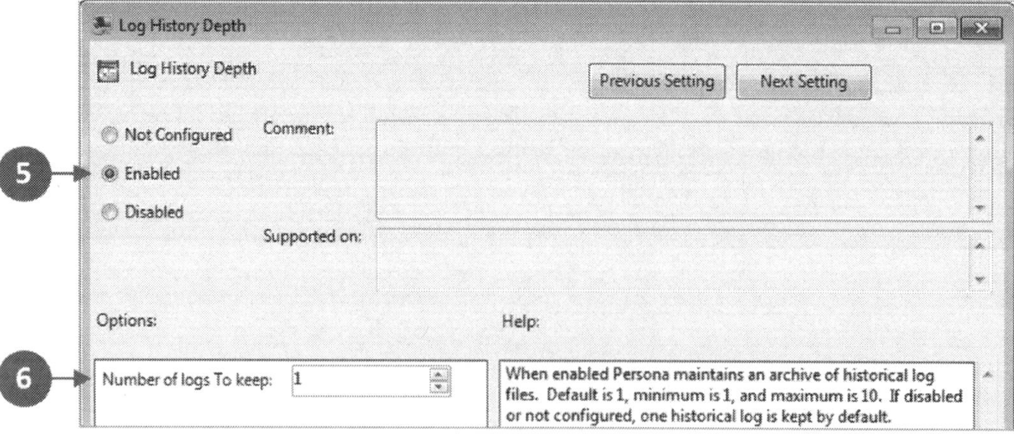

4. The **Log History Depth** page configures how many logfiles are archived. You can have up to 10 logfiles.
5. Click on **Enabled** (**5**) to switch this policy on. Then, in the **Number of logs To keep** box (**6**), enter the number of logfiles you want to archive.
6. Click on **Next Setting** to configure the next policy.
7. In the **Logging destination** policy configuration box, you can configure where you want to store the logfiles.
8. Click on **Enabled** (**7**) to switch this policy on. Then, if you want to send messages to the logfile, check the box for **Send log messages to the log file.** (**8**). If you want to send them to the debug port, check the box for **Send log messages to the debug port.** (**9**), as shown in the following screenshot:

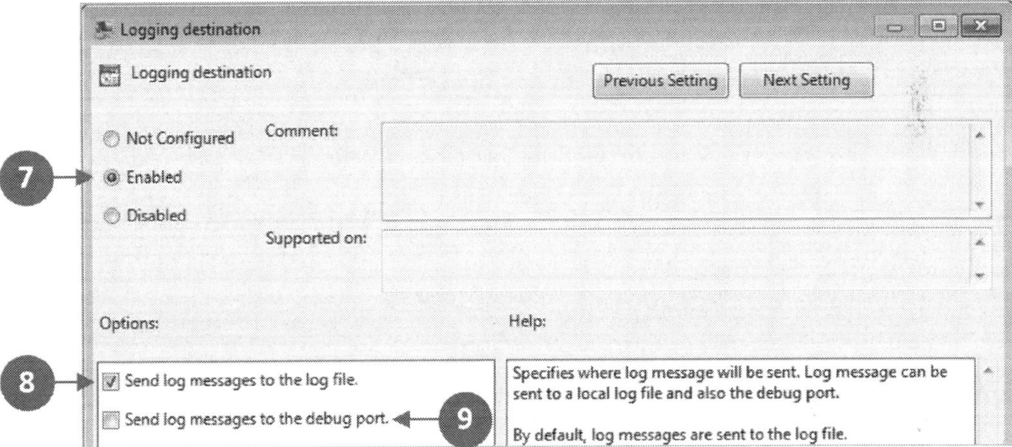

9. Click on **Next Setting** to configure the next policy.
10. In the **Logging filename** policy configuration box, you can configure the path and filename for the logfile.

11. Click on **Enabled** (**10**) to switch this policy on. Then, in **Local log file pathname** (**11**), enter the path to the location where you want to store the logfile. Don't forget to add the filename in the path; don't use a UNC path:

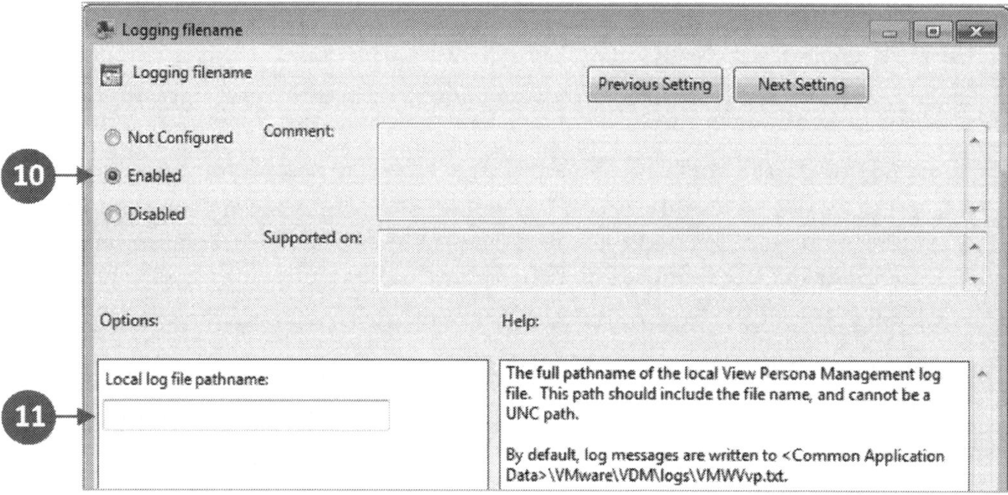

12. If you enable the policy and leave the **Local log file pathname** field blank, the logfile will be saved to `ProgramData\VMware\VDM\logs\VMWVvp.txt`.
13. Click on **Next Setting** to configure the next policy.
14. The next policy to configure is the **Logging flags** policy. This allows you to choose which type of messages get stored in the logs.
15. Click on **Enabled** (**12**) to switch this policy on. Then check the box for each type of information you want to add to the log, as shown in the following screenshot:

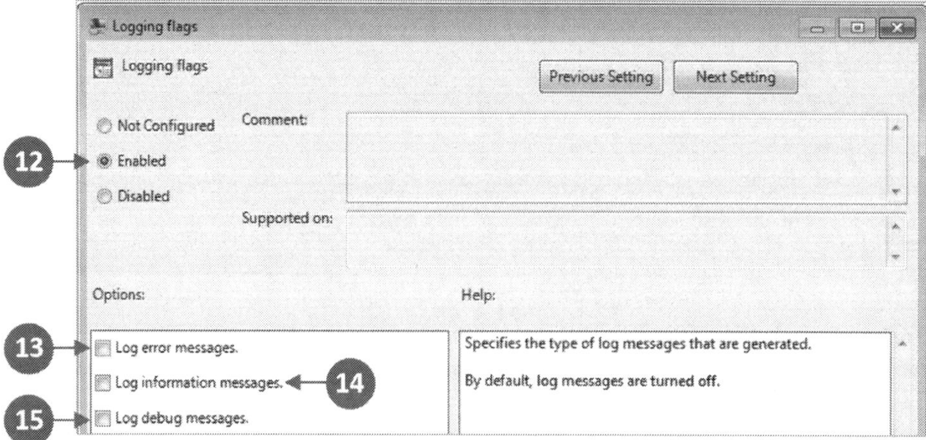

16. You can choose from the following options:
    - **Log error messages.**
    - **Log information messages.**
    - **Log debug messages.**
17. By default, just the error messages and information messages are logged. Click on **Next Setting** to configure the next policy.
18. The final policy to configure is the **Upload log to network** policy. This policy allows you to configure a network share on which the logfile is to be uploaded.
19. Click on **Enabled (16)** to switch this policy on. Then, in the **Network share path:** box, enter the details of the UNC path to the share the path you want to use:

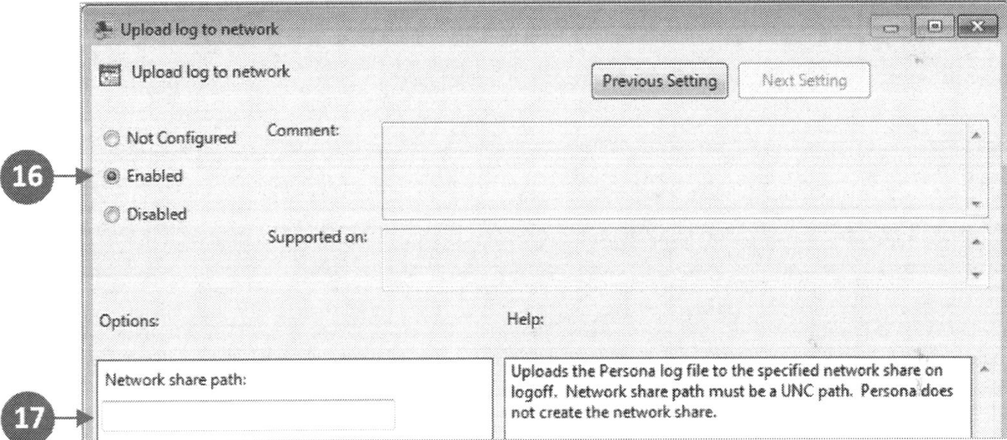

20. With all the policies now configured, click on **Apply** to save the policy configurations. Close the configuration box.

We have now completed the Persona Management policy configurations for the parent image virtual desktop machine. The next step is to prepare the updated parent image for delivery to the end users, as covered in the *Preparing the Virtual Desktops for delivery* section in *Chapter 6, Building and Optimizing the Desktop Operating System.*

Basically, we have to make sure we have an updated snapshot, based on which our linked clone desktops will be built, and an updated template to create our dedicated desktops, which now include the Persona Management policy configurations.

In the next section, we will configure the Persona Management Group Policy for the domain controller in our AD.

Installing the ADM template in AD

We are now going to turn our attention to the AD domain and configure Group Policy for use with Persona Management:

1. To start with, log in to the domain controller with administrative privileges that allow you to create and edit group policy. Once logged in, click on **Start** and go to **Administrative Tools**. Then, from the menu options, double-click on **Group Policy Management**. You will then see the **Group Policy Management** dialog box, as shown in the following screenshot:

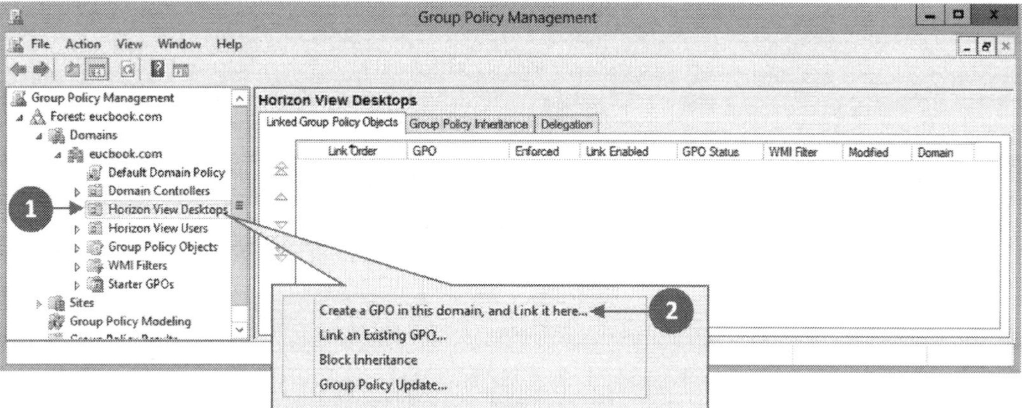

2. Click on the **Horizon View Desktops** (**1**), which we previously created. Right-click and then, from the menu options, click on **Create a GPO in this domain, and Link it here...** (**2**). You will now see the **New GPO** dialog box, as shown in the following screenshot:

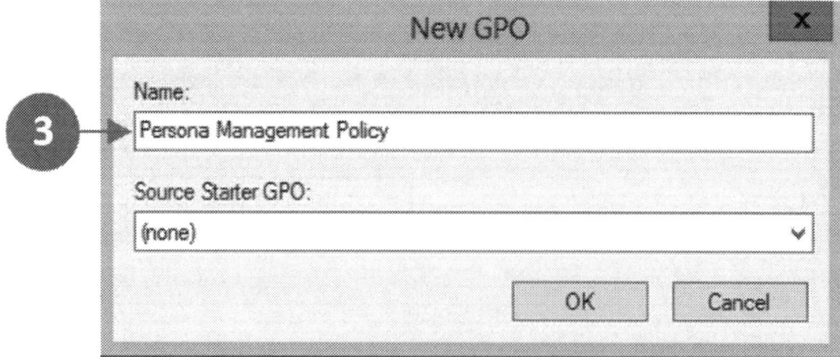

3. Type in a name for this new policy in the **Name:** box (**3**). In our example, we name it `Persona Management Policy`. Once you have typed in the name, click on **OK**.

4. You will now see that the policy has been created within the **Horizon View Desktops** OU. The next task is to edit and configure the policy. First, add the **Persona Management ADM template**. Click on the newly created policy to highlight it (**4**), then right-click on it. From the menu options, click on **Edit** (**5**):

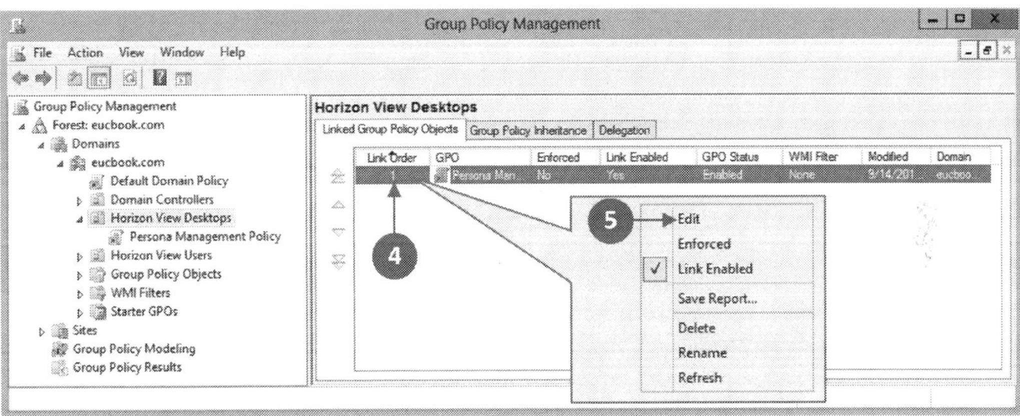

5. The **Group Policy Management Editor** dialog box is displayed, as shown in the following screenshot. Click on **Administrative Templates Policy definitions** (**6**) and then right-click. From the menu options, click on **Add/ Remove Templates...** (**7**).

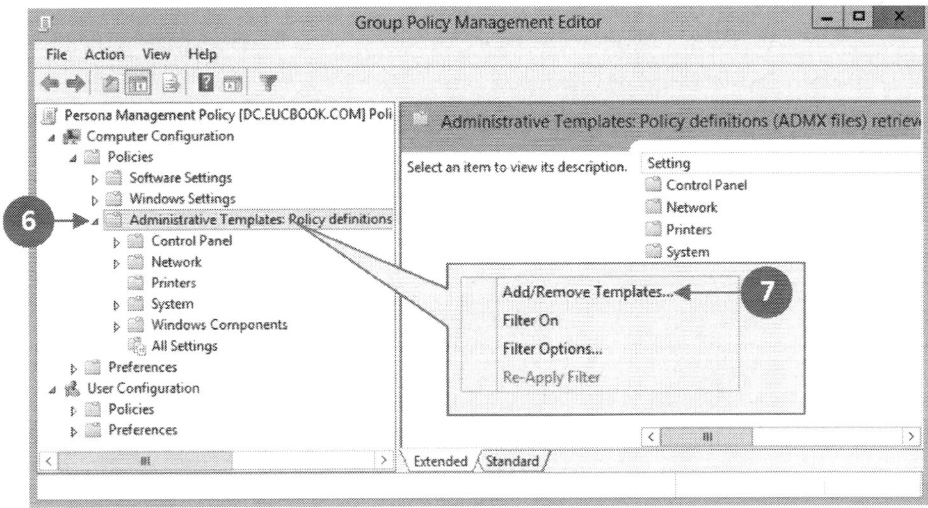

6. You will now see the **Add/Remove Templates** dialog box where we can add the ADM template for Persona Management.

   You might have done this already when you imported the other View ADM templates. In that case, you can skip this section or use it as a reminder. We are just going to create a policy for Persona Management.

7. In the **Add/Remove Templates** dialog box, click on **Add...** (**8**), as shown in the following screenshot:

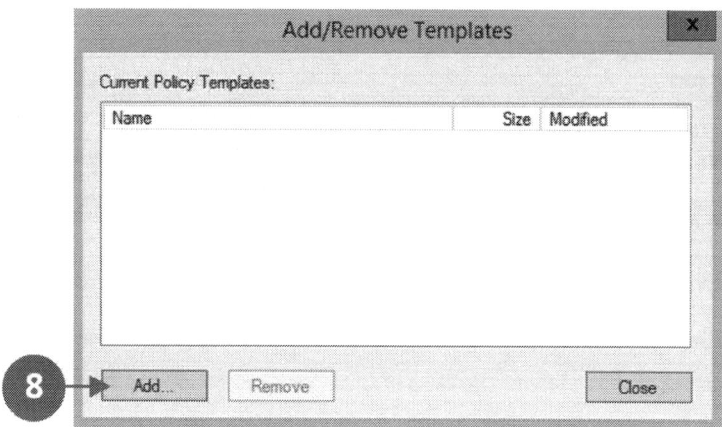

8. A **Windows Explorer** box will open, where we can browse to the location of the template we want to add.
9. We are adding the Persona Management template, just as we did when we configured the virtual desktop machine (basically, it's the same policy that we are going to add).
10. Click on **ViewPM.adm** (**9**) and then click **Open** (**10**), as shown in the following screenshot:

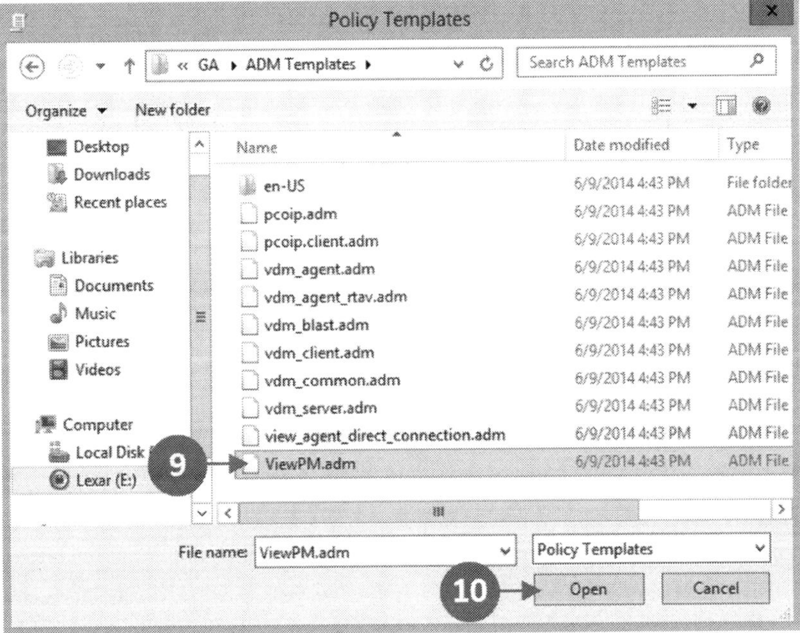

11. You will now see that the policy has been added (**11**).
12. Click on **Close** (**12**) to complete the task of adding the template, as shown in the following screenshot:

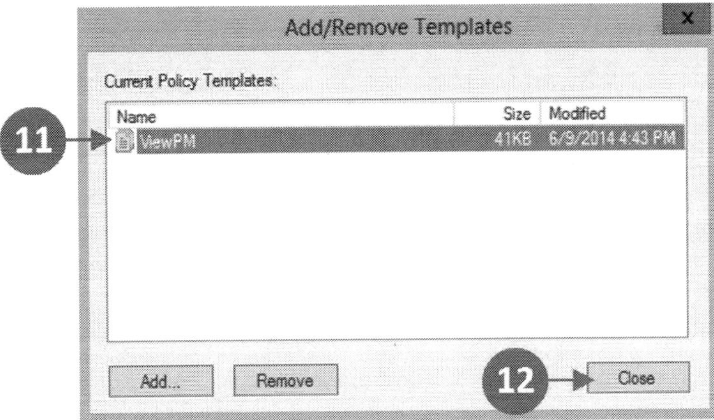

13. You will return to the **Group Policy Management Editor** screen, where we can check whether the Persona Management template has been successfully added.

14. Navigate to **Classic Administrative Template (ADM)** (**13**) | **VMware View Agent Configuration** (**14**) | **Persona Management** (**15**). You will see the Persona Management policy configuration options shown, as we described in a previous section of this chapter:

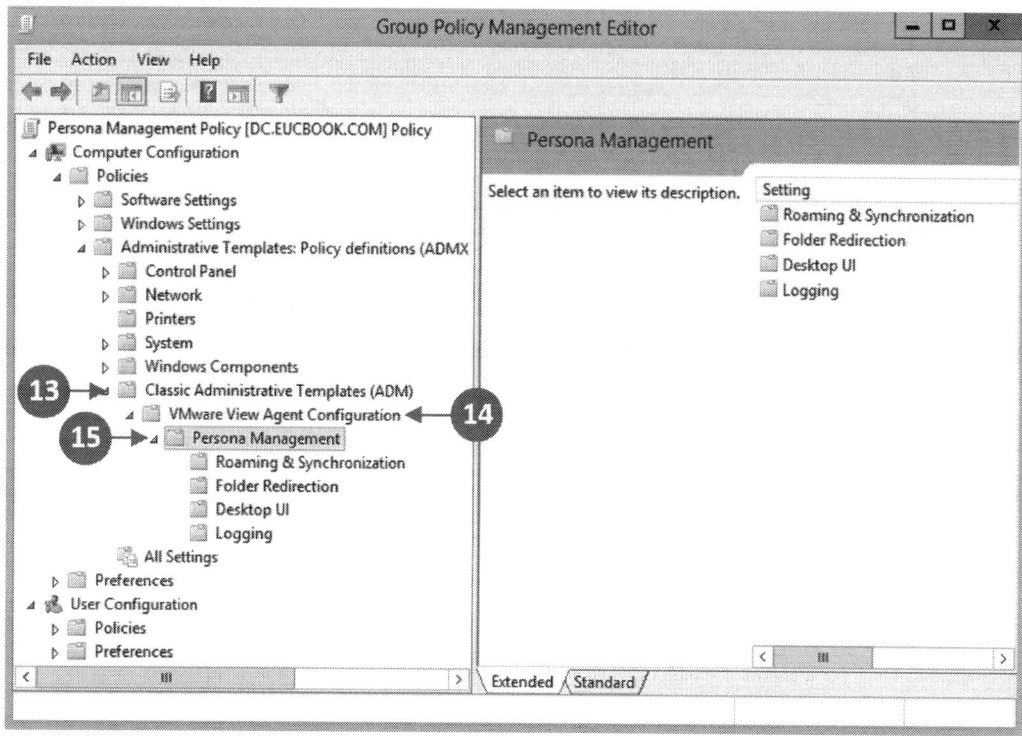

Now, you have successfully added the Persona Management Group Policy to the domain. The next task is to configure the various policy options, as we did in the *Configuring Persona Management on the virtual desktop* section earlier in this chapter. As we have mentioned before, the ADM template we used for the domain policy is identical to that used on the virtual desktop machines. Therefore, it contains exactly the same policy configuration options.

Installing the View Agent with Persona Management

So far in this chapter, we have discussed in detail how to configure the Persona Management policy settings, but what else needs to be installed? Basically, we need to ensure that the Persona Management Agent is on the virtual desktop machine.

The Persona Management Agent is one of the options that you need to install when installing the View Agent, as shown in the following screenshot:

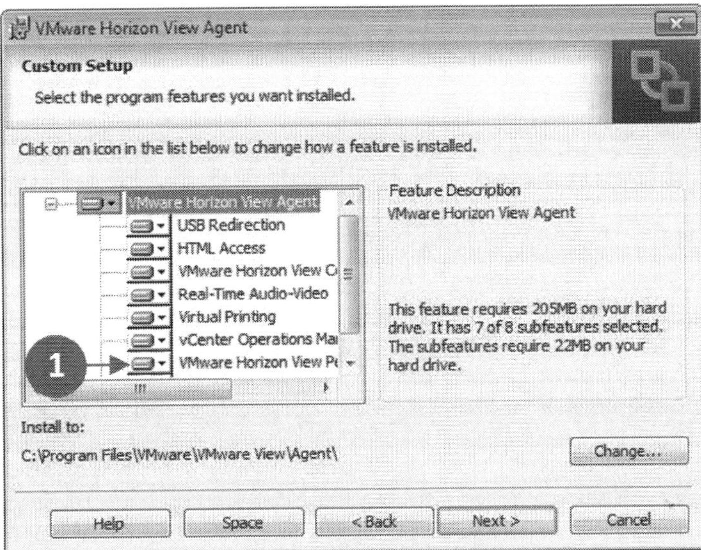

During the installation of the View Agent, ensure that you have selected the option to install the Persona Management Agent. We have already covered the installation of the View Agent in *Chapter 6, Building and Optimizing the Desktop Operating System*.

One last thing to point out when installing Persona Management is that you need to run the optimization script. And there is a specific script to be used when you are deploying virtual desktop machines with Persona Management enabled. Again, we covered this back in *Optimizing the guest operating system* section, in *Chapter 6, Building and Optimizing the Desktop Operating System*.

Installing Persona Management on physical PCs

Persona Management is all about managing a user's profile and data when using the Windows operating system. It makes no difference whether the instance of the Windows desktop operating system is physical or virtual. So the same is true for the VMware View Persona Management tool. It can be used to manage both virtual desktop machines and physical PCs/laptops.

In this section, we will cover how to install Persona Management on a physical device so that we manage the user's profile in the same way as we do for the virtual desktop machines in our environment.

The first task we need to perform is to check that we have configured our Group Policy for Persona Management on the domain controller. We also need to make sure we have a separate OU configured for physical devices managed with Persona Management. We don't want to add these physical devices to our existing virtual desktop machine OU as there are a number of other policy settings that do not apply to physical devices.

We then need to install the Persona Management agent onto the device. As part of the Horizon View software download bundle, you should see two applications for Persona Management. One for 32-bit operating systems and the other for 64-bit operating systems.

So, let's get on with the installation of Persona Management:

1. Locate the installation files, choose the appropriate operating system version, and double-click to launch it. In our example, we have a 64-bit desktop that will launch an install application named **VMware-personamanagement -x86_64-6.1.0-2509221**, as shown in the following screenshot:

Name	Date modified	Type	Size
VMware-viewconnectionserver-x86_64-6.1.0-2509221	3/18/2015 1:53 PM	Application	175,837 KB
VMware-viewcomposer-6.1.0-2506641	3/18/2015 1:57 PM	Application	32,084 KB
VMware-viewagent-x86_64-6.1.0-2509441	3/18/2015 1:56 PM	Application	161,800 KB
VMware-viewagent-direct-connection-x86_64-6.1.0-2509221	3/18/2015 1:57 PM	Application	15,144 KB
VMware-viewagent-direct-connection-6.1.0-2509221	3/18/2015 1:57 PM	Application	13,719 KB
VMware-viewagent-6.1.0-2509441	3/18/2015 1:54 PM	Application	122,825 KB
1 VMware-personamanagement-x86_64-6.1.0-2509221	3/18/2015 1:56 PM	Application	18,387 KB
VMware-personamanagement-6.1.0-2509221	3/18/2015 1:56 PM	Application	12,478 KB
VMware-Horizon-View-HTML-Access-2.6.0-2329873	3/18/2015 1:58 PM	Compressed (zipp...	1,869 KB
VMware-Horizon-View-Extras-Bundle-3.3.0-2491779	3/18/2015 1:57 PM	Compressed (zipp...	2,694 KB

2. You will now see the **Welcome to the VMware Horizon View Persona Management Setup Wizard**, as shown in the following screenshot:

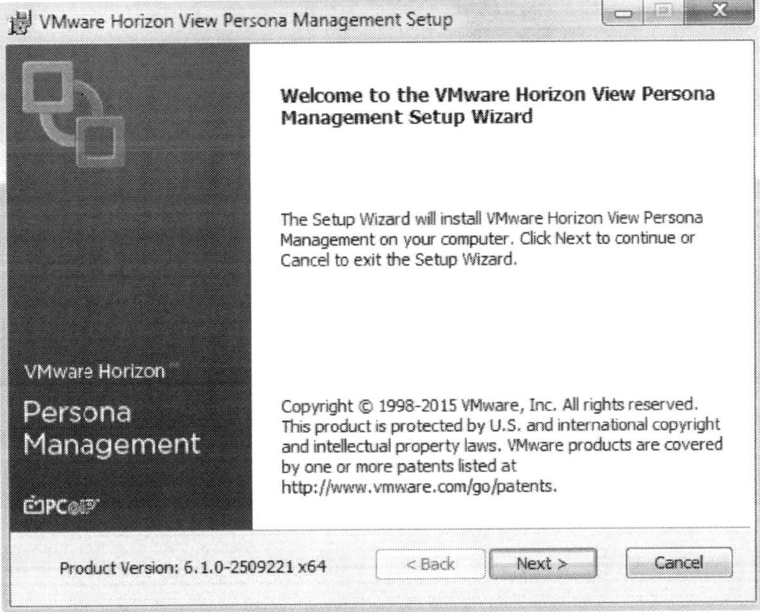

3. Click on **Next >** to continue the installation.
4. On the **End-User License Agreement** page, check the box to accept the terms (**2**):

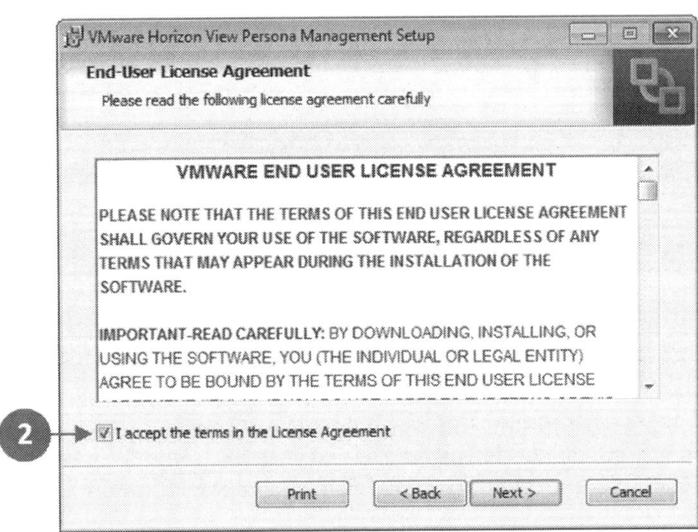

5. Click on **Next >** to continue the installation.
6. There are no configuration or setup options when installing Persona Management. So, click on **Install**, as shown in the following screenshot, to start the installation and copy the file:

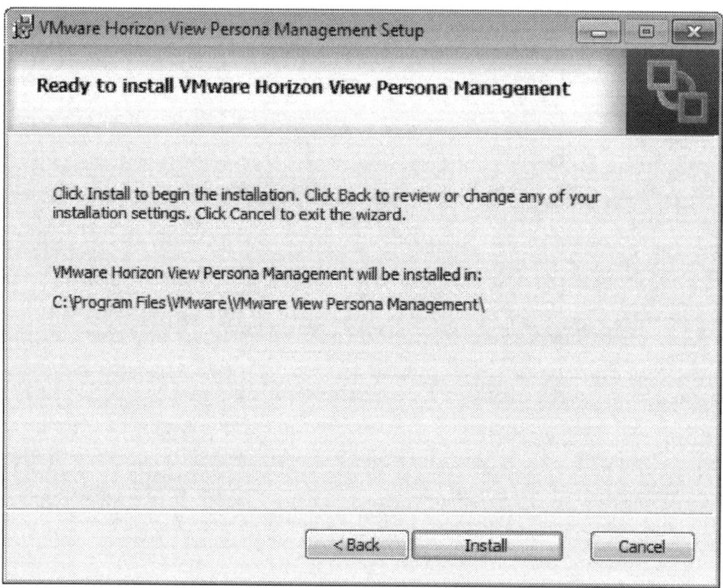

7. Once the installation is complete, you will see the following dialog box that will prompt you to reboot the machine:

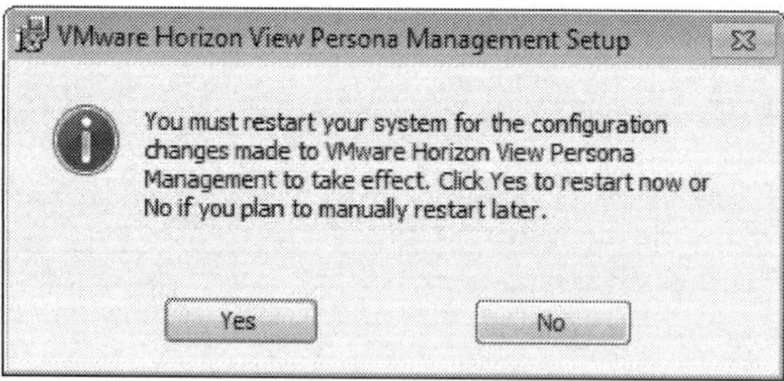

8. Click on **Yes** to reboot. The installation of Persona Management is now complete.
9. Once the machine has rebooted, and it is back up and running, check that Persona Management is running. To do this, click on **Start** and then on **Run**. Then, in the **Run** dialog box, type `services.msc` to open the services screen:

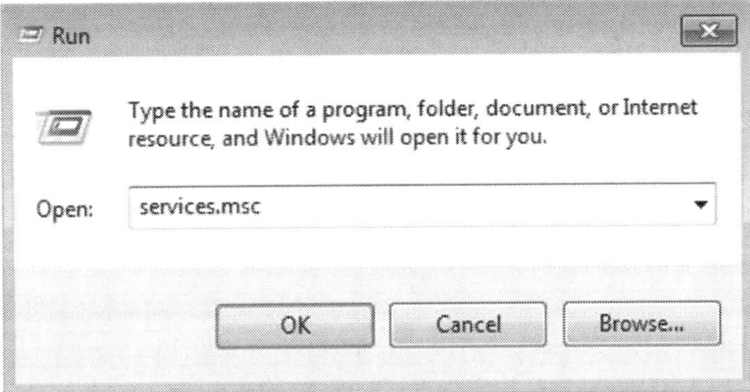

10. Click on **OK**.
11. In the **Services** window, scroll down until you find an entry for **VMware Horizon View Persona Management** (3), as shown in the following screenshot, and check whether the service has started:

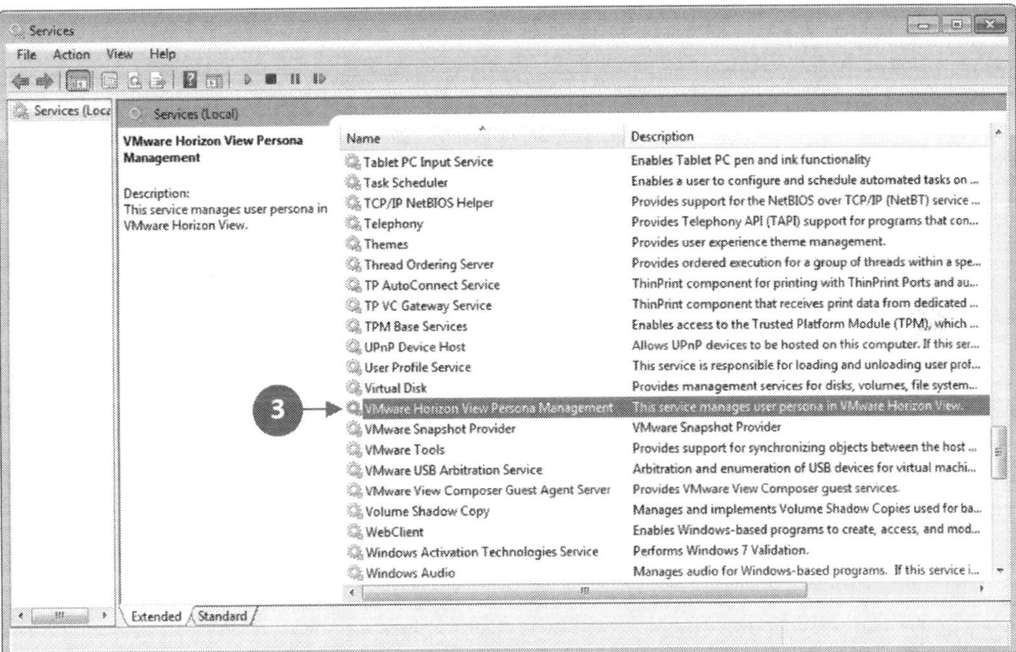

In our example, Persona Management is running and so, the user's profiles and data are being managed.

Testing Persona Management

Now that we have Persona Management running on our virtual desktop machines and physical devices, we have to make sure that it is working correctly.

To do this, we will log in as a user and make sure the files and folders are being redirected. In our example, we have logged on to a virtual desktop machine as the user PVO and created a test file on the desktop of the machine.

To check whether Persona Management is working, we will now switch back to the server that is hosting the central repository and make sure the user's folder has been created and that files have been redirected as per the policy we configured.

On the server hosting the Persona Management central repository, open Windows Explorer and navigate to the shared folder that we configured earlier in this chapter to store user profiles and data. This folder is `PM_UserProfiles`.

In the path to the shared folder (**1**), you will now see that the username that we logged in as for the test, PVO, is part of the path. Now if you click and open the **Desktop** folder, you can see the document we created and saved on the desktop (**2**):

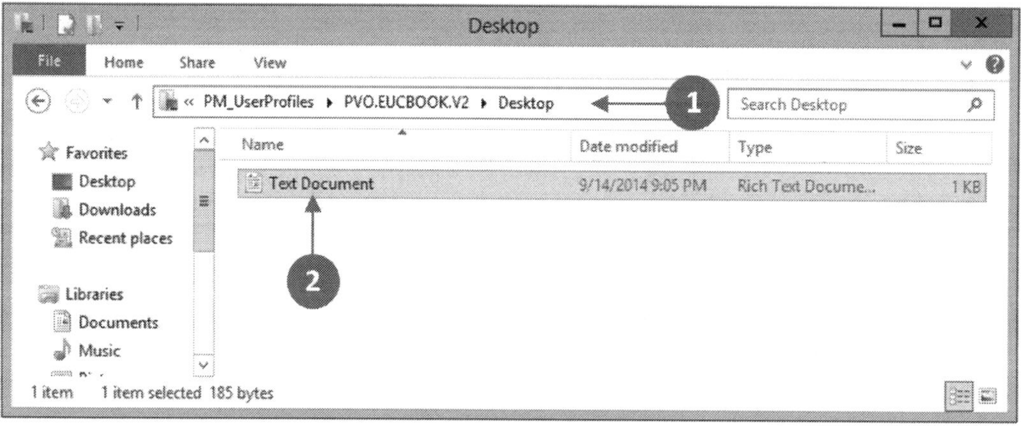

We have now successfully deployed View Persona Management in our environment.

In the next section, we will take a look at some of the best practices to consider when deploying Persona Management.

Best practices

In this section, we will highlight some of the best practices to work with Persona Management. We have covered some of these throughout the chapter, so we will just summarize these.

Removing local user profiles at logout

The default setting for this is that the user profiles do not get deleted when the users log off their desktops. This helps with reducing the amount of I/O.

However, if you are using floating virtual desktop machines and they are configured to refresh or delete when a user logs off, then you need to set the **Remove local persona option at log off** to disable. As the virtual desktop machine is refreshed by View anyway, there is no need for Persona Management to do it.

Persona Management and Windows roaming profiles

If you are using Persona Management to manage your Horizon View virtual desktop machine and also using Windows roaming profiles for physical devices, it's best practice to configure different profiles for each environment.

When AD Group Policies are being used to manage this, make sure you enable the **Persona repository location** policy and select the **Override Active Directory user profile** path.

Configuring redirected folders

When you configure Folder Redirection, ensure that the folder path includes the `%username%` variable added at the end of the redirected folder's name.

In our example, we configured this as: `\\DC\PM_UserProfiles\%username%\`.

Using antivirus with Persona Management

When using an **antivirus** (**AV**) application with Persona Management, configure it with the default behavior and ensure you do not set it to scan offline files. If you need to perform a virus scan for the desktop, then you need to make sure that the files and folders are preloaded.

Backing up the central repository

VMware recommends that you use your standard practice when it comes to backing up the shared folder that is used to store the profile repository. Avoid things like Windows Volume backup services as that could cause data loss or corruption.

Using persistent disks

If you have virtual desktop machine users that create large amounts of data, and have a dedicated desktop assignment, then it's best practice to use persistent disks for these particular users.

When you configure a persistent disk, it is used to preserve the user data and settings; even when you run a refresh or recompose using Horizon View Composer. The persistent disk acts as a cache for the user profiles and, therefore, limits the amount of I/O traffic.

However, when you use persistent disks, make sure you set the **Remove local persona at log off** policy to be disabled. If you do not, then the policy will delete the user data from the persistent disk when a user logs off, regardless of the fact that it's a persistent disk. The Persona Management policy will take precedence.

Summary

In this chapter, we introduced you to Horizon View Persona Management, what it is, and why you would want to deploy it. We then went on to examine how it is driven by standard AD Group Policy and took an in-depth look at the policies.

Finally, we installed and tested Persona Management, before looking at some of the deployment best practices.

In the next chapter, we will look at how Horizon View can deliver published applications.

10
Delivering Remote Applications with Horizon Advanced

So far in this book, we have concentrated on the delivery of virtual desktop machines. However, with Horizon View 6, you now have the ability to also deliver remote applications (or published applications as it's more commonly known) and session-based desktops from the same platform.

In this chapter, we will dive deeper into the features of Horizon Advanced Edition. We will look at how Horizon View publishes an application directly into the Horizon View Client without the need to launch a full virtual desktop machine.

This also means that, from View Client, you can launch applications on an operating system that wouldn't normally be able to run this application. For example, you can run the Microsoft Windows version of Word on your iPad using View Client.

The infrastructure required for this is Microsoft Remote Desktop Services, which is running at the backend. However, as Horizon View is brokering the applications or desktop sessions, it uses PCoIP as the delivery protocol, giving you all the benefits of using the protocol, which we discussed previously.

Architecture overview

So what does the architecture look like and how does application remoting work in comparison to the Standard View virtual desktop machine brokering? In terms of architecture, delivering remote applications is handled in pretty much the same way as virtual desktop machines are managed and brokered.

Horizon View acts as the broker. However, instead of brokering a virtual desktop machine that would run on the ESXi host server, it is now brokering an application session that runs on a Microsoft Windows server, configured with the RDSH role and the applications installed on it.

The following screenshot gives you a detailed outline of the architecture:

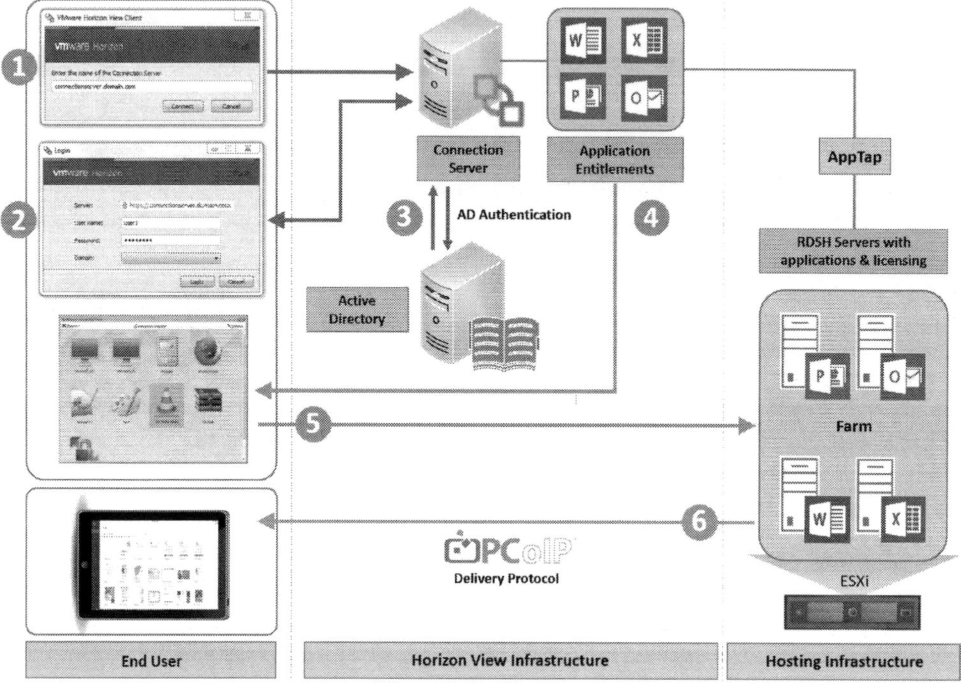

So, how does it work?

1. To begin with, as you do when connecting to a View virtual desktop machine, you launch the View Client and log in to the Connection Server. You enter the details of the View Connection Server you want to connect to (**1**), enter your username and password (**2**), and then authenticate against the AD.
2. Once authenticated, the client sends a `<get-launch-items>` request to the Connection Server to request a list of all the entitled application sessions, applications, and desktops for that user. The response contains the following details:
    - `<app-sessions>`, `<desktops>`, `<applications>`
    - Absolute paths to the icons
3. The client fetches any icons it hasn't cached already via HTTPS, using the paths that were provided by the Connection Broker when it sent the response.
4. Access to the icon for **uniform resource identifiers** (**URI**) needs to be authenticated. The Connection Server performs an entitlement check and only returns an icon if that user is entitled to at least one application that has an icon associated with it. For applications that don't have any icons, the client will provide a default icon.
5. A list of entitled desktops and application pools is then displayed to the end user in the View Client (**4**).
6. The end user then double-clicks on an application to launch it (**5**). The connection is made and the application opens in a new window (**6**).

In the next section, we will take a closer look at what happens during the process to connect the user to the application or desktop session they requested; we have briefly touched this in steps of the previous tasks.

Application connection sequence

The following screenshot illustrates the process to connect the user to the application:

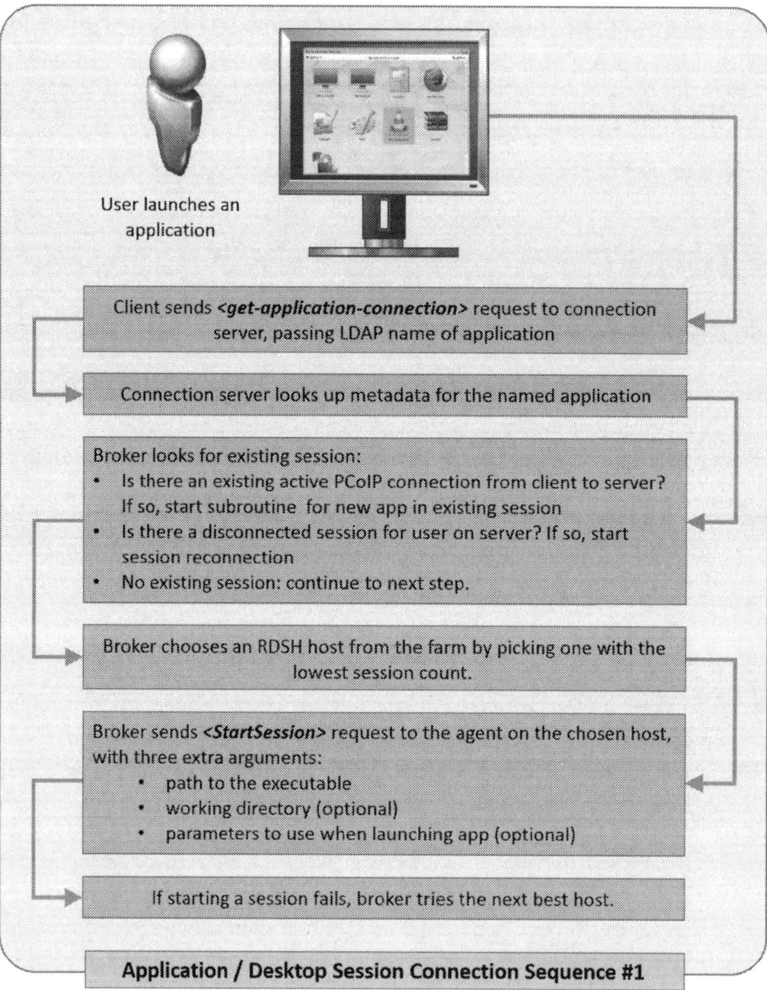

So, now we have a user who has made a request via the client to the Connection Server to launch an application. The next phase of the connection process is for the Connection Broker to talk to the View agent installed on the RDS server. The following screenshot illustrates the process:

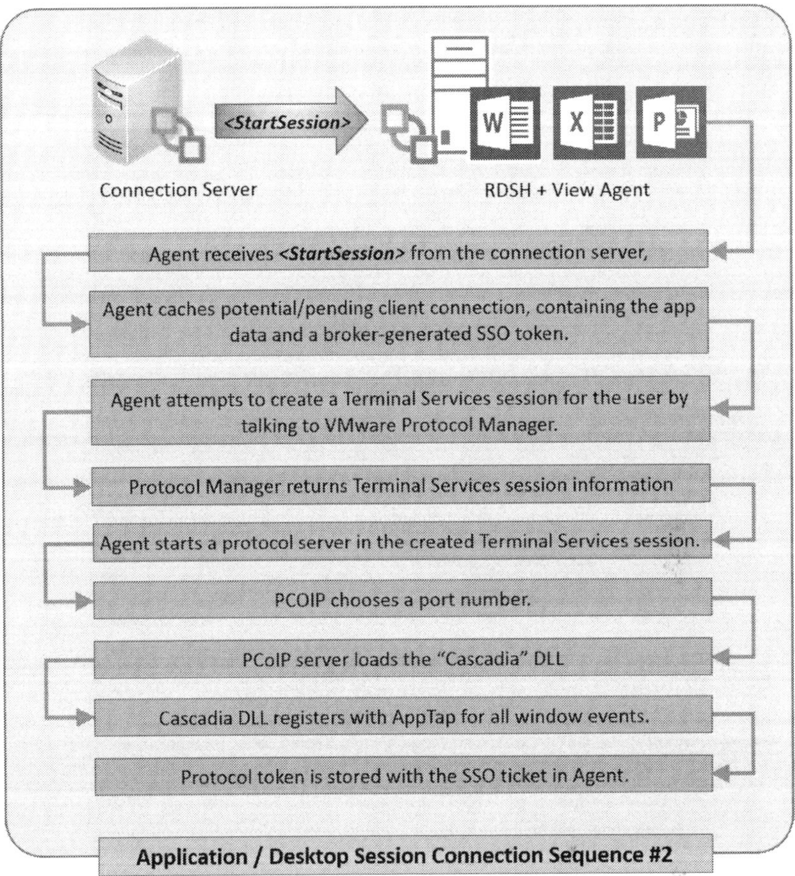

Application / Desktop Session Connection Sequence #2

The next step in the connection process is to set up the secure connection to the **PCoIP Secure Gateway (PSG)** server. A tunnel is set up by the View agent on the RDS server by talking to the PSG. The details of this connection are then forwarded via the Connection Server back to the client. This is pretty much the same way that this process works when connection to a virtual desktop machine is hosted on an ESXi host server.

The final part of the process is to log the end user in and connect them to the application they requested. The following screenshot illustrates the final steps in the process:

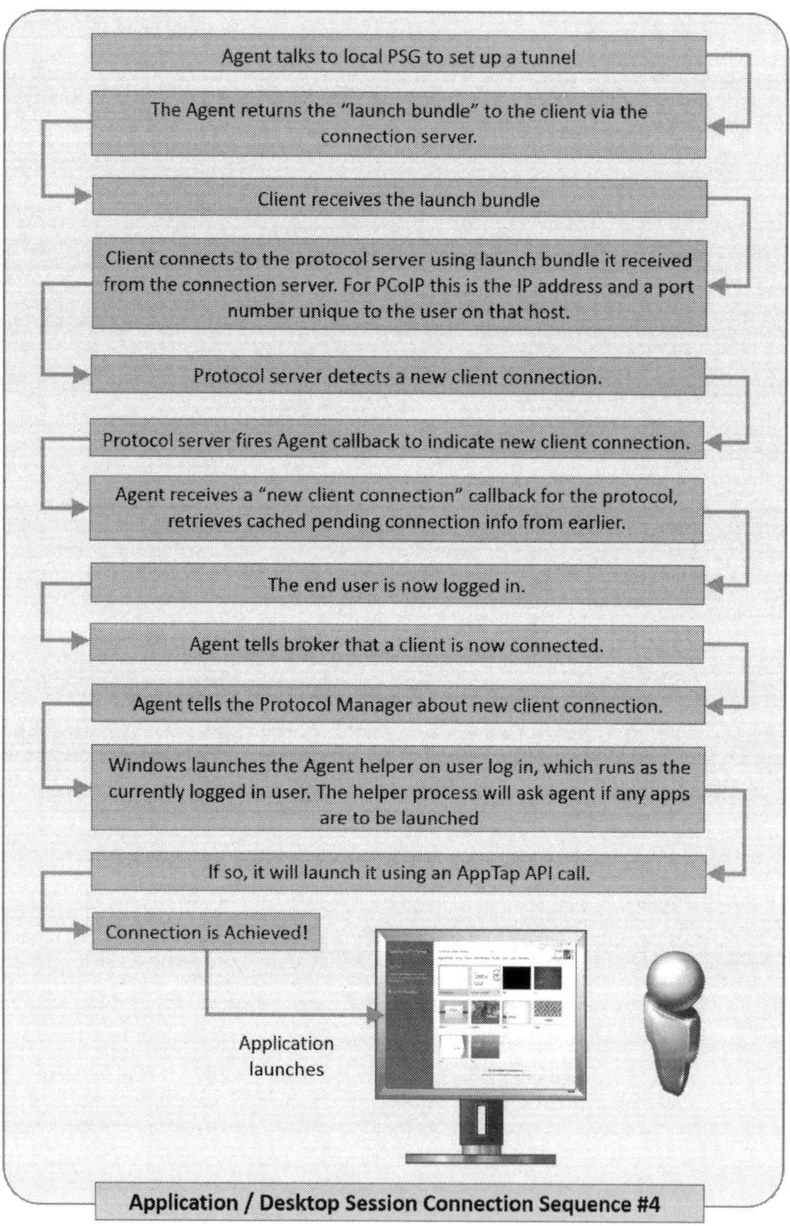

We have now covered how the process to connect the end user to their remote applications works. In the next section, we will look at some of the specifics for the RDS roles in this environment, starting with some sizing guidelines.

RDSH sizing guidelines

As with the sizing of View for virtual desktop machines, configuring the right specification for the RDSH servers is also key. We will look at different user types, similar to the way in which we considered desktop sizing. The VMware recommendation for the user workloads and the memory requirements is as follows:

User Workload Requirements	Memory	Use Case
Light User	512 MB	Basic application user such as Microsoft Office applications and some web browsing
Medium User	768 MB	Running multiple Microsoft Office applications and light user of multi-media, and more intensive web browsing
Heavy User	1 GB	Advanced application user running 3D-based applications and multi-media, and heavy web-browsing

For the total memory in each RDSH server, VMware recommends that a virtual machine configured as an RDSH server should be provisioned with a 64 GB memory. In terms of CPU requirements, the VMware recommendation is to create virtual servers for the RDSH roles and configure each role with four vCPUs. Make sure that you do not over commit the number of cores.

For example, if you have a virtual machine running as an RDSH server configured with 64 GB of memory, and have heavy users hosted on it, you can host a maximum of 64 sessions on that server.

For the hardware configuration, let's say you have a physical ESXi host server configured with a two-socket CPU, which had 12 cores, giving you a total of 24 cores. This would allow a maximum of six RDSH servers as we are going to provision virtual machines for the RDSH role that each of the 4 cores plays (24 cores/4 cores per server). This means that the physical server also needs to be configured with 384 GB of memory in total (64 GB x 6 RDSH host servers).

These figures are only guidelines and based on VMware-recommended best practice. It is always best to run an assessment on your environment to work out the optimum configuration.

Load balancing application publishing in View

The next thing we will cover is how the Connection Broker decides which of the RDSH host servers in the farm is going to deliver the application. There is no real complicated science behind the load balancing from a View perspective. It is purely based on how many sessions are available on any given RDSH server. So, when the user logs in and launches a remote application, the application is delivered from the server that has the maximum number of free sessions available, that is, the one which is the least busy. This is shown in the following screenshot:

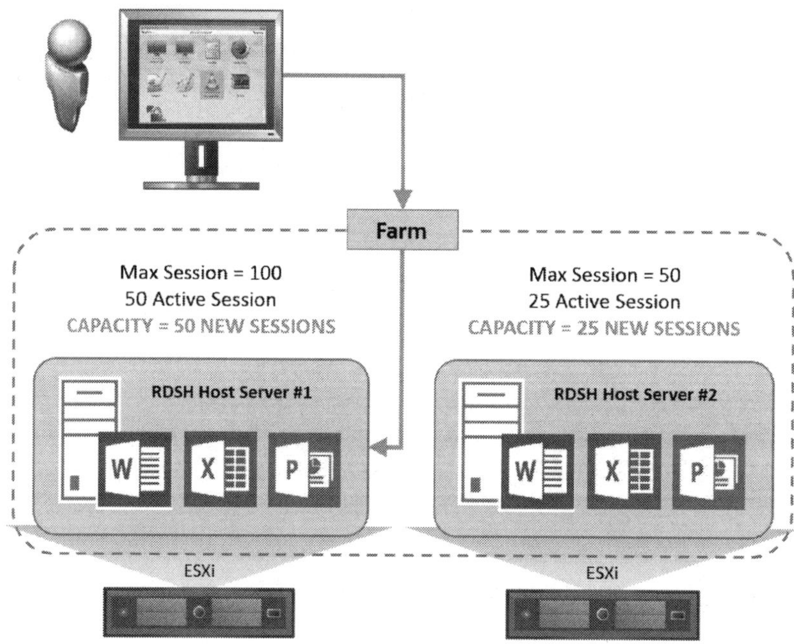

Now that we have covered how delivering published applications from Horizon View works, and also looked at the architecture and sizing, in the next section, we will start the installation and get our environment up and running.

Installing and configuring remote applications in View

We will now start the installation process. We start by configuring the servers that we will use to remote our applications and add the RDSH role to them. In our example lab, we already have two Windows Server 2012 servers built, namely EUC-RDSH-01 and EUC-RDSH-02, to perform this role.

The installation process is straightforward and can be summarized with the following screenshot:

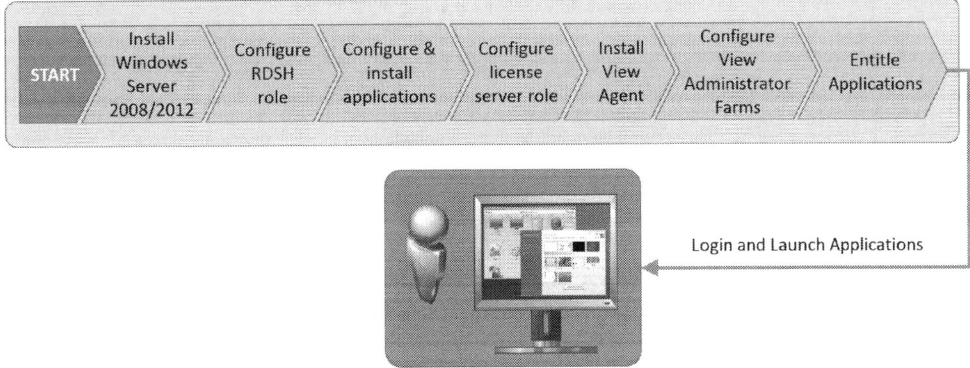

In the next section, we will walk through this process in more detail.

Configuring the RDS server role

The first thing that we will do is configure our first RDSH server and use this for our remote applications. The server we are going to configure is EUC-RDSH-02:

1. From the **Server Manager Dashboard** page, click on **Add roles and features** (**1**), as shown in the following screenshot:

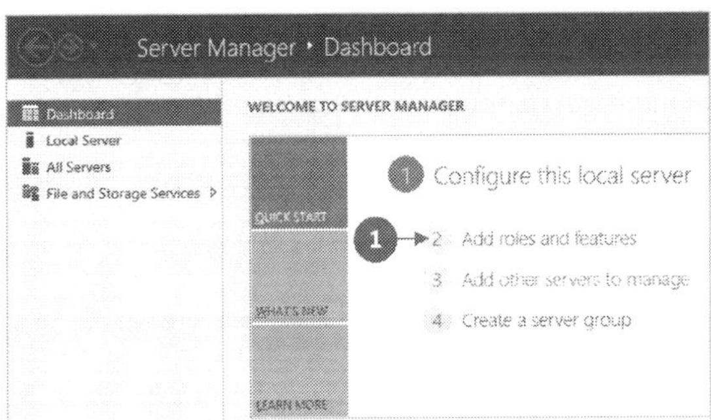

2. The **Add Roles and Features Wizard** page will now launch. Now click on the **Next >** button (**2**) to continue the configuration, as shown in the following screenshot:

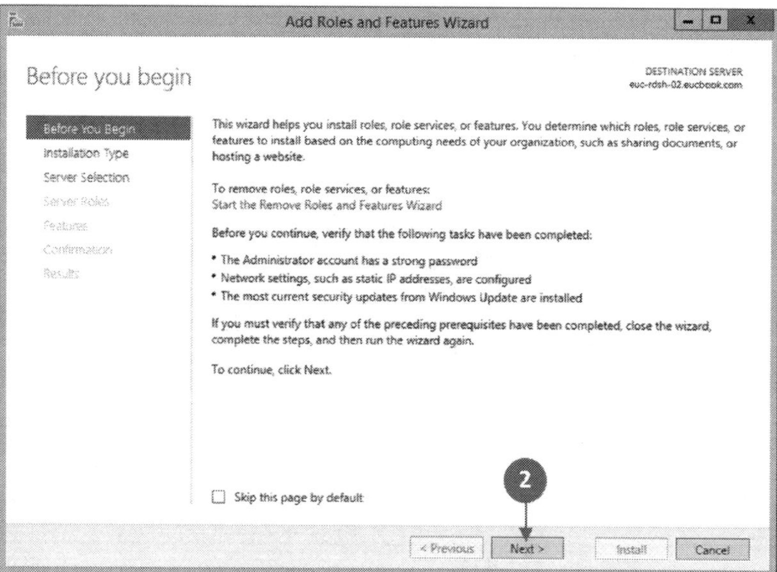

3. You will see the **Installation Type** page. Click on the radio button for **Remote Desktop Services installation** (**3**). Then, click on the **Next >** button (**4**) to continue, as shown in the following screenshot:

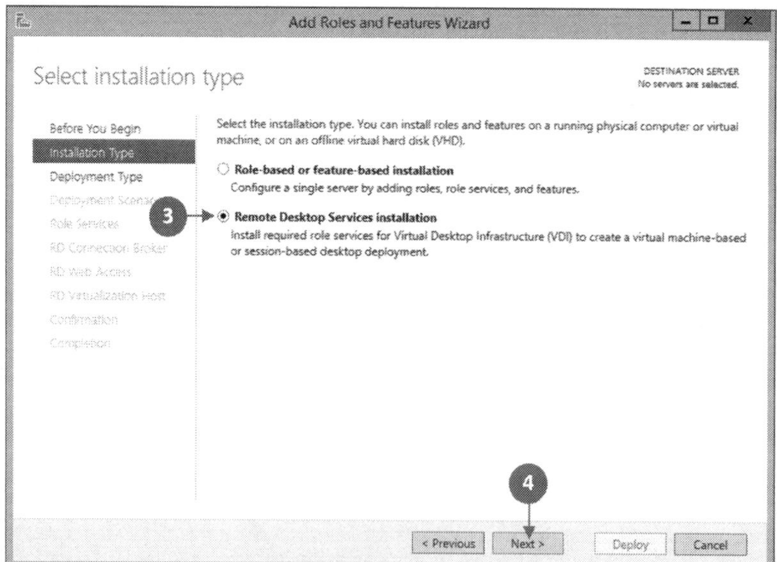

4. In the **Deployment Type** page, click on the radio button for **Quick Start** (**5**) and then click the **Next >** button (**6**):

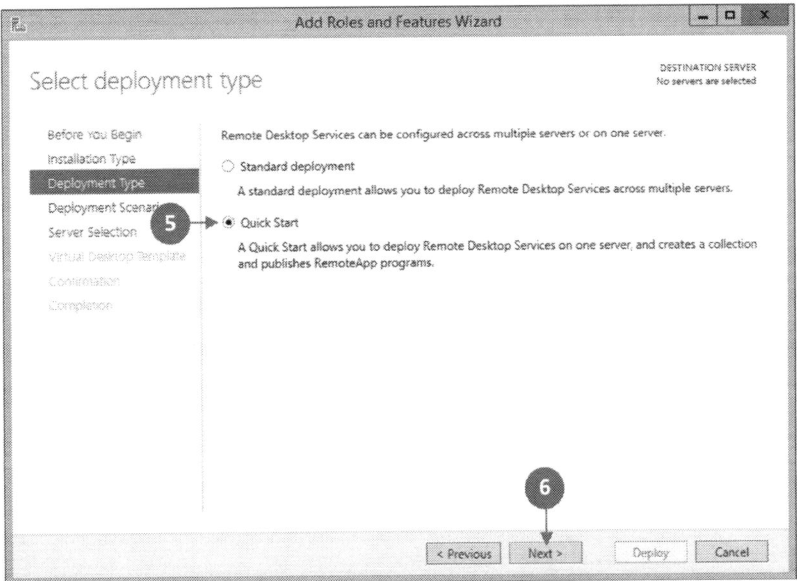

5. Click on the radio button for **Session-based desktop deployment** (**7**). Then, click on the **Next >** button (**8**) to continue to the configuration for **Server Selection**, as shown in the following screenshot:

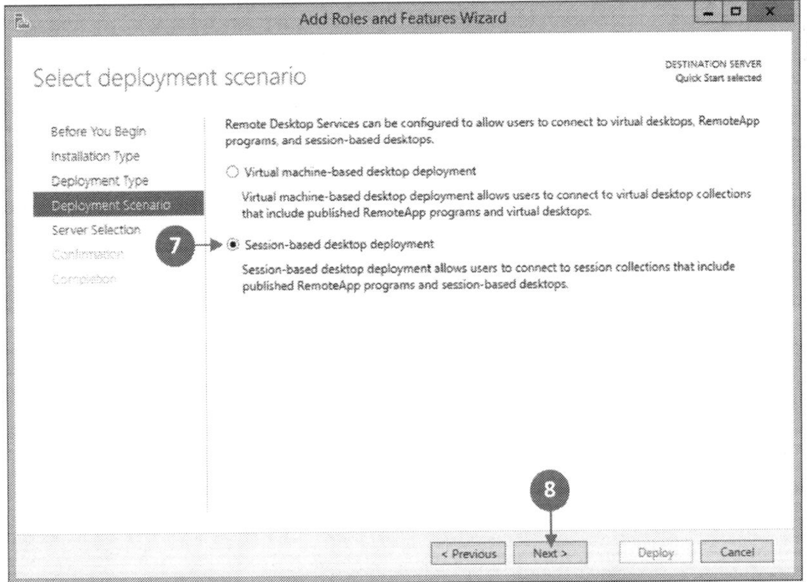

6. Click on the server you want to configure **(9)** and click on the arrow **(10)** to add the server to the **Selected** list. Click on the **Next >** button **(11)** to continue:

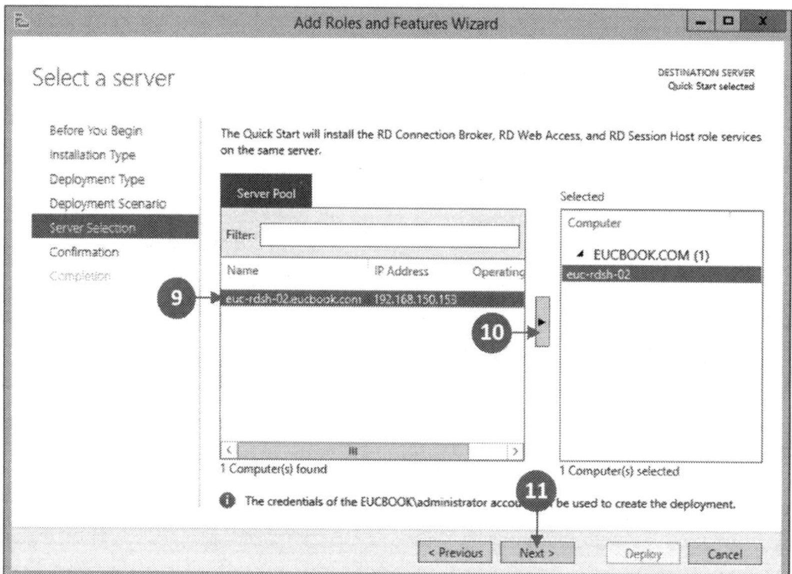

7. On the **Confirmation** screen, check that the correct roles are going to be installed. Then, make sure that the box for **Restart the destination server automatically if required** (12) is ticked. Now, click on the **Deploy** button **(13)**:

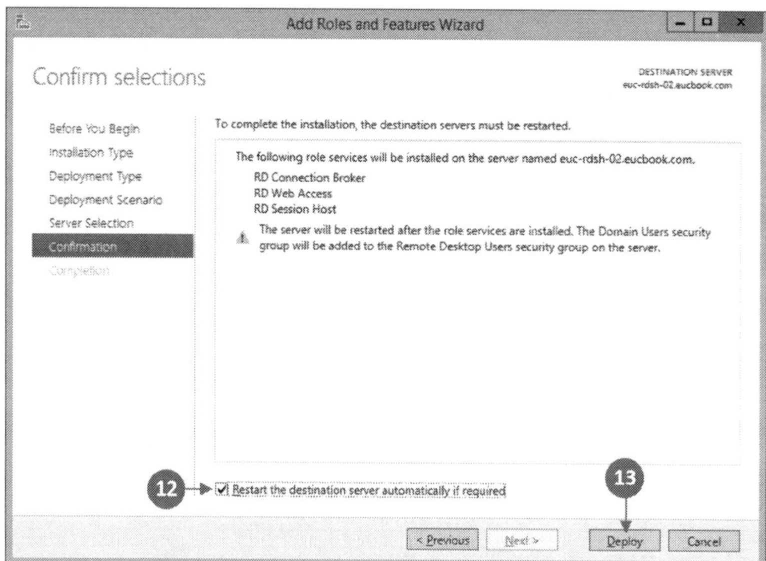

8. You will see the following screenshot. The server will reboot during the installation process and then continue until the installation is complete:

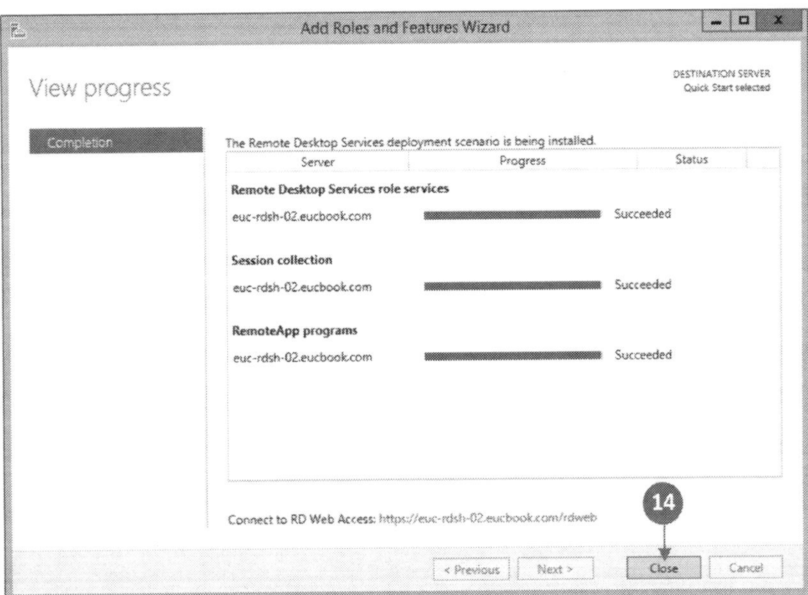

9. Click on **Close** (**14**) to complete the installation of the RDS server role. In the next section, we will configure the applications to be made remote.

Testing with the standard remote applications

The first applications that we will configure for the session-based remote access are those that are integrated into the Windows operating system and configured by default when you create the RDSH server role. This includes applications such as Calculator and Notepad.

We will test whether these applications work as remote applications, by first checking whether they have been configured, and then checking whether or not we can access them remotely, for that perform the following steps:

1. From the **Server Manager Dashboard** page, click on **Remote Desktop Services** (**1**), as shown in the following screenshot:

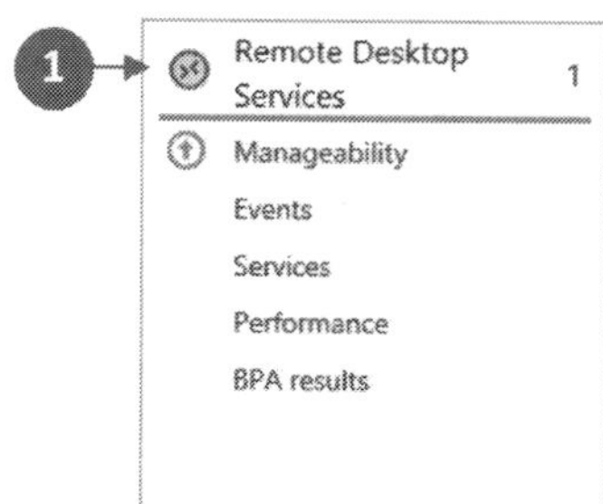

2. You will then see the list of servers that are configured with the RDSH role. In our example this is the **EUC-RDSH-02** server. Click on this server (**2**), and then click on **QuickSessionCollection...** (**3**), as shown in the following screenshot:

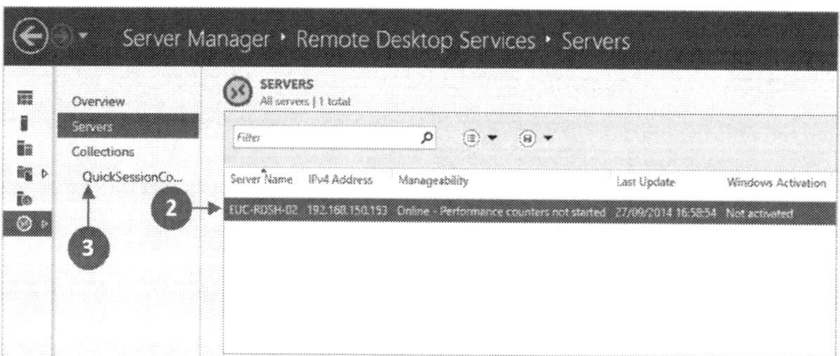

3. You will now see the **REMOTEAPP PROGRAMS** box as shown in the following screenshot, which should have **WordPad**, **Paint**, and **Calculator** as listed applications:

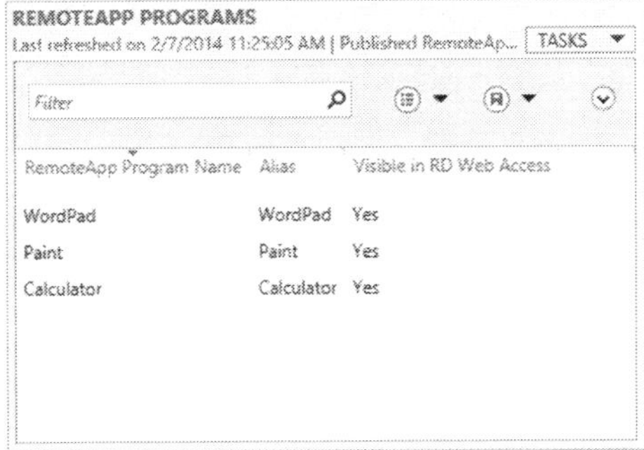

So, now that we have the standard applications available for remote sessions, we will try connecting using the RD Web Access web portal.

4. To do this, open a browser either from your desktop or from the server itself. It's best to test from a remote desktop rather than the server. In the browser, got to the URL for the RDSH server. In our example lab, this address is: `https://euc-rdsh-01.eucbook.com/rdweb`. The following login page is displayed:

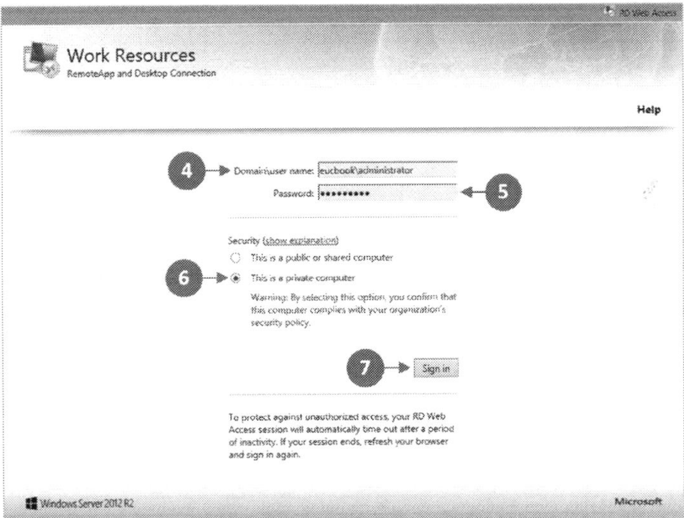

5. Enter the username in the requested format of **Domain\username (4)**, and then enter the password **(5)**. Click on the **This is a private computer** radio button **(6)** and then click on **Sign in** (7), as shown in the previous screenshot.

6. You will now see the following web page, which displays the available applications:

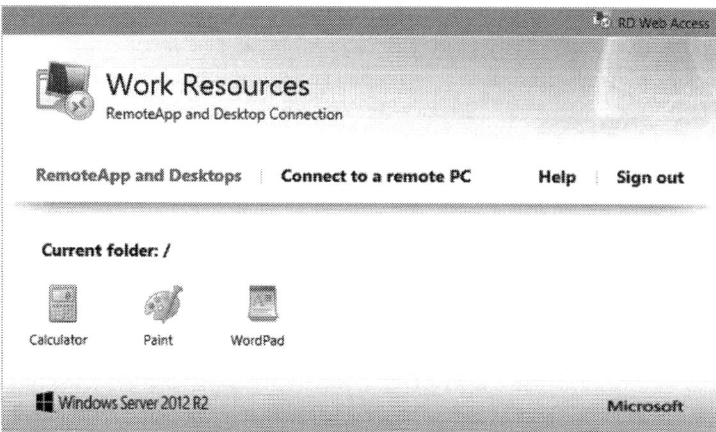

7. You will also see that you are connected to the RemoteApp work resources:

In the next section, we will add some additional applications, namely Microsoft Office applications.

Installing additional applications

Installing applications is almost identical to installing applications on any other Windows operating system. However, there are a few subtle differences, given that this is a remote session host server. Let's run through the process quickly:

1. From the RDSH server on which you want to install the applications, open **Control Panel**, as shown in the following screenshot. Click on **Programs** (**1**):

2. In the **Programs** box, click on **Install Application on Remote Desktop...** (**2**):

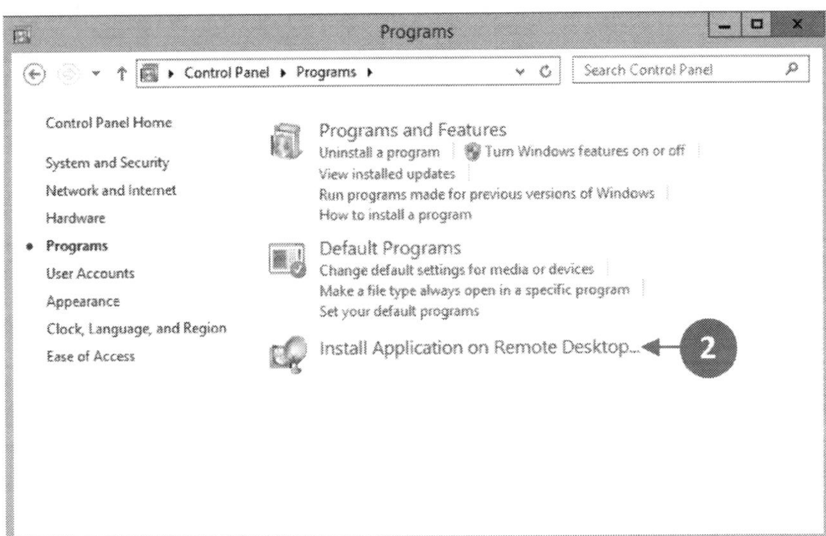

3. The **Install Program From Floppy Disk or CD-ROM** dialog box appears, as shown in the following screenshot:

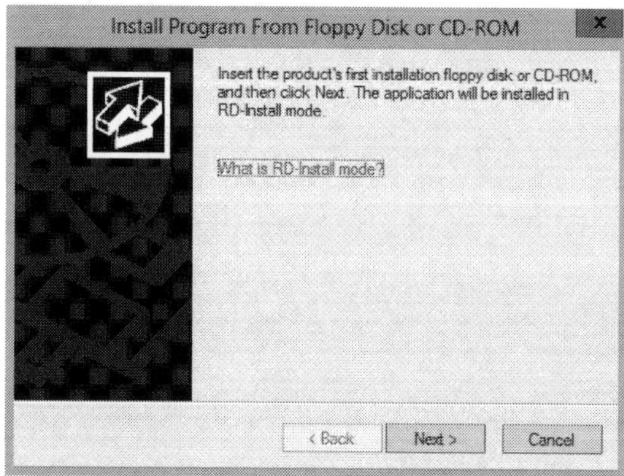

4. The dialog box mentions **What is RD-Install mode?**

   To install an application on an RDSH host server, it needs to be switched into a special install mode known as RD-Install to make sure that the applications are able to run in a multiuser environment. Once you have installed the applications on the RDSH server, the server needs to be switched back into, what is called, execution mode or RD-Execute, so that users can remotely connect to the server and the applications running on it. This can also be done on the command line using the following commands:

   ```
   change user /install
   change user /execute
   ```

   You can check the current install mode of your RDSH server using the following command:

   ```
   change user /query
   ```

   The easiest was to install applications is by installing them from the Programs option in Control Panel, which is how we are going to do it in this example. This option takes you through the installation process by automatically switching the server to RD-Install mode, installing the program, and switching the server back to the RD-Execute mode once the installation is complete.

5. Now, click on **Next >** to start the installation. The server automatically checks for the installation media and installation files, first on the `A` drive and then the `E` drive. If it doesn't locate any media, then the **Run Installation Program** dialog box is displayed, as shown in the following screenshot:

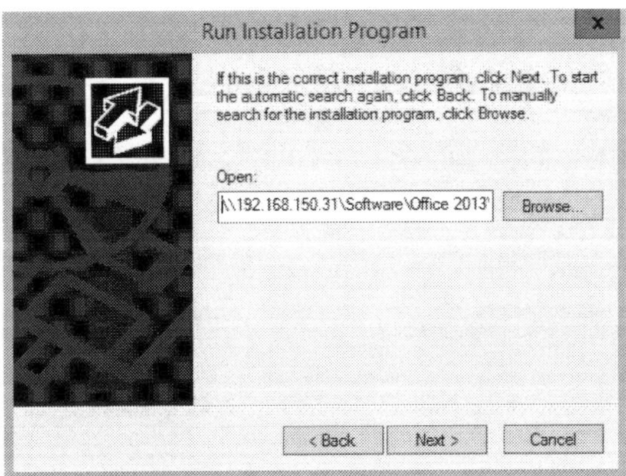

6. Type the location of the installation media in the **Open:** box or click on the **Browse...** button to open a **Windows Explorer** dialog box, where you can navigate to the software, as shown in the following screenshot. In our example, we will install MS Office:

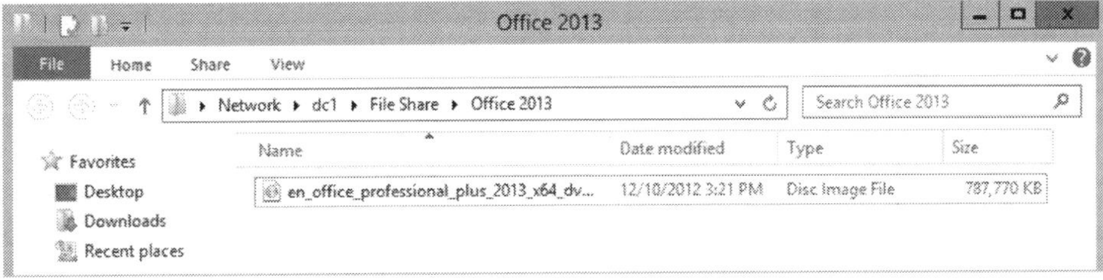

7. Double-click on the installer file to launch it. As the installer launches, you will see the **Finish Admin Install** dialog box, as shown in the following screenshot:

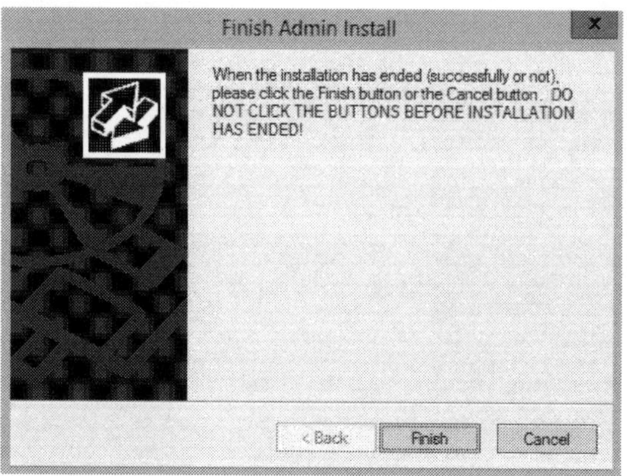

Ignore this dialog box for now. Make sure that you *do not* click on **Finish** at this point. We will come back to this after the application has installed.

8. Now, we will install Microsoft Office. Double-click on **setup** and then click on the **Install Now** button. This is exactly how you would install Microsoft Office on any other machine:

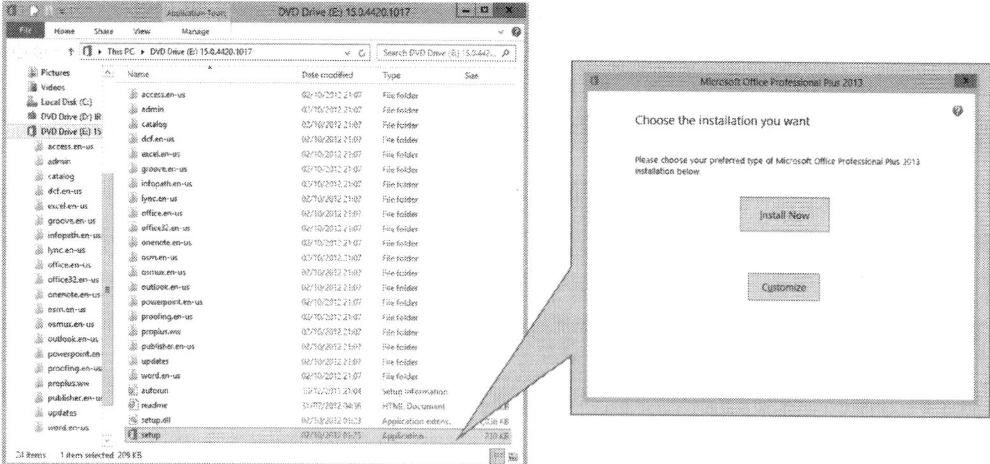

9. Once Microsoft Office has been installed, we can return to the **Finish Admin Install** dialog box, as shown in the following screenshot:

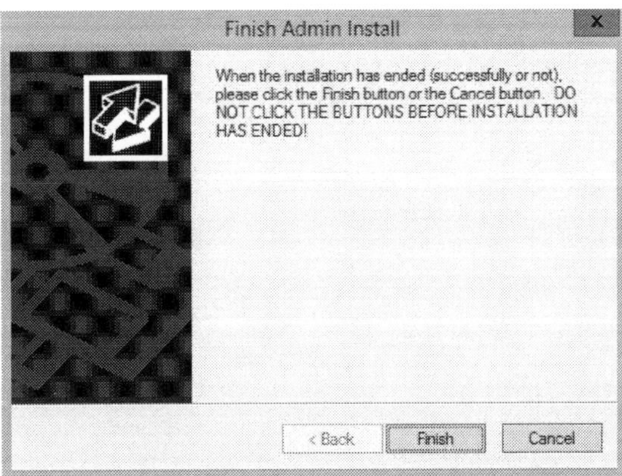

10. You can now click on **Finish**.

So, now that we have installed Microsoft Office on the RDSH server, we need to go back and configure which of the Office applications will be available to the users as remote applications:

1. The first step is to launch the RDS configuration from the **Server Manager** console. Click on **Remote Desktop Services**, highlight the RDSH server you want to configure and then click on **QuickSessionCollection** (**3**), as shown in the following screenshot:

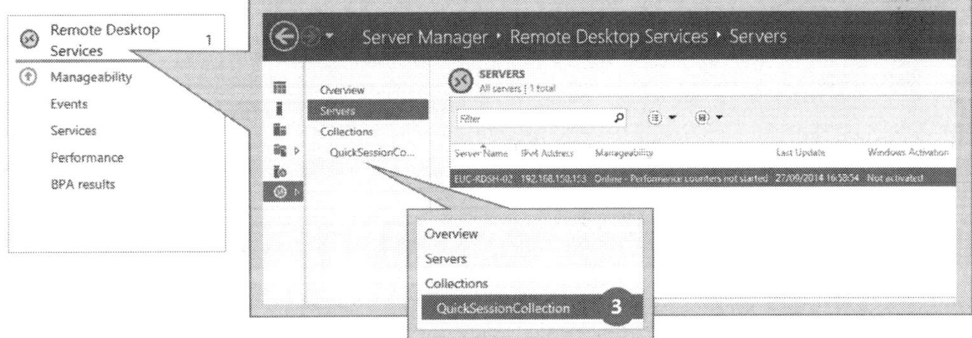

2. You will now see the **REMOTEAPP PROGRAMS** dialog box. Click on the down arrow on the **TASKS** button at the top-right corner (**4**), and then click on **Publish RemoteApp Programs** (**5**), as shown in the following screenshot:

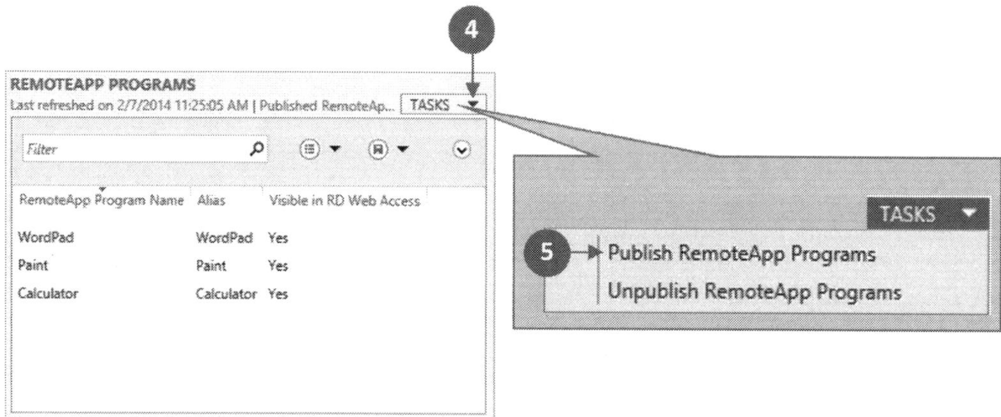

3. You will now see the **Publish RemoteApp Programs** dialog box, where we can select which application we want to make available remotely to the users.
4. Check the boxes next to the applications you want to add (**6**). In our example, we will check the boxes for the following applications:
   - **Excel 2013**
   - **OneNote 2013**
   - **Outlook 2013**
   - **PowerPoint 2013**
   - **Publisher 2013**
   - **Word 2013**

Once you have selected all the applications you want, click on **Add...** (7), as shown in the following screenshot:

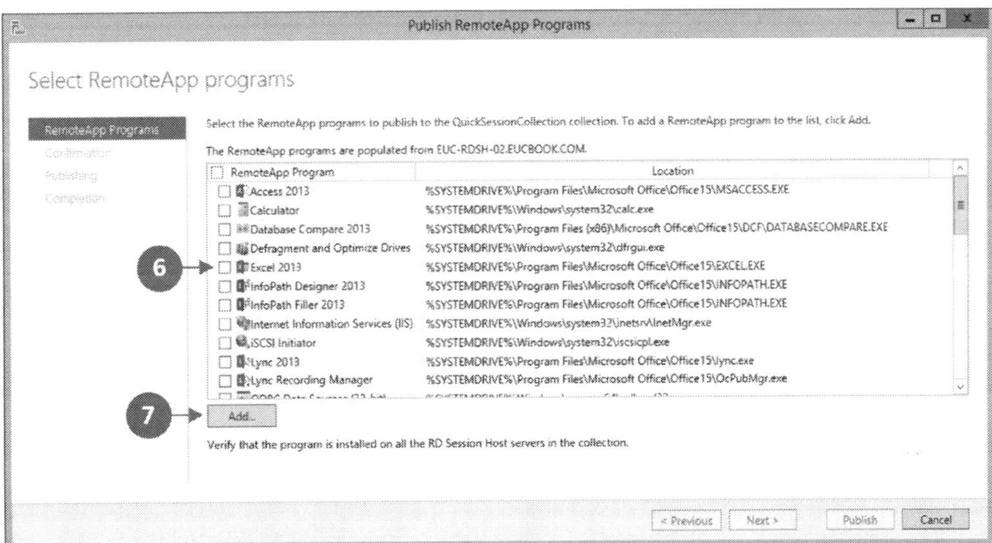

5. You will now see the confirmation box for the applications you selected. Click on **Publish** (8):

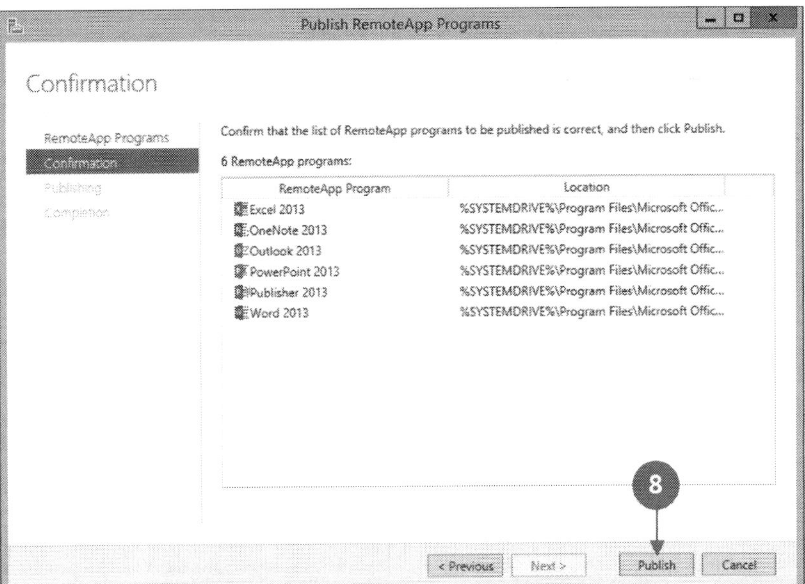

6. You will then see a progress bar detailing that the applications are now being published. Once completed you will see the following screenshot telling you that the applications were successfully published, here click on **Close** (**9**) to complete the publishing process:

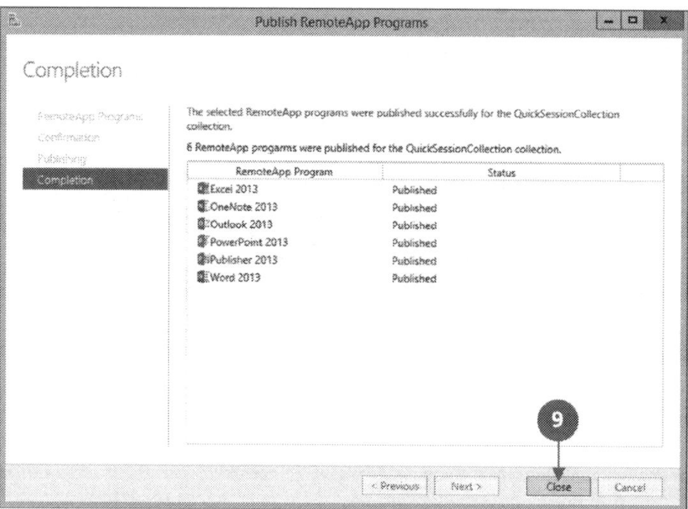

7. As we did previously, we will test whether the applications are available from the web access portal. Open a browser and go to: `https://euc-rdsh-01.eucbook.com/rdweb`. You will see the following screenshot from the RD Web Access portal, showing the newly published application:

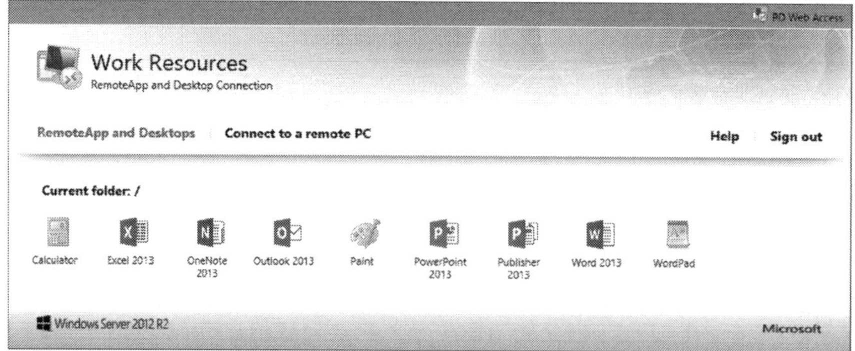

8. Click on **Sign out** to exit.

In the next section, we will configure the final role, the licensing role.

Configuring the licensing role

The next role we need to configure is the remote desktop licensing role. Unlike a Microsoft RemoteApp deployment, Horizon View only requires this licensing role and the RDSH role, which is very much simplified from that of the Microsoft deployment. For the configuration perform the following steps:

1. From the **Server Manager Dashboard** page, click on **Add roles and features** (**1**), as shown in the following screenshot:

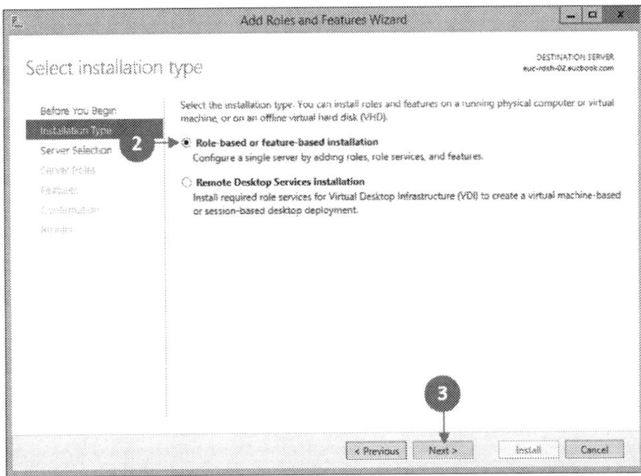

2. The **Add Roles and Features Wizard** page will now launch, as shown in the following screenshot. Click on the radio button for **Role-based or feature-based installation** (2), and then click on the **Next >** button (**3**):

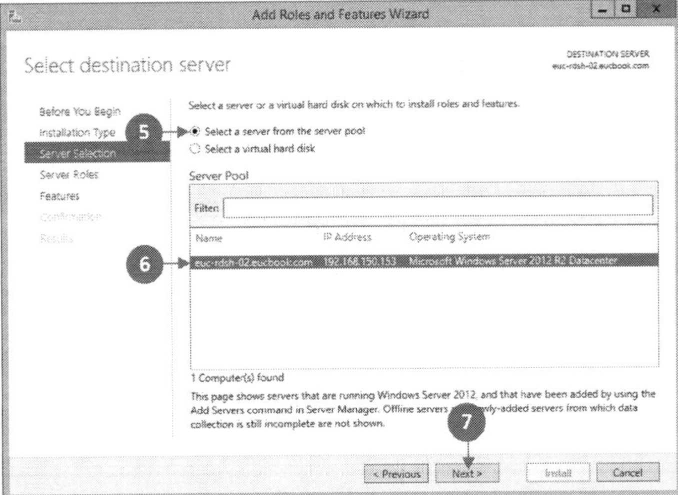

3. In the **Server Selection** screen click on the radio button for **Select a server from the server pool** (5) and then select the server you want to use. In our example, we will choose the **euc-rdsh-02 server** (6):

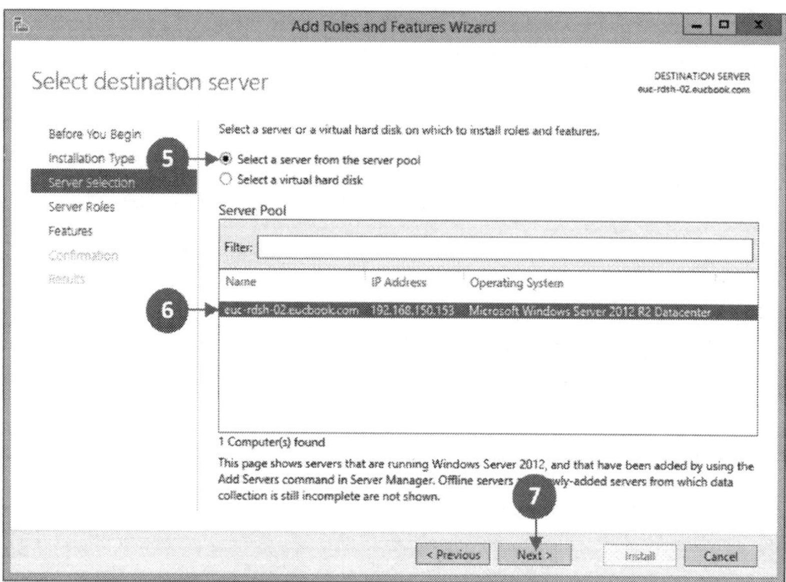

4. Click on the **Next >** button (7) to continue to the **Server Roles** screen. Expand the **Remote Desktop Services (3 of 6 installed)** option (8) and then tick the box for **Remote Desktop Licensing** (9):

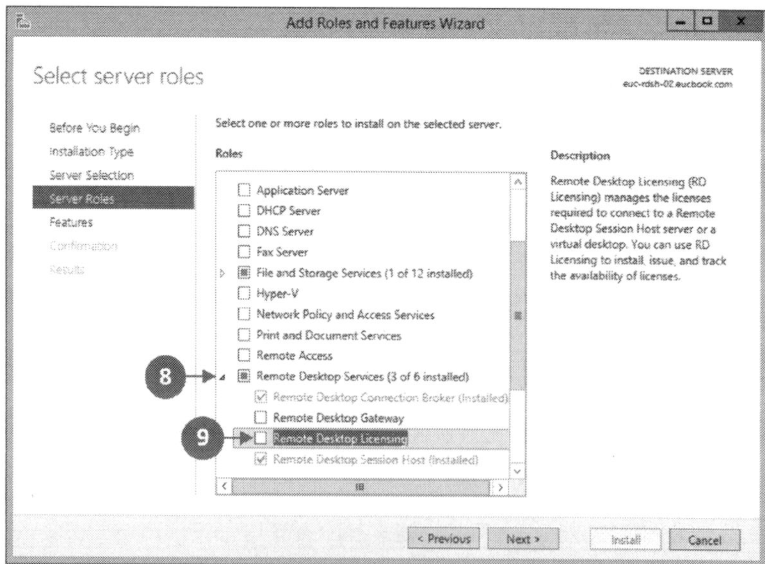

5. You will then see the following dialog box. Click on **Add Features** (**10**):

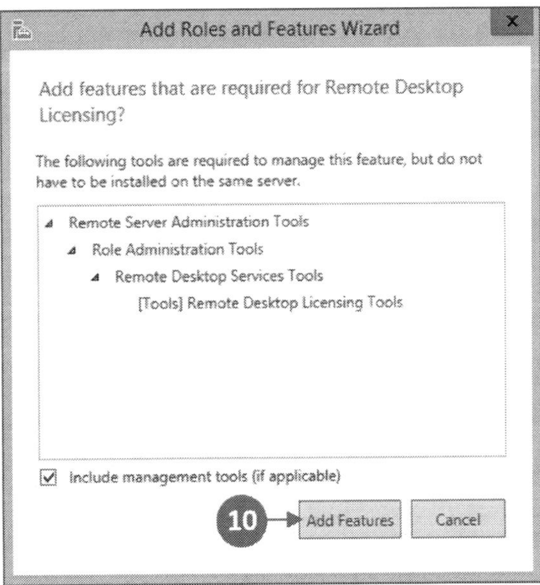

6. On the **Features** screen, click on **Next >** to continue to the **Confirmation** screen:

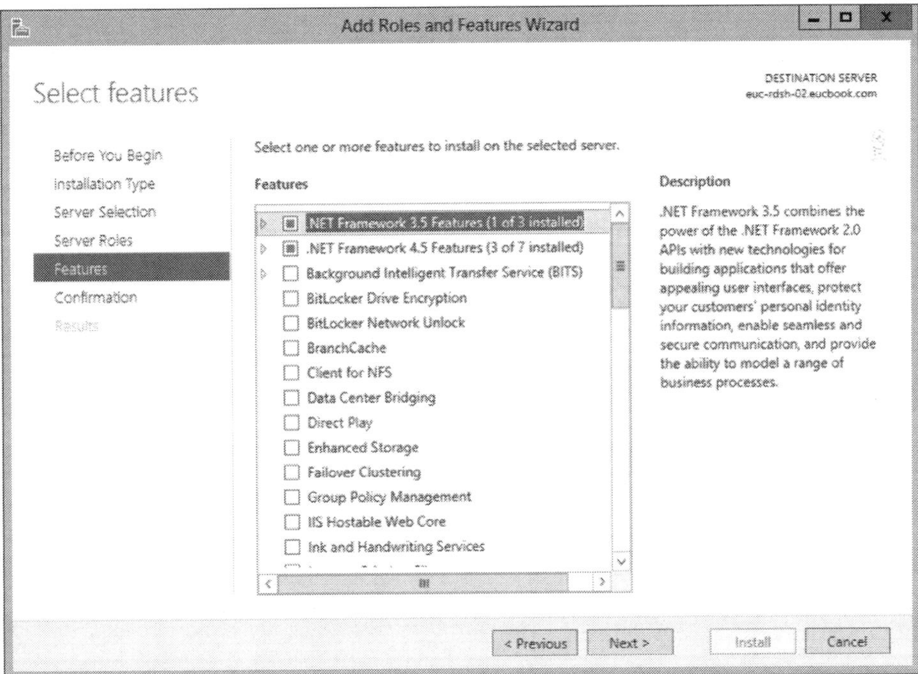

7. On the **Confirmation** screen, ensure that the box is ticked for **Restart the destination server automatically if required (11)**, as shown in the following screenshot:

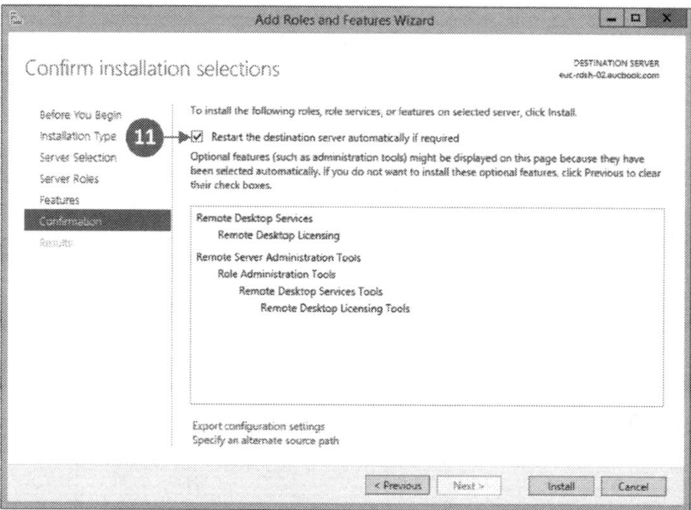

8. Click on the **Install** button to install the features. The features will now be installed, as shown in the following screenshot:

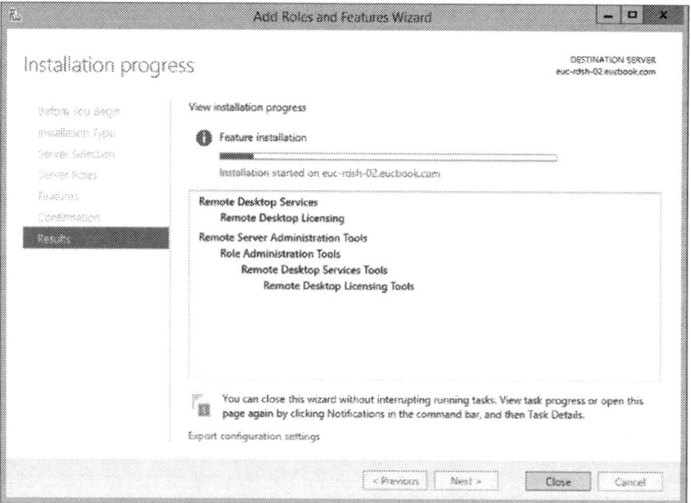

9. Once the features have been installed, click on the **Close** button.

The next stage of the installation process is to activate the licensing server.

Activating the licensing role

Now that we have the license server role added, the next step is to activate it:

1. On the **Server Manager** page, click on **Remote Desktop Services**.
2. Highlight the RDSH server **EUC-RDSH-02** and right-click. From the menu, click on **RD Licensing Manager** (**2**):

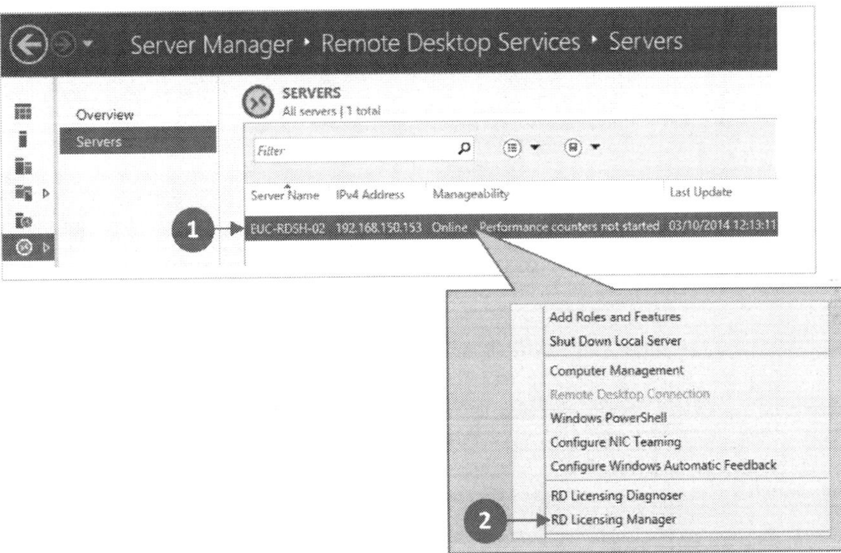

3. You will then see the **RD Licensing Manager** dialog box, as shown in the following screenshot. Click on the **EUC-RDSH-02** server (**3**) to highlight it. Right-click and select **Activate Server** (**4**) from the menu options :

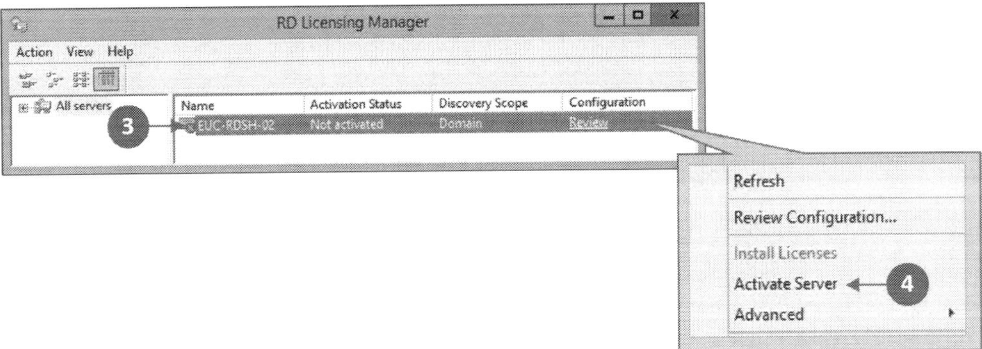

4. The **Activate Server Wizard** page will now launch, as shown in the following screenshot:

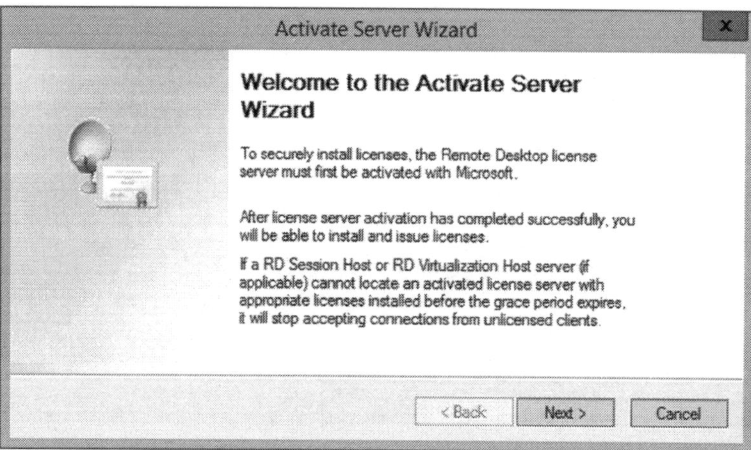

5. Click on **Next >** to continue.
6. You will now see the **Connection Method** dialog box, as shown in the following screenshot. Ensure that you have selected **Automatic connection (recommended)** from the **Connection method** drop-down box. Click on **Next >** to continue:

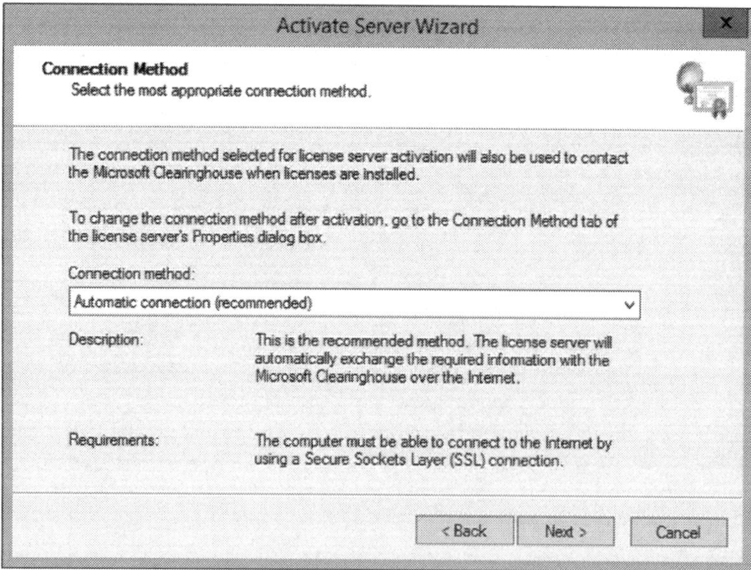

7. You will now see the **Company Information** dialog box, where you can enter your company's details. This is shown in the following screenshot. Click on **Next >** to continue:

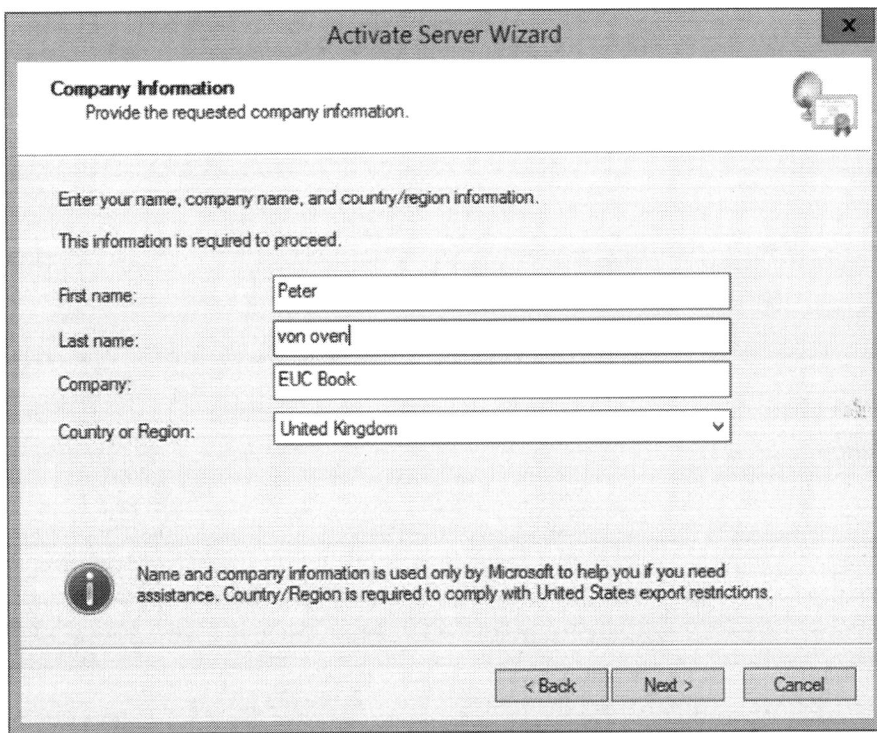

8. You will now see a second **Company Information** dialog box. The information for this page is optional, so we can leave it blank. Click on **Next >** to continue.

9. Finally, you will see the **Completing the Activate Server Wizard** screen. Ensure the box is ticked for **Start Install Licenses Wizard now** so that we can install RDS licenses.

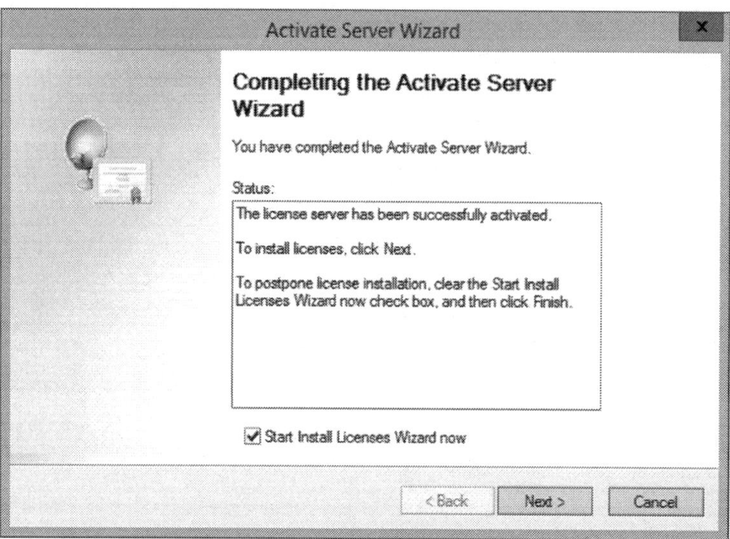

10. Click on **Next >** to continue. The **Install Licenses Wizard** page will now launch, as shown in the following screenshot:

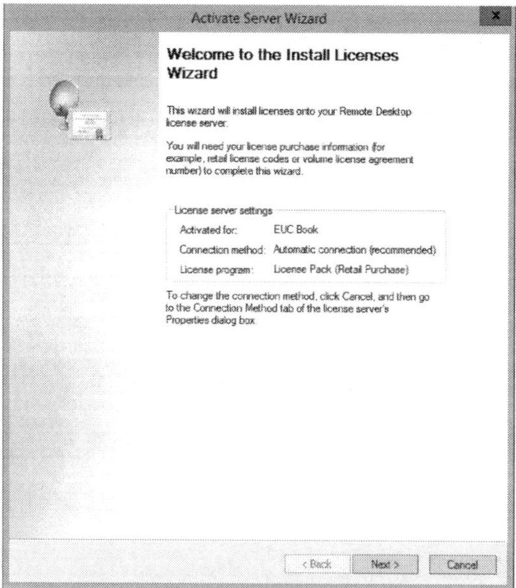

11. Click on **Next >** to continue. You will now see the **License Program** dialog box, where you can choose the licensing model that is appropriate for your environment. Click on **Next >** to continue.
12. In the next dialog box, enter your agreement number and click on **Next >** to continue.
13. You will now see the **Product Version and License Type** dialog box from where you can choose the product type and license type, as shown in the following screenshot:

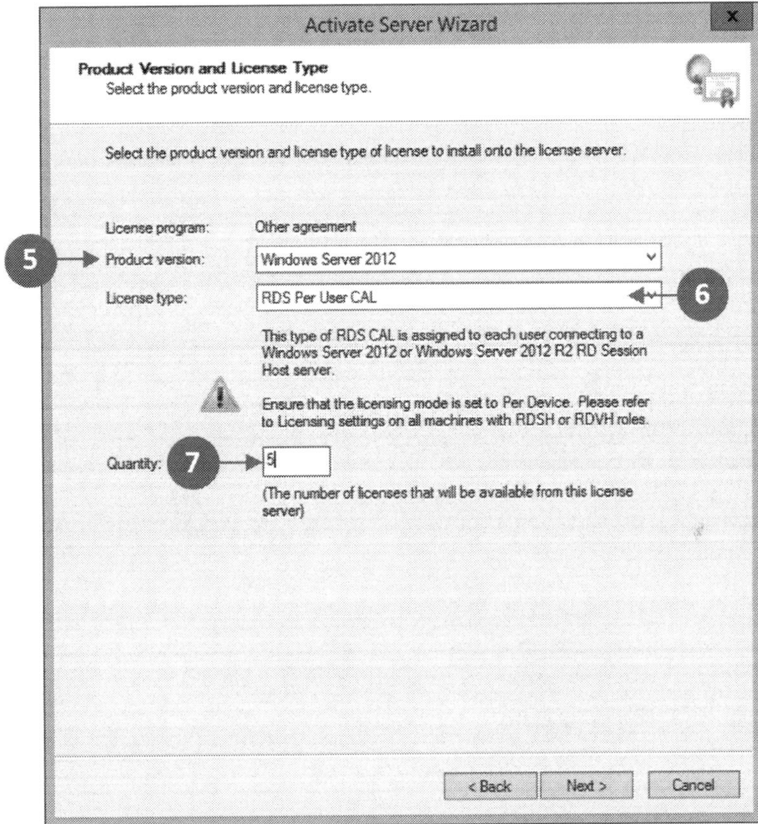

14. Click on **Next >** to continue.

The licenses are now installed on the server and ready to be used.

Installing the Horizon View Agent

In this section, we will install the Horizon View Agent on the RDSH server. The agent is exactly the same agent as the one we would install on the virtual desktop machines.

Browse to the shared software folder and navigate to the agent installation application (**1**), as shown in the following screenshot. The file we are looking for is `VMware-viewagent-x86_64-6.1.0-2509441`. The seven-digit number at the end of the filename refers to the build version, and so, you might have a different number, depending on the build version you are using.

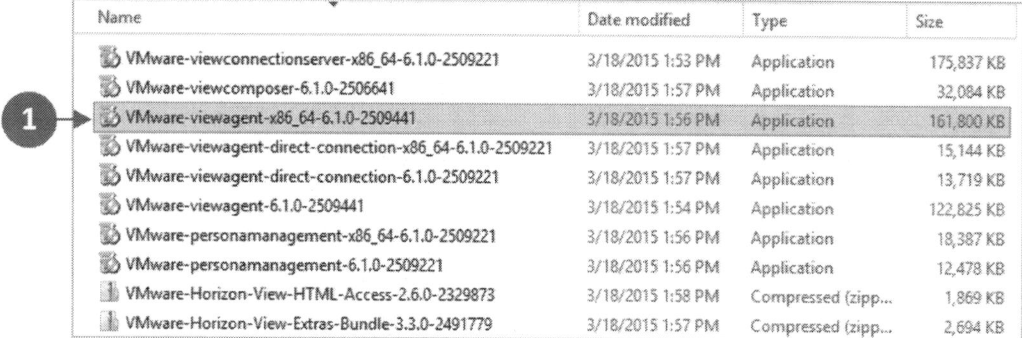

We now begin with the process:

1. Double-click on the file to launch the installation. Click on **Next >** to start the installation:

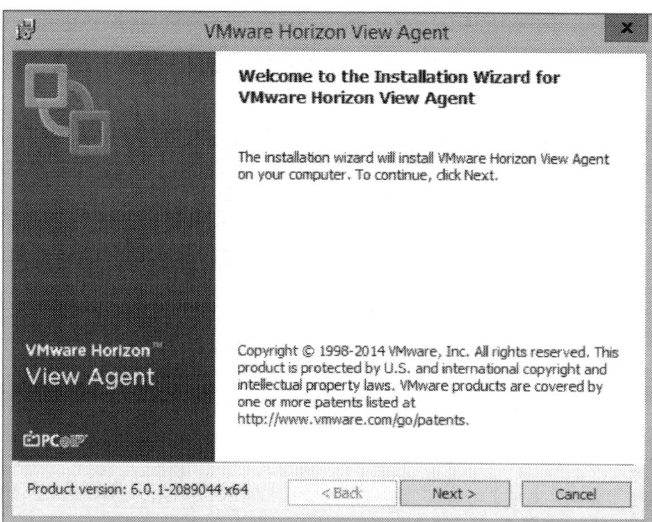

2. Click on the radio button (**2**) to accept the EULA:

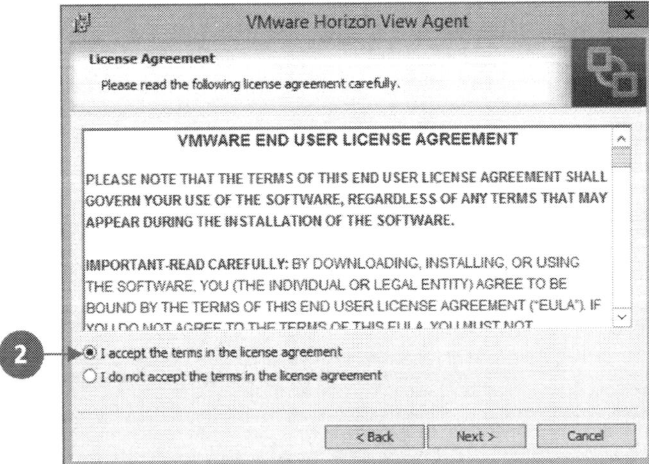

3. On the **Custom Setup** configuration screen, you can select which options to install:

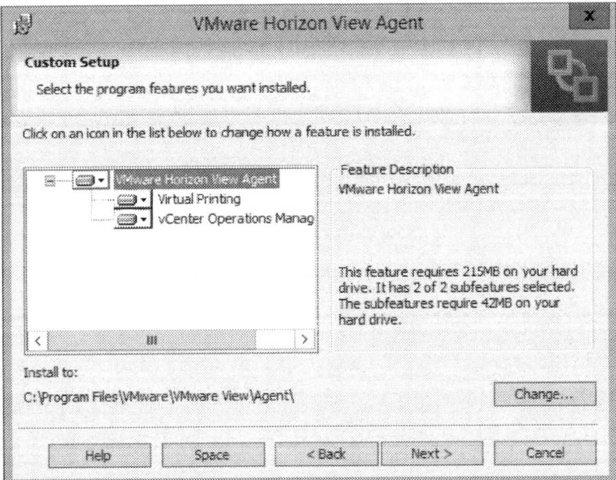

4. You can choose to install the virtual printing elements and the agent for vCenter Operations Manager. We will accept the defaults. There are also a number of features that get installed by default. These are as follows:
    - **PCoIP Agent**: This allows end users to connect to published applications and session-based desktops using PCoIP as the display protocol

- **Unity Touch**: This provides flexibility for users to use their Windows applications, which are running on a remote desktop, on their tablets and smart phones
- **PSG Agent**: This installs the PSG on the RDSH server to allow the desktop and application sessions running on the RDSH server to be delivered to the end user
- **VMwareRDS**: This is the VMware implementation of RDS

Click on **Next >** to continue.

5. In the **Register with Horizon View Connection Server** configuration screen, we will configure the agent to talk to our Connection Server. This allows the Connection Server to read the published applications from the RemoteApp catalog and allow you to create pools within View:

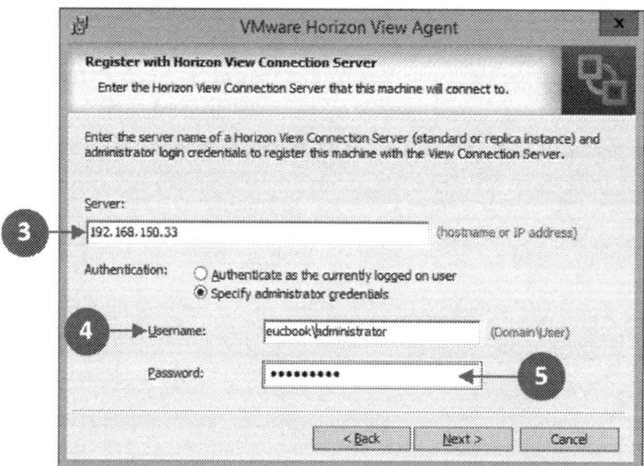

6. In the **Server** box (**3**), enter the name of the Connection Server. In our example, we will use a Connection Server called `euc-vcs01`. In the **Authentication** section, click on the radio button for **Specify administrator credentials**. Then, in the **Username** box (**4**), enter the name of the user account you want to use to connect to the Connection Server, followed by the password in the **Password** box (**5**).

Make sure you use the domain\user format to enter the username. Also make sure that the account has the correct privileges to access the Connection Server.

7. Click on **Next >** to continue.

8. On the **Ready to Install the Program** screen, click on **Install** to start the process.
9. Once successfully installed, you will see the **Installer Complete** screen. Click on **Finish** to quit the installation.

One of the most common reasons the installation of the agent fails is due to the configuration of the RDSH server. More often than not, there are no sound drivers loaded on the Windows Server running the RDSH role. If this is the case, then the installation of the agent will fail and automatically roll back. If that happens, it's worth checking this first.

You will need to reboot the server once the installation is completed. We have now completed the first part of the Horizon View configuration. In the next step of the process, we will turn our attention to the View Administrator and configure our application pools.

Configuring app publishing in the View Administrator

The next stage in the installation and configuration process is performed in the View Administrator console. Like the standard View setup, it involves creating pools and entitlements. However, rather than creating pools for virtual desktop machines, this time, we will configure application pools. First, we will set up a farm that contains our newly built RDSH server.

Creating a published application farm

So, the first step of the configuration process in the View Administrator is to create an application pool, as described in the following steps:

1. Open a browser and connect to the View Administrator. In our example lab, the address for the View Administrator is `https://euc-vcs01.eucbook.com/admin/`.

2. Log in to the **View Administrator** using the administrator account and password, as shown in the following screenshot:

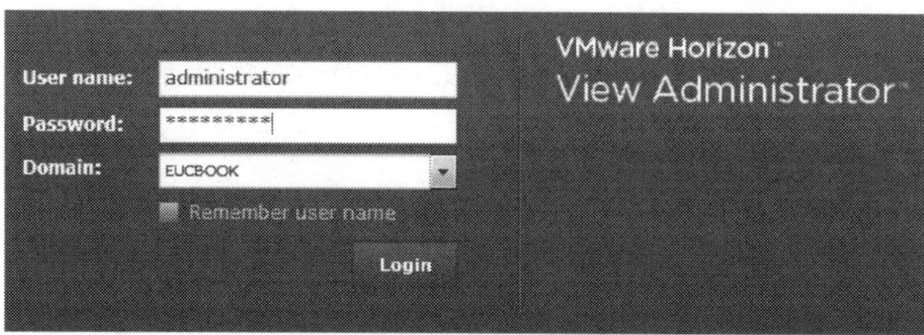

3. From the **Dashboard** screen, navigate to **Resources** | **Farms (1)** | **Add... (2)**, as shown in the following screenshot:

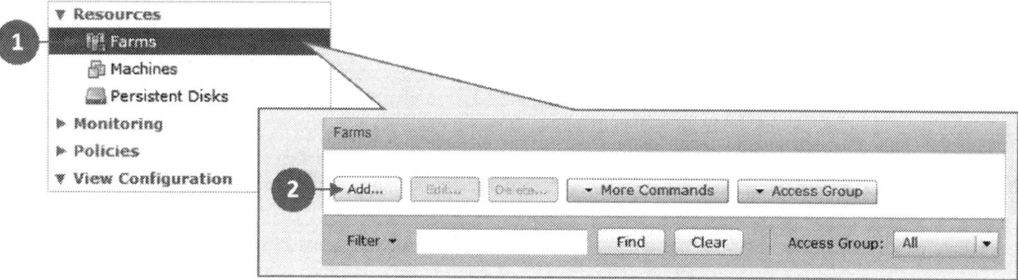

4. You will see the **Add Farm** configuration screen, as shown in the following screenshot:

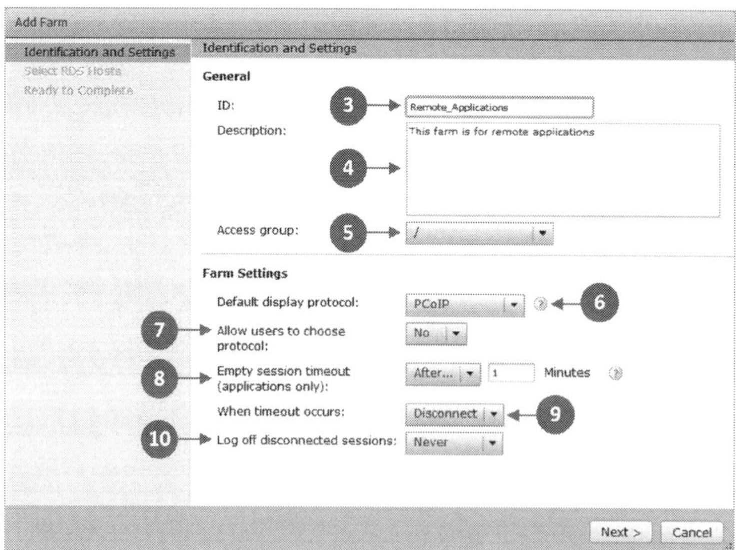

5. In the **ID** box (3), enter an ID for the farm that will be used by View to identify it.

> You cannot use spaces for the ID. Only letters (upper and lower case), numbers (0-9), and the - (minus) and _ (underscore) characters are allowed.

6. In the **Description** box (**4**), enter an optional description for the farm. Then, from the **Access Group** drop-down (**5**), select an access group if you have one.
7. Next, under **Farm Settings**, set **Default display protocol:** to **PCoIP** (**6**). From **the Allow users to choose protocol:** drop-down (**7**), select **No**.
8. The **Empty session timeout (applications only):** (**8**) is not applicable to desktop sessions, so you can ignore this setting.
9. Finally, select the setting for the **When timeout occurs:** (9) and **Log off disconnected sessions:** (**10**) options.
10. Once you have completed the options on this screen, click on **Next >** to continue.
11. On the next configuration screen, we will select the RDSH server that we want to add to this farm. Click on **euc-rdsh-01.eucbook.com** (**11**), as shown in the following screenshot:

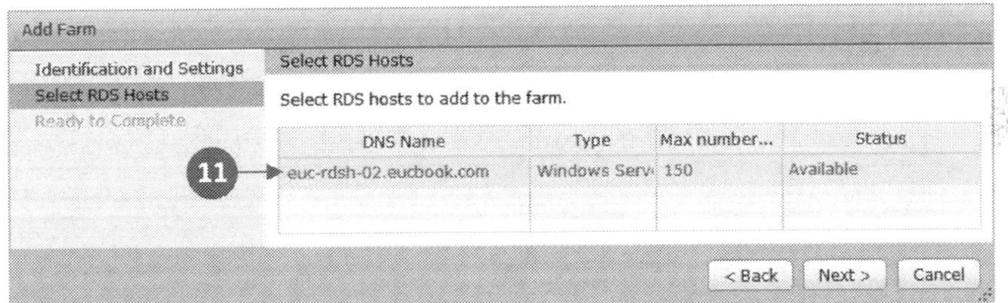

12. Click on **Next >** to continue. You will now see the **Ready to Complete** screen, as shown in the following screenshot:

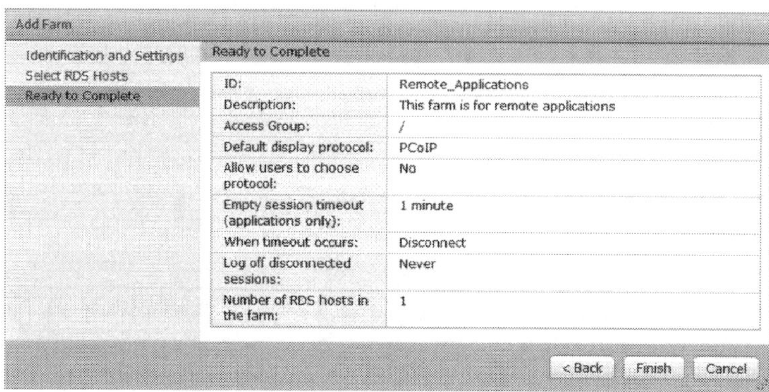

13. Check that the settings you have entered are correct and click on **Finish**.

We have now successfully created the farm configuration for our published applications. In the next section, we will create an application pool.

Creating a published application pool

In this section, we will create an application pool. This basically allows us to create a pool that contains a number of different applications. For example, you might want to create application pools to reflect different departments, for that perform the following steps:

1. In the **View Administrator** section navigate to **Inventory | Catalog | Application Pools (1)**. From the **Application Pools** menu, click on **Add... (2)**, as shown in the following screenshot:

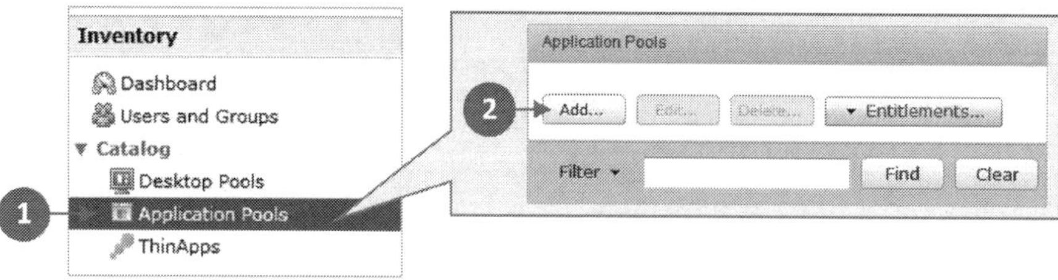

2. You will now see the **Add Application Pools** configuration screen:

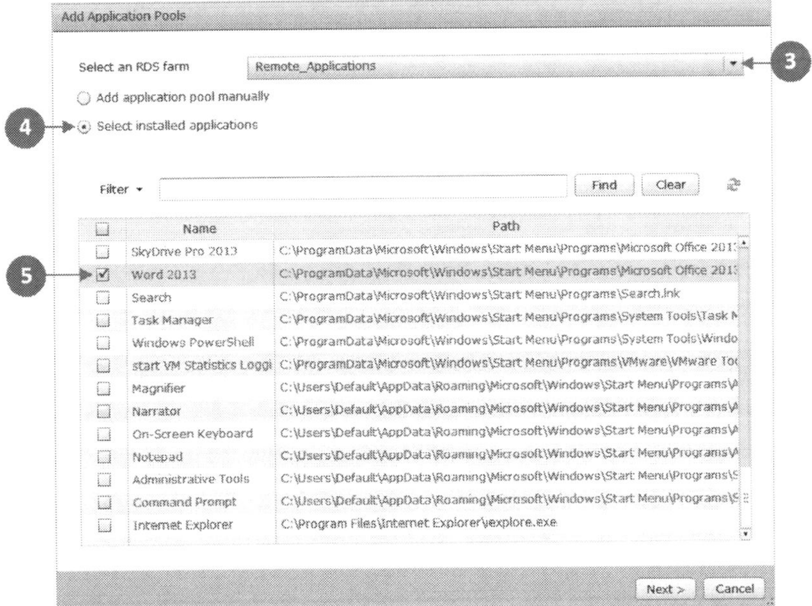

3. From the **Select an RDS farm** drop-down menu (**3**), select the farm that we created previously for our published applications. In our example, we select the **Remote_Applications** farm from the menu.
4. Click on the radio button for **Select installed applications** (**4**). This will automatically list all the applications that are installed on that particular RDSH server. We can also add an application pool manually.
5. From the list of applications displayed, tick the box next to each application you want to add to the application pool. In our example, we will add the following applications:
    - Calculator
    - Paint
    - Excel
    - PowerPoint
    - Word
6. When you have selected all the required applications, click on **Next >** to continue.

7. You will now see the **Edit ID and Display Name of the selected applications** screen, as shown in the following screenshot:

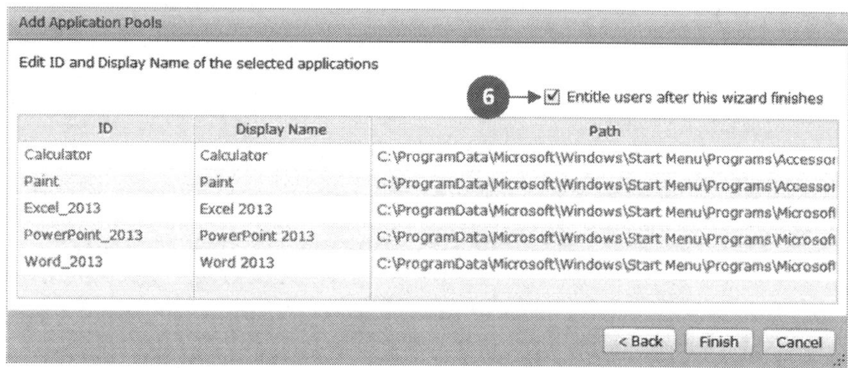

8. You can choose to edit the ID and the display name for the applications. Once you have completed this, tick the box for **Entitle users after this wizard finishes** (**6**) so that we can go straight into entitling users to the published applications.
9. Click on **Finish**.

Now we have our application pool all set up and ready to go. The next step is to entitle end users to the pool to allow them to launch an application.

Entitling users to application pools

We will entitle a user to be able to access desktop sessions. In the last section, as we ticked the box to launch the **Entitlement** configuration screen, perform the following steps:

1. Click on **Add...** (**1**) to add a new user entitlement.

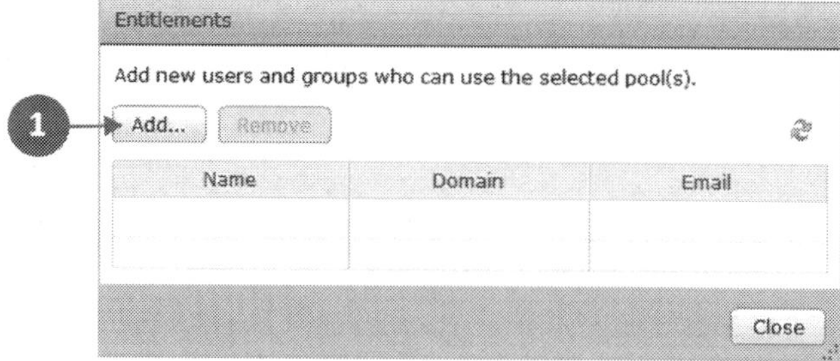

2. You will now see the **Find User or Group** configuration screen, as shown in the following screenshot:

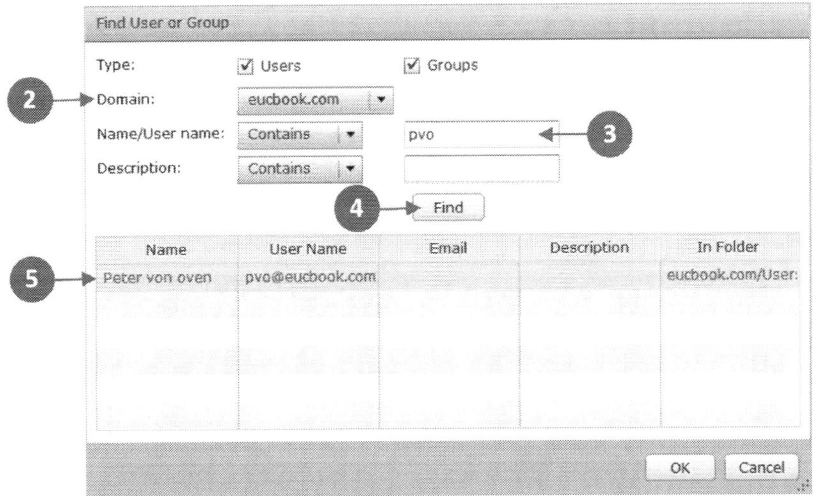

3. From the **Domain:** drop-down menu (**2**), select the domain for the user you want to entitle. In our example, we will use the **eucbook.com** domain.
4. In the **Name/User name:** box (**3**), enter the user details you want to entitle. In our example, we will entitle a user called `pvo`. Click on **Find** (**4**) to search for the user in the **eucbook.com** domain.
5. We should have found the user by now with their details displayed in the table shown (**5**). Select the user and then click on **OK**.
6. You will now see the **Add Entitlements** screen again, but this time, with our newly added user listed. From here, you can insert additional user entitlements or, as in our example, you can add just one user. Click on **OK** to continue:

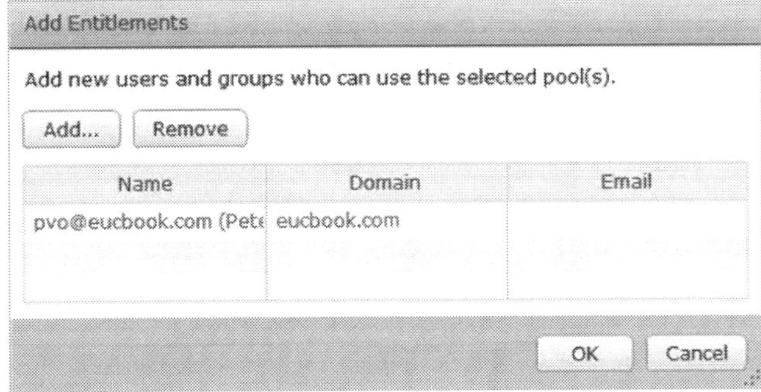

7. The **Entitlement** screen is displayed. Click on **Close** to finish adding user entitlements. As a final check, we will ensure that we have user entitlements. Under the **Inventory** section, click on **Users and Groups**. You will now see the following screenshot:

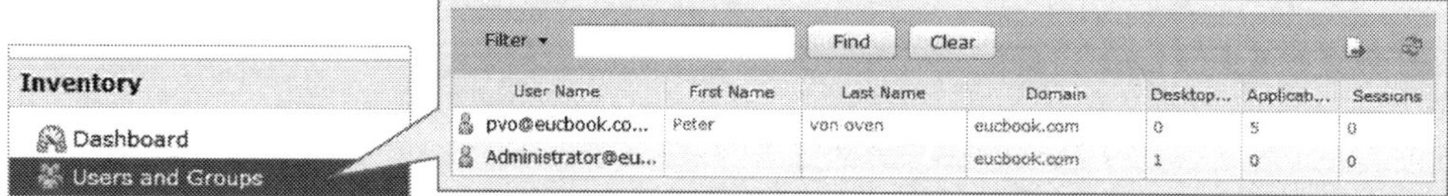

Here, you can see that the user PVO has been entitled to five applications. The next test is to check whether the user can access these applications. To test this, we will launch the Horizon View Client, log in, and then launch one of the applications.

> Make sure you are using one of the latest versions of Horizon View Client (Version 3.0 or later). Older versions will still work with VDI desktops, but will not show published applications.

8. Launch the Horizon View Client and make sure that you have added the address of the Connection Server. In our example, we will use the address of our security server as we are connecting externally **(6)**:

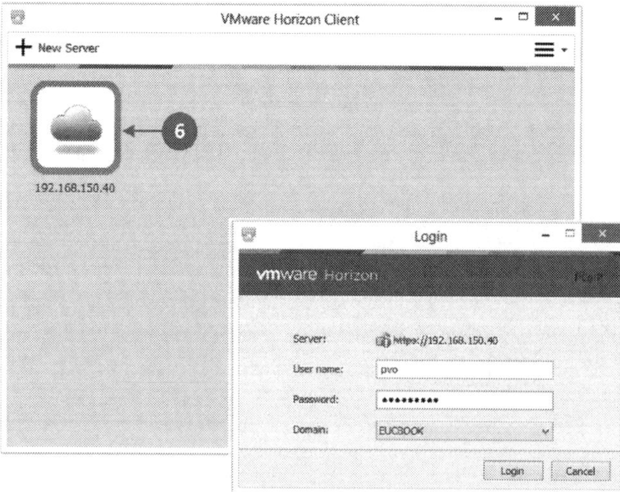

9. Log in as the end user that we just entitled. In our example, the username is `pvo`. Once you have successfully logged in, you will see the applications displayed in the Horizon View Client, as shown in the following screenshot:

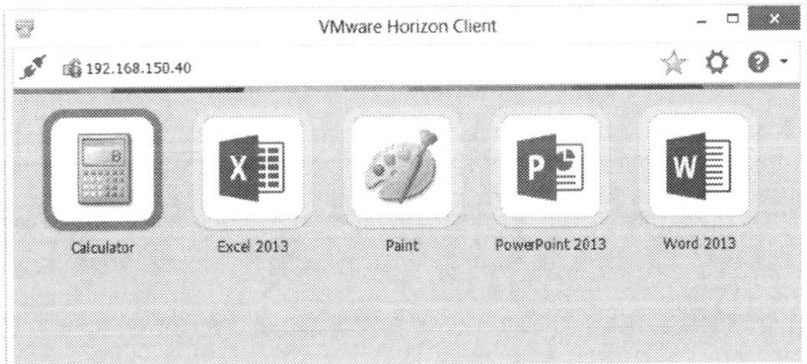

10. Double-click an application to make sure it launches.

Summary

In this chapter, we discussed how to deliver remote/published applications with Horizon View. We started off by looking at the architecture and seeing how it works. We then walked through the installation and configuration process for both the Microsoft RDSH components and the Horizon View components.

In the next chapter, we will look at how we apply the same methodology to deliver session-based desktops.

11

Delivering Session-based Desktops with Horizon View

Following on from the previous chapter—where we configured Horizon View to deliver published applications hosted on a Microsoft RDSH environment—in this chapter, we will cover the other half of View's remoting functionality and take a look at the ability of View to deliver session-based desktops from a Microsoft RDSH host server. The key advantage of this feature is that you don't need to deploy a full VDI-based desktop to the user, they just use a session from the host.

As with the published applications we covered in *Chapter 10, Delivering Remote Applications with Horizon Advanced*, the desktop sessions will be delivered using the Horizon View Client. We will cover the installation of the RDSH role and the configuration of the desktop sessions.

Architecture overview

So, let's take a look at the architecture and how session-based desktops work in comparison to the standard View virtual desktop machine brokering. In terms of architecture, delivering desktop sessions is pretty much the same as delivering published applications.

Horizon View acts as the broker, but instead of brokering a virtual desktop machine that is running on the ESXi host server or an RDSH published application, it is now brokering a desktop session that is running on a Microsoft Windows Server. This server is configured with the RDS role and some customizations to make the Windows Server GUI interface look more like that of the Windows 8 desktop operating system.

A farm in Horizon View terms is a collection of servers that host applications or desktops. These servers can be Windows Server 2008, 2012, or a mix of both.

The following diagram gives you an outline of the architecture:

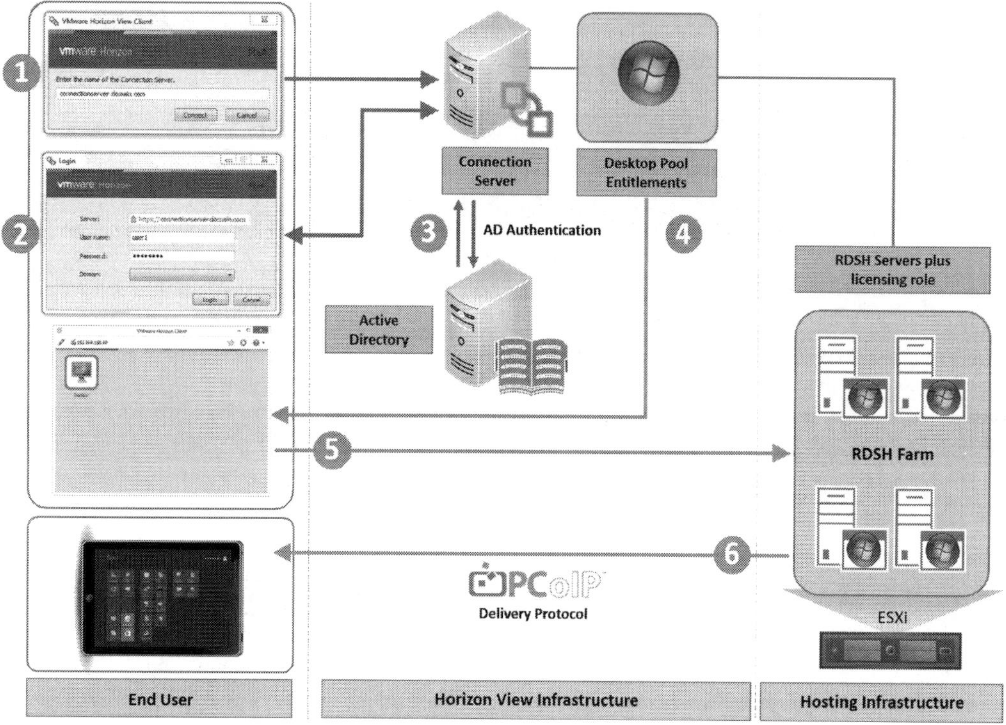

So, how does the architecture work? Basically, in exactly the same way as we have already discussed in *Chapter 10, Delivering Remote Applications with Horizon Advanced*, but now we are delivering remote desktop sessions rather than applications.

Rather than covering the same thing again by describing in detail how this solution works and the system requirements, please refer back to that chapter and in particular the *Application connection sequence* section.

Load balancing session-based desktops in View

The next thing we are going to cover is how the connection broker decides which of the RDSH host servers in the farm will deliver the desktop session.

There is no real complicated science behind load balancing from the perspective of View. It is purely based on how many sessions are available on any given RDSH server. So, when the user logs in and launches a remote application, the application is delivered from the server that has the freest amount of sessions available, that is, the one that isn't the busiest. This is shown in the following diagram:

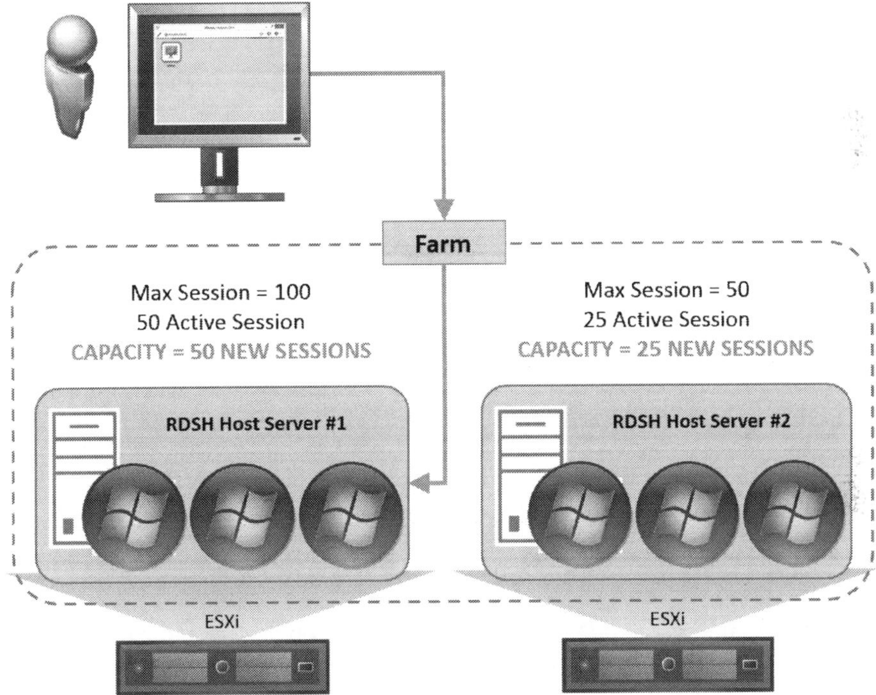

Now that we have covered the architecture, in the next section, we are going to start the installation and get our environment up and running.

Installing and configuring desktop sessions in View

We are now going to start the installation process, starting with configuring the servers that we are going to use for remoting our applications and adding the RDSH role to them.

The installation process is straightforward and can be summarized with the following schematic diagram:

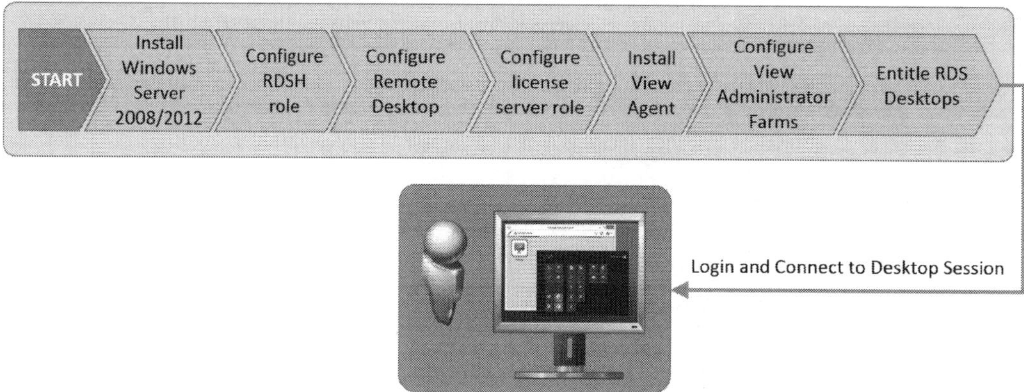

In our example lab, we already have two Windows Server 2012 servers built, `EUC-RDSH-01` and `EUC-RDSH-02`, to perform this role. `EUC-RDSH-02` was used for the published applications, so we will use `EUC-RDSH-01` for the desktop sessions.

> You can only have either desktop sessions or published applications per session collection on an RDSH host server. There is a workaround to have both, however, it is not supported. For our example lab, we are going to configure a separate RDSH host for each session type just to make it easier.

In the following sections, we are going to walk you through the installation and configuration process in more detail.

Configuring the RDSH role

In this section, we will cover the installation of the RDSH role to host our desktop sessions. We will assume that you already have a new server built for this purpose. In our example lab, the server named `euc-rdsh-01` is going to be used for this role.

The first thing that we are going to do is to configure the RDSH role as follows:

1. On the **Welcome to Server Manager** page, click on **Add roles and features** (**1**), as shown in the following screenshot:

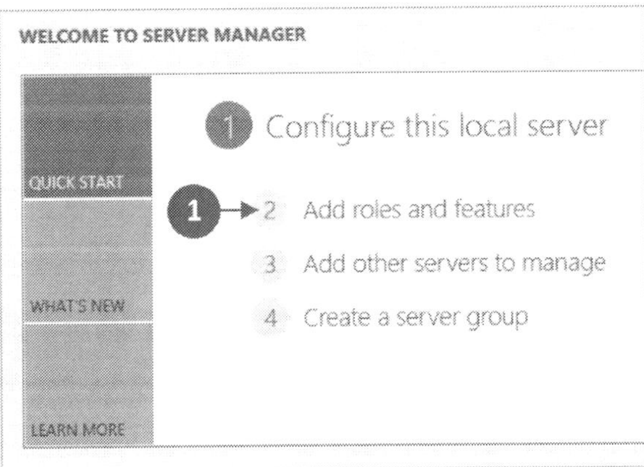

2. The **Add Roles and Features Wizard** page launches, as shown in the following screenshot. On the **Before you begin** page, click on **Next >** (**2**):

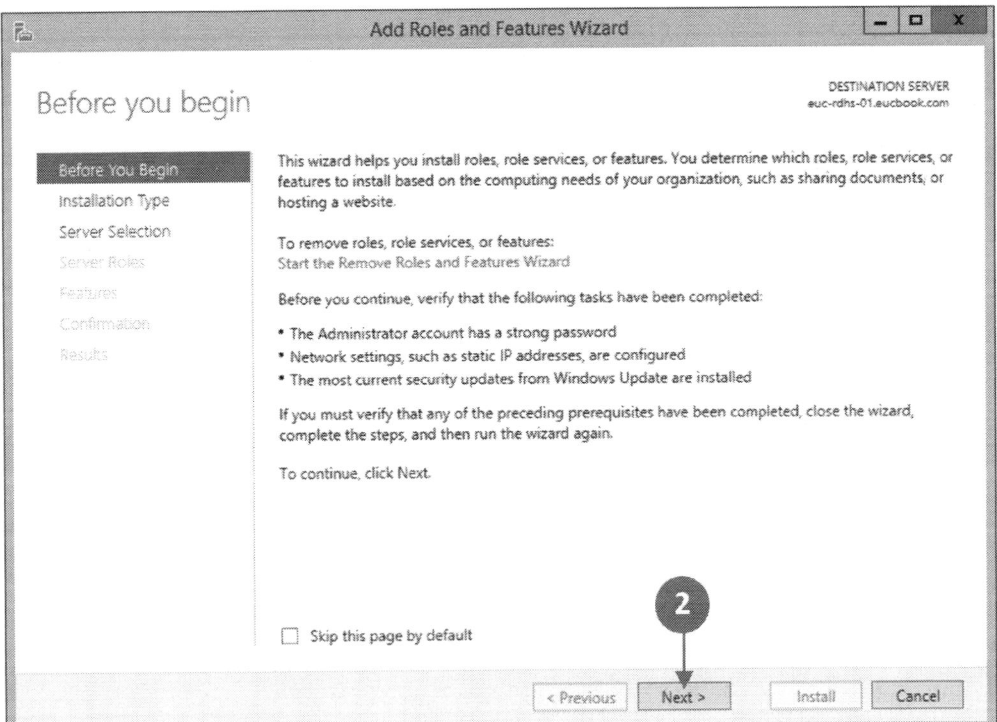

3. Now, choose the **Installation Type** option. Click on the radio button for **Remote Desktop Services installation** (3).
4. Click on **Next >** (**4**) to continue to the next configuration page, as shown in the following screenshot:

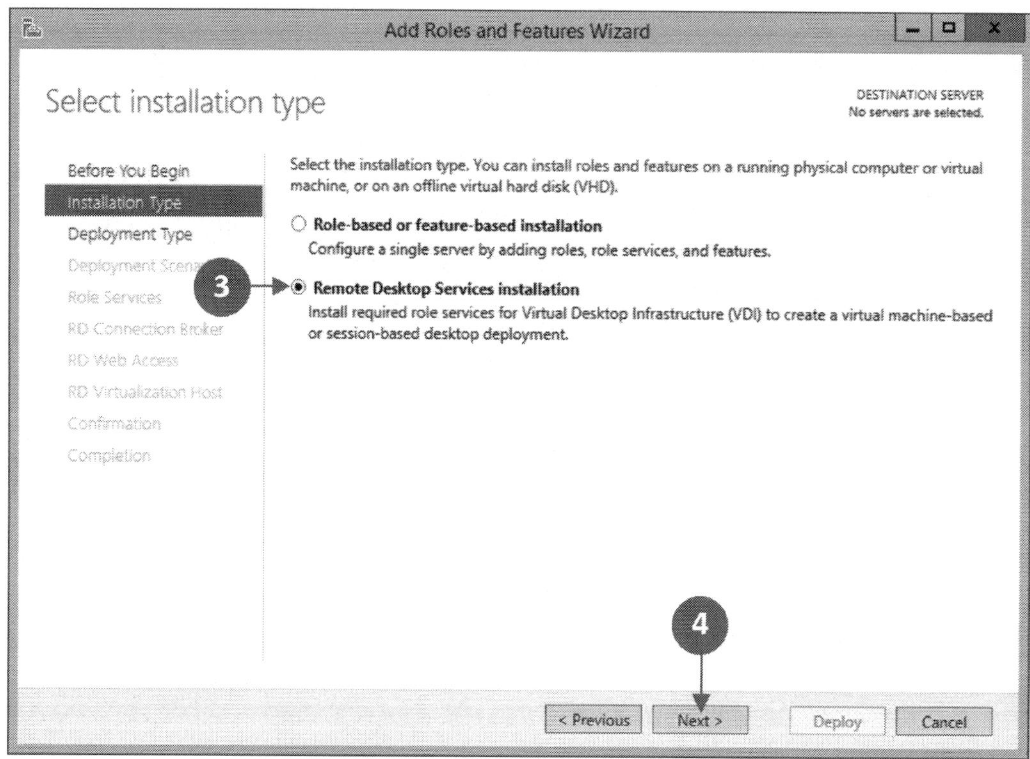

5. On the **Deployment Type** page, click on the radio button for **Quick Start** (**5**).
6. Click on **Next >** (**6**) to continue to the next configuration page, as shown in the following screenshot:

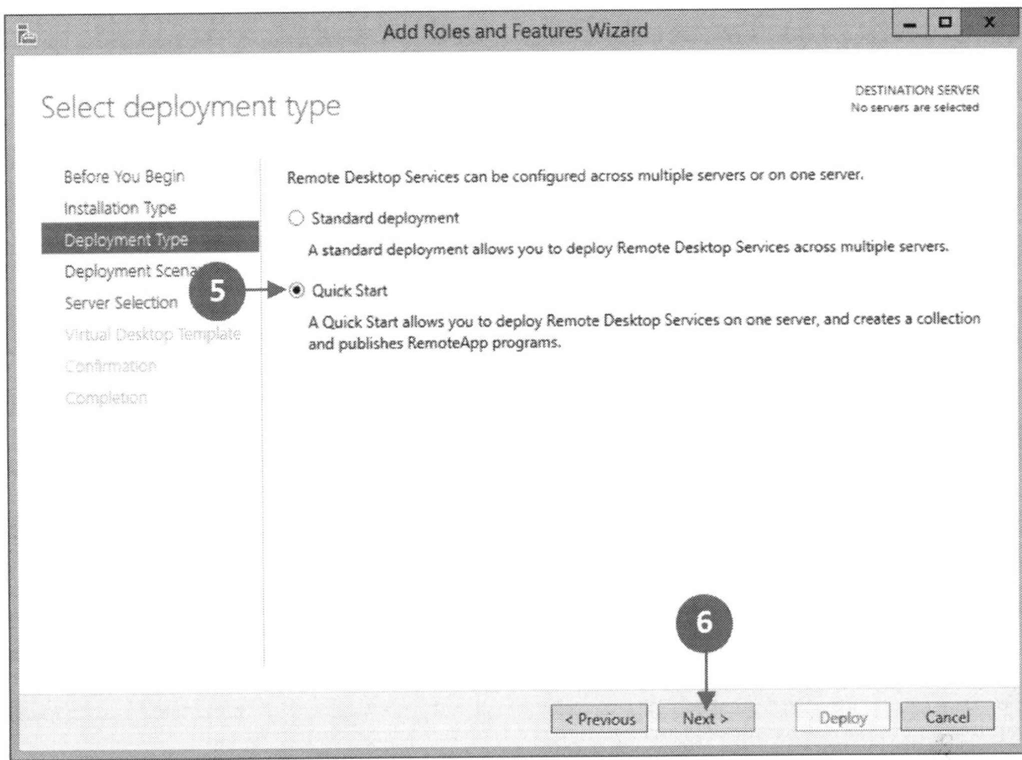

7. On the **Deployment Scenario** page, click on the radio button for **Session-based desktop deployment** (**7**).

8. Click on **Next >** (**8**) to continue to the next configuration page as shown in the following screenshot:

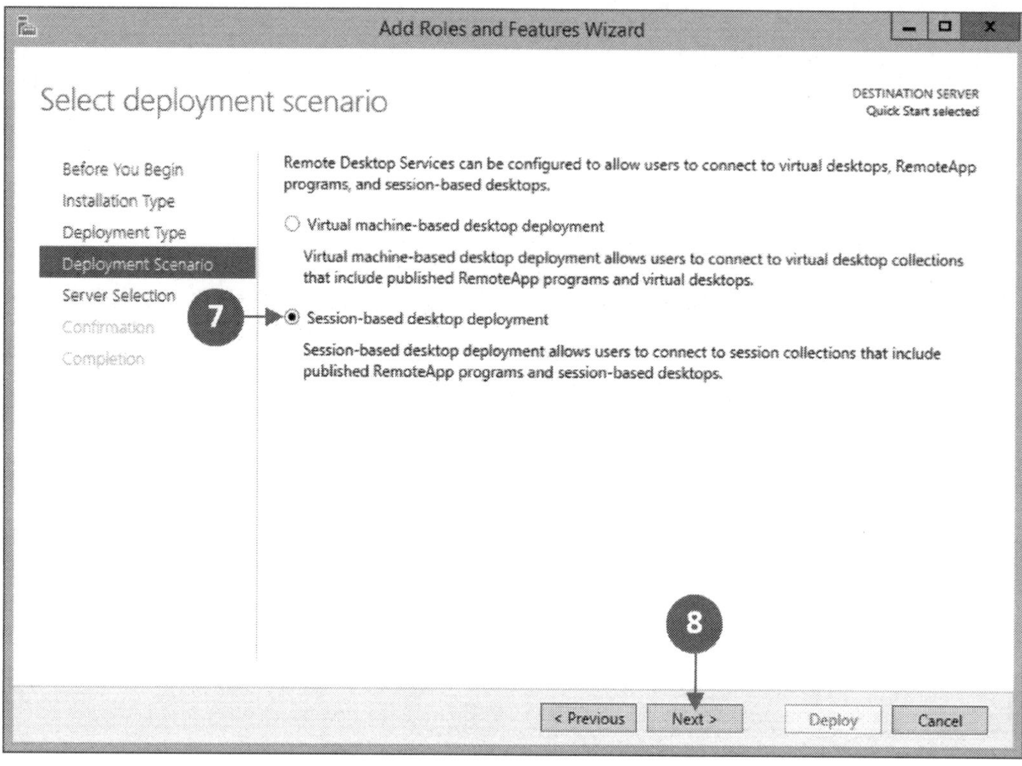

9. Now, select the server onto which you want to add this role. In our example, we only have one server, **euc-rdsh-01**, so click on it to highlight it (**9**), and then click on the arrow to add it to the **Selected** list (**10**), as shown in the following screenshot:

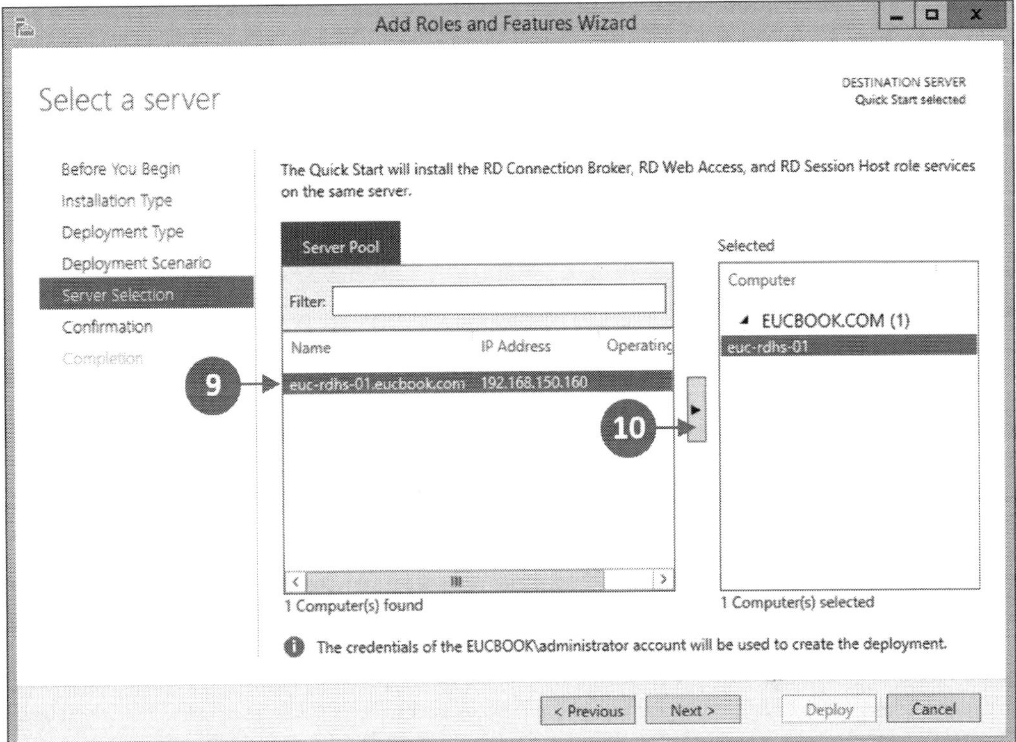

10. Click on **Next >** to continue to the next configuration page.

11. You are now ready to complete the RDSH role, so ensure that everything you want to install is listed in the confirmation box and, once happy, click on **Deploy** (**11**), as shown in the following screenshot:

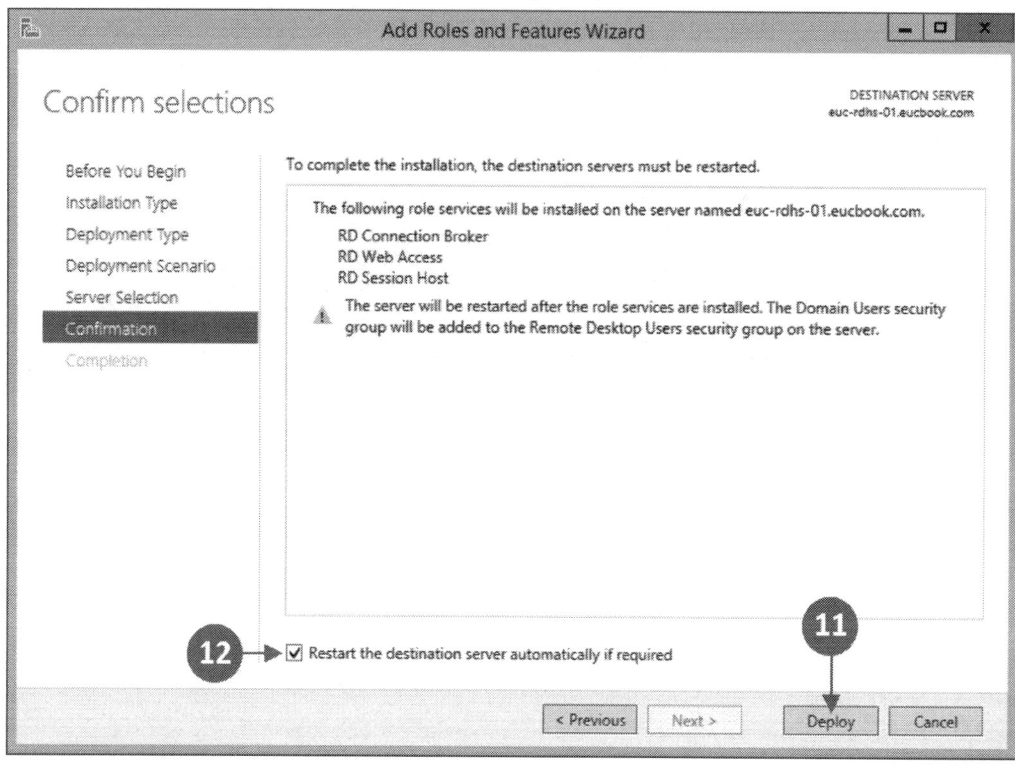

12. You should also tick the box for **Restart the destination server automatically if required** (**12**) as shown in the preceding screenshot.

13. The **View progress** page is displayed showing the installation progress. Click on **Close** (**13**) once the installation has succeeded, as shown in the following screenshot:

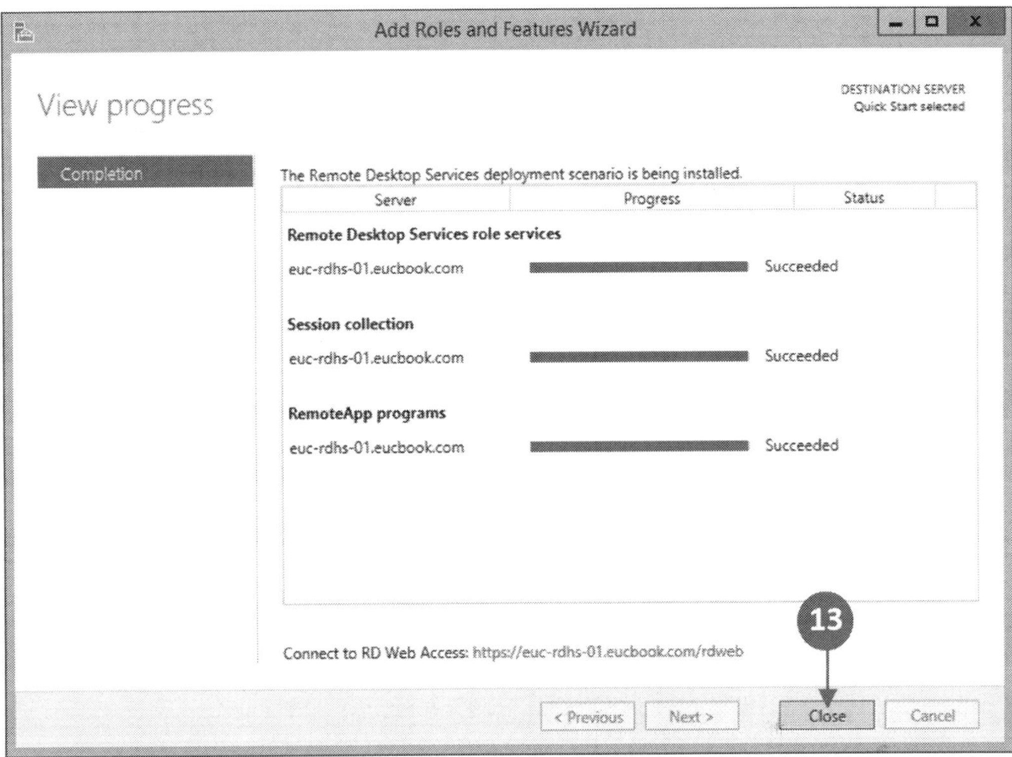

We now have a server configured with the RDSH role. In the next section, we will configure the server for session-based desktops

Configuring RDSH for desktop sessions

As we used the QuickStart installation method for setting up our RDSH role, it also included configuring some published applications. As we are going to use this RDSH host server for just desktop sessions, the first thing we are going to do is unpublish those applications.

Unpublishing the existing applications

To unpublish the applications, we perform the following steps on the **Welcome to Server Manager** page:

1. Click on **Remote Desktop Services** (**1**).
2. Then, on the configuration screen, click on **Servers** (**2**), and then click on the server we are going to use for our session desktops. In our example, we are using **EUC-RDSH-01** (**3**).
3. Finally, click on **QuickSessionCollections** (**4**), as shown in the following screenshot:

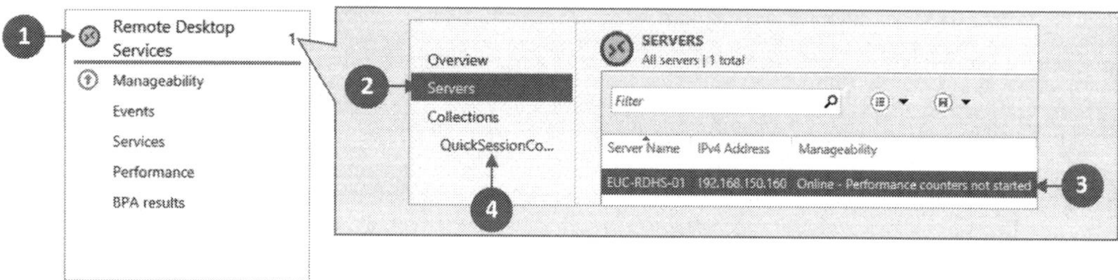

4. In the **RemoteApp Programs** section of the screen, click on **TASKS** (**5**), and then from the displayed menu options, select **Unpublish RemoteApp Programs** (**6**), as shown in the following screenshot:

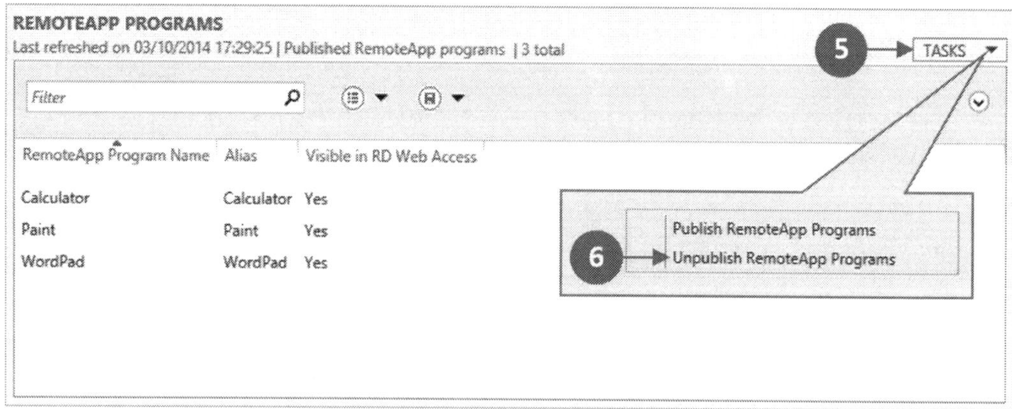

5. On the **RemoteApp Programs** screen, click the applications to unpublish (**7**), as shown in the following screenshot. Click on **Next >** (**8**) to continue:

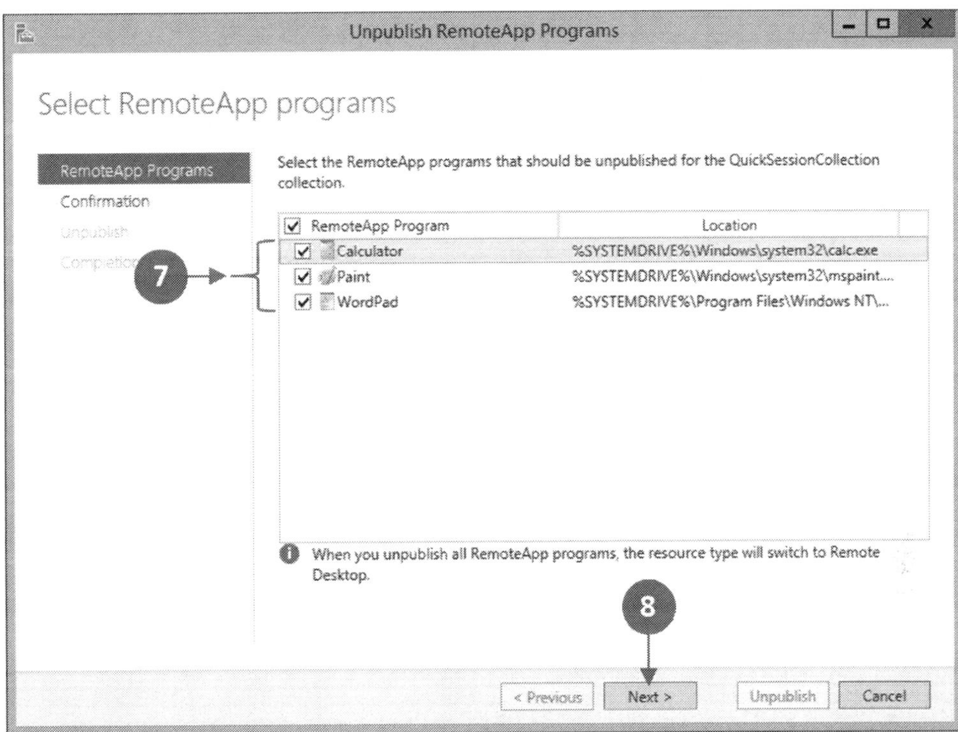

6. On the **Confirmation** screen, ensure the correct applications are listed and, once happy, click on **Unpublish** (**9**), as shown in the following screenshot:

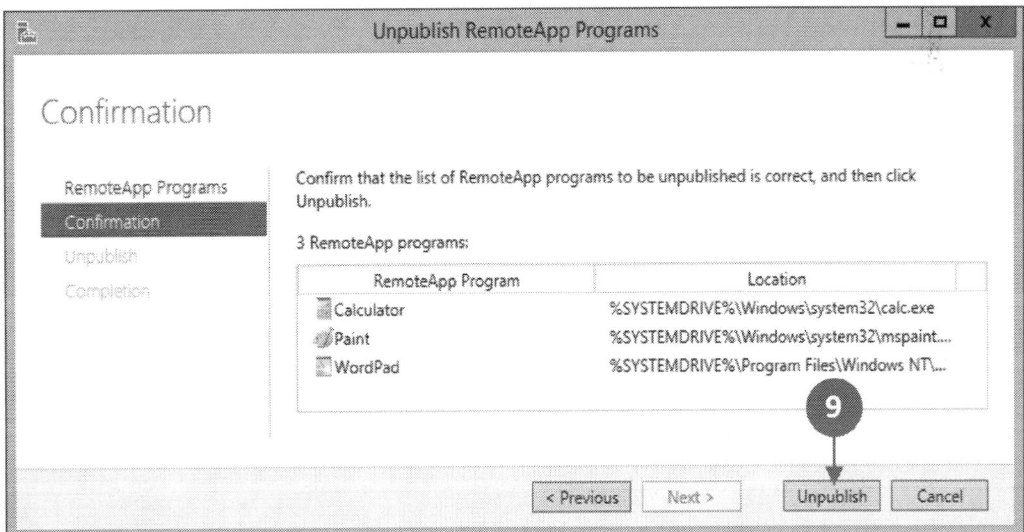

7. Click on **Close** (**10**) on the **Completion** screen to finish the unpublishing task, as shown in the following screenshot:

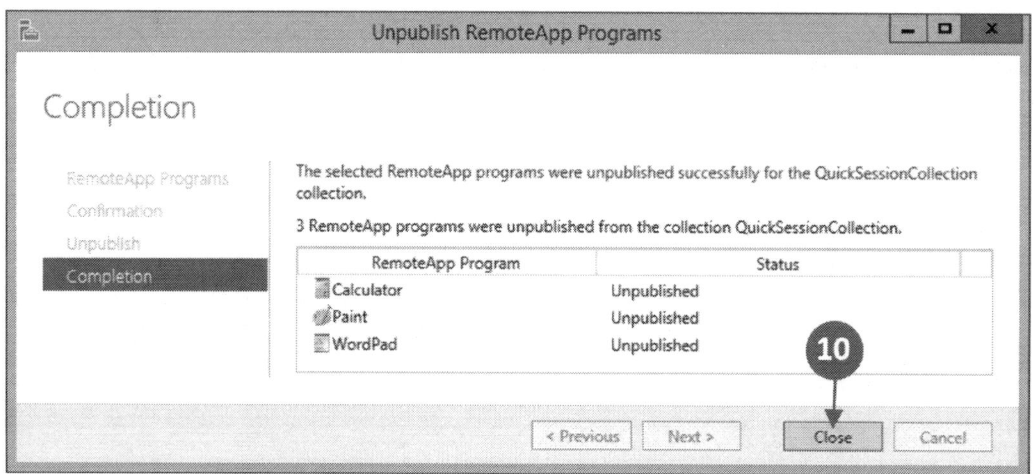

Now, we have unpublished the applications that were configured as part of the installation process, we can now move on and add the desktop sessions as a RemoteApp.

Adding the RemoteApp for desktop sessions

In this section, we are going to add the Remote Desktop Connection application as a RemoteApp. Perform the following steps for that:

1. Click on **Remote Desktop Services** (**1**).
2. Then, from the configuration screen, click on **Servers** (**2**), and then click on the server we are going to use for our session desktops. In our example, we are using **EUC-RDSH-01** (**3**).
3. Finally, click on **QuickSessionCollections** (**4**), as shown in the following screenshot:

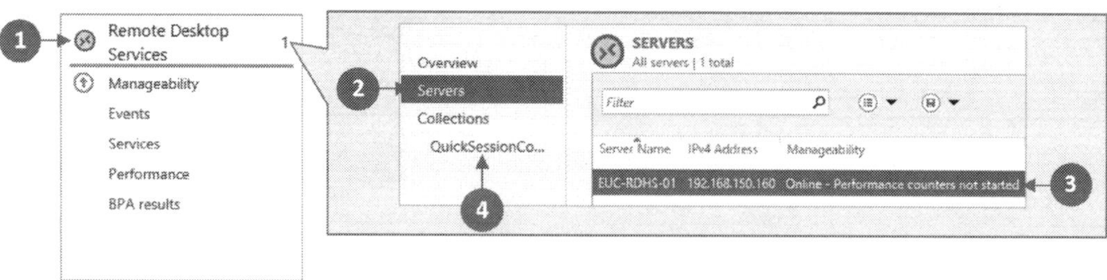

4. In the **RemoteApp Programs** section of the screen, click on **TASKS** (**5**), and then from the displayed menu options, select **Unpublish RemoteApp Programs** (**6**), as shown in the following screenshot:

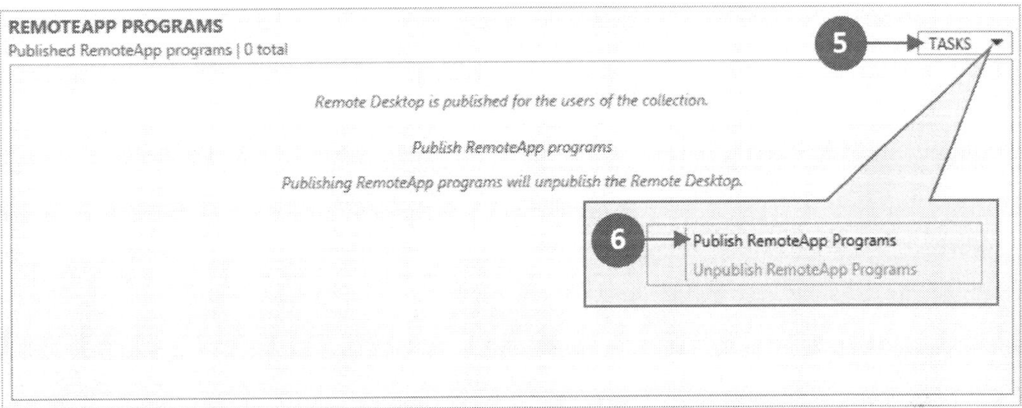

5. Click on **Remote Desktop Connection** (**7**), and then click on **Next >** (**8**) as shown in the following screenshot:

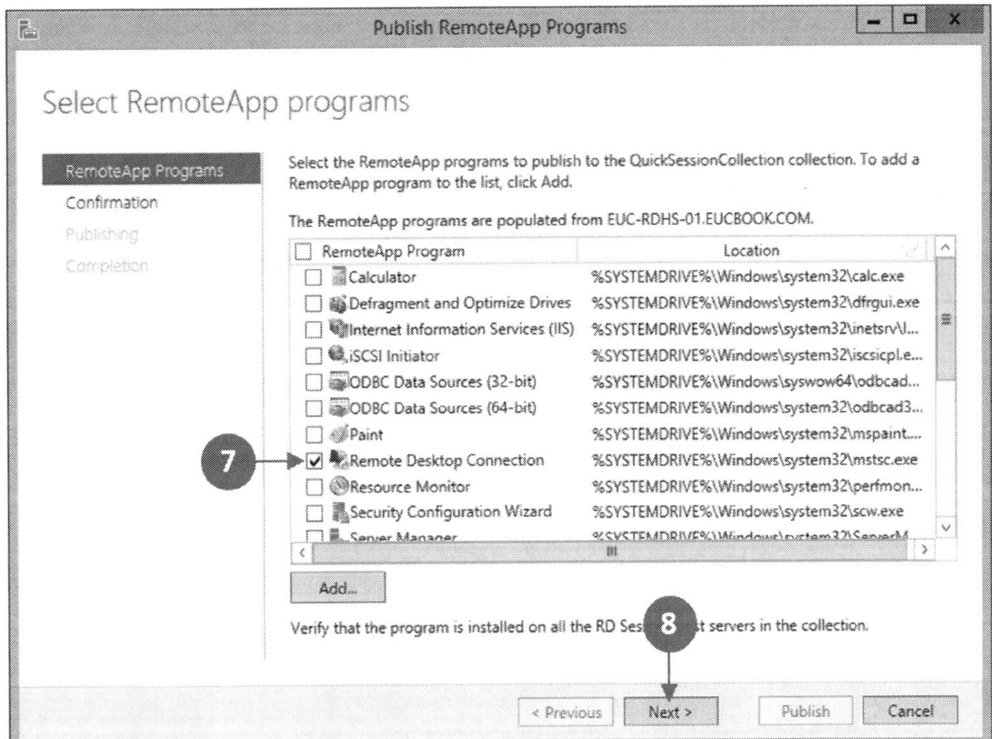

6. In the **Confirmation** box, check that **Remote Desktop Connection** is listed, and then click on **Publish** (9), as shown in the following screenshot:

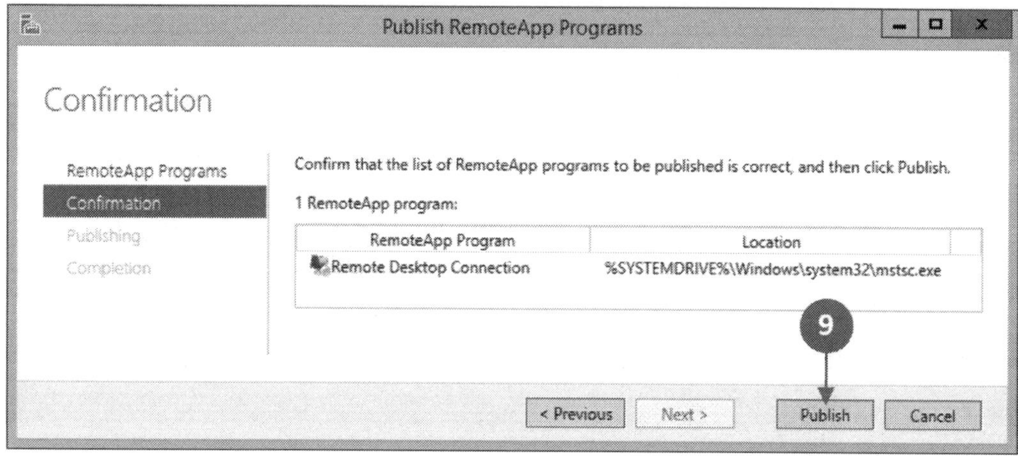

7. Click on **Close** (10) on the **Completion** screen to finish adding the Remote Desktop Connection applications, as shown in the following screenshot:

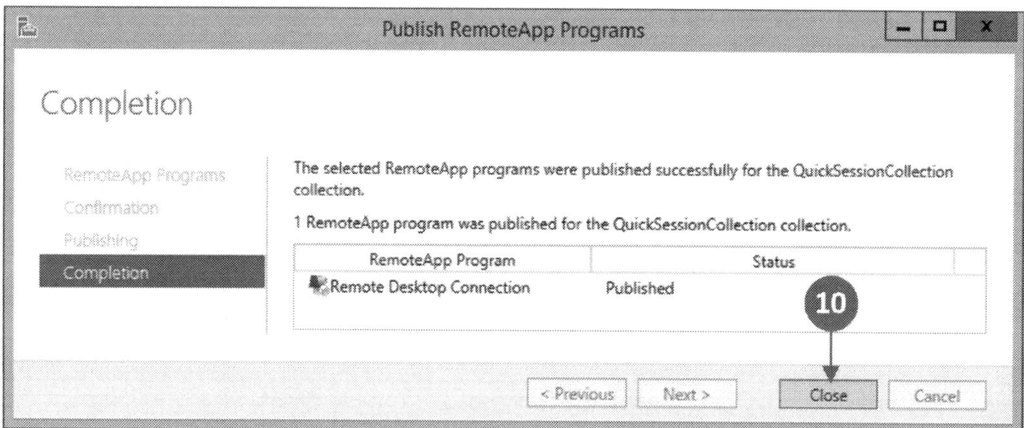

We have now completed the configuration for setting up a desktop session-hosting role on our RDSH server.

The final thing that we need to do from a Microsoft Windows Server perspective is to add the licensing role. As we have already covered the installation of this role in *Chapter 10, Delivering Remote Applications with Horizon Advanced*, please refer to the *Configuring the licensing role* section in the chapter for details on how to perform this task.

With the RDSH platform now in place, configured, as well as up and running, the next steps are to look at the Horizon View elements of the configuration, starting, in the next section, with the installation of the Horizon View Agent onto the RDSH server.

Installing the Horizon View Agent

We are going to install the Horizon View Agent onto the RDSH server. The agent is exactly the same as the one we would install on the virtual desktop machines, by performing the following steps:

1. Browse to the shared software folder and navigate to the agent installation application (**1**), as shown in the following screenshot:

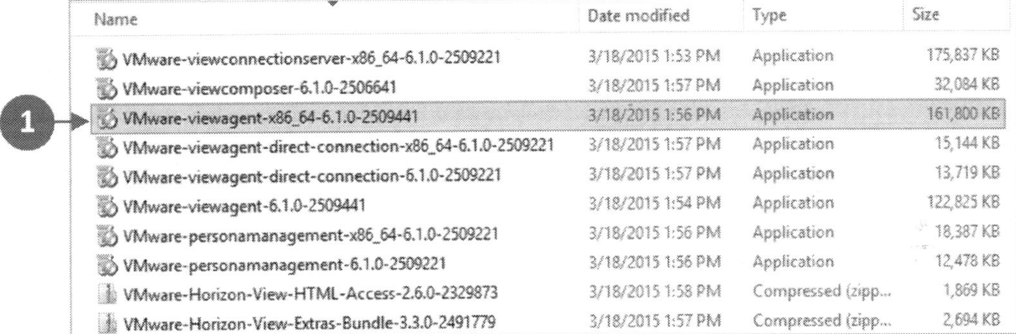

The file we are looking for is `VMware-viewagent-x86_64-6.1.0-2509441`. The seven-digit number at the end of the filename refers to the build version, so you may have a different number, depending on the build version you are using.

Let's begin with the installation process now:

2. Double-click on `VMware-viewagent-x86_64-6.1.0-2509441` to launch the installation, as shown in the following screenshot:

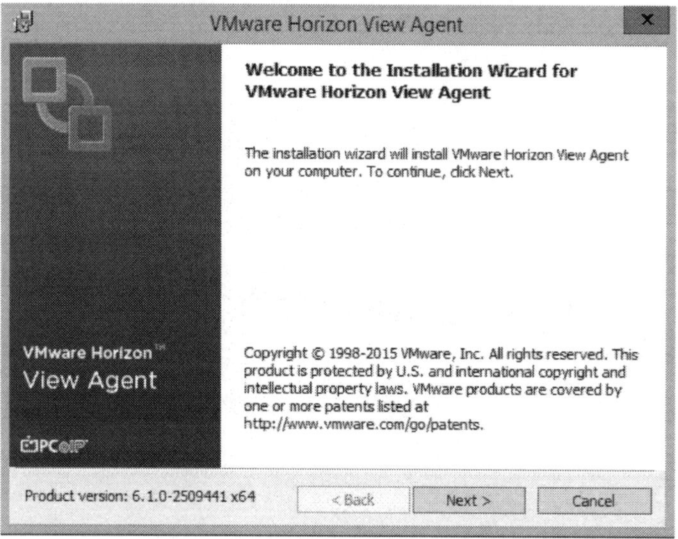

3. Click on the radio button (**2**) to accept the EULA.
4. Click on **Next >** to start the installation, as shown in the following screenshot:

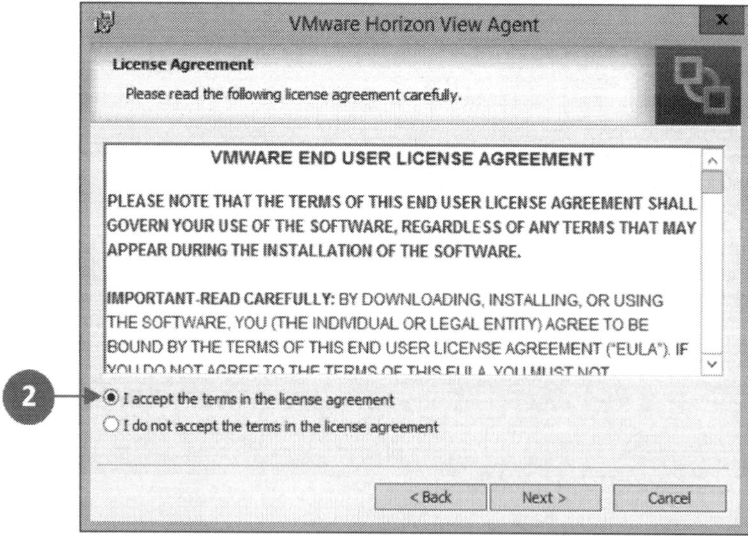

5. On the **Custom Setup** configuration screen, you can select which options to install, as shown in the following screenshot:

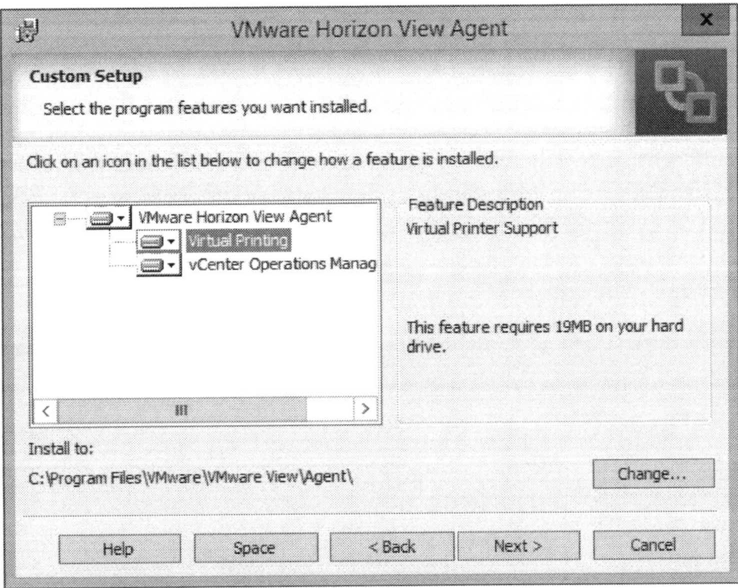

6. By selecting **Virtual Printing** and **vCenter Operations Manager**, you can install the virtual printing elements and the agents for operations manager.
7. There are also a number of features that get installed by default. These are listed as follows:
    - **PCoIP Agent**: It allows end users to connect to published applications and session-based desktops using PCoIP as the display protocol
    - **Unity Touch**: It provides functionality for tablet and smartphone users to use their Windows applications running on a remote desktop
    - **PSG Agent**: It installs the PCoIP Secure Gateway on the RDSH server to allow the desktop and application sessions running on the RDSH server to be delivered to the end user
    - **VMwareRDS**: It is the VMware implementation of RDS

8. Click on **Next >** to continue, and you will see a screen similar to the one shown in the following screenshot:

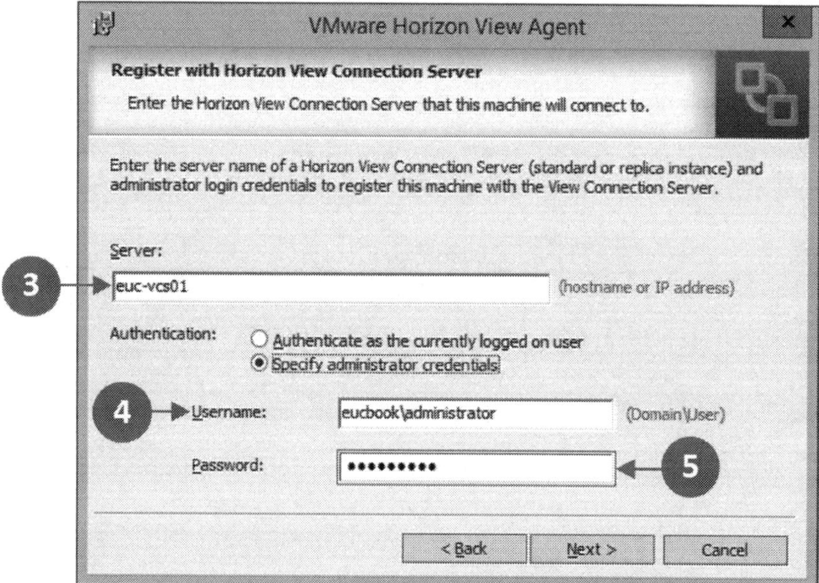

In the **Register with Horizon View Connection Server** page, we are going to configure the agent to talk to our Connection Server. This allows the Connection Server to read the published applications from the RemoteApp catalog and allows you to create pools within View.

9. In the **Server** box (**3**), enter the name of the Connection Server. In our example, we are using the Connection Server called **euc-vcs01**.
10. In the **Authentication** section, click on the radio button for **Specify administrator credentials**, and then in the **Username** box (**4**), enter the user account you want to use to connect to the Connection Server, followed by the password in the **Password** box (**5**).

Make sure you use the format domain\user to enter the username, and also that the account has the correct privileges to access the Connection Server.

11. Click on **Next >** to continue.
12. On the **Ready to Install the Program** screen, click on **Install** to start the process.

13. Once successfully installed, you will see the **Installer Complete** screen. Click on **Finish** to quit the installation.

> One of the most common reasons that the installation of the agent fails is due to the configuration of the RDSH server. More often than not, there are no sound drivers loaded on the Windows Server running the RDSH role. If this is the case, then the installation of the agent will fail and automatically roll back. If that happens, it's worth checking this first.

You will need to reboot the server once installation has completed. We have now completed the first part of the Horizon View configuration. In the next step of the process, we will turn our attention to the View Administrator.

Configuring desktop sessions in Horizon View

The next stage in the installation and configuration process is performed in the View Administrator console and, like a standard View setup, involves creating pools and entitlements. First, we will set up a farm that contains our newly built RDSH desktop session server.

Creating a farm for desktop sessions

To create a farm for desktop sessions, we perform the following steps:

1. Open a browser and connect to the View Administrator. In our example lab, the address for the View Administrator is `https://euc-vcs01.eucbook.com/admin/`.
2. Log in to the **View Administrator** using the administrator account and password, as shown in the following screenshot:

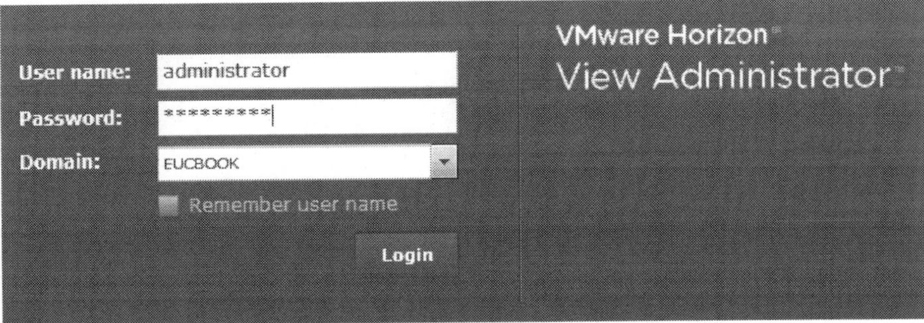

3. On the dashboard screen, navigate to **Resources** | **Farms (1)** | **Add... (2)**, as shown in the following screenshot:

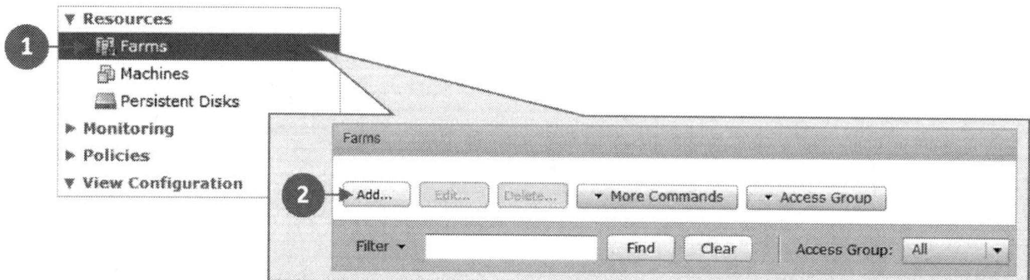

4. You will now see the **Add Farm** configuration screen, as shown in the following screenshot:

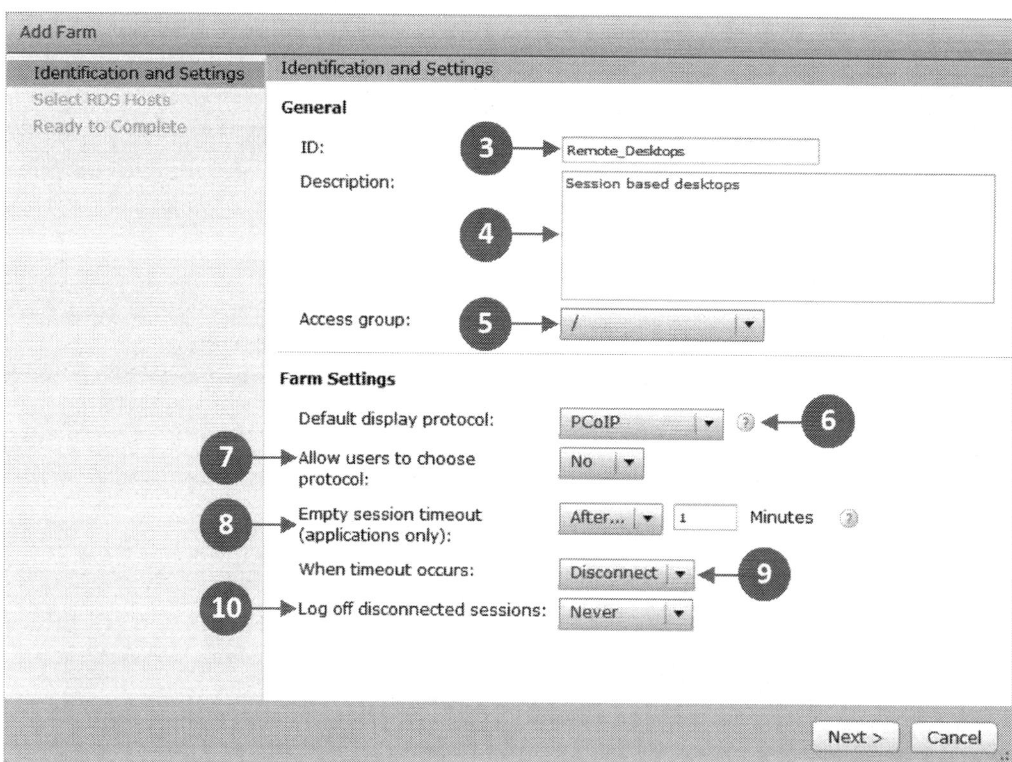

5. In the **ID** box (**3**), enter an ID for the farm that will be used by View to identify it.

You cannot use spaces for the ID, only letters (upper and lower case), numbers (0-9), and – (minus) or _ (underscore) characters.

6. In the **Description** box (**4**), enter an optional description for the farm, and then from the **Access group** drop-down (**5**), select an access group, if you have one.
7. Next, under **Farm Settings**, set the **Default display protocol** to **PCoIP** (**6**), and from the **Allow users to choose protocol** drop-down (**7**), select **No**.
8. The **Empty session timeout (applications only)** (**8**) is not applicable to desktop sessions, so you can ignore this setting.
9. Finally, select what to do **When timeout occurs** (**9**) and whether or not to **Log off disconnected sessions** (**10**).
10. Once you have completed the options on this screen, click on **Next >** to continue.
11. On the next configuration screen, we are going to select the RDSH server we want to add to this farm.
12. Click on **euc-rdsh-01.eucbook.com**, as shown in the following screenshot:

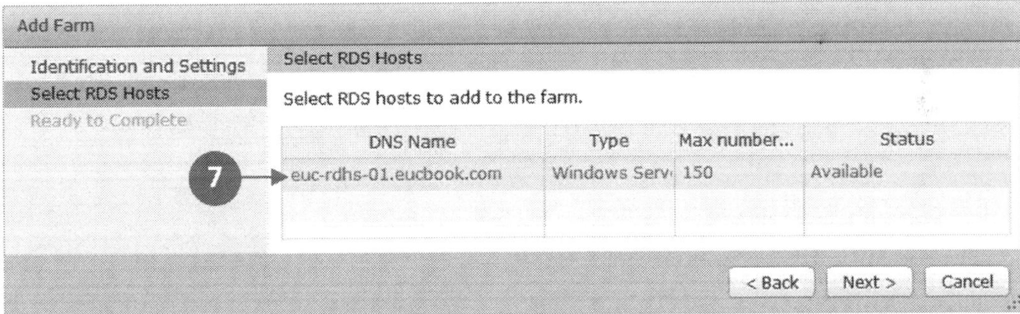

13. Click on **Next >** to continue.

14. You will now see the **Ready to Complete** screen as shown in the following screenshot. Check that the details are all correct:

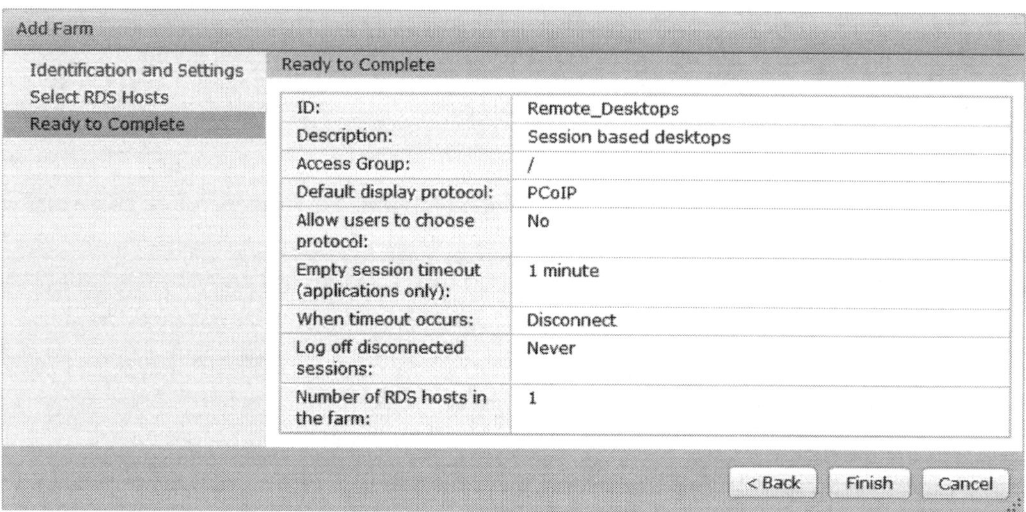

15. Once you are happy with the details, click on **Finish**.
16. Once the farm has been created, you will see the following screenshot, showing the **ID** of the Farm, along with the number of connections possible and that the farm is enabled:

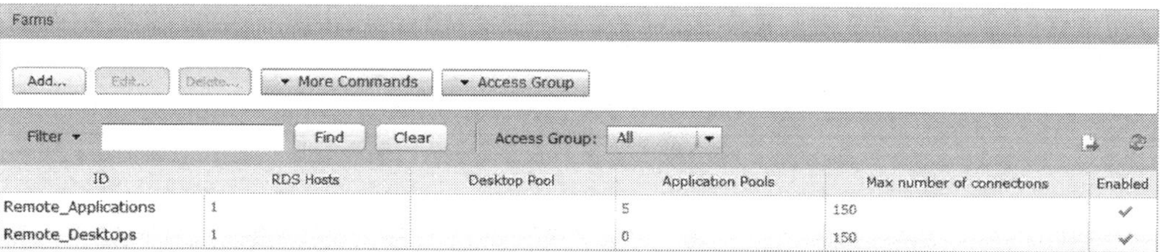

We now have a configured farm. The next step is to create a pool for our session-based desktops.

Creating a desktop pool for desktop sessions

The next stage in the configuration is to create a desktop pool for our session-based desktops. You need to perform the following steps for that:

1. On the View Administrator dashboard, navigate to **Inventory** | **Catalog** | **Desktop Pools** (**1**). Then, click on **Add...** (**2**), as shown in the following screenshot:

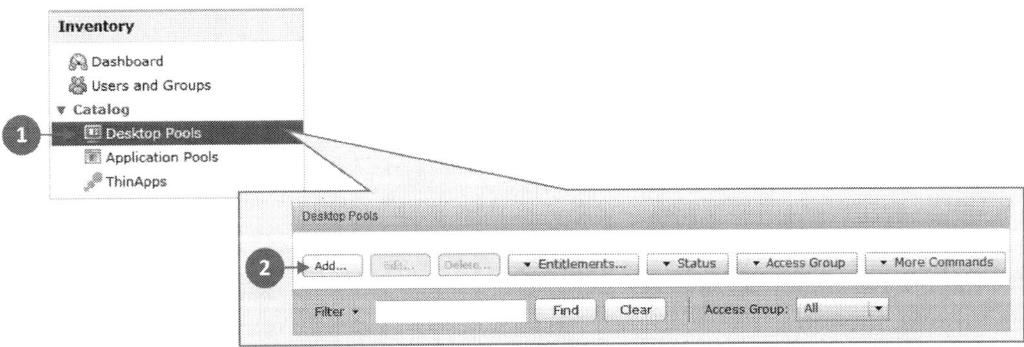

2. You will now see the **Add Desktop Pool** configuration screen, and the first thing we will configure is the type of pool.
3. Click on the radio button for **RDS Desktop Pool** (**3**), as shown in the following screenshot:

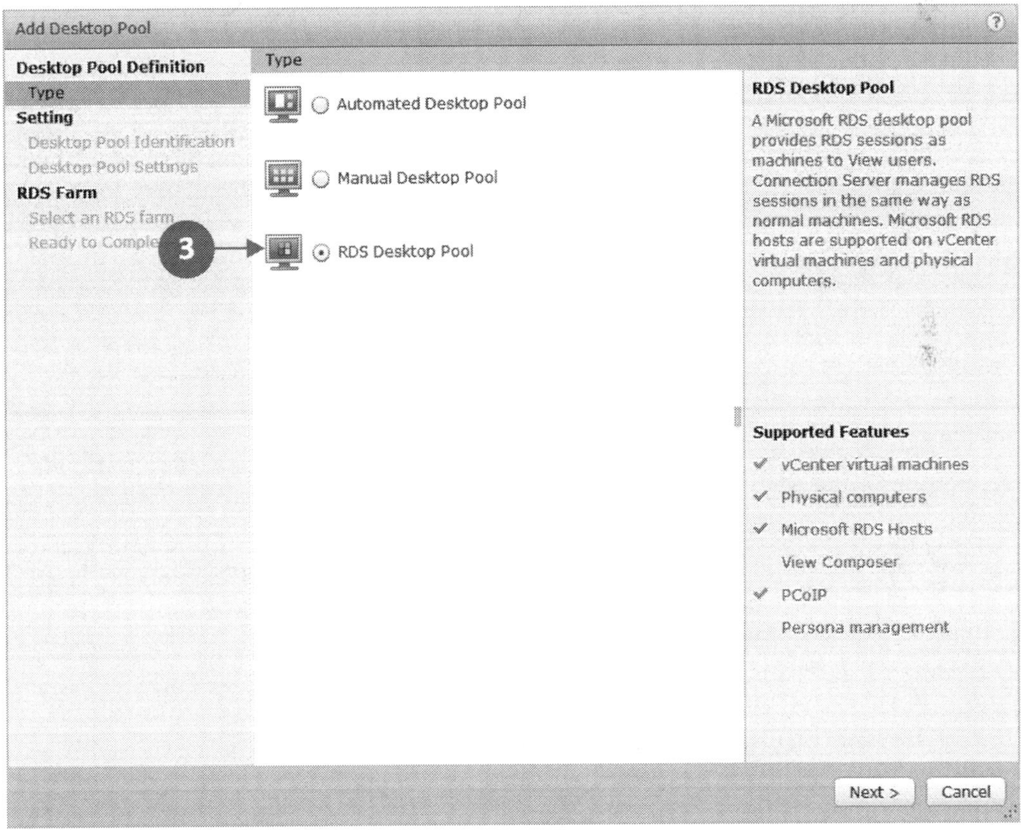

4. Click on **Next >** to continue.
5. You will now see the **Desktop Pool Identification** screen, as shown in the following screenshot:

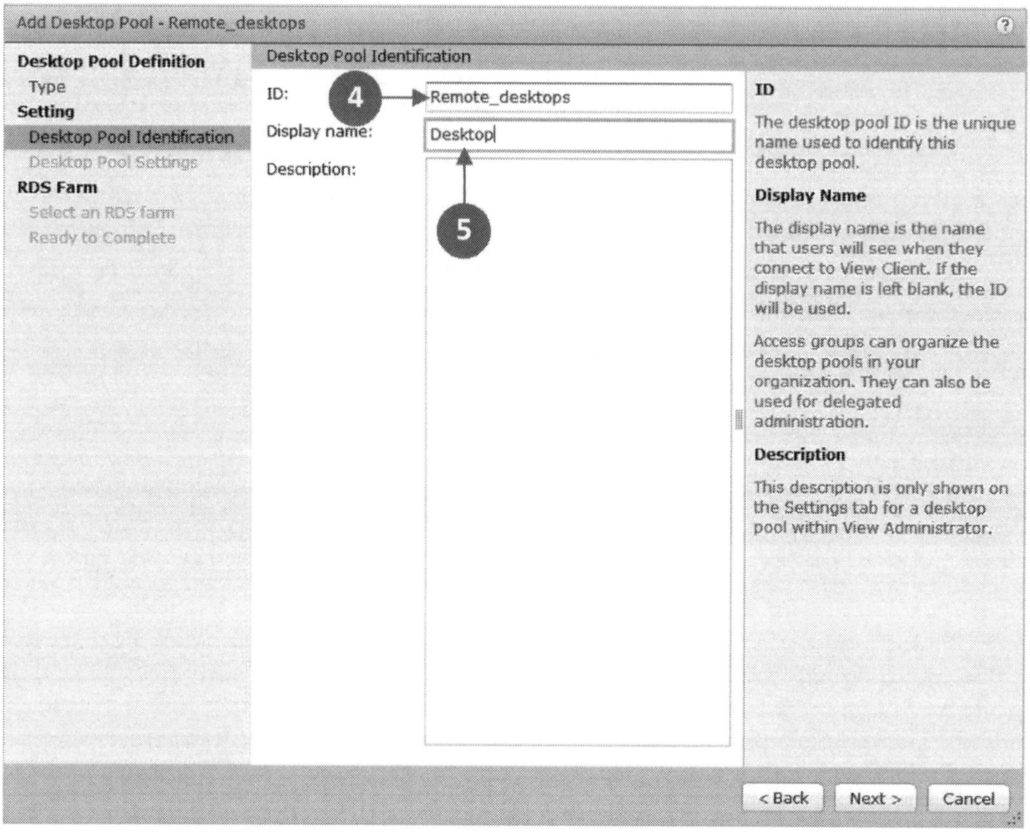

Add Desktop Pool - Remote_desktops

Desktop Pool Definition
Type
Setting
Desktop Pool Identification
Desktop Pool Settings
RDS Farm
Select an RDS farm
Ready to Complete

Desktop Pool Identification

ID: (4) Remote_desktops
Display name: (5) Desktop
Description:

ID

The desktop pool ID is the unique name used to identify this desktop pool.

Display Name

The display name is the name that users will see when they connect to View Client. If the display name is left blank, the ID will be used.

Access groups can organize the desktop pools in your organization. They can also be used for delegated administration.

Description

This description is only shown on the Settings tab for a desktop pool within View Administrator.

< Back | Next > | Cancel

6. In the **ID** box (**4**), enter an ID for the pool. In our example, we are going to call the pool `Remote_desktops`.

> As with the Farm ID, you cannot use spaces for the ID, only letters (upper and lower case), numbers (0-9), and - (minus) or _ (underscore) characters.

7. In the **Display name** box (**5**), enter a name that will be displayed to your users in the View Client and their Horizon Workspace portal.
8. Click on **Next >** to continue.

9. You will now see the **Desktop Pool Settings** screen, as shown in the following screenshot:

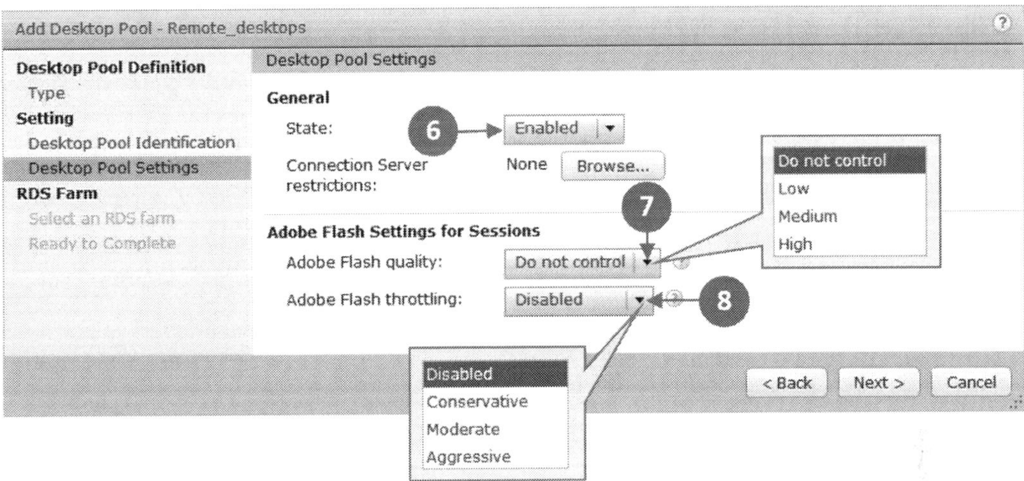

10. In the **State** box (6), from the drop-down, select **Enabled** to enable this pool.
11. Next, we will configure the **Adobe Flash Settings for sessions** section. On the **Adobe Flash Quality** drop-down (7), select **Do not control**. The other options available are:
    - **Do not control**: It allows the web page to determine the best setting
    - **Low (default)**: Low quality means less bandwidth consumption
    - **Medium**: Medium quality means average bandwidth consumption
    - **High**: High quality means more bandwidth consumption
12. From the **Adobe Flash throttling** drop-down (8), select **Disabled**. The other options available are:
    - **Disabled**: Throttling is turned off
    - **Conservative**: Update interval set to 100 milliseconds
    - **Moderate**: Update interval set to 500 milliseconds
    - **Aggressive**: Update interval set to 2500 milliseconds

    Adobe Flash updates the screen by default using a timer service to determine the update interval. By changing this time interval setting, you can control the frame rate of the screen updates and, therefore, reduce the bandwidth requirements.

13. Click on **Next >** to continue.
14. You will now see the **Select an RDS Farm** screen from where we can select the server for this pool, as shown in the following screenshot:

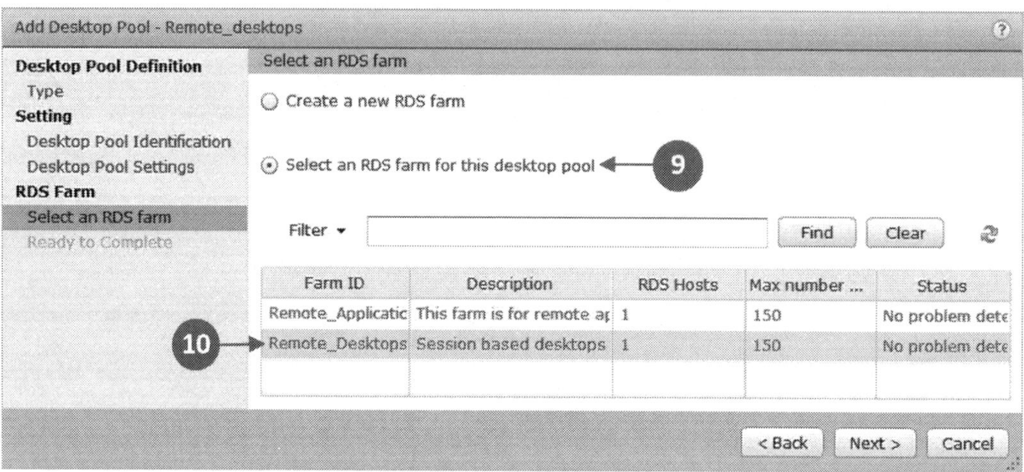

15. Click on the radio button for **Select an RDS farm for this desktop pool** (**9**), and then from the listed servers, select the **Farm ID** for `Remote_Desktops` (**10**).
16. Click on **Next >** to continue.
17. You will now see the **Ready to Complete** screen, as shown in the following screenshot. Tick the checkbox for **Entitle users after this wizard finishes** (**11**) to automatically launch the entitlement configuration screen so that we can add a user entitlement to be able to use the newly created desktop sessions:

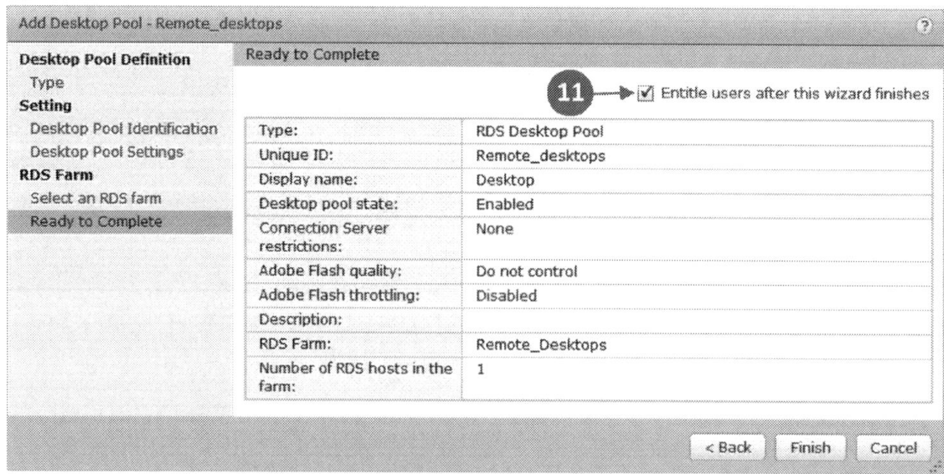

18. Once you are happy that the configuration information is correct, click on **Finish**.

In the next section, we are going to entitle a user to be able to connect to a desktop session.

Entitling users to desktop sessions

We are now going to entitle a user to be able to access desktop sessions. Perform the following steps:

1. From the last section, the **Entitlement** configuration screen should be automatically displayed, as shown in the following screenshot:

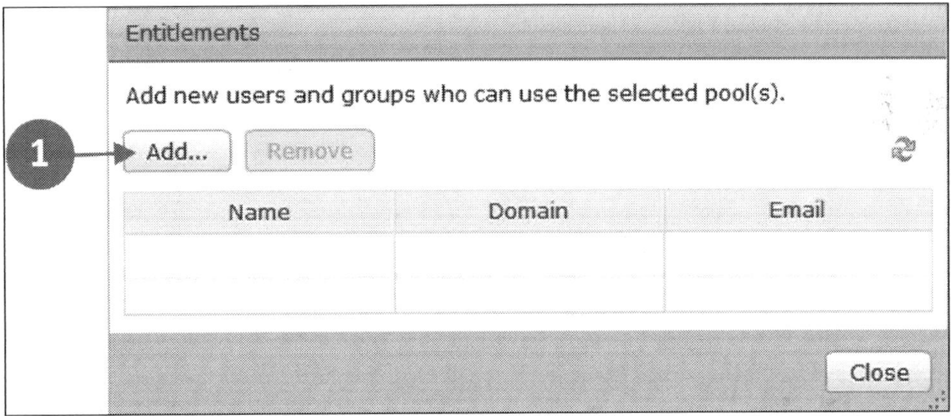

Now, we will begin with the entitling process.

2. Click on **Add...** (**1**) to add a new user entitlement. You will now see the **Find User or Group** configuration screen, as shown in the following screenshot:

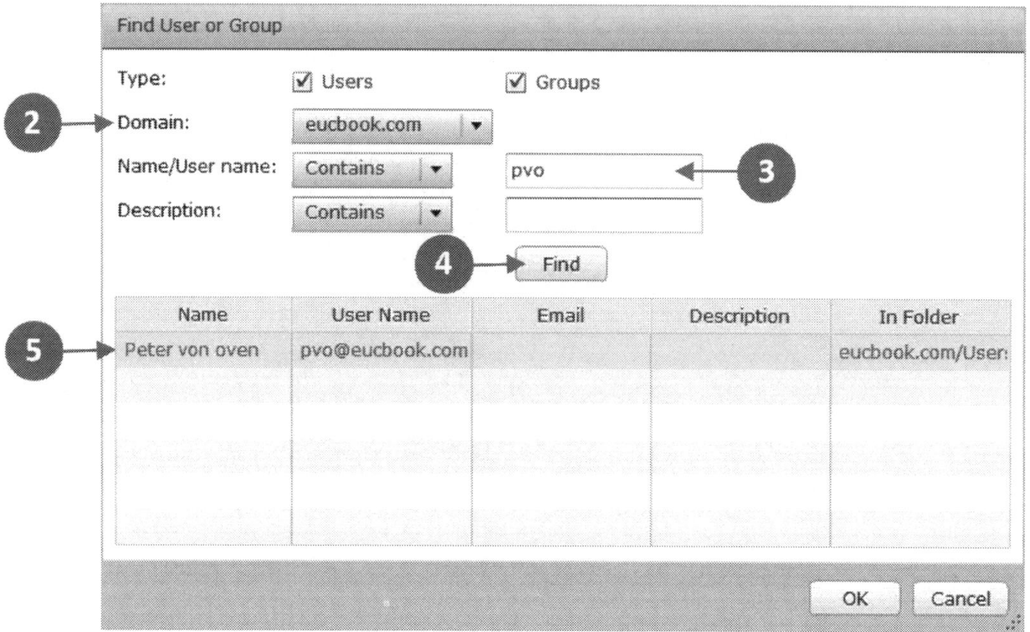

You can search by both users and groups by ticking the **Users** and **Groups** boxes at the top of the screen. We will leave them both ticked.

3. From the **Domain** drop-down menu (**2**), select the domain for the user you want to entitle. In our example, we are going to use our **eucbook.com** domain.
4. In the **Name/User name** box (**3**), enter the user details you want to entitle. In our example, we are going to entitle the user called `pvo`. Click on **Find** (**4**) to search for the user in the specified domain.
5. We should now have found the user, and their details will be displayed in the table shown (**5**). Click on the user and then click on **OK**. You will see that the user has been added, as shown in the following screenshot:

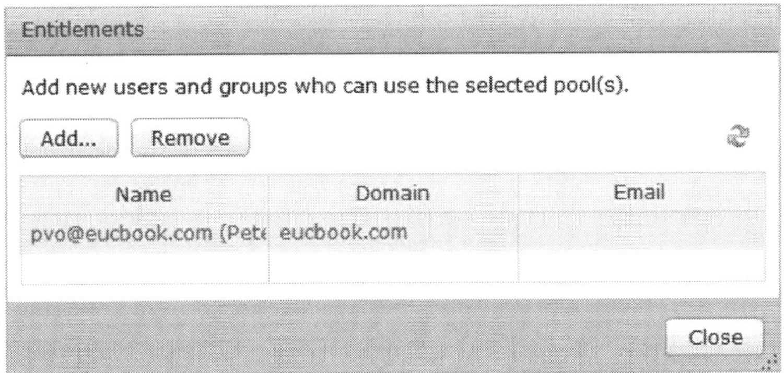

6. Click on **Close** to complete the adding of a user entitlement.

   Next, we are going to test and make sure that the entitled user can log in and access their desktop session.

7. From your desktop, launch the Horizon View Client. If you haven't already added it, enter the address of your View Connection Server or security server. In our example lab, we are using the IP address of our security server.
8. Double-click the icon for the Connection Server (**6**), as shown in the following screenshot:

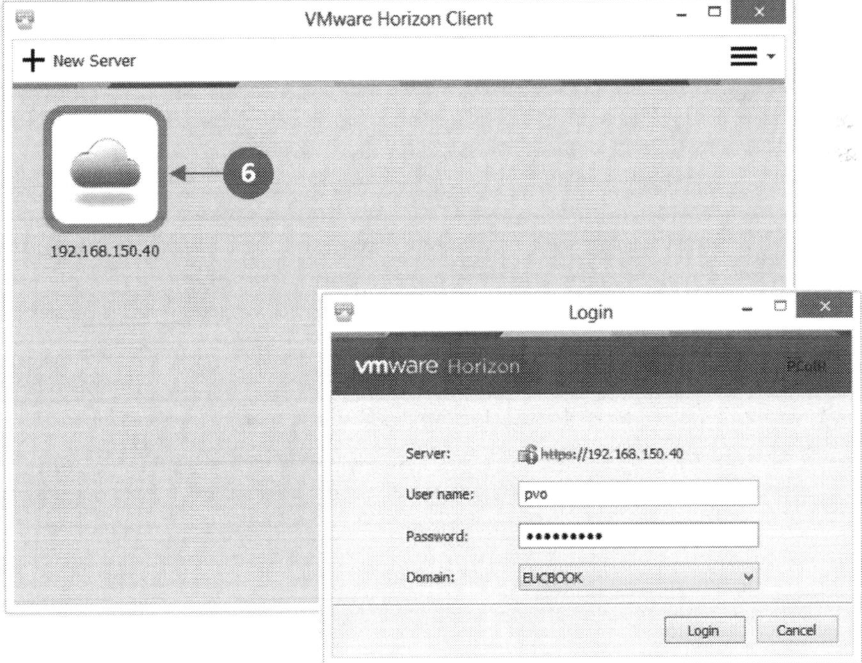

9. In the **Login** dialog box, enter the **User name** for the user that we just entitled and the user's password. Make sure the **Domain** option reflects the domain for the user.
10. Click on **Login**. You will then see the following screenshot showing the entitled desktop session:

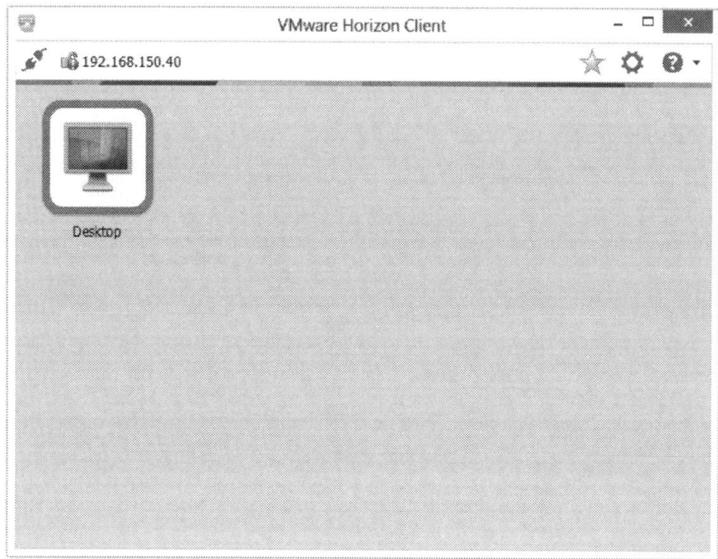

11. Double-click the icon to make sure that a desktop session is launched.
12. Once you have successfully connected to a desktop session, log out and then disconnect from the Connection Server, and then close the View Client.

As you would have just seen, the desktop session that you were connected to looks and feels like Windows Server 2012, basically because that's exactly what it is! There are some additional configuration tasks that you can perform to make it look more like a Windows 8 desktop. We will cover a couple of these in the next section.

Enhancing the end user experience

In Windows Server 2012, there are some configuration steps you can take to make the desktop GUI look like a Windows 8 desktop, which is much better for the user experience and stops them having access to server-based tools.

We are only going to cover a couple of the basics as examples, as configuring Windows Servers is out of the scope of this book, and given that there are many options, that could end up being a whole book in its own right.

Desktop experience

The first thing we can configure is to add the Desktop Experience feature to our Windows Server. We do this by performing the following steps:

1. Launch the Server Manager on the RDSH server and then in the top-right menu, navigate to **Manage | Add Roles and Features (1)**, as shown in the following screenshot:

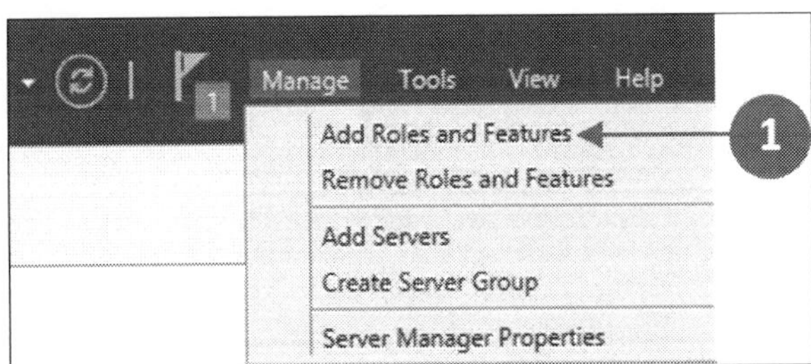

2. On the **Before you begin** screen, click on **Next >**.
3. On the **Installation Type** screen, click on the radio button for **Role-based or feature-based installation**, and then click on **Next >**.
4. On the **Server Selection** screen, click on the radio button for **Select a server from the server pool**, and then click on the server you want to add this feature to. In our example, we will select the `euc-rdsh-01.eucbook.com` server. Click on **Next >**.
5. On the **Server Roles** screen, click on **Next >**.

6. On the **Features** screen, scroll down to **User Interface and Infrastructure (2 of 3 installed)** (2) and then tick the box for **Desktop Experience** (3), as shown in the following screenshot:

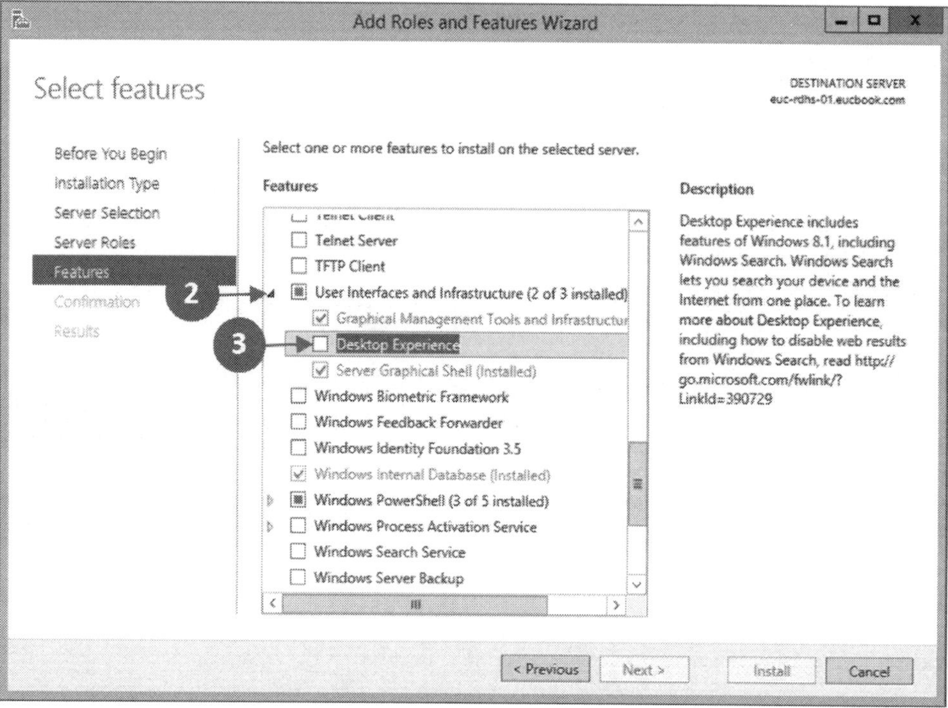

7. When you tick the box, another dialog box may appear asking you to add other features that are required by the **Desktop Experience** feature. Click on the **Add Features** button to add these features.
8. On the **Confirmation** screen, check the feature components that are going to be installed and also ensure that the box for **Restart the destination server automatically** is ticked. Click on **Install** to start the feature installation.
9. You will now see the **Installation Progress** screen, showing you how the installation is progressing. Once the installation is complete, click on **Close**.
10. You have now installed the Desktop Experience feature. Restart the server to invoke this feature. When the server reboots, you should be able to configure the appearance of the desktop interface, by adding background themes and so on.

The final thing we are going to cover is how to turn off the Server Manager.

Configuring the Server Manager

As we are using the session as a desktop, we want to prevent the Server Manager from launching.

Launch the **Server Manager** on the RDSH server. Then, from the menu in the top-right of the screen, navigate to **Manage** | **Server Manager Properties** (**1**), as shown in the following screenshot:

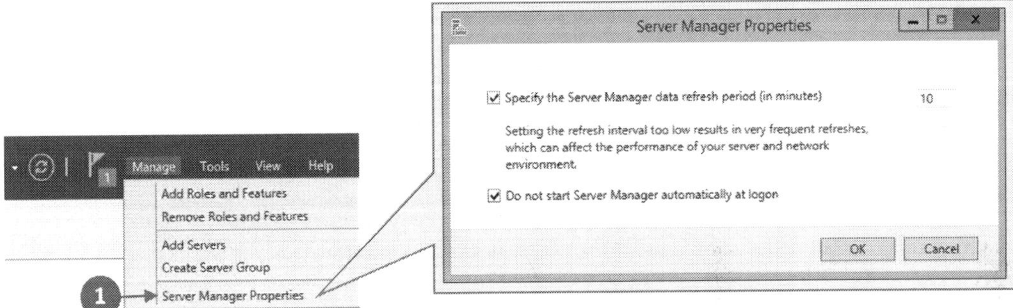

From the dialog box, tick the box for **Do not start Server manager automatically at logon**.

Summary

In this chapter, we configured the RDSH server role in order to deliver session-based desktops. We then went on to configure the View Administrator and create a farm for our desktop sessions; then, we entitled a user to be able to log in and connect to a desktop session.

Finally, we touched upon a couple of things to start you off on configuring the RDSH session to look and feel more like a desktop operating system, rather than a server operating system.

In the next chapter, we will take a closer look at the different View Client options.

12
View Client Options

This chapter will discuss the options for the View Client, both hardware and software. The View Client is used to receive and display virtual desktops and applications on the end users' devices. We will discuss the various options and why you will choose one over the other based on the use case.

Software clients

To get the best user experience, users connect to their virtual desktop from their client device using a piece of software called the Horizon View Client. The Horizon View Client is a piece of software that is installed onto the local client device and allows users to enter their login credentials, select a desktop pool, and then establish the connection to the virtual desktop.

In recent versions of Horizon View, the software client has been unbundled from the major View releases, which means that the client downloads are updated more often and without waiting for the next version of View. This reflects the fast pace at which new devices come to the market.

There are a number of different platform versions available, depending on the choice of end point device. In this section, I am going to give you a high-level overview of each of the available versions along with any specific requirements. The download page can be found at `http://www.vmware.com/go/viewclients`.

Windows client

The Horizon View Client for Windows allows you to access your Windows virtual desktop from a Windows-based device and delivers the best possible user experience on either a LAN or a WAN connection. The following screenshot shows the Horizon Client for Windows; we can see two VDI desktops and a number of published RDSH applications:

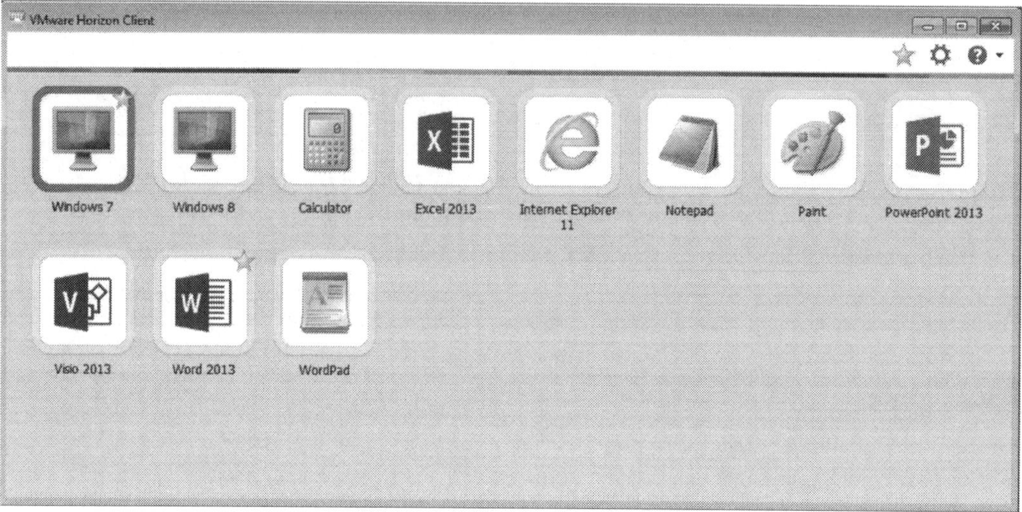

With the latest client and the latest versions of View, USB 3.0 redirection is supported from the guest to the VDI desktop, among other improvements in performance, printing, and ease of use.

VMware Horizon View Client 3.3 for Windows requires one of the following operating systems:

- 32-bit or 64-bit Windows 8, 8.1, or 8.1 Update, Enterprise, or Pro Edition
- 32-bit or 64-bit Windows 7 SP1 or no service pack, Home, Enterprise, Ultimate, or Professional Edition
- 32-bit Windows Vista SP2, Home, Enterprise, Ultimate, or Business Edition
- 32-bit Windows XP SP3, Home or Professional Edition

VMware Horizon Client for Windows is supported with the latest maintenance releases of VMware View 4.6.x, 5.0.x, or 5.1.x; Horizon View 5.2.x or 5.3.x; or VMware Horizon 6.0 or 6.0.1.

> The Horizon View Client requires SSL for connections to the View Connection Server. Therefore, you must enter a fully qualified domain name for the View Connection Server, rather than just its IP address, in the View Server field of the Horizon View Client.

Android client

The Horizon View Client for Android-based devices, like the Windows client, allows you to access your Windows virtual desktop from an Android tablet or smartphone device and delivers the best possible user experience on either a LAN or a WAN connection. It can be downloaded from the Google Play Store.
In the following screenshot, we can see the Horizon Client for Android that displays two VDI desktops and two RDS desktops as well as a number of RDSH published applications. In the screenshot on the left-hand side, we can see Microsoft PowerPoint and Adobe Reader running as RDSH-published applications alongside the Unity Touch feature being used, allowing you to easily run applications from the slide-in menu on the left:

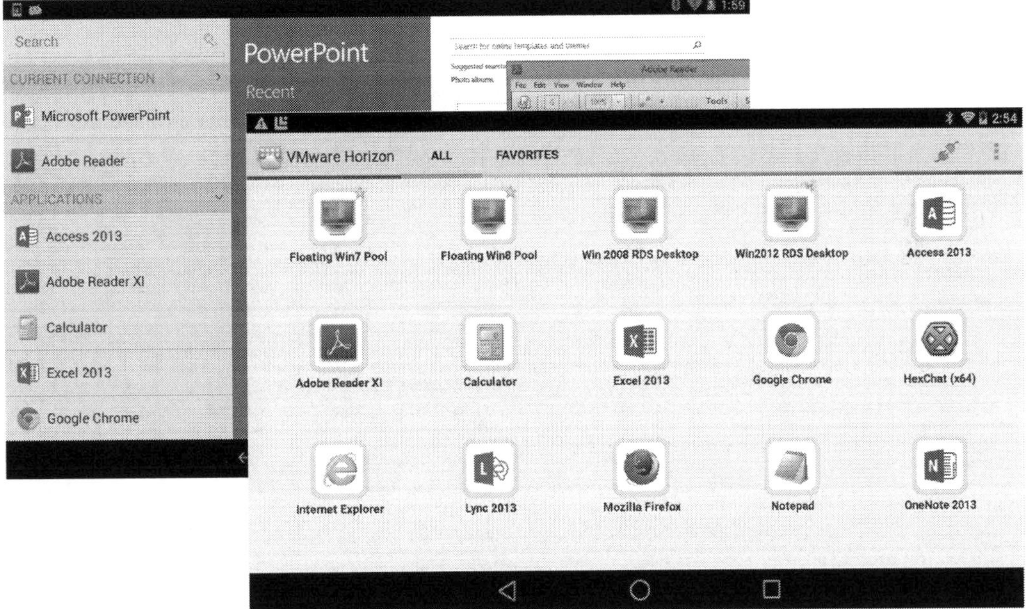

The Horizon View Client supports native Android gestures for quick and easy navigation around the desktop. When working on a Windows desktop, the fullscreen touchpad feature lets you touch anywhere on the screen to move the mouse pointer around the Windows virtual desktop. The Unity Touch sidebar makes it easy to browse, search, open, close Windows applications and files, as well as switch between running applications, all without using the Windows start menu or taskbar.

The Horizon Client supports features in Horizon View such as Unity Touch, fullscreen mode, dictation (Android 4.x), and better language and localization support.

The Horizon Client for Android requires the Android 2.3.3 (Gingerbread) or later operating system and is supported on VMware View 4.6.1 or later.

The iPad and iPhone iOS clients

The Horizon View Client for iOS allows you to access your Windows virtual desktop from an Android tablet or smartphone device and delivers the best possible user experience on either a LAN or a WAN connection. In the following screenshot, we can see three screens taken from the iOS Horizon Client. In the first screen, we are connecting to the Horizon Connection Servers, the second screen shows the desktops that are available to us, and the final screen shows us connected to the Windows desktop with the input options menu open, allowing us to change settings and change the mouse mode as well as display the keyboard and more:

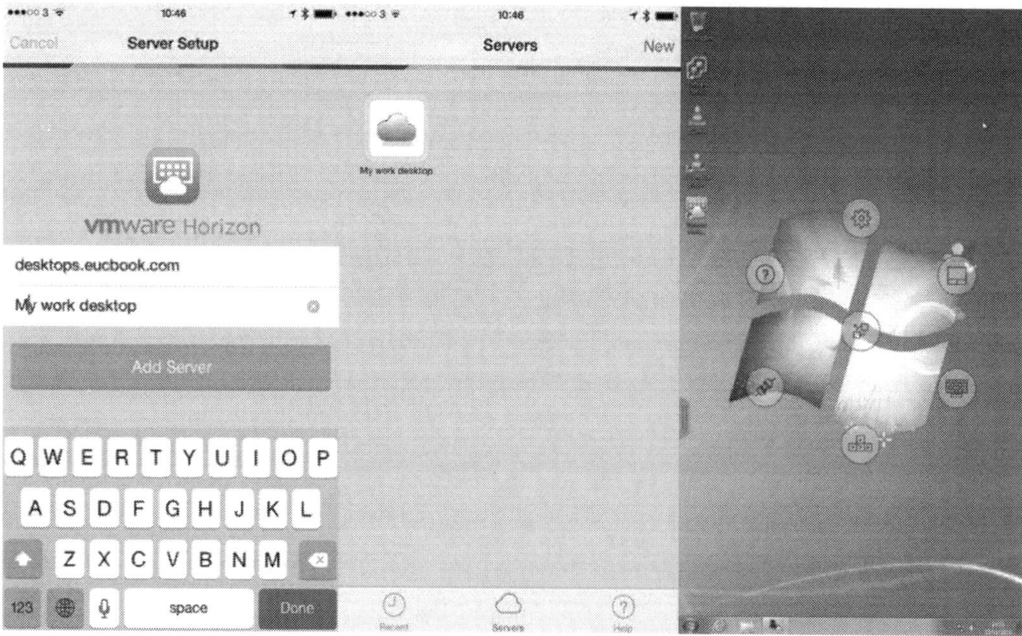

The Horizon View Client for the iPad and iPhone supports native iPad and iPhone gestures for quick and easy navigation around your desktop. As with the Android client, when working on a Windows desktop, the fullscreen touchpad feature lets you touch anywhere on the screen to move the mouse pointer around the Windows virtual desktop. The Unity Touch sidebar makes it easy to browse, search, open, close Windows applications and files, and switch between running applications, all without using the Windows start menu or taskbar.

The Horizon Client supports features in Horizon View such as Unity Touch (iOS 5 or later), fullscreen mode, iOS dictation, better language, localization support, and an enhanced presentation mode, allowing you to use an external monitor or AirPlay to show your View desktop while your iPad or iPhone turns into a keyboard and touchpad.

The Horizon View Client for iOS requires the iOS 6.0 or later operating system and is supported on the following devices:

- iPhone 4, 4S, 5, 5S, 5C, 6, 6 Plus, and iPad 2 and iPad (3rd generation)
- iPad (4th generation), iPad mini, iPad mini with Retina display, and iPad Air

The Horizon View Client for iOS is supported with VMware View 4.6.1 or later. To install and/or upgrade your Horizon View Client for iOS, you can either download from the VMware client download page or go to the Apple store and download it like any other application.

Linux client

The Horizon View Client for Linux allows you to access your Windows virtual desktop from a Linux device and delivers the best possible user experience on either a LAN or WAN connection using the PCoIP protocol.

The Linux Client has the following requirements:

- 32-bit Ubuntu Linux 12.04 or 14.04 operating system
- Supported with VMware View 4.6.1 or later

In the latest 3.1 release, the Linux client now supports a hosted RDSH application within Horizon View and USB 3.0 support.

Mac OS X client

The Horizon View Client for Mac allows you to access your Windows virtual desktop from a Mac and deliver the best possible user experience on either a LAN or WAN connection using the PCoIP protocol.

The following screenshot shows the Mac OS X client for Horizon, it also demonstrates the Real Time Audio and Visual functionality available in this client alongside the Linux and Windows clients, allowing us to pass through the webcam and microphone to the View desktop:

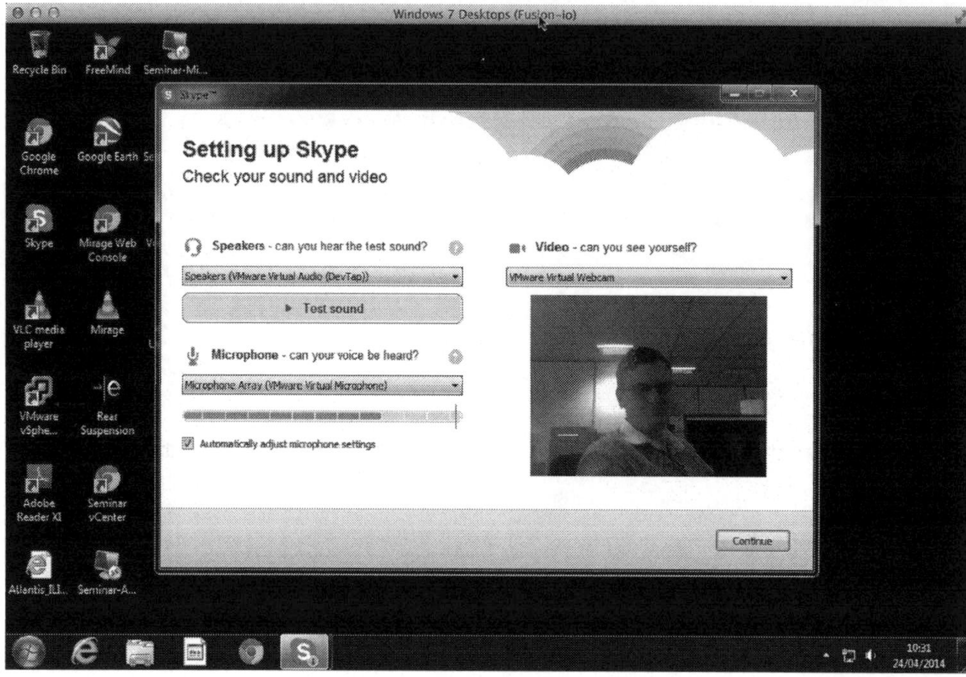

The latest 3.0 release of the Mac Client supports the following operating systems:

- Mac OS X Snow Leopard (version 10.6.8)
- Mac OS X Lion (version 10.7)
- Mac OS X Mountain Lion (version 10.8)
- Mac OS X Mavericks (version 10.9)

The Mac client supports the following feature set, including:

- RSA SecurID
- Single sign-on
- PCoIP display protocol
- RDP display protocol
- USB access
- Real Time Audio and Video (as per the preceding screenshot)
- Location-based printing and more

In the latest version, the feature set has been further expanded to include USB 3.0 Support, automatic reconnection after sleep, and more. You are able to utilize webcams and audio input devices with the Mac client; there are a number of configuration options you are able to set such as the quality of the image received from the webcam. By default, the webcam will be configured to use a resolution of 320 x 240; however, you are able to customize this using the terminal application on the Mac, the following example would set a resolution of 1024 x 768:

```
defaults write com.vmware.rtav srcWCamFrameWidth 1024
defaults write com.vmware.rtav srcWCamFrameHeight 768
```

You are able to check your current configuration by running the following command within the terminal application:

```
defaults read com.vmware.rtav
```

Hardware clients

One of the things I hear a lot from speaking with customers is that the endpoint device is irrelevant when connecting to a virtual desktop, so that means I can buy the cheapest device possible and that will be fine, right? The correct answer is that it depends on the use case for the users and what their requirements around features and functionality are. Then, you can choose the most suitable endpoint device to connect from.

The other confusion that I see is what is the difference between a thin client and a Zero client, and is there actually a difference?

In this section, I am going to cover the different types of hardware clients available and the use case for which one to choose.

Thin clients

A thin client is a hardware endpoint device that's used to connect to a network and deliver a remote desktop session. Unlike a typical PC or "fat client", that has the memory, storage, and computing power to run applications, a thin client relies on the computing power residing on servers in the datacenter to do the processing.

Typically, a client device will have just enough processing power and resources to access and use the computing resources of the server. They have no storage and more importantly no moving parts, which means they don't go wrong very often. Due to the reduced CPU and memory capacity, a thin client will draw a fraction of the power that a PC would normally need, meaning that thin clients should be cheaper to run and manage, as well as have longer life cycles.

One thing they do have in common with a PC is an operating system. A thin client will have its own local operating system installed, typically embedded on a flash card, and would be running the vendor's own cut-down version of Linux distribution such as Dell Wyse ThinOS or Microsoft Windows Embedded. In addition, it would be running the appropriate client software to connect to the appropriate virtual desktop—that is, PCoIP for View and ICA for Citrix, and so on. Usually, a thin client will have them all installed giving you the choice.

Now, this is where you need to make the right choice of device, as the operating system will be embedded onto the device. The use case for the user will typically dictate the type of device. For example, if you are going to deploy unified communications with Microsoft Lync 2013, then you will need a Windows Embedded operating system, as it will more than likely require some of the Windows multimedia functionality. Always check before going off and buying the cheapest device.

There are also a couple of other points to bear in mind with thin clients. If the device is running on a local operating system, this will still need to be managed and maintained. The other consideration is around licensing and the fact that you will need a Windows VDA license if you are connecting from a non-Windows device. This needs to be taken into account when looking at cost models.

Zero clients

A Zero client performs the same functionality as a thin client; however, instead of an operating system, a Zero client will have a highly tuned on-board processor specifically designed for one of the VDI protocols (PCoIP, HDX, or RemoteFX). For VMware View, a Zero client would use the on-board Tera2 hardware chipset such as a Dell Wyse P25 or a 10ZiG V1200. These devices are still small, light, have no moving parts, and consume minimal power, just like a thin client.

Most of the decoding and display processes take place on dedicated hardware and therefore are more efficient and deliver better performance than using a software client, and a standard CPU and GPU setup as with a thin client.

Zero clients have bootup speeds of just a few seconds and are immune to viruses, decreasing the overall downtime of the device and increasing the productivity to the end user. The Zero client device requires very little maintenance and rarely needs an update, unless there is a significant change/enhancement to the VDI protocol or the occasional BIOS-related update.

There are a couple of things to watch out for. First is the licensing, as these devices are not running an operating system, you need to look at VDA licensing for using a non-Windows device. The final thing is that if you change your VDI infrastructure from PCoIP to a new protocol, then the device is not able to be used with a different protocol, so you lose the flexibility that you get with a thin client. However, you will get much better performance.

Repurposed PCs (thick clients)

It is also possible to re-purpose existing physical PCs to be used as "thick clients"; there are a number of ways to achieve this, but you must ensure it is simple for the user to use and does not confuse the usage of the virtual desktop.

The two most popular ways of creating a thick client would be, first, to use local policy or Group Policy to lock down the Windows PC and to change the shell to the Horizon Client only, and, second, to use third-party software such as Devon IT's VDI Blaster technology; this allows a simple thin client operating system to be deployed and configured on the users' machines.

Don't forget, if going for the first option and keeping Windows installed on the thick client, you may need to consider anti-virus software and security policies more so than with a cut-down and restricted Linux-based thin client operating system. . Another option is TinyCore Builder for VMware View, which allows you to create a TinyCore Linux ISO image to boot your end point devices from. It includes the View Client and the build is automated so that you can pre-populate the ISO with the details of your environment. To create a build follow this link: `http://repurpose.vmwarecloud.at/`

HTML5 browser desktop access

In the previous sections, we have talked about either using a software-based or hardware-based client to access our virtual desktop from, but there is also a third method and that's by using an HTML5-enabled browser on any device. The key use case for using this method is when installing client software on an endpoint device is not possible. For example, you might want to use a Chromebook (there is no client for the Chrome OS today) or you might want to use a public-facing endpoint in a hotel lobby, for example, where the device is locked down and you cannot install the client software. This is where this use case comes in, allowing you to access your virtual desktop machine using an HTML5-enabled web browser, which also requires no additional plugins or software to be downloaded and installed. The HTML desktop access is what is referred to as the VMware Blast protocol.

To connect to your virtual desktop machine using the browser, open the browser, and in the address bar, type the address of your Connection Server. In our example lab, the address is `https://desktops.eucbook.com`.

Before you access your virtual desktop machine, you will first see a web page that displays two options. You can either download the Horizon View Client or you can continue and connect via HTML. This is shown in the following screenshot:

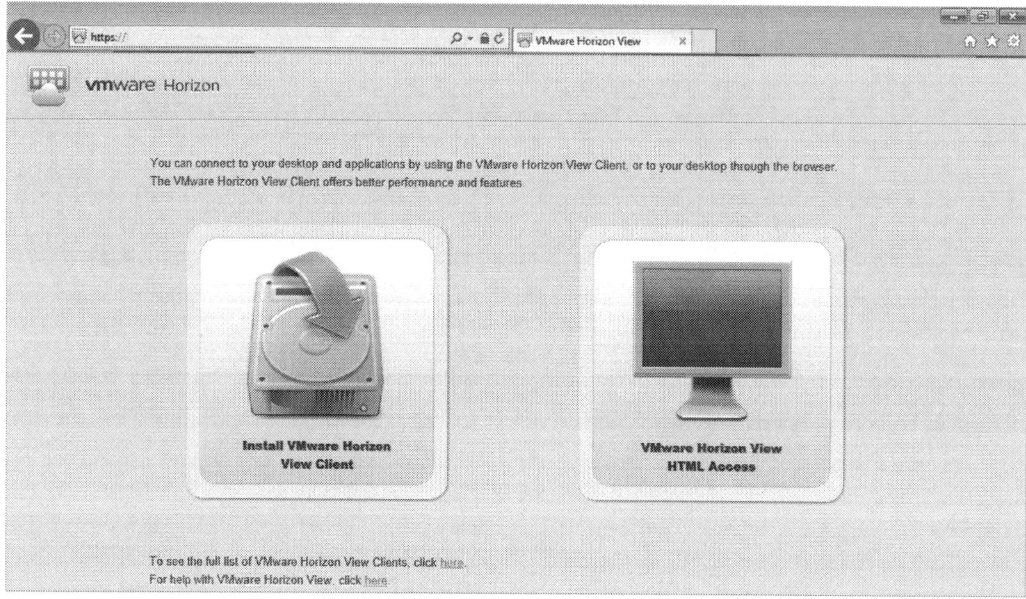

This web page is configurable, allowing you to personalize it to your own specific environment. You can configure the following:

- Hide the HTML Access icon
- Hide the View Client icon
- Change the URL of the web page for downloading the View Client
- Create links for specific View Client installers
- Configure other links on the page

In this example, we are going to use the HTML access method, so click on the **VMware Horizon View HTML Access** button. You will then be prompted to log in using the credentials you would normally use for logging in to the network. This is shown in the following screenshot:

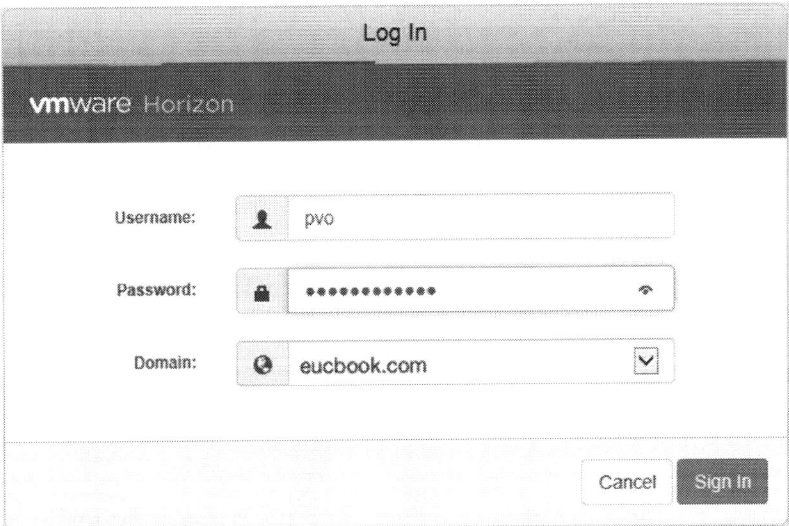

In the following screenshot, you have the option of selecting the virtual desktop machine that you want to access. The virtual desktops displayed relate to the desktop pools to which you are entitled to. In this example, the user is entitled to the Windows 8 desktop pool.

If you click on the **Windows 8.1 Desktop** option, you will now see another browser tab open. In this tab, you will see that your virtual desktop machine is being displayed in the browser, as shown in the following screenshot:

To use the HTML access feature, you need to run a supported browser. The currently supported browsers are:

- Chrome 28 or later
- Internet Explorer 9 or later
- Safari 6 or later
- Mobile Safari on iOS devices running iOS 6 or later
- Firefox 21 or later

You also need to make sure that you have enabled the desktop pool for HTML access as well as have the remote experience agent installed on the virtual desktop.

Summary

In this chapter, we took a closer look at the options for connecting to the virtual desktop machine from our endpoint device. We discussed software-based clients, hardware-based clients, and the HTML access feature. We also looked at the pros and cons of each type of access method and why you might choose one over the other. In the next chapter, we will discuss how to upgrade from a previous version of Horizon View to Horizon View 6; you will also be able to take the learnings from the next chapter for future upgrades.

13

Upgrading to Horizon View 6

In this chapter, we will cover the upgrade process and recommendations for upgrading your VMware View 5.3 environment to VMware Horizon View 6.0. We will start by discussing the elements that need to be considered before undertaking the upgrade, how we should undertake the upgrade to ensure there is minimum disruption to our users, and finally the step-by-step process to complete the upgrade.

Compatibility and the upgrade procedure

The first element that we should be aware of is that with Horizon View 6.1, the View Transfer Server role has been discontinued. The View Transfer Server role enables you to be able to change the mode of VDI desktops to offline to be used in scenarios with no Internet connectivity when used in conjunction with the View Client with Local Mode. As such, if you are currently using this feature, you will need to understand how this is going to affect your users and put suitable alternatives in place. As an alternative VMware recommend using VMware Mirage to manage physical desktops and in combination with Horizon Flex this solution can be used to deliver containerized desktops that can be used offline.

Before undertaking any upgrades, you should start by reading the release notes and the upgrade guide for the product in question; this does not differ from Horizon View. With a number of interdependent components, we need to ensure that we undertake the upgrade in the correct order to minimize the risk of failure and disruption to our users.

VMware publishes a product compatibility matrix as shown in the following screenshot that really sets the picture of how the upgrade needs to be performed:

	Connection Server 5.3.x	Security Server 5.3.x	View Composer 5.3.x	View Client (Windows) 5.x
Connection Server 6.1	Only during upgrade	Only if paired before upgrade	No	Yes
Security Server 6.1	No	N/A	No	Yes
View Composer 6.1	Only during upgrade	Only during upgrade	N/A	N/A
View Agent 6.1	Only during upgrade	No	No	Only during upgrade
Horizon Client 3.3	Yes	Yes	Yes	N/A

As such, the process by which the upgrade needs to take place is as follows:

- View Composer upgrade
- View Connection Server upgrade
- View Security Server upgrade
- Upgrading Group Policies
- Upgrading vCenter (if required)
- Upgrading ESXi Hosts and Virtual Machine Hardware/Tools (if required)
- Upgrading View Agents
- Recomposing desktop pools

We will also need to think about the impact of any upgrade that may need to be undertaken on our users; for instance, we will not want to upgrade a View Connection Server in the middle of a working day with potentially 2,000 users connected through it. As such, we will normally schedule the upgrades out of hours or ensure that each View Connection Server is removed from the load balancer the night before the planned upgrade. We can also decide to build new View Connection Servers rather than upgrading and simply removing the old Connection Servers once complete.

Upgrading View Composer

You are going to start your upgrade to your Horizon View installation by upgrading the View Composer Server.

Prerequisites to upgrade

We need to perform the following steps prior to commencing with the upgrade to the View Composer Server:

1. Check the prerequisites with the VMware Horizon View installation guide to ensure all components to be upgraded meet the minimum requirements for resources, operating system, and applicable database versions.
2. If your View Composer Server is installed in a virtual machine, snapshot the virtual machine.
3. Back up your vCenter and View Composer databases.
4. Back up the folder containing the SSL certificates on your View Composer Server at `%ALLUSERSPROFILE%\Application Data\VMware\VMware VirtualCenter`.
5. Document the IP address and hostname of your vCenter Server.
6. Ensure the user names and passwords are documented for the accounts used to access your composer database.

7. For all linked clone desktops, disable provisioning of new virtual desktop machines, as shown in the following screenshot. Navigate to **Pools** (**1**) | **Status** (**2**) | **Disable Provisioning...** (**3**).

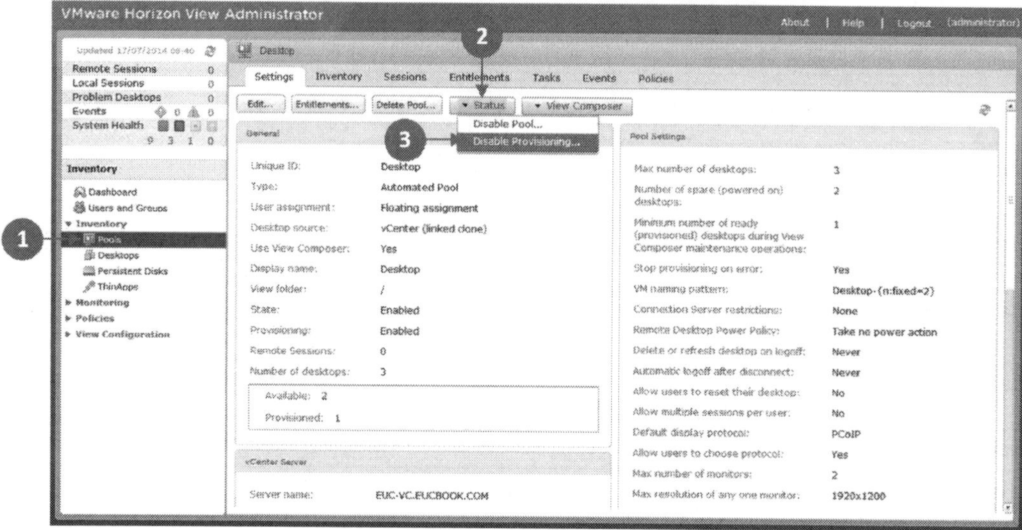

8. Modify any desktop pools that are set to refresh on logoff to ensure they are set to never refresh. Select **Pools** (**4**) from the **Inventory** pane, right-click and select **Edit...** (**5**), as shown in the following screenshot:

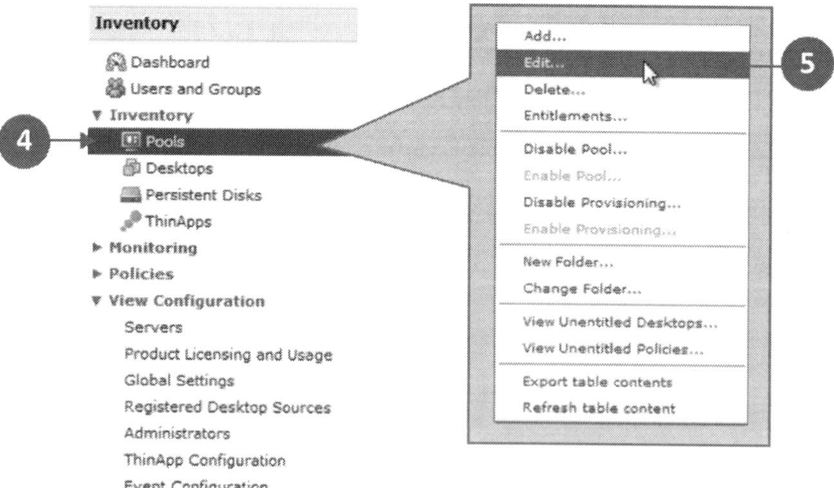

9. Click on the box for **Delete or refresh desktop on logoff:** box (**6**), and select **Never** (**7**), as shown in the following screenshot:

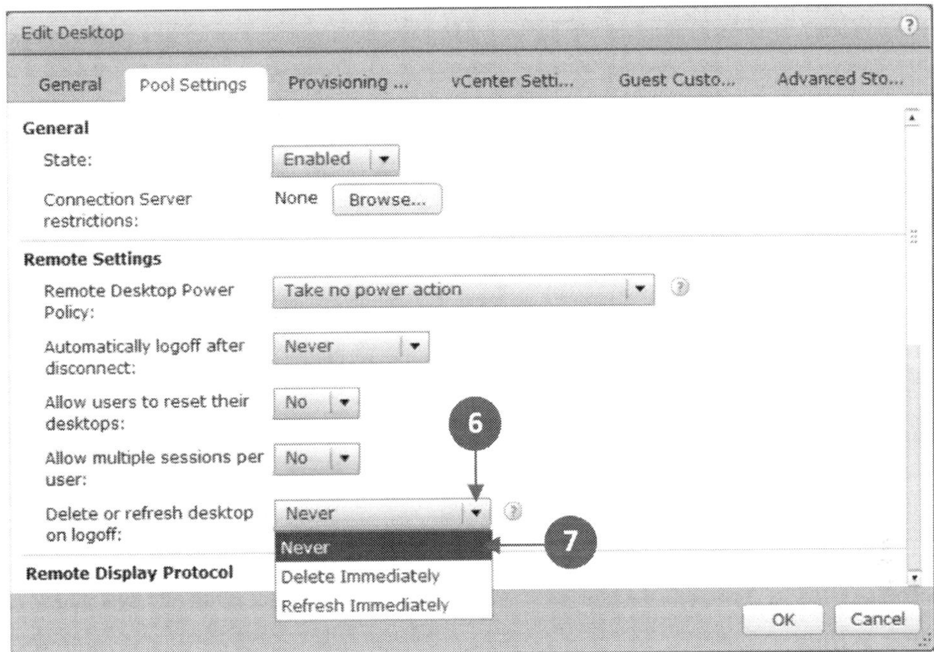

10. Cancel any tasks for desktops that have been scheduled to refresh or recompose. Click on **Pools** (**8**), and select the **Tasks** tab (**9**). Select **Cancel task...** (**10**), as shown in the following screenshot:

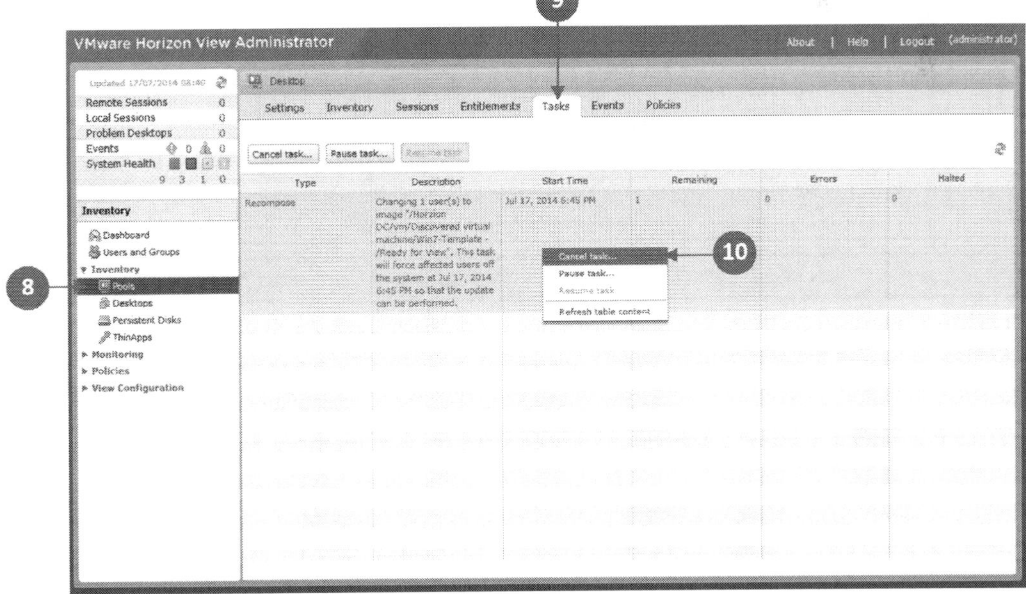

Completing the View Composer upgrade

Once we have completed all the prerequisites, and we have planned the upgrades as to have the minimal effect on the end users, we are able to start the upgrade procedure by upgrading view composer. First-off, ensure you have carried out all the prerequisites, and perform the following steps:

1. On your View Composer Server, find and launch the VMware View Composer 6.1 installer, as shown in the following screenshot:

Name	Date modified	Type	Size
VMware-viewconnectionserver-x86_64-6.1.0-2509221	3/18/2015 1:53 PM	Application	175,837 KB
VMware-viewcomposer-6.1.0-2506641	3/18/2015 1:57 PM	Application	32,084 KB
VMware-viewagent-x86_64-6.1.0-2509441	3/18/2015 1:56 PM	Application	161,800 KB
VMware-viewagent-direct-connection-x86_64-6.1.0-2509221	3/18/2015 1:57 PM	Application	15,144 KB
VMware-viewagent-direct-connection-6.1.0-2509221	3/18/2015 1:57 PM	Application	13,719 KB
VMware-viewagent-6.1.0-2509441	3/18/2015 1:54 PM	Application	122,825 KB
VMware-personamanagement-x86_64-6.1.0-2509221	3/18/2015 1:56 PM	Application	18,387 KB
VMware-personamanagement-6.1.0-2509221	3/18/2015 1:56 PM	Application	12,478 KB
VMware-Horizon-View-HTML-Access-2.6.0-2329873	3/18/2015 1:58 PM	Compressed (zipp...	1,869 KB
VMware-Horizon-View-Extras-Bundle-3.3.0-2491779	3/18/2015 1:57 PM	Compressed (zipp...	2,694 KB

2. We are now going to follow the steps in the Composer installation wizard. Launch the View Composer installer and click on **Next >** on the welcome screen, on the following screen accept the EULA, and then accept the default installation folder location.

3. On the **Database Information** page, we will need to enter the details for the DSN for the View Composer database. Enter the name of the DSN (**1**), followed by the username (**2**) and the password for that user (**3**), as shown in the following screenshot:

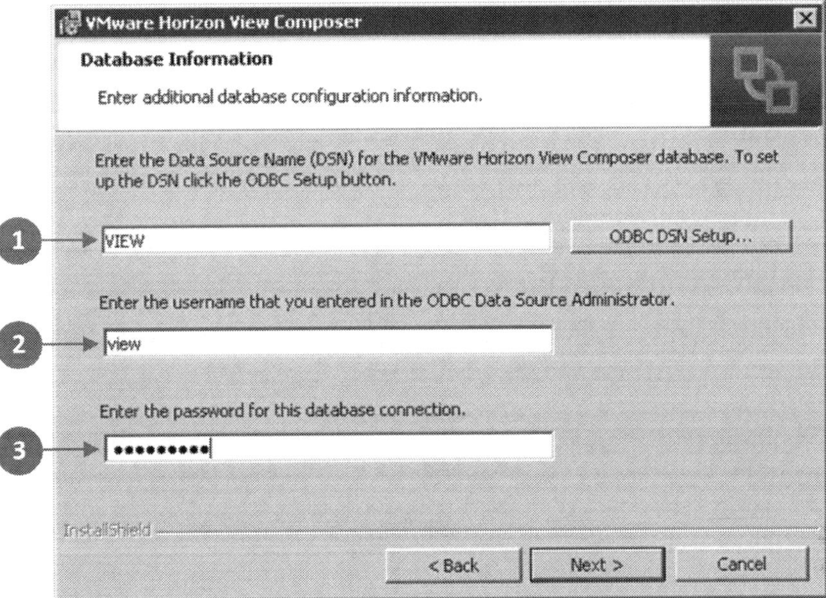

4. We should be able to leave the **SOAP Port:** as is it, unless it has previously been changed and isn't reflected correctly, as shown in the following screenshot:

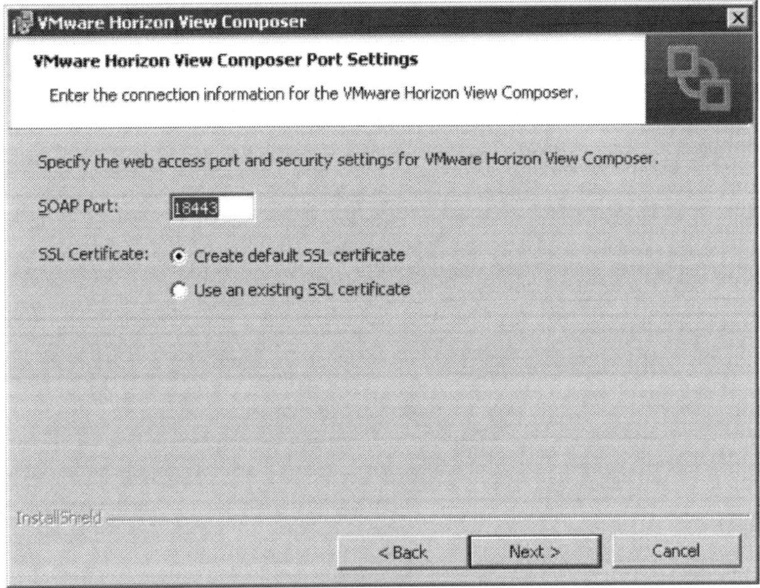

5. Finally, we are going to click on **Install** to start the installation, as shown in the following screenshot:

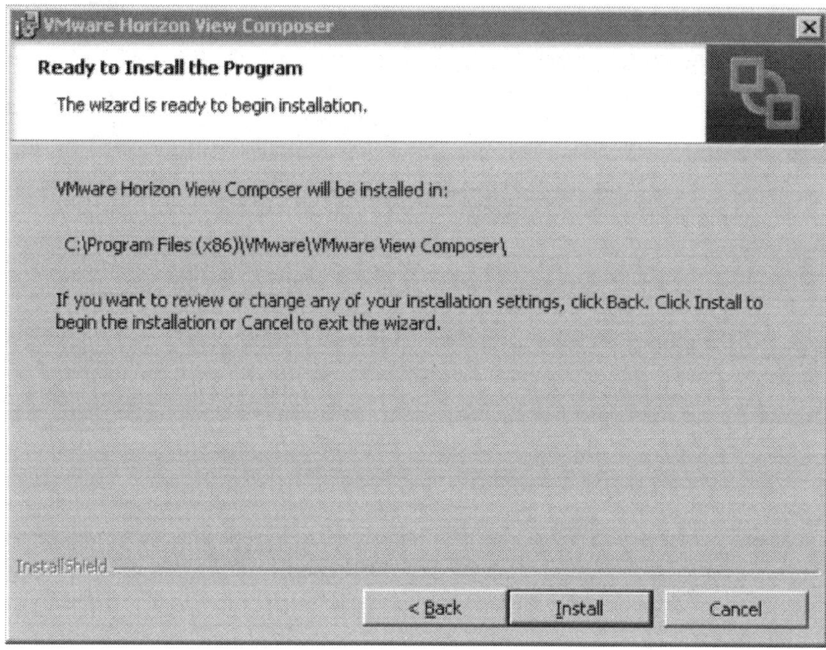

6. The upgrade will run through and once completed we will be asked to restart the server, as shown in the following screenshot:

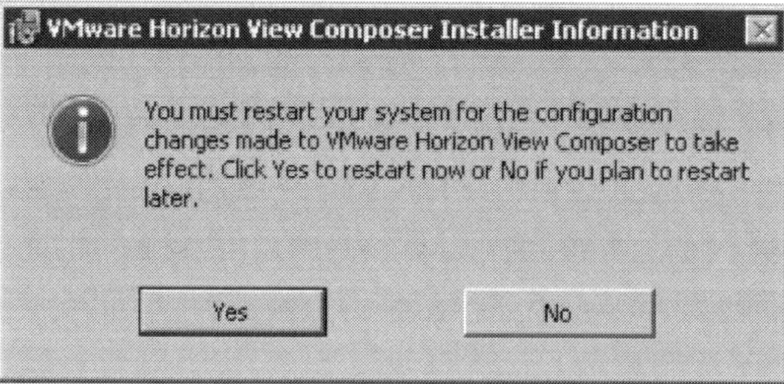

7. As the Horizon View Composer Server doesn't have a GUI associated with it, it can be hard to see whether the upgrade completed successfully. The easiest place to check this is within the Windows **Program and Features** page checking the version number noted at the bottom when selected, as shown in the following screenshot (**1**):

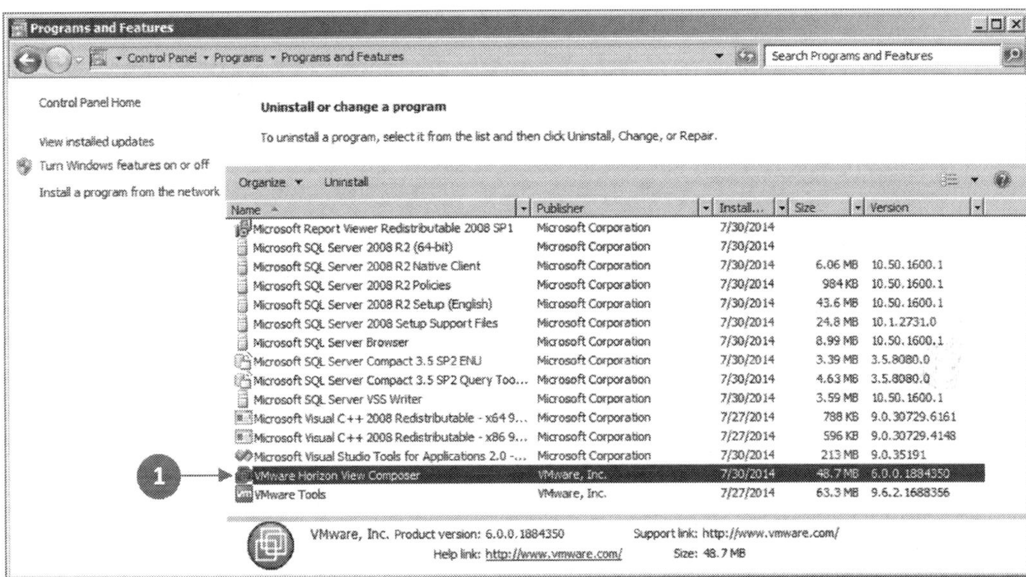

8. We should also check that the relevant services have started ok, as shown in the following screenshot:

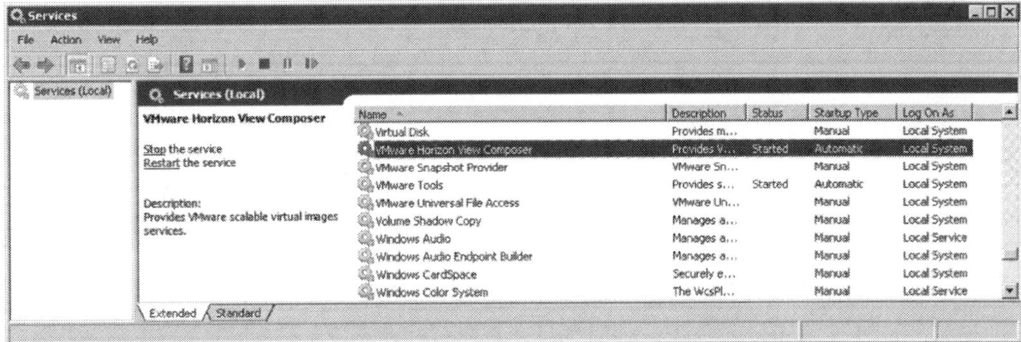

9. You also need to run through the View Composer verification wizard from inside the View Administrator Console, by logging into the web interface, selecting **View Configuration**, and then clicking on **Servers**. Click on the **vCenter Servers** tab and select your vCenter from the list. Click on **Edit...**, as shown in the following screenshot:

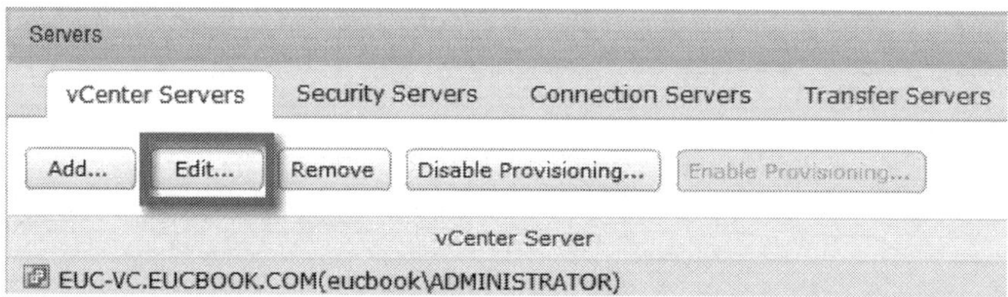

10. Then click on **Edit...** (**1**) to edit the **View Composer Server Settings** option, as can be seen in the following screenshot; finally, we will select **Verify Server Information** (**2**), before closing the boxes by selecting **OK**. This will confirm that the View Connection Server is talking to the newly upgraded Composer Server:

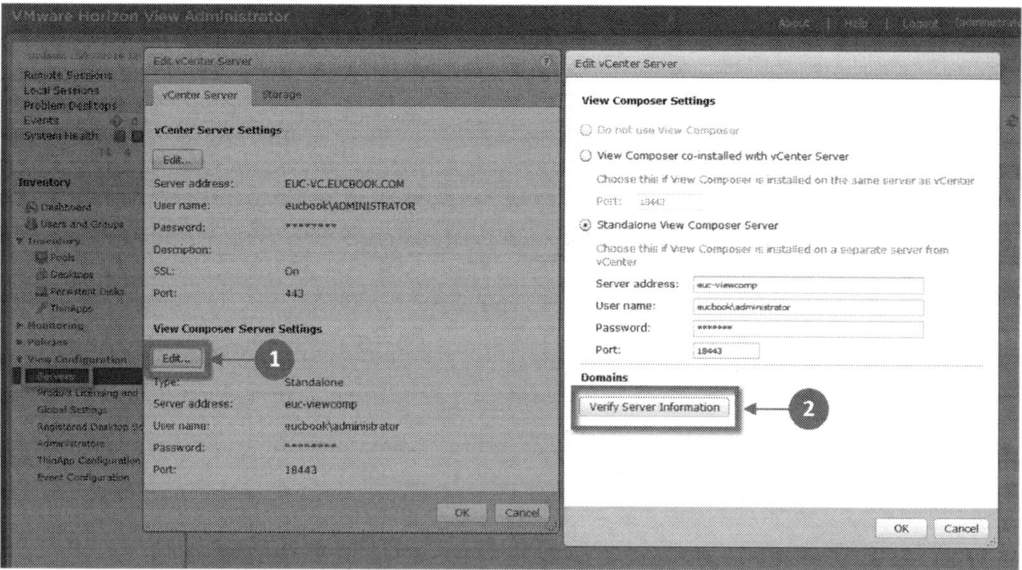

The upgrade procedure for the View Composer Server is now complete. Obviously, if you are using multiple Composer Servers, you will need to repeat these steps on all Composer Servers.

Upgrading the View Connection Server

You are now in a position to move onto upgrading all the View Connection Servers within your infrastructure.

Prerequisites to upgrade

Prior to starting with the upgrade, there are a number of prerequisites we need to check:

1. Check the prerequisites with the VMware Horizon View installation guide to ensure all components to be upgraded meet the minimum requirements for resources, operating system, and so on.
2. If your View Connection Server is installed in a virtual machine, snapshot the virtual machine. Please note, if you need to recover this snapshot, you will first need to uninstall any replicated Connection Servers before reverting the master to the snapshot.
3. Ensure that local mode is not utilized within your View deployment, if it is, ensure all users' desktops are checked in, and then remove the transfer server from View. To do this, click on **Servers** (**1**) and then on the **Transfer Servers** tab (**2**). Right-click on the **Transfer Server** and select **Remove...** (**3**), as shown in the following screenshot:

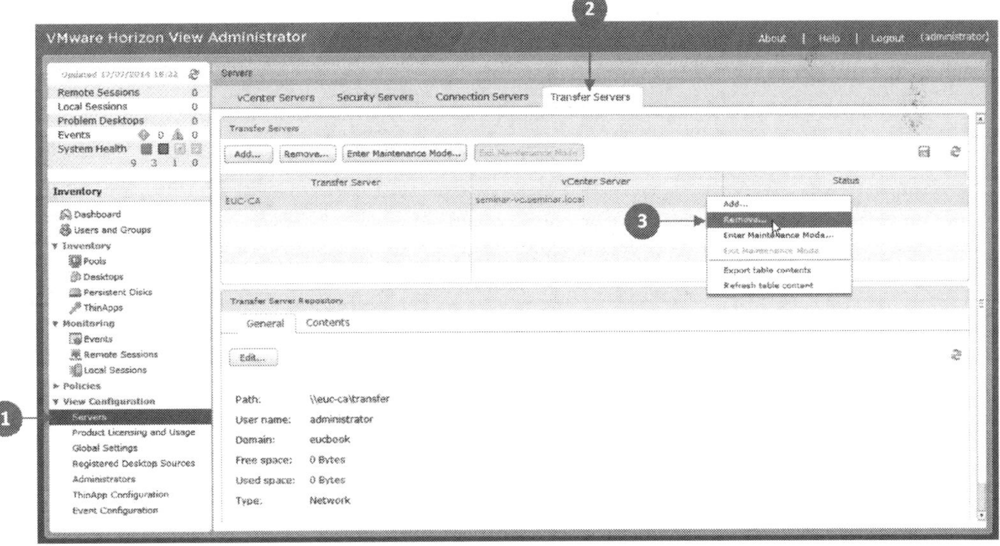

4. Ensure your documentation is up to date, including pool configuration, global configuration settings, IP addresses, batch files, SQL credentials for the event database, and load balancer configuration. To check this, click on **Global Settings** (**4**), as shown in the following screenshot:

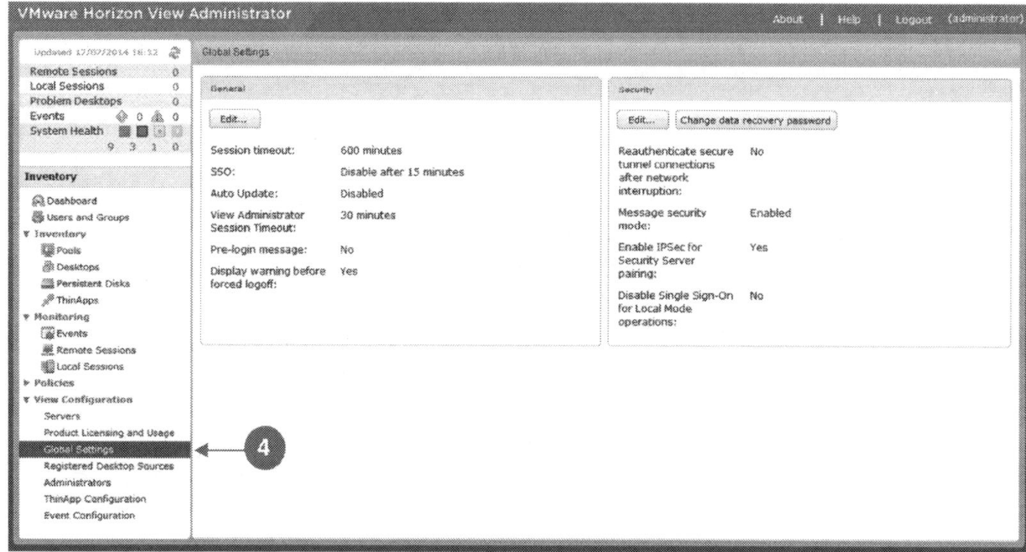

5. Use the `vdmexport.exe` command line utility to back up the existing configuration help within the LDAP database. From the command line, run the following command:

```
vdmexport > {backup location\filename.ldf}
```

In our example, it looks something like the following screenshot:

Completing the View Connection Server upgrade

Please perform the following steps to complete the View Connection Server upgrade:

1. Ensure you have carried out all the prerequisites.

2. On your View Connection Server, locate the VMware View Connection Server 6 installer, as shown in the following screenshot:

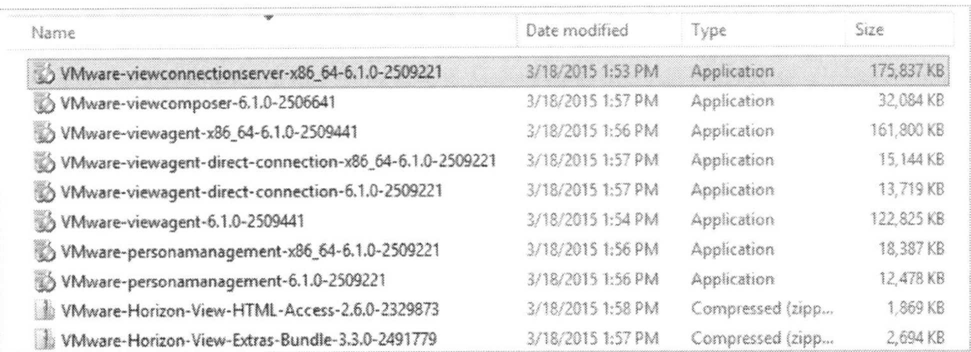

3. We are going to start the installer to proceed with the upgrade process. Click on **Next >** to continue, as shown in the following screenshot:

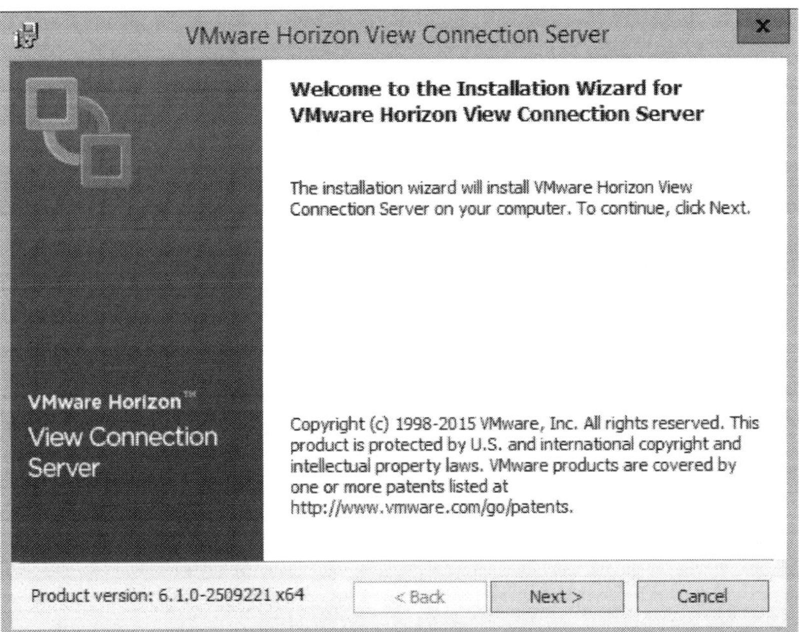

4. We are going to accept the EULA and then select **Install** to begin the upgrade process, as shown in the following screenshot:

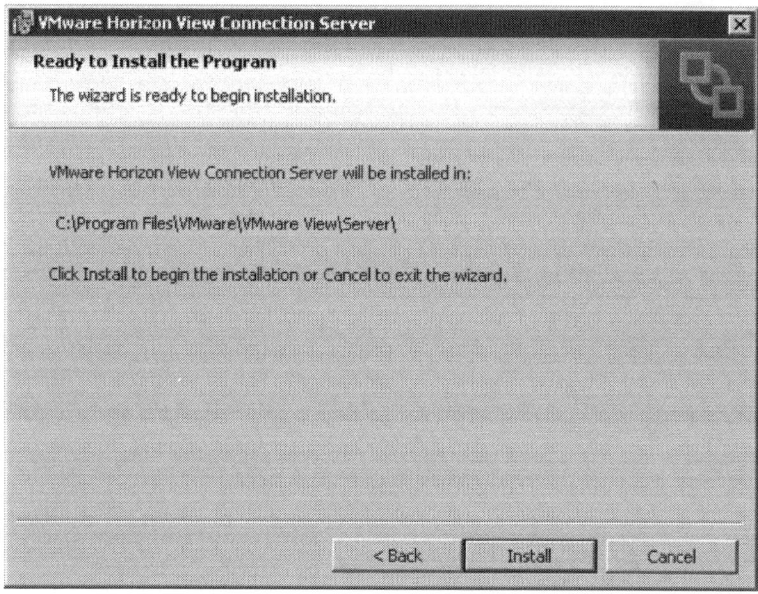

5. We will see that the installation process effectively uninstalls and reinstalls the View. Due to the configuration being held within the lightweight directory services database, the configuration will remain unaffected:

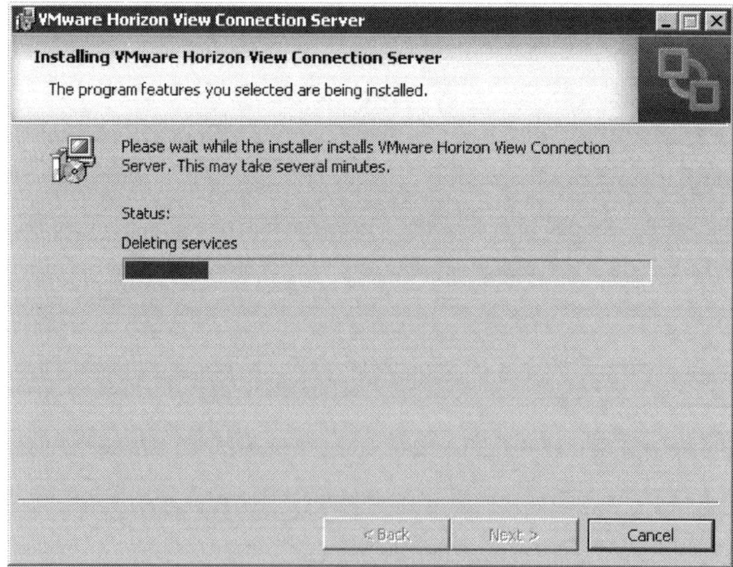

6. Finally, the installation will be completed, so click on **Finish**. Although you are not prompted, you should reboot the server at this point, as shown in the following screenshot:

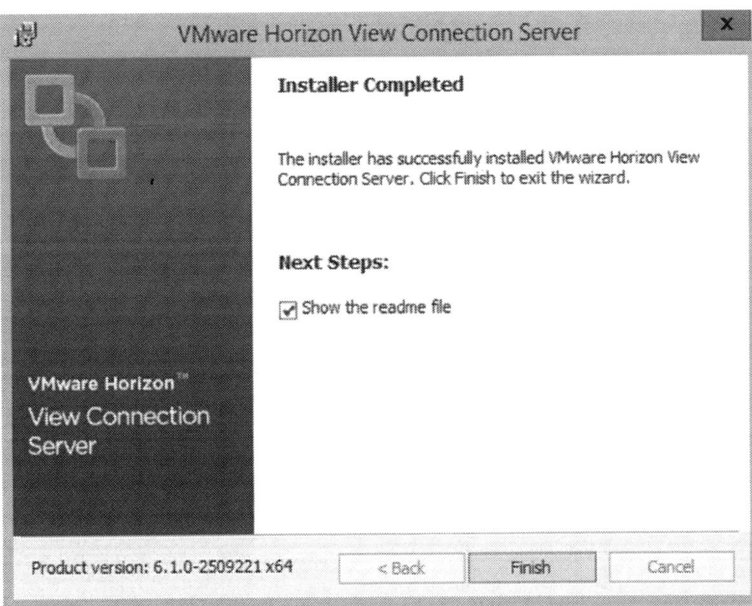

7. Once rebooted, you should be able to see that the upgrade has completed successfully by accessing the View Administrator Console, navigating to **Servers | Connection Servers**, and checking the version number for the associated Connection Server, as shown in the following screenshot:

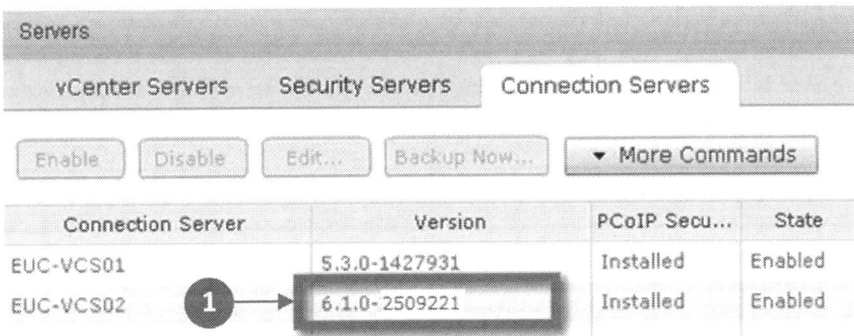

8. We are also able to see that the end user landing page has the new Horizon View look as well, as shown in the following screenshot:

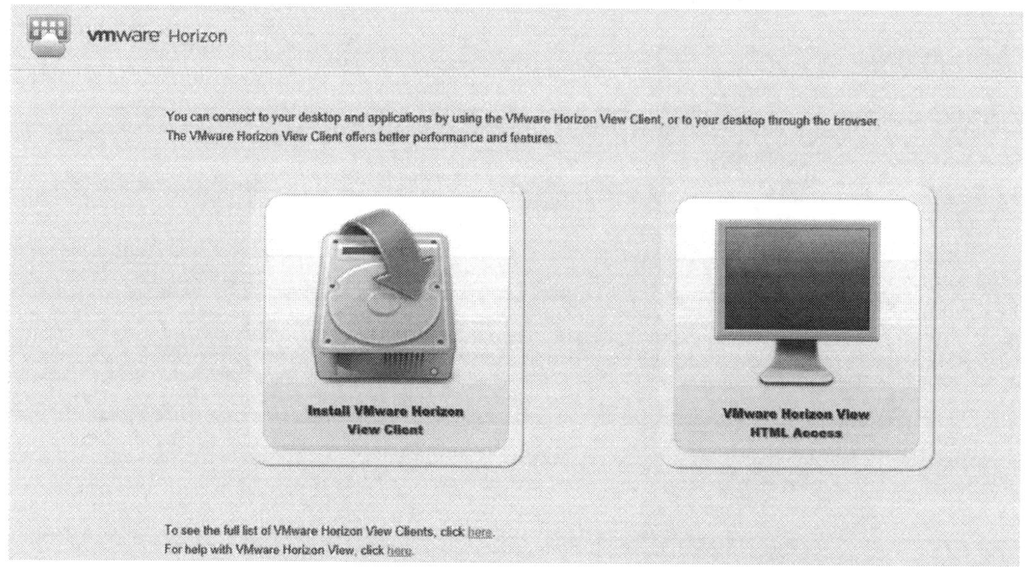

You will need to repeat this process for all the View Connection Servers used within your infrastructure.

An alternative method for upgrading View Composer

There may be a scenario where you decide to upgrade View Connection Servers by adding new Horizon 6 Connection Servers to your existing Horizon 5.3 Connection Servers and load balancers, and then remove the old Connection Servers from the configuration, when applicable. We aren't going to cover the procedure for the installation of the new replica View Connection Servers here, as this is extensively covered in *Chapter 4, Installing and Configuring Horizon View 6 Infrastructure*, but it is important to understand how to remove the old View Connection Servers correctly, by performing the following steps:

1. Once you have installed the new Connection Server and are ready to remove your first 5.3 Connection Server, you will need to ensure that the View Connection Server to be removed has been removed from any load balancers and is no longer in use by the users.

2. You will then need to uninstall the **AD LDS Instance VMwareVDMS** (1) and **VMware View Connection Server** (2) from the View Connection Server to be removed, as shown in the following screenshot:

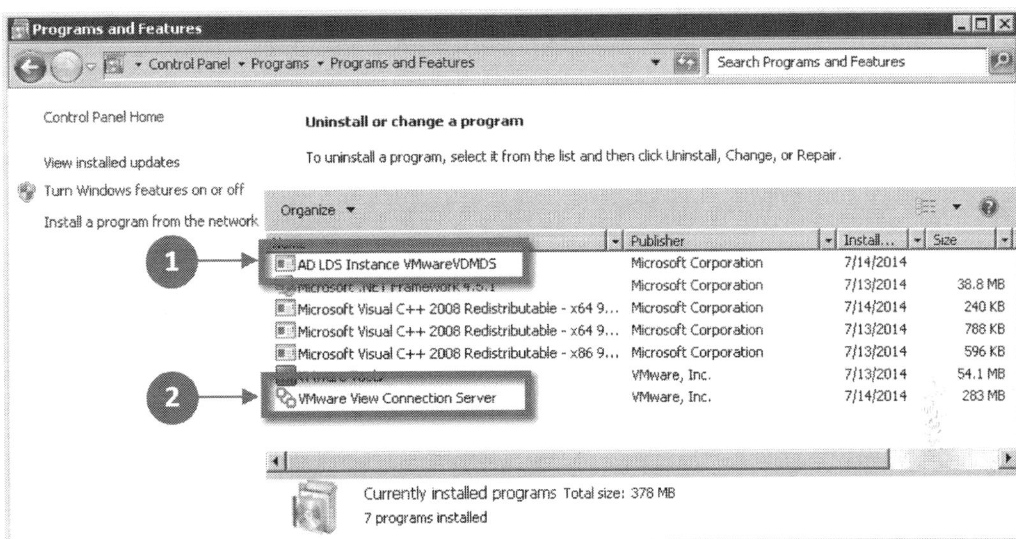

3. Once completed, you will need to connect to any of your remaining Connection Servers and run the following command:

```
"C:\Program Files\VMware\VMware View\Server\tools\bin\vdmadmin.
exe" -S -r -s server_name
```

For example, the command in our environment is shown in the following screenshot:

4. You will then get confirmation of the scheduled removal and the server will no longer display in the View Administrator:

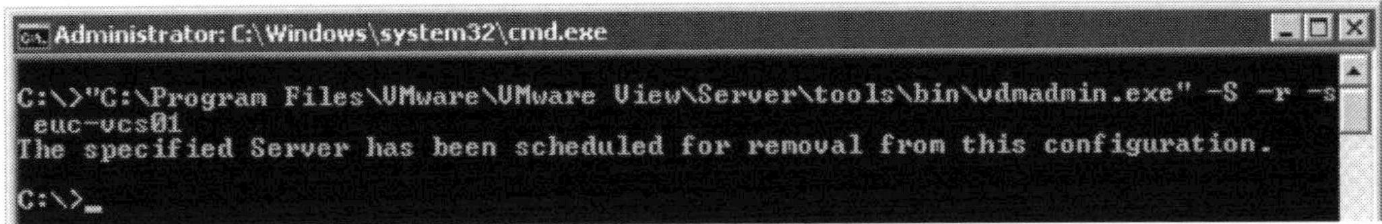

Upgrading the View Security Server

The next step in upgrading your Horizon View environment is to upgrade the Security Servers that will be used for the external users to connect to their desktops. Keep in mind, this won't be added to your domain, so you will need to log in using local credentials.

Prerequisites to upgrade

You will need to complete the following prerequisites prior to commencing with the upgrade:

1. By default, in View 5.3, traffic between the Security Server and Connection Server is governed by IPSEC rules: when you complete an upgrade of a View Security Server, these rules will need to be recreated, and if the existing rules still exist, this will fail.
2. As such, VMware has built-in functionality to clear the IPSEC rules prior to the upgrade being undertaken. From the **View Administrator** page, click on **Servers** and then on the **Security Servers** tab (**1**).
3. Right-click on the Security Server you wish to upgrade, and select **Prepare for Upgrade or Reinstallation...** (2), as shown in the following screenshot:

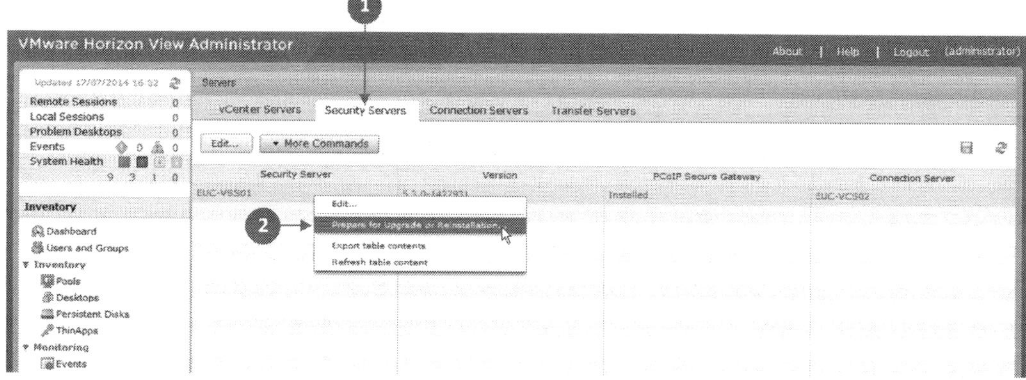

4. Upon clicking this, the Security Server is no longer able to communicate with the Connection Server, so ensure this is only completed as part of planned maintenance to the Security Server to avoid disruption.

Completing the View Security Server upgrade

Now we will be completing the View Security Server upgrade, by performing the following steps:

1. Ensure you have carried out all the prerequisites.
2. Connect to your View Administrator console, select **Servers**, and then click on the **Connection Servers** tab (**1**). Select your View Connection Server (**2**), and then right-click and select **Specify Security Server Pairing Password...** (**3**), as shown in the following screenshot:

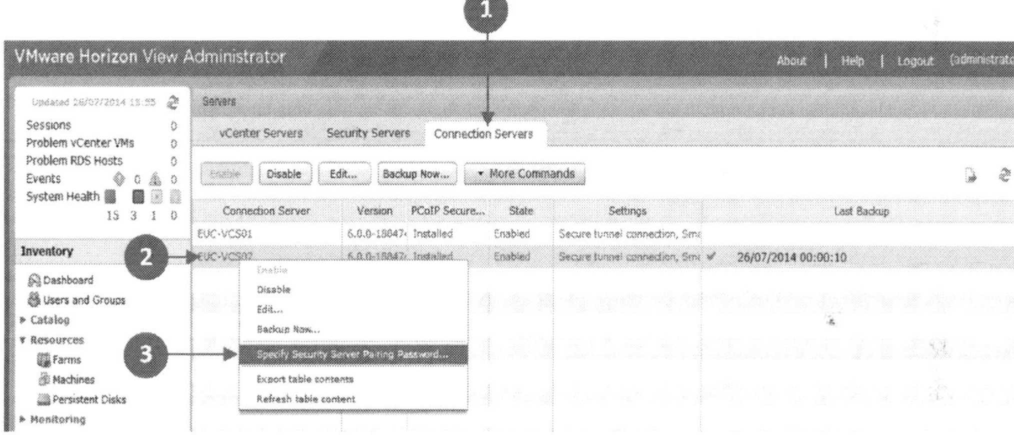

3. Here, you will need to set a password that you are going to use to re-pair the Security Server to the Connection Server, as shown in the following screenshot:

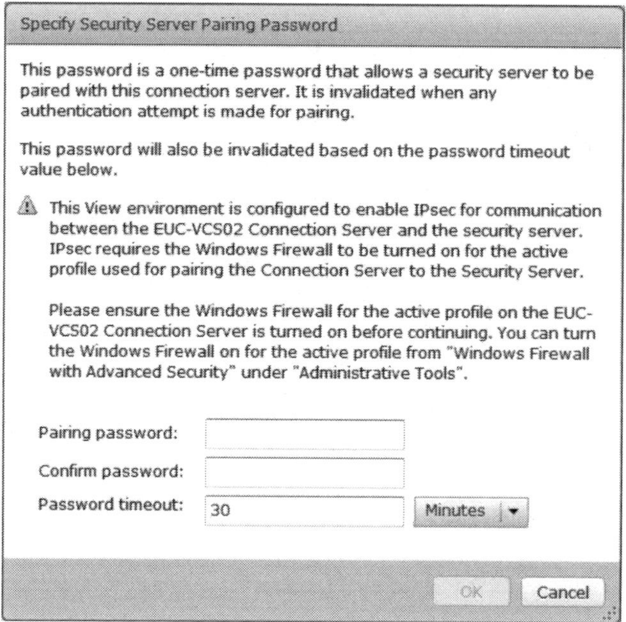

4. On your View Security Server, locate and launch the VMware View Connection Server 6 installer, as shown in the following screenshot:

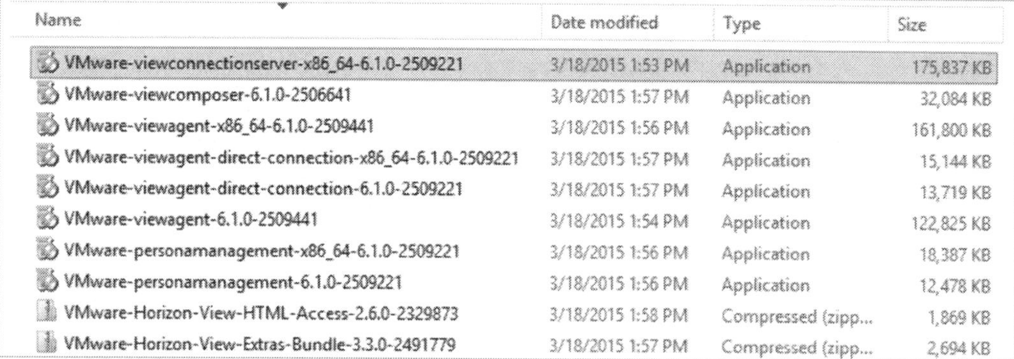

Name	Date modified	Type	Size
VMware-viewconnectionserver-x86_64-6.1.0-2509221	3/18/2015 1:53 PM	Application	175,837 KB
VMware-viewcomposer-6.1.0-2506641	3/18/2015 1:57 PM	Application	32,084 KB
VMware-viewagent-x86_64-6.1.0-2509441	3/18/2015 1:56 PM	Application	161,800 KB
VMware-viewagent-direct-connection-x86_64-6.1.0-2509221	3/18/2015 1:57 PM	Application	15,144 KB
VMware-viewagent-direct-connection-6.1.0-2509221	3/18/2015 1:57 PM	Application	13,719 KB
VMware-viewagent-6.1.0-2509441	3/18/2015 1:54 PM	Application	122,825 KB
VMware-personamanagement-x86_64-6.1.0-2509221	3/18/2015 1:56 PM	Application	18,387 KB
VMware-personamanagement-6.1.0-2509221	3/18/2015 1:56 PM	Application	12,478 KB
VMware-Horizon-View-HTML-Access-2.6.0-2329873	3/18/2015 1:58 PM	Compressed (zipp...	1,869 KB
VMware-Horizon-View-Extras-Bundle-3.3.0-2491779	3/18/2015 1:57 PM	Compressed (zipp...	2,694 KB

5. You are now going to start the installer to proceed with the upgrade process:

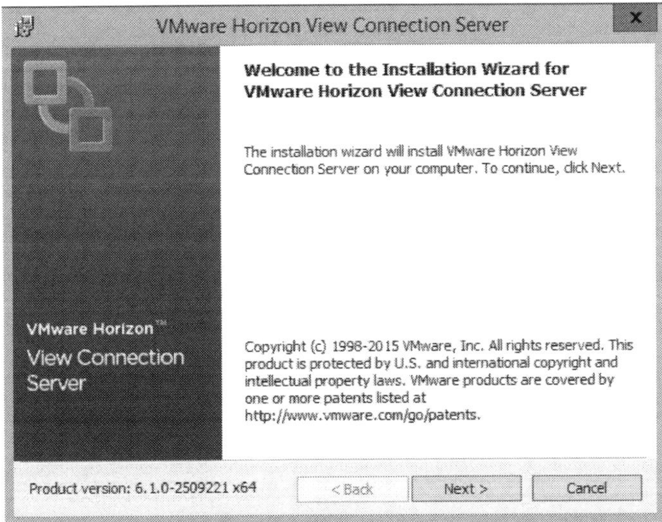

6. You are going to accept the EULA and then we will need to confirm which View Connection Server the Security Server is paired with:

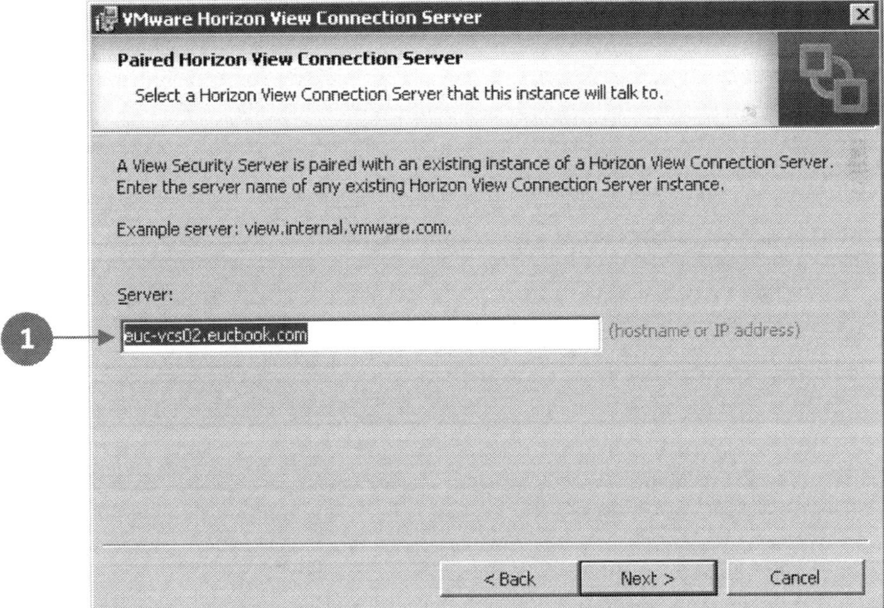

7. You will now need to enter the password that you set through the View Administrator Console, as shown in the following screenshot:

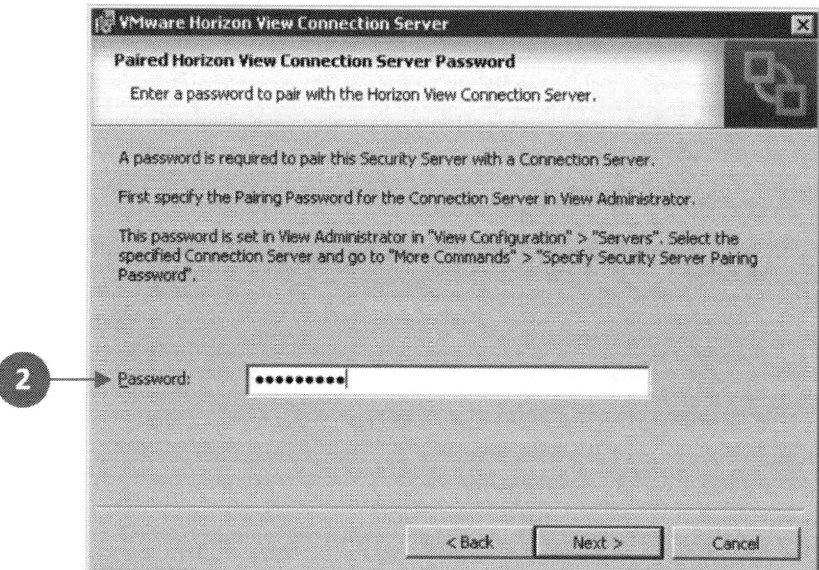

8. You will now be asked to confirm the external URLs for the Security Server, as shown in the following screenshot:

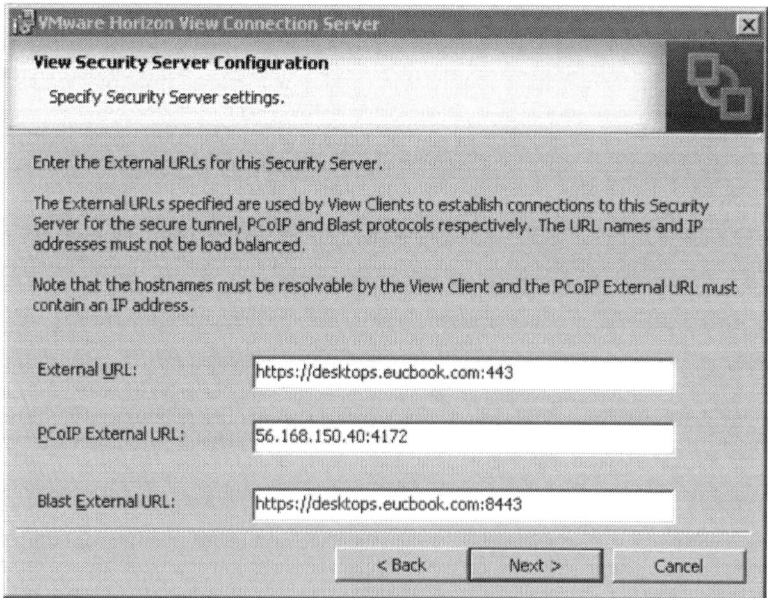

9. You will now confirm the details on the final pages of the installation wizard and select **Install**.
10. Finally, the installation will be completed, although, not prompted, we would reboot the server at this point.
11. You will need to repeat this process for all View Security Servers used within your infrastructure, as shown in the following screenshot:

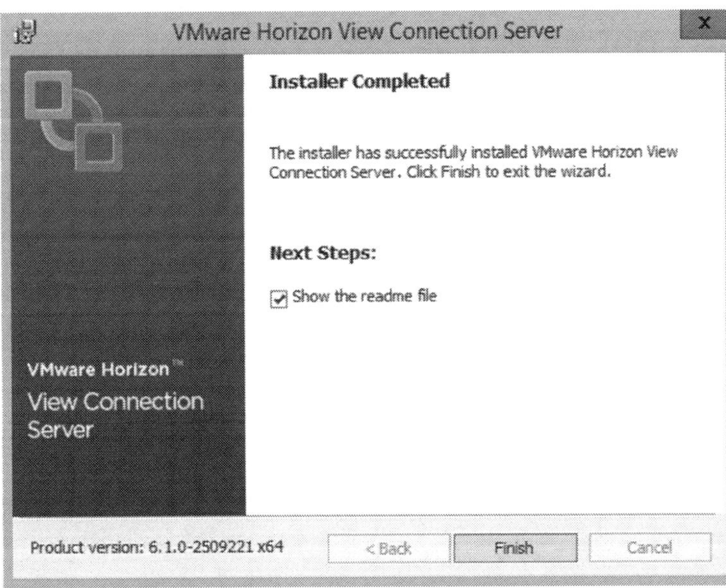

12. Once rebooted, you should be able to see that the upgrade has completed successfully by accessing the View Administrator Console, navigating to **Servers** | **Security Servers**, and checking the version number for the associated Security Server, as shown in the following screenshot:

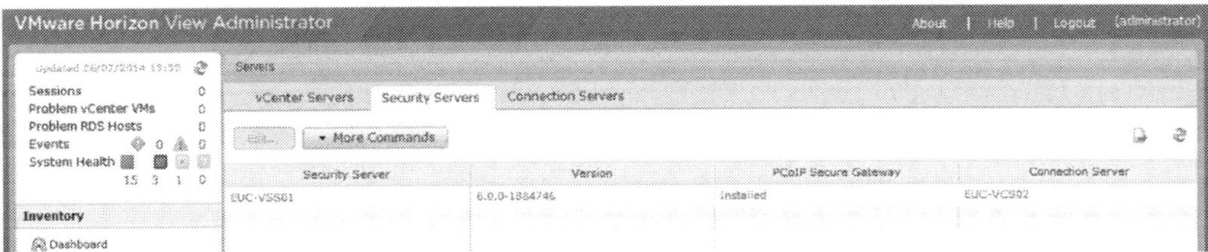

Upgrading Group Policy templates

You will need to upgrade the Group Policy Administrative templates to the latest version when upgrading to Horizon View 6; this is easily achieved through the Group Policy Object Editor within your domain controllers, by performing the following steps:

1. From within the **Group Policy Object Editor**, select the relevant policy used to apply the View settings:

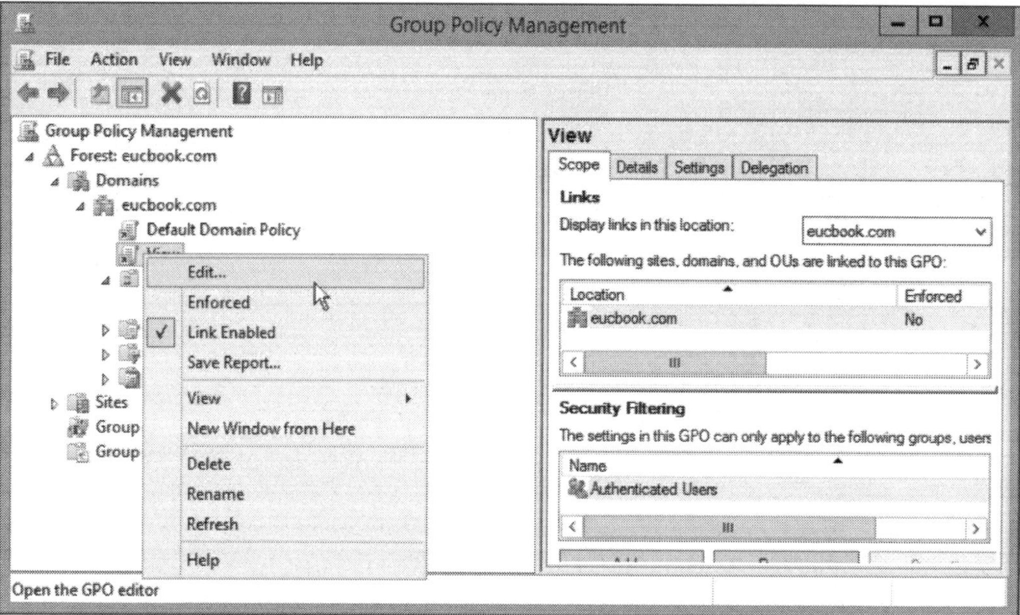

2. Navigate to **Computer Configuration** | **Policies** | **Administrative Templates**, right click on **Administrative Templates** and choose the **Add/Remove Templates...** option, as shown in the following screenshot:

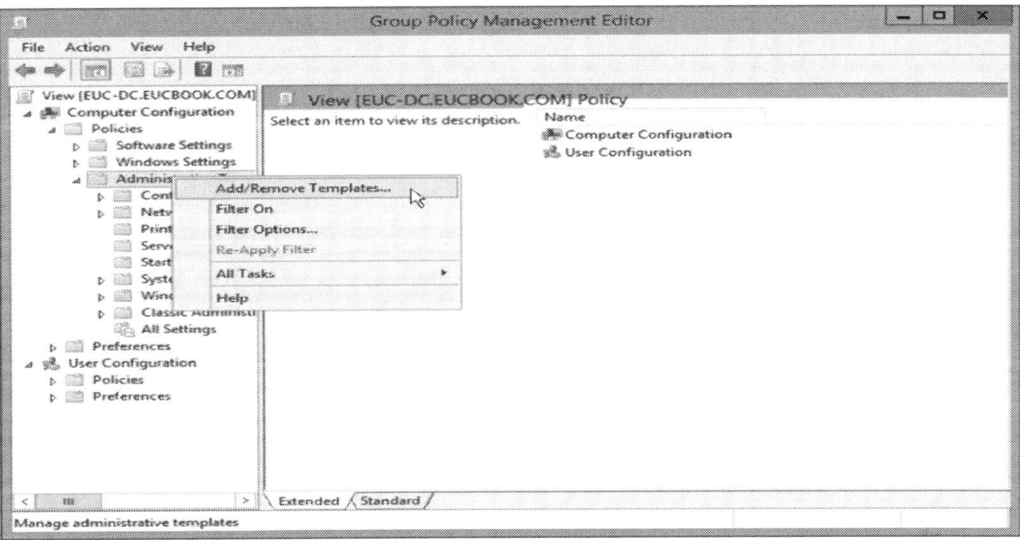

3. You will see here your existing templates listed; do not remove them but select **Add...** and add in the updated templates that you downloaded alongside Horizon View 6, as shown in the following screenshot:

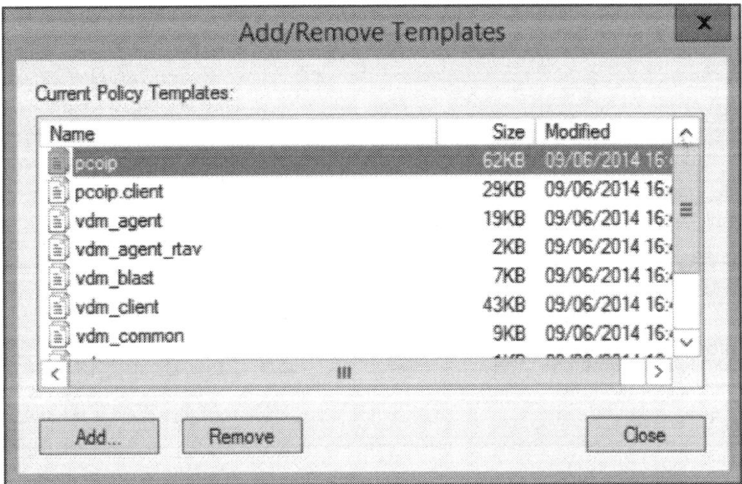

4. When you have added the new templates, you will see the following message, and you will need to select **Replace the files in the destination**:

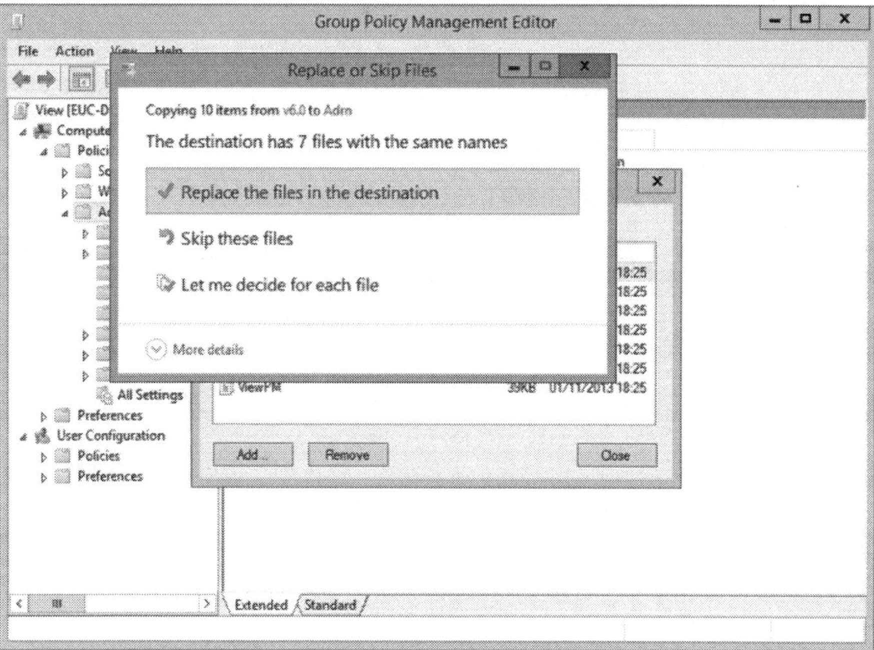

5. Once completed, you will see that the modified dates for the templates have now been updated; there are also more templates for Horizon 6 than there were for 5.3, as shown in the following screenshot:

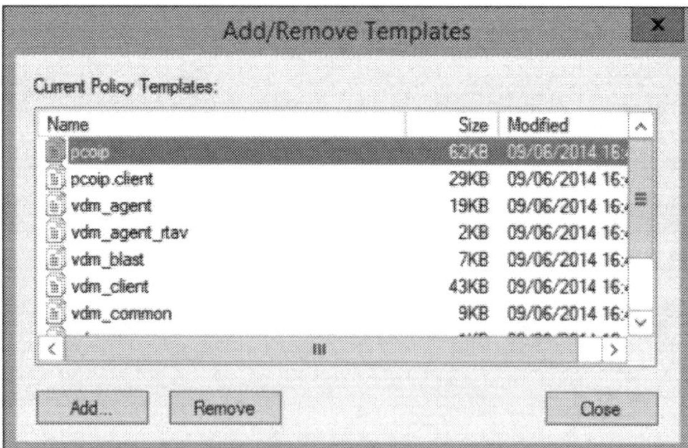

6. This process will now need to be repeated for the User Configuration Administrative Templates in the same process.
7. Once completed, you will need to review the policies to see whether any reconfiguration of policies is needed after the upgrade.

Upgrading Horizon View Agent

Upgrading the Horizon View Agent is probably one of the simplest tasks of the upgrade process. We are going to need to upgrade the agents in all of our golden images and then recompose the pools. With nonpersistent desktops, this is a relatively simple task of upgrading the agent, taking a new snapshot, and recomposing all the pools. With persistent desktops, you may need to take further consideration into the effect of recomposing the pool, or alternatively manually upgrading the agent on each or complete with a third-party management tool of some kind, by performing the following steps:

1. To upgrade the agent, either copy the Horizon View 6 Agent to the golden image or run from a network share.

2. As we run through the wizard, we will get to the **Custom Setup** screen. This is a good opportunity to review the components we are going to install, and options such as **Real-Time Audio-Video** and **Persona Management** can be installed at this time, if required, as shown in the following screenshot:

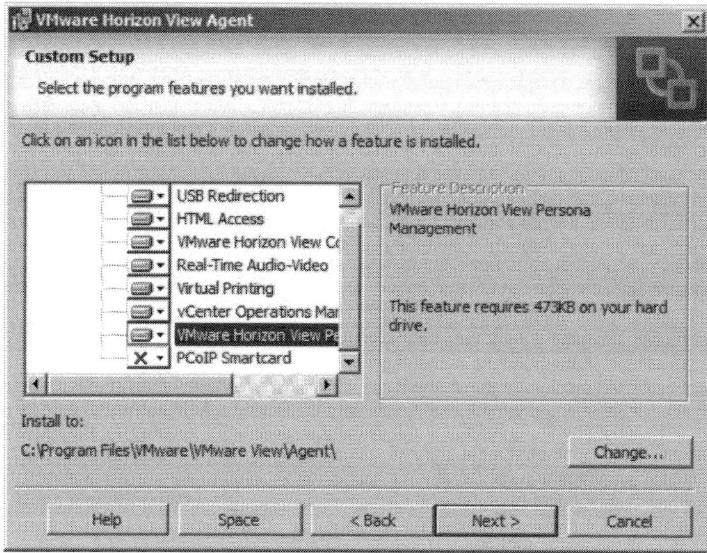

3. Finally, we are going to complete the installation to commence the upgrade:

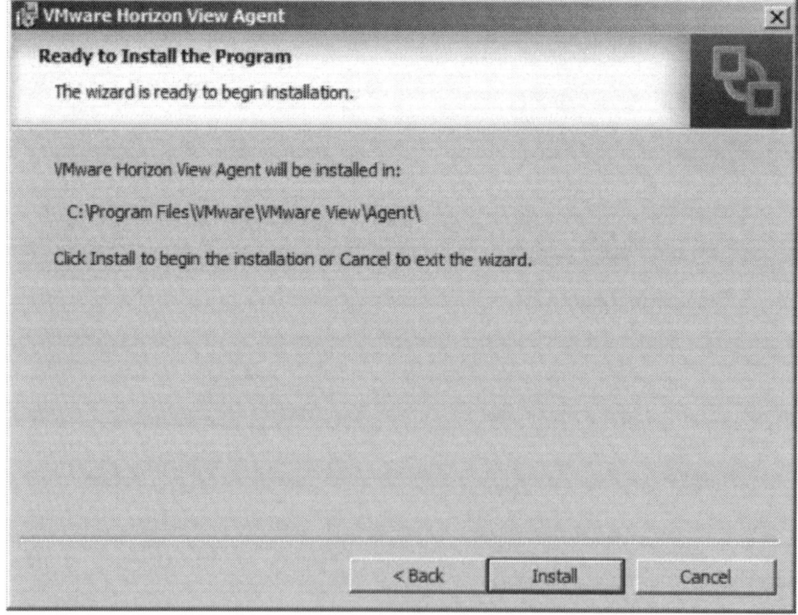

4. Once completed, your will be asked to reboot the VM, as shown in the following screenshot:

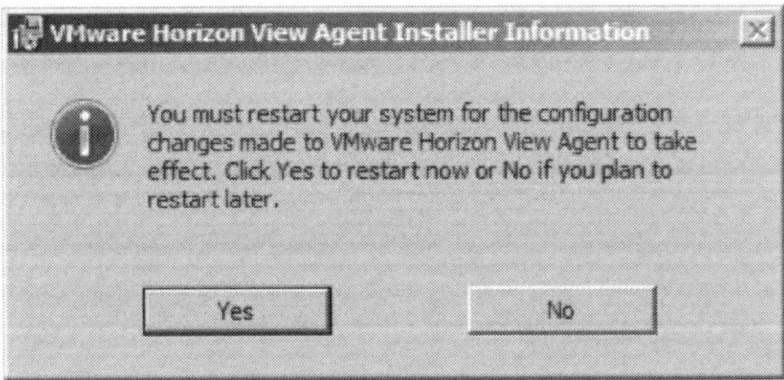

5. Once the VM has been rebooted, you can check the version of the agent in the Windows **Programs and Features** page, as shown in the following screenshot:

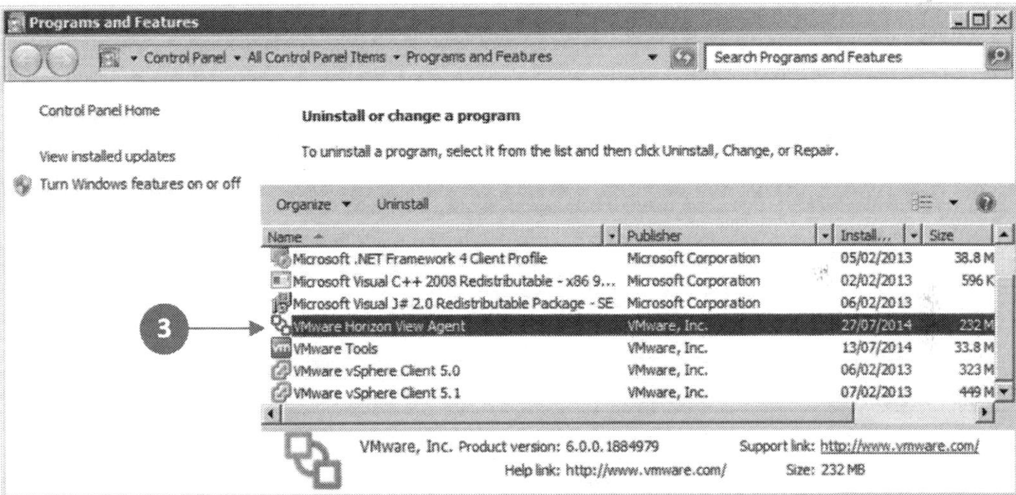

6. With the upgrade complete you should now perform some housekeeping and clear up the virtual desktop image ready for it to be used. Remove any old installation programs and delete any temporary files, including any browser history. When you have completed that the final task is to release the IP address by running ipconfig /release at the command. The virtual desktop is now ready to have a snapshot taken.

Upgrading Horizon View Clients

There is no built-in method to upgrade the Horizon View Clients, but with Horizon 6 upgrading, clients can be more important than ever. With the new Horizon View Clients, we are able to gain access to the RDSH-published applications.

If you are running thin clients as end user devices for your users, the upgrade procedure is usually easily managed with the management software that comes with the thin clients. If you are using reprovisioned PCs or maybe laptops to connect to the Horizon View environment, you are going to need to either manually update the client, direct your users to do so, or use a third-party tool to complete the upgrade. If you are using Horizon Mirage to manage the laptops or PCs, it will be possible to update the image or the software layer and then apply to the devices.

Summary

In this chapter, we covered the process of upgrading your VMware View 5.3 environment to Horizon View 6.0. We discovered that the actual upgrade process itself is relatively easy, but we must take the time to check and complete the prerequisites first. We also learned about the importance of planning the update to minimize the effect on users. In the next chapter, we will take a look at the additional products and features available within Horizon Suitee Advanced.

14

Horizon 6 Advanced Edition

In this chapter, we will cover some of the other features that are part of Horizon's Advanced Edition. The key features of this edition are listed as follows:

- Mirage
- Workspace Portal
- Virtual SAN
- Application publishing

In the next sections, we will cover VMware Mirage with Fusion Pro and the VMware Workspace Portal products in a little more detail. We have already covered application publishing in *Chapter 10, Delivering Remote Applications with Horizon Advanced*, and we will cover **Virtual SAN (VSAN)** in more detail in *Chapter 16, Introduction to VSAN for VDI*.

Introducing VMware Mirage

Let's start with VMware Mirage and give an overview of how this product fits into the Horizon product suite and what it delivers.

Starting at a high level, VMware Mirage is a Windows desktop image management solution that works by centralizing a copy of each Mirage-managed desktop image on the Horizon Mirage Server infrastructure that is hosted in the data center. This allows you to manage Windows desktop images and provide a solution to deliver and manage images for the following three key use cases:

- Horizon View desktops for the management of VDI-based desktop images
- Physical desktop and laptop image management, backup, and recovery for Microsoft Windows-based endpoints
- Delivering a virtual Windows desktop machine onto a device running VMware Fusion Professional or VMware Player

The following screenshot illustrates these key high-level use cases:

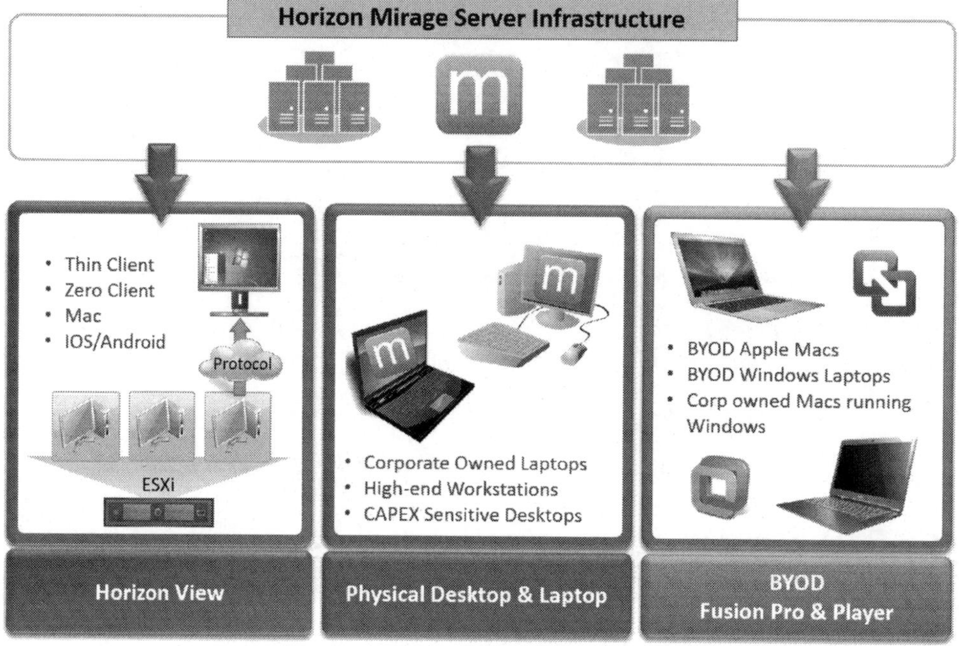

Horizon Mirage makes use of layering technology that categorizes the image into logical layers and copies the desktop image. It's like adding a level of abstraction between the image components (for example, operating system, applications, and user data) but without a hypervisor. These layers fall into the following two categories:

- Owned and managed by the end user
- Owned and managed by the IT department

This allows the IT-managed layers, such as the operating system, to be independently updated, while leaving the end users' files, profiles, and applications, which they have installed, intact and untouched by any other operation.

These layers are continuously synchronized with the image that's stored in the data center, creating either full desktop snapshots or snapshots based on the upload policy applied to that particular device. The upload policy can be used to determine what does and what does not get centralized from the end user's device. The snapshots that get created are backed up and are ready to recover a corrupt or missing file or are used to perform a complete rebuild in the event of a failure of the endpoint device.

The following screenshot provides a high-level overview of the layering technology employed by Mirage:

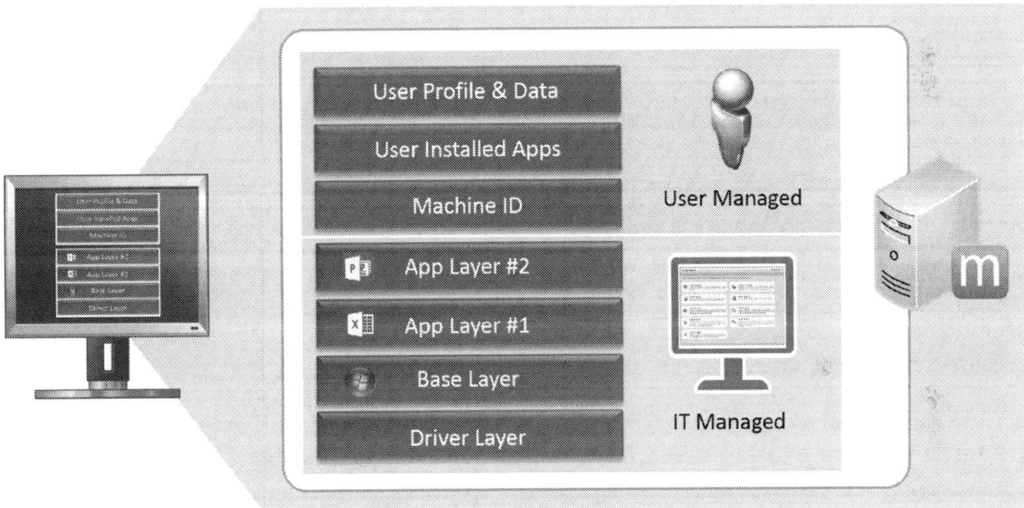

So the question is, how is this different from VDI, and does that mean I don't need Horizon View virtual desktop machines anymore?

To answer this question, there are a couple of things that highlight the differences. Firstly, as we said previously, Mirage does not require a hypervisor to operate; it's an image management tool that can manage an image on a physical desktop PC or laptop. In fact, one of the use cases for Mirage is to provide an end user with an IT-managed Windows desktop when there is little or no connectivity, or limited bandwidth between the data center and the local site. It might also be the case that the end user needs to work offline. It can also be used to manage persistent virtual desktop machine images. The following screenshot illustrates the key differences between Mirage and VDI:

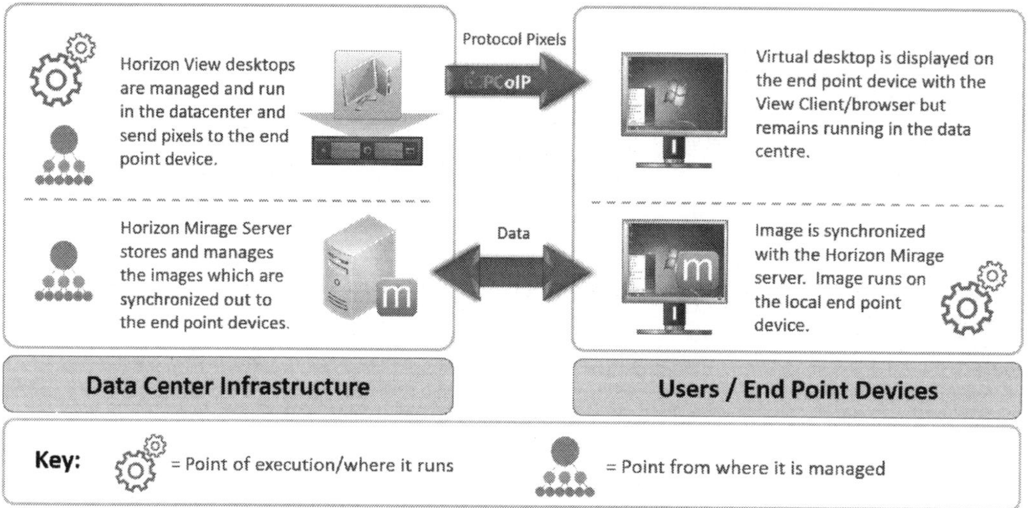

The other difference, and probably the biggest one, is where the image executes. By execute we mean where does that desktop actually run?

As we have seen in this book, in a VDI environment the desktop runs as a virtual desktop machine hosted centrally on a server, in the data center running a hypervisor. This gives us both central management and central execution.

In a Mirage deployment the desktop is now a physical endpoint device rather than a virtual desktop machine. This means that the operating system is running natively on that device, and managed using Mirage. This gives us central management, but local execution.

VMware Mirage use cases

In this section, we are going to cover some of the key use cases for Mirage. There are a number of use cases, and we have broken them down into three categories to reflect the key objective of each one: **manage**, **migrate**, and **protect**.

Manage

These features and components are all about delivering image management to your endpoint devices.

Endpoint repair

As the user's desktop is backed up in the data center, it's very easy to replace missing or corrupt files from the backed up image in the data center back down to the endpoint device. This could be fixing a single file, application, or directory folder, or a complete restore of the endpoint.

Single-image management

As we touched on previously, with Mirage you have the ability to create a layered approach to the operating environment by abstracting operating systems, applications, drivers, user data, and so on. This allows you to manage fewer images, the idea being that you have only one core operating system image or base layer as your starting point for any machine.

To build a complete endpoint, you assign additional layers to the operating system layer, with different layers relating to different applications, or different drivers to reflect different endpoint devices.

Application layering

With this feature, you have the ability to deliver an application as an individual layer. Application layers can be added to a user to create a complete desktop with the correct applications for the user based on their entitlement or the department that they work in. This is similar to how VMware ThinApp delivers applications; however, Mirage does not build a virtual application package like ThinApp. Instead, a Mirage application layer natively installs the application onto the endpoint device.

Remote office management with Mirage Branch Reflectors

Remote office locations have always been a problem for a traditional VDI solution because connectivity is usually limited or, in some cases, non-existent. So how can you deliver a centralized image with limited connectivity or slow WAN connections?

With Branch Reflectors, you can nominate a desktop PC in the remote location to act as an intermediary between the local endpoints and the data center. The local endpoints connect locally to a Branch Reflector rather than the Mirage Server and, in turn, the Branch Reflector synchronizes with the data center, downloading only the differences between the IT-managed layers and the local endpoints.

Migrate

The second category, migrate, covers two migration areas: one for the desktop operating system and the second for hardware refresh projects or migrating between platforms.

Windows XP/Windows 7/Windows 8

Probably, the most important feature of Mirage today is its ability to migrate operating systems. By using a layered approach to desktop images, Mirage is able to manage the operating system as a separate layer and can therefore update this layer while leaving the user data, profile, and settings all in place. The migration process is also less intrusive to the end user because the files are copied in the background, keeping the user downtime to complete the migration to a minimum.

Hardware refresh

Similar to the way in which Mirage can migrate an operating system using a layered approach, it can also manage drivers as a separate layer. This means that Mirage can also be used if you are refreshing your hardware platform, allowing you to build specific driver profiles to match different hardware models from multiple vendors. It also means that, if your endpoint device becomes corrupt, unusable, or is even stolen, you can replace it with something entirely different, while still using the same image.

Protect

The third and final category is protection. This is something that doesn't typically get deployed for desktop and laptop estates. It's usually left to the end users to make sure that their machine is backed up and protected.

Centralized endpoint backups

By installing the Mirage client onto an endpoint device, meaning that the endpoint is now be managed by Mirage, the first thing that happens is that the endpoint is centralized and the data copied to the Mirage Server in the data center.

In addition to this, Mirage can create snapshots of the image and create points in time from which to roll back.

Desktop recovery

Backing up desktops is only half the story; you also need to think about the restoration process. It's no good backing up if you can't get the files and data back again.

Mirage offers the option of restoring specific layers, while preserving the remaining layers. You can restore an endpoint to a previous snapshot without overwriting user data. If a computer is stolen, damaged, or lost, you can restore the entire image to a replacement desktop computer or laptop. It doesn't even need to be the same make and model. Or, you could just select which layers to restore. For example, if a particular application becomes corrupt, you can just replace that application layer.

In this use case, it doesn't just apply to the physical machines. You could restore a physical computer to a virtual desktop machine either temporarily or as a permanent migration, maybe as a stepping stone to deploy a full VDI solution.

Mirage architecture

In this section, we are going to take a look at the different components that make up the Mirage solution and how they all fit together.

Mirage Management Server

Mirage Management Server controls and manages the Mirage Server or cluster, if you have deployed a clustered solution. It also interfaces with the Mirage SQL database, which is also shared with Mirage Server.

Mirage Server

The Mirage Server manages all Mirage operations and objects. It's the central point from which **centralized virtual disks (CVDs)**, base layers, and application layers are all managed.

During installation, you will be prompted to configure a local cache, which is used to store common data blocks. These data blocks are used to perform data de-duplication over the WAN. When large files are transferred, their file blocks are stored in the cache as they are transferred across the WAN, meaning that next time similar files need to be transferred, the Mirage Server uses the cache to get the blocks instead of transferring them over the network. Best practice would be to use fast storage for the cache, such as a local SSD drive. The default size for the cache is 100 GB.

The Mirage Server and Mirage Management Server can be installed on the same machine or separate machines, depending on your design configuration, but they need to meet the following requirements:

- Windows Server 2008 R2 (Standard or Enterprise) 64-bit
- Windows Server 2012 Standard Edition 64-bit

- Microsoft .NET Framework 3.5 SP1
- Must be Domain member

Mirage Database

The Mirage Server and the Management Server both need to connect to a database. Mirage supports the following database engines:

- SQL Server 64-bit R2 Express, Standard, and Enterprise
- SQL 2012 SP1 Express, Standard, and Enterprise

File Portal

The File Portal is an optional component to Mirage that allows users to connect, via a web-based interface, to their files stored on the Mirage Servers in the data center. This self-service portal allows users to access and download their files.

It can be installed on the actual Mirage Server but, if not, it will need to be installed onto a server that is joined to the Domain and meets the following requirements:

- Windows Server running IIS 7.0 or newer
- ASP.NET components are needed
- IIS 6 Management Compatibility Role

Mirage client

The Mirage client is installed onto all the endpoints that you want Mirage to manage. It ships as a 5 MB Windows Installer Package (MSI) that can also be installed silently. The endpoints need to meet the following requirements:

- Microsoft .NET Framework 3.5 SP1
- Windows XP 32-bit Service Pack 3
- Windows 7 32-bit or 64-bit (Professional or Enterprise)
- Windows Vista 32-bit or 64-bit (Business or Enterprise)
- Windows 8.0 and 8.1 32-bit and 64-bit (Professional or Enterprise)

Mirage Management console

The Management console is an MMC snap-in that provides a graphical user interface to centrally manage the endpoints and Mirage Server infrastructure. It can be installed either on the Mirage Server or an administrator's desktop. From the console you can manage the base layers, application layers, drivers, and the backup of endpoints. It is also the place where you initiate updates from. To run the Management console, you need the following to be installed:

- Microsoft .NET Framework 3.5 SP1
- Microsoft Management Console Version 3.0 (MMC)

Branch Reflector

Branch Reflector is almost like having a remote deployment of a Mirage Server at the branch office site, used for when the remote location has poor connectivity back to the data center. You can assign any endpoint on the remote site to be a Branch Reflector. As it has to be an endpoint running the Horizon Mirage client, you cannot use a server, meaning you don't need dedicated infrastructure. Just don't choose a laptop as it might not always be available in the office.

Branch Reflector serves the local endpoints in the branch office and allows those endpoints to have their base layer and application layers updated without having to connect to the Mirage Server in the data center, saving on your network requirements. A Branch Reflector assigned endpoint should have as a minimum:

- A dual-core CPU
- 2 GB memory
- Enough disk space for the cache (approximately 20 GB)

Web Management Console

The Web Management Console uses a web interface to provide a console specifically designed for the IT help desk and therefore gives access to help desk-based tasks to manage endpoint devices. Tasks such as restoring an endpoint from a backed up copy or from a snapshot are available.

Mirage Gateway server

The Mirage Gateway server acts as a secure gateway server that is typically deployed in the same data center as the rest of the Mirage infrastructure; however, it sits within the DMZ. It allows Mirage-managed endpoints to access the Mirage infrastructure securely over the Internet, ensuring that your security and firewall requirements are met.

The Mirage Gateway server is deployed as a virtual appliance based on the SUSE 11 SP3 operating system and integrates into the Mirage infrastructure.

The following diagram illustrates the Mirage infrastructure and how the components fit together:

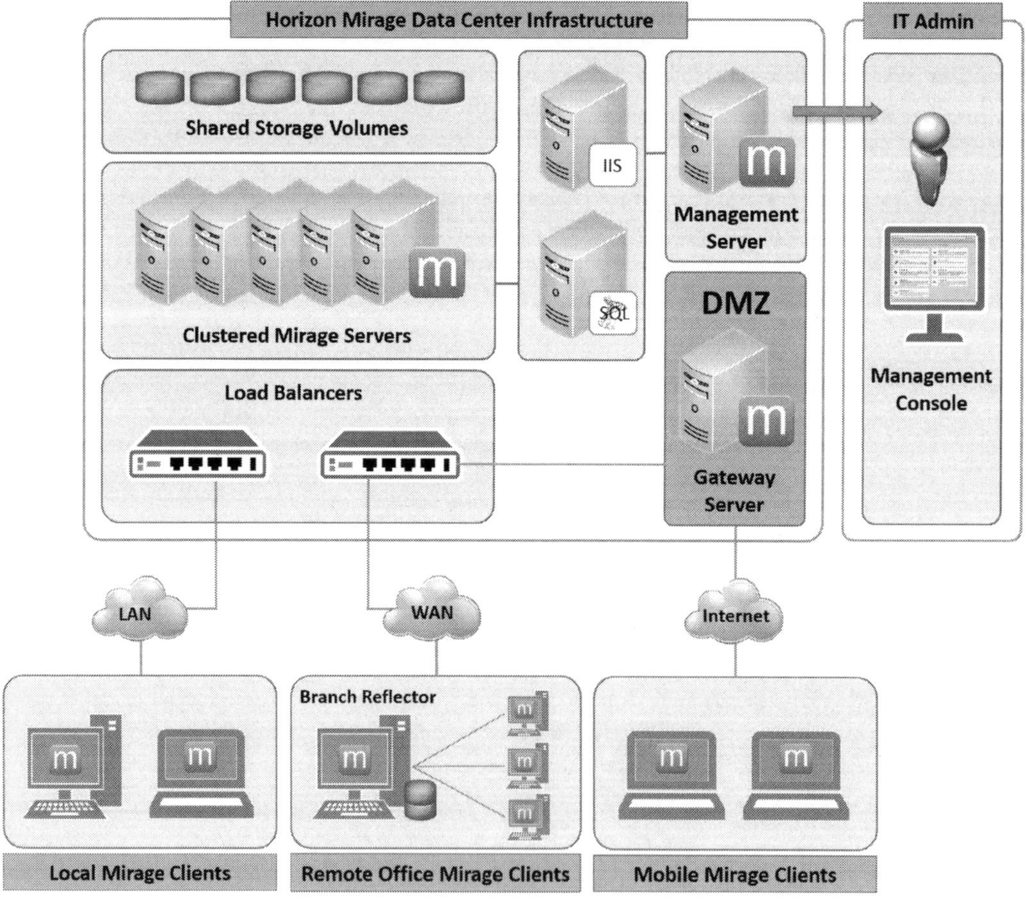

Hardware requirements

In the previous section, we covered the minimum software requirements. This section details the hardware requirements for running Mirage. We will configure this as virtual servers.

VMware Mirage Server

The following configurations will support up to 1,500 endpoint devices in steady state. You may need more capacity for the initial centralization process.

For Mirage to support the 1,500 endpoints, you will need a virtual server that meets the following requirements:

- **Minimum memory**: 16 GB
- **Minimum CPU**: 8 x vCPU
- **Minimum system storage**: 150 GB (includes 100 GB for the Mirage cache)
- **Minimum networking**: 2 x gigabit Ethernet ports

VMware Mirage Management Server

The Mirage Management server should meet the following requirements:

- **Minimum memory**: 8 GB
- **Minimum CPU**: 4 x vCPU

VMware Mirage Gateway Server

The Mirage Gateway server is deployed with the following configuration:

- 4 core CPU, 2.26 GHz Intel core speed or equivalent
- 4 GB RAM
- 40 GB available disk space
- 1 x gigabit Ethernet port

The Horizon Mirage client

The endpoint running the Horizon Mirage client should meet the following requirement:

- **Minimum memory**: 512 MB for Windows XP, 1 GB for Vista, Windows 7, and, Windows 8
- **Storage**: Minimum of 5 GB storage space

Storage requirements

If you are running a standalone Mirage Server, then you can use either DAS, SAN, or NAS storage. For a clustered deployment, you will need some form of shared storage with a CIFS network share that supports **Alternate Data Streams** (**ADS**).

ADS is a feature of NTFS that contains metadata to locate a specific file by author or title. It is supported by all versions of Windows from Windows NT onwards.

For storage capacity, an average of 15 GB should be allowed per user for storing their CVD. You can also enable compression to save disk space; however, do not enable compression or de-duplication on the local cache. Horizon Mirage is already optimized for hardware-level deduplication on its storage volumes.

Mirage Server example sizing

The following screenshot shows four different sizing examples for a single Mirage Server instance, based on best practices. The examples cover from 100 users up to a maximum of 1,500 users (the limit for one Mirage Server). The blue-shaded section denotes a Mirage Server running as a VM:

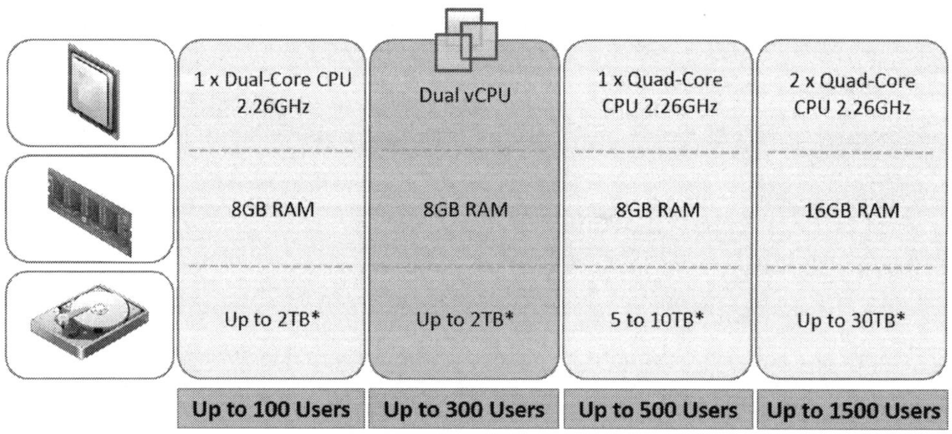

The storage requirements shown in the previous diagram are only rule of thumb and include space for snapshots, base layers, user data, driver libraries, and profiles. To work out the total storage requirements, we should take the information gained from our assessment for the size and number of CVDs and apply the following equation:

*(Average size of CVDs * Number of CVDs) + 30% Snapshot*

So, if you have 1,000 users each with a 15 GB CVD, then this is how your storage requirements will look:

*(15 GB * 1000 CVDs) + 30% = 19 TB*

VMware Workspace Portal 2

VMware Workspace Portal provides end users an easy way to access all of their applications from a single, browser-based workspace on any device they choose to connect from. Whether that's a Windows desktop, Mac, iPad, or Android device, or all of them, it really doesn't matter.

The user experience is consistent no matter which device they use with the same look and feel across all device types. Users will also only see the applications that are relevant to them based on their entitlement policy, type of device, or location, so they are context-aware. For example, once they have logged in using workspaces **single sign-on** (**SSO**) capabilities, they may be using a Mac, so, they will not see any ThinApp applications in their workspace. Why? Simply because you cannot run a ThinApp on a Mac OS. Or it might be a question of location. For example, the application you want to run contains sensitive information and therefore it can only be launched when you are on the corporate network.

It's not just the end users that benefit from this way of working. For the IT administrators, all user entitlements are centrally managed and fully integrated into the existing directory structure. This means that applications can quickly be added to a user's workspace or self-service catalog, and equally all entitlements can be removed in one go should that user leave your organization.

As the user only sees the application in their workspace, how that application is actually delivered may vary due to how IT want to deliver it. For example, the end user sees the Microsoft Excel icon in their workspace, and today when they launch it, Excel may be delivered as a XenApp published application. IT may then implement Horizon View published applications. In this case, all they need to do is update where that icon points to. As for the users, they neither know nor care how it's delivered. All they are interested in is that, when they click on **Excel**, it just launches and runs.

We use the example of a light switch. All you care about is that when you flick the switch, the lights come on. You don't care how the electricity is generated, by who, or how it gets from the power station to your home. You just care that the light comes on.

We often hear the Workspace Portal referred to as the switch board of the Horizon solution, as it is the first place a user goes to in order to be directed to their applications. It's not just VMware technology that workspace brokers, it also integrates with Citrix XenApp, Microsoft Office 365, and SaaS-based applications too. This gives the user one place to go to in order to consume all of the applications, no matter how they are provisioned and delivered.

The following screenshot highlights the brokering capabilities of Workspace, showing the unified view for the end user:

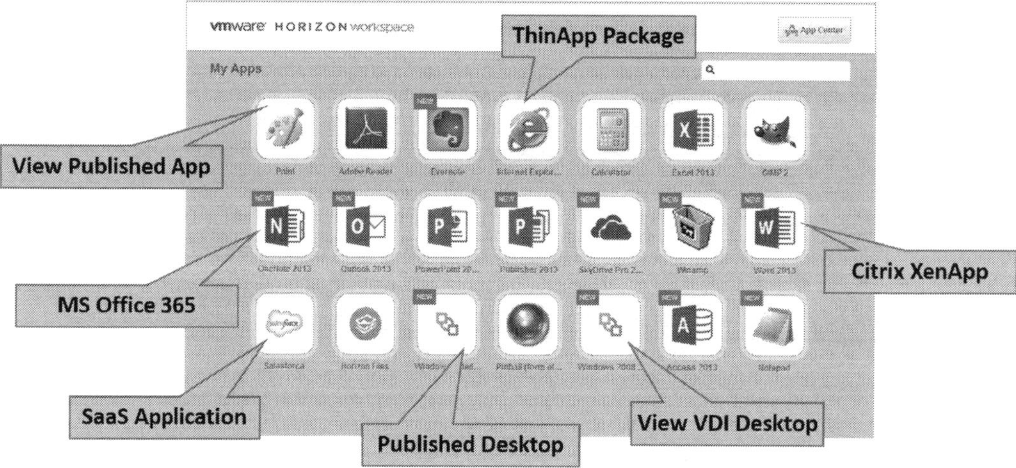

In the following sections, we are going to look a little deeper into some of these capabilities.

Citrix XenApp Integration in Workspace Portal

In order for Workspace to be able to integrate into an existing Citrix environment, you need to also deploy the Workspace Integration Broker. The Integration Broker is a separate application that is installed on a Windows Server within your environment and that talks to your Citrix XenApp infrastructure.

Workspace Portal only supports XenApp Versions 5.0, 6.0, and 6.5 for published applications and desktops. Citrix XenDesktop is not supported.

Once installed and configured, the Workspace Portal virtual appliance synchronizes with the Citrix XenApp farm via the Integration Broker and the user entitlements are then added to the application catalog on the Workspace Portal.

The IT department can configure a generic user settings template and an ICA launch template for the resources. This template is saved in the Workspace data store. An example of this configuration is shown in the following screenshot:

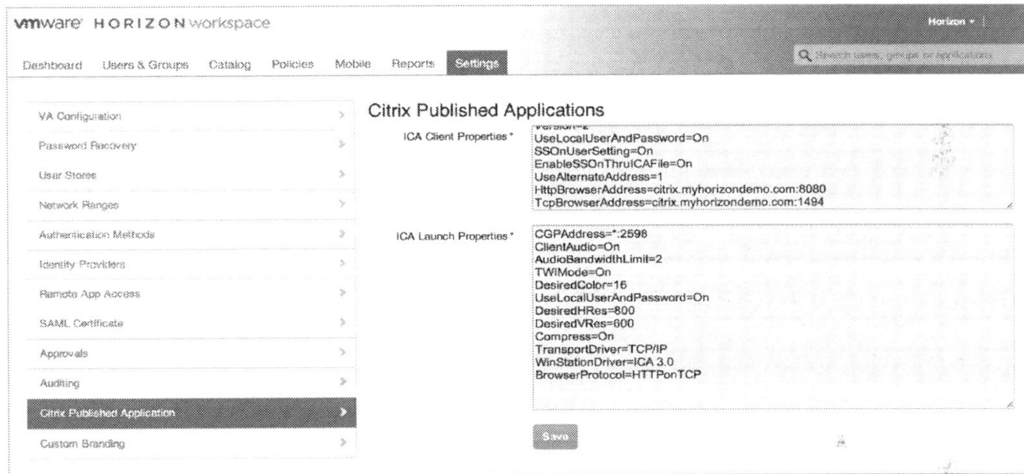

When a user launches a Citrix published application, the request is made from the Workspace Portal to the Integration Broker to initiate the session, which, in turn, talks to the Citrix XenApp Web Interface SDK to create a session. This means that a user can still take advantage of SSO to the Citrix published application.

As with a Citrix environment, an ICA file is sent to the user's endpoint device containing the details of how to launch the application and any specific configuration settings. For this to work, the endpoint device must be running the Citrix Receiver application.

The following screenshot illustrates the process:

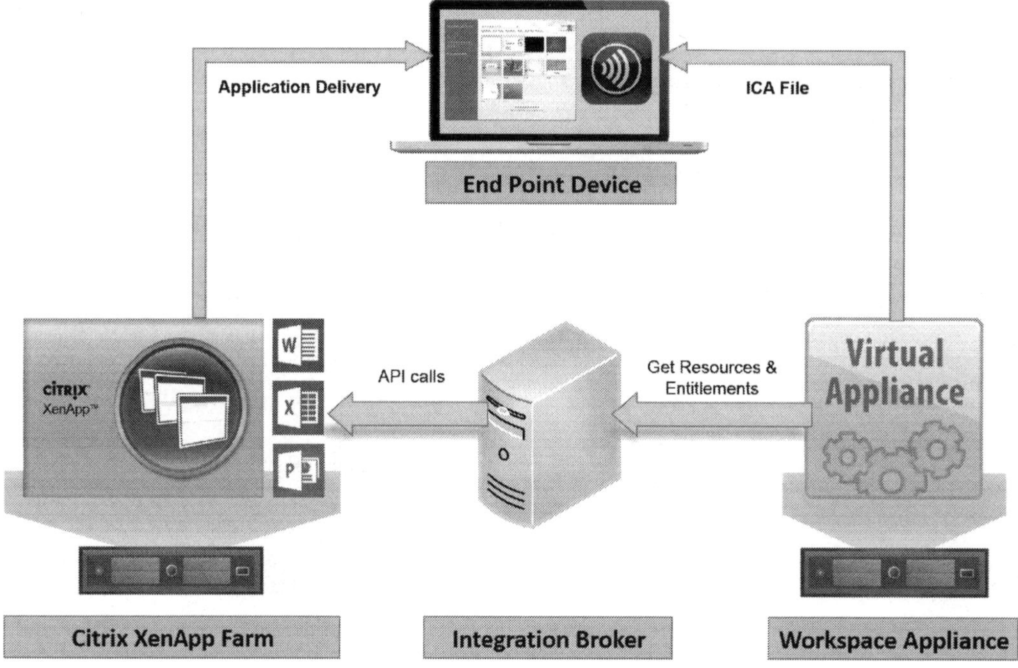

In the next section, we will look at how Horizon View virtual desktops and View published applications integrate with the Workspace Portal.

Horizon 6 published applications and VDI desktops

In a similar way in which the brokering with Citrix XenApp works, Workspace Portal can reflect the catalog information from the View Connection Servers and display that within the Workspace. Any user entitlements to virtual desktop machines, View published applications, or View session-based desktops will be presented to the users based on their entitlement.

This means that a user can launch any of these from their Workspace Portal, taking advantage of SSO. The SSO in this case is based on SAML 2.0 authentication, which is configured on the View Connection Servers to accept the SAML tokens from the Workspace Portal appliance.

An example of the SAML configuration for the View Connection Server is shown in the following screenshot:

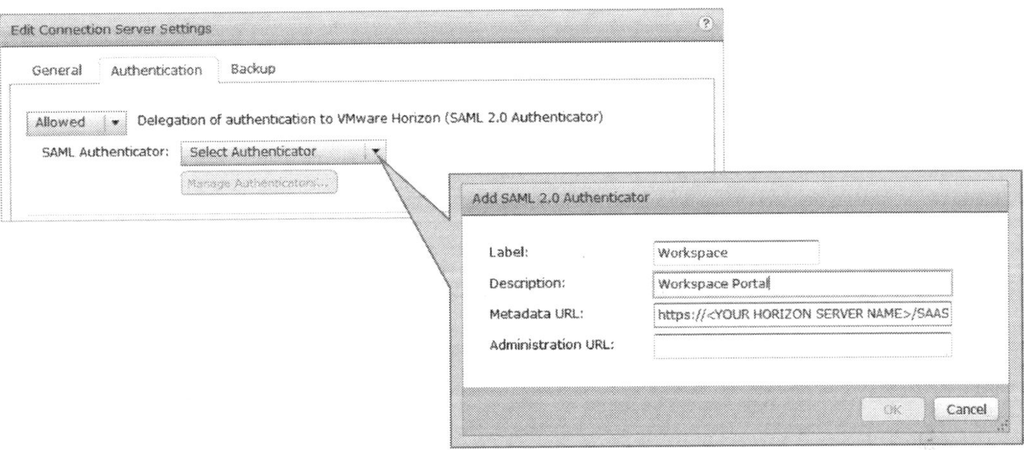

The Workspace Portal synchronizes with the View Connection Server at configurable set periods to determine any updates and/or new applications or desktop pools; these are then displayed to the end user via their browser, as shown in the following screenshot:

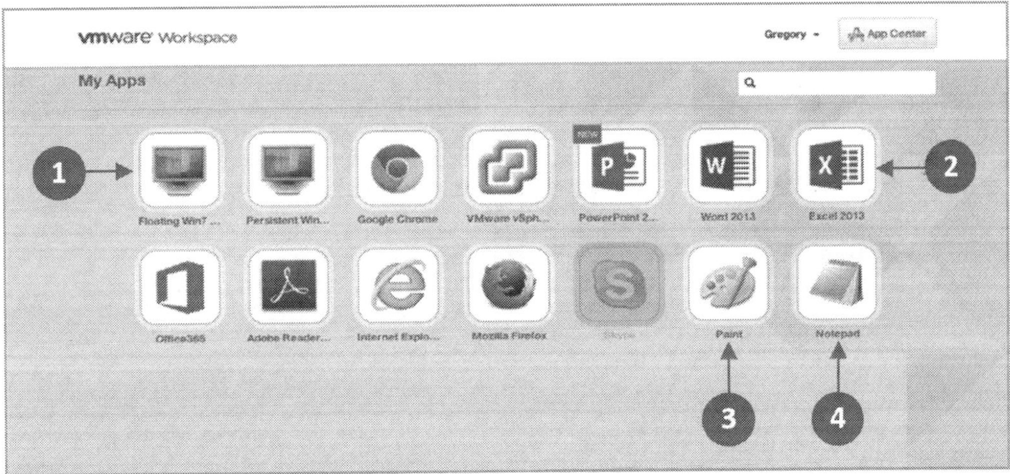

To launch an application or virtual desktop machine, the user simply clicks the icon.

In order to launch a View virtual desktop machine or a View published application, the end user must have the latest version of the View Client installed on their endpoint device.

Depending on how you have configured your View environment, the end user could also have the option to launch their virtual desktop machine in their browser.

The following diagram illustrates a high-level architecture overview:

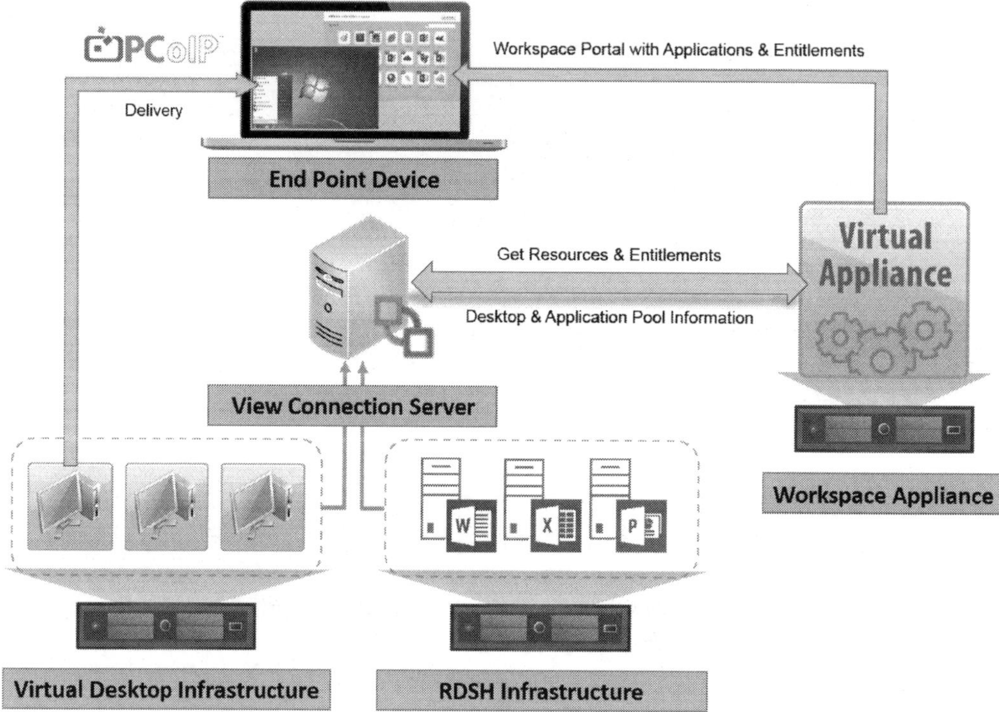

In the next section, we will look at how ThinApp packages can be integrated.

ThinApp integration

When it comes to delivering ThinApp packaged applications, you have a number of choices. They can be delivered as part of a View virtual desktop machine. However, if you are looking at a solution for simply delivering applications, then ThinApp packages can be presented from the Workspace portal. From a delivery perspective, the ThinApp could be a native ThinApp package or a ThinApp that's published using View published applications.

To the user, the application will look just like any other application.

A couple of things to note—remember you need to package your applications for use with the Workspace Portal by checking the Workspace box during the setup capture. This means that you need to have the Workspace client installed on the device as this checks your entitlements for launching the ThinApp.

Native ThinApp packages will only launch on a Windows platform. View published ThinApp packages will launch on other platforms such as Mac or iOS using the View Client.

To setup ThinApp brokering in Workspace, it's just a case of configuring Workspace to read the package details directly from the file share on which they are stored. All your ThinApp packages will be stored centrally. Published ThinApp packages will be presented from the Horizon View Connection Server.

SaaS/Web application integration

You have two options for adding web-based applications to the Workspace Portal.

The first is to just simply add a static link that places an icon in the Workspace and then points to a URL. For example, this could be a link to an internal intranet page.

The second is to provide an SSO feature to SaaS applications, such as `www.salesforce.com` or `www.workday.com`. For example, in this scenario, if you are setting up `www.salesforce.com`, you are effectively changing the authentication method for `www.salesforce.com` to accept SAML tokens from Workspace. The end user can only login by going through their Workspace Portal as `www.salesforce.com` will only accept logins from this authenticator and not via the standard web page. This means that you are able to add policy for when and where they can log in to `www.salesforce.com`.

Microsoft Office 365

The other SaaS-based application that can be integrated with the Workspace Portal is Office 365. With Office 365, the authentication method is different as it uses WS-Fed rather than SAML, which allows for SSO to Office 365 applications.

Application Center/Catalog

To give users the feeling that they are able to self-serve applications, one of the features of the Workspace Portal is the App Center.

Here, a user will see a range of applications that they can consume via self-service; clicking an application from the App Center will place that icon onto the Workspace home page. If a user deletes an icon from the home page, it will go back into the App Center. The following screenshot shows the App Center:

Although the applications that appear in the App Center look to be self-service, and they are, the IT department has put them in the catalog in the first place and basically has given the end users the ability to choose whether or not they actually want the applications.

Management Console

Most of what we have discussed up to now has been very end user-centric, but the same integrated, single-experience ethos applies to the management side of Workspace Portal too, as shown in the following screenshot:

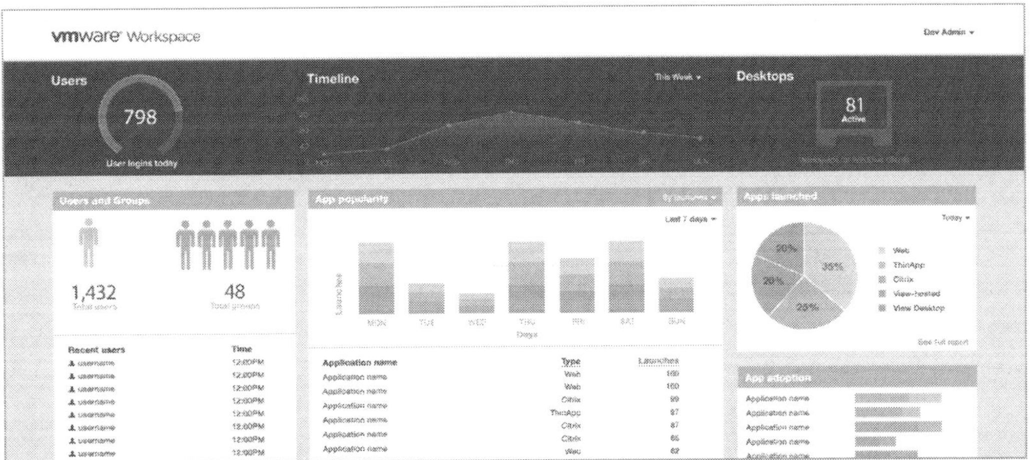

The IT administrators log in into a single management console from where they can quickly see all the available resources and, more importantly, who is using them. From here, they can quickly entitle a user or group of users to a particular resource, whether that's a virtual desktop machine, a ThinApp package, or a SaaS-based application.

Some of the other functions include customization of the portal screen, where you can do the following:

- Change the logo for login prompts and the application launcher
- Change the favicon
- Add a background picture
- Add branding such as company name and product name

Reporting is another key component in Workspace Portal, and you can report on things such as audit details, actions, statistics, launched applications, and so on.

Workspace appliance architecture and sizing overview

The Workspace Portal is driven by a single virtual appliance that is deployed on your vSphere infrastructure in the data center. The virtual appliance consists of services, as illustrated in the following screenshot:

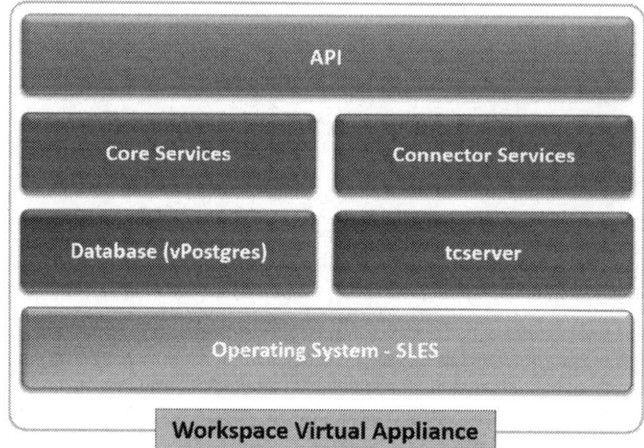

The Workspace appliance's recommended sizing is as follows:

- 8 x vCPU
- 8 GB RAM
- 72 GB available disk space

With this configuration, you will be able to support around 30,000 users with 40 applications. The sizing of the hard drive will be sufficient for around 6 months of Elasticsearch queries.

Summary

In this chapter, we introduced you to some of the additional features that come as part of the Horizon Advanced Edition.

We described at a high level how VMware Mirage and the Workspace Portal products work and what they deliver. For more information on Mirage, you can read *VMware Horizon Mirage Essentials, Peter von Oven, Packt Publishing*.

In the next chapter, we will focus on the additional features that come as part of Horizon Enterprise Edition.

15
Introduction to App Volumes

In this chapter, we will give you an introduction to **App Volumes**, one of the newest features of Horizon, which is now part of the Horizon Enterprise edition.

What is App Volumes?

In August 2014, VMware acquired a start-up company called CloudVolumes. The CloudVolumes technology provides a virtualized, real-time application delivery engine for virtual desktop infrastructures. In December 2014, CloudVolumes was rebranded and named App Volumes and offered as part of the Horizon Enterprise edition.

So, what does App Volumes give you? App Volumes provides a real-time application delivery and life cycle management solution that is used as a delivery system for your virtual desktops.

To create an application that can be delivered by App Volumes, you start by installing the application into a VMDK file, called **AppStack**, to deliver the application to the virtual desktop machines; this AppStack VMDK file is then mounted on to the virtual desktop machine. As the VMDK file is read-only, you can mount this on multiple virtual desktop machines.

An App Volumes Agent runs on the virtual desktop, making the application appear as if it is fully integrated and installed locally, rather than running from an additional drive.

ThinApp, Mirage, or App Volumes?

Which technology should you use and when? We often hear people ask whether or not App Volumes is going to replace ThinApp and Mirage and are these technologies still required?

All three technologies are key to the VMware vision and strategy and won't be going anywhere in the foreseeable future, so let's quickly discuss which one you will need, why you will need it, and then show how they are complimentary.

Let's start with Mirage, which we covered in *Chapter 14, Horizon 6 Advanced Edition*. Mirage is a Windows image management solution, primarily designed to manage physical desktop PCs and laptops. It is also used to deliver the containerized desktop solution, **Horizon FLEX**, for delivering virtual desktops in a BYOD environment.

Let's talk about ThinApp now. ThinApp is an application virtualization/packaging technology that is primarily used when you need isolation between applications. For example, you might need to deploy an older version of an application that doesn't run on your current operating system version. You may also need to run multiple versions of applications; for example, you may need to run different versions of Internet Explorer. Mirage and App Volumes cannot provide this.

We mentioned that these three technologies—App Volumes, Mirage, and ThinApp—are also complimentary, and depending on your use case, you can use them in combination.

When it comes to managing a physical desktop environment or delivering containerized desktops with Horizon FLEX, then Mirage is the technology you will use. If you have applications that need to be isolated, then you will combine them with ThinApp to create Mirage application layers, which will contain those ThinApp packages.

If we now take virtual desktop environments and, in particular, those that are built using linked clones and have a floating user assignment, then App Volumes will be the ideal solution for this use case. End users will be assigned a vanilla desktop from a pool of floating desktops when they are logged in. Their applications will then be deployed by simply mounting the relevant VMDK file, containing the applications in real time.

That's the model for nonpersistent, linked clone desktops, but what about virtual desktops that are built using full clones and have a persistent assignment? With this use case, all three solutions can be combined: Mirage to manage the operating systems element, App Volumes to deliver the applications, and the applications potentially being packaged using ThinApp, if you require the isolation between applications.

There is another use case to discuss, and that's when we will talk about hosted or published applications. App Volumes not only works by mounting the AppStack within a virtual desktop machine, but also mounts AppStack on a Windows RDSH server and then publishes those applications using the features of Horizon Advanced Edition. Essentially, you are creating a stateless RDSH server.

As you can see, there are several use cases that lend themselves to the different technologies, and that's the key to deciding which ones to use and when. The following diagram summarizes the different approaches:

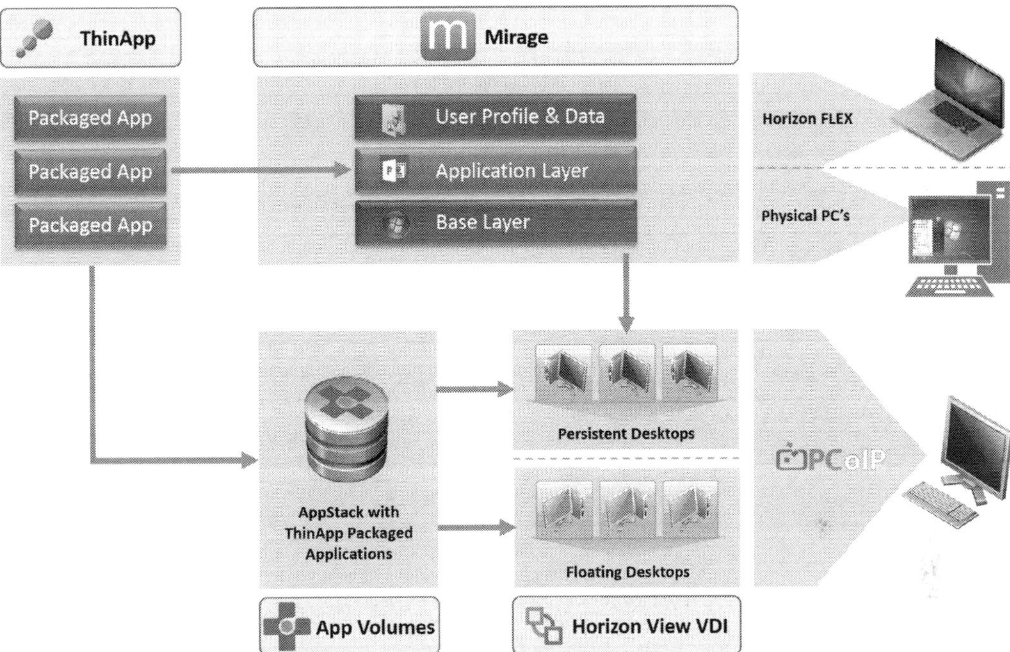

Now that we understand where App Volumes fits and some of its use cases, in the next section, we will take a look at the architecture components and how it works.

The architecture and components of App Volumes

Before we get into what the architecture looks like, let's first understand what the different components are and what they are used for. The App Volumes solution consists of the following:

- **App Volumes Manager**: This is the management and configuration console where the App Volumes Agent breaks the application assignments and writeable volumes.
- **App Volumes Agent**: The agent provides the filesystem and registry abstraction layer and is installed on the virtual desktop machines. It also virtualizes the filesystem writes, if you have deployed a writeable volume to this user.
- **AppStack Volume**: This is the read-only volume that contains the applications. A user can be assigned more than one AppStack, and an AppStack can contain more than one application.
- **Writeable Volume**: This is used as a read/write volume for the users to save any changes they make. Each user has their own writeable volume that follows them if they use nonpersistent desktops. It gets mounted in the same way as an AppStack does.

Now that we understand the components, the following screenshot shows a high-level architecture for App Volumes:

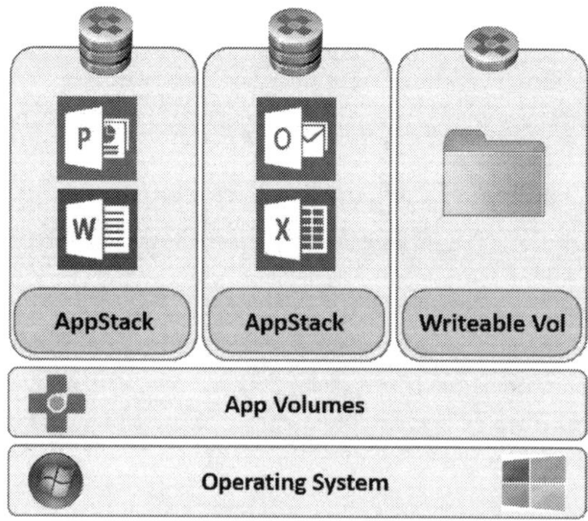

Next, we will take a look at the infrastructure required for App Volumes. A typical enterprise deployment is shown in the following screenshot:

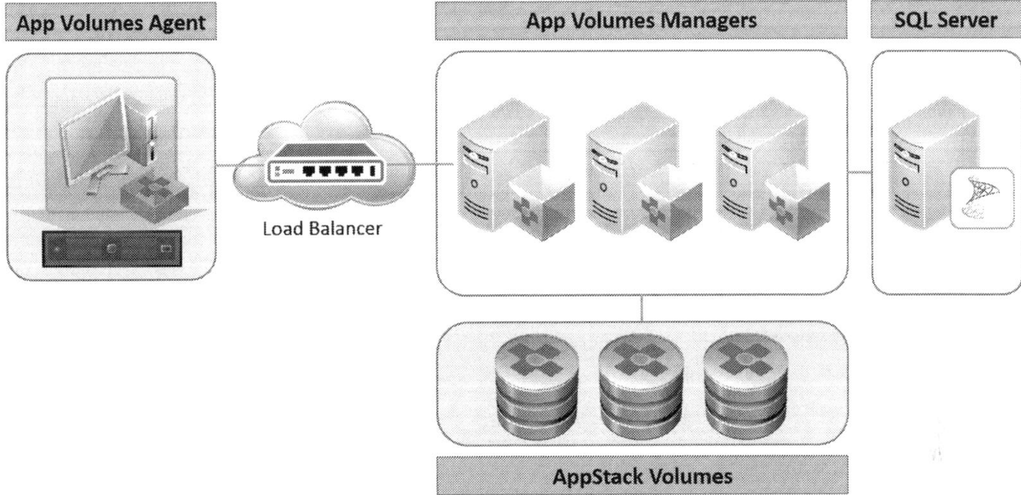

The App Volumes Manager is a Windows application that installs onto either a Windows Server 2008 R2 or Windows Server 2012 operating system. The management console is based on a browser and supports the following browsers:

- Internet Explorer 9 and 10
- Firefox 10 and 11
- Safari 5.1x

In addition, you will also need either a SQL 2008 R2 or 2012 database. In terms of system requirements, you will need the following specification to run the App Volumes Management server:

- 2 x vCPUs minimum (4 x vCPUs recommended)
- 4-GB memory
- 1-GB hard disk space

For the virtual desktop machines, you need to be running Microsoft Windows 7 and later to be able to install the App Volumes Agent.

There are also some maximum limits that you need to bear in mind. These are basically vSphere limits, as you would find in any virtual environment. These maximums are as follows:

- 2048 virtual disks per host server
- 2048 powered-on virtual desktop machines per VMFS volumes
- 60 SCSI devices attached per virtual desktop machine
- 1 AppStack per 2000 virtual desktop machines (recommendation)
- Up to 20 AppStack volumes per virtual desktop machine

Installation

In this section, we will cover the installation process and the initial configuration that you will need to perform after the installation.

Before you start the installation, ensure that you have the details of your AD, ESXi hosts server, and/or vCenter Server, as you will need them in the configuration phase of the installation.

First, we are going to run through the install on the App Volumes Manager.

App Volumes Manager

To install the App Volumes Manager, locate and launch the setup file, as shown in the following screenshot:

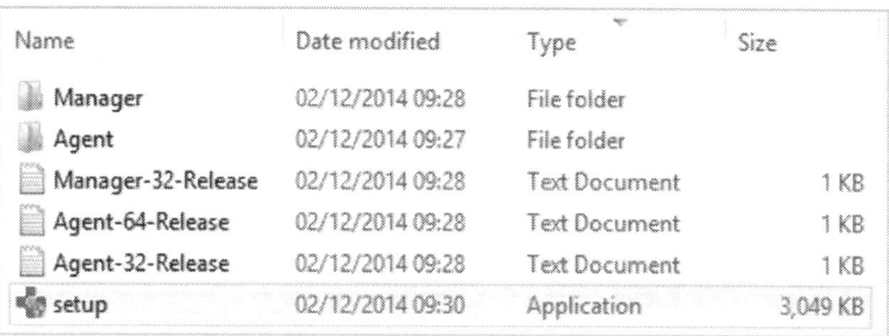

Then, follow the process as described in the following steps:

1. On the **VMware App Volumes Installation Wizard** page, click on **Next >** to start.
2. Next, click on the **I accept the terms in the license agreement** radio button, and then click on **Next >**.
3. On the **App Volumes Install** page, click on the radio button for **Install App Volumes Manager**, and then click on **Install**.
4. Next, you need to choose a database. Click on the radio button for **Install local SQL** if you want the App Volumes installer to install a SQL Express database, or click on the radio button for **Connect to an existing SQL Server** if you already have SQL in your environment and want to use this, and then click on **Next >** to continue. If you have opted for SQL Express, this will now be installed.
5. On the **Database Server** page, enter the details for your database. If you chose the **SQL Express** option, then the details will have already been completed. Click on **Next >** to continue.
6. Next, you have the **Choose Network Ports** page. The default port for HTTP is 80, and for HTTPS it's 443. Click on **Next >** to continue.
7. On the **Destination Location** page, select the features you want to install. You also have the option to change installation folder location. Leave these as default and click on **Next >** to continue.
8. You now see the **Ready to Install the Program** page. Click on **Install** to continue.
9. Once installation has been successfully completed, you will see the **App Volumes Wizard Completed** page. Click on **Finish** to close the installation.

You have now successfully completed the first part of the installation. You will now see the **App Volumes Manager** icon on your desktop, as shown in the following screenshot:

The next step is to launch the App Volumes Manager either from the local machine you installed it onto, that is, the server, or from a browser from your laptop. In our example, we will launch it locally on the App Volumes Manager server.

You will now see the following **Welcome to App Volumes Manager** page, as shown in the following screenshot:

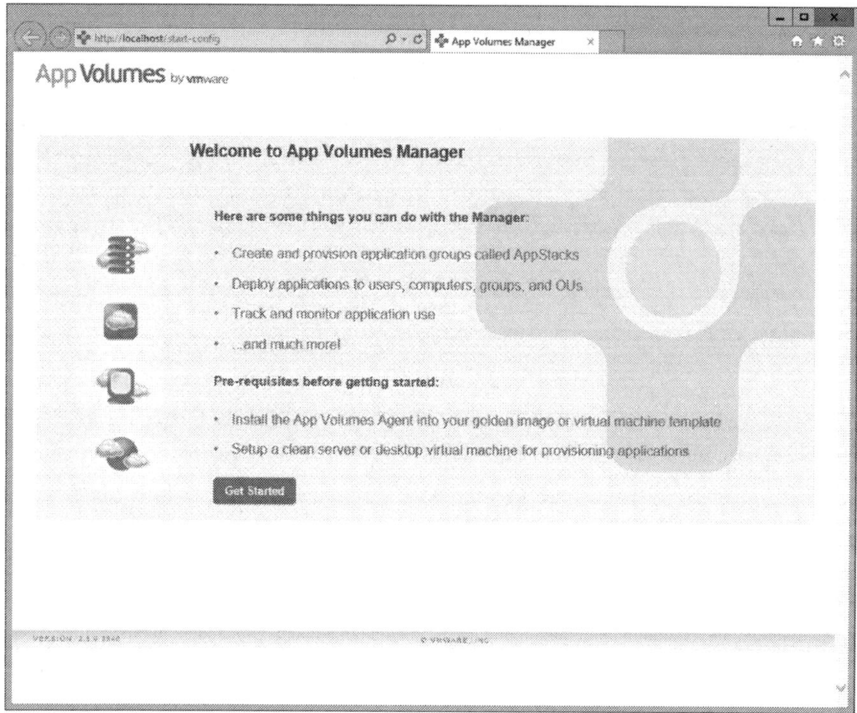

Click on **Get Started** to start the configuration process. This is described in the following steps:

1. On the **License Information** page, you will see the default licensing for 10 users. If you have a license key file, then click on **Edit**, enter the details to browse to the license file, and then click on **Upload**. Click on the **Next** button to continue.
2. You will now see the **Active Directory** page. Enter the details for your **Domain**, **Domain Controller**, and then the details for an account that has read-only access to AD. In our example, we are going to use the **Administrator** account. On this screen, you also have the option to allow an AppStack to be mounted to a non-domain joined virtual desktop machine. If you want to allow this, then check the **Allow non-domain entities** box. Click on the **Next** button to continue.

3. On the **App Volumes Administrators Group** page, select the AD group that contains all the users who you want to have access to the App Volumes Manager. Click on the **Next** button to continue.
4. Next, we need to enter the details of our hypervisor on the **Hypervisor Credentials** page. From the **Hypervisor** drop-down menu, you can choose to have a single ESX host, a vCenter Server, or a VHD, if you use a non-VMware environment. In our example, we are going to choose **ESX (single host)**, and then enter the host name of our ESX server, and the username and password. Click on the **Next** button to continue.
5. On the **Storage** page, enter the storage locations for the AppStacks and the Writeable Volumes. In our example, we are going to use the default VMFS datastore on our ESX host. When you click on the **Next** button, you will see a dialog box pop up to confirm the storage settings. Click on the radio button to choose to either import volumes immediately or to do it in the background. Click on the **Set Defaults** button to continue.
6. Next, you will see the **Upload Prepackaged Volumes** page. Check the boxes for each volume you want to upload, and then click on the **Upload** button.
7. The final page is the **Summary** page. Check that the settings are correct, and then click on the **Next** button to finish.

You have now completed the installation and configuration of the App Volumes Manager. You will now see the following screenshot, where we can start to manage our AppStacks:

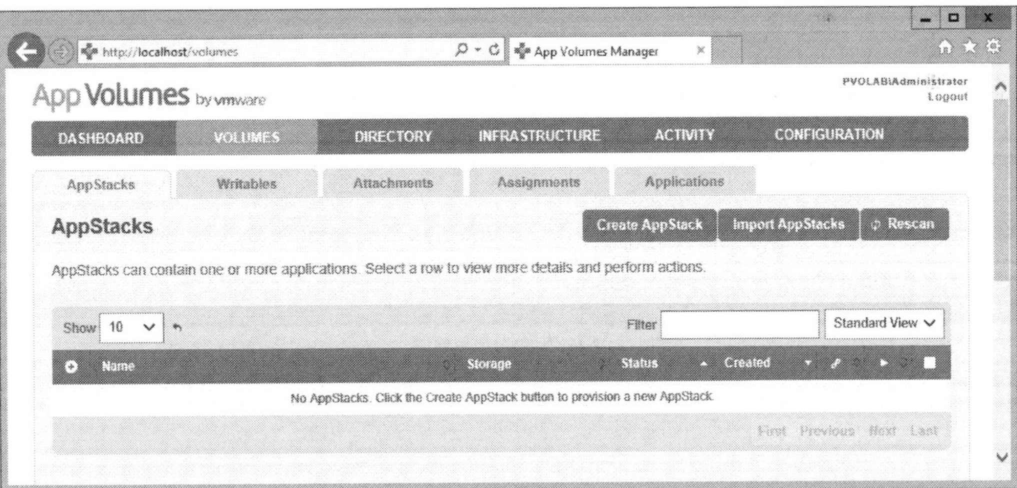

Before we do this, we need to install the App Volumes Agent on the desktop we are going to use for capturing the AppStack. The agent will also need to be installed on all of our virtual desktop machines for which you want to provision applications to.

App Volumes Agent

In this section, we will install the App Volumes Agent on our capture machine. Log on to the virtual desktop machine that you are going to use as your capture machine, locate the installation software, and launch the **App Volumes Agent** installer, as shown in the following screenshot:

Once the installer has launched, perform the following steps:

1. On the **App Volumes Agent Installation Wizard** screen, click on **Next >** to start.
2. Next, click on the **I accept the terms in the license agreement** radio button, and then click on **Next >**.
3. You will now see the **Server Configuration** page. Enter the address of your App Volumes Manager. Leave the default port setting, and then click on **Next >**.
4. On the **Ready to Install the Program** page, you will see a summary of the configuration. Click on **Install** to start the installation.
5. Once completed, you will see the **App Volumes Wizard Completed** page. Click on **Finish** to close the installation.
6. You will then be prompted to reboot. Click on **Yes** to restart your machine.

You have now successfully installed the App Volumes Agent on the virtual desktop machine that you wish to use as your capture machine. You will need to follow the same process to install the App Volumes Agent on the virtual desktop machines that you wish to deliver applications (AppStacks) to. In the next section, we will create an AppStack.

Creating, assigning, and delivering an AppStack

We have now covered all the infrastructure requirements for setting up App Volumes, but before we create our first AppStack, we need to make sure we have a clean build of the operating system on which to build the AppStack. This machine will become our capture machine, and in our example we have a clean Windows 7 build we are going to use.

Best practice would be to create the AppStack on the same operating system that it is going to be deployed on. So, if you are deploying an AppStack to a Windows 7 virtual desktop machine, then create the AppStack on Windows 7.

The following diagram details the process of creating and delivering AppStacks:

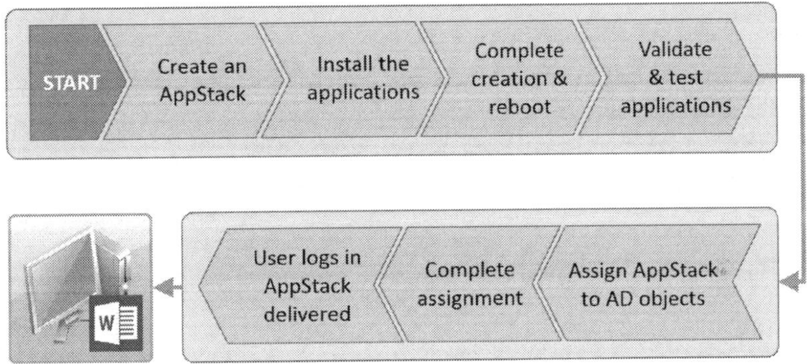

In the next section, we will create our first AppStack.

Creating an AppStack

To start the AppStack creation process, from the App Volumes Manager, perform the following steps:

1. Click on the **VOLUMES** tab (**1**), and then click on the **Create AppStack** button (**2**), as shown in the following screenshot:

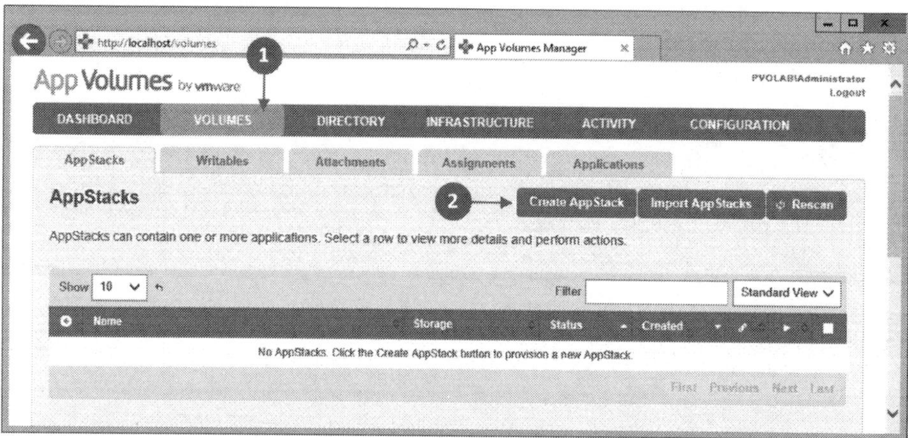

2. Next, fill in the **Name** field for the AppStack (**3**), and a **Description** of what the AppStack contains (**4**). Leave the **Storage**, **Path**, and **Template** locations as default.
3. Click on **Create** (**5**), as shown in the following screenshot:

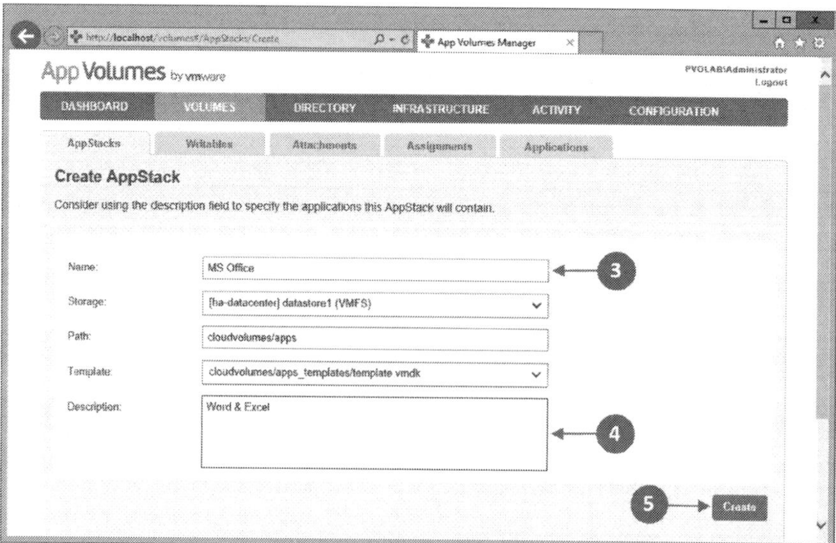

4. You will now see the following dialog box for **Confirm Create AppStack**:

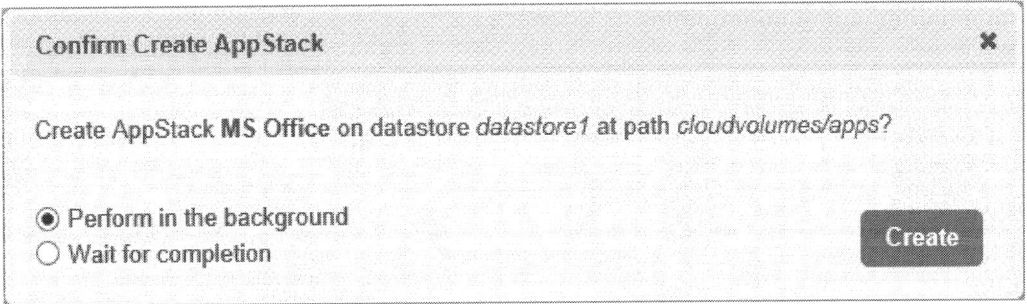

5. Click on the radio button for **Perform in the background**, and then click on the **Create** button.
6. Once the AppStack has been created, you will see the following screenshot showing the details of the AppStack:

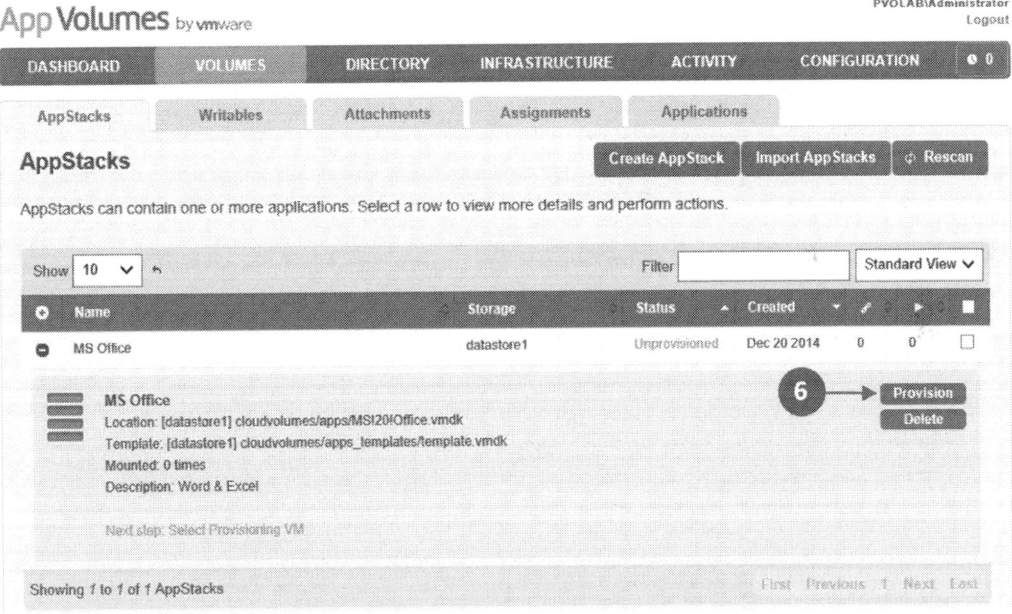

Next, we need to provision the AppStack. This means we are going to mount this AppStack (VMDK file) to our capture machine. At this stage, the AppStack is an empty container ready for us to install the application into.

7. Click on the **Provision** button (6) to continue to the provisioning stage.
8. You will now see the **Provision AppStack: MS Office** page, as shown in the following screenshot:

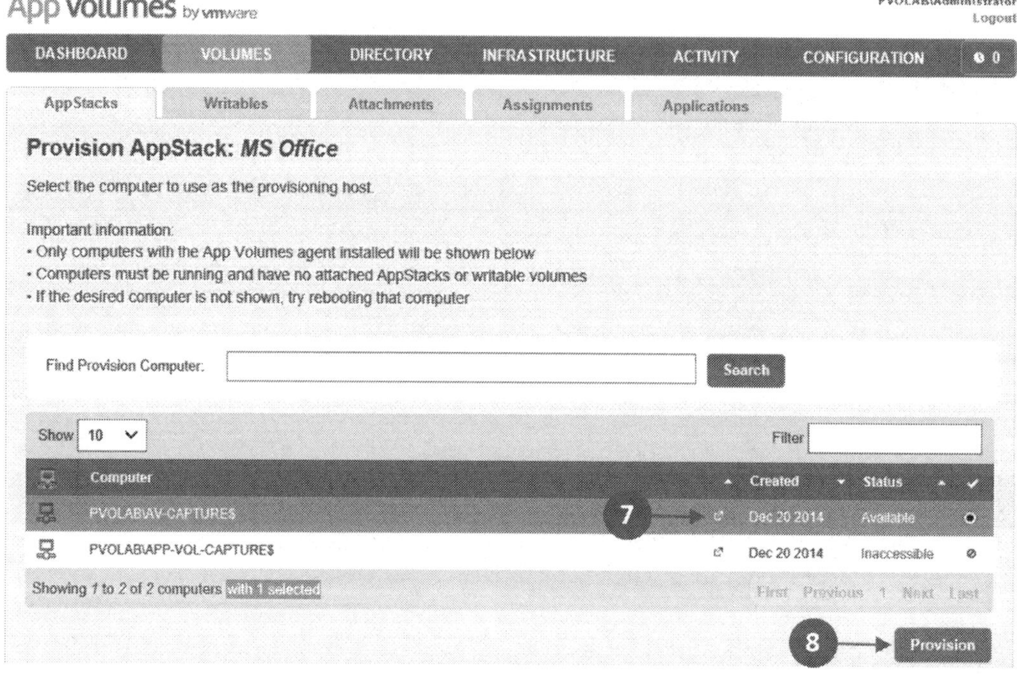

9. The next step is to locate the capture virtual desktop machine so that we can mount the AppStack to it.

The capture virtual machine must have the AppVolumes Agent installed.

10. In the **Find Provision Computer** box, enter the name, or part of the name, of the capture machine, and click on the **Search** button. A list of results/matches will be displayed.
11. Click on the radio button next to the machine you want to use. In our example, it's the machine called **PVOLAB\AV-CAPTURES**, so click on the radio button (7).
12. Now, click on the **Provision** button (8).

13. You will see the **Confirm Start Provisioning** message, as shown in the following screenshot:

14. Click on the **Start Provisioning** button. You will now return to the **AppStacks** page of the App Volumes Manager, as shown in the following screenshot:

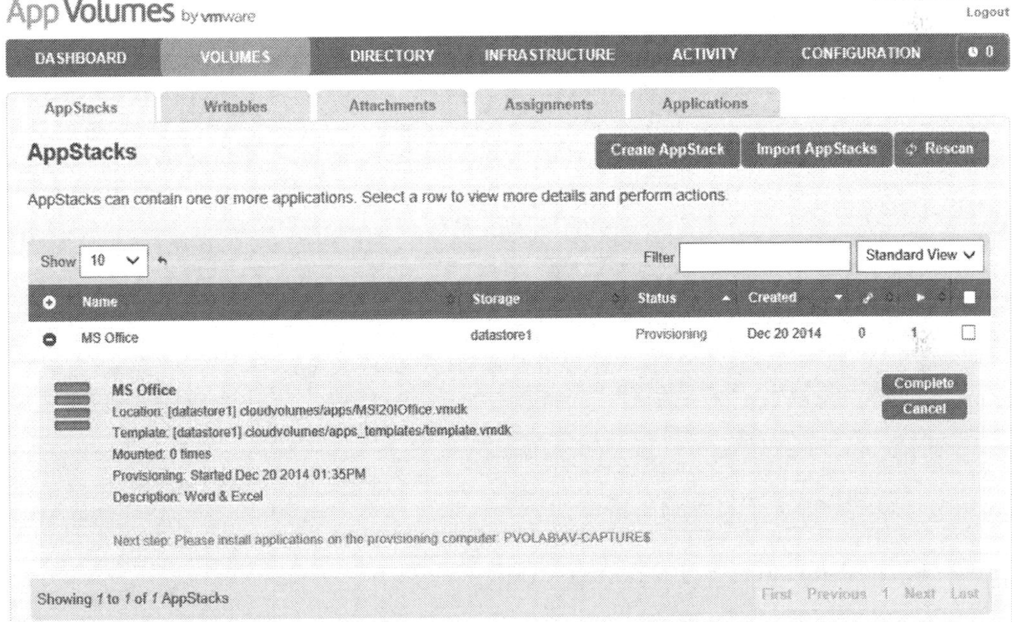

Do not click on the **Complete** button on this page! Follow the instructions for creating the AppStack, and the process will complete automatically.

15. Now, switch to the capture machine. You will now see that it has been put into the provisioning mode, as shown in the following screenshot:

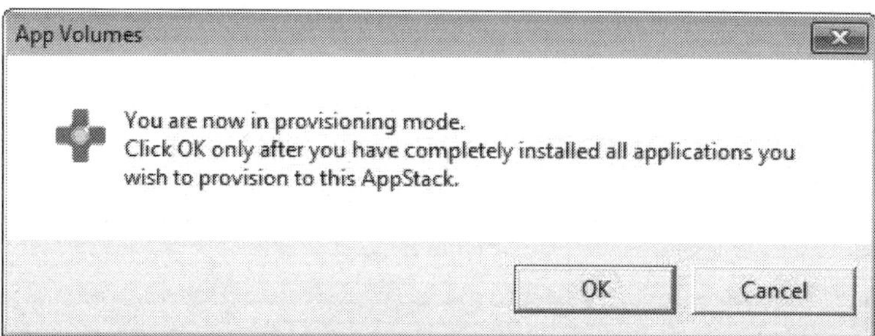

Do not click on **OK** until you have completed the installation of your applications.

Now you can install the application as you would normally install it. App Volumes has at this point mounted an empty AppStack, which will be used to capture the application into. If your application installation requires a restart, then App Volumes will just continue the capture process after the restart. In our example, we are just going to install a couple of the Microsoft Office applications, Word and Excel.

16. Once you are happy that your application has installed correctly, then you can now click on **OK** to complete the provisioning process. You will see the following message:

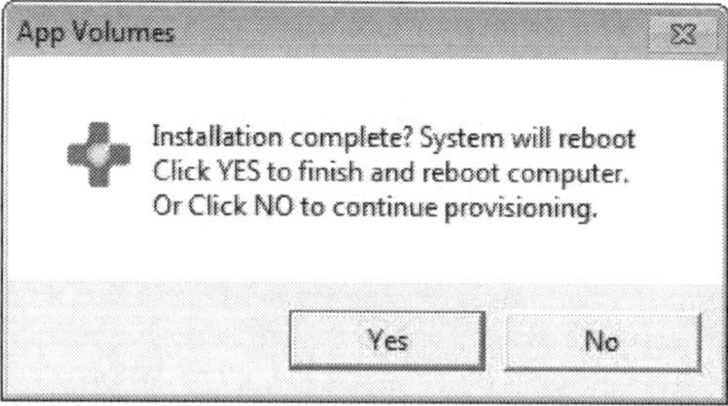

17. Click on **Yes** to restart the capture machine. Once it restarts, log in and you should see the following message:

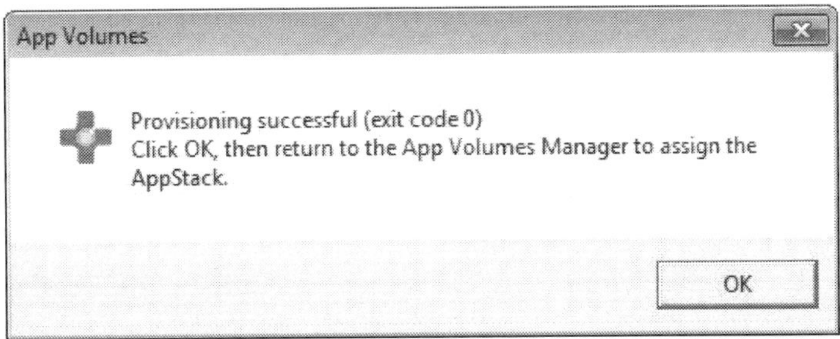

18. Click on **OK**. You can now return to the App Volumes Manager to assign this AppStack to a user. You will see that the AppStack now appears as enabled and provides you with a summary of the applications, file size, and assignments.

Next, we are going to assign this AppStack.

Assigning an AppStack

To assign an AppStack, perform the following steps:

1. From the **App Volumes Manager** screen, click on the **Assign** button (**1**), as shown in the following screenshot:

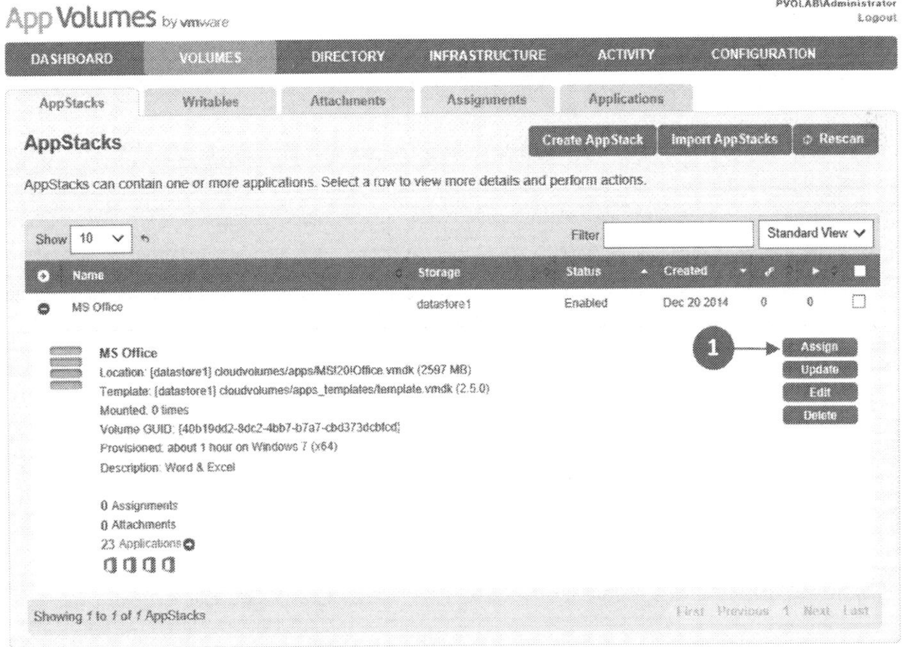

2. From the **Assign AppStack: MS Office** page, you need to search for the AD group to which you want to assign this AppStack. In our example, we have a group called **AppStack**.
3. In the **Search Active Directory** field, enter the first part of the name of the group, and then click on the **Search** button (**2**). You will see the results listed.
4. Check the box for the group you want to use for assignment, in our example it's the **PVOLAB\AppStack** group, and then click on the **Assign** button (**4**), as shown in the following screenshot:

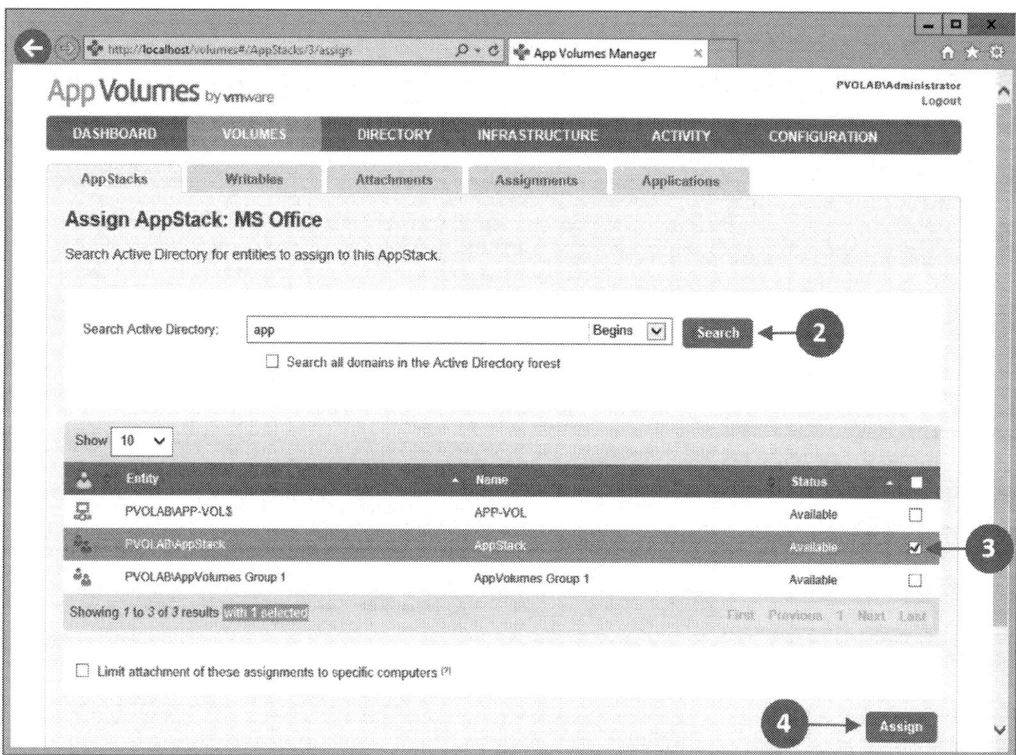

5. You are now prompted to either **Attach AppStacks on next login or reboot**, or **Attach AppStacks immediately**. Click on the radio button for **Attach AppStacks on next login or reboot**, and then click on the **Assign** button, as shown in the following screenshot:

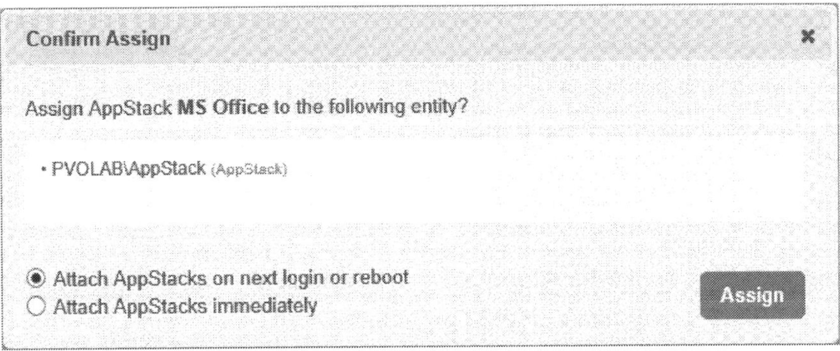

6. Once assigned, you will return to the **AppStacks** page, where you can see that the AppStack has now been assigned.

Next, we will log in as a user and test that we have Microsoft Word and Excel available. Make sure that the user you log in as is in the AD group you assigned, in our case the group called AppStack.

Delivering an AppStack

Log in to the virtual desktop machine, and navigate to **Start** | **All Programs**. You will see a folder for **Microsoft Office 2013** and, if you open the folder, you will see that you have Microsoft Word and Excel available, as shown in the following screenshot:

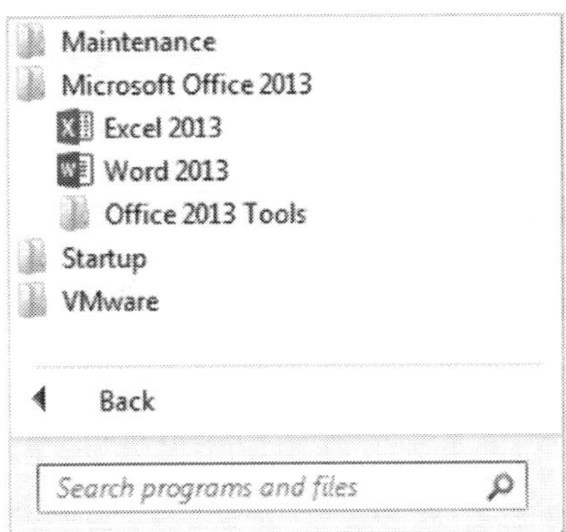

App Volumes has mounted the Microsoft Office AppStack that we created as an additional virtual disk file. You can see this by logging into your host or vCenter Server and looking at the properties of the virtual desktop machine, as shown in the following screenshot:

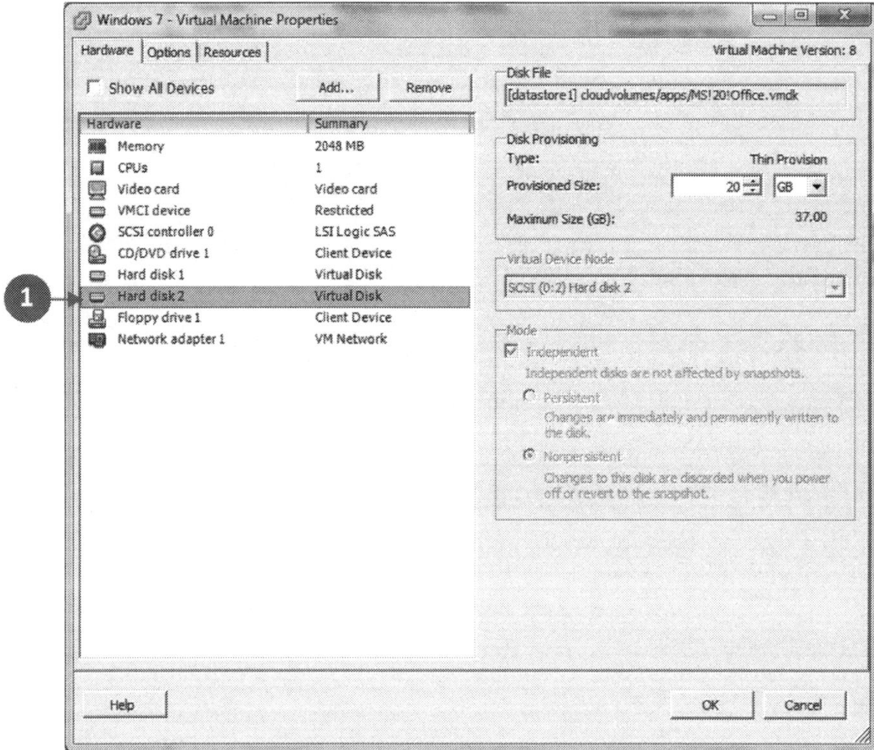

You can see that a second virtual hard disk has been attached to the virtual desktop machine (**1**), and if you take a look at the **Disk File** details, you will see that it is our Office AppStack, shown as a VMDK file.

Best practice

As this is an introduction to App Volumes, we are going to quickly highlight a few of the best practices that you need to keep in mind when deploying the technology. These are listed as follows:

- Install any kernel mode drivers in the base image of the virtual desktop machine (the parent image), not in an AppStack
- Applications that need to run when a user is logged out should also be installed in the base image

- For DR, use a third-party tool to replicate the App Volumes folders across datacenters
- If an application has a dependency on another application, then both the applications should be installed in the same AppStack
- For enterprise deployments, you should have a minimum of two App Volumes Managers with a load balancer in front
- For backup and recovery, ensure that you back up the SQL database (for enterprise deployments, it is recommended that you have clustered SQL), the AppStacks, and writeable volumes, if you have deployed them
- When you come to restoring, it's a simple case of restoring SQL; install the App Volumes Manager software and then import the App Stacks

Summary

In this chapter, we gave you a brief introduction to App Volumes. We then guided you through the installation process before creating our first AppStack and then delivering it to a virtual desktop machine.

We finished this chapter by covering a few of the best practices for deploying App Volumes in a production environment.

In the next chapter, we will take a look at VMware VSAN and how it works within a virtual desktop environment.

16
Introduction to VSAN for VDI

Since Horizon View 5.3.1, Horizon View has supported VMware's Virtual SAN technology for use with VDI desktops. In this chapter, we will review the functionality of **Virtual SAN (VSAN)** and how it integrates with Horizon View. VMware claims that by utilizing VSAN technology with your VDI deployment, you could save up to 50 percent of your capital investment in comparison to traditional SAN storage. VSAN can be used in place of the traditional shared storage in most situations when deploying Horizon View, as long as it is designed accordingly to meet your performance requirements. Although, the form factor for your servers may dictate whether VSAN can be used or not, with blades or 1U servers, you may struggle to design an appropriate solution with VSAN for your Horizon View environment.

VSAN overview

VSAN is a software-defined storage capability included directly within the vSphere 5.5 hypervisor, allowing you to create SAN storage by utilizing spinning disks and SSDs contained within some or all of your hosts within your cluster. Each host that will be contributing to the cluster will need at least one flash device and one spinning disk; normally, there will be a number of spinning disks (maximum seven), but there is a limitation of one flash device per disk group. However, within your host, you could have multiple disk groups made up of a single SSD and a number of spinning disks each. Within your cluster, there can be up to 32 servers with some or all of them contributing to the VSAN, but all are able to consume the VSAN capacity and performance, there does need to be a minimum of three servers in the VSAN cluster for availability reasons.

All writes coming into the VSAN will be delivered through the flash devices within the cluster and a proportion of the reads, with all capacity being delivered by the spinning disks within the cluster.

Data protection across the VSAN is provided by storage policies that can be configured on a per virtual machine basis; these policies control elements such as the stripe size, failures to tolerate, and percentage of the SSD to reserve as a read cache. By configuring these policies, you are able to configure the redundancy within the system if there should be a host or disk group failure, as well as controlling the granularity of the performance characteristics by customizing the read cache reserve.

Horizon View 6 integrates directly with VSAN and through vCenter to configure the correct storage policies on the relevant disks created for your virtual desktops.

The following screenshot illustrates the architecture of the VMware VSAN when deployed into your vSphere infrastructure:

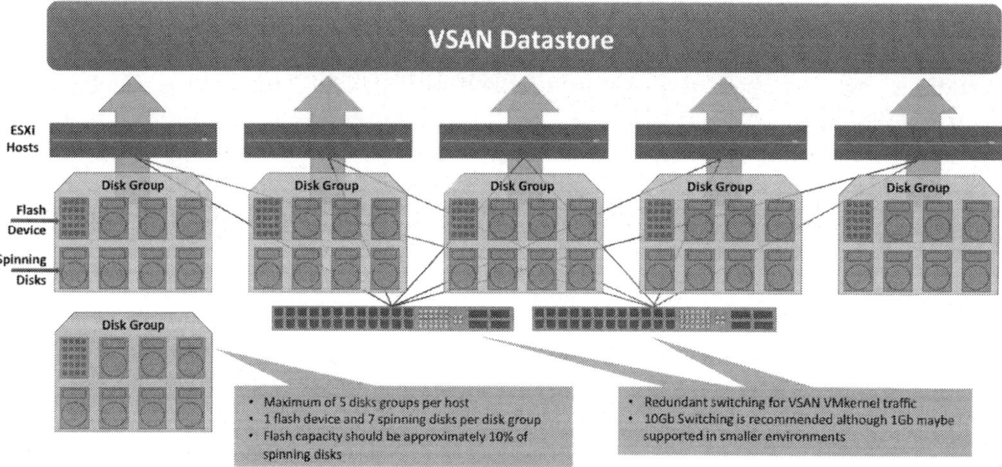

VSAN licensing with Horizon View

VSAN is bundled with Horizon View Advanced and later configurations, allowing you to reduce the overall cost of your VDI implementation, and you are also able to purchase VSAN for desktops on a per concurrent connection basis, if you wish to use VSAN with Horizon View Standard.

Designing a VSAN

There are three ways to create a VSAN solution for use with your VDI desktops:

- Designing your own solution
- VSAN Ready Nodes
- VMware EVO: RAIL

Whichever way you decide to go, you should ensure you have carefully considered the design to ensure it will meet the performance and capacity needs for your VDI environment, especially during a failure scenario. When building your own solution, consider each component carefully, ensuring that it is on the VMware HCL for VSAN and it is going to deliver the performance/capacity required by your design. Important consideration should go to the storage controller, particularly the queue depth—which has been known to cause issues if insufficiently sized, particularly in failure scenarios when rebuilding while still trying to serve I/O. With VSAN Ready Nodes, each OEM manufacturer has many different configurations for different purposes. So, ensure again that you check the VMware's HCL and select a VSAN Ready Node that the manufacturer recommends for desktop workloads. With the EVO: RAILS solution, there is only a single configuration available from the OEM manufacturers, so consider the suitability of this solution for your configuration.

Creating a VSAN cluster

We are now going to run through the process of creating a vSphere Cluster, which has VSAN storage enabled. We are going to assume that you have already built your hosts with the specific hardware requirements for VSAN and have vCenter running in a management cluster, ready for you to create your new VSAN cluster inside.

From within the vSphere web client, we will want to create a new cluster within an existing datacenter, for that perform the following steps:

1. Select the icon for Hosts and Cluster view (**1**), expand your vCenter (**2**), and then right-click on the datacenter (**3**).

2. Select **New Cluster...** (**4**) from the menu, as shown in the following screenshot:

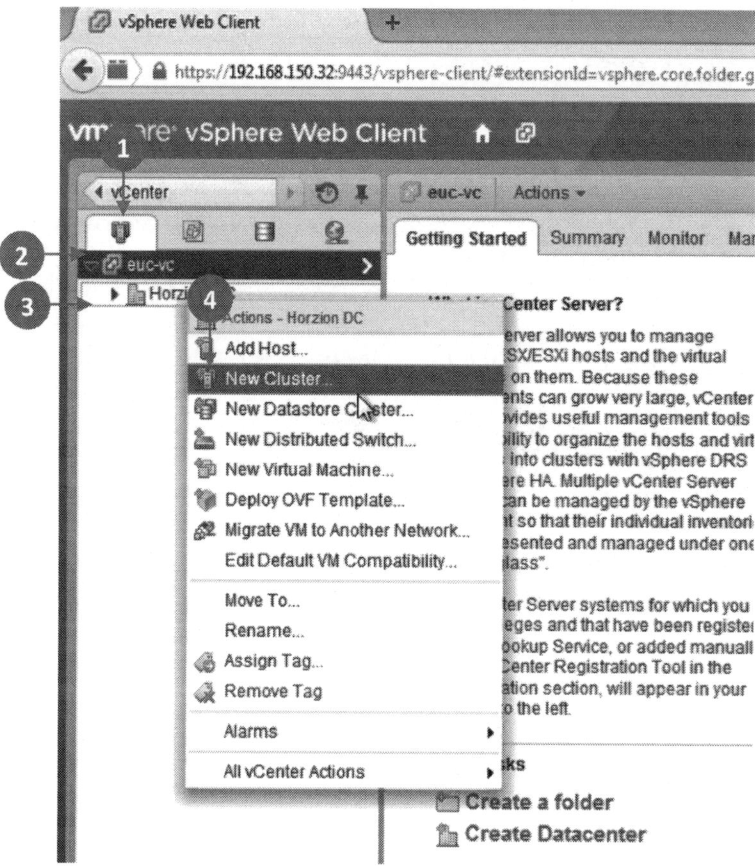

3. You now need to complete the **New Cluster** wizard as normal, naming your cluster (**1**) and selecting the appropriate options for the DRS (**2**) and HA (**3**) configurations. You will also need to select the tick box to **Turn ON** VSAN and choose **Automatic** from the **Add disks to storage** drop-down menu. This will automatically add all suitable empty disks to your VSAN configuration, as shown in the following screenshot:

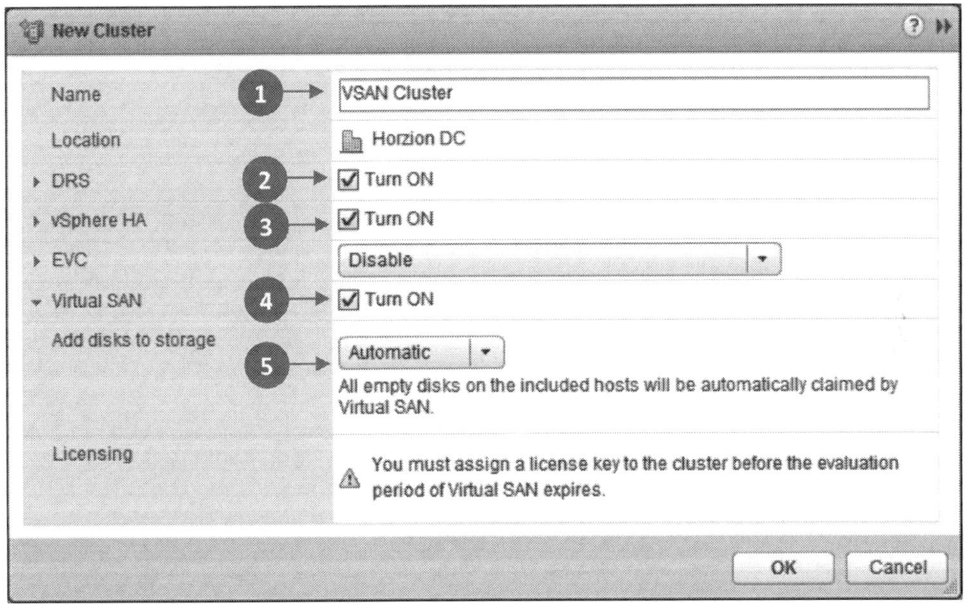

4. You will now add your VSAN hosts to the cluster in the usual manner; from within the web client, hosts and clusters view, expand your vCenter, the relevant datacenter and right click the new **VSAN Cluster** (**1**), from here select **Add Host...** (**2**), as shown in the following screenshot:

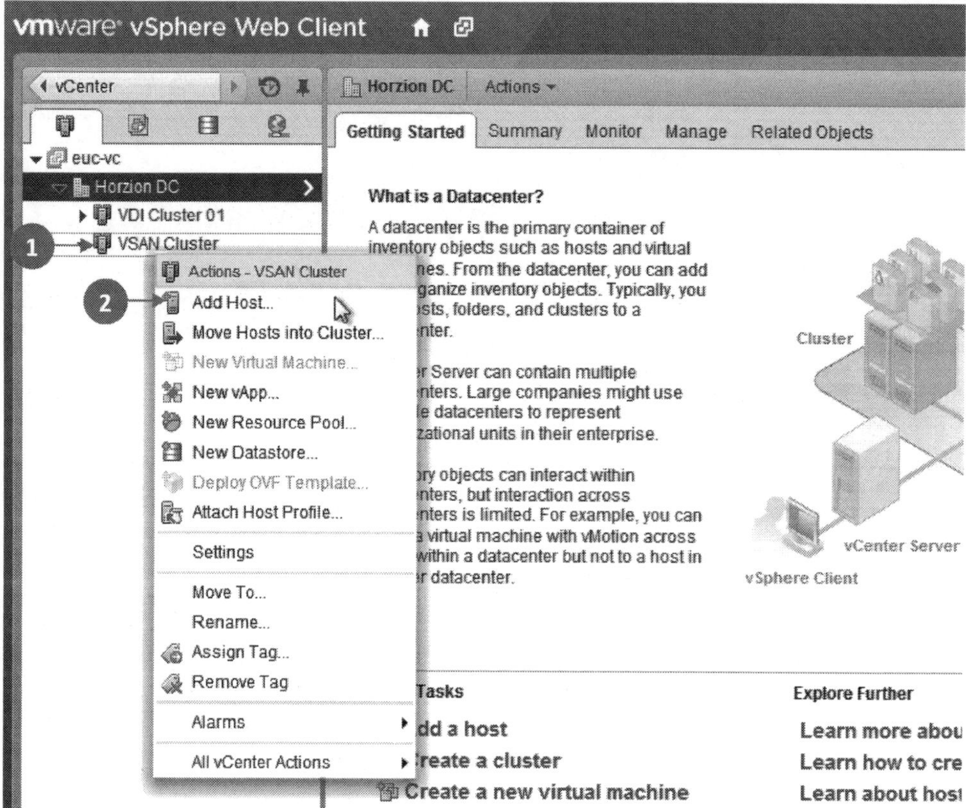

5. You will now be presented with the **Add Host** wizard that will need to be completed in the usual manner, as shown in the following screenshot:

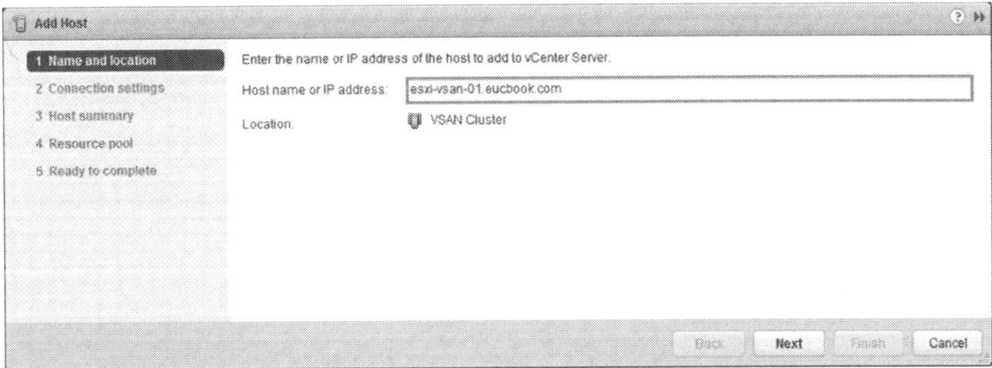

6. Once complete, you will be able to see your VSAN configuration by selecting your cluster and navigating to **Manage** | **Settings**. Here, expand the **Virtual SAN** option on the left-hand side and select **General**.

   In the following example, you can see we have three hosts in our VSAN cluster, with three SSDs in use and three data disks, providing a total of just under 500 GB of available space. We are using nested ESXi hosts to test the VSAN technology, hence the small capacity available within our environment:

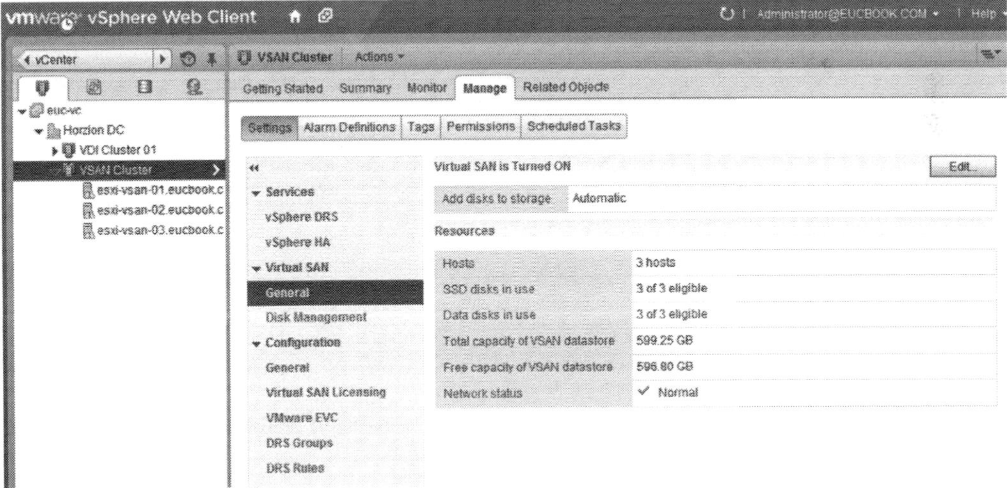

7. In the following screenshot, you are able to see that when you expand the **Disk Management** view, you are able to see each host and the resource it is contributing to the VSAN cluster:

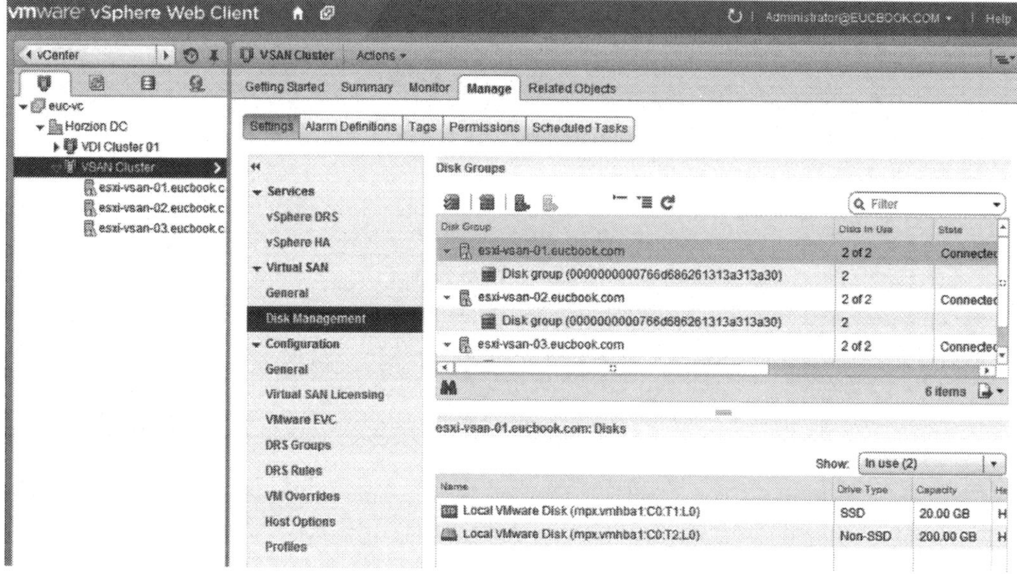

8. Finally, by viewing the **Datastores** for the cluster, we can see the presented **vsanDatastore**, as shown in the following screenshot:

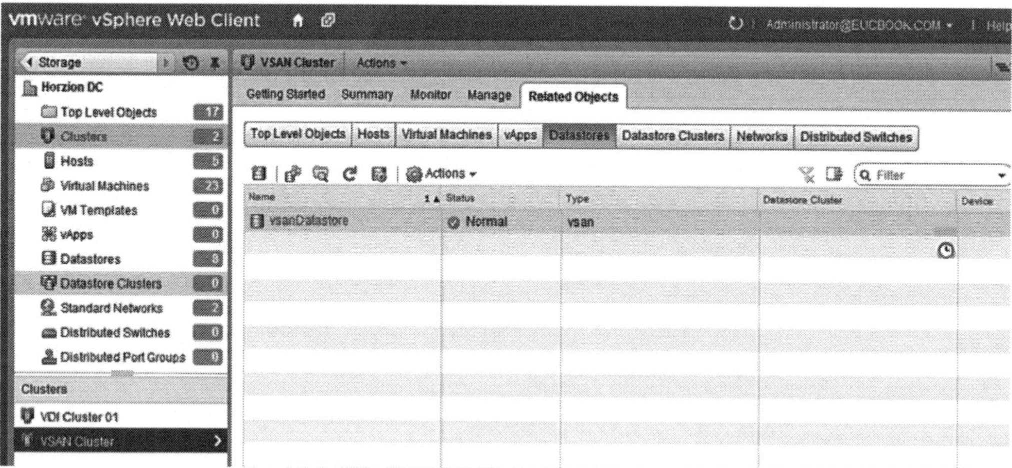

Creating a View pool on a VSAN cluster

You should create your desktop pool using the process discussed in *Chapter 7, Managing and Configuring Desktop Pools*, and when you get to the **Storage Optimization** page, select **Use VMware Virtual SAN**, as shown in the following screenshot:

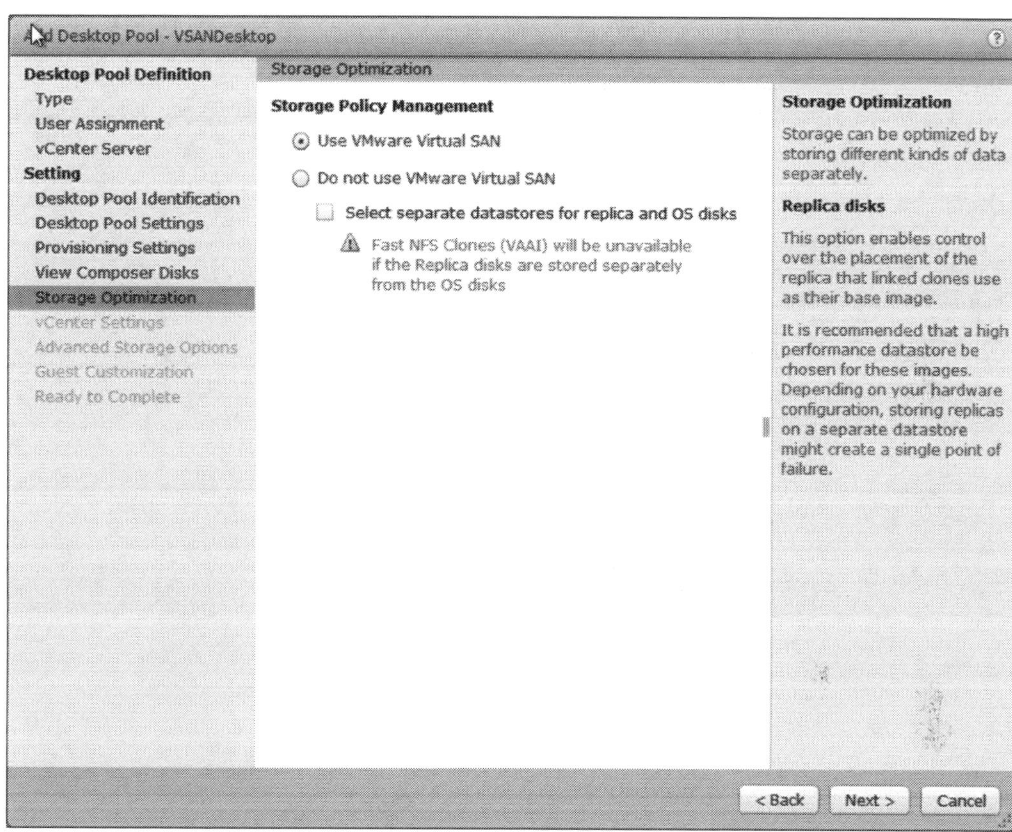

On the **vCenter Settings** screen, you will choose the relevant options, including choosing the relevant vCenter and cluster to place your desktop pool to utilize the VSAN and the relevant datastore to place your desktops on the VSAN storage, as shown in the following screenshot:

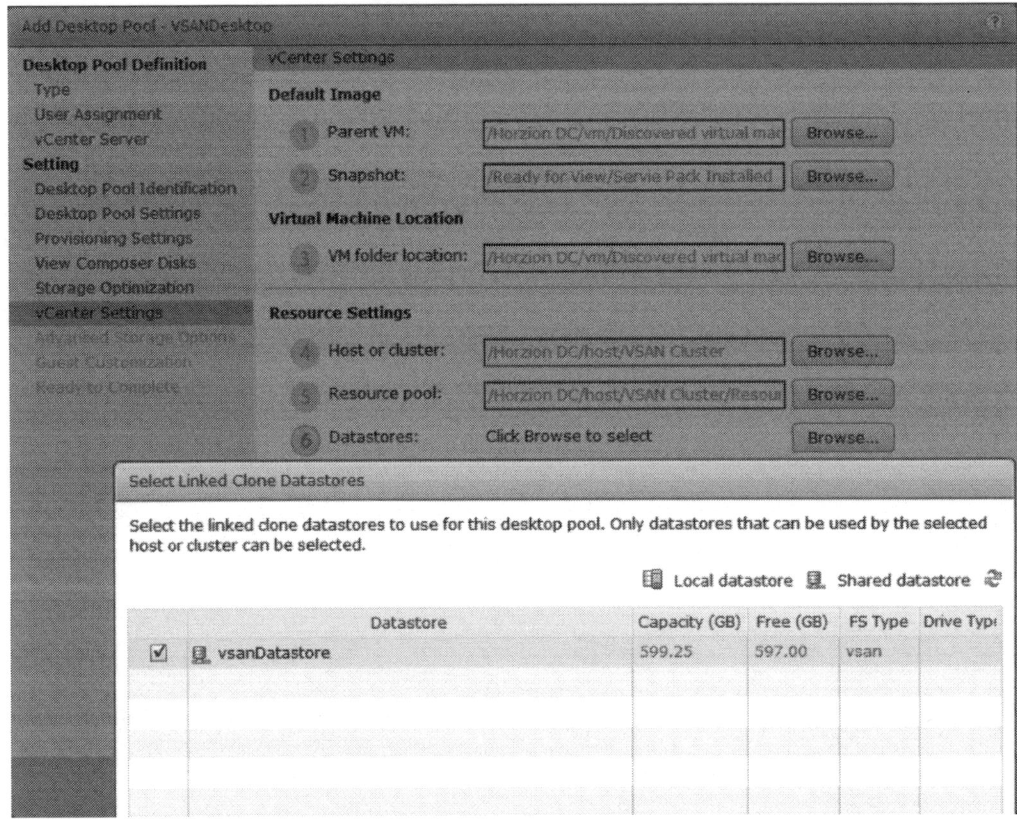

You will now complete the wizard in the usual way and finish by entitling your users. Now you have created your first VSAN-enabled pool, and you are able to see that there are a number of VM storage policies created within your vCenter, as illustrated in the following screenshot. There is a storage policy created for each type of virtual hard disk, and the default policies have been created for each to ensure the relevant protection levels:

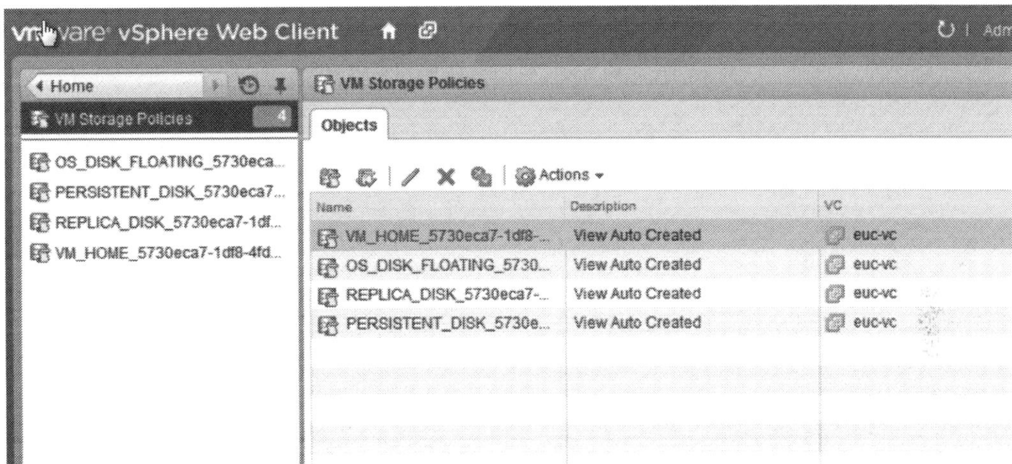

Summary

In this chapter, we have given a brief overview of the VMware VSAN technology, how it is architected, and how you go about creating a VSAN-enabled cluster. Once you created your VSAN-enabled cluster, we reviewed the process of creating your first desktop pool of VSAN storage, and when creating the desktop pool, we saw that View automatically created the relevant storage policies for use with VSAN. In the next chapter, we will discuss troubleshooting for your Horizon View environment; your VDI environment is made up of many components and being able to get to the bottom of an issue often involves having the correct understanding and methodology to get to the bottom of the problem quickly.

17 Troubleshooting

As you have learned throughout this book, a successful VDI or EUC project is made up of many components, and its success boils down to user experience; it's not just a question of whether it's working or not. As such, it is important to have a well-defined methodology and the tools to be able to adequately diagnose and fix issues within your environment. In this chapter, we are going to cover troubleshooting techniques and the methods to use within Horizon View.

Looking at the big picture

The common issue when introducing any VDI technology is that it can quickly become the point of blame when any issue arises with any component in the infrastructure. Remember that the Horizon View technology is only one component of the desktop that the user utilizes, and just because the desktop is sitting within a VDI environment, it isn't going to be trouble- or blame-free.

When a user reports an issue or you notice an issue within the infrastructure, you will need to think logically as to which component within the infrastructure can be the likely cause and where you should start your troubleshooting journey.

Is the issue affecting more than one user?

A good place to start understanding any issue within your environment is by understanding who is experiencing the issue and has more than one user reported the same issue. If you try and recreate the issue, do you get the same results? Can another user, with the same permissions and resources, recreate the issue?

If you find that the issue is related to a single user, consider where the issue will reside by asking yourself the following questions:

- What device are they connecting from?
- What connection are they connecting over?
- Can it be a bandwidth or connection reliability issue?
- Can a port be blocked?
- Have they used PCoIP, RDP, and/or HTML5?
- Do they have specific application or permission requirements?

If you believe that the issue has something to do with their desktop, consider refreshing it. This is the beauty of VDI; you should use it. Don't spend hours trying to troubleshoot and fix application or OS issues if a simple refresh can resolve it.

If the issue is affecting more than one user, consider checking whether a fix can be applied to the base image and then rolled out to your desktop pools in order to simplify the process of resolving the issue.

Performance issues

This is probably one of the widest subject areas; performance issues can be related to many areas, aspects, and personal opinions as well.

Users reporting performance issues

If users report poor performance, ask them to be specific; keep an issue journal, listing the time and issue, if it is a prolonged issue, and ask them following questions:

- How are they measuring performance?
- What time of the day do they experience the problem?
- Are they doing something specific when they experience the problem?
- Are they connecting from somewhere specific or from a specific device when they have the issue?

Where possible, visit the user and understand their issue in person; this will enable you to the get to the bottom of the issue with ease.

Non-VDI issues

Performance issues on a desktop may be caused by many elements, regardless of whether they are virtualized or not. The common areas for consideration include the following:

- Extended logon times
- Application crashes
- Long application load times
- Operating system crashes
- Poor application performance
- Permission errors

Many of these issues can and will occur, irrespective of whether the desktop is virtualized or not; of course, in a virtualized environment, they may be easier to resolve. For example, if you find you are getting OS or application crashes, consider patching these elements to the latest updates and recomposing the image for all the users. This can take a lot longer and can be a lot more difficult with a physical desktop estate. Maybe login times or application load times are suffering due to a CPU performance issue; with physical desktops, you will be stuck with the hardware unless you replace or upgrade, and in a VDI environment, you can consider tweaking the spec at the push of a button.

The important point to understand here is that generic desktop issues still exist, so use the VDI platform to your advantage. We have worked with so many users where, once VDI is implemented, they forget about generic desktop support and spend too much time digging deep into the VDI architecture when there may be a simpler answer.

Bandwidth, connectivity, and networking

Networking-related issues can often be the most difficult to get to the bottom of; where possible, ensure that you work with your networking team in order to ensure that there is suitable end-to-end monitoring in place.

While your users are connecting on a LAN, you would hope there will be plentiful bandwidth, latency will be low enough, and connectivity will be reliable. If you are struggling on a LAN, consider the following:

- Has anything on the network changed?
- Is the user connecting via a wired or wireless network?
- Have you configured PCoIP for QoS on your switching?

- Is the network currently reliable?
- Are you seeing any of the following dropped packets:
  - Clients to core switching
  - Clients to servers
  - Clients to VDI desktops
- Is the latency as expected?
- Even on the LAN in larger environments, bandwidth could be an issue. Have you considered the sum of the bandwidth required from your client devices to VDI desktops?
- Are you routing between networks? Do the routers work at a suitable performance level?
- Are the load balancers sized correctly for your environment?

When your users are connecting over a WAN, it can sometimes be more difficult to troubleshoot or guarantee connection quality. For remote or branch offices, ensure that the Internet connection is suitably sized; where possible, ensure that you have configured QoS for the PCoIP protocol end-to-end. Ensure that you have suitably configured the PCoIP policy to cope with the reduced bandwidth available.

When troubleshooting issues, investigate the relevant logs on the client and on the View Connection Servers, as well as any intermediary components such as the load balancers and routers.

The users will experience the following:

- **Black screens**: This is commonly caused by ports blocking the PCoIP Protocol, somewhere in the chain
- **Disconnections**: High latency and dropped packets will cause the users to be disconnected from their desktops
- **Poor resolution images**: Due to the nature of the protocol, if there is low bandwidth permanently, users may complain about low-quality images

Compute issues

CPU and memory issues on your hosts have a large knock-on effect on the experience of your users. As with most technical solutions, we would recommend that while you are going through your initial testing and roll out, you document your baseline for key performance characteristics, such as CPU and memory utilization, and deeper metrics such as CPU Ready times.

With these baselines in your toolkit, it makes it easier to compare when you have issues to find out what could be causing the problem. Likewise, using technology such as vRealize Operations for Horizon will help you understand performance utilization over time.

Within your VDI infrastructure, you don't want to be experiencing any memory overcommit, considering how much memory is allocated to your virtual desktops and the total memory within your hosts; ideally, you want to ensure that your total allocated memory is less than the total in your hosts minus one host in case of failure or maintenance. If you are experiencing performance issues to do with memory or CPU, check if memory is being swapped for the VMs, and is there any ballooning with the environment. Understand what your CPU Ready characteristics are. The acceptable CPU Ready within your VDI environment will vary based on the environment and users, and generally you are going to want to keep CPU Ready below 5 percent per allocated CPU with 10 percent at a peak.

When scaling your VDI environment from the initial design through to production, it can be easy to forgot to keep an eye on these metrics and failure to do so will often lead to performance related issues.

Disk performance

As we have previously mentioned, disks are key to a successful VDI solution, and being able to keep an eye on the disk performance is crucial to avoiding issues in the future.

As we can see in the following screenshot, within our environment we are using a **nimblestorage** array and we are able to use **InfoSight** to granularly review the performance statistics over time; tools like these are invaluable for you to avoid performance issues; when the worst does happen, they are able to quickly identify where the issue lies. Ensure you understand the tools that are available to you with your storage vendor:

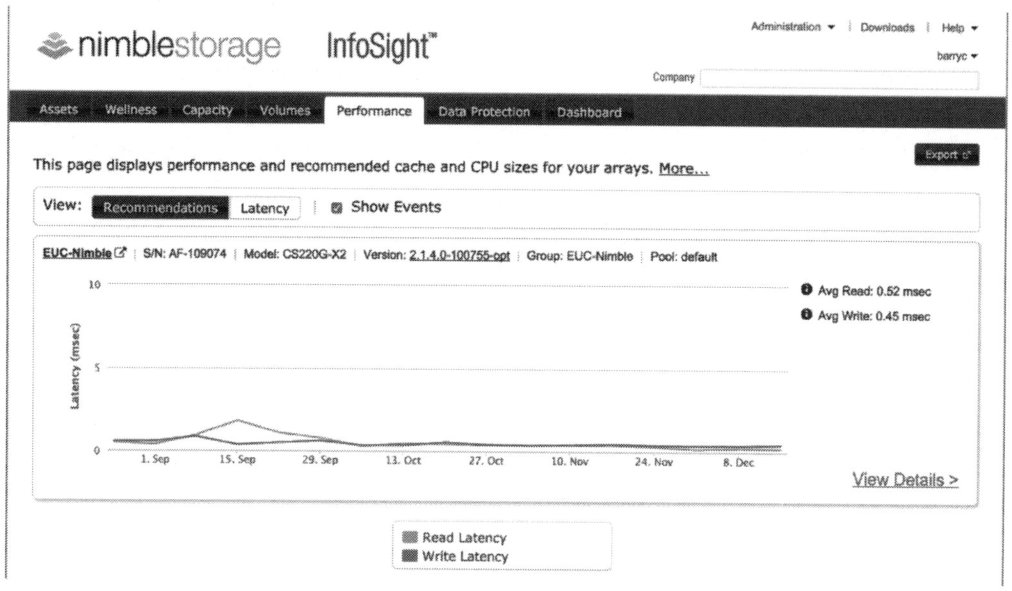

How much latency is acceptable within your environment is going to very much depend on the users, and also consider what will happen as you scale up the solution. While we may say that disk latency of less than 25 milliseconds is generally acceptable, it doesn't mean that a user who has been using a system with sub-millisecond latency would be happy, or not notice, if all of a sudden they were experiencing 25-millisecond latency. Likewise, if a user is completing disk-intensive processes, 25 milliseconds may be simply too much for the user to start with.

Horizon View-specific issues

There are a number of components that you now understand make up your Horizon View infrastructure, and while they are generally very reliable, they can, of course, all fail at some point with knock-on effects. Wherever possible, you should be ensuring that your solution is highly available, and where not possible, ensure that the components are sufficiently monitored using components such as vRealize Operations for Horizon.

Infrastructure issues

The first port of call when troubleshooting your Horizon View infrastructure should be the event log within the Horizon View Administrator console. You can quickly and easily access the event log by clicking alerts on the top left-hand corner of the screen, as shown in the following screenshot:

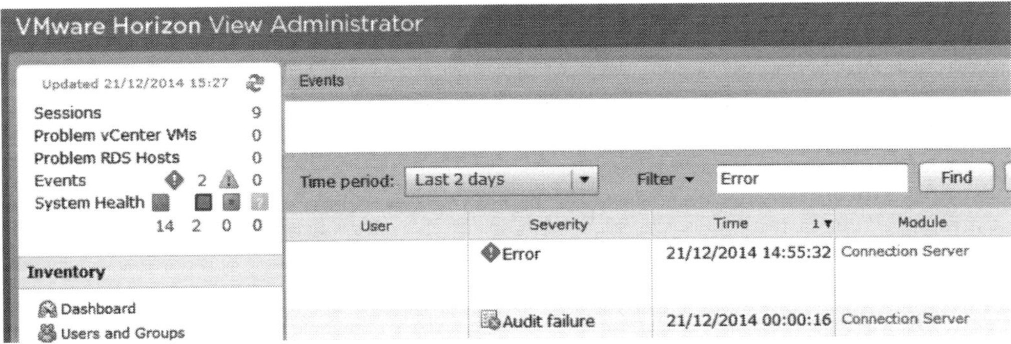

You should also utilize the dashboard to get a quick overview to understand the health of your environment. From the following screenshot, we can see health of all the key components within our infrastructure, such as vCenter, Hosts, View Connection Servers, View Security Servers, Desktops, RDS Hosts, Datastores, and more. This is a great resource to start troubleshooting infrastructure issues within your Horizon View environment:

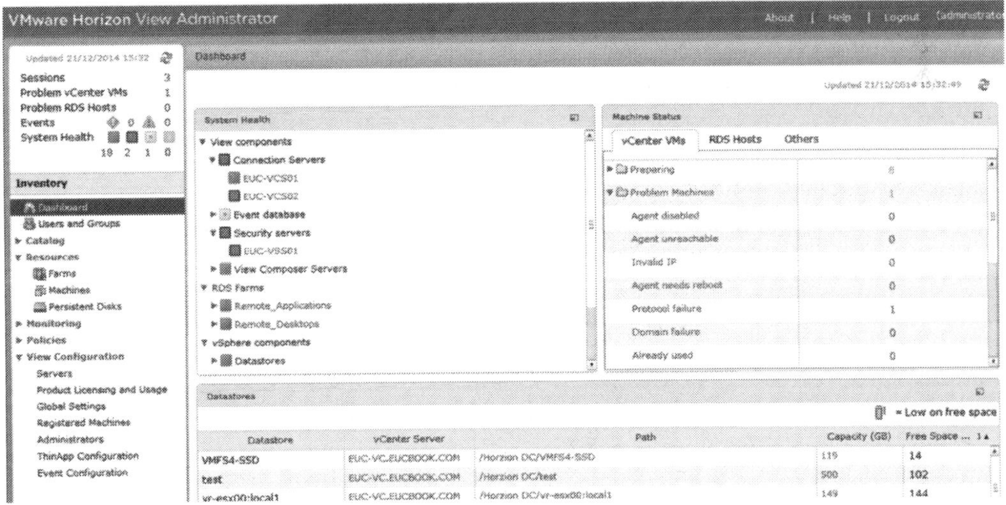

You should also not forget the simplest of troubleshooting steps when experiencing issues with your Horizon View infrastructure:

- Are all the servers, desktops, hosts, and so on, contactable on the network?
- Are all the required services started?
- Is there sufficient free space on all servers?
- Are the memory and CPU maxed out?
- Have you checked all the events logs?

Consideration also needs to be given to the backend database systems and the effect if they were to go offline. Ensure your SQL solutions are reliable and the same as all other components. If you are having issues with maybe your vCenter or View Composer, ensure you check the SQL Server for the following:

- Are resources sufficient?
- Are the services started?
- Are the correct ports open?
- Is there enough free disk space for the database and logs?

Component issues

Of course, there may be issues that arise that are outside the remit of all the areas we have discussed so far. In these situations, Horizon View's error reporting is generally very good, allowing you to pinpoint the issue quickly and easily. Unfortunately, sometimes the corrective actions can be quite cumbersome. Issues you may see that may require specific corrective actions are as follows:

- Manual removal of a View Connection Server or Security Server after loss of a component or OS corruptions
- Manual removal of VDI desktops or whole pools
- Recovery of Horizon View from a backup
- Recovery of a persistent disk from a backup
- Persistent disks running out of space for users

We aren't going to cover the specific corrective actions for these processes here, as there are some great knowledgebase articles on VMware's KB at `http://kb.vmware.com/`.

vRealize Operations for Horizon

vRealize Operations for Horizon are available as part of Horizon Enterprise or separately, and where vRealize Operations differs from most monitoring tools is its analytics engine. Most monitoring tools are based around setting thresholds for key values such as CPU or memory consumed. The issue with this kind of alarm simply is that stumbling over a threshold value doesn't mean there is necessarily an issue; sometimes it is within the normal parameters of the applications in use or potentially the problem could be a resource not being consumed when it should be. With the analytics engine included within vRealize Operations, it is able to learn and understand what the normal working parameters of your environment are, and from this it is then able to alert you when an error occurs that falls outside these parameters. It is also able to track growth and consumption over time to pre-empt an issue prior to its occurring.

vRealize Operations for Horizon should be installed where possible; at the beginning of your project, vRealize Operations is deployed simply via a single vApp, and when deployed and configured, it starts listening and learning your environment. There are three key metrics tracked with vRealize Operations, these are:

- **Health**: It reports on the current health status of your environment; items that could affect health include high packet loss, component failure, disk capacity at a critical level, and more.
- **Risk**: It indicates an issue within your environment that, if left unintended, could very well impinge on the health of your environment.

- **Efficiency**: It reports on considerations such as overprovision that, if rectified, could help you get more out of your environment to maximize the investment. An example of this would be VMs with overprovisioned CPU or memory. The following screenshot depicts the VMware vRealize Operations Manager dashboard displaying the Health, Rick and Efficiency metrics:

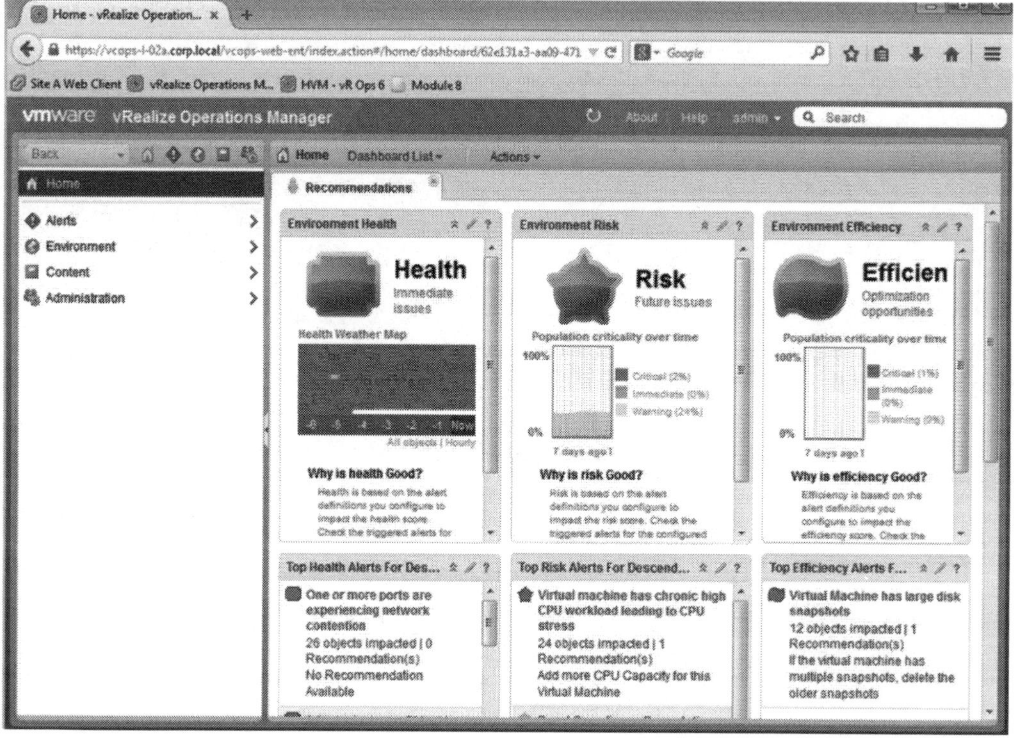

vRealize Operations for Horizon includes specific features to ensure that you fully understand the health of your Horizon View environment, including the full visibility in the PCoIP protocol, as well as integration for health monitoring with the View Connection Server, View Security, and more.

vRealize Operations will use the analytics engine to learn your environment and understand what is normal, raising alarms based on dynamic thresholds for your environment rather than meaningless static thresholds.

Within vRealize Operations 6, it also incorporates smart alerts, allowing you to quickly understand the root cause of an issue within your infrastructure and the recommended remediation actions to resolve the issue. The following screenshot illustrates a smart alert and recommendation inside VMware vRealize Operation Manager:

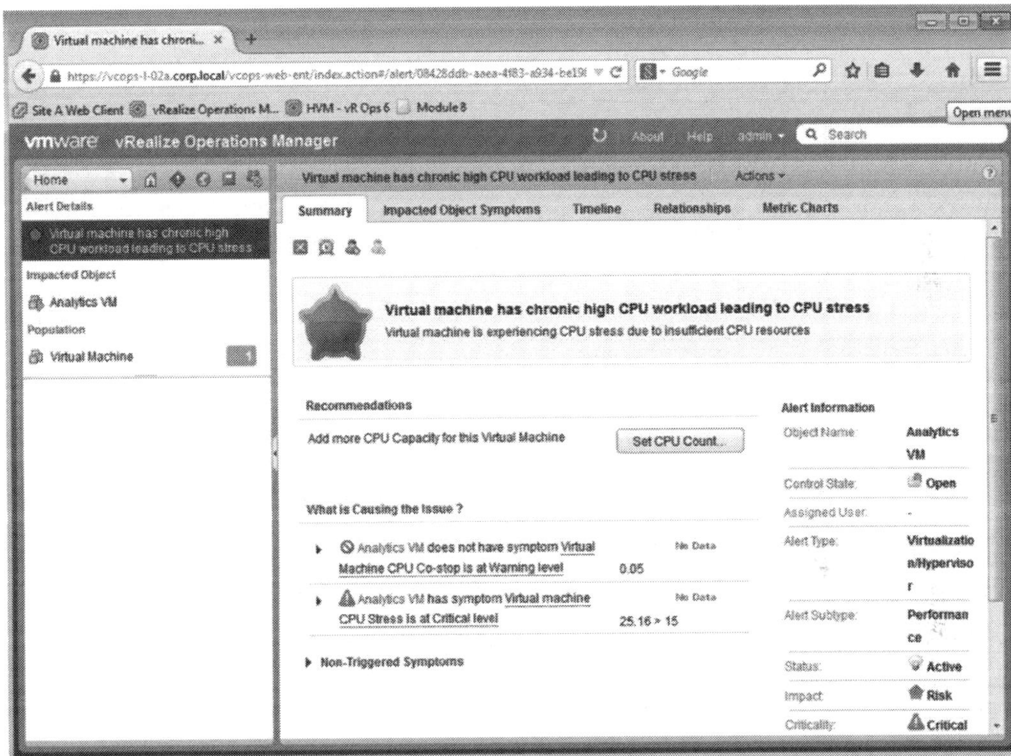

Getting further help

There are a number of resources available, if you are struggling to get to the bottom of an issue within Horizon View; first and foremost, we recommend logging a call as early as possible with VMware support to get the best assistance possible to resolve your issue.

There are also a large amount of resources online, such as blogs, Google "VMware Planet V12N" for a list of VMware Bloggers that may have suitable resources. The VMware community also has a wealth of resources available at `https://communities.vmware.com`. Possibly the most useful resource is the VMware Knowledge Base; at the time of writing, there are 300 specific support topics related to Horizon View, including video how-to guides alongside step-by-step resolution guides. The home page is shown in the following screenshot:

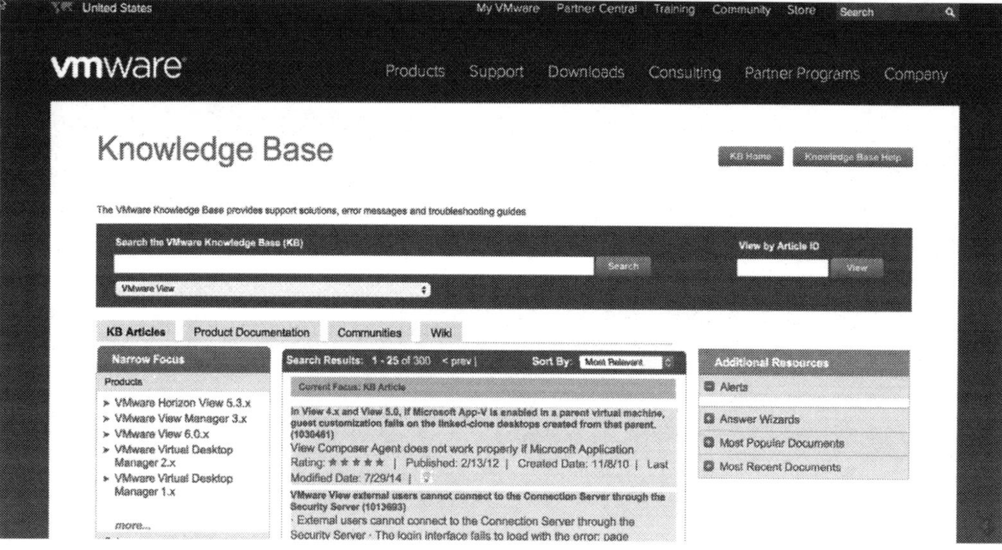

Summary

In this chapter, we covered some of the methods and areas to be considered when troubleshooting issues within your Horizon View environment. Consideration should be given to the bigger picture, ensuring that you fully understand the issues that the user is facing and which area of the user's desktop experience might be causing these issues. Where possible, use monitoring tools such as vRealize Operations for Horizon to find the root cause of the problem. There are a number of areas within Horizon View that you should check if you believe you have infrastructure problems, and these include the dashboard within the Horizon View Administrator and the event log within the Horizon View Administrator. Finally, we covered getting further help from the VMware Knowledge Base.

We have now reached the end of this book; at this point, you should have an understanding of the architecture of the Horizon Suite and how to design your EUC solution. You should understand the stages and details involved in rolling out Horizon View for your users, including installing the various components and configuring, designing, and building the desktop images and pools. You have learned about various methods to layer your applications to your desktops using technology such as ThinApp, RDSH published applications, and App Layers.

Designing and rolling out any EUC solution to any organization is a task that must be under taken with care and understanding, and we hope that the elements we covered within this book will better equip you for the tasks ahead.

Index

A

B

C

D

E

F

G

H

I

J

K

L

M

N

O

P

R

S

T

U

V

W

Z

Thank you for buying

Mastering VMware Horizon 6

About Packt Publishing

Packt, pronounced 'packed', published its first book, *Mastering phpMyAdmin for Effective MySQL Management*, in April 2004, and subsequently continued to specialize in publishing highly focused books on specific technologies and solutions.

Our books and publications share the experiences of your fellow IT professionals in adapting and customizing today's systems, applications, and frameworks. Our solution-based books give you the knowledge and power to customize the software and technologies you're using to get the job done. Packt books are more specific and less general than the IT books you have seen in the past. Our unique business model allows us to bring you more focused information, giving you more of what you need to know, and less of what you don't.

Packt is a modern yet unique publishing company that focuses on producing quality, cutting-edge books for communities of developers, administrators, and newbies alike. For more information, please visit our website at `www.packtpub.com`.

About Packt Enterprise

In 2010, Packt launched two new brands, Packt Enterprise and Packt Open Source, in order to continue its focus on specialization. This book is part of the Packt Enterprise brand, home to books published on enterprise software – software created by major vendors, including (but not limited to) IBM, Microsoft, and Oracle, often for use in other corporations. Its titles will offer information relevant to a range of users of this software, including administrators, developers, architects, and end users.

Writing for Packt

We welcome all inquiries from people who are interested in authoring. Book proposals should be sent to `author@packtpub.com`. If your book idea is still at an early stage and you would like to discuss it first before writing a formal book proposal, then please contact us; one of our commissioning editors will get in touch with you.

We're not just looking for published authors; if you have strong technical skills but no writing experience, our experienced editors can help you develop a writing career, or simply get some additional reward for your expertise.

VMware Horizon Mirage Essentials

ISBN: 978-1-78217-235-2 Paperback: 166 pages

Manage your entire desktop environment with a single management tool – VMware Horizon Mirage

1. Deliver a centralized Windows image management solution for physical, virtual, and BYOD.
2. Migrate seamlessly to new versions of operating systems with minimal user downtime.
3. Easy-to-follow, step-by-step guide on how to deploy and work with the technology.

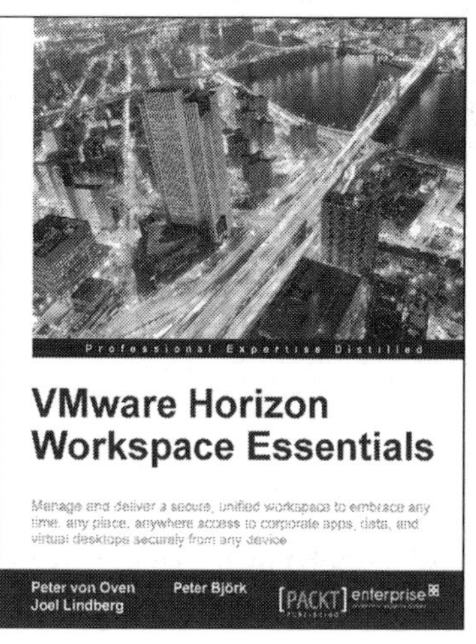

VMware Horizon Workspace Essentials

ISBN: 978-1-78217-237-6 Paperback: 158 pages

Manage and deliver a secure, unified workspace to embrace any time, any place, anywhere access to corporate apps, data, and virtual desktops securely from any device

1. Design, install, and configure a Horizon Workspace infrastructure.
2. Deliver a user's workspace to mobile devices such as Android and iOS.
3. Easy to follow, step-by-step guide on how to deploy and work with Horizon Workspace.

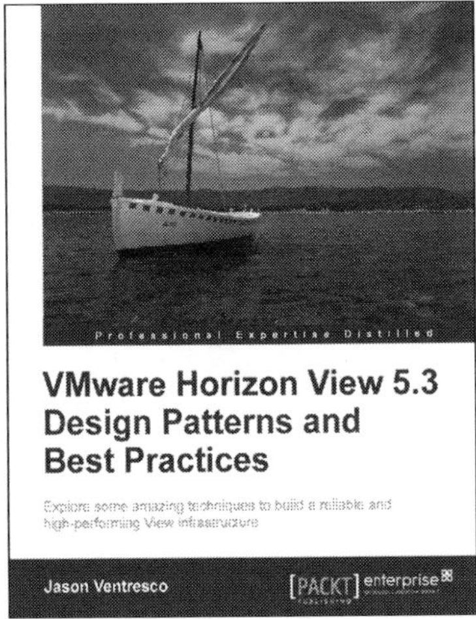

VMware Horizon View 5.3 Design Patterns and Best Practices

ISBN: 978-1-78217-154-6 Paperback: 124 pages

Explore some amazing techniques to build a reliable and high-performing View infrastructure

1. Identify the reasons why you are deploying Horizon View, a critical step to identifying your metrics for success.
2. Determine your Horizon View desktop resource requirements, and use that to size your infrastructure.
3. Recognize key design considerations that should influence your Horizon View infrastructure.

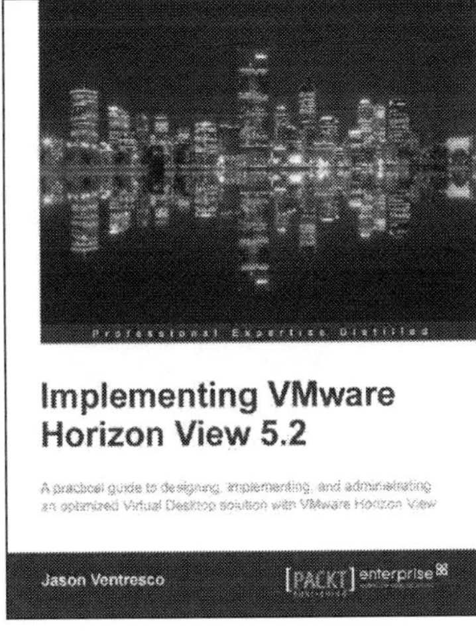

Implementing VMware Horizon View 5.2

ISBN: 978-1-84968-796-6 Paperback: 390 pages

A practical guide to designing, implementing, and administrating an optimized Virtual Desktop solution with VMware Horizon View

1. Detailed description of the deployment and administration of the VMware Horizon View suite.
2. Learn how to determine the resources your virtual desktops will require.
3. Design your desktop solution to avoid potential problems, and ensure minimal loss of time in the later stages.

Please check **www.PacktPub.com** for information on our titles

Made in the USA
Lexington, KY
11 December 2015